GunDigest PRESENTS

THE
BALLISTICS
HANDBOOK

Factors Affecting Bullet Flight from Muzzle to Target

BY PHILIP P. MASSARO

Published by

Gun Digest® Books, an imprint of Caribou Media Group, LLC
Gun Digest Media
5583 W. Waterford Ln., Suite D
Appleton, WI 54913
gundigest.com

To order books or other products call 920.471.4522
or visit us online at gundigeststore.com

CAUTION: Technical data presented here, particularly technical data on handloading and on firearms adjustment and alteration, inevitably reflects individual experience with particular equipment and components under specific circumstances the reader cannot duplicate exactly. Such data presentations therefore should be used for guidance only and with caution. Caribou Media accepts no responsibility for results obtained using these data.

ISBN-13: 978-1-959265-28-3

Edited by Andrew Johnson and Corey Graff
Interior Design by Em Coo

Printed in the United States of America

10 9 8 7 6 5 4 3 2 1

DEDICATION

This book is dedicated to Tim Fallon, Doug Prichard and the entire crew of the FTW Ranch in Barksdale, Texas, who have been more than kind in both word and deed, and who were instrumental in the development of this book. Without the SAAM Shooting School, I would still be in the dark ages.

ACKNOWLEDGMENTS

Along the way, certain people come into your life and make a definite impact. I have been lucky to meet many of my heroes, as well as major players in the firearms industry, and now call them friends. In addition, a book of this magnitude takes up a huge amount of time—time that would normally be spent with family. I'd like to thank my darling wife Suzie, and my daughter Angelina, for being so understanding during the writing process.

I'd like to thank Marty Groppi for all of his help during this project; Marty is always there to help test new products or load some ammo for evaluation. Thanks bud, you've been invaluable. Robin Sharpless, at Redding Reloading, is possibly the best-educated man I know when it comes to ballistics, and if you've ever met Robin, you know what a kind soul he is. J.J. Reich and Jake Edson at Vista have been more than kind, providing insight and information; gentlemen, I can't thank you enough. Chris Hodgdon, of Hodgdon Powders is another fellow I'm proud to call a friend. Chris, I truly appreciate all that you do. Then there are the ammunition and bullet companies that strive to keep us all shooting. Neal Emery at Hornady, Zach Waterman at Nosler, Ron Petty at Norma, Dan and Samantha Smitchko at Cutting Edge Bullets, Kristof Aucamp at Peregrine, Carroll Pilant at Sierra, and too many others to name; you guys and gals work very hard, and I am most grateful. Katie Godfrey at Kestrel, Ryan Muckenhirn at Vortex, Chris Sells at Heym USA, and too many others to name, thank you for your kindness and generosity. If I've neglected to mention your name, please accept my apologies; gun writers have only so much room on the mental hard drive.

Lastly, I'd like to thank Dave Fulson of Safari Classics Productions, firstly for being the clown that he is, and secondly for his unceasing efforts in promoting and preserving the positive images of hunters and shooters worldwide. Father Fulson, you're one of the good guys.

TABLE OF CONTENTS

INTRODUCTION

The *Merriam-Webster's Dictionary* defines ballistics as *1. The science of the motion of projectiles in flight, 2. The study of the processes within a firearm as it is fired.* This book will expound on both definitions.

The study of ballistics can be daunting. The deeper one delves into understanding a spinning projectile—and the effects of our atmosphere upon it—the more things start to sound like Chinese algebra. We humans thrive on quantifications and the mathematical formulas used to represent a projectile's speed, energy, and attributes. Still, like most things in life, they don't tell the complete story.

While we will have to get technical sooner or later, all efforts will be made to offer the science in a palatable manner without writing a book that is a legal cure for insomnia.

Our study involves three sections: interior, exterior and terminal ballistics. Interior ballistics is the study of those processes that happen from the instant you pull the trigger, and the firing pin strikes the primer until your projectile leaves the barrel's muzzle. Exterior ballistics covers the bullet's journey from the muzzle to the target, whether a long flight of several hundred yards or a short jaunt measured in feet. Finally, terminal ballistics covers what happens when a projectile strikes a target and the various types of bullet construction. I'll discuss various cartridges, how they function, and why they've gained (or lost) popularity, plus dispel some myths and compare and contrast cartridges and certain bullet types and weights. We'll examine the conformation and configuration of the various metallic cartridges to make better-informed decisions and suit our hunting or shooting needs best. And lastly, we'll look at bullet designs and explain their function in the real world.

While science is used to best explain the world around us and the numerous factors that affect how things behave, this book will not be a definitive essay on the art of ballistics. I call it an art because there is much more involved than a white lab coat and a Ph.D. to make a distant shot or place several bullets on the bullseye; we as humans are ultimately in control of the inanimate object that is the firearm, and I think the human conditions affecting a bullet's path warrant discussion.

Some folks (we call them ballisticians) devote their life to studying a projectile's journey from cartridge to target, and they may be much better qualified to speak on some issues than this author. "Every man must know his limitations," the saying goes, and where I feel there are those whose knowledge is greater than mine, I have contacted them for their wisdom and insight. I learned a lot during this project and am grateful for those kind people's input and insight.

The successes you experience behind the trigger are rarely made by accident. Instead, they result from hours of diligent practice and the desire to expand your knowledge of firearms and how to use them best. The same can be said for the associated tools that aid you in delivering the bullet on target: you must understand the applications to put them best to use.

Let us begin the study.

SECTION

I

INTERIOR BALLISTICS

SECTION I GUNDEX®

CHAPTER 1
Interior Ballistics Overview

T he sequence that a fired metallic cartridge undergoes is a small wonder in and of itself. The design hearkens back to the mid-19th century, and with the exception of the composition of the components, not all that much has changed. Yes, the propellants have become small scientific wonders (we're going to get to that shortly), while the projectiles of today are engineering marvels. However, the actual processes aren't that much different when comparing 2024 and 1876, and they aren't altogether strange when compared to those 140 years ago.

For all of our centerfire cartridges, the basic process is as follows: The loaded cartridge is secured into the chamber of the firearm, where the rear and sides of the cartridge are sealed within the steel chamber; the only exit point is down the barrel. The firing pin strikes the primer—located in the center of the cartridge case head—and the chemical compound is smashed against an interior anvil, resulting in a shower of sparks. Those sparks are forced through the flash hole, a term which reaches back to the days of flintlock rifles, and ignites the powder charge located inside the large chamber of the cartridge. Once that powder charge is ignited, the burning powder generates all kinds of pressure, and there is only one possible result: the bullet (which is pressed into the cartridge case) is forced out of the case, and sent down the barrel, where it has an inevitable meeting with the rifling of the barrel, and begins rotating rapidly.

The rimfire cartridge works in the same manner, except that the priming is contained in the rim of the cartridge and integral with it. Muzzleloading firearms use the actual breech to form a chamber, with the spark coming from an external source, be it a pan full of flash powder, a No. 11 percussion cap or, in the case of the modern muzzleloders, a 209 shotgun primer.

In any of these cases, the load can only generate the amount of pressure that the steel chamber can adequately handle. Now, while that may sound relatively simple, there are a multitude of factors that can have both negative and positive effects on the consistency and performance of the resultant flight of the bullet. Powder burn rate, powder charge weight, primer heat, chamber volume, bullet weight—the list goes on and on. We'll carefully compare and contrast those features.

There are volumes that have been written about the size, shape and performance of certain cartridges, so much so that these stories have evolved into a sort of gospel, and with some people there's no point in discussing it because no amount of explanation or logic is going to change their minds. Whether the cartridge is one of the U.S. military adoptees or Grandpa's favorite meat-maker, it's the be all and end all. Let's take a look at certain cartridges with a clean slate, try to draw some logical conclusions as to why they have a particular reputation—good or bad—and attempt to draw some educated conclusions about some of the cartridges that are often overlooked.

Keep in mind that any cartridge is just a combustion chamber, at least when looking at it from the view of the projectile, and while there are those cartridges that may feed better than others, or that may result in a lighter weight rifle or handgun, the bullet doesn't give a hoot; it just knows that there is a particular powder charge and pressure created that has just propelled it from zero to pretty-damned-fast, and that it has met the rifling to start spinning on its journey to glory.

The shape and construction of the bullet will have a definite effect on the interior ballistics, almost an equal effect as will be found during exterior and terminal ballistics phases. The powder will have a correlative effect, in the amount of pressure developed and the velocity at which the bullet is launched. The length and configuration of the barrel can and will have a definite effect on how that bullet will fly, too, and you need to know those specifications to best match the ammunition to the barrel, to get the best performance out of your firearms.

So, your chamber is loaded with a cartridge, and the sear has released the firing pin. That primer is just about to be crushed, and that's where we'll pick up our study.

There are many things simultaneously happening inside your action and barrel when you pull the trigger. Having an understanding of interior ballistics can demystify exterior and terminal ballistics issues encountered later.

CHAPTER 2
THE CARTRIDGE CASE

The little brass wonder we call the cartridge case is the basis for the whole shebang. It contains the primer, powder charge and bullet. There have been many fantastic designs since things became pretty well standardized by the 1870s. Some of these designs are still popular, like the .45 Colt (1873), the .45-70 Government (1873), the .44-40 WCF (1873), the 7x57mm Mauser (1892), .303 British (1889) and the .30-30 WCF (1895). The early 20th century saw some radical developments in bullet design and powder composition, which directly affected the design of the brass cartridge. Many of those early designs became the classics that we all know very well, cartridges like the .30-06 Springfield, .375 Holland & Holland Magnum, .404 Jeffery, .250/3000 Savage, .45 ACP, .38 Special and .35 Remington, all released between 1900 and 1915. The trend showed that as the higher pressures became attainable—from the advent of smokeless powders coupled with the strength of the copper-jacketed bullet—cartridges in general started to shrink in both bore diameter and case capacity, yet they got the job done.

As anyone with experience with different calibers will attest, there are very, very few hunting situations that couldn't be handled with one of the cartridges that I've listed above. As a matter of fact, they are all still available in modern production rifles a century later, and they comprise an irrefutable set of classic cartridges.

Between the World Wars, cartridge development continued and we saw velocities climb in cartridges like the .270 Winchester and the .300 Holland & Holland Magnum, both in 1925. After the Second World War, even the U.S. Government began to make the shift toward smaller cases using powders that generated higher pressures. The military was seeking to replace the .30-06 Springfield with a cartridge just as effective ballistically, yet cut down in size and weight so the soldier could carry more ammunition in the field. The resulting T-52—or as we know it in its civilian form, the .308 Winchester—came to fruition after testing began with the .300 Savage cartridge. It morphed into the .308 Winchester we all know and love and delivered the exact parameters the government was after: a lighter, higher-pressure .30-06, delivering muzzle velocities so close that it didn't really matter in a combat situation.

The 1950s and 1960s were a veritable renaissance of cartridge development, and the faster/shorter/lighter trend continued. Winchester released its foursome of belted cartridges, the .264 Winchester Magnum, .338 Winchester Magnum, .458 Winchester Magnum and lastly, the .300 Winchester Magnum, all based on the .375 H&H case shortened to .30-06 length. Remington followed suit with the 7mm Remington Magnum. (Remington wasn't quite done though, taking the short-fat idea to unprecedented levels with the 6.5 Remington Magnum and .350 Remington Magnum, both based on the H&H belted case, but cut to fit into a .308 Winchester-length action.) The short, squat trend had begun, but it would take until the late 1990s for it to make another commercial appearance when Winchester announced the arrival of their Short Magnum series, including .270, 7mm, .30 and .325 calibers. These WSM cases were a derivative of the Remington Ultra Magnum, a .375 H&H-length cartridge based on a blown-out .404 Jeffery. Winchester then took it to an altogether new level with the Winchester Super Short Magnum—in .223, .243 and .25 calibers—for a cartridge that resembles a fire hydrant.

Then there are the cartridges designed specifically for punching paper and delivering serious accuracy. The .22PPC and 6mm PPC, designed by Dr. Louis Palmisano and Ferris Pindell really set the benchrest world on its proverbial ear in the 1970s, breaking nearly every record possible. Then the Fl folks discovered the 6.5-284 Norma, and long-range accuracy took on a new meaning. The 6mm Bench Rest Norma and Remington cases produced some fantastic results, as well as David Tubbs' 6mmXC.

So, as we take this cursory look at cartridge history, you can see that things are constantly evolving in an attempt to create the most efficient design possible. I find it humorous and almost ironic when I see someone print a tiny group with a .30-06 Springfield; it almost seems to have been all for naught. However, I do feel that there is room for all of the different variations, just as long as someone identifies with it. We shooters have spent way too much time and energy debating the minute differences in energy and velocity figures, instead of learning how to maximize the rifle/cartridge combination that we've chosen in the field or at the range.

There is a theory among cartridge designers, and those Louis Palmisano-designed PPC cartridges come immediately to mind, that a short, fat powder column will burn more efficiently than will a long, skinny column. To a degree, I can buy that, especially in reference to the .308 Winchester, .300 WSM and 6.5 Creedmoor, as the primer's spark will reach a larger cross-section of the powder in that configuration than in the long, narrow cartridges. But on the flip side, I've seen some incredible performance from the longer cartridges such as the .300 Remington Ultra Magnum, .300 Winchester, and 6.5-284 Norma.

The .300 H&H Magnum, or Holland's Super .30 as it's also known, has a long, sloping 8-degree 30-minute shoulder, and headspaces off of the belt at the cartridge base, but it was used by Ben Comfort to win the Wimbledon Cup at Camp Perry in 1935 and again another 1,000 yard match in 1937. But yet, few would consider it to be an efficient, well-designed target cartridge. That .300 H&H has, in more than one rifle I've shot and/or loaded for, proven to be an exceptionally accurate cartridge. Conversely, I've seen some rifles chambered for the .300 Winchester

Short Magnum—a cartridge often touted for its inherent accuracy, and the holder of a few 1,000-yard records—that didn't even give mediocre accuracy, regardless of measures taken to improve it. It really depends on what your requirements are in a cartridge, and what your ultimate goal is. Is it a target gun, with which you need to reach out to 600, 700 or 1,000 yards? Is it a hunting gun, which will only be asked to perform within sane hunting ranges? Perhaps it will be some combination of both attributes. We will discuss cartridge features, and how they affect the interior ballistics of the rifle to help you make a better-informed decision.

The same concepts can easily be applied to pistol cartridges. While the pressures are often lower than their rifle counterparts, the design of the cartridge itself, and how it functions within the process of discharging the firearm, affect its performance. Wheelguns, generally speaking, can withstand a much higher chamber pressure than most of the semi-automatics, yet both are highly useful in their respective applications. The cartridges are generally of two designs: the rimmed cartridges (.38 Special, .357 Magnum and .44 Remington Magnum) and the rimless cartridges (9mm Luger, .40 S&W and .45ACP). Again, speaking in generalities until we delve a bit deeper, the rimmed pistol cartridges use that rim for headspacing, while the rimless pistol cartridges use the case mouth for headspacing.

What is Headspacing?

Headspacing requires some discussion, as it can have an effect on the way a cartridge works within the firearm's chamber and can definitely impact the accuracy of your firearm.

Headspace is the distance from the base of the cartridge case to the point on the cartridge case that prevents the cartridge from moving any farther forward in the chamber.

To put this into real-world, appreciable terms, I'll give some examples.

A rimmed cartridge, whether straight-walled, tapered or bottlenecked, uses the thickness of the cartridge rim for its headspacing. It is a positive method of headspacing, resulting in very uniform results, yet these cartridges don't often feed well in bolt- or pump-action magazine rifles. They do very well in lever-action rifles and revolvers, as well as single-shot and double rifles. Examples include the .30-30 Winchester, .45-70 Government, .22 Long Rifle, .38 Special and .357 Magnum.

Rimless bottleneck cartridges such as the .223 Remington, .308 Winchester, .30-06 Springfield and .270 Winchester, have an extractor groove cut into the base of the case, just north of the case head. As a result, these cartridges use the shoulder of the bottleneck for headspacing. The shoulder is typically quite steep, upwards of 15 degrees (though there are exceptions like the .404 Jeffery) to prevent the cartridge from moving any farther forward in the chamber. The rimless bottleneck design works perfectly in almost all repeating rifles, from lever to bolt to semi-automatic to the military's fully automatic, belt-fed machine guns. So long as the firearm is properly headspaced, this bottlenecked rimless design will work as intended. The groove allows for excellent extraction, too; it's a design common among many of our most famous cartridges.

The original quartet of Winchester Magnums, the .300, .264, .338 and .458.

Rimless bottleneck rifle cartridges.

Rimless, straight-walled cartridges comprise the most common choices for modern, semi-automatic pistols. This style of cartridge uses the same extractor groove as its bottlenecked cousins, but because there is neither rim nor shoulder, it headspaces off the case mouth. Note that this feature is especially important to those who handload this style of cartridge, as the projectiles cannot be roll-crimped into the case; they must be taper crimped or held in place by the use of a special die which squeezes the side wall of the cartridge around the shank of the bullet. In this type of cartridge, the case length is of utmost importance as that distance is the sole dimension responsible for setting the headspacing. If you've ever picked up a 9mm Luger or .45 ACP that has a rather 'sooty' look around the mouth of the case, it is an example of poor (excessive) headspacing, either from the firearm's chamber being too long, or the ammunition being too short. The .40 Smith & Wesson, as well as the 9mm Luger and .45 ACP, are all examples of pistol cartridges that headspace off of the case mouth.

The belted cartridges, based on the famous Holland & Holland design of the early 1900s, are a hybrid of the rimmed and rimless design. Because the rimmed design gave such fantastic headspacing, but didn't feed very well from a box magazine, and the London firm didn't want to rely on a steep shoulder for headspacing (both the .375 H&H and .300 H&H have gentle, sloping shoulders), they built a small shelf, or belt of brass into the case wall, just above the extractor groove. So, in essence, the H&H belted cartridges use a "rimmed-rimless" case, which feed perfectly in repeating rifles, yet headspace off of the rim. Thus, the shoulder dimension is irrelevant. While it is commonly thought that the .375 H&H Rimless Belted Magnum—the .375 H&H we all know and love—was the first cartridge released that featured the now-famous belt, that isn't true. In 1905, Holland & Holland released the .400/.375 Belted Nitro Express, also known as the .375 Velopex, but its performance was poor in comparison to other Nitro Express cartridges of the era, so it didn't last long. Additionally, when the .375 H&H was released in 1912 it wasn't alone. The .275 Holland & Holland Magnum, with a 2.500-inch case length and the same belt was released simultaneously. Firing a 7mm projectile at some very familiar velocities, the .275 H&H Magnum is, in theory, the 7mm Remington Magnum. It just took 50 years for the shooting world to realize they wanted it!

Since the belt on any belted cartridge is there for headspacing and has nothing to do with case strength, these cases show a tendency to stretch upon the initial firing, sometimes as much as 0.020 inch. Now, I know what you're thinking. In the last half of the 20th century, no self-respecting "magnum" cartridge would be caught dead without its belt. It's a very good point, but I think that the .375 H&H case was used as the basis for the brood of offspring ranging from the .257 Weatherby up to the .458 Lott—not for the strength of the belt or for headspacing issues, but for the case capacity of the parent cartridge.

Let's break the cartridges down, based on their rim types. There are five main classifications of rims, as follows:

Rimmed

This cartridge has a rim that extends beyond the diameter of the case body (bet you never saw that coming!), which serves to hold the case in the chamber. It also serves as a positive depth guide for headspacing. The earliest cartridge designs were rimmed, designed for single-shot and early lever-action rifles, and the first revolvers. Some rimmed cartridge examples are the venerable .30-30 WCF, .357 Magnum, .303 British, .32 Winchester Special and .45-70 Government.

Rimless

Rimless cartridges use a rim the same diameter as the case body, with a groove machined into the area just in front of the case head. Rimless cases headspace on either the cartridge shoulder (for a bottlenecked case) or the case mouth (for some straight-walled cases). The firearm's extractor grabs the case by the groove in front of the case head. This design greatly facilitates cartridge feeding from a spring-loaded magazine. These cartridges saw the light of day in the late 1880s. Some examples are the .308 Winchester, .30-06 Springfield, 5.56mm NATO, .45 ACP, .40 S&W, 7x57mm Mauser, and .25-06 Remington.

Semi-Rimmed

Possibly the rarest type, semi-rimmed have a very small amount of rim extending past the diameter of the case body, but not nearly as much as a rimmed case. They were designed for the positive headspacing capability of the rimmed cartridge, while coming close to achieving the ease of feeding from a magazine that the rimless cartridges possess. Examples of semi-rimmed cases are the .25 ACP and the .444 Marlin.

Rebated Rim

This is a case that uses a rim dimension smaller than the diameter of the case body, with the rim only serving the purpose of extraction. This is a feature seen on the Winchester Short Magnum series and the Remington Ultra Magnums, and is designed to have huge case capacity for high velocities. Other examples of rebated rim cartridges are the .50 Beowulf, .500 Jeffery, 6.5-284 Norma and .284 Winchester.

Belted Magnum

The belted magnum case dates back to 1910. It has a "belt" of raised brass ahead of the extractor groove, yet a case head designed similarly to the rimless cases. The theory behind this design was to provide easy feeding from a rifle's box magazine (a la rimless), while offering the positive headspacing from the rim, and not the shoulder (a la rimmed). The British firm of Holland & Holland first offered it in their .375 Velopex (which never caught on) and used it again in their .375 Belted Rimless Nitro-Express in 1912, better known as our African classic .375 H&H Magnum. This case led to the development of the Super .30, or .300 Holland & Holland Magnum in 1925, and it was this belted-case design that would be the basis for nearly every case that had "magnum" in its name, including the Weatherby line, until the Winchester Short Magnums and Remington Ultra Magnums came along at the turn of the 21st century. These newer magnum cases are primarily based on the beltless .404 Jeffery.

Case Capacity: How Much is Too Much?

As time goes by, and smokeless powder continues to develop slower burn rates, both the velocities and pressures of our cartridges continue to increase. It really doesn't matter what category of cartridges we are discussing, things are getting faster. The .17 Winchester Super Magnum in the rimfire world; the 6.5-300 Weatherby and .300 Remington Ultra Magnum in the medium centerfire realm; the .460 Smith & Wesson in the pistol department; one can easily see how the love affair with speed has not wavered in the least. But, there are circumstances where even though we've created a cartridge that has the potential for unprecedented velocity, we may have reached the point of diminishing returns. Obviously, to reach these unprecedented figures, you must use a considerable amount of slow burning powder. Can all that powder be burned in a barrel of manageable length? Does that powder charge generate such incredible pressures (recoil) that the average shooter will deem it unshootable?

I know for certain that some of the faster magnum cartridges—the .257 Weatherby being one of the culprits—will produce a visible 12- to 18-inch muzzle flame at high noon on a bright sunny day. That flame is produced, in part, by unburnt powder. I've seen the same thing from my .300 Winchester Magnum and factory loads that use lighter bullets at a high velocity; while the ammo was wonderfully accurate, it turned the rifle into a fire-breathing dragon. Now, that isn't necessarily a bad thing if the velocity/bullet combination is suitable for the job at hand, be it a game animal or distant bullseye, but there are certain caveats that must be addressed.

First, launching a bullet at velocities of about 3,300 fps or faster can have a significant effect on the throat and barrel of a rifle, especially if the shooter fires a number of shots in succession. Cartridges like the .264 Winchester Magnum, .26 Nosler, 6.5-300 Weatherby, .300 Remington Ultra Magnum and their ilk have been responsible for short barrel life, throat wear, and a reputation for a degradation of accuracy in less than 1,000 shots. I use some of these cartridges in hunting rifles (not target rifles), but I'm very careful to avoid heating the barrel excessively.

Additionally, in the search for flat trajectories and the highest velocities possible, powder consumption drastically increases. If you're shooting factory ammunition, this may be a moot point, but to the handloader it represents a serious increase in costs. Let's look at three differing .30 caliber cartridges, at three distinct levels of performance. We'll use the loads for a good old 180-grain bullet—a popular choice for big game—and powders that are well-suited to each cartridge. The .30-06 Springfield, which has long proven itself to be the benchmark of .30 caliber cartridges, uses just about 60 grains of suitable powder before the load becomes compressed and the grain structure of the powder runs the risk of being broken. Velocities run between 2,700 fps and 2,800 fps, depending on your rifle and chosen powder. The .300 Winchester Magnum, which has long represented the most you could get out of a standard long-action rifle (until the .30 Nosler came along) can cram just about 76 grains of powder before compression, giving velocities in the neighborhood of 3,050 fps to 3,100 fps—a definite increase in both velocity and trajectory. Bump up to the .300 Remington Ultra Magnum, and you'll easily run 95 grains of slow burning powder, with pressure becoming excessive before you're able to fill the case. The .300 RUM obtains velocities of up to 3,350 fps with that huge powder charge, but it's not hard to see why long shooting sessions with a cartridge like this will definitely heat up your barrel, as well as put a strain on a bullet as it jumps from the cartridge mouth into the rifling. With this class of cartridge, I prefer to keep my groups to three shots. If I'm getting serious about hunting accuracy, I allow the barrel to cool to ambient temperature between shots, to assess what the rifle will do with a cold barrel, which represents most of the hunting scenarios.

Does this mean that these cartridges are trouble? Or at least that they aren't worth the fuss? I don't think so, but you need to realize that the interior ballistics of these super-magnums can have an effect on the rifle, and that they need to be treated a bit differently than, say, a .308 Winchester or .35 Whelen.

Case Function and Interior Ballistics Effects

The brass cartridge case is nothing more than a combustion chamber. It is designed to withstand a prescribed amount of pressure when housed within the steel chamber of the rifle or pistol. That pressure, generated by the burning powder within the case, is what forces the bullet

The semi-rimmed .25ACP.

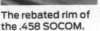
The rebated rim of the .458 SOCOM.

Belted magnums.

down the barrel. The case is subjected to the violent forces of the process and expands from the standard dimension to become a mirror of the firearm's chamber. If the pressures are too great, the case will become stuck in the chamber and will be difficult to extract. There are tell-tale signs of this scenario: primers that are flattened and/or cratered, where you can see the metal of the primer cup molded around the firing pin imprint, showing that the powder ignition created a pressure so great that the primer metal was violently pressed rearward toward the bolt face. You may see the brass of the case head flowing around the extractor of the bolt face; this is another indication of extreme pressures. Difficult extraction, as stated above, is an obvious sign that things are getting dangerous. Heck, I've seen people use a mallet to beat open a bolt-action rifle when using ammunition that reached dangerously high pressures.

For the best accuracy, things need to be uniform, and that includes the cartridge case and powder charge. In order to launch bullets in a uniform manner, you need to generate the most consistent pressures possible. If there are variations in the cartridge case dimensions, the size of the combustion chamber changes and the pressures (read velocities) will vary accordingly. Those pressure changes can result in a loss of accuracy, even if you do your part as a shooter. This is the idea behind match-grade cases; they strive to give the most uniform dimensions possible, to keep things consistent. Serious benchrest shooters tune their cartridge cases, turning the case necks to a constant dimension, reaming the flash holes to a uniform diameter, and use the best sizing dies so all the cases maintain a consistent configuration. If you shoot only factory ammunition, you're at the mercy of the production techniques of the manufacturer, but if you've experimented with Federal's Gold Medal Match line, Norma's wonderful ammunition, Nosler's Handloaded Series or the Hornady Match stuff, you've more than likely seen an increase in accuracy. Now, that's not to say that the traditional ammunition is inaccurate, but a more consistent production technique leads to a more uniform (accurate) product, all things being equal.

Load density within the case can have an effect on the accuracy of your chosen combination. While a heavily compressed load in a rifle case can break the grain structure and slightly vary the pressure—especially with an extruded stick powder—a load that best fills the case will provide the best accuracy. Again, there will be exceptions to this rule, but it's what I'm looking for as a handloader.

In a pistol case, it will be nearly impossible to fill the case, and as the cases are so much shorter than their rifle counterparts, the load density doesn't pose as great of an issue. The load density of factory loaded ammunition, which can and does use a blended powder mixture, is out of your control, and as the factories are loading ammo for a broad range of firearms, it's easy to understand why not every gun likes all types of ammunition (we'll get to this further when we discuss barrels and their harmonics).

Case Capacity and Pressure
Not all brass cartridge cases are created equal, and if you're a reloader you may already be familiar with this. If you're shooting factory ammunition, you'll want to experiment with different

types and brands to find what your gun likes best, preferably by obtaining a large quantity of that ammo from the same lot. That way you can keep things as uniform as possible.

If you reload, become a brass hoarder; every single empty cartridge should be snatched up for future use. As you develop your pet loads, closely following your recipe for all the accuracy you can muster, keep detailed notes regarding all of the components and their performance. On more than one occasion, I've had fellow reloaders tell me that a load that has worked well for a period of time has suddenly lost accuracy or sent a flier (a shot that prints out of the normal group size) without explanation. Or, the cartridge cases show signs of excess pressure, perhaps cratered primers, sticky extraction, or brass flowing around the extractor on the case head. And, quite often, the answer is a cartridge case of different brand, giving a different capacity. That difference in capacity yields a different pressure, and therefore a different velocity (in the case of a flier) or raises the pressure generated up to an unsafe level, should the case capacity be smaller than that with which the load was developed.

Again, as with all aspects of accuracy, uniformity is paramount. Many shooters that enjoy the popular military rifle calibers—5.56 NATO, 7.62 NATO and .30-06 Springfield—have access to surplus ammunition and brass cases. As a general rule of thumb, military brass cases are quite a bit thicker than sporting ammunition, and if you were to use the same powder charge that worked in a Federal case, for example, I wouldn't be shocked if you saw both a change in point of impact and possibly excessive pressures. For this reason, I keep all of my brass cases sorted by brand, and the nickel-plated cases separate from the plain brass variants.

I found out early on that nickel-plated cases show a change in point of impact when compared to brass cases, even if from the same manufacturer. I ran into this first when loading for my .300 Winchester Magnum before a caribou hunt. That particular rifle had given me very good accuracy over the years, so I was a bit confused when the rifle printed a ¾-inch group, but three inches high and right. At first, I simply figured the scope had been bumped, but I grabbed three rounds of brass-cased ammo to double check. That stuff drilled the bull, so there was nothing wrong with the scope. Three more nickel-cased rounds grouped where the first three had gone. I think that the nickel coating slightly reduced the case capacity, and increased the pressure and velocity, while still giving good accuracy.

I've had other instances where the nickel cases completely changed the accuracy of a rifle. My Legendary Arms Works Big Five rifle, chambered in .404 Jeffery, likes a particular load of Alliant's Reloder 15, printing three 400-grain Hornady DGX bullets into a 1.5-inch group at 100 yards when using Norma brass. That same load, in Nosler nickel-plated cases, opened up to 4 inches, which is completely unacceptable. Now, that's not to say that the Nosler cases are bad, but it does demonstrate that the load would need to be revised if I were to use that type of brass. Very small variations in case volume can dramatically affect downrange accuracy, and you should do your best to keep things as uniform as possible.

Again, when shooting factory ammo you are at the mercy of the company that loaded it, but through reloading can control many of the variables that affect both interior and exterior ballistics.

To Crimp or Not to Crimp?

I'm sure you've run across some ammunition where you've seen the very end of the case mouth rolled around a groove in the bullet. This is roll-crimping, a process designed to firmly hold the bullet in place, and in some instances, provide a bit of resistance to generate pressures. This is especially prevalent in straight-walled rifle and revolver cartridges. It works for any cartridge that doesn't use a square case mouth for headspacing, as do many pistol cartridges. In the instance of the rimless pistol cases, like the 9mm Luger, .40 Smith & Wesson, and .45 ACP (among others), the case mouth must not be rolled over, as it's used to properly headspace the ammunition; instead, a taper crimp must be employed. Taper crimping involves squeezing the sidewalls of the case tightly around the bullet to prevent it from moving in or out of the cartridge case during the violent chambering operation of an autoloading pistol.

There are instances where you may see a bottlenecked rifle cartridge use a roll crimp, and that's fine, as long as you're consistent. Personally, if the case has enough neck tension to properly hold a bullet in the case, I generally don't crimp, as it really works the brass case and diminishes the amount of times it can be reloaded. But, for our purposes here, know that a heavy roll crimp can and will increase pressure, so observe your factory ammo to make sure things are consistent. If you're rolling your own, make a decision whether to crimp or not, and stick with it.

As an example, when making .44 Magnum ammunition I've seen a crimp die come out of adjustment and put a very heavy crimp on the case mouth. This became painfully evident when the revolver was putting bullets all over the target. We inspected the ammo and made a correction, and the Model 29 was back delivering the fantastic groups we knew it was capable of producing. There is a delicate balance between enough crimp to prevent the projectile from extending out of the case mouth (and preventing the cylinder from spinning), and excessive crimp that creates a pressure issue.

Indeed, the form and style of the cartridge case will affect performance once things get ignited.

Traditional Boxer-primed cartridge.

Flash Holes: Boxer v. Berdan

Almost all American ammunition uses a centralized flash hole, or what we refer to as a Boxer cartridge. You'll find some European cartridges that use an offset, multi-holed design to deliver the spark into the powder charge, known as a Berdan cartridge. While it really doesn't matter to a shooter who uses only factory ammunition, it is of particular importance to reloaders, as the Boxer cartridge is easily reloadable, yet the Berdan configuration is a much more difficult matter. Ironically, the Boxer design is a European development, while the Berdan hails from America. It is a mystery how things seem to have gotten switched around.

Berdan primer flash hole.

CHAPTER 3

The Projectile

That small blob of metal we call the bullet gets so little of the glory, yet does such a huge percentage of the work. Whether it's a round lead ball like those used by our forefathers, a cup-and-core jacketed bullet, or a monometal design that seems futuristic, the bullet—and only the bullet—is what gets the job done. There are a multitude of designs and construction methods, some of which have a definite effect on interior ballistics and play a role in the way your chosen cartridge performs within the bounds of the firearm.

Let's look at a couple of terms that will be important to us as we examine these projectiles. Firstly, we need to know a bullet's sectional density, or SD. The sectional density of a bullet is nothing more, and nothing less, than a mathematical figure that represents the ratio of a bullet's weight to its diameter. The actual formula is this: The bullet's weight (in pounds) is divided by the bullet's diameter (in inches) squared.

$$SD = \text{Bullet weight in pounds} \div \text{Bullet diameter in inches}^2$$

Because bullets are measured in grains, you need to convert to pounds by dividing by 7,000, as there are 7,000 grains in a pound. For example, to derive the sectional density of a .308 caliber 180-grain projectile, divide 180 by 7,000, yielding a weight in pounds of 0.02571. Then square the diameter of 0.308 to get a figure of 0.09486. Divide the first figure by the second to arrive at a sectional density figure of 0.27103 or, as it is commonly represented out to three decimal places, 0.271. This figure has a large effect on the exterior and terminal phases of the bullet's flight, and relevancy in correlating the length of a bullet to its diameter as we look at the amount of bearing surface that will be engaging the rifling. Of course, at that point in time the design of the bullet comes into play, thus understanding sectional density is important.

Secondly, every bullet has a ballistic coefficient, or BC. This is a mathematical figure used to describe how well a bullet will resist atmospheric drag and the effects of crosswind. It is a figure typically represented by a decimal less than one, but in extreme cases above one, that represents a comparison to one or more standard bullet models. Ballistic coefficient, generally speaking, is the ratio of a bullet's sectional density to its coefficient of form. This math is long and drawn out and will come into play much more once our metallic hero leaves the muzzle, but for most applications the listed BC will suffice.

Anatomy of a Bullet

You should become familiar with bullet design, so you can understand which parts make a difference in performance once they are put into action. A bullet's nose—or meplat, (pronounced *mee-plah*), French for 'flat'—comes in a variety of designs: pointed, round, flat, hollow, etc. The ogive of the bullet is the transitionary section where the meplat turns into the bearing surface at caliber dimension. Sometimes the ogive is a straight line, as in the case of a truncated cone pistol bullet, but most often it's a curve of some

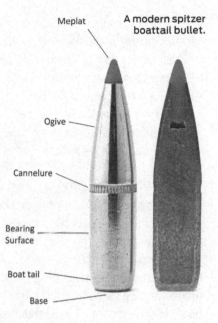

Meplat

A modern spitzer boattail bullet.

Ogive

Cannelure

Bearing Surface

Boat tail

Base

sort. The bullet's bearing surface, or shank is comprised of two parallel sides at specific caliber dimension, and it is this section of the projectile that engages the rifling of the barrel. The heel and base of the bullet finish out the design and can range from a square, flat arrangement, to one of the sleek, tapered boattail designs that will resist atmospheric interference best. Knowing the anatomy allows you to choose which type of bullet will work best for your particular shooting needs.

These .308 caliber bullets—150 grains on the left, 180 on the right—clearly demonstrate the difference in sectional density.

The Construction Zone

A bullet's makeup will definitely affect its ability to perform. And its construction is an important factor when considering interior ballistics. For example, a hardcast lead bullet can be pushed to a velocity of around 1,800 fps before things start to fall apart; the lead isn't hard enough to take the rifling and spin at that rate, so it sort of skids down the barrel. Performance becomes erratic, and the smeared lead in your bore becomes an issue quickly.

Put a copper jacket around that lead bullet, and you can increase velocity dramatically. Yes, I've seen some copper cup lead-core projectiles come apart from extremely high muzzle velocities (we couldn't figure out why the bullets weren't hitting the 100-yard target, until we saw the bark missing on a tree 15 yards down range) but they are rather strong and can handle most sane velocities. Copper is a harder material than lead, yet is still soft enough to allow the steel rifling to impart the proper spin on the bullet. A copper jacket, or cup, also helps to slow down expansion upon impact, but that will be discussed in the terminal ballistics section. What we are concerned about here is that a jacketed bullet, or as I prefer to call them a 'cup-and-core bullet, can withstand much higher velocities than a lead bullet.

Should that cup-and-core bullet have its core chemically bonded to the jacket, all the better. Should it be an all-copper monometal design, there's even less worry of jacket separation, because there is no jacket to separate during the trip down the barrel.

The Shapes of Things

Form is extremely important when considering interior ballistics. The bullet's shape will definitely affect the amount of pressure built, the way it engages the rifling in the throat section of the barrel, and how the bullet will feed from a magazine. There are a multitude of profile shapes when it comes to today's bullets. And these profiles will come into play with regard to interior and exterior ballistics. There are models, set as the benchmark standards, which will be used to describe the bullet in flight. However, even before unguided flight begins (read in the barrel, or interior ballistics), these standard shapes will give an idea as to how things will go.

Let's take a look at some of the popular bullet profiles so we can identify and get a feel for their effects. That way, we'll be familiar with them for all phases of the shot.

Round Nose

Round-nose bullets are aptly named, for they feature a round (hemispherical) or rounded nose profile. Almost all round-nose bullets are flat-based, meaning the shank of the bullet meets the base at a right angle. This style of bullet is popular in auto-loading pistols and big-bore safari rifles, as the nose profile isn't exactly the best for retaining energy and velocity at longer ranges, but feeds very well and hits with authority.

Flat Nose

Flat-nose bullets are defined by a flat, blunted meplat. They work very well in most handguns as their effective range tends to be short (in relation to the high-powered rifles). This style of bullet is also popular in many of the lever-action rifles with tubular magazines, as the flat point eliminates the possibility of a magazine detonation caused by a pointed bullet striking the primer of the cartridge in front of it. Again, many of the lever guns are short- to mid-range affairs, so there isn't a huge limiting factor with a flat-nosed bullet.

Spitzer

Derived from the German word *spitzgeschoss*—literally meaning pointed projectile—spitzers have a flat base with a nose profile that terminates in a pointed end; the transition from the shank or bearing surface to the end is a curve. Such bullets were one of the first designs that attempted to maximize velocity and energy figures. The spitzer design will cut through the atmosphere much more efficiently than will a flat- or round-nose projectile. While there are some spitzer bullets designed to be used in the larger bore revolvers, spitzers are generally reserved for rifles.

Boattail

Ballistic experiments dating back to the end of the 19th century observed that a spitzer bullet's effectiveness improves when used in conjunction with a boattail, which allows the air to flow more easily around the bullet in flight. Used primarily in conjunction with a spitzer nose profile (though Peregrine Bullets from South Africa makes some excellent dangerous game flat-nosed bullets that use a boattail) to make the ultimate aerodynamic design, the spitzer boattail is highly popular with the long-range target and hunting crowd.

Truncated Cone

Self-defining, the truncated cone bullet uses an ogive profile that doesn't curve, but features the straight line of a cone, terminating in a flat meplat, hence truncated. These bullets are popular in pistol cartridges, as well as in cast lead bullets for rifles. They work well in that all lead configuration, as well as the full metal jacket style.

Wadcutter

Wadcutters are a purely cylindrical bullet, being square at the ends, and are designed for cutting perfect holes in paper targets. The wadcutters score targets very easily. They are rather inexpensive and among the simplest to produce. Typically reserved for revolvers, these square-nosed bullets don't really feed well in any of the autoloaders, but work just fine in a revolver's cylinder. The wadcutter is sometimes employed as a defensive bullet style, giving all sorts of frontal diameter, yet not diminishing exterior ballistics when used in short-barreled revolvers like my sweetheart Smith & Wesson Model 36 in .38 Special.

Semi-wadcutter

Blending the simplicity of the wadcutter design with a truncated cone or a slightly curved ogive, semi-wadcutters make a good choice for an all-around bullet for handgun hunters and shooters. The famous 'Keith' bullet, which was popularized by gun writer Elmer Keith, features a flat nose of 70 percent caliber dimension, and a curved ogive—in order to keep the bullet's weight forward—meeting almost all the requirements for an all-around bullet for the target shooter, hunter and plinker alike. I've seen these bullets perform very well in revolvers and autoloaders, as well as rifles and carbines that were chambered for pistol cartridges.

Hollowpoint

The idea of reducing weight by hollowing out the nose portion of the bullet, which also enhances expansion, dates back to the 19th century and still holds water today. The hollowpoint

The Nosler Ballistic Tip, a modern cup-and-core bullet design, using a polymer tip.

bullet is a staple in the industry in both pistol and rifle communities, for equally different reasons. The handgun folks truly appreciate and rely upon the radical expansion and threat-stopping capabilities of the hollowpoint pistol bullet, as do varmint hunters looking to create the red mist, while the rifle target crowd absolutely loves the accuracy and aerodynamics of the hollowpoint spitzer boattails.

Whichever feature you employ or enjoy, the hollowpoint bullet is one that is here to stay. It gives great expansion for good terminal ballistics, and is among the most accurate designs available. I suppose you could include the polymer-tipped bullets in this group, as the general gist is that the hollowpoint has been filled with a polymer tip (both to increase the ballistic coefficient and to initiate expansion) yet the goal still remains the same: to provide accurate, precise shot placement and generate all sorts of expansion.

Comparing and contrasting these bullet profiles will demonstrate the different applications for the various types. There is a tool for every job, and a job for every tool. Each design has its advantages and its weaknesses, and depending on your shooting requirements, you may choose to employ several, if not all of these designs.

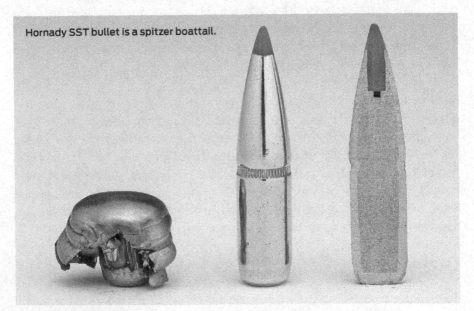

Hornady SST bullet is a spitzer boattail.

Take for example a bullet that's .308 caliber, 180 grains, with a flat base and a round-nose design. If you were to compare it to a flat-base spitzer, you could easy see how and why there would be less bearing surface on the sharp bullet—the bullet needs to interrupt the bearing surface to make room for the long, sharp nose. Again, look at a spitzer bullet, but this time put a boattail on it, and you can see how the bearing surface (that portion of the bullet which engages the rifling) is further reduced based on the design itself, in turn affecting the pressure data.

Even closer scrutiny will reveal that when looking at the most aerodynamic designs—bullets scientifically engineered to provide the least amount of air drag possible—you'll find that the nose profile curve that gives the least resistance may not be the profile curve that behaves the best between chamber and muzzle. So, you need a balance of performance between interior and exterior ballistics. In other words, it's no good having a bullet that defies the effects of gravity and wind drift if it doesn't give repeatable results (accuracy) that allow the shooter to actually hit the target.

When you look at those models or benchmarks that verily define ballistic capability, and compare them with the projectiles available for the calibers and cartridges you own, it will help you make an educated decision regarding the range of projectiles for your hunting and shooting applications. These models are known commonly as the G1 and G7 models; G1 being a flat-base spitzer bullet, while the G7 is a more modern, sleek design that correlates to the latest developments in bullet technology. It's like comparing a Ferrari coupe to a box truck. One would yield one set of data, which would seem radically impressive, yet if we put that Ferrari in its own class—say compare it to the Corvette design—the discrepancy won't be so dramatic, but will be much more accurately represented.

A round-nose Woodleigh Weldcore in the .318 Westley Richards.

These bullets are 200-grain flat points in .348 Winchester.

The truncated cone projectile.

Hollowpoint bullets are extremely popular in modern handgun cartridges.

You'll find that most bullet companies tend to reference the G1 model; it's universal and easily understood. That model, when used as a reference, yields impressive figures that work well in the marketing department. Any which way you want to slice it, when you compare these benchmark figures to the bullet you're using, it will indeed give you a feel for both interior and exterior ballistics. Longer bullets with better BC figures invariably take up more space in a cartridge case with a SAAMI-specified overall length dimension. That factor will eat up case capacity and needs to be balanced out when it comes to manageable pressures.

However, longer bullets give a desirable effect once they leave the barrel, but that's for later. In the interior ballistics world, the longer, sleeker bullets come with a particular set of issues that should be understood. The ogive of such bullets, for reasons we will be examining in the exterior ballistics section, is typically of a secant curve profile, instead of the tangent ogive of the G1 model. Such are known as VLD, or Very Low Drag bullets. While VLDs fly through air better than their tangent curve counterparts, they don't engage the rifling as well. Berger's Hybrid line of bullets, designed by ballistician Bryan Litz, use a blend of secant curve from the nose through a good portion of the ogive, yet transition into a tangent curve to best guide the bullet into the throat of the barrel.

The same thing can be said for the boattail angle of the bullet. Looking at the interior section of the bullet's path, a boattail has a base that is a measurable dimension smaller than caliber, and the burning gas from the powder charge surrounds the base of the bullet up to the bearing surface. If, as I've had happen in some of my rifles, this gas doesn't exit equally around the muzzle or crown of the barrel, accuracy can be affected. Should the crown be imperfect, gas will escape faster on one edge of the circle than the others and you'll see inaccurate results in as little as 100 yards. It's certainly not the boattail bullet's fault, and these symptoms can actually be masked by a flat-based bullet. However, as in the case of my Ruger .22-250, a re-crown will solve the problem.

As the boattail angle becomes steeper, the internal problem can get magnified; just as well as the benefits can be magnified on the opposite end of the muzzle. Again, while the long-range shooting crowd relies on a low drag, steeply boat-tailed bullet to flatten trajectory and retain velocity, it does come with a set of issues that must be dealt with in order to make things work properly.

This is the very dilemma that many hunters will face: while the long-range style bullet certainly shines for shots out past 300 yards, sometimes a flat-base bullet would better serve your needs, especially in the hunting fields. Again, a tool for every job, and a job for every tool. I like a flat-base bullet, which will seal the gas best and keep things as equal as possible, for shots within 300 yards; this comprises about 95 percent of my hunting shots. For my long-range work, I totally rely on the multitude of spitzer boattails to make things go easier.

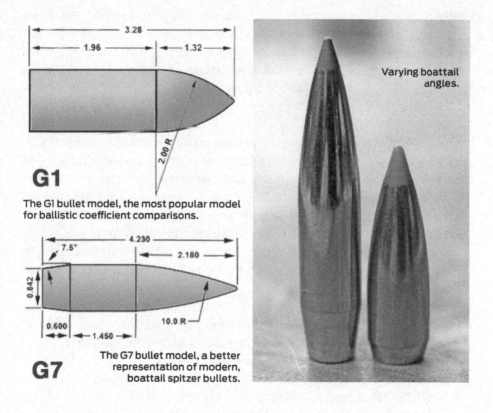

Varying boattail angles.

G1

The G1 bullet model, the most popular model for ballistic coefficient comparisons.

G7

The G7 bullet model, a better representation of modern, boattail spitzer bullets.

CHAPTER 4
The Ignition System

The spark and fuel system of a cartridge case can make or break accuracy. The primers and powders of today are the most reliable and consistent we shooters have ever had. The primer, seated in the center of the cartridge case head of centerfire cartridges, or in the case rim of rimfire cartridges, uses a chemical compound that delivers a shower of sparks through the flash hole when struck by the firing pin.

Primer Styles

There are two types of centerfire primers for our purposes: rifle primers and pistol primers. Each variety comes in large and small sizes and each size has a hotter spark magnum variant. Rifle primers have a thicker metal cup due to the higher pressures at which they operate. Pistols operate at much lower pressures, and therefore, the primer cups are thinner. Large rifle and large pistol primers are 0.210 inches in diameter, while small rifle and small pistol primers are 0.175 inches. I've heard the myth of a "medium" primer, made by the Frankfort Arsenal in Pennsylvania, which is said to measure 0.204 inches, but I've never seen one with my own eyes. Col. Townsend Whelen refers to these being used in the early .45ACP cartridges, but for our purposes they are a moot point.

The designation of primers can be confusing. If you handload your ammunition, you must make a habit of checking and double checking your reloading manual so you have the right ones for the ammunition you are loading. Here are some examples of primer nomenclature:

- Large Rifle: CCI 200, Federal 210, Remington 9 ½, Winchester WLR
- Large Rifle Magnum: CCI 250, Federal 215, Remington 9 ½ M, Winchester WLRM
- Small Rifle: CCI 400, Federal 205, Remington 6 ½, Winchester WSR
- Small Rifle Magnum: CCI 450, Federal 250M, Remington 7 ½
- Large Pistol: CCI 300, Federal 150, Remington 2 ½, Winchester WLP,
- Large Pistol Magnum: CCI 350, Federal 155, Winchester WLPM
- Small Pistol: CCI 500, Federal 100, Remington 1 ½, Winchester WSP
- Small Pistol Magnum: CCI 550, Federal 200, Remington 5 ½, Winchester WSPM

There are also several varieties of match primers available, giving the most consistent results, which are readily embraced by the target shooting community. For example, the Federal 210 Large Rifle primer is available in match form, as the GM210M, or Gold Medal 210 Match primer. Several companies produce military primers, which have the thickest cups; these are designed for use in the AR platform and other military-type rifles and are made to military specifications. The CCI 34 (large rifle) and CCI 41 (small rifle) are two examples. These primers are designed to avoid a slam fire infrequently associated with the protruding firing pins found on some military firearms.

As mentioned, always use the type of primer called for in the reloading manual you are using, as a change in primers can result in a change in pressure. It is also a good idea to have only one type of primer on your reloading bench at one time to avoid any confusion and a possibly dangerous situation at the bench.

So, these little wonders are the first spark in the chain of combustion events that cause a bullet to be launched. The spark is created by the reaction of lead, barium nitrate and other chemical compounds being struck against the anvil located in the primer cup. This explosion sends sparks through the flash hole and into the powder charge. The first percussion cap used in the muzzleloading rifles of the mid-19th century needed to be struck against an anvil, in this case the nipple on the percussion lock. The modern configuration of primers for centerfire cartridges feature a self-contained anvil within the primer assembly. Years ago, the priming compound contained fulminate of mercury, a corrosive substance.

Large rifle primer.

A large rifle magnum primer in the case head of a .375 H&H Magnum.

Care must be taken when firing old (WWII-era or earlier) military ammunition. While commercial sporting ammunition made the switch to non-mercuric primers around the turn of the 20th century, the U.S. military did not make the official switch until after the Second World War. If you use this type of ammunition, be sure to clean your rifle with a good solvent after shooting it. When my pal Kevin Hicks first bought his sweetheart .30-06, we had a surplus of WWII military ammunition on hand for practice and sighting in. After taking the rifle to the range, he decided to clean it several days later. He could barely fit a patch down the bore because of the corrosion caused by those old primers. Hours of scrubbing and brushing later, he had things back in order and he was concerned about the condition of the bore. That was the last time we shot them without cleaning immediately! Thankfully, today's primers are non-corrosive.

Certain types of factory ammunition—Federal comes quickly to mind—use a primer sealant to prevent any moisture from making its way into the combustion chamber. While it certainly doesn't hurt, I've never personally used a sealant on any of my ammo, and (knock on wood) I've never had any issues.

Powder, the Fuel System

The burning powder charge is what generates the pressure that drives your bullet out of the cartridge case and down the barrel. The smell of burning powder is among my favorite scents; it brings me back to my youth, spending time with my father, learning to shoot. In order to better understand how the different types of powder affect the performance of your firearm, let's look at the history of this amazing stuff.

Friar Roger Bacon was the first European to record the mixture for gunpowder in the 13th century, although it is a widely held belief that Chinese culture had it long before that. Regardless, that blissful blend of sulphur, charcoal and saltpeter called blackpowder certainly changed the world. It ruined the effectiveness of metal armor, diminished the security of the castle, and leveled the playing field between strong, brave soldiers and their more diminutive counterparts.

Blackpowder has not really changed in its makeup over the last century and is still going strong. However, it burns dirty and leaves a corrosive residue throughout the bore, which must be removed quickly to prevent rusting and pitting. There are cleaner burning substitutes available that have made the job of cleanup easier. Blackhorn 209, as well as Hodgdon's Pyrodex and 777 are among these. Blackpowder is generally measured by volume, not weight, and the substitutes are measured this way as well. It's graded and identified by the coarseness or fineness of the granules. Fg is the very coarse cannon and shotgun powder, FFg and FFFg are more fine and used in many rifles and pistols, and the finest, FFFFg is typically reserved for priming the flintlock action.

Progress was made in the scientific field of powder in the 1840s, when nitric acid was put upon cellulose to produce nitrocellulose. This was known as gun cotton. It was capable of producing pressures and velocities much greater than blackpowder, and it took time to develop steel that could withstand the pressures generated. Later, in 1887, Alfred Nobel invented nitroglycerine. When mixed with nitrocellulose, this created a plasticized substance that was a stable compound. Cordite, an early British version, was the propellant du jour for many of our classic cartridges. One of cordite's little peculiarities was the fact that it was extremely sensitive to temperature fluctuation. Those cartridges that were developed in England and Continental Europe often had pressure increases when brought to steaming hot Africa and India. The heat of the Tropics quickly brought out the flaws of cordite, from extraction troubles to cracked receivers and this is why some of the huge cases like the .416 Rigby and the .470 Nitro Express came about. They needed that volume to keep the pressure low.

Modern single- and double-base smokeless powders have resolved that issue, and the temperature sensitivity has been diminished greatly. Single-base powders are comprised mostly of nitrocellulose. Double-base is a mixture of nitrocellulose and nitroglycerine. The powder is coated with a deterrent and a stabilizer. The deterrent slows the burn rate to a desired amount, and the stabilizer slows down the self-decomposition of the compound. Taking things even further, Hodgdon—which produces smokeless powder under their own brand, as well as IMR and Winchester—recently introduced the 'Enduron' line of powders, which have been engineered to provide very uniform burn rates to minimize the effects of temperature fluctuation upon muzzle velocities. I've used these powders in temperatures ranging from single digits, up to 112°F in Africa, and they've performed flawlessly.

Powder Structures and Nomenclature

The shape of the powder granules can be one of three types—flake, stick and spherical. Flake powder is shaped like miniature pancakes. Many shotgun and pistol powders are in this configuration, and some contain color-coded flakes. Alliant's Green-Dot, Bullseye and Unique are three examples of flake powder.

Stick powder is one of the most popular shapes in rifle propellant. The compound is extruded into long spaghetti-like rods and is cut to the desired length. Examples of stick powder include IMR 4064, IMR 4350, IMR 4451, Hodgdon's Varget and H4831SC, and Alliant Reloder 25.

Spherical powder is a round ball, or a slightly flattened round ball. It takes up less space than stick powder and can help achieve good velocities in a case with limited capacity. Some of the spherical powders include Hodgdon's H380 and BL-C(2), Winchester's 760, and Accurate Powder's No. 9.

Powder is measured in *grains*, not to be confused with grams, a metric unit of weight. There are 7,000 grains to the pound. Depending on the cartridge being loaded (and especially pistol cartridges), a variation of as little as 1/10th of a grain can make the difference between a safely loaded cartridge and a dangerous one that produces excessive pressures. IT IS IMPERATIVE THAT YOU STRICTLY ADHERE TO THE LOAD DATA PUBLISHED BY REPUTABLE MANUFACTURERS! I cannot stress that point enough. The various reloading manuals are a product of months or years of pressure testing under strict laboratory conditions and an attempt to exceed the published values can result in your untimely demise. Start at the published minimum charge weight, and carefully increase the charge, stopping when you see the first sign of excessive pressure.

The powders available to the handloader are referred to as canister grade. They are each unique in their burn rate. Fast-burning powders are (generally) used in shotshells, small-case rifle cartridges and many of the pistol cartridges. The medium burn rate cartridges work well in standard rifle cartridges and some of the bigger caliber magnums. The newly developed slow-burning powders really shine in the huge overbore cases. Velocity kings like the .30-378 Weatherby, 7mm STW, .338 Remington Ultra Magnum and .338 Lapua all develop their high speeds from very slow-burning powders that develop the high pressure necessary to push bullets fast.

Today's powders go by many different names, and it can be confusing, bordering upon dangerous. Some are just names like Bullseye, TiteGroup, Varget, Red Dot or Unique. Others are just numbers, such as (Accurate Arms) No. 5, (Winchester) 760 and 748. Yet others still are a combination, such as IMR 7828, H380, N160, Reloder 15, etc. It is important that you are well versed in powder nomenclature to avoid confusion and possible injury. An example: There are three different powders, from three different manufacturers that contain '4350' in their name. IMR 4350 (Improved Military Rifle), H4350 (Hodgdon) and AA4350 (Accurate Arms), and all have slightly different burn rates AND ARE NOT INTERCHANGEABLE. Strict attention must be paid to ensure that you have the right powder called for by the reloading manual. This rule must be followed.

Storing powder is not a big deal. Common sense should prevail. It should be stored in a cool place, with no risk of open flame and far away from children. I store my powder in a clearly labeled wooden box with a lockable lid. You never want to store it in a container that will contain pressure; in the event of a fire powder that is not under pressure will burn rapidly, but put it under pressure and you've made a bomb. A gun safe is the absolute wrong idea for storage. Always store powder in its original canister; never try to relabel another container. I mark the date of purchase and the date I opened the canister, so I can use the powder in the order in which it was purchased.

Choosing a powder can be time-consuming. Often, reloading manuals will offer several selections per cartridge/bullet combination, sometimes highlighting or recommending the powder *that worked best in their test rifle or pistol*. All barrels are different, and while the most accurate load in the manual may work well in your firearm, sometimes you may need to experiment. Not all manuals test every powder that would be suitable for your cartridge, so inevitably you will end up owning more than one manual.

Some powders can be used in many different applications. For example, among pistol cases I use Unique and TiteGroup in many different cartridges, from 9mm Luger to .45 Long Colt. The .308 Winchester is the first cartridge I learned to reload. My Dad, Grumpy Pants, insisted that a 165-grain bullet on top of IMR 4064 was the only way to go, and anything else was blasphemy. In his world, at that time, there was no other powder, or cartridge for that matter. I have used IMR 4064 (because we had a ton of it!) in .22-250 Remington, .243 Winchester, 6.5x55 Swedish, .270 Winchester, 7x57 Mauser, .308 Winchester, .30-06 Springfield, .300 Winchester Magnum,

.375 H&H Magnum and my sweetheart .416 Remington Magnum. This doesn't mean it's the only powder that will work, nor the best powder in each of those cartridges. It just means that it is a powder which has a wide range of applications.

Conversely, a single cartridge may be served well by a large number of different powders. The venerable .30-06 Springfield, that classic of classics, can be fed a wide range of powders, with innumerable burn rates, and still provide great results. For example, depending upon bullet weight, the following powders are well-suited for use in the .30-06: IMR 3031, IMR 4064, IMR 4320, IMR 4350, IMR 4895, IMR 7828; Hodgdon VARGET, H414, H380, H4350 and BL-C(2); Alliant Reloder 15, Reloder 17, Reloder 19, Reloder 22, Reloder 25 and 4000-MR; Winchester 748, and 760, you get the idea. There are many like it. Read the manuals and choose wisely. It may take several attempts before you find that accuracy you so desire.

Burn Rates and Interior Ballistics

Not all gunpowder burns at the same rate. One quick glance at a burn rate chart will reveal that there are many different powders, for many different applications. Factory-loaded ammunition may or may not use a canister-grade powder; some of the companies use a blend of powders to achieve higher velocities; this is something that reloaders must not do, as the factories have developed this practice under strict laboratory conditions, and any attempt at blending powder types by a reloader is begging disaster. The canister grade powders should suffice to achieve your goals. While it is often difficult to match or exceed the factory loaded ammunition's velocities, the uniformity of handloaded ammunition can often lead to an increase in accuracy.

The large, fast cartridges—for example, the .30-378 Weatherby Magnum, .300 Remington Ultra Magnum and the 7mm STW—begin to shine when using the slowest burning powders, which generate the highest velocities. These cartridges will also perform best when using a longer barrel, say 26 inches or more, in order to burn as much of the huge powder charge as possible, generating the highest velocities for which they have been chosen. The term overbore is used to describe a cartridge that may not be able to burn its powder charge within a barrel length common to that cartridge. As an example, my pal Dave deMoulpied has a .257 Weatherby Magnum that will produce a visible flame at the muzzle of about 12 inches, even at noon on a sunny day. While the .257 Weatherby is certainly a flat-shooting, hard-hitting cartridge, the case may be classified as having a powder charge too large to be burned in the 26-inch barrel. That doesn't make it a bad cartridge, but it's fair to say that it isn't one of the more efficient designs.

Burn Rate Chart

Ultimately, what you're looking for from your firearm is accuracy, and accuracy is most definitely a product of uniformity. Taking the shooter out of the equation, I like my gear to operate as best as possible, making me the weak link in the chain. Accuracy is also obtained through repeatability, and that requires all things to be as equal as possible for every shot. Some of my

Table 4-1 RELATIVE BURN RATES FROM FASTEST TO SLOWEST *(Rev. Nov '23)*

#	Powder	#	Powder
1	Norma R1	48	VIHTAVUORI N350
2	VIHTAVUORI N310	49	VIHTAVUORI 3N38
3	ALLIANT EXTRA-LITE	50	WINCHESTER 572
4	ACCURATE NITRO 100	51	ALLIANT BLUE DOT
5	ALLIANT e3	52	ACCURATE NO. 7
6	HODGDON PERFECT PATTERN	53	ALLIANT PRO REACH
7	HODGDON TITEWAD	54	HODGDON LONGSHOT
8	RAMSHOT COMPETITION	55	ALLIANT 410
9	ALLIANT RED DOT	56	ACCURATE TCM
10	ALLIANT PROMO	57	ALLIANT 2400
11	HODGDON CLAYS	58	RAMSHOT ENFORCER
12	ALLIANT CLAY DOT	59	VIHTAVUORI N105
13	HODGDON HI-SKOR 700-X	60	ACCURATE NO. 9
14	ALLIANT BULLSEYE	61	ACCURATE 4100
15	ALLIANT SPORT PISTOL	62	ALLIANT STEEL
16	HODGDON HIGH GUN	63	NORMA R123
17	HODGDON TITEGROUP	64	VIHTAVUORI N110
18	ALLIANT AMERICAN SELECT	65	HODGDON LIL' GUN
19	ACCURATE SOLO 1000	66	HODGDON H110
20	ALLIANT GREEN DOT	67	WINCHESTER 296
21	RAMSHOT TRUE BLUE	68	ACCURATE #11 FS
22	WINCHESTER WST	69	IMR 4227
23	HODGDON TRAIL BOSS	70	ALLIANT POWER PRO 300-MP
24	WINCHESTER SUPER HANDICAP	71	ACCURATE 5744
25	HODGDON INTERNATIONAL	72	ACCURATE 1680
26	VIHTAVUORI N320	73	ACCURATE LT-30
27	ACCURATE NO.2	74	HODGDON CFE BLK
28	RAMSHOT ZIP	75	NORMA 200
29	HODGDON HP-38	76	ACCURATE 2200
30	WINCHESTER 231	77	ALLIANT RELODER 7
31	ALLIANT 20/28	78	ACCURATE LT-32
32	VIHTAVUORI N32C - TIN STAR	79	IMR 4198
33	WINCHESTER 244	80	HODGDON H4198
34	ALLIANT UNIQUE	81	VIHTAVUORI N120
35	HODGDON UNIVERSAL	82	NORMA 201
36	ALLIANT POWER PISTOL	83	ALLIANT POWER PRO 1200-R
37	VIHTAVUORI N330	84	VIHTAVUORI N130
38	ALLIANT HERCO	85	HODGDON H322
39	WINCHESTER WSF	86	ACCURATE 2015BR
40	VIHTAVUORI N340	87	ALLIANT RELODER 10X
41	ALLIANT BE-86	88	IMR 3031
42	ACCURATE NO. 5	89	VIHTAVUORI N133
43	HODGDON HS-6	90	HODGDON BENCHMARK
44	WINCHESTER AUTOCOMP	91	HODGDON H335
45	HODGDON CFE PISTOL	92	RAMSHOT X-TERMINATOR
46	RAMSHOT SILHOUETTE	93	ACCURATE 2230
47	VIHTAVUORI 3N37	94	ACCURATE 2460

95	IMR 8208 XBR
96	ALLIANT AR COMP
97	RAMSHOT TAC
98	ALLIANT POWER PRO VARMINT
99	HODGDON H4895
100	VIHTAVUORI N530
101	IMR 4895
102	VIHTAVUORI N135
103	ALLIANT RELODER 12
104	ACCURATE 2495
105	IMR 4166
106	IMR 4064
107	NORMA 202
108	ACCURATE 4064
109	ACCURATE 2520
110	ALLIANT RELODER 15
111	NORMA 203B
112	VIHTAVUORI N140
113	HODGDON VARGET
114	WINCHESTER 748
115	WINCHESTER StaBALL Match
116	HODGDON BL-C(2)
117	VIHTAVUORI N540
118	HODGDON CFE 223
119	ALLIANT RELODER 15.5
120	ALLIANT POWER PRO 2000-MR
121	HODGDON LEVEREVOLUTION
122	HODGDON H380
123	RAMSHOT BiG GAME
124	VIHTAVUORI N150
125	ALLIANT POWER PRO 4000-MR
126	WINCHESTER 760
127	ACCURATE 2700
128	NORMA URP
129	VIHTAVUORI N550
130	IMR 4350
131	IMR 4451
132	ALLIANT RELODER 16
133	HODGDON H4350
134	ALLIANT RELODER 17
135	ACCURATE 4350
136	NORMA 204
137	HODGDON HYBRID 100V
138	WINCHESTER StaBALL 6.5
139	HODGDON SUPERFORMANCE
140	ALLIANT RELODER 19
141	IMR 4831

142	RAMSHOT HUNTER
143	VIHTAVUORI N160
144	VIHTAVUORI N555
145	NORMA 205
146	HODGDON H4831 & H4831SC
147	VIHTAVUORI N560
148	IMR 4955
149	NORMA MRP
150	ALLIANT RELODER 22
151	NORMA MRP2
152	ALLIANT RELODER 23
153	VIHTAVUORI N165
154	IMR 7828SC
155	ALLIANT RELODER 25
156	VIHTAVUORI N565
157	VIHTAVUORI N170
158	ACCURATE MAGPRO
159	IMR 7977
160	ALLIANT RELODER 26
161	HODGDON H1000
162	RAMSHOT GRAND
163	NORMA 217
164	HODGDON RETUMBO
165	WINCHESTER StaBALL HD
166	IMR 8133
167	VIHTAVUORI N568
168	RAMSHOT LRT
169	VIHTAVUORI N570
170	ALLIANT RELODER 33
171	VIHTAVUORI 24N41
172	HODGDON H50BMG
173	HODGDON US869
174	ALLIANT RELODER 50
175	VIHTAVUORI 20N29

Hodgdon Brand Powders
IMR Brand Powders
Winchester Brand Powders
Accurate Brand Powders
Ramshot Brand Powders
Alliant Brand Powders
Vihtavuori Brand Powders
Norma Brand Powders

most accurate rifles and ammunition have one thing in common: the muzzle velocities, when measured with an accurate chronograph, have a very low standard deviation. For example, my Savage Model 116, chambered in 6.5-284 Norma, maintains 1/3MOA groups out to 500 yards. While this is certainly influenced by the fact the rifle is well-constructed, it is also due to the fact that the ammunition gives extremely uniform results. My Oehler Model 35P chronograph has shown that these loads give an extreme velocity spread of no more than 8 fps, up or down, from the average. Most of my accurate handloaded ammunition has demonstrated the same trait, and I firmly believe there is a direct correlation between accuracy and uniform velocity, especially when the distance to the target increases. While some loads with a wider velocity spread may show more than acceptable accuracy at 100 yards, they tend to open up when you take things out to 300 yards and beyond. That 6.5-284 of mine likes several different bullets, but definitely shows a preference for Hodgdon H4831SC powder, which has a burn rate that works well in this case. I've tried other powders, and while I obtained accurate results that were more than acceptable, H4831SC gave the best results by far; yet, in other 6.5-284 rifles, this particular load didn't work nearly as well. Point is, each barrel is slightly different and may react differently to a particular powder charge, playing a significant role in accuracy. If you don't handload and use factory ammunition, you'll have to experiment with many different brands until you find the combination of bullet and powder charge that will show the full potential of your rifle or handgun. You'll see a particular type of ammunition either praised as being the best or slagged as being terribly inaccurate on many Internet forums, but realize that more often than not all

Some good pistol powders, yielding desired velocities for a hunting cartridge.

that's represented is the experience of one shooter with one firearm. You may find an entirely different result in your gun.

I've also seen shooters complain that something has gone terribly wrong with their firearm, because Brand X ammunition, loaded with a particular bullet, which has historically produced fantastic results, suddenly throws bullets all over the target. The problem didn't lie with the firearm, or even the shooter; what happened was the Brand X Ammunition Company changed the powder type and/or load for that line of ammo, and the firearm didn't shoot the new load well. Many shooters, when they find a load that their rifle or handgun shoots well, will do their best to obtain as much of that ammo as possible, often trying to stay within the same lot number, to keep things as uniform as possible.

Powder Charges: Weight vs. Volume

There are a couple of ways to think about powder charges, and you'll see a dichotomy when you compare a serious handloader with a benchrest shooter. As a handloader, I was taught to weigh all of my powder charges to keep things as uniform as possible. But many of the benchrest shooters who achieve fantastic accuracy load their powder by volume, not weight. Which is the better method? That depends. Again, experimentation is key, but if your firearm shows better accuracy with one method over another, go with it.

Pistol Cartridges and Powder Charges

Pistols can be a different animal altogether, especially since so many of their cases have a capacity which can hold a double charge of powder, and that will result in terrible things happening. The progressive presses, which are highly efficient for those situations where you need a whole bunch of ammunition for pistol competitions, use a case-activated powder thrower to dispense powder into the newly resized case. Care must be taken to properly adjust the dispenser, due to the fact that pistol charges are relatively light, and an overcharge of 0.2 grains can result in excessive pressure. The common powders for pistols cartridges—including Bullseye, Unique, 700X and TiteGroup—all meter very well, but again, it's not easy to detect a slight overcharge that could cause trouble.

Most of the pistol powders are fast-burning and generally use the flake or ball powder shape. This gives them lots of surface area for burning and generates a (generally) lower pressure when compared to centerfire rifle cartridges. Things tend to get a bit slower burning when you get into the bigger revolver cartridges that are so popular among handgun hunters. The .44 Magnum, .45 Colt and .454 Casull are all prime examples of great handgun hunting rounds, and while they will run on many of the standard powders, they really perform best with the slower powders that wrings that last bit of velocity from the big cases. Hodgdon's H110, Ramshot's Enforcer and Accurate Arms No. 9 will certainly fuel the fire, and when loaded behind a premium bullet, deliver the goods on the hunting fields. Once again, a good reloading manual will give you a feel for what powder will work best in your cartridge.

CHAPTER 5
The Barrel

The barrel is the rifle's delivery system, the steel guidance mechanism that sends the projectile spinning toward the target. Barrel technology has come leaps and bounds in the last century, to the point where the accuracy has become both highly predictable, as well as repeatable. It's important to know how barrels work in order to better understand how a bullet will perform within its confines.

The Throat

Starting at the breech end, your barrel has three or four main parts, depending on the type of firearm. For rifles, as well as semi-automatic pistols, there is a chamber, throat or leade, and the rifling itself, all terminating at the crown. The chamber is a mirror image of the cartridge to be fired and is sealed by the breech bolt or block to ensure all the burning gas pushes things toward the muzzle end of the barrel. The throat, or leade, is the area between the chamber of the barrel and the point where the rifling begins. The length of the throat can vary greatly, from less than 1/16 inch, to as much as ½ inch, depending on the cartridge and manufacturer. The throat is exposed to burning powder and hot gas, and when shooting a high-velocity cartridge is often the first part of the firearm to show wear and erosion. Some of the fastest cartridges, like the .300 Remington Ultra Magnum and .264 Winchester Magnum, can show throat wear in as little as 1,500 rounds. I make a conscious effort not to heat my barrels excessively, to help keep wear and tear to a minimum. Some companies (Weatherby for example) purposely extend the throat of their barrels to give room for the bullet to jump. This is known as free-bore, and can help increase accuracy. You never want a modern cartridge to have the projectile touching the rifling; dangerous pressures can easily develop. At the end of the throat, the rifling begins.

Rifling

Rifling is the set of twisted ridges you'll see when you look down the bore of the firearm. It imparts a spin on the bullet, keeping it stable in flight. Those ridges, properly called lands, engrave their imprint into your bullet, and are machined at a smaller diameter than the bullet itself. The corresponding valleys, or grooves, are designed to be at caliber dimension to properly seal the gas and build pressure. The number of lands and grooves can vary, from the two-groove U.S. Army Springfield rifles of the early 20th century, to the Marlin MicroGroove barrel that used 16 or more, and all sorts in between. (Note: some handgun companies today employ polygonal rifling, which is a bit of a different geometry, yet works fine for their purposes.) Almost all common barrels use a static twist rate, meaning that the grooves are cut in a specific manner to maintain a consistent spin on the bullet. When researching rifles, note the barrel specs listed as 1:10 or 1:7 twist rate. This is simply a means of telling you how fast or slow the barrel will cause the bullet to spin. The example twist rates given above work like this: a barrel with a 1:10 twist rate will have a bore in which the lands make a complete revolution in 10 inches of barrel ("one in ten"), while the 1:7 barrel will make that same complete revolution in just 7 inches of barrel, therefore imparting more spin on the bullet. The higher the sectional density figure of a particular bullet (read that as a longer bullet), the faster it must be spun in order to maintain gyroscopic stability throughout its flight. While the numbers may be deceiving, a 1:10 barrel is called a slower twist than is 1:7, and with many of today's bullets becoming longer and heavier for caliber, the fast twist rate barrels are becoming more desirable to take advantage of these bullets.

One of my favorite varmint rifles is a Ruger Model 77 MkII, chambered in .22-250 Remington. This big case is the old .250-3000 Savage necked down to hold .224-inch diameter bullets, and there is plenty of powder capacity to push the bullets to high velocity. However, because the .22-250 uses a relatively slow twist rate—either 1:12 or 1:14—the heaviest bullet I can use in this rifle is a 55-grain slug. While there are plenty of good, heavy bullets for hunting and/or target work available in this caliber right up to 80 grains and more, my rifle can't stabilize them with that slower twist rate. My dad's .223 Remington, with its 1:8 twist rate, can shoot most of the heavier designs without issue, even though it has much less case capacity. My .22-250 serves me well, and can really reach out and touch the coyotes and woodchucks, but I'd love to be able to utilize the longer bullets.

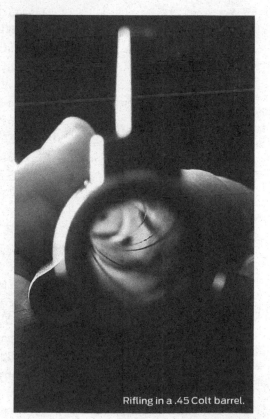

Rifling in a .45 Colt barrel.

For years, I used a .308 Winchester exclusively as my big game rifle here in Upstate New York. I shot a .308 because Dad shot a .308, and we always discussed the reasons that we couldn't use the heavy, 220-grain round-nosed slugs common in the .30-06 Springfield. He insisted it was a case capacity issue, but I found out that the .308 Winchester was originally released with a 1:12 twist, as opposed to the Springfield's 1:10, so it couldn't stabilize bullets heavier than 200 grains. (The .30-06 Springfield, normally supplying a 1:10 twist, can stabilize the heavy 220-grain bullets, but the .308 Winchester with a 1:12 cannot.) To prove my point, I borrowed a .308 Winchester with the faster twist rate, and loaded up some 220-grain pills. Much to my father's chagrin, they worked just fine.

Here's a chart of many common twist rates, from popular manufacturers. Of course, there may be some variations, but this should give you a good starting point.

Common Twist Rates for Rifle Calibers

.17 Mach II	1:9
.17 Hornady Magnum Rimfire	1:9
.17 Winchester Super Magnum	1:9
.17 Hornet	1:9
.17 Remington	1.9
.204 Ruger	1:12
.22 Long Rifle	1:16
.22 Winchester Magnum Rimfire	1:16
.22 Hornet	1:14
.222 Remington	1:14
.223 Remington	1:7, 1:8, 1:9, 1:12
.223 WSSM	1:10
.22 ARC	1:7
.224 Valkyrie	1:7
.22-250 Remington	1:12, 1:14
.220 Swift	1:12, 1:14
6mm Remington/.244 Rem	1:9, 1:12
.243 Winchester	1:10
.243 WSSM	1:10
.240 Weatherby Magnum	1:9.5
6 Norma BR	1:8
6mm ARC	1:7
6mm Creedmoor	1:7.7, 1:8
.25-'06 Remington	1:10
.257 Roberts	1:9.5, 1:10

.250/3000 Savage	1:10, 1:14
.25 WSSM	1:10
.257 Weatherby Magnum	1:9.5
.260 Remington	1:8, 1:9
6.5 Grendel	1:8
6.5 Creedmoor	1:8
6.5x55 Swedish Mauser	1:7.5
6.5-284 Norma	1:8, 1:9
6.5 PRC	1:8
.264 Winchester Magnum	1:8, 1:9
.26 Nosler	1:8
6.5-300 Weatherby Magnum	1:8
.270 Winchester	1:10
.270 Winchester Short Magnum	1:10
.270 Weatherby Magnum	1:10
6.8 SPC	1:9.5, 1:11, 1:12
6.8 Western	1:7.5, 1:8
.27 Nosler	1:8.5
7x57 Mauser	1:8, 1:9, 1:10
7-30 Waters	1:9
7mm-08 Remington	1:9.25
.280 Remington	1:9.25
7x64 Brenneke	1:9
.284 Winchester	1:9
7mm Winchester Short Magnum	1:9.5

7mm Weatherby Magnum	1:9.25, 1:10
.28 Nosler	1:9
7mm PRC	1:8
7mm Remington Ultra Magnum	1:9.25
7mm STW	1:9.25, 1:10
.30 Carbine	1:16
.30-30 WCF	1:12
.30 T/C	1:10
.30/40 Krag	1:10
.308 Winchester	1:10, 1:12
.300 Savage	1:10
.30-'06 Springfield	1:10
.30 Nosler	1:10
.300 Winchester Magnum	1:10
.300 Winchester Short Magnum	1:10
.300 Remington Ultra Magnum	1:10
.300 Weatherby Magnum	1:10
.30-378 Weatherby Magnum	1:10
.300 Holland & Holland Magnum	1:10
.308 Norma Magnum	1:10
.300 Remington SAUM	1:10
.300 PRC	1:8
.300 Norma	1:8
.303 British	1:10
7.62x39mm	1:10
.32 Winchester Special	1:16
.325 Winchester Short Magnum	1:10
8x57mm Mauser	1:9.25
8mm Remington Magnum	1:10
8x68S	1:11
.338-06 A-Square	1:10
.338 Federal	1:10
.338 Winchester Magnum	1:10
.338 Remington Ultra Magnum	1:10
.338/378 Weatherby Magnum	1:10
.340 Weatherby Magnum	1:10
.33 Winchester	1:12
.338 Lapua	1:9
.35 Remington	1:16

.358 Winchester	1:14, 1:16
.35 Whelen	1:14, 1:16
.358 Norma Magnum	1:12
.350 Remington Magnum	1:16
.357 Magnum (rifle)	1:16
9.3x62mm	1:10, 1:14
9.3x64mm	1:14
9.3x74mmR	1:10, 1:14
.375 Holland & Holland Mag	1:12, 1:14
.375 Ruger	1:12
.375 Remington Ultra Magnum	1:12
.375 Weatherby Magnum	1:12
.378 Weatherby Magnum	1:12, 1:14
.375 Dakota	1:12
.375 Winchester	1:12
.405 Winchester	1:14
450/400 3" NE	1:15
.404 Jeffery	1:14, 1:16.5
.416 Rigby	1:14
.416 Ruger	1:14
.416 Weatherby Magnum	1:14
.416 Remington Magnum	1:14, 1:16.5
.416 Barrett	1:11
.500/416 NE	1:14
.44 Magnum (rifle)	1:20, 1:38
.444 Marlin	1:20
.45-70 Gov't	1:20
.458 Winchester Magnum	1:14
.458 Lott	1:14, 1:16
.450 3 ¼" NE	1:16
.450 Rigby	1:10
.458 SOCOM	1:14, 1:18
.450 Marlin	1:20
.460 Weatherby Magnum	1:16
.470 NE	1:21
.50 BMG	1:15
.500 NE	1:15
.500 Jeffery	1:17
.505 Gibbs	1:1

The target crown of the author's Savage Model 116.

So, it's important to know what the twist rate of your barrel so you can choose the proper ammunition for your gun. There's an easy way to observe or verify the twist rate of your barrel. Using a cleaning rod, affix a tight patch and get it started down the bore. With a magic marker make a small mark at the base of the rod at the top, and another one where it meets the breech (or the muzzle in the case of a lever gun, slide, etc.). Push the rod down the bore until the mark makes one complete revolution, and make another mark at the same reference point (breech or muzzle). Measure the distance between the marks to determine how many inches it took to make one revolution, and voilà! you've got the twist rate.

If you look at some of the long-range bullets, like the Nosler AccuBond Long Range, or some of the Berger offerings, they will indicate the required twist rate needed to stabilize their particular bullet. If you want a bit more information, or should the bullet be marginal for your twist rate, you can consult the Berger website (bergerbullets.com/twist-rate-calculator/) and plug in all of your information. Based upon the Miller Twist Rule (more about that in the exterior ballistics section), the Berger calculator will provide you with the level of stability (or instability) of your particular barrel/cartridge/bullet combination. It's a very useful tool, which can help you optimize your setup.

The Crown

The final point of the barrel, where the bullet exits, is referred to as the crown. A uniform, even crown is invaluable for good accuracy, as it is the very last thing that your bullet will touch before embarking on its journey through the atmosphere. You'll need to know about the varying types of crowns and how they affect the flight of the bullet. Looking at the end of your barrel, you may see a simple, rounded end and be able to feel the lands and grooves with the pad of your finger. Or you may see a square-cut, recessed affair, known as a target crown. In any instance, you'll definitely want to be careful with the crown of your firearm; it plays a very important role in its accuracy. I've seen my fair share of well-worn lever-action rifles, which need to be cleaned from the muzzle end, sporting worn or nearly eroded crowns from years of swabbing with a filthy aluminum rod. I'm sure if their owners, who were tough as nails and certainly knew how to shoot those guns, saw us today with our polymer bore guides and ball-bearing-handled, nylon-coated cleaning rods, they'd certainly have a chuckle. However, if they could see the difference in accuracy between a healthy crown and a worn one, they'd have no choice but to admit that our methods preserve rifle accuracy better.

An imperfect crown can be the demise of accuracy. I went mildly insane trying to figure out what was wrong with that .22-250 Remington of mine, as I simply couldn't figure out why it wouldn't shoot boattail bullets. I mean, I tried factory ammunition, handloads, you name it. Because it is a flat-shooting cartridge, I wanted the 53- and 55-grain boattail match bullets to work. My pal Donnie Thorne, better known as Col. Le Frogg, weighed in on the matter, and found the cure in one simple sentence: "Try some flat-base match bullets."

Long story short, once I switched to flat-base bullets, the rifle was printing 1/3 MOA groups out to 200 yards, which makes up a huge portion of my shots with this rifle, unless the coyotes are posing across the hay lots. The crown of this Ruger rifle is less than perfect, and the escaping gas was being pushed on one side or the other of the exiting boattail. Switching to a flat-base bullet improved the accuracy immensely and was not a handicap as far as wind deflection and trajectory were concerned. To be honest, the combination of the imperfect crown and slow twist rate should warrant re-barreling the rifle. But I love the way it handles, so I'll wait a while until I feel it's time to do so.

Twist Direction

Most of today's barrels use a right-hand twist; that is, the bullet is spun in a clockwise motion. However, you can come across a left-hand twist barrel, spinning bullets in a counterclockwise motion, and when the distances get out beyond 500 yards or so, the spin direction of the barrel comes into play. A right-hand twist barrel will cause the bullet to drift a measurable degree to the right when the time of flight increases. Conversely, the opposite is true for a left-hand twist barrel, and these considerations must be accounted for when trying to accurately place your bullets on a distant target. Many of the ballistic calculators incorporate twist direction as one of the parameters for long range dope, so it's important to know. One glance down your barrel and you can easily verify the direction of twist.

Barrel Construction

Steel has long been the chosen material for barrels. It is rigid enough to withstand the intense pressures generated by modern cartridges, yet flexible enough to allow the bullet down the barrel without cracking or shattering. The two most popular types of steel barrels produced are chrome-moly (a chrome-molybdenum alloy steel) and stainless steel. I've had excellent results with both, and I honestly feel that either will make a suitable choice for a barrel. Both give long life and are equally accurate, at least in my experiences. Stainless is a bit less susceptible to rust (though not impervious), and chrome-moly can be a bit lighter, but I own and like both types. More important to me is the construction method used to create the barrel.

Cut vs. Hammer-Forged vs. Button-Rifled

Most factory barrels in production today are hammer-forged, cut or button-rifled. All three methods have positive and negative attributes. Personally, I've found good and bad in all three types along the way, and as long as a barrel does its job, I'm good with it. The cut barrels are probably the most labor intensive, as the rifling is cut one groove at a time in a reamed bore. Krieger, who made the barrel for my .318 Westley-Richards, makes cut barrels. The button-rifled barrels are made in a similar fashion, in that a drilled bore at less than caliber size is utilized to guide the cutting button down the bore. Button rifling is popular with many custom rifle companies like Shilen, as well as Savage rifles—both of which have an impeccable reputation for accuracy. So, with both cut and button rifling, a smaller-than-caliber hole is drilled through the centerline of the bore, and a tool is used to put the finishing touches on the barrel.

Hammer-forged barrels work in the opposite manner. They start with a barrel blank that gets reamed to a dimension larger than the desired caliber, and then a mandrel that is a perfect mirror of the desired bore dimension is inserted into the reamed hole. At that stage, a series of hammers are used to forcefully mold the steel around the mandrel, so that the resulting bore comes out perfect. Undoubtedly, hammer-forged barrels are both cost-effective and accurate, yet some folks feel that they are the least accurate type of barrel. I've had some of the best—and worst—accuracy with a hammer-forged barrel, yet I feel it's due to the fact that they represent such a large portion of the barrels produced each year. My Heym Express .404 Jeffery uses a hammer-forged Krupp barrel, and yet it gives sub-MOA accuracy consistently. Likewise, I've got a trio of Winchester Model 70s (.300 Win. Mag., .375 H&H and a .416 Remington Magnum) and all have exhibited excellent accuracy, accompanying me on hunts all over the world. Likewise, my favorite revolver, a Ruger Blackhawk in .45 Colt, uses a 7.5-inch hammer-forged barrel that allows me to hit targets as far as I can hold accurately. The hammer-forged method occasionally gets a bad rap because it is associated with mass production, but that's not fair. Heym rifles, makers of some of the finest safari guns available, make approximately 6,000 hammer-forged barrels annually, but only consume about 2,000 for their own in-house use. The remainder are sold to other fine rifle companies, and I've yet to meet a Krupp barrel from Heym that didn't perform very well.

Down the Rabbit Hole

When the cartridge is fired, the primer sends a shower of sparks into the powder charge, which is burned. The resulting expanding gas creates lots of pressure. This sends the bullet in the path of least resistance: down the barrel. It's also when things get interesting, as the entire situation changes in an instant. Once the bullet passes the throat and engages the rifling, the torque creates a wave of distortion that causes the barrel to swell just in front of the bullet. The barrel will—although minutely—swell and return to original shape as the bullet passes down the bore. In addition, the barrel will 'whip,' as if you were holding a fishing pole in your hand and quickly shook your wrist. Barrel flexure is minimized with a larger diameter barrel of shorter length, but those shapes come at the cost of velocity loss and increased weight. In addition, if your barrel is not free floating, meaning that it is touching the stock at some point, accuracy can be affected. Like all things in life, there are no absolutes, and I've seen rifles with Mannlicher stocks where the stock extended to the muzzle and touched almost all the way exhibit excellent accuracy. Many military rifles such as the M1 Garand or M98 Mauser have stocks that extend much farther than do our common hunting and target rifles. Yet, these have shown some amazing capabilities in competition shooting ... in no small part to the men behind the trigger. That aside, I prefer my rifles to have barrels free floated so they can swell and torque and whip without interference. That keeps things as accurate as possible. You can test your rifle's barrel channel by placing a dollar bill under the barrel, and run it up along the stock toward the receiver as a feeler gauge to see if the stock is touching the barrel at any point. If it is, remove a small amount of material from the barrel channel in order to let the barrel move freely during the shot.

The idea of reducing barrel whip by using a stiffer (larger diameter) barrel isn't a new one, but it definitely works. It not only dissipates heat better, but reduces the amount of flexure to give a more repeatable result, promoting accuracy. The bull barrel is a staple of the target community, as well as being a popular choice among varmint hunters who must hit distant, tiny targets. However, they are heavy to carry, and can be very unwieldy to shoot offhand. Now, I don't mind a barrel on the heavier side of things, particularly the semi-bull barrels that make a good blend of portability and stability, but I don't want a bull barrel on the mountain hunts of the Adirondacks and Catskills, nor do I want one when in the African game fields, where the daily walks are measured in miles. There is a way to get the best of both worlds using a light, rigid, carbon fiber. Starting out with a featherweight steel barrel, carbon fiber is wrapped around it, until it achieves the diameter of a bull barrel approaching one inch or more in diameter. This combination is lightweight like a slim steel barrel, but has the rigidity of a bull barrel. The carbon also dissipates heat very well, and it keeps your barrel cooler, longer.

When a barrel gets too hot, it'll tend to print a bit higher on the target. This occurs because the steel expands and the bore diameter is slightly reduced, creating a higher pressure and thereby more velocity. Heating your barrel to the point that it is impossible to touch without pulling your hand away is never a good idea, as it will lead to premature barrel wear and throat erosion. Allow things to cool, and a barrel should give nearly a lifetime worth of service.

Harmonics

The manner in which a barrel whips, torques and contorts is referred to as barrel harmonics. The idea of accuracy is simply a set of repeatable barrel harmonics. If you use the centerline of the bore as the baseline for your observations, you would see a wave in which the barrel would rise and fall, equally above and beyond the baseline. The thinner and longer a barrel is, the further from the baseline the barrel will whip. Again, a short, thick barrel will have a much smaller deviation from the baseline. Accuracy is optimized when harmonics are repeatable, and when the various pressure waves align in such a fashion that the muzzle diameter is kept at a uniform dimension. Um, what? How can the muzzle diameter change? Allow me to explain a complicated theory in simple terms.

I ran across a theory, presented by radio communications engineer Chris Long, which makes a whole lot of sense and explains some ideas I knew to be true, but had no idea how to nail down scientifically. It also changed the way I look at my own handloaded ammunition. Long purports that a series of crossing waves can, will and do have a great effect on the barrel and its ability to produce a repeatable point of impact (known to us as a tight group). While I am not a scientist (cue Star Trek music: "Dammit Jim, I'm a surveyor not an engineer!"), Long's theory boils down to this: the ignition of the powder charge creates pressure that sends a shockwave down the barrel, to the muzzle and back again, in a repeating fashion much like the plucking of a guitar string. This ignition stress shockwave can and will move the steel enough to cause a distortion in the bore diameter. Subsequently, when the bullet engages the rifling, a second force—the swelling of the barrel ahead of the bullet—starts to travel toward the muzzle. According to Long's sound theory, if those two waves collide when the first wave is affecting the muzzle, the groups will open up as if the crown were out of round, much like my .22-250 Remington was behaving. If you can find the load with which the two waves are separated, the group size will indeed shrink.

Now, there are many variables in Long's equation, including the amount of powder and the load density, as well as the seating depth of the bullet, and while this isn't a book on reloading ammunition, this theory makes perfect sense to me as a handloader. It can easily explain how changing the powder charge a mere 0.1 or 0.2 grains would so dramatically affect group size, as I've seen for decades in my own handloaded ammo. In addition, the Chris Long theory also explains why some barrels like a particular brand of ammunition, yet others can't get it to work at all. I think it also explains the drastic changes in group size that can occur when changing seating depth and cartridge overall length. (Which incidentally has been a little trick of mine for years, though I didn't understand exactly why it worked, I just knew that it did.) The variations in seating depth will definitely affect the barrel harmonics and their timing.

A Seating Depth Experiment

With this information in hand let's run a little experiment using a proven rifle that is capable of 1/2 MOA accuracy, to see how important of a role seating depth plays in the barrel/accuracy equation. Marty Groppi and I took a proven load and varied the seating depth of the bullet in increments of 0.005 inches to see whether or not it made a significant difference. We knew what this gun would do at 100 yards, so to magnify the differences in group size we took things out to 300 yards for the test. My pal Mark Nazi was kind enough to lend his Remington 700 in .308 Winchester, and we headed to the reloading bench to cook up the ammo we'd need. This rifle shines with a particular load of Hodgdon's Varget powder and a Federal GM210M large rifle primer. To keep things as uniform as possible, we used Kinetic Industries' match .308 brass, full-length re-sized in a good set of Redding Competition dies. For a bullet, we used the Sierra 168-grain Tipped MatchKing; again, I wanted an accurate, uniform projectile for test purposes, and it's really hard to beat the Sierra TMK. So, being limited by the design of the bullet ogive, we started at the SAAMI overall length of 2.800 inches, and then set the bullets out longer in 0.005-inch incre-ments until we reached 2.835 inches—first verifying that the longest load was not touching the lands and grooves. Mark's rifle has a particularly long throat, and our longest cartridge was still in the clear. Below is a chart, but I'll describe the chain of events that led to the results.

I put my buddy Manny Vermilyea on the trigger and we first affirmed zero at 100 yards, and checked the five-shot group size. As expected, it was just over 1/2MOA, so we then started with the shortest load (that is, the SAAMI dimension load) at 300 yards. The first group printed just shy of 3 inches, or 1 MOA at that distance, with an average velocity of 2,638 fps, proving two things: that even though outside air temps pushed 90°F the load was performing as we ex-pected, and Manny was shooting properly.

As the seating depth increased in increments up to 2.815 inches, we saw an increase in ve-locity (to be expected as you seat bullets out further) and we saw a definite degradation in accuracy. The 2.805- and 2.810-inch groups opened up to 5.25 and 4 inches, respectively, and maintained the slight increase in velocity. At 2.815 inches, the five-shot group came back down to 3 inches, with another velocity bump up to 2,660 fps. However, at 2.825 inches we found a sweet spot; the velocity dropped down to an average of 2,644 fps, with the lowest standard deviation on velocity, and a group size of exactly 2 inches. We had found the proper barrel har-monics for this rifle/bullet combination. Further retesting showed similar results in both group size and uniform velocities. At an overall length of 2.830 inches our velocities bumped back up to 2,652 fps and the group size opened up to just over 4 inches. It got worse with the 2.835-inch load, where we saw the first signs of high pressure in some slightly flattened primers.

.308 Winchester Federal GM210M primer	Kinetic Match Brass 43.5 gr. Hodgdon VARGET	Redding Competition Dies Oehler 35P chronograph
Cartridge Length (inches)	Avg. Velocity (fps)	Five-shot group size @ 300 yds. (inches)
2.800	2,638	3.0
2.805	2,644	5.25
2.810	2,650	4.0
2.815	2,656	3.0
2.820	2,660	2.5
2.825	2.644	2.0
2.830	2,652	4.0
2.835	2,657	4.75

Our cartridges only changed a grand total of 0.035 inches in length, yet the same powder charge and components showed a radical shift in accuracy. Thinking about Chris Long's hypothesis, his barrel harmonic theory made perfect sense. The minute changes in seating depth cut the group size in less than half at 300 yards, without any changes to the powder charge. Barrels, they are finicky creatures indeed.

During load development for my 6.5-284 Norma, I found the same effect of seating depth on the rifle's accuracy. From the time I opened the box, this rifle would put many different types of ammunition into less than 1 MOA without issue. As my load development got more experimental, I tried radically changing the seating depth. This particular rifle was ordered from the Savage Custom Shop on the Model 116 action, much longer than you'd traditionally need for the 6.5-284 Norma, but I wanted the ability to seat the bullets out as long as the throat would allow. That gun likes H4831SC powder, and it likes it a lot. However, when using the Hornady ELD-Match 140-grain bullets and the same load of H4831SC, I tried seating them out so far that the bullet's shank was just at the bottom of the case neck—giving good neck tension, but using a much longer overall length than normal. The accuracy fell apart. When I returned to the shorter seating depth that I'd stumbled onto during earlier experimentation, things tightened right back up.

Barrel Length and Its Effects

For years, it was a common assumption that longer barrels were more accurate than shorter ones. It's an arguable point, but I've seen evidence that points to the fact that both can be equally accurate. I do believe that when discussing iron-sighted guns, a longer sighting radius will usually result in an ability to place the shot better, but in a scientific world—say using a machine rest—I'm not certain that the longer barrel will always come out on top.

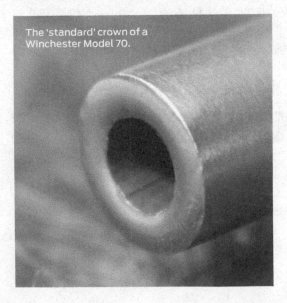

The 'standard' crown of a Winchester Model 70.

There is a definite increase in velocity when using a longer barrel, as the longer pipe will build more pressure. The generally accepted velocity loss/gain when comparing barrel lengths is 25 fps per one inch of barrel length. While I've never had the opportunity to actually measure the velocity loss of one particular barrel by cutting off an inch at a time, I've seen studies where this test was performed and that rule was more or less proven. For example, my 6.5-284 Norma is a popular choice among F-Class shooters, and many of those rifles take advantage of the case capacity by using a barrel length of 28 or even 30 inches. My own Savage Model 116 with a 25-inch barrel doesn't quite match some of the advertised velocities because of the shorter tube, and I'm OK with that. It's a hunting rifle, and while I normally don't mind longer barrels, toting a 28-inch barrel through the woods and fields seems a bit excessive to me. So, when I ordered the rifle, I figured the 25-inch length would make a good balance of velocity and portability. The choice is ultimately up to you, whether you want a compact rifle for ease of carry, or the long barrel for additional velocity, but it's important to know that the measured velocity of Brand X ammunition in your gun may not equal advertised velocities due to the difference in the test gun's barrel length and the length of your barrel.

When I first started to handload ammunition, I didn't understand why a particular load prescribed by the reloading manual didn't obtain the velocity shown in the data. I followed the recipe exactly. Used the test data's primer, powder charge, case, and bullet and seating depth. But I was still 125 fps below the manual. Then I glanced at the test rifle information. This company had used a universal receiver and a 26-inch barrel to arrive at their data, and my rifle sported a 22-inch barrel. Barrel length was the factor.

Pistol barrels can and will have a similar effect on the performance of ammunition. Many of the micro-carry, or pocket pistols, give lower velocities than their full-sized counterparts due to the decreased barrel length. Ammunition companies have made an effort to optimize the cartridges for best performance in the shorter barrels. Federal Premium HST ammo has a 'Micro" line that is designed to function properly in the shorter barrels of concealed carry pistols, and it works very well. My own carry gun—a Smith & Wesson Model 36 in .38 Special—has the 1 7/8-inch snubnose barrel and, while the velocities certainly aren't what you'd get from a 4- or 6-inch target gun, I knew that when I purchased it. For distances at which I feel comfortable using a short-barreled pistol, I'm fine with the velocity loss in exchange for ease of carry and concealment.

These are things to keep in mind when purchasing a rifle or pistol. Does a .308 Winchester need a 26-inch barrel? Probably not, because the case capacity can be utilized in a 20- or 22-inch barrel, and if it's made properly, should offer fine accuracy. Can you get the most from a 7mm Remington Magnum with a 22-inch pipe? Not likely. This is an example of a cartridge needing a bit more barrel length to achieve optimum results, due to the increased case capacity. Will a short-barreled handgun be as accurate as a longer barreled one? Maybe, but it has more to do with balance and the ability to aim the firearm than actual function of the barrel and its length. Will a 20-inch barreled Winchester 94 carbine, in .30-30 WCF, perform as well as the 26-inch octagon-barreled rifle of your grandfather's era? For the distances at which a .30-30 is most commonly shot, I'd vote yes, but again, that longer sighting radius of the bigger rifle may cause it to appear more accurate than the carbine, so it would take a machine rest to verify the results. For a hunting application, either is more than acceptable if you practice diligently with an iron-sighted gun (which seems to be a lost art these days), so if you appreciate the compact design of the carbine, have at it.

SECTION

II

EXTERIOR
BALLISTICS

SECTION II GUNDEX®

CHAPTER 6

Exterior Ballistics Explained

T he primer has been struck, the powder burned, and the bullet acted upon in a most violent chain of events. Yes, our proud little metallic fledgling has left the nest! Into free air it is sent, rotating rapidly, on its course to an unknown destination. Immediately, a multitude of alien forces begin to act upon it as it rolls with the punches and reacts accordingly.

Obviously, not all bullets are built in the same fashion, and each of them react differently to the forces of their particular environment. Some are sleek and streamlined, like a fighter jet, designed for the utmost speed and efficiency, while others are built like a tank, square and strong, to breach the strongest defenses. As with mechanized implements on the battlefield, the two extremes in bullet design use completely different means to the same end and have different applications.

Exterior ballistics deals with that portion of the bullet's flight from the moment it leaves the muzzle until it impacts its target—whether that target is paper, steel or flesh. In a handgun, especially a defensive arm, the flight of the bullet is rather short, and the atmosphere and laws of physics have less opportunity to influence things. In a high-powered rifle, these forces have plenty of time to show their effects. To be able to put that bullet precisely on target, you need to fully understand how the bullet will react to your environment at a wide variety of ranges. Entire lifetimes have been spent in pursuit of the accurate prediction of bullet trajectories. While the answers are out there, the science of ballistics is constantly evolving, and our ability to quantify and predict the values associated with the bullet's path is improving all the time.

There are scientific terms associated with exterior ballistics, and they can be confusing at times. The most prevalent term we'll need to understand is ballistic coefficient, or BC as we'll see it abbreviated, a term that describes the bullet's ability to resist the effects of atmospheric drag and wind drift, as compared to the base models of bullet shapes as defined by the Commission d'Experience de Gavre. That was where a series of tests were performed at the Aberdeen Proving Ground, Maryland, by the U.S. Army in the early 1880s, and the G1 bullet form (G in honor of Gavre) was adopted as the model for comparative purposes. Almost all of today's bullets are labeled with a BC based on the G1 model, although there are newer and different models that better serve the shooter (we'll get into detail about that later in this section).

The accuracy of a particular firearm is most often measured in the arc subtended by a minute of angle, abbreviated as MOA. One minute of angle is 1/60th of one degree on a circle, and is equal to 1.047 inches at 100 yards. For our general purposes, assume that figure as one inch. Thus one MOA is one inch at 100 yards, two inches at 200 yards, three inches at 300 yards, and so forth. A rifle that is said to shoot MOA will print a group of shots that measure no more than one inch of extreme spread at 100 yards. Since group size is measured in a function of a projecting cone, the further the distance the target is from the muzzle, the wider the arc subtended by that angle. For hunters facing shots inside of 400 yards, an MOA rifle should print a group measuring four inches at the 400-yard mark.

Wind drift is the effect of any crosswind during the bullet's flight. It is a tricky proposition learning to 'dope' the wind, but it is necessary to hit distant targets in real world situations. Wind will certainly blow a bullet off its course in a horizontal direction, but in certain situations it will have a vertical effect as well. Wind drift is typically represented in inches, but I've seen it in MOA as well. I personally prefer inches, but the two are easily converted. MOA is an important value for precisely adjusting telescopic sights.

Now, the trajectory of a bullet is based on more than one factor. Shortly after Sir Isaac Newton had his noodle rocked by that fateful piece of fruit (I'm thinking back to the wonderful Schoolhouse Rock cartoons of my youth), he did his best to explain the laws of gravity. The resultant accepted formulas state that, with the effects of atmospheric drag aside, all small bodies will fall to the earth at the same rate. This applies to projectiles as well. Whether fired at Mach III or simply dropped from your hand, the bullet falls to the ground in the same amount of time. When a rifle is described as flat shooting, it is because it generates a higher than normal muzzle velocity, and the bullet is allowed to cover more ground before gravity pulls it earthward. The flattest shooting cartridges have the shortest time of flight (abbreviated TOF), so that the represented curve of the bullet path looks much flatter than the slower cartridges. Combine this gravitational effect with the effects of air drag, crosswind and atmospheric conditions, and your projectile has much to overcome before it tears out the bullseye. You can now see why the science of ballistics is so in-depth.

There is a common misconception about trajectory that can be easily misconstrued from looking at the trajectory curves printed on the back of ammunition boxes. I've had many people argue until they were red in the face that a bullet rises once it leaves the muzzle and starts to drop in a rainbow-like curve. That, dear reader, is simply not the truth, though it is necessary to adjust the way you use your firearms to have that be the end result. If you were to hold any firearm so that the line of the bore were perfectly level (perpendicular to gravitational pull), your bullet would immediately start to drop below the line of the bore, essentially never striking a

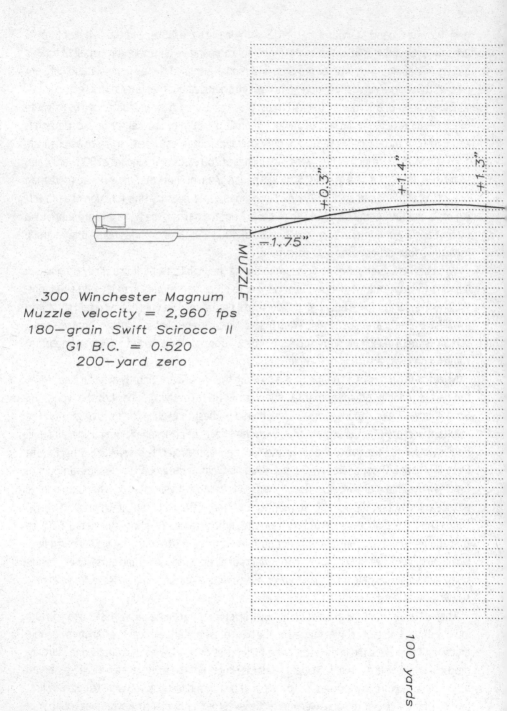

.300 Winchester Magnum
Muzzle velocity = 2,960 fps
180—grain Swift Scirocco II
G1 B.C. = 0.520
200—yard zero

MUZZLE

−1.75"

+0.3"

+1.4"

+1.3"

100 yards

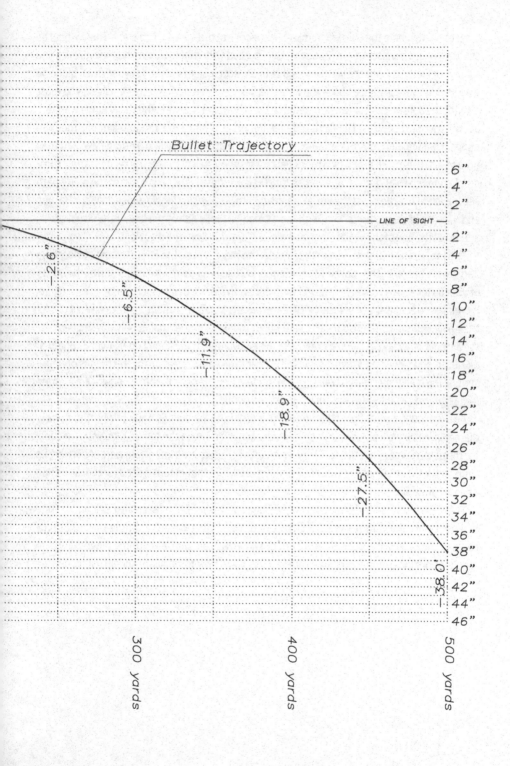

target exactly where the bore was aiming, irrespective of distance to the target. There would be some (perhaps minuscule) gravitational pull. Coupled with that idea, the manner in which you sight your firearms—whether with iron sights or telescopic sights—requires your visual plane be elevated at some distance above the bore line. So, with those two factors involved, you must elevate the bore at a certain angle upward so that the bullet path and the visual plane will cross at two specific distances. The flight of the bullet must begin below the visual plane, then rise above it, and finally cross the visual plane once again after gravity and air drag have had their time to act. The distance at which the bullet crosses the visual plane for the second time is commonly referred to as 'zero.' A rifle zeroed for 200 yards means that the curve of the bullet path will leave the muzzle, cross the visual plane at 25 to 50 yards (strongly dependent on the type and velocity of cartridge you're using), rise a small distance above the line of the visual plane, and meet the line of the visual plane at exactly 200 yards from the muzzle.

The farther the bullet gets from the muzzle, the more drastic the effects of the atmosphere and gravity become. That ballistic coefficient or BC figure—again, the comparison of the ability of your bullet to overcome air drag and wind drift with a particular model—is not a static figure; it changes over a range of velocities. Often when the bullet manufacturer lists a BC figure for their bullet, it is in comparison with the G1 bullet model (a model that simply doesn't best describe most of today's bullets) as well as being an average of the changing BC over a variety of distances and velocities. While it serves as an approximation, there are better means of representing the highly specialized bullets of the modern era, the ones that truly require an accurate representation as they are used for long-distance work.

As a reminder, the sectional density, or SD, is a ratio of the bullet's mass (weight) to its bore diameter. While we'll be using this characteristic much more in the terminal ballistics section, for the purposes of external ballistics your bullet's SD figure is an important part of deriving its form factor, in comparison to a G1 or G7 bullet model, and that in turn is used for the derivation of an accurate BC.

There are also the rotational effects of a bullet that need to be taken into account for true long-range accuracy. That same spin that the barrel's rifling imparted on the bullet not only keeps it stable in flight, but causes an effect known as spin drift at extreme ranges. If you're serious about long-range shooting, you'll want to know how to calculate and adjust for it.

CHAPTER 7

Factors Affecting the Bullet in Flight

O nce that projectile leaves the muzzle of the barrel spinning at a prescribed rate, having received all the propulsion it possibly could have from the specific powder charge that was designed for it, there are a number of forces that begin to act. Gravity, friction (caused by the atmosphere into which it was delivered), and wind drift being chief among the culprits, the poor bullet isn't quite sure what to do. Hopefully, the bright-eyed humans who designed the launching tube—that piece of steel we call a barrel—have understood the physics of their environment well enough that the projectile is spinning at a rate sufficient to provide a smooth, stable flight, with as little interference as possible during its journey.

Gravity

Gravity has a definite effect on bullet flight. All objects fall toward the earth's center at the same rate. If you were to drop a stone from your hand, it will fall at the same rate as if you threw it as hard as you could on a line perpendicular to the line of gravity.

The same principal can be applied to projectiles. As explained earlier, when we say that a particular cartridge is flat-shooting, it is due to the fact that a higher than normal muzzle velocity allows for the bullet to cover more ground before it begins to fall due to gravity. The more aerodynamic the bullet, the less it will be affected by the friction of the atmosphere. Concurrently, an aerodynamic projectile will be less affected by crosswind drift. As I stated earlier, the quantification for the aerodynamic properties of a certain shaped bullet is called its ballistic coefficient. This figure is rather difficult to describe and harder to understand, as it is a comparison to a particular model, not a static number. The figure is represented as a definite number by many of the bullet companies (Sierra Bullets gives a varying BC figure for different velocity ranges) but is actually a variable, affected greatly by velocity, and changing throughout the velocity spectrum. In other words, though it may only be a slight change, a bullet's BC will indeed change throughout the entire course of its flight. For true long-range work, you should be able to compute these figures to best hit a distant target, and some of the ballistic calculating programs can be a great aid in these calculations.

Again, let's not lose sight of the big picture. What kind of shooter are you? If you've purchased this book, you have an interest in long-range ballistics, or at least ballistics in general. If you're like me and limit yourself to what I call sane hunting ranges, say 350 to 450 yards, the more minute points of ballistic coefficient may be lost on you. Yes, at ranges beyond 200 or 250 yards the boattail bullet begins to show its benefits with respect to both trajectory and wind drift; but I can tell you with certainty that I've made shots out past 350 yards with what most would consider the most unfavorable bullet profile. Not to say that it's all bunk, and those of us who stay within 450 yards need not understand the minutiae, but realize that once you get out past 500 yards the small details make a much bigger difference. There are many different hunting and/or shooting situations in the world, and each has a different application.

Me? I limit myself to ranges inside 450 yards, and then only under perfect conditions. As a target shooter, I absolutely love the long-range game, but local conditions limit the distances to 500 yards. So, as a result of many different conditions here in my home state of New York, in addition to the multitude of situations that I'm faced with as a global hunter, I have to adapt the ammunition and bullet choices to the job at hand.

Wind, the Unseen Enemy

Wind drift is a more difficult parameter with which to deal than is gravity. The effect of crossing winds on a bullet's flight path is dramatic, and often less easy to predict than the effects of gravity. The weight and speed of your projectile come into play here, as well as its shape. I grew up hunting in Upstate New York, where the effects of the wind are negligible at best, unless you were a dedicated woodchuck hunter who prowled the hay lots and orchards; even then the truly windy days didn't give a lot of action. I was on safari in the Orange Free State of South Africa in 2004, hunting eland with my prized Winchester Model 70 in .375 H&H Magnum. We had tracked a herd for nearly a mile when we caught sight of them, but there was a problem. They were feeding slowly across a wide open plain, but were 400 yards out with no cover available whatsoever to make an approach possible. We laid down next to a small termite mound and had a brief, curt discussion. My Professional Hunter firmly believed I could make the shot and encouraged me to use my pack for a rest to be as steady as possible. Now, I know that rifle very well and had carefully handloaded all the ammunition and knew the gun was MOA out to 250 yards, even prepared a drop chart out to 400, but we had a 20 to 25 mph crosswind, right to left. I knew the vertical holdover to compensate for bullet drop, but that wind! With a muzzle velocity of 2,500 fps on the button, I knew it didn't have the frozen rope trajectory of some of the lighter caliber magnums, but the 300-grain bullet wouldn't be horrible in the wind. The Swift A-Frame is a semi-spitzer design, with a decent ballistic coefficient as compared to the round-nosed bullets, but it isn't exactly optimum for true long-range work. However, this was the shot that presented itself, and we discussed these factors as we waited for the big bull to come clear of the cows. I did my best to recall all the data I'd looked at for this bullet combination, and figured 12–14 inches of lead would have worked just fine. As I started the squeeze, a small cow stepped into view and I backed off from the shot. I'm glad I did, as it gave me an opportunity to reevaluate the situation. I looked at the stunted grass near the eland herd, and saw the wind was blowing much harder at the eland than it was where we were lying in wait.

When the bull cleared again, I adjusted the windage to give a full 20 inches of lead into the wind, and caressed the trigger. The sound that floated back on that wind was glorious; a bone-smashing *crack*—and once the rifle had recoiled I saw he'd taken that A-Frame right on the shoulder. We walked to within 200 yards and finished him. However, had that cow not interrupted the first shot, I'd have invariably hit him too far back, and might have lost him.

The second story I'd like to relate to demonstrate the point is a prairie dog shoot in South Dakota, where I had an opportunity to use many different rifles during the course of a week. My friend JJ Reich of Vista Outdoors had invited me and several other writers on a hunt to unveil several new types of ammunition and rifles out on the Rosebud Reservation. The Dakotas have some of the biggest prairie dog towns I've ever seen, and as trees come at a premium on the open prairie, the wind was certainly going to be a factor. We were using small-bore rifles: .17 HMR, .17 WSM, .17 Hornet, .22 Hornet, .22 Long Rifle, .22 WRM, .223 Remington and .22-250 Remington. In three full days of shooting, we had about two hours of truly calm conditions, so this was a great opportunity to observe and educate ourselves about the effect of wind drift. Rifles were zeroed at varying ranges, depending on their trajectory, and our guide Cliff would be helping us call the shots on the little rodents. We had shooting benches available, and I was paired with my friend Eric Conn, then Editor in Chief of *Gun Digest the Magazine*. Conn and I set up on the top of the small hill overlooking a dog town that stretched out to 600 or 700 yards. This experience opened my eyes to the wind's effects like no other shooting I've ever done. We had all sorts of Federal Premium and American Eagle ammunition, in varying configurations.

Velocity was key on this hunt, to minimize the time of the bullet's flight, and therefore minimize the effect of wind drift. The .17 HMR is considered a decent long-range rimfire cartridge, pushing a 17-grain polymer-tipped bullet at a muzzle velocity of 2,650 fps, while the .17 Winchester Super Magnum launches a 20-grain pill of similar profile and construction to a muzzle velocity of 3,000 fps. While using both cartridges, the .17 WSM showed a distinct superiority in the wind. And despite only a 350 fps difference between the cartridges, the WSM's wind lead was measured in inches, while the HMR's was measured in feet when both were shot in a stiff crosswind. While each bullet had enough striking power to quickly dispatch any dog with a solid hit, the hits were easier with the faster cartridge.

The same conclusion can be drawn when comparing the .17 Hornet with the venerable .22 Hornet. While the .22 Hornet has been with us since my grandfather's generation and is a well-respected varmint cartridge, the younger sibling made the old guy look anemic. If I had to pick a second favorite cartridge on this particular trip—second by a nose to my old friend the .22-250

Remington—it would be the .17 Hornet. The 20-grain bullet driven to a muzzle velocity of 3,650 fps proved itself an absolute champion while working in the Dakota breeze, giving wind-bucking performance on par with the .223 and .22-250 within 300 yards. The .22 Hornet was solid within 150 yards or so, but the heavier, semi-spitzer design we were using began to drift severely outside that distance.

The .223 Remington also enlightened me on this trip, as we had two different loads to compare in the field. The 50-grain hollowpoint load from the American Eagle Varmint and Predator line was on hand, as well as the Federal Premium 62-grain Trophy Bonded Tip load. The American Eagle load runs at a muzzle velocity of 3,325 fps, while the Federal 62-grain bullet exits the barrel at 3,050 fps, and one would think that the higher velocity bullet would hold the advantage in the heavy crosswind. That wasn't what I found to be true. The 62-grain slug needed several less inches of wind dope when shot in the same conditions in order to kill the dogs, despite being almost 300 fps slower than the 50-grainers.

After burning up over 1,000 rounds of ammunition, at distances varying from 45 to 450 yards and wind conditions changing from near calm to gale force, I knew after three days of nonstop shooting that I needed to know more about these parameters and how they affect the bullet flight path of my favorite rifles and cartridges. It was quite an education seeing the dust puff up from my misses, as well as having a guide with good optics and an incredible set of eyes to call my hits. It piqued my curiosity to learn more about these effects so I could better predict the outcome of my shots.

Other Culprits

About a month later, I had pulled up to the front door of Tim Fallon's FTW Ranch near Barksdale, Texas, as a student of the SAAM (Sportsman's All-Weather All-Terrain Marksmanship) Shooting course. The FTW is comprised of 12,000 acres of draws and canyons, with numerous shooting ranges that would combine distance, crosswind, elevation differences, and both moving and stationary targets. The instructors are Navy Seals, well-versed and experienced in all types of precision shooting, as well as being very familiar with the heavy bore safari rifles that would comprise a part of the training. These boys are shooters and great teachers, as well.

I spent equal time with a medium-caliber 6.5 Creedmoor and my old safari friend: a Heym Express bolt-action rifle in .404 Jeffery. The first thing I found was a dope card for the rifles, giving all sorts of information about the downrange trajectory and wind-bucking capabilities of the two rifles, in addition to the necessary information about the riflescope reticles I would be using, and how to reference certain points to make a long-range shot much easier.

In the classroom, instructor Doug "Dog" Prichard delved into the data used to prepare these cards. A computer program asked for a variety of parameters to best calculate a trajectory and give a baseline for wind drift, taking into account air density, elevation and spin drift caused by the rifling. Notable was the difference in trajectory while shooting in air of varying densities. It made logical sense that as elevation above sea level increases, the air becomes thinner and a projectile would meet less resistance in this type of air. Correspondingly, thicker air—nearer to sea level—would create more friction and change the trajectory. Humidity and barometric pressure have an effect on a bullet's path. Humid air is actually thinner than dry air, and will increase the BC of your bullet, something that will change the point of impact of a particular load when distance increases. If you routinely shoot at ranges over 500 yards, or are practicing for a sheep hunt or other circumstance where a long shot may be required, it is important to know how the conditions of the atmosphere will affect your shot.

Knowledge is power, and there are tools available to provide it, like the Kestrel Elite Weather Meter, which allows you to measure and combat atmospheric effects to place the bullet where it needs to be. You need to know how to use these tools, and how to derive the changes in trajectory. Depending upon the particular weather conditions at your location, the atmosphere will affect your bullet's flight path. I can adjust elevation higher or lower than the baseline information.

There is also the *Coriolis Effect*, which comes into play when distances get truly long. Summed up for our purposes, Coriolis is the effect of the rotation of the earth on a bullet in flight. The earth rotates (at the equator) at about 1,040 miles per hour. Converted to feet per second (fps) that's a velocity of 1,525 fps. This speed is significantly less as you move toward either of the poles, because less ground is covered per revolution. This difference in ground speed, if you will, pushes a bullet's point of impact to the right in the northern hemisphere, left in the southern hemisphere. The horizontal correction for Coriolis is negligible until you get out to 1,000 yards and over.

Additionally, Coriolis will change the vertical point of impact if you are shooting along the east-west directional lines. Long-range shots to the east will hit higher than those fired to the west, because of the direction of the earth's rotation. What is actually happening is this: a target east of your muzzle is actually sinking away from the bullet's path as the earth rotates, so the impact on the target will hit higher than if it were fired in a north-south direction (where this effect is negated), while shots fired westward hit low, because the earth's spin is causing the target to rise.

You see, the longer the time of flight of a bullet, the more time the earth has to spin. This vertical effect is maximized at the equator, minimized at the poles. For both horizontal and vertical correction, your latitude must be known to make the proper correction. While this correction is too small to be significant for most hunting situations, the long-range target crowd will appreciate the correction values, and some of the ballistic software we're going to discuss will help make that correction in your dope.

Let's take a look at each of these factors in depth.

CHAPTER 8

Gravity

I f you've ever accidently dropped a drinking glass while doing the dishes, the resulting shards are a result of good ol' gravity. Earth has a definite force known as gravity, which pulls all objects toward its center whether at rest or in motion. All objects, if we ignore the effects of atmospheric resistance, fall to the ground at the same speed. Yes, there are minute variations, but for our purpose of understanding the trajectory of a projectile assume that all bullets are going to be drawn toward the planet's center at the same rate. The same rate, in fact, as if you simply held them against the muzzle and let them fall to the ground (this would be absolute in a vacuum, but it's close enough for this discussion, the atmospheric forces actually tend to give a bullet in flight a tiny bit of lift.)

In order to reach a distant target, you must propel the projectile from your barrel at a certain speed in order to cover more horizontal distance before the gravitational pull brings it down to the ground. Otherwise, you'd be resorting to climbing trees and dropping heavy rocks on your prey from above, and that's not much fun at all. So, assuming a standard, uniform projectile, whether a sleek spitzer boattail or a round ball fired from a muzzleloader, the faster the projectile is launched, the more horizontal distance it will cover. Let's look at an example.

Imagine a projectile launched from the muzzle of a rifle at dead level, perpendicular to the gravitational force, and launched at a velocity of 2,000 fps. It would cover a certain amount of distance, which we'll call X, before it falls to the earth, yet will fall at the same rate as if you had dropped it. Now imagine the same projectile launched at 3,000 fps. It, too, will fall at the same prescribed rate but will cover a different amount of distance, call it Y. It's rather plain to see that the 'X' distance (of the slower bullet) must be less than the 'Y' distance due to the latter's greater speed. The faster you propel a bullet (assuming the weight and dimensions are uniform), the more ground it will cover before dropping to the earth.

This is the very reason magnum cartridges give a flatter trajectory than do their standard-velocity counterparts: the bullet is simply moving faster and covers more ground in the time it takes gravity to pull it downward.

When you use a firearm, you are never perfectly aligning the bore to the line of sight. You are constantly fighting the effects of the gravitational force, and must therefore elevate the muzzle of the firearm with respect to the line of sight, giving the bullet's trajectory some amount of arc. Most of the time, your sight plane is above the bore (laser-sighted handguns are the only exception I can think of), so the bullet starts out at a certain distance below the bore from the word go. Once the powder is burned and the bullet leaves the muzzle it will cross the sight plane at a certain distance—typically 25 to 30 yards for rifle bullets—then rise above the sight plane only to cross that plane again at the zero distance.

It is the second crossing of the sight plane, the zero distance, which you use to reference your trajectory curve. When we say that a rifle is zeroed for 200 yards, it means that the bullet will cross the line of sight at exactly 200 yards. Within that distance, there will be a slight rise, the amount depending on the shape and velocity of the bullet. Past the zero distance the parabolic curve is generated by the slowing of the bullet and the effects of gravity, and represents a trajectory that will show how the bullet will drop.

One of my favorite big game cartridges is the .300 Winchester Magnum, and my best load for that rifle pushes a 180-grain Swift Scirocco II bullet at a velocity of 2,960 fps. I use a 200-yard zero for this rifle, as that best serves my needs for most of my hunting situations. Once I plug the data into the Hornady Ballistic Calculator (www.Hornady.com) the trajectory is as follows. The bullet starts out at 1.75 inches below the sighting plane (a Leupold riflescope), and first crosses the line of sight at about 30 yards. Remember, I have sighted this rifle to have the bullet hit spot-on the bullseye at 200 yards, so there will be some elevation between 40 yards and 200 yards. The highest that bullet will rise in its trajectory curve is 1.6 inches at 125 yards.

Once it crosses the sighting plane again at 200 yards, it begins to drop below the line of sight. At 250 yards, the bullet will strike 2.6 inches below the line of sight, and at 300 yards it has dropped 6.6 inches. Take it out a bit farther, and you'll find it dropped 12.1 inches at 350 yards, 19.1 at 400 yards, and 27.8 at 450 yards. At extreme ranges, you'll get a feel for how quickly trajectory drops off. At the 600-yard mark, the bullet drops 65 inches, and at 700 yards a full 101 inches. You can easily see why it is difficult to hit those distant targets! Now, the .300 Winchester Magnum is considered a flat-shooting cartridge, yet even this trajectory requires a precise knowledge of the distance to the target when shooting past 200 yards. Because I use this rifle for hunting, I can accept a vertical deviation of about 2.5 inches up or down and still be confident in striking the vitals of a game animal, so I will call this rifle "dead-on" to 250 yards; meaning that my bullet will neither rise nor fall more than 2.5 inches from the line of sight.

Once distances exceed 250 yards, the effect of gravitational pull forces me to make an adjustment in my sighting plane to account for the bullet's drop. There is plenty of accurate data available to predict the effect of gravitational pull, and if you intend to shoot at distances past the point at which your rifle is zeroed, I'd highly recommend you take a look at it.

RANGE(YARDS)	VELOCITY(FPS)	ENERGY(FT.-LB.)	TRAJECTORY(IN)
Muzzle	2,960	3,502	-1.75
50	2,868	3,288	0.5
100	2,779	3,086	1.5
150	2,691	2,894	1.4
200	2,605	2,712	0
250	2,521	2,540	-2.6
300	2,438	2,375	-6.6
350	2,357	2,220	-12.1
400	2,277	2,072	-19.1
450	2,198	1,932	-27.8
500	2,122	1,799	-38.3
550	2,046	1,674	-50.8
600	1,973	1,555	-65.3
650	1,901	1,444	-82.1
700	1,831	1,339	-101.2
750	1,762	1,241	-123
800	1,696	1,149	-147.5
850	1,631	1,063	-175.1
900	1,569	984	-205.9
950	1,509	910	-240.3
1000	1,451	842	-278.5

Angle Shooting

All of these figures I've shown you are relative to a flat-shooting plane, where the muzzle and target are at the same elevation. If you raise or lower the target, the amount of drop necessary will appear to change. Let's say I'm using my .300 Winchester to shoot at a target 400 yards away, but at a downhill angle of 20 degrees. The above information will indicate that I need to hold 19.1 inches above the bullseye, in order to allow for the drop over that distance. However, I'd hit the target about 4 inches higher than I aimed. Now, perhaps that would still be a lung hit, or maybe it would not be a vital hit at all. Why?

When measuring the effect of gravity on a bullet's trajectory, it needs to be done on a level line, perpendicular to the line of gravity. When shooting uphill or down, you need to know the level distance. It's not hard to calculate this difference; simply observe the angle of deviation from level (in our instance, 20 degrees), and take the cosine of that angle. Multiply those results by the slope distance (like you'd observe on some laser rangefinders) and you'll have the level distance. In the case above, where my .300 Winchester was 19.1 inches low at 400 yards, I should've held for 375 yards—the level distance—where the bullet will strike 15.5 inches low.

Here's the math:

$$\text{Cos (20 deg.)} = 0.939 \quad 0.939 \times 400 \text{ yards} = 375.8 \text{ yards.}$$

As the shooter, you need to know both the distance (again the range finder is your friend), and angle, either up or down. There are a couple of methods I recommend. Many of today's smartphones provide an app that will act as a level, providing a measurement of the angle up or down from level; I use one that acts as a clinometer (I'm a mild-mannered land surveyor by day) and is rather accurate. If I have a severe uphill or downhill shot, especially at the distances where the reduction in range becomes significant, I should have time to use my phone to observe the angle and make the necessary adjustment. Many of today's laser rangefinders, such as the Bushnell Elite 1 Mile, also provide either a level distance to the target, doing the mathematics for you, or the angle from the shooter to the target. If you don't like the electronic gizmos, you can spend some time in the field judging some severe slopes where the level distance to the target will be affected most and develop a good idea of what a 10-degree slope looks like in comparison to a 20- or even 30-degree slope. When things get to 30 degrees and more, you'll usually find climbing requires a hands and knees position. It's very common for most folks to judge a slope as more severe than it truly is, so some practice will come in handy for reducing those distances to level. While few of us carry a cosine chart around in our heads, here's a good reference piece to give you the amount of reduction necessary, in percentages.

5-10 degree slope = 98% of slope distance
15-20 degree slope = 95% of slope distance
25-30 degree slope = 90% of slope distance
35-40 degree slope = 80% of slope distance
45 degree slope = 70% of slope distance

For the rifle, where we have the benefit of using sleek, sharp bullets that resist gravity's effects efficiently, the gravitational drop is a manageable figure, especially within common hunting distances. For the handgun hunter, where velocities are significantly lower—coupled with using projectiles that traditionally have a much lower BC—knowing the distances even within 150 yards becomes paramount.

For personal defense guns, the distances at which you are likely to shoot are close enough to negate the major effects of gravitational pull. That said, I like to take my carry guns out to distances where I see a definite drop in my group, so I know what's going on. The same principals we discussed for rifle bullets apply to handgun bullets, except the scale shrinks a bit.

As a side note, while all of this mathematical wizardry probably won't make much of a difference to the hunter whose shots are taken within 200 yards (which I feel represents a great deal of the shots taken at game annually), there is a movement in the hunting world to take shots at game at distances that seem to increase with every television season. While I realize that shots out past 500 yards can certainly be executed by a shooter who is highly experienced and

SLOPE SHOOTING

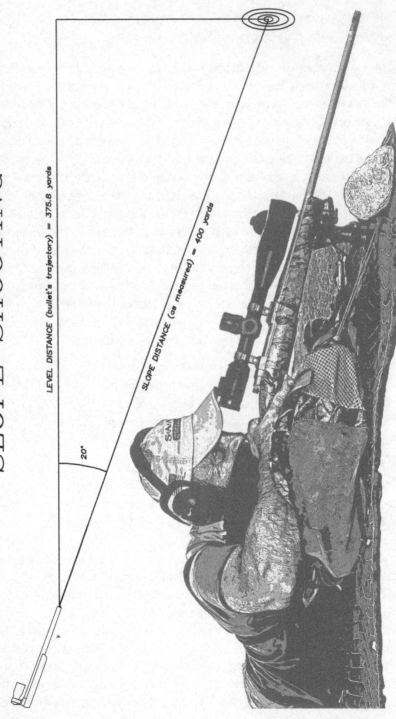

LEVEL DISTANCE (bullet's trajectory) = 375.8 yards

SLOPE DISTANCE (as measured) = 400 yards

20°

knows his or her gear inside and out, the portrayal of routine shots taken out past 700 yards, at unwounded game, is not only unethical, but will result in a multitude of wounded game. As I demonstrated with the drop figures alone—saying nothing of the effects of wind deflection—a misjudgment in distance of as little as 25 yards can result in a wounded and/or lost animal. I highly suggest you find your own personal limits with respect to distance, based upon your own shooting abilities, and stay true to that figure. It's one of the instances where you'll have to police yourself. Should you realize that the distance is too great to make a confident hit, simply say no to the shot and get closer. Purchasing the best long range optics, and a cartridge/rifle combination that is theoretically capable of connecting, does not make it a wise decision to take the shot. I don't want to sound like I'm preaching, but I'm not comfortable with the way some outdoor personalities act blasé about shots past 500 yards at game; there's an awful lot that can go wrong.

So, with an accurate drop chart available, how can you make those shots that require a certain amount of holdover? Gravity is relentless, and you need to fight that effect, even at 250 or 300 yards.

In this great technological age you'd be foolish not to take advantage of electronic calculators. A ballistic drop compensated (BDC) reticle in a riflescope is another means. This is a reticle with more than just crosshairs, but a series of smaller horizontal lines on the lower vertical wire at a predetermined interval, providing a specific aiming point out at certain distances. For example, my 6.5-284 Norma wears a Swarovski Z5 3.5-18x44mm riflescope, with the BRH reticle. This optic features a duplex reticle on three of the four wires (up, left and right) and a ballistic compensated reticle on the lower vertical wire. In addition to the crosshair point, which I use for a 200-yard zero, there are five additional, smaller crosswires, and four small dots on that lower wire, as well as a point where the thin wire thickens. In that rifle with 140-grain handloads, it works like this: my traditional crosshair is set to hit at 200 yards (and at any range shorter than that I'll confidently hit an animal's vitals), using the next lower crosswire it will hit at 270 yards, and the dot below that will impact at 330 yards. Should an even 300-yard shot present itself, I simply hold between the first crosswire and first dot.

Holding at the next crosswire down causes the rifle to hit at 390 yards (I use this for 400, calling it close enough) while the next dot lower is for 450 yards. Continuing down the line, the next line is an even 500 yards, and the dot below that will strike at 550 yards. The fourth wire down strikes at 590 yards (so close to 600 it'll scare you) and the dot below impacts at 640 yards. The lowest crosswire is designed to hit at 680 yards, but we're already considerably past my hunting ranges. I much prefer to stay within 400 yards, but certain hunts may require a longer shot. However, it sure is fun to play with steel plates and paper targets at those distances. Now, I've found this reticle works within reason at these distances, and Swarovski has put a considerable amount of research into it. And while this is only one of their available options, I think it makes a good choice for a hunter whose ranges concur with my own, or don't plan to take shots much past 600 yards (where things can get tricky due to the winds, but that's for later).

Trust Then Verify

However well your trajectory projections are, you must verify your point of impact v. point of aim in actual field conditions. This is called truing the rifle, and it's an important part of knowing how your measuring device (reticle) works at extended ranges. While Swarovski has done an exorbitant amount of homework, barrels are finicky little buggers, and slight variations of barrel performance or ammunition can result in a different distance at which those crosswires and dots will strike. Swarovski provides several blank stickers, with a reticle diagram, for those who perhaps shoot a cartridge/bullet combination that doesn't mate up to one of the standard profiles, or for those who wish to tweak and fine-tune the reticle measurements. After all, those crosswires are nothing more and nothing less than a series of reference points for holds on distant shots, rather than the "hold the top of the back and send it" method. Note, because this reticle works in the second focal plane, these measurements will only work when the riflescope is at maximum power, in my case at 18x. By the way, those small crosswires each have a vertical tick mark to demonstrate 10 and 20 mph crosswinds, but that's another discussion that will be handled in an upcoming chapter.

Another method that is frequently employed for hitting distant targets is to dial-up the elevation turret the required amount to move the crosshairs to the necessary point of aim. These are the riflescopes with the huge turrets, replete with finger grooves for quick turning. They are designed to quickly dial an elevation change, based upon a dope card that matches your particular ammunition. For example, if you zero a rifle such as my .300 Winchester Magnum at 200 yards, the elevation drop for further distances can be compensated for by dialing up a particular amount of minutes of angle, or a particular amount of milliradians, or mils on the elevation turret. Again, an example:

When I hand you my favorite .300 Winchester, you take a few shots at the 200-yard target and verify it hits the bullseye. You are then presented with a shot at 450 yards, and are forced to use only the elevation turret to make the adjustment, so as to hold the crosshairs directly

Many smartphones offer an app for measuring slope angle.

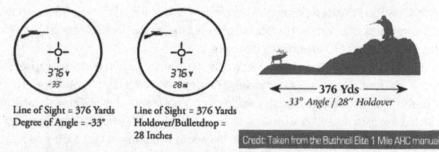

Line of Sight = 376 Yards
Degree of Angle = -33°

Line of Sight = 376 Yards
Holdover/Bulletdrop =
28 Inches

376 Yds
-33° Angle / 28" Holdover

Credit: Taken from the Bushnell Elite 1 Mile ARC manual

The Bushnell 1 Mile rangefinder helps establish the shooting angle.

on the target in order to make the shot. Consulting the same ballistic chart you did earlier, you would see that the Hornady program says you'd need an additional 5.9 MOA in order to have your trajectory curve strike the line of sight at 450 yards. Assuming you set the elevation turret to read zero when you hit the 200-yard bullseye, it would be a simple adjustment of dialing up to 6.0 MOA (rounding the 5.9 up to 6.0, as the scope takes adjustment in 0.25 MOA increments), and a confident, yet gentle squeeze of trigger to make a solid hit. Using this dial-up method is a quick learning curve, allowing you all sorts of flexibility if you know the range. This method, as well as the Ballistic Drop Compensated reticle, requires a definitive knowledge of the range at which you are shooting, or all is for naught.

The distance to the target, whether sloped or level, is a required variable in the equation of holdover to defeat gravitational force. A good laser rangefinder is a very important piece of gear to the hunter or shooter who needs to make that distant shot on a target at an unknown distance. In addition, measuring reticles can also be used to approximate distance, if the size of the game animal is known.

At any rate, the effects of gravity are predictable and can be compensated for. Of all the effects that will be placed upon a bullet once it's launched from the barrel, gravitational pull is the easiest with which to deal. However, your riflescope's reticle must be perfectly aligned with the centerline of your rifle's bore. Any sort of a cant in the alignment of the vertical hair, and your bullets will not drop in a line along the vertical crosshair, they will be hitting in the direction that the top of the scope is canted. This can be frustrating, especially with an accurate rifle that *should* be hitting where you aim. I highly recommend a scope level; there are many styles available, and they can be an invaluable tool for long-range work, ensuring that your bullets fall along the line of the vertical crosswire. If you keep things precise before you pull the trigger, it will become much easier to hit a distant target.

Choosing a Zero

At what distance you choose to zero your rifle is both subjective and personal. Different hunting or shooting scenarios call for different zero distances. Firstly, where do you hunt? Is it in the thick forests of the northern West Coast, or the arboreal forests of the Northeast, where most of your shots are within 100 paces? Or are you a western hunter, where shots can vary from up-close-and-personal to across a distant canyon? All of these situations call for a different zero, and you should look at some of the reasons for the choice.

Starting with a woods gun, like a .30-30 Winchester, it really wouldn't make sense to set the zero at 200 yards, like you would with many of the common centerfire rifle cartridges. That's because the severe arc of its trajectory would cause a rise of 4.2 inches at 100 yards, which is a bit much in thick vegetation. More sensible would either be a 100-yard zero, which is actually about the longest shot you're likely to get in the woods anyhow, or at best a 150-yard zero if you're concerned about a longer shot.

From the Federal Premium Ballistics Calculator:	
Load Number:	3030B
Zero Range:	150 yd.
Caliber:	.30-30 Win.
Temperature:	59 °F
Bullet Style:	Soft Point RN
Wind Speed:	10 mph
Bullet Weight:	170 gr.
Altitude:	0 feet
Ballistic Coefficient:	0.254
Max Range:	300 yd.
Muzzle Velocity:	2,200 fps
Test Barrel:	24 in.
Sight Height:	1.5 in.

Range (yd.)	Drop (in.)	Wind Drift (in.)	Velocity (fps)	Energy (ft.-lb.)
0	-1.5	0	2,200	1,827
25	0.1	0.1	2,121	1,698
50	1.2	0.4	2,044	1,577
75	1.8	1	1,968	1,462
100	1.8	1.8	1,894	1,354
125	1.3	2.9	1,822	1,253
150	0	4.3	1,753	1,159
175	-2	6.1	1,685	1,072
200	-4.7	8.1	1,619	990
225	-8.2	10.4	1,556	913
250	-12.6	13	1,494	843
275	-18	16	1,435	777
300	-24.5	19.4	1,380	719

This kind of scenario is pretty close to the old "inch-and-a-half-high-at-a-hundred" recommendation to which my grandfather subscribed. He felt it covered all the bases, and it does. I actually prefer to zero my .30-30 Winchester at 75 yards, because that's about the longest shot I get in the areas I most frequently use my old lever gun to hunt. My trajectory looks more like this, again from Federal:

From the Federal Premium Ballistics Calculator:	
Load Number:	3030B
Zero Range:	75 yd.
Caliber:	.30-30 Win.
Temperature:	59 °F
Bullet Style:	Soft Point RN
Wind Speed:	10 mph
Bullet Weight:	170 gr.
Altitude:	0 feet
Ballistic Coefficient:	0.254
Max Range:	300 yd.
Muzzle Velocity:	2,200 fps
Test Barrel:	24 in
Sight Height:	1.5 in.

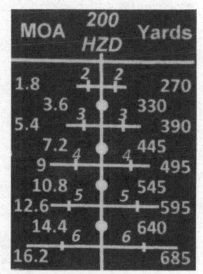

The author's dope card for the Swarovski Z5 reticle.

Range (yd.)	Drop (in.)	Wind Drift (in.)	Velocity (fps)	Energy (ft.-lb.)
0	-1.5	0	2,200	1,827
25	-0.5	0.1	2,121	1,698
50	0	0.4	2,044	1,577
75	0	1	1,968	1,462
100	-0.5	1.8	1,894	1,354
125	-1.7	2.9	1,822	1,253
150	-3.6	4.3	1,753	1,159
175	-6.1	6.1	1,685	1,072
200	-9.5	8.1	1,619	990
225	-13.6	10.4	1,556	913
250	-18.6	13	1,494	843
275	-24.5	16	1,435	777
300	-31.6	19.4	1,380	719

While I may be 6 inches low at 175 yards, I don't feel comfortable taking a shot at that distance with an iron-sighted carbine anyhow, so I prefer the one-inch window trajectory. That way I don't have to think about drop at all, within woods range.

Let's look at a .308 Winchester, with a bit more muzzle velocity, and a bullet that has a form better suited to the longer ranges. I generally zero a rifle in this class at 200 yards; that gives me a dead hold to somewhere around 250 yards on a deer-sized target. Let's look at the Federal Trophy Bonded Tipped factory load, at 165-grains.

From the Federal Premium Ballistics Calculator:

Load Number:	P308TT4
Zero Range:	200 yd.
Caliber:	.308 Win. (7.62x51mm)
Temperature:	59 °F
Bullet Style:	Trophy Bonded® Tip
Wind Speed:	10 mph
Bullet Weight:	165 gr.
Altitude:	0 feet
Ballistic Coefficient:	0.45
Max Range:	500 yd.
Muzzle Velocity:	2880 fps
Test Barrel:	24 in.
Sight Height:	1.75 in.

Range (yd.)	Drop (in.)	Wind Drift (in.)	Velocity (fps)	Energy (ft.-lb.)
0	-1.8	0	2,880	3,039
25	-0.5	0	2,828	2,929
50	0.5	0.2	2,776	2,823
75	1.2	0.4	2,725	2,721
100	1.6	0.7	2,675	2,621
125	1.6	1.1	2,625	2,524
150	1.4	1.6	2,575	2,430
175	0.9	2.2	2,527	2,339
200	0	2.9	2,478	2,250
225	-1.2	3.6	2,431	2,164
250	-2.8	4.5	2,383	2,081
275	-4.8	5.5	2,337	2,000
300	-7.2	6.7	2,290	1,922
325	-10	8	2,245	1,846
350	-13.3	9.3	2,200	1,773
375	-17.0	10.8	2,155	1,701
400	-21.1	12.5	2,111	1,633
425	-25.8	14.2	2,067	1,566
450	-30.9	16	2,024	1,501
475	-36.6	18.1	1,982	1,439
500	-42.6	20.1	1,939	1,377

Again, you see the "inch-and-a-half-high-at-a-hundred," with a respectable trajectory at the longer hunting ranges. What if you wanted to flatten the trajectory a bit, by using a 250-yard zero? What would that do to your closer shots? Here's the dope:

Ballistics Calculator:	
Load Number:	P308TT4
Zero Range:	250 yd.
Caliber:	.308 Win. (7.62x51mm)
Temperature:	59 °F
Bullet Style:	Trophy Bonded® Tip
Wind Speed:	10 mph
Bullet Weight:	165 gr.
Altitude:	0 feet
Ballistic Coefficient:	0.45
Max Range:	500 yd.
Muzzle Velocity:	2880 fps
Test Barrel:	24 in
Sight Height:	1.75 in

Range (yd.)	Drop (In.)	Wind Drift (in.)	Velocity (fps)	Energy (ft.-lb.)
0	-1.8	0	2,880	3,039
25	-0.2	0	2,828	2,929
50	1	0.2	2,776	2,823
75	2	0.4	2,725	2,721
100	2.7	0.7	2,675	2,621
125	3.1	1.1	2,625	2,524
150	3.1	1.6	2,575	2,430
175	2.9	2.2	2,527	2,339
200	2.2	2.9	2,478	2,250
225	1.3	3.6	2,431	2,164
250	0	4.5	2,383	2,081
275	-1.7	5.5	2,337	2,000
300	-3.8	6.7	2,290	1,922
325	-6.4	8	2,245	1,846
350	-9.3	9.3	2,200	1,773
375	-12.8	10.8	2,155	1,701
400	-16.6	12.5	2,111	1,633
425	-21	14.2	2,067	1,566
450	-25.8	16	2,024	1,501
475	-31.2	18.1	1,982	1,439
500	-37	20.1	1,939	1,377

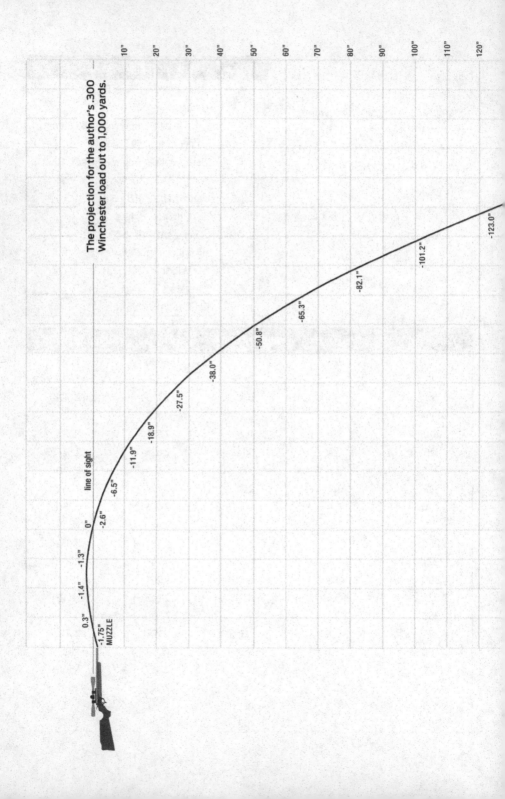

The projection for the author's .300 Winchester load out to 1,000 yards.

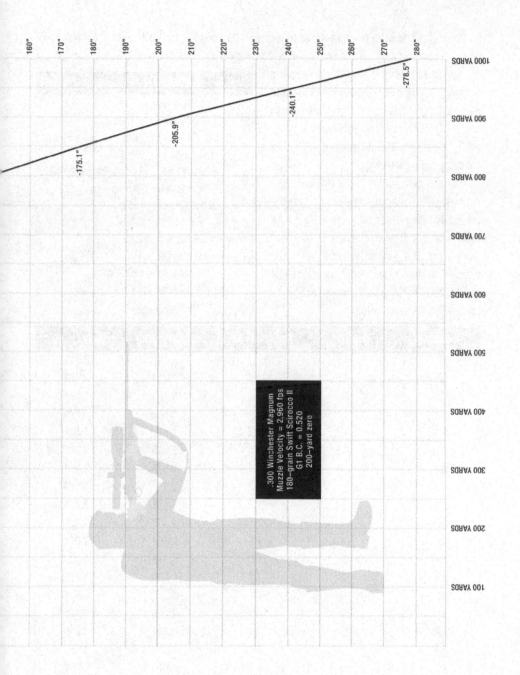

.300 Winchester Magnum
Muzzle Velocity = 2,960 fps
180-grain Swift Scirocco II
G1 B.C. = 0.520
200-yard zero

The highest point in the mid-range trajectory is 3.1 inches, which is tolerable, especially on an open country hunt. This bullet travels to lower than 3 inches out to 290 yards. Considering the size of a deer's vital area, that represents a dead hold out to 300 yards. I know that the Federal Premium load develops a rather high muzzle velocity, but it is legitimate, so when you're shooting a .308 Winchester you have a solid big-game cartridge.

There are times when I use a 100-yard zero with my .308, especially when hunting in the thicker wooded areas of Upstate New York when I need to 'thread the needle' on those tight shots. But, I need to know what will happen on the longer shots, even if it's just out to 200 or 250 yards. Here's that same load with a 100-yard zero:

Ballistics Calculator:	
Load Number:	P308TT4
Zero Range:	100 yd.
Caliber:	.308 Win. (7.62x51mm)
Temperature:	59 °F
Bullet Style:	Trophy Bonded® Tip
Wind Speed:	10 mph
Bullet Weight:	165 gr.
Altitude:	0 feet
Ballistic Coefficient:	0.45
Max Range:	500 yd.
Muzzle Velocity:	2880 fps
Test Barrel:	24 in.
Sight Height:	1.5 in.

Range (yd.)	Drop (in.)	Wind Drift (in.)	Velocity (fps)	Energy (ft.-lb.)
0	-1.5	0	2,880	3,039
25	-0.7	0	2,828	2,929
50	-0.2	0.2	2,776	2,823
75	0.1	0.4	2,725	2,721
100	0	0.7	2,675	2,621
125	-0.4	1.1	2,625	2,524
150	-1	1.6	2,575	2,430
175	-2	2.2	2,527	2,339
200	-3.4	2.9	2,478	2,250
225	-5	3.6	2,431	2,164
250	-7.1	4.5	2,383	2,081
275	-9.5	5.5	2,337	2,000
300	-12.4	6.7	2,290	1,922
325	-15.6	8	2,245	1,846
350	-19.4	9.3	2,200	1,773
375	-23.5	10.8	2,155	1,701
400	-28.1	12.5	2,111	1,633
425	-33.2	14.2	2,067	1,566
450	-38.7	16	2,024	1,501
475	-44.9	18.1	1,982	1,439
500	-51.4	20.1	1,939	1,377

Let's bump things up to the magnum class cartridges with a look at the .300 Winchester Magnum, loaded with the same 165-grain Trophy Bonded Tip, and a 250-yard zero.

Ballistics Calculator:	
Load Number:	P300WTT2
Zero Range:	250 yd.
Caliber:	.300 Win. Magnum
Temperature:	59 ºF
Bullet Style:	Trophy Bonded® Tip
Wind Speed:	10 mph
Bullet Weight:	165 gr
Altitude:	0 feet
Ballistic Coefficient:	0.45
Max Range:	500 yd.
Muzzle Velocity:	3050 fps
Test Barrel:	24 in.
Sight Height:	1.5 in.

Range (yd.)	Drop (in.)	Wind Drift (in.)	Velocity (fps)	Energy (ft.-lb.)
0	-1.5	0	3,050	3,408
25	-0.1	0	2,996	3,288
50	1	0.1	2,942	3,171
75	1.8	0.3	2,889	3,058
100	2.4	0.6	2,837	2,948
125	2.8	1	2,785	2,841
150	2.8	1.5	2,734	2,738
175	2.6	2	2,683	2,638
200	2	2.7	2,633	2,540
225	1.2	3.4	2,584	2,446
250	0.0	4.2	2,535	2,354
275	-1.5	5.2	2,487	2,265
300	-3.4	6.1	2,439	2,179
325	-5.6	7.2	2,391	2,095
350	-8.2	8.5	2,345	2,014
375	-11.2	9.9	2,298	1,935
400	-14.6	11.4	2,253	1,859
425	-18.5	13	2,207	1,785
450	-22.8	14.7	2163	1713
475	-27.6	16.6	2,118	1,644
500	-32.8	18.5	2,075	1,577

The trajectory flattens out, from the increased muzzle velocity. In comparing the trajectory between the .308 Winchester and .300 Winchester Magnum, it may not seem that there is a huge advantage given to the magnum, but realize that the .308 load is hot (about 125 fps higher than standard), and the .300 Magnum load is a standard velocity. It pays to seek out the faster loads, if you want the most out of a standard rifle.

Let's look next at the .300 Remington Ultra Magnum, in the Federal Trophy Bonded Tip, but switch to the heavier 180-grain bullet. The 180 grainer will maximize the additional muzzle velocities.

Ballistics Calculator:	
Load Number:	P300RUMTT1
Zero Range:	250 yd.
Caliber:	.300 Rem. Ultra Magnum
Temperature:	59 ºF
Bullet Style:	Trophy Bonded® Tip
Wind Speed:	10 mph
Bullet Weight:	180 gr.
Altitude:	0 feet
Ballistic Coefficient:	0.5
Max Range:	500 yd.
Muzzle Velocity:	3200 fps
Test Barrel:	24 in.
Sight Height:	1.5 in.

Range (yd.)	Drop (in.)	Wind Drift (in.)	Velocity (fps)	Energy (ft.-lb.)
0	-1.5	0	3,200	4,092
25	-0.3	0	3,149	3,964
50	0.7	0.1	3,099	3,839
75	1.5	0.3	3,050	3,717
100	2.1	0.5	3,001	3,599
125	2.4	0.8	2,952	3,484
150	2.4	1.2	2,905	3,372
175	2.2	1.6	2,857	3,263
200	1.8	2.2	2,810	3,157
225	1	2.8	2,764	3,053
250	0	3.5	2,718	2,953
275	-1.3	4.3	2,673	2,855
300	-3	5.2	2,628	2,760
325	-4.9	6.1	2,584	2,668
350	-7.1	7.1	2,540	2,578
375	-9.8	8.3	2,496	2,490
400	-12.6	9.4	2,453	2,404
425	-15.9	10.7	2,410	2,321
450	-19.6	12.1	2,368	2,240
475	-23.7	13.6	2,326	2,162
500	-28.2	15.2	2,284	2,085

Even with the heavier bullet, the .300 RUM offers the flattest trajectory of all, and is definitely worthy of the 250-yard zero. It's a dead hold to 300 yards.

Personally, if I were rockin' a .300 RUM, I'd opt for a 275-yard zero, for this trajectory curve. It would be the optimum curve for long-range big game hunting. It'd look like this:

Ballistics Calculator:	
Load Number:	P300RUMTT1
Zero Range:	275 yd.
Caliber:	.300 Rem. Ultra Magnum
Temperature:	59 °F
Bullet Style:	Trophy Bonded® Tip
Wind Speed:	10 mph
Bullet Weight:	180 gr.
Altitude:	0 feet
Ballistic Coefficient:	0.5
Max Range:	500 yd.
Muzzle Velocity:	3200 fps
Test Barrel:	24 in.
Sight Height:	1.5 in.

Range (yd.)	Drop (in.)	Wind Drift (in.)	Velocity (fps)	Energy (ft.-lb.)
0	-1.5	0	3,200	4,092
25	-0.2	0	3,149	3,964
50	1	0.1	3,099	3,839
75	1.9	0.3	3,050	3,717
100	2.6	0.5	3,001	3,599
125	3	0.8	2,952	3,484
150	3.2	1.2	2,905	3,372
175	3.1	1.6	2,857	3,263
200	2.7	2.2	2,810	3,157
225	2.1	2.8	2,764	3,053
250	1.2	3.5	2,718	2,953
275	0	4.3	2,673	2,855
300	-1.5	5.2	2,628	2,760
325	-3.3	6.1	2,584	2,668
350	-5.4	7.1	2,540	2,578
375	-7.9	8.3	2,496	2,490
400	-10.7	9.4	2,453	2,404
425	-13.9	10.7	2,410	2,321
450	-17.4	12.1	2,368	2,240
475	-21.4	13.6	2,326	2,162
500	-25.7	15.2	2,284	2,085

Assuming a 6-inch vital zone, I'm all set to about 325 yards, with the heavier bullet giving me additional energy thanks to the huge RUM case.

You can see how changing the zero of your rifle can be an important means of optimizing the performance of a particular load, and how different hunting situations may require an adjustment of your scope. Once you find a type of factory ammunition or handload that gives you the accuracy you're after, simply plug it into one of the ballistic calculators to see what zero will work best for your hunting situation. Just remember, you need to keep an eye on what happens between the muzzle and the zero distance, so that a 100- or 125-yard shot doesn't hit too high. Keep things within 2 or 3 inches above the line of sight, and you should be good to go.

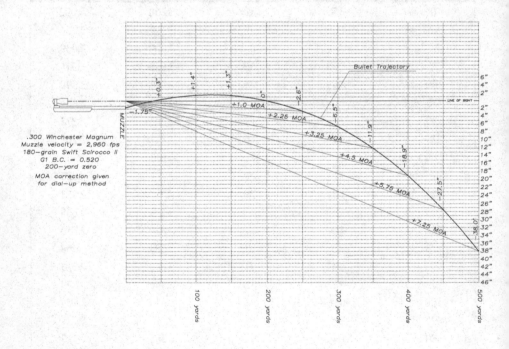

.300 Winchester Magnum
Muzzle velocity = 2,960 fps
180-grain Swift Scirocco II
G1 B.C. = 0.520
200-yard zero
MOA correction given
for dial-up method

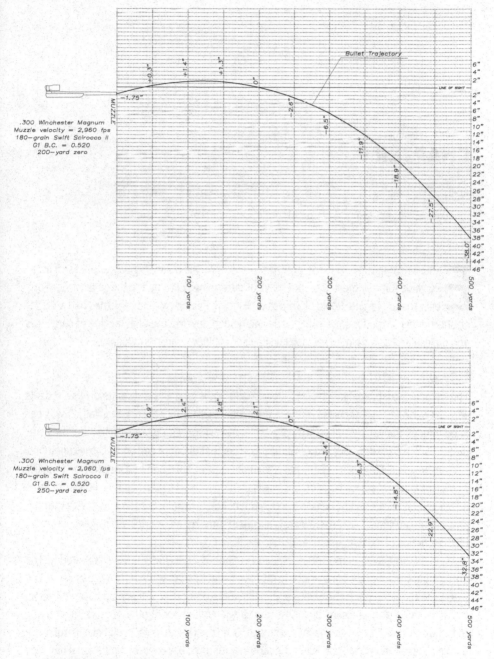

Example of how changing the zero on the author's .300 Winchester Magnum affected its long-range trajectory.

CHAPTER 9

Ballistic Coefficient

E xplaining ballistic coefficient, or BC is no easy task. The bullet companies publish a listed BC value for their projectiles, but how is it determined? I turned to the sage wisdom of a dear friend of mine, Robin Sharpless of Redding Reloading. Sharpless has had a distinguished career in the firearms industry, having helped develop the CheyTac line of cartridges and projectiles. I asked him to help explain ballistic coefficient and its influences.

BC: Art, Science and Alchemy by Robin Sharpless

The list of searchable definitions of ballistic coefficient is long and truly quite diverse. It deals with drag, slipperiness and ease of the bullet's movement through air. Historically, it was defined through the variance of velocity of a bullet at two specific distances. That is a static approach, which only really gives you an indication over that distance and under those conditions.

From Wikipedia: (n) ballistics, the ballistic coefficient (BC) of a body is a measure of its ability to overcome air resistance in flight. It is inversely proportional to the negative acceleration—a high number indicates a low negative acceleration. This is roughly the same as saying that the projectile in question possesses low drag, although some meaning is lost in the generalization. BC is a function of mass, diameter and drag coefficient.

There are literally hundreds of articles and variations of BC formulas available today. The bottom line in all of this is not so much to rate one bullet against another for a higher value. The true value to the hunter is the ability to predict where that bullet will end up based on velocity, wind, barometric pressure, humidity, slant angle and a host of other factors when trying to humanely take a game animal at a distance. BC is the critical driver in all ballistic software and can in itself thumbnail one bullet over another for this crazy concept of relational negative acceleration.

Actually, BC was derived from U.S. military research long, long ago, and the coefficient is a comparison to a specific fictitious projectile used at that time. This is the basis of the G1 BC model. Years later, a more efficient boattail bullet was used as the basis for comparison creating the G7 Model that we see today. In either case, you are comparing to a fictitious projectile at the time.

Your real interest in ballistic coefficients is to use them as a basis in conjunction with either software or mathematical calculations to predict where a projectile at a given speed with a given ballistic coefficient will be at the end of its flight to target. You add to this a variety of other environmental and physical factors that affect the bullet's flight to create a set of adjustments for your optical sighting device. This allows you to correct for all of the variables, including BC, and with some measure of luck (hence the alchemy term) to score solid hits on the target.

Time and technology have changed, and the advent of high-speed Doppler radar units and heavy-duty computing power for backend processing has shown us a very different view of BC. Today, it is not simply a measure of how the bullet travels through the air under varying circumstances and conditions. We've learned that BC is not a constant, but a variable with some basis in velocity and a host of other impacting factors. Today we know that the BC as a constant model is false as the actual slipperiness (BC) of the projectile changes at varying velocities throughout its flight profile.

My experience with this came during a time when I was involved with an advanced sniper weapons system company, and we used the high-speed Doppler units at both the Yuma and Aberdeen proving grounds to develop the firm's ballistic computer system and prove the concept behind a radical (for the time) new projectile. The Doppler radar units showed us BC in as little as 1-yard increments over 3,500 yards of flight. It also showed us the real effects of *precession*, that is, how the bullet's nose climbs up into the wind with a specific twist rotation and wind resistance on the nose of the bullet. Further, it allowed us to see the true effect of over-stabilization in the early flight of the bullet and its highly degrading effect on the potential BC of a specific bullet.

BC as a Transitory Function of Velocity

Historically, BC was calculated from a pair of velocities over a specified distance and the change, or delta, which occurred. As time progressed, refinements were added for air pressure and other variables. The difficulty here is that the velocity data was derived only from the change that occurred within a given distance and range of velocities. One chronograph at the muzzle and another at a given range would produce two velocity readings that would be used with a formula to determine a numerical BC value based on one of the existing models. However, the work done on the Doppler radar has shown the flaw in a static BC model. This becomes a larger and larger problem as distance increases. BC changes with velocity and, therefore, a static number becomes a greater negative in predictive capability for shots at longer distances.

The best ballistic computer systems now work with velocity respective sets of BC values and are providing far better predictive capabilities at long range.

Precession

As mentioned, precession is the term for the nose of the bullet climbing up and into a wind based off of the rotational energy. Doppler radar can actually be used to model the bullet in three dimensions throughout its flight. When we model against the actual flight path, we can see the bullet is not in axial profile with its flight direction. When this occurs, the bullet is presenting to the wind with an inherent amount of yaw, which increases drag and changes the outcome of the BC model. The bullet is spinning in either a right- or left-handed rotation if there is a wind quarter value on the nose. The direction of the rotational force of the spin causes the nose of the bullet to precess or climb into that wind. You end up with a bullet not traveling along its intended axial path, but presenting to the air ahead of it a non-conformal profile and adding an amount of drag again changing its true BC moment from the published BC. This drag slows the projectile at a higher than anticipated or predicted rate, causing rounds to strike lower than intended.

Over-Stabilization or Yaw

Twist rates traditionally must be established so that there is enough remaining rotational energy to stabilize the bullet at the end of its flight, especially for a long-range cartridge. This means that the bullet is over-stabilized at the start of its travel downrange. You can see this when a quarterback throws a football. Everyone wants a nice, tight spiral, but if he puts too much spin on the ball, it wobbles for the early part of its flight. This wobble is called yaw and it is a function of too much rotational energy as relates to the linear energy—the movement of the football forward. As the rotational energy degrades, the football regains balance between rotational and linear energy and will fall into a tight spiral.

As this relates to firearms, designers must over-stabilize the bullet at the beginning of its flight so that it "settles down" over the intended range of use. How this relates to BC is really quite simple. Yaw keeps the bullet constantly shifting off of its intended path when compared to its optimal shape—the center axis of the bullet is not at the center of the intended flight path. Once again, you're presenting the bullet in its less than optimal shaped form against the oncoming air, creating additional drag which modifies—actually degrades—the BC. One company, CheyTac, patented a bullet with balanced flight. This was unique, and the Doppler radar proved this lack of over stabilization and yaw in its early flight profile. The bullet had an extremely high BC based on the G7 model and retained an incredible amount of energy downrange when compared to more traditional projectiles like the 50 BMG.

The proof of this was found in the trace produced by the Doppler. The CheyTac balanced flight bullet produced a very clean and smooth line throughout the duration of its flight with a small dip as it went transonic on the downside, meaning that it did yaw slightly as it went through the sound barrier transiting from supersonic to subsonic. Traditional bullets tracked on the Doppler show a fuzzy or hazy initial trace, until the axial energy and rotational energy fall into alignment, producing the clean spiral just like that of the football with too much spin.

Unfortunately, balanced flight has yet to come to the vast majority of hunting bullets and you are saddled with over-stabilization and yaw at the beginning of these bullets' flight profiles. If you look back historically at many earlier BC calculations, you may assume that they could even be low based upon the numbers being taken over a distance where the bullet has yet to settle down. Until the advent of Doppler radar, we unfortunately did not have a good handle on what ballistic coefficient really was.

BC in 3D

Throughout the years, the shooting public has generally viewed BC as a linear function relating to drag loss of velocity in bullet drop over distance. The other fascinating effect is that high BC bullets are less affected by the wind in all three dimensions. This means that a higher BC bullet not only travels through the air more efficiently from point A to point B, but also that same level of efficiency allows it to fight crosswind. Therefore, a higher BC bullet in general will buck the wind much better and need less left or right correction downrange. That is important for the target shooter seeking a bullet for hunting in a high wind area, for the higher BC may allow you a much easier correction.

I'm reminded of a particular training session in Idaho where we were working with the high BC CheyTac bullets and a group of Marines who were training with us shooting 50 BMG sniper rifles. The day became very interesting as the winds came up and they ultimately ran out of the ability to correct for drift based on limitations of their scopes. Conversely, in the same range and conditions, the CheyTac bullet—with its extremely high BC—was only requiring 12 minutes of correction and scoring solid hits.

Factors Impacting BC

BC can be impacted by a wide range of things like those listed above. But there are some constants that will provide interplay with the published ballistic coefficient. By constants I refer to variables that will always be there. Wind may or may not cause precession based upon its angle and speed, or lack thereof. But two items you encounter every day will always have an impact on your data tables or software—barometric pressure and slant angle of shot. In the case of barometric pressure, you're impacting the media through which the bullet must fly, thereby modifying the effects of drag and the BC as well. In the case of slant angle, while the distance remains the same, shooting up or down changes the effect of gravity which, while not directly relating to BC, does change the amount of correction necessary to place the bullet on its intended target.

Barometric Pressure

Barometric pressure is the measure of air density through which the bullet must travel. Air is not air. You want to always reflect upon barometric pressure as actual barometric pressure not corrected sea level pressure. You need to think of air as the medium through which the bullet must transit. Like any medium, changes occur that can affect the bullet's flight through it. Low barometric pressures like those found at higher altitudes provide far less resistance to a projectile at a given speed. Conversely, higher air and barometric pressures such as at sea level create a denser or thicker medium through which to pass. Think of this in terms of two glasses, each filled with liquids of different viscosity, the idea being to insert a straw into each glass. I've used this demonstration a number of times working with snipers around the world to illustrate the effects of air density or barometric pressure. In the first case, you have iced tea, representing a very low barometric pressure. In the second glass, honey—still liquid, though much, much thicker and therefore resistant to an object passing into and through it. In these demonstrations, the students take two straws and force them into the glasses. One goes very quickly and easily into the iced tea, while in the other the resistance is obvious and more pressure is needed to pass the straw through the thick honey.

Let's consider this with the bullet traveling through dense or thin air with a higher barometric pressure like what you find at sea level or when a high pressure front comes through—it's a lot like the bullet transiting through a medium more consistent with something like honey than iced tea. When hunting or shooting at high elevation where the air becomes thinner, there is far less resistance on the bullet as it transits through the medium of air. So, in each of these cases, ballistic coefficient is modified by density in terms of its ability to be predictive.

Slant Angle

When shooting up or down hill, the curve of the bullet's flight path is modified due to slant angle. While this does not truly impact the BC of a bullet, you will see less drop due to the angle. It has the given effect of increasing BC in a practical sense, requiring you to aim lower than you normally would in a flat-shooting scenario.

Target Reference Points

TRPs, or Target reference points, are a tool of the military sniper, and the concept becomes quite applicable to the modern hunter. In a sniping situation, TRPs are developed along paths of ingress or egress where the opposing force may appear. The same concept is applied to the hunter when working from a specific point overlooking a valley from a ridge or in any place where you have determined game may transit. You can establish mobile TRPs and use them in conjunction with ballistics software as identified locations where you anticipate a shot may take place. You can run your scenarios on each location based upon environmental factors like slant angle and wind speed, building a small cheat sheet or dope sheet for each. That will give you a strong indication of required holdover for that location on a game animal. If you're working with a spotter, he too should be aware of these and use a numbered system to call the TRP in question when game appears. Through this method, you will have a quicker, more accurate response time for a shot. Again, this drifts off of the general BC concept but reaches into the realm of practical application in real-world hunting situations.

All of the above are items for you to consider in your practical application of ballistic coefficient to real-world firing solutions and situations. There are a number of great software packages available for use in assisting with predictive solutions for scope correction. One of the best uses of these packages is at the range under varying conditions to determine how your individual projectile and rifle perform against the predictions as generated. Once this is done, you can build your discrete fudge factor in using the BC and software available. The use of a handheld device and a good software package—especially those based in Doppler radar—will positively impact your hunting situations and rates of success. Technology has come a long way in our field, and its benefits can be realized all over the world.

Doppler radar has changed the way in which we think about our bullets and the way they fly. A good ballistic computer system is not only helpful in the field, but also makes a great resource when sitting at home to run scenarios and truly learn what your rifle and projectile combination are capable of under a wide variety of circumstances.

CHAPTER 10

Bullet Stability and Spin Drift

The concept of spinning a bullet to keep it stable goes back to the days of muzzleloading rifles, when the English, armed with smoothbore Brown Bess muskets, saw the advantages of the Pennsylvania and Kentucky rifles. While the Brown Bess was not what you'd describe as an accurate firearm, lacking any rifling at all, the Continental rifles were extremely accurate for their time, and gave the Revolutionaries a definite advantage.

The spinning motion of a projectile keeps it stable in flight, but exactly how much spin is required for each projectile? This question is important for those who want to utilize the long, sleek bullets that give such good trajectory and wind-deflection performance. Invariably, the modern bullet trend has gone longer and heavier within each caliber, but the barrels of rifles produced over the last century can only spin a bullet so fast. If you try to exceed the capability of the barrel's twist rate, your bullet will lose gyroscopic stability, and you'll see your accuracy fall apart. Your bullets will hit the target sideways, creating what is known as a keyhole.

Certainly, the ballistic engineers of yesteryear couldn't have envisioned this trend, and the barrel you own will dictate the bullets you can use. As I've related elsewhere in this book, I own a couple of rifles that are handicapped, if you will, by the twist rate of their barrels. My .22-250 Remington comes quickly to mind, and though I would love nothing more than to use 69- and 77-grain Sierra MatchKing bullets in this rifle, my 1:14-inch twist rate simply won't stabilize them.

First, the twist rate of your firearm must be known, and I've described that process in the interior ballistics section (chapter 5). You can use some mathematics to determine exactly how heavy a bullet a given barrel will stabilize. The Miller Twist Rule, developed by Don Miller, uses the following factors for determining the proper stabilization rate for a bullet. You'll need to know the mass (m) of the bullet in grains, and that's easy enough. You'll need the bullet's diameter in inches (d) and its length in calibers (l), plus the twist rate of your barrel in calibers (t). The equation works like this:

$$s = 30m/(t^2 d^3 l (1+l^2))$$

The s figure that you're solving for is the gyroscopic stability factor, which will indicate just how stable the bullet will be during flight. Any bullet that ends up with an s factor greater than 1.5 (this number has no units) will be stable, while a figure ranging between 1.0 and 1.5 is considered to have marginal stability. If the figure is less than 1.0, the bullet will be unstable. Some examples:

Let's consider a 180-grain Swift Scirocco II, with a G1 BC of 0.520, and a length of 1.435 inches, fired from my .300 Winchester Magnum with a 1:10 twist rate. Converting the bullet length to calibers (1.435/.308) yields a figure of 4.659. Converting the 1:10-inch twist rate into calibers (10/0.308) gives you 32.468. Plugging these values into Miller's equation results in an s factor of 1.67; indicating that this bullet will have good stability when fired from this barrel.

Supposing I wanted to use the 62-grain Swift Scirocco II in my .22-250 Remington with a 1:12 twist rate, the bullet having a length of 0.928 inches, I'd first check the stability factor in this rifle. Multiplying the weight of the bullet in grains by the constant factor of 30 (which Miller derived to give an approximation of velocity, and happens to work rather well) gives you 1,860 on the top of the equation. Convert the bullet length into caliber and you get 4.143, while the twist rate converted into calibers per turn (t) is 53.571. Calculate the squares, cubes, multiplication and division, and you'll end up with an s value of 0.72, far below the desired minimum of 1.00. Were I to load this bullet in my rifle, I'd see lousy accuracy. The bullet would hit the target sideways, as it begins to yaw coming out of stable flight.

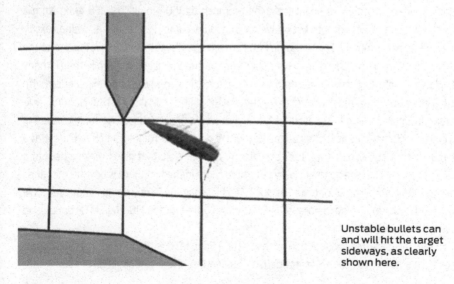

Unstable bullets can and will hit the target sideways, as clearly shown here.

Let's now check the bullet that has worked in my rifle for so long—the Sierra 53-grain flat-base MatchKing. This bullet measures 0.694 inches, considerably shorter than the 62-grain Scirocco, though it's only 9 grains lighter due to the flat base and lack of polymer tip. Crunching the numbers in the Miller formula, I obtain an s factor of 1.41, indicating that I've got good stability. This has been proven for years, as I've used this load for varmints and predators out to 400 yards and beyond.

These results can be enlightening. Certain cartridges can be blessed or cursed by the twist rate of the barrel and other factors like case capacity. This has long been an issue (which I could not understand as a younger man) with the .270 calibers. Why would the .284-inch (7mm) cartridges be able to handle bullets up to 175 grains, yet drop the bore diameter down by just 0.007 inches, and bullet weights top out at 150 grains. It just didn't make a lick of sense. Well, based on Miller's equation, the answer is simple. The barrels of almost all the .270 cartridges use a 1:10 twist rate, and that twist simply won't stabilize a bullet heavier than 150 grains. Change the twist rate to 1:8 and you could use bullets as heavy as 170 grains, and that would certainly be a nice prospect for larger game, or for a high BC choice for long-range work. Berger makes the Extreme Outer Limits Elite Hunter in .277 at 170 grains, which won't work in conventional barrels, but if you were to order a custom .270, I'd recommend the faster-than-normal twist rate so you can take advantage of the design. That's true as well of the older Barnes original round-nose at 170 grains. I guess this issue with the .270 might explain why they make a good hunting cartridge, but haven't been used very often as a true long-range target rifle.

Utilizing the bullet's length in the Miller Twist Rule is an important factor. It can make the difference in choosing a bullet that may seem like it will work, yet will actually be unstable—and one that truly is a tack-driver. My 6.5-284 Norma with its 1:8 twist barrel will easily handle a conventional cup-and-core bullet weighing as much as 160-grains. The 156-grain Norma Oryx and 160-grain Hornady InterLock have given good accuracy in this rifle, as well as excellent terminal performance. The 140-grain bullets work equally well, and within this group the 140-grain North Fork hollowpoints have ruined more than one deer's day, while the Hornady ELD-Match bullet has given the best accuracy of all from this gun. My previous experiences with Cutting Edge Bullets sparked a desire to try their 140-grain MTH (Match Tactical Hunting) bullet. I simply figured that a 140-grain lead-free bullet would pose no issue, but while discussing this choice with the folks at Cutting Edge, they informed me that I'd need a 1:7.5 twist rate at a minimum and that this bullet wouldn't stabilize in my rifle. Well, that didn't make a heck of a lot of sense, until I ran the numbers (why I doubted them in the first place is beyond me) and I came up with a stability factor of just about 1.27. This would be barely marginal and certainly not a good choice in my rifle for long-range shooting. I opted for the 130-grain MTH bullet, and I'm very happy with the results.

You see, the lead-free construction of the Cutting Edge MTH is the culprit here, and it's not necessarily a bad thing. Copper is less dense than lead, so the 140-grain MTH is 1.505 inches long, as compared to the 140-grain ELD-Match at 1.380 inches. But the center of gravity is much farther rearward in the Cutting Edge than in the Hornady. Based on the difference in length and center of gravity, the Hornady bullet gives me a stability factor of 1.63, which is much better suited to my purposes.

There is a fantastic tool available on the Berger website, a twist-rate calculator (http://www.bergerbullets.com/twist-rate-calculator). It allows you to enter the pertinent data relating to your bullet/rifle combination, and delivers not only the stabilization factor—which they refer to as SG—but indicates whether or not your BC is optimized for your bullet. This website is a gem and worthy of a bookmark on your favorites bar. It does note that the Miller Twist Rule may come up inaccurate for flat-based bullets as the rule bases its mathematics on a projectile profile shaped like a football, and offers some suggestions for calculations regarding flat-based bullets.

More On Over-Stabilization

How does a faster twist rate affect standard bullets? I've read the theories that purport that spinning a bullet too fast will have a dramatic effect on the velocity—that the energy is eaten up by the revolutions of the bullet. However, I have found no evidence to prove this point while doing testing and research for this book, and all scientific data points to the fact that any reduction in velocity caused by bullet spin is so minimal as to be disregarded.

However, I have seen a barrel with a fast twist rate take a light-for-caliber bullet—these were of a highly frangible varmint design—and spin the jacket out from around the lead core. Come to think of it, I've actually seen this in a couple of calibers, namely a .223 Remington and .264 Winchester Magnum, and in both instances the bullets were on the light side of the spectrum. That .264 Magnum was launching 85-grain hollowpoints and, if I recall correctly, they were Sierra Varminter bullets that wouldn't hit the 100-yard target at all. On the third shot, I saw bark fly about 15 yards down our backyard range, five or six yards to the right. While the Sierra Varminter certainly delivers near-explosive results on woodchucks and prairie dogs (and has proven to be an accurate bullet over the years), this combination of high velocity and a twist rate on the faster side ended up being just too much for the little 85-grain pill. I wish I still had the rifle to observe the twist rate, but I'd bet it was in the neighborhood of 1:8. That rifle had no issues with the 129- and 140-grain bullets. On the other hand, 85-grain bullets didn't work out so well after all.

The bottom line to all of this? I'd much rather have a bullet over-stabilized than under-stabilized, especially for long-range shooting. However, as valuable as a fast rate of twist is to stabilizing a longer projectile, it will magnify any flaws in the construction of the bullet. Should you have a small void in the lead core or a jacket that is not perfectly concentric, a faster twist rate will surely bring this out, and I firmly believe that the inexplicable flier—that one shot that ruins your group size when you feel certain that you'd held perfectly—can sometimes be attributed to a slight deformation in bullet construction.

Range (yds.)	Velocity (fps)	Energy (ft.-lb.)	Trajectory (in.)	ComeUp (MOA)
0	2580	2070	-1.75	0
25	2,545	2,015	-0.2893	-1.1052
50	2,511	1,961	0.8337	1.5923
75	2,477	1,908	1.6128	2.0536
100	2,443	1,857	2.0384	1.9467
125	2,410	1,806	2.1003	1.6046
150	2,376	1,756	1.7875	1.1381
175	2,343	1,707	1.0913	0.5955
200	2,310	1,660	0	0
225	2,277	1,613	-1.4988	-0.6362
250	2,245	1,567	-3.4157	-1.3048
275	2,212	1,522	-5.7625	-2.0012
300	2,180	1,478	-8.5537	-2.7229
325	2,148	1,435	-11.8016	-3.4678
350	2,116	1,392	-15.5195	-4.2346
375	2,084	1,351	-19.7216	-5.0224
400	2,052	1,310	-24.4248	-5.8314
425	2,021	1,270	-29.6425	-6.6609
450	1,990	1,231	-35.3907	-7.5107
475	1,958	1,193	-41.6884	-8.3816
500	1,927	1,155	-48.5516	-9.2734
525	1,896	1,118	-55.9986	-10.1864
550	1,865	1,081	-64.0494	-11.1213
575	1,834	1,046	-72.7245	-12.0786
600	1,802	1,010	-82.0449	-13.0589
625	1,771	975	-92.0322	-14.0626
650	1,740	941	-102.714	-15.0911
675	1,709	908	-114.111	-16.1446
700	1,677	875	-126.251	-17.2243

Spin Drift

The very act of spinning a bullet results in a downrange phenomenon known as spin drift. At longer distances the spin that keeps the bullet in a nose-forward flight pattern will cause it to drift in the direction in which it is spinning. Put simply, if you have a right-hand twist in your barrel, your bullets will drift right, the opposite for a left-hand twist. How much the bullet will drift is based upon the stability factor of the bullet and the time of flight. While left-hand twist barrels are a rarity these days, most of our rifles will spin toward the right. Where wind is a variable, and our ability to judge it is limited, spin drift is a predictable effect. Bryan Litz, in his excellent

Wind Drift (in.)	Wind Drift (MOA)	Spin Drift (in.)	Spin Drift (MOA)	TOF (sec.)
0	0	0	0	0
0.0348	0.1329	-0.0027	-0.0102	0.0293
0.1396	0.2666	-0.0108	-0.0206	0.0589
0.3158	0.4021	-0.0246	-0.0313	0.089
0.5649	0.5395	-0.0441	-0.0421	0.1195
0.8886	0.6789	-0.0696	-0.0532	0.1504
1.2887	0.8205	-0.1013	-0.0645	0.1817
1.7665	0.964	-0.1392	-0.076	0.2135
2.3239	1.1097	-0.1837	-0.0877	0.2458
2.9628	1.2575	-0.2347	-0.0996	0.2785
3.6849	1.4076	-0.2927	-0.1118	0.3116
4.4918	1.5599	-0.3577	-0.1242	0.3453
5.386	1.7145	-0.4299	-0.1369	0.3794
6.3697	1.8717	-0.5097	-0.1498	0.4141
7.445	2.0314	-0.5971	-0.1629	0.4493
8.6144	2.1938	-0.6924	-0.1763	0.485
9.8806	2.359	-0.7958	-0.19	0.5213
11.2458	2.527	-0.9076	-0.2039	0.5581
12.7126	2.6979	-1.0279	-0.2181	0.5955
14.284	2.8718	-1.1572	-0.2327	0.6335
15.9625	3.0488	-1.2956	-0.2475	0.6721
17.7517	3.2291	-1.4434	-0.2626	0.7113
19.6555	3.4129	-1.6008	-0.278	0.7512
21.678	3.6004	-1.7681	-0.2937	0.7918
23.8232	3.7919	-1.9455	-0.3097	0.833
26.0954	3.9874	-2.1333	-0.326	0.875
28.4996	4.1873	-2.3319	-0.3426	0.9177
31.0398	4.3916	-2.5414	-0.3596	0.9612
33.721	4.6005	-2.7623	-0.3769	1.0055

book, *Applied Ballistics for Long Range Shooting*, has derived the equation for computing the predicted spin drift, and he puts it like this:

$$Drift = 1.25(SG+1.2)tof^{1.83}$$

In this equation, drift is measured in inches, SG is what Litz refers to as the stabilization factor as determined by the Miller Twist Rule, and *tof* is the time of flight in seconds. It isn't difficult to find information regarding time of flight in a good reloading manual or on a component bullet company's website. We've already derived the stability factor, so the equation isn't very difficult

Range (yds.)	Velocity (fps)	Energy (ft.-lb.)	Trajectory (in.)	ComeUp (MOA)
700	1,677	875	-126.251	-17.2243
750	1,615	811	-152.875	-19.4662
800	1,553	750	-182.827	-21.8251
850	1,491	692	-216.378	-24.3109
900	1,430	636	-253.835	-26.9349
950	1,368	582	-295.537	-29.7096
1000	1,308	532	-341.879	-32.6499
1050	1,247	484	-393.297	-35.7719
1100	1,188	439	-450.297	-39.0948
1150	1,130	397	-513.448	-42.6396
1200	1,080	363	-583.389	-46.4295
1250	1,044	339	-660.752	-50.4833
1300	1,017	321	-746.064	-54.8094
1350	997	309	-839.755	-59.4078
1400	981	299	-942.16	-64.2726
1450	967	291	-1053.57	-69.395
1500	953	283	-1174.25	-74.7665

to solve. Personally, when the shots get long enough that I need to take spin drift into consideration, I consult my Kestrel Anemometer to arrive at the adjustment. While it sounds like a cop-out and a dependence on technology, I will say that with all the other factors involved in long-range shooting it's difficult to keep another chart in my head. The Kestrel has made the art of long-distance shooting much more manageable.

In a hunting situation (unless you fully intend to pursue unwounded game at ranges over 500 yards, something I personally won't do and would advise against) the spin drift values are negligible and can almost be taken out of the equation. For a shot at the outer limits of my hunting ranges (keeping in mind that all of my rifles are outfitted with right-hand twist barrels) I will reduce the amount of wind hold in a right-to-left wind—as the wind deflection is fighting the spin drift—and give a bit more hold at longer distances in a left-to-right wind, as the wind will work in conjunction with the spin drift effect. On the other hand, if you fully intend to play the long-range game, you'll want the best tools available, and a handheld ballistic computer ranks right up there as one of the best, so long as you have a working knowledge of what effects are happening.

I plugged my 6.5-284 Norma parameters into the Hornady 4 Degrees of Freedom ballistic calculator and got the following dope chart for my gun:

I have underlined the 500-yard mark, as that is where most hunters would draw the line in the hunting fields, and you can see in column for spin drift that the 500-yard value is 1.30 inches

Wind Drift (in.)	Wind Drift (MOA)	Spin Drift (in.)	Spin Drift (MOA)	TOF (sec.)
33.721	4.6005	-2.7623	-0.3769	1.0055
39.5271	5.0331	-3.2397	-0.4125	1.0967
45.9626	5.4868	-3.7665	-0.4496	1.1914
53.0767	5.9633	-4.346	-0.4883	1.2899
60.9246	6.4648	-4.9817	-0.528	1.3926
69.5677	6.9934	-5.678	-0.5708	1.4999
79.0749	7.5516	-6.4399	-0.615	1.612
89.5193	8.142	-7.2726	-0.6615	1.7295
100.9817	8.767	-8.1808	-0.7102	1.8527
113.5444	9.4291	-9.1681	-0.7614	1.9822
127.2461	10.1266	-10.2348	-0.8145	2.1182
141.9153	10.8423	-11.3854	-0.8698	2.2597
157.3492	11.5591	-12.627	-0.9276	2.4055
173.3752	12.2646	-13.9678	-0.9881	2.5546
189.8739	12.9521	-15.415	-1.0515	2.7065
206.7869	13.6193	-16.9737	-1.1179	2.8606
224.0946	14.2673	-18.6482	-1.1873	3.017

(as rounded up). I'm not a bad shot, yet I'm no sniper, but for me to honestly say that I can hold within an inch-and-a-quarter at 500 yards would be severely stretching the truth. Spin drift is a factor in exterior ballistics, but it is a small factor in the hunting world in comparison to the effects of gravity and wind deflection.

Take it out past 700 yards, and you'll see where the spin drift can become an issue. Again, from the Hornady calculator shown above.

At exactly 1,000 yards the simple act of spinning the 140-grain Hornady ELD-Match causes a drift (to the right due to the right-hand twist of the barrel) of almost 6-1/2 inches; more than enough to push it off the edge of 12-inch plate if not accounted for. At 1,500 yards, you'll be off the right side of a 36-inch plate. In order to put your bullet where you want to at long range, you need to figure in this phenomenon.

CHAPTER 11
Density Altitude

While many effects on a bullet in flight are predictable—leaving the ever-changing wind as a definite variable—the atmosphere itself can and will change, to further affect its flight path. If you take a look at most of the ballistic calculators, they use a baseline temperature of 59°F, and a barometric pressure of 29.92 inches of mercury, at mean sea level. This apparently random set of data is based on the International Civilian Aviation Organization's Standard Atmosphere, and can be adjusted from there. The ICAO figures do not account for the humidity levels of the atmosphere, but reflect the changes in both temperature and pressure, with respect to elevation. Let's look at one set of data for a .300 Winchester Magnum, using a Hornady 178-grain ELD-X at 2,960 fps, at the ICAO baseline atmosphere:

Now let's change the data to mimic a Texas whitetail deer hunt, at 2,000 feet above sea level, at 80°F, at 26.50 Hg, assuming the same muzzle velocity:

Next, let's take our rifle to Montana, for a bighorn sheep hunt (since we're pretending, I can actually afford this hunt!) at 9,000 feet above sea level, at 32°F, with a pressure of 21.50 Hg:

Lastly, let's take our rifle to the Alaskan coast (let's say for a brown bear, while we're dreaming), where the elevation is at mean sea level, pressure is 27.50 Hg, and temperature is 40°F.

If you examine the way that bullet, at the same muzzle velocity, performs in different environments, you'll see that there is definitely a trajectory shift, especially approaching 400 and 500 yards. The change is a result of the density of the atmosphere, due to the combined effects of elevation and temperature.

There's a simple rule: when the elevation is up, bullet trajectory is up. If the temperature is up, the bullet's trajectory is up. The reverse applies as well. If you're traveling to a new hunting destination, ask the outfitter for the data (elevation, average temperature, etc.) and prepare a new dope card for your hunt. A Kestrel Elite weather station/ballistic computer will also capture the environment of your new hunting location, and adjust your trajectory curve accordingly.

Humid Air vs. Dry Air

The one aspect of the atmosphere that ICAO neglects to take into account is the humidity of the atmosphere, which needs to be considered for trajectory purposes. The atmosphere is comprised of roughly 78% nitrogen and 20% oxygen, with some carbon dioxide and minimal amounts of other trace gases thrown into the mix. What I'm about to tell you will defy common sense, but it is true. When the air gets humid—you know those summer days when you're stuck to your clothes and just can't seem to cool off—the air is actually thinner than it is on those nice, dry days. It took me a while to wrap my head around it, as it defied logic, but the water vapor in the air on a humid day is lighter than nitrogen, thus the air is lighter and thinner when it is saturated with water vapor.

As we saw with the trajectory charts above, thinner air at a higher elevation is easier for the bullet to fly through, resulting in a flatter trajectory. The humidity of the air has the same effect. If the air at a given location is humid, the resulting trajectory will be a bit flatter than if the air was dry.

The effect isn't huge, until you get out past the 500-yard mark, and any good ballistic calculator will reveal the difference with your chosen load.

Humidity and density altitude play significant roles in ballistics. Thinner air at a higher elevation is easier for the bullet to fly through, resulting in a flatter trajectory.

Mean Sea Level, 59°F, 29.92Hg

Range (yds.)	Velocity (fps)	Energy (ft.-lb.)	Trajectory (in.)	ComeUp (MOA)
0	2,960	3,464	-1.75	0
50	2,876	3,270	-0.3503	-0.6691
100	2,793	3,084	0	0
150	2,711	2,905	-0.7638	-0.4863
200	2,629	2,733	-2.7082	-1.2932
250	2,549	2,568	-5.9106	-2.2579
300	2,469	2,410	-10.4487	-3.3262
350	2,390	2,259	-16.4104	-4.4777
400	2,312	2,114	-23.8933	-5.7045
450	2,236	1,976	-32.9989	-7.0031
500	2,160	1,845	-43.8426	-8.3739

2,000 ft. elevation, 80°F, 26.50Hg

Range (yds.)	Velocity (fps)	Energy (ft.-lb.)	Trajectory (in.)	ComeUp (MOA)
0	2,960	3,464	-1.75	0
50	2,888	3,297	-0.3496	-0.6678
100	2,816	3,136	0	0
150	2,746	2,980	-0.7422	-0.4725
200	2,675	2,829	-2.6328	-1.2572
250	2,605	2,684	-5.7344	-2.1905
300	2,536	2,543	-10.1191	-3.2213
350	2,468	2,408	-15.8535	-4.3257
400	2,400	2,278	-23.0117	-5.4941
450	2,333	2,153	-31.6777	-6.7227
500	2,267	2,032	-41.9414	-8.0108

9,000 ft. elevation, 32°F, 21.50Hg

Range (yds.)	Velocity (fps)	Energy (ft.-lb.)	Trajectory (in.)	ComeUp (MOA)
0	2,960	3,464	-1.75	0
50	2,897	3,318	-0.4063	-0.7759
100	2,835	3,176	0	0
150	2,773	3,039	-0.6719	-0.4278
200	2,711	2,907	-2.5	-1.1938
250	2,651	2,778	-5.5156	-2.107
300	2,590	2,653	-9.7656	-3.1087
350	2,530	2,531	-15.2891	-4.1717
400	2,471	2,414	-22.1953	-5.2991
450	2,412	2,300	-30.5156	-6.4761
500	2,354	2,190	-40.3281	-7.7027

Wind Drift (in.)	Wind Drift (MOA)	Spin Drift (in.)	Spin Drift (MOA)	TOF (sec.)
0	0	0	0	0
0.1297	0.2477	-0.0098	-0.0188	0.0514
0.5259	0.5022	-0.0403	-0.0385	0.1043
1.2016	0.765	-0.0929	-0.0591	0.1589
2.1709	1.0366	-0.1693	-0.0809	0.215
3.4502	1.318	-0.2714	-0.1037	0.273
5.055	1.6092	-0.4011	-0.1277	0.3328
7.003	1.9108	-0.5604	-0.1529	0.3945
9.3132	2.2235	-0.7514	-0.1794	0.4583
12.0046	2.5476	-0.9763	-0.2072	0.5243
15.0983	2.8838	-1.2375	-0.2364	0.5925

Wind Drift (in.)	Wind Drift (MOA)	Spin Drift (in.)	Spin Drift (MOA)	TOF (sec.)
0	0	0	0	0
0.111	0.212	-0.0098	-0.0186	0.0513
0.4491	0.4289	-0.0398	-0.038	0.1039
1.024	0.652	0.0914	-0.0582	0.1578
1.8462	0.8816	-0.166	-0.0792	0.2132
2.9266	1.118	-0.2649	-0.1012	0.27
4.2773	1.3616	-0.3899	-0.1241	0.3284
5.91	1.6126	-0.5425	-0.148	0.3883
7.8375	1.8712	-0.7243	-0.1729	0.4499
10.074	2.1379	-0.9371	-0.1989	0.5133
12.6328	2.4129	-1.1827	-0.2259	0.5785

Wind Drift (in.)	Wind Drift (MOA)	Spin Drift (in.)	Spin Drift (MOA)	TOF (sec.)
0	0	0	0	0
0.0966	0.1845	-0.0099	-0.0188	0.0512
0.3904	0.3729	-0.0401	-0.0383	0.1036
0.8885	0.5656	-0.0918	-0.0585	0.1571
1.5978	0.7629	-0.1663	-0.0794	0.2118
2.5261	0.965	-0.2649	-0.1012	0.2677
3.6818	1.172	-0.3888	-0.1238	0.325
5.0746	1.3847	-0.5395	-0.1472	0.3836
6.7135	1.6028	-0.7186	-0.1716	0.4436
8.6081	1.8268	-0.9277	-0.1969	0.505
10.7696	2.057	-1.1685	-0.2232	0.5679

Mean Sea Level, 40°F, 27.50 Hg

Range (yds.)	Velocity (fps)	Energy (ft.-lb.)	Trajectory (in.)	ComeUp (MOA)
0	2,960	3,464	-1.75	0
50	2,880	3,280	-0.3519	-0.6721
100	2,802	3,104	0	0
150	2,724	2,934	-0.7549	-0.4806
200	2,647	2,771	-2.679	-1.2792
250	2,571	2,613	-5.8431	-2.2321
300	2,496	2,462	-10.3199	-3.2852
350	2,421	2,317	-16.1917	-4.418
400	2,347	2,178	-23.5435	-5.621
450	2,274	2,044	-32.4729	-6.8915
500	2,202	1,917	-43.0823	-8.2287

Wind Drift (in.)	Wind Drift (MOA)	Spin Drift (in.)	Spin Drift (MOA)	TOF (sec.)
0	0	0	0	0
0.1225	0.234	-0.0099	-0.0189	0.0514
0.4963	0.474	-0.0404	-0.0386	0.1042
1.1331	0.7214	-0.093	-0.0592	0.1585
2.0445	0.9762	-0.1693	-0.0808	0.2143
3.2446	1.2395	-0.271	-0.1035	0.2718
4.7478	1.5114	-0.3999	-0.1273	0.331
6.5696	1.7926	-0.5581	-0.1523	0.3921
8.7259	2.0833	-0.7475	-0.1785	0.455
11.2346	2.3842	-0.9702	-0.2059	0.5199
14.1138	2.6957	-1.2286	-0.2347	0.5869

CHAPTER 12

Wind Deflection

If there is one factor that is the most difficult to deal with when it comes to a long-range shot, it is the wind. Gravity is a predictable effect. Spin drift and the other, less dramatic effects don't really come into play until the distances get out past 700 or 800 yards. Wind, however, is an ever-changing problem, and its effects aren't always taken at face value. It's one of those things that you can't see, only its effects. If you intend to become any sort of long-range shooter, you're going to need to get a pretty good handle on calling the wind and adjusting for it.

The term wind drift is often used, though wind deflection is the proper terminology. Frankly, I don't care which you use, so long as you understand it, and I'll use both here. The effects of crosswind drift are dependent on the velocity of the wind, the velocity of the bullet and the bullet's ballistic coefficient. That effect is predictable to a certain degree if you know for certain what the wind speed and direction are all the way from muzzle to target. Truthfully, knowing all the wind characteristics along the bullet's flight path is highly improbable on a target range, and nothing short of impossible in a hunting situation, unless you can verify that there is no wind whatsoever. But there are tools and methods you can use to help defeat the wind's effects and properly place the bullet on target. Learning to call the wind is equal parts science and art; you'll need to spend some time in the field doing nothing more than watching, and if you can get the opportunity to sit next to an experienced wind caller, definitely take advantage of that. I had the privilege of spending eight days at the FTW Ranch outside of Barksdale, Texas, with none other than Douglas "Dog" Pritchard, and I learned a ton from that man. My time was spent equally divided as the shooter and the spotter, engaging targets from 200 out to 1,800 yards into and across the broken Texas canyons, all the while discussing the wind calls with Pritchard. While I cannot garner the wisdom and experience of his Navy Seal training in eight days, I do know I'm much better at calling wind than I ever imagined I could be.

I'll say this several times throughout this book: if you're serious about long-range shooting or hunting, the SAAM course at the FTW Ranch is a worthy investment.

There is a definite difference between shooting long-range steel or paper targets, and long-range hunting. If ever I could make a case for the most precise wind calls possible, it is in the hunting fields. Should you miss the steel plate at 800 yards due to an incorrect wind call, the only thing that gets hurt are your feelings. Make that same mistake on an elk, moose or other game, and you could end up with a wounded, unrecoverable animal. Long-range hunting is in vogue right now, promulgated by several television shows that make it seem easy to hit an animal out to 700 yards, and I feel this is simply wrong-headed. I don't put down anyone's method of hunting, so long as it's legal and ethical, but there are so many unseen wind variables at those distances that a wind call that is off by a mere 2 mph can cause havoc, even if the shooter is disciplined and well-practiced.

That said, there are certain hunts that will call for a shot much longer than the average. Mountain goat, Dall sheep and Marco Polo argali fall into this category, as can pronghorn antelope. There are times where you just cannot get closer, and you'll need to be prepared for a distant shot. In addition to knowing the trajectory of your chosen cartridge, you will definitely need to know how to dope the wind. All the high BC bullets and baby bottle-sized cartridges won't combat a misread wind call, so you need all the advantages you can get to make it happen. I'm generally not a huge electronic gizmo guy, but the tools available to the long-range shooter—particularly those used to measure the wind—are not only extremely helpful, but I've found them to be an integral part of my gear, just like my riflescope or choice of bullets. I rely on a Kestrel Elite, which has not only the weather station features, but also comes with the Applied Ballistics computer to wrap things up into one convenient hand-held package. As with any electronic device, batteries can die at the most inopportune time, and capacitors can suffer from the "ghost-in-the-machine" syndrome, so I make a backup chart that I carry with me. Sometimes a hard copy is invaluable, even if you have to make adjustments on the fly. Let's first look at how wind drift works, then how to use visual clues in the field to get as close to the true wind call as possible.

Basic Wind Effects

Any projectile, be it a ping-pong ball, arrow or high-speed bullet, will be affected in some manner by crosswind, even if the amount of deviation is minute. For our purposes there is an accepted margin of error within which we may still hit the target. In order to best understand how wind drift affects a bullet in flight, we'll pick a constant wind speed—let's use 10 mph for convenience—and a particular bullet at a known speed. Just because I love the rifle/cartridge combination, let's use a .300 Winchester Magnum, driving a 180-grain Swift Scirocco II at a muzzle velocity of 2,960 fps (my own personal rig). For demonstrative purposes, the wind will be left to right, at the full 10 mph value. Let's look at the chart, and observe the wind drift at every 50 yards out to 500 yards, a reasonably sane limit for any hunting shot.

While some of this may be obvious to an experienced shooter who's spent time out past 300 yards, it may be demonstrative to those hunters who spend most of their time inside 200 yards, as I do more often than not in the deer woods. If you're headed out West for an elk, antelope or prairie dog hunt, this will give you an idea of the mayhem that crosswinds can create. This rifle is considered to be among the most flat-shooting setups, and the Swift Scirocco II, with a G1 BC of 0.520, has no flies on it as a hunting bullet, yet you can easily see that at only 300 yards a wind deflection of 5.4 inches may be enough to push your shot out of the vital area. Take things out to

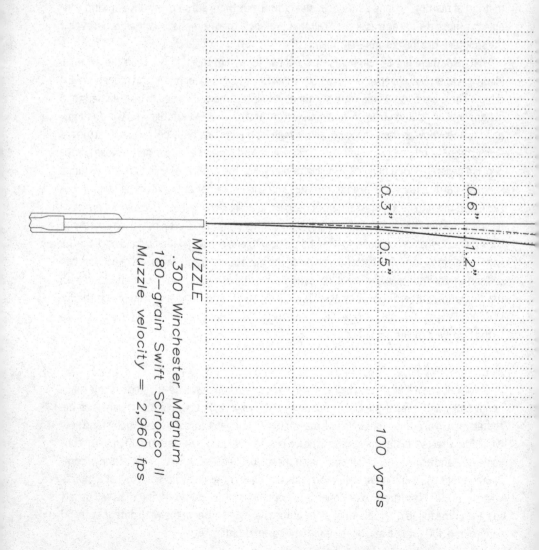

400 yards, and you'll see the drift jumps out to an even 10.0 inches, which is definitely trouble. I think you're getting the idea as to how important the wind is when it comes to hunting at longer ranges. At 500 yards, I've got just over 16 inches of wind drift, which will make for some serious contemplation, especially when you compound that figure with the 34 inches of drop—and that's using a hunting zero of 250 yards. There's an awful lot of thinking that goes into a shot at this distance, and then you've probably got a less-than-ideal shooting position from which to work, as well as the heart-pounding excitement generated by the chance at bagging your trophy.

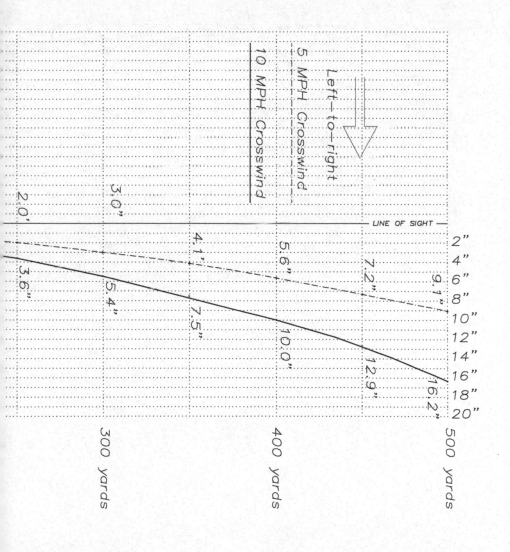

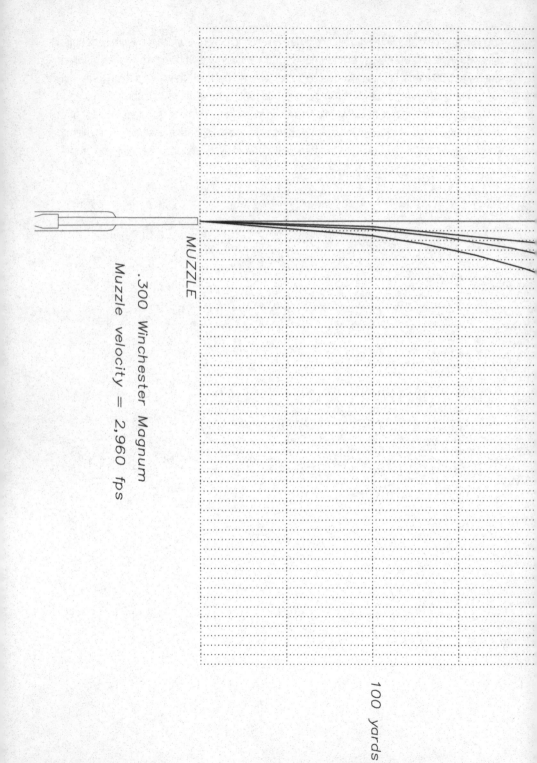

MUZZLE

.300 Winchester Magnum
Muzzle velocity = 2,960 fps

100 yards

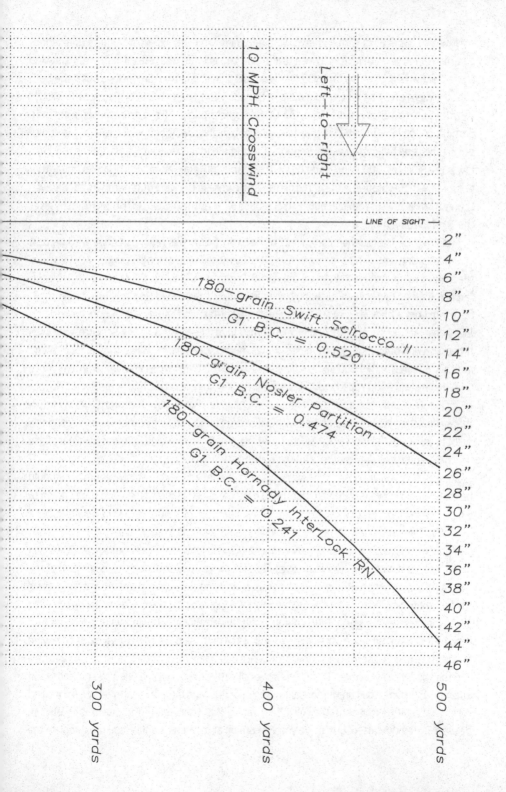

Left-to-right

10 MPH Crosswind

LINE OF SIGHT

2"
4"
6"
8"
10"
12"
14"
16"
18"
20"
22"
24"
26"
28"
30"
32"
34"
36"
38"
40"
42"
44"
46"

180-grain Swift Scirocco II
G1 B.C. = 0.520

180-grain Nosler Partition
G1 B.C. = 0.474

180-grain Hornady InterLock RN
G1 B.C. = 0.241

300 yards

400 yards

500 yards

Now, you are dealing with a known wind and a known distance. Most hunters think about distance in terms of trajectory, concentrating on the gravitational effect, but this little wind chart clearly demonstrates that you need to start thinking in two dimensions, with the horizontal dimension being much more difficult to deal with than the vertical. Reduce the muzzle velocity, as with a .308 Winchester or .30-06 Springfield, and you'll see an increased wind drift. Same fact applies with a bullet that has a lower ballistic coefficient; which is why the choice of cartridge and bullet play a very important role in the long-range game. Here's the rub: Let's lower the BC in my .300 Winchester by switching to a 180-grain Nosler Partition—a bullet that has a fantastic reputation in the game fields—and compare the wind drift numbers above. Even though the Partition is a spitzer bullet, its flat base reduces the G1 BC to 0.361, and thereby gives the wind the advantage.

The lower BC figure, when compared to the Swift Scirocco II, requires about a 50 percent increase in wind hold to hit the target, as well as increased drop at longer ranges. At 400 yards, the Scirocco deflects 10 inches, while the Partition moves 15.4 inches; this is an appreciable difference. Change things even further by using a good, old-fashioned Hornady 180-grain round-nose InterLock with a G1 BC of 0.241 and you'll see horrific wind values. The round-nose moves 13.3 inches at 300 paces, and 25.6 inches at 400 yards! Compared to the Scirocco, that's 2.5 times the wind deflection, which makes things much more difficult. While the ballistics aren't radically affected within 200 yards where I most often use this style of bullet, anything much past that distance and you'll be doing some math. Should I even remotely think of shooting out to 250 or 300 yards, I'd opt for a different choice of bullet. Funny how important that wind factor can be, especially when combined with bullet drop factor. And while these charts seemingly point to using a bullet with a high BC value all the time, there are factors in the terminal phase which will come into play that may influence the decision.

So, assuming you've chosen the high BC Scirocco in the .300 Winchester Magnum, you should take a look at wind values that are not the 10 mph baseline. Reducing the wind speed down to 5 mph, the wind drift is cut just about perfectly in half. So, your 500-yard shot now requires a hold of 9 inches into the wind rather than 16 inches—a significant difference.

Inside 300 yards, the 5 mph wind becomes much less influential, especially if you're talking about game animals and their vital zones. But, for the hunting shots on the longer end of the spectrum, even a 5 mph wind requires a compensatory hold. Another derivation of the chart is the fact that the wind drift for the 500-yard shot is highly dependent upon knowing the wind speed, because you've got a 7-inch difference between those two wind values. Should that wind be less than full value, you'll need to adjust the hold even farther. Let's look at how wind that isn't perpendicular to your shot will influence deflection.

If the wind is blowing directly at your face or directly at your back, it will have no horizontal effect on your shot. You can simply negate the effect of wind deflection altogether. If the wind is perpendicular to your shot, the full-effect values that I showed in the previous charts can be used as demonstrated. But, if the wind is coming at a different angle, you must reduce the values by the cosine of the angle, in order to arrive at the correct dope. Looking at your situation as if it were a clock face, you can better estimate the value of the wind, with reference to your baseline, where the winds are perpendicular to the line of flight. Again, assuming the 10 mph baseline for the .300 Winchester Magnum and a distance of 400 yards where the full-value wind drift would be 10 inches, you can adjust the value to a certain percentage of that number based upon the cosine of the angle. Let's say that 6x6 elk is standing at 400 yards, with the wind blowing at 45 degrees from your left, or somewhere between 10 and 11 o'clock on the dial. The math would work like this:

Sin45°, or, 0.707 x 10 in.(full value) = 7.1 inches

Change that wind position to exactly 10 o'clock on the dial and you'll find the wind value will increase to 86 percent of the full-value wind effect.

Sin60°, or 0.866 x 10 in.(full value) = 8.7 inches

You can simplify this a bit for field purposes, as winds are rarely a static value, and may change slightly within a matter of seconds while lining up the shot. Taking an average of wind direction, and based on the sine functions of the angle, you can arrive at a basic chart that is easy to remember in the field.

This concept, combined with a baseline wind chart, will allow you to place your shots much more accurately in the field than "Kentucky windage" ever would. You'll need to prepare a wind drift chart for each of your chosen calibers, and for each bullet/velocity combination you use within that caliber. When it comes to long-range shooting and "bucking the wind" (to use the vernacular) the bullets with the best BC values will keep the wind deflection to a minimum. If you like to use the semi-spitzer, round-nosed or flat-base bullets (as I often do) the wind will present more of a problem, as the BC values drop significantly. The longer time of flight and drop in velocity will allow the crosswind to have more time to work on the bullet. My example, based around the .300 Winchester Magnum and a sleek 180-grain bullet, is one that does rather well in the wind. Let's take a look at the same idea for a few different calibers, with popular bullet choices, to understand why certain cartridges have been touted as good long-range choices.

You can see the difference in performance, and how even though some of the lighter cartridges start out with a much higher muzzle velocity, their bullets, with lower BC figures, simply will not stand up to the wind as well as the high BC bullets. Now, the 7mm Remington Magnum is a good choice for a long-range hunting cartridge, but take a look at the figures for that 6.5 Creedmoor. There seems to be something magical about the 6.5mm bullet; it possesses a good balance of sectional density and ballistic coefficient, and comes in quite a few cartridge choices that are easy on the shoulder, yet generates enough muzzle velocity to work very well for long-range work. Depending on your hunting situation, you'll want to look for the bullet that best serves your needs, but if you feel your ranges could exceed 300 yards, the higher BC bullets will

SINE WIND VALUES

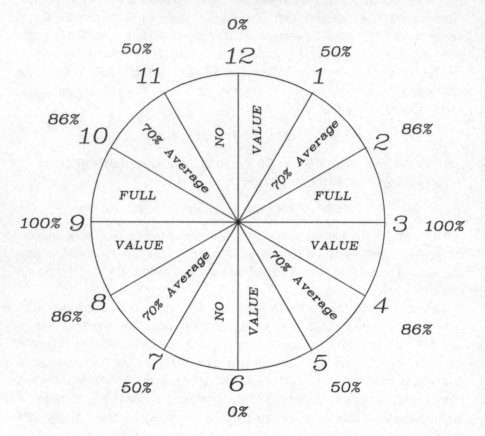

make your shots in windy conditions much easier. Let's address some of the points regarding good wind bullets briefly.

Hunting Bullets and Windy Terrain

Most of the bullets that behave well in the wind have a common trait: a G1 BC above .500. In some cartridges, the common twist rate prevents the use of a bullet with a BC figure this high, and that's a good indicator of why they're not often chosen for long-distance shooting. To be clear, I'm still talking hunting cartridges and bullets, so the requirements also include the terminal phase; we'll get to some target bullets in just a bit. As mentioned, I've long been a fan of the Swift Scirocco II, as the bullet is very uniform and holds together well at a wide range of impact velocities. I've had excellent accuracy with it in a variety of calibers, and its high BC values (for most calibers) make it a good choice. The bullet's bonded core and thick jacket give me a bunch of confidence if I'm holding a magnum caliber in hand and the shot is close. Some of the thinner jacketed bullets, which perform equally well in the wind, will make a bit of a mess on the close shots. The Nosler AccuBond has certainly proven itself in the hunting fields, too, as has the Ballistic Tip. Both have a high BC for windy conditions. The Ballistic Tip makes a great deer bullet (especially in the high BC, heavy for caliber slugs) and the AccuBond has a great reputation for its terminal ballistics. Yet, I really like the AccuBond Long Range line of bullets, which have a steeper boattail, and revised ogive to give an even higher ballistic coefficient. The new 142-grain 6.5mm ABLR has a G1 BC of 0.719, and the .30-caliber 210-grain bullet a BC of 0.730! There's a pair of winners if I ever saw them, blending all the attributes of a great hunting bullet: good in the wind, decent trajectory, and solid terminal performance. Fans of the .270 can get the 150-grain ABLR with a B.C. of 0.625, and the 7mm crowd has three choices—150, 168 and 175 grains, with G1 BCs between 0.611 and 0.672. Bullets like these are changing the game: A .270 Winchester with the ABLR is certainly not your grandfather's gun, and it makes a perfectly viable elk rifle, even shooting across windy canyons.

Sierra, famous for the MatchKing target bullet, has some offerings in the GameKing line that provide a good hunting BC for windy country. The 175-grain 7mm and 200-grain .308 bullet work very well, and while they are definitely heavy for caliber (check your barrel's twist rate!), they minimize the effects of wind deflection while offering enough sectional density to get the job done neatly.

Berger is one of those companies who've staked their claim in the long-range game, and they've done it well. Walt Berger started a company based upon benchrest precision, and it has evolved into producing some of the most innovative projectiles for both hunting and target shooting ever designed. You'll be reading more about these bullets in the target bullet section, but Berger has some damned fine hunting bullets as well. Almost all of the Berger offerings are sleek, boattailed affairs, with the VLD, or Very Low Drag bullet being the flagship of the hunting fleet. The VLD is accurate, and performs well on game, in addition to sporting a profile that resists wind deflection. However, Bergers tend to be considerably longer than some of the more traditional hunting bullets and can pose a challenge when it comes to staying within the SAAMI maximum length and functioning through normal-sized magazine boxes. However, if you can get them to function properly through your rifle, you'll find you've got serious medicine in your hands. If you're serious about a high BC bullet, take a look at Berger's Extreme Outer Limits Elite Hunter line, designed for true long-range hunting applications. Note, these do require a fast twist rate. They are heavier than normal, to obtain that high BC figure and resist crosswind deflection. The .277-inch diameter EOL bullet is 170 grains, and the 7mm is 195 grains. Serious business for certain, and though you may not have good results with a pre-'64 Model 70, long-range hunting requires specialized gear. Odds are you're going to be looking into a specialized rifle for this style of hunting. I know serious sheep hunters who've built rifles just to handle the longest bullets to be able to connect on those long shots.

For small-bore rifles like the .223 Remington and .22-250 right up through the 6mm, wind plays a more dramatic role in the hunting fields, especially with smaller targets like prairie dogs

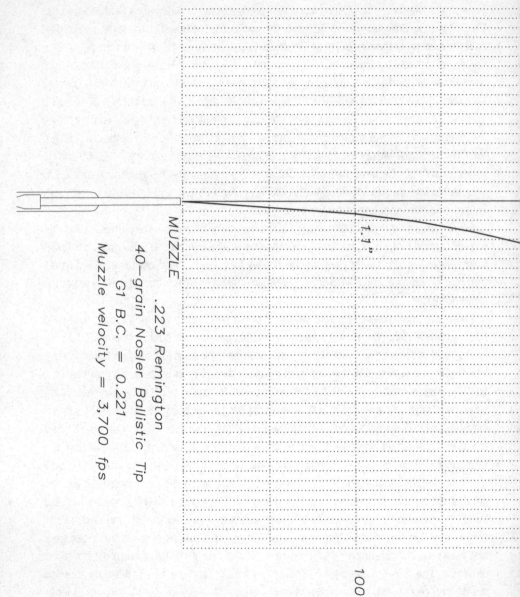

MUZZLE

.223 Remington
40-grain Nosler Ballistic Tip
G1 B.C. = 0.221
Muzzle velocity = 3,700 fps

1.7"

100 yards

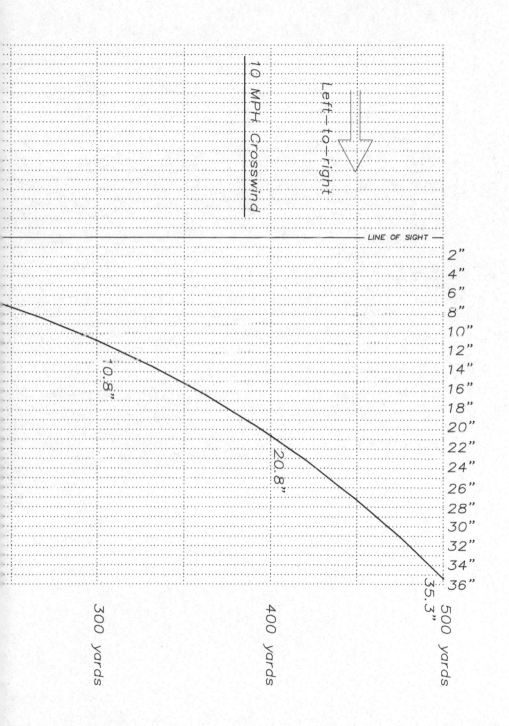

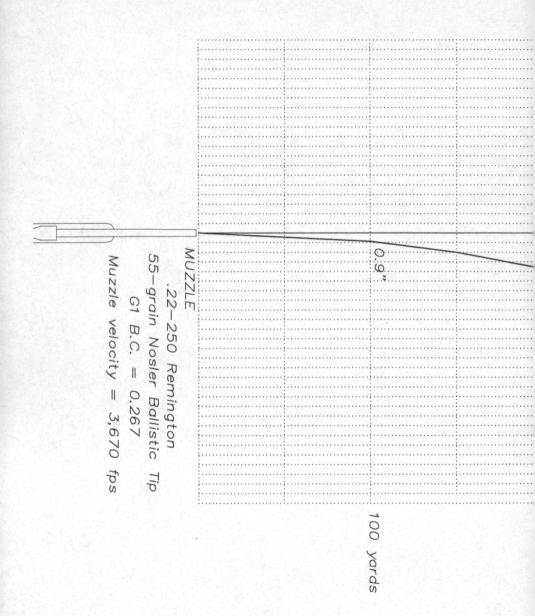

MUZZLE
.22–250 Remington
55–grain Nosler Ballistic Tip
G1 B.C. = 0.267
Muzzle velocity = 3,670 fps

0.9"

100 yards

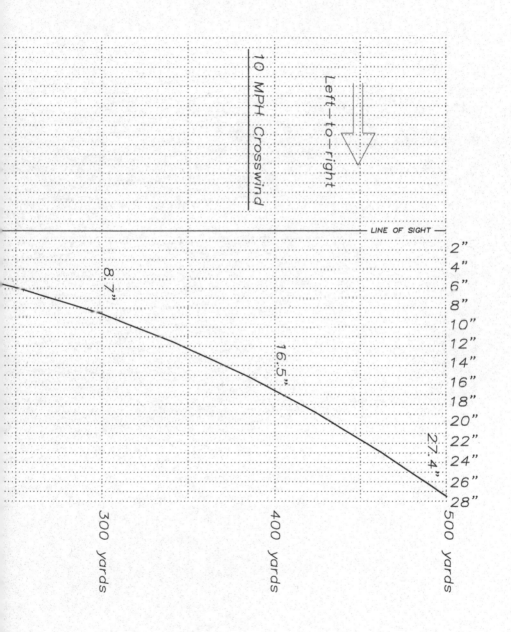

LINE OF SIGHT

Left-to-right

10 MPH Crosswind

2"
4"
6"
8"
10"
12"
14"
16"
18"
20"
22"
24"
26"
28"

8.7"

16.5"

27.4"

300 yards

400 yards

500 yards

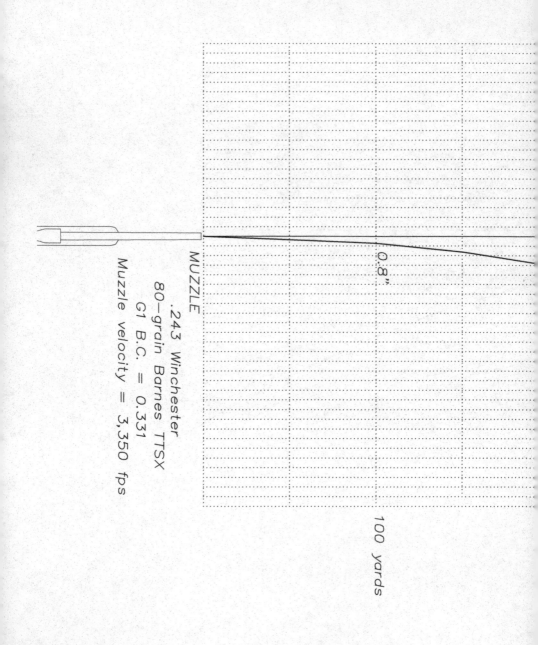

MUZZLE
.243 Winchester
80—grain Barnes TTSX
G1 B.C. = 0.331
Muzzle velocity = 3,350 fps

0.8"

100 yards

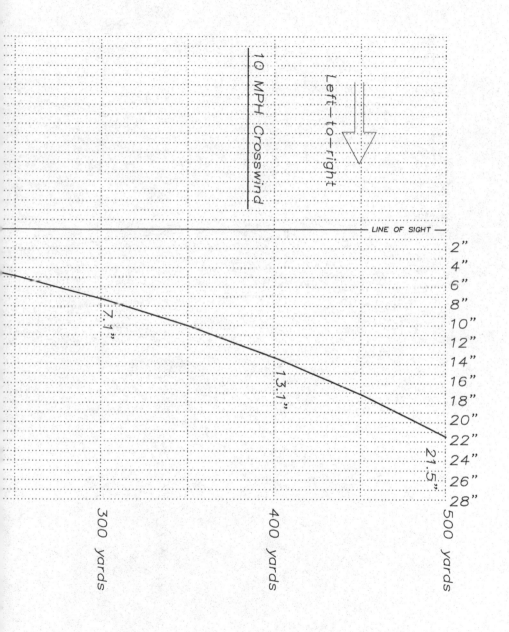

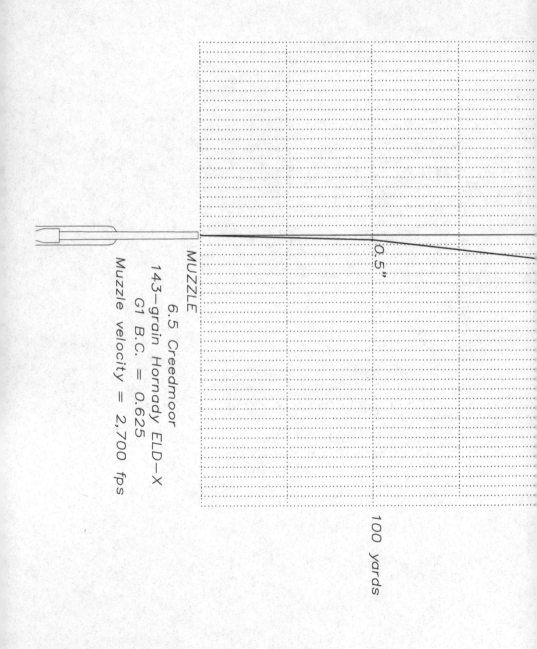

MUZZLE

6.5 Creedmoor
143–grain Hornady ELD–X
G1 B.C. = 0.625
Muzzle velocity = 2,700 fps

0.5"

100 yards

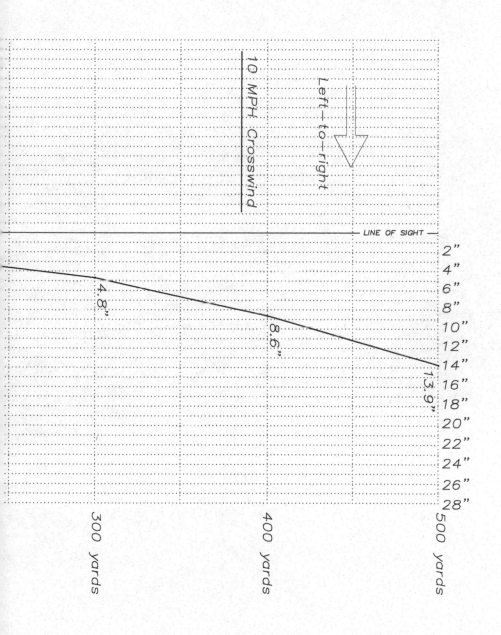

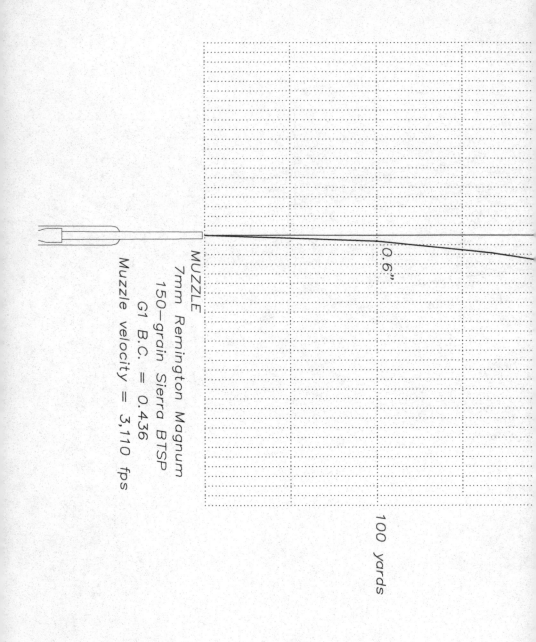

MUZZLE
7mm Remington Magnum
150—grain Sierra BTSP
G1 B.C. = 0.436
Muzzle velocity = 3,110 fps

0.6"

100 yards

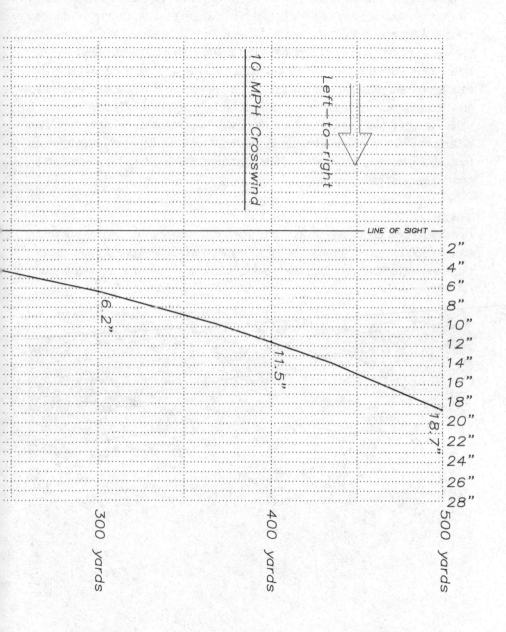

or woodchucks. The G1 and G7 BC values drop off in these cartridges, largely due in part to the weight of the bullets, and though they may be of similar geometry to their larger counterparts, they are more susceptible to wind drift. Despite having a muzzle velocity of 750 fps faster than the .300 Winchester Magnum, the 40-grain Nosler Ballistic Tip as loaded in .223 Federal Premium ammunition has twice the wind deflection at 400 yards than the .30 caliber 180-grain bullet. Even at 200 yards, the .223 Remington drifts 4.5 inches in a 10 mph crosswind, which will definitely cause a miss on a prairie dog-sized target. Even the .22-250 Remington, which has a great reputation as a flat-shooting round, drifts almost 4 inches at just 200 yards when using a muzzle velocity similar to the .223, but with the heavier 55-grain Ballistic Tip. Accordingly, wind deflection must be known and accounted for if you want to hit those little flea-ridden varmints. By increasing the BC figures for either of these cartridges, you can reduce the wind deflection and make your life easier.

Target Bullets and 1,000 Yard Wind

I personally don't take shots at unwounded game beyond 400 or, under absolutely optimum conditions 500 yards, but I'm only speaking for myself. If you routinely practice past that distance, and are comfortable, I'm not one to disagree. However, I know my own limitations, and

The Nosler AccuBond Long Range 142-grain 6.5mm bullet has a high BC, allowing it to buck the wind and shoot flat—yet it's a bonded bullet and tough enough to take game at long distances.

between 400 and 500 yards things get too iffy for my comfort level. Shooting targets, now that's a whole different ballgame! I absolutely love to ring steel out to 1,500 yards or more, if the opportunity affords. Here in the Northeast, those opportunities are limited, but I've spent some time in Texas where the vast expanses of land and broken terrain allow for a safe shooting condition, with targets out to 1,800 yards and more. I'll warn you upfront: check your ego at the door when the distances get to four figures, as it can be a very humbling experience. I've seen excellent shots in the game fields who've become frustrated, flustered and downright pissed when it came to hitting a 1,200-yard steel gong.

Invariably, knowing the exact drop of your cartridge is very important at those four figure distances, as is proper shooting form, but man!—the wind becomes difficult. At 1,000 yards, some of the highly popular target cartridges have gone subsonic and are travelling through the dirty air that affects a bullet between Mach 1.2 and the speed of sound. Even if the bullet remains supersonic, it has slowed down considerably and has had a much longer time of flight than has a hunting bullet, so the wind has a greater opportunity to work on the bullet's flight path. While the Scirocco is a great hunting bullet, perhaps you would be better served by a match-grade target bullet. There are many available, from the Sierra MatchKing—which has pretty much become the benchmark bullet for this application—to the Berger target projectiles and their fantastic J4 jackets, to the Lapua Scenar and Scenar-L, and the Cutting Edge MTH with its Seal-Tite band that will give some of the best velocities available. All of these have the capability of producing excellent long-range accuracy, provided you can do your part to take advantage of their wind drift resistant capabilities. I've had great results with the Hornady ELD-Match bullet in my 6.5-284 Norma on targets out to 1,400 yards. I took my time, testing the rifle's accuracy out to 500 yards where, with my handloads, the rifle can and will maintain 1/3 MOA, and used this bullet to test my own shooting abilities out to four-figure distances. At 140 grains, the ELD-Match has a G1 BC of 0.610, more than acceptable for targets at the distances I've described. While the muzzle velocities were not remarkable, it did give extremely uniform results. My particular rifle gives better velocities using a flat-base 140-grain bullet, but the accuracy using boattail match-grade bullets is unparalleled, at least in my barrel. Such accuracy makes life much easier when attempting to ring steel at 1,000 yards and more. Accordingly, this rifle wears two hats in that, for my hunting loads, I actually prefer the balance of trajectory and terminal performance of the premium flat-base 140- and 160-grain slugs, but when it comes to target work, the higher BC bullets get the call.

On more than one occasion I've used match-grade bullets to develop a load for a rifle, assessing what I feel to be the true accuracy potential, and adjusting fire accordingly when choosing a hunting bullet. I feel comfortable saying this: if you intend to use a rifle for target work, especially long-range target work, you're best served by choosing two or three different types of high BC match bullets and trying them in your rifle. These designs—whose job is to punch paper targets or ring steel discs—will invariably resist wind deflection best. As the distance increases, they will retain their energy and keep the time of flight to a minimum.

Range (yds.)	Velocity (fps)	Energy (ft.-lb.)	Trajectory (in.)	ComeUp (MOA)
0	2,580	2,070	-1.75	0
25	2,545	2,015	-0.2893	-1.1052
50	2,511	1,961	0.8337	1.5923
75	2,477	1,908	1.6128	2.0536
100	2,443	1,857	2.0384	1.9467
125	2,410	1,806	2.1003	1.6046
150	2,376	1,756	1.7875	1.1381
175	2,343	1,707	1.0913	0.5955
200	2,310	1,660	0	0
225	2,277	1,613	-1.4988	-0.6362
250	2,245	1,567	-3.4157	-1.3048
275	2,212	1,522	-5.7625	-2.0012
300	2,180	1,478	-8.5537	-2.7229
325	2,148	1,435	-11.8016	-3.4678
350	2,116	1,392	-15.5195	-4.2346
375	2,084	1,351	-19.7216	-5.0224
400	2,052	1,310	-24.4248	-5.8314
425	2,021	1,270	-29.6425	-6.6609
450	1,990	1,231	-35.3907	-7.5107
475	1,958	1,193	-41.6884	-8.3816
500	1,927	1,155	-48.5516	-9.2734
525	1,896	1,118	-55.9986	-10.1864
550	1,865	1,081	-64.0494	-11.1213
575	1,834	1,046	-72.7245	-12.0786
600	1,802	1,010	-82.0449	-13.0589
625	1,771	975	-92.0322	-14.0626
650	1,740	941	-102.714	-15.0911
675	1,709	908	-114.111	-16.1446
700	1,677	875	-126.251	-17.2243

A dope card for the 6.5-284 Norma, from the Hornady 4 Degrees of Freedom Ballistic Calculator, using the 140-grain ELD-Match.

Handguns, Lever Guns and Wind

The idea of time-of-flight being a controlling factor in wind deflection is important. It explains why so many of the handgun bullets can easily get away with a round- or flat-nosed projectile: They just aren't out there in the atmosphere long enough to be affected. Same can be said for many of the woods guns, like the venerable .30-30 WCF and .32 Winchester Special, guns typically employed for shots within 100 to 150 yards. Wind will have very little effect at those distances. If you do choose to use one of these style cartridges, or even a hunting handgun out to similar distances, you will begin to understand why the Hornady LeveRevolution ammunition

Wind Drift (in.)	Wind Drift (MOA)	Spin Drift (in.)	Spin Drift (MOA)	TOF (sec.)
0	0	0	0	0
0.0348	0.1329	-0.0027	-0.0102	0.0293
0.1396	0.2666	-0.0108	-0.0206	0.0589
0.3158	0.4021	-0.0246	-0.0313	0.089
0.5649	0.5395	-0.0441	-0.0421	0.1195
0.8886	0.6789	-0.0696	-0.0532	0.1504
1.2887	0.8205	-0.1013	-0.0645	0.1817
1.7665	0.964	-0.1392	-0.076	0.2135
2.3239	1.1097	-0.1837	-0.0877	0.2458
2.9628	1.2575	-0.2347	-0.0996	0.2785
3.6849	1.4076	-0.2927	-0.1118	0.3116
4.4918	1.5599	-0.3577	-0.1242	0.3453
5.386	1.7145	-0.4299	-0.1369	0.3794
6.3697	1.8717	-0.5097	-0.1498	0.4141
7.445	2.0314	-0.5971	-0.1629	0.4493
8.6144	2.1938	-0.6924	-0.1763	0.485
9.8806	2.359	-0.7958	-0.19	0.5213
11.2458	2.527	-0.9076	-0.2039	0.5581
12.7126	2.6979	-1.0279	-0.2181	0.5955
14.284	2.8718	-1.1572	-0.2327	0.6335
15.9625	3.0488	-1.2956	-0.2475	0.6721
17.7517	3.2291	-1.4434	-0.2626	0.7113
19.6555	3.4129	-1.6008	-0.278	0.7512
21.678	3.6004	-1.7681	-0.2937	0.7918
23.8232	3.7919	-1.9455	-0.3097	0.833
26.0954	3.9874	-2.1333	-0.326	0.875
28.4996	4.1873	-2.3319	-0.3426	0.9177
31.0398	4.3916	-2.5414	-0.3596	0.9612
33.721	4.6005	-2.7623	-0.3769	1.0055

took off so well: the soft, rubbery tip is safe to use in a tubular magazine, but more importantly the BC values dramatically increased. This gives not only a much more desirable trajectory, which immediately jumped out at most consumers, but also greatly reduced wind deflection.

I mentioned earlier in this chapter that I use the Hornady 180-grain round-nose InterLock in my .300 Winchester Magnum, especially in the forests of the Catskill and Adirondack mountains. I've had fellow hunters look at me as if I'd lost my mind; with so many good spitzer boattails available, why in the world would I choose that throwback style bullet? Well, I like the way it imparts energy, but looking at it in a different light, I'm really not concerned about wind deflection or long-range trajectory. I zero this particular load at 150 yards, which gives me the ability to hold dead on out to 200 yards, and within those ranges I'm not concerned about drop or wind drift since the time of flight is so short that the bullet will strike the vital area even on the windiest of days. The round-nose bullet hits hard, penetrates well, and is accurate in my gun.

This theory also applies to many of the African safari bullets—even those that may be loaded in a cartridge like the .300 Winchester, or others that are capable of long-range work. In Africa, a shot past 200 yards is the exception, not the rule, unless you're hunting one of the areas like the Kalahari Desert or the swamps of Bangweulu, and these are specialized affairs to begin with. As a result, most of the Professional Hunters I know prefer the round- or flat-nosed projectiles for the "bushveld" shots. Yes, I realize I told you about that eland that stood at 400 yards, with no possibility of getting closer, but that was a rare exception, and I was prepared for that by making a dope card for my .375 H&H. For certain, most dangerous game is taken inside of 150 yards, as the PH wants an accurately placed shot and to impart all the energy available into an animal. Most of the double rifle calibers like the .450 Nitro Express, .470 Nitro Express and .450/400 3-Inch Nitro Express, are designed for short-range work and will rarely be used past 150 paces, plus the ammunition is more often than not loaded with round- or flat-nose projectiles. The wind deflection values of these cartridges do look abhorrent past 200 yards, but such ranges don't typically come into play.

Hornady LeveRevolution ammo offers improvements in both trajectory and wind drift values.

On the flip-side of that coin are some big bores that can be used as longer-range rifles. Certainly the .375 H&H falls into this category, as it will generate respectable muzzle velocities, especially with some of the new bullet designs between 230 and 260 grains, yet can be used at distances out to 400 yards and beyond. That cartridge represents one of the few do anything, anywhere choices, with enough horsepower to handle the heavyweights like elephant, buffalo, grizzly and hippo, but makes a decent choice for elk and moose when loaded with the higher BC bullets. A 260-grain Nosler AccuBond performs very well in windy conditions, maybe not as good as a fast .30 caliber, but certainly workable for a rifleman who practices with it. This bullet has a G1 BC of 0.473, which makes it comparable to many of the .30 caliber hunting bullets, and you'll see from the graph that the 400-yard wind drift is only 12.5 inches in a 10 mph wind; not too far off from the .300 Winchester's 10.0 inches. Many hunters are surprised when they actually look at the ballistics of the .375 H&H, as they eventually recognize (as I did) that the trajectory mimics the .30-06 Springfield, only on a larger scale. Couple that with the fact that the 300- and 350-grain bullets can be employed for dangerous game work, and you'll see why so many hunters have come to rely on the venerable cartridge for so long, and why it remains as popular as it is to this day. The .375 Ruger, its ballistic twin, is fully capable of the same accolades. You can also understand why a hunter who pairs his .30-06 deer rifle with a good .375 bore will be very comfortable: the two behave very similarly in the field, the difference being the payload delivered. Should you own a .375 and want to use it for elk, moose or other distant shots, look to bullets like the 260-grain AccuBond or the 235-grain Cutting Edge Raptor and you'll have a relatively flat-shooting, wind-defiant big bore.

POINTS TO REMEMBER ABOUT WIND DEFLECTION

> More than gravity, wind deflection can cause errant shots and at ranges out beyond 300 yards must be accounted for.

> Wind is most definitely a variable, and knowing how your bullet will perform in a variety of different wind conditions will vastly improve your marksmanship skills.

> Using a bullet of the highest BC value possible will definitely reduce the effects of the wind.

> Higher muzzle velocities (read shorter time of flight) will also deny the wind the opportunity to push your bullet off course.

> Inside 200 yards, the wind has very little effect in a hunting situation, rarely pushing the bullet out of the vital area on a big game animal.

SECTION
III
TERMINAL
BALLISTICS

SECTION III TERMINAL BALLISTICS

CHAPTER 13

Terminal Ballistics Overview

That little blob of metal, so content in its metallic case, has been sent screaming down the barrel, spinning until it's dizzier than a 2-year-old on sugar, sailing through the air faster than, well I was going to say a speeding bullet, but, it's going pretty damned fast. Then, instantly, violently, the journey ends. At the gun range it just rips paper and meets its untimely demise in a sand bank or dirt berm. Perhaps it smashed through hide, bone and vital tissue, putting dinner on the table for a family all winter. Or maybe it was built like a racecar and got to fly long and high, only to end in the sweet ringing of steel. Best of all, that bullet may have saved someone's life. Whatever the case, the end of a bullet's life is an important part of our study, or what we call terminal ballistics—what happens when it makes impact.

Whether in a defensive situation or on a dangerous game hunt, there are times when the construction and terminal performance of a bullet means life or death. In the case of hunting bullets, you want a quick, humane kill—after all, the bullet's job is to reach the vital organs to destroy tissue. No matter how many trajectory charts you've memorized, no matter how many lines-per-inch the checkering on your AAA Circassian walnut features, it is the bullet, and only the bullet, that touches a game animal and delivers the death blow.

At this stage of the game you've managed to place the shot where it belongs, and now you need to consider what's going to happen after impact. Will the bullet penetrate sufficiently? Will it expand properly? Was it of suitable construction to handle the task at hand? Did you choose the proper type of bullet to meet the requirements you need? All these questions and more fall under the heading of terminal ballistics.

In this section, the handgun will receive much more attention than it has previously. While the exterior ballistics of handgun bullets aren't nearly as complex as that of rifles, the terminal

Expanded handgun bullets have come a long way today. All three of these examples exhibit excellent expansion.

ballistics of a handgun are very interesting. Handgun hunting bullets have come an awful long way, and there are some absolutely incredible personal defense choices out there, too. Their performance needs to be analyzed to best choose a handgun caliber, as well as settle some old arguments.

Rifle bullets have changed for the better as well, having many new designs available. Some of these designs are a far cry from the cup-and-core bullet of our grandfathers' era and deliver some outstanding performance, almost forcing us to rethink the old cartridge and caliber recommendations. These innovations implore you to take a new look at how much cartridge/bullet is really needed to get the job done. I am always intrigued about new bullet designs, and I've had the opportunity to test some of these around the globe on animals small, medium and large.

There is much demand placed upon the rifle bullets of today. You expect your modern rifle bullet to be a death-ray. If you do our part in holding the rifle on the right spot and squeeze the trigger properly, you expect instantaneous results. The bullet needs to be accurate, retain almost all of its energy downrange, expand well enough to create a huge wound channel, and penetrate deep enough to destroy the vitals from any angle. Oh, and you want it cheap, too! No worries!

Well, the bullets of today can meet most of those parameters, but not all. There are some that will certainly deliver the goods, but the materials and manufacturing costs are higher than the bullets of yesteryear. While some of the tried and true hardcast lead and cup-and-core bullets still perform wonderfully in certain situations, there are those times when the cost of a hunt or the scarcity of a coveted tag warrant the investment in the best projectile money can buy, no matter which of the attributes listed above is most important.

The birth of the premium bullet industry hearkens back to 1948 in Canada, when John Nosler experienced terrible bullet failure while trying to relieve a large-bodied moose of its life with a .300 Holland & Holland Magnum. The cup-and-core bullets that Nosler was using simply weren't strong enough to handle the high impact velocity of the Super .30 and had prematurely expanded on the moose's shoulder, giving poor penetration. His idea of a dual-core bullet separated by a copper partition really set the hunting world on its ear and created an entire market for premium projectiles. Fast forward to the 21st century, and you have monometal bullet designs that would certainly make my grandfather cock an eyebrow. Some of these newcomers use a funky sort of nipple at the front end to cause trauma via a cavitation bubble, delivering straight-line penetration and a cylindrical core of trauma. Some designs, like the aforementioned Nosler Partition, have been with us for decades and have their devout followers.

Whatever the case, there is now a proper tool for the job at hand. You, as the hunter, shooter and consumer, need to be honest with yourself about the requirements of your shooting situation to choose a bullet that will give you the results you're after. We will start the study of terminal ballistics by dealing with a bit of bullet history and how bullet performance so heavily influenced the reputation of the cartridges themselves. We'll then examine how the projectiles of the 21st century could and should change the way we think about cartridge requirements.

The Nosler Partition is still the benchmark by which all modern bullets are measured. Photo courtesy Nosler.com

John A. Nosler pioneered bullet construction and is perhaps best known for the tough Partition bullet. Photo courtesy Nosler.com

CHAPTER 14

The History of Terminal Ballistics

The first projectiles for the firearm were round lead balls, slightly smaller than bore diameter, to be "patched" for a tight seal. Lead was the chosen material, not for its durability upon impact, but for its malleability in forming the projectiles. Lead is easy to work and shape, melts at a relatively low temperature and is plentiful. This was perfect for the early users of the cartridge guns, as many firearms were sold with a set of molds of appropriate caliber and bullet weight for that firearm. Think of the buffalo hunters on the Great Plains, hunting all day and sitting by their campfire at night, melting lead and casting their own lead bullets for the next hunt. However, lead has several shortcomings, especially with modern firearms and propellants.

Your goal as a hunter (we'll get to the self-defense bullets soon enough), is to deliver a quick, humane kill to minimize the suffering of the game animal. For most of your hunting, with the exception of solid bullets or a shot column from a shotgun, you depend on the bullet to create massive hemorrhaging by destroying as much vital tissue as possible. The expansion of a bullet—if it is designed to expand—creates hydraulic shock, which destroys tissue as well. Now, when a material as soft as lead impacts hide, bone and water-rich flesh at an appreciable velocity, you can have very rapid expansion. Your projectile will certainly meet enough resistance to flatten a round ball or rapidly deform the meplat of a lead bullet. So the lead ball or bullet must be of sufficient weight and diameter to properly penetrate into an animal's vitals in order to guarantee a quick kill, and the velocity must be kept to a reasonable level, say below 2,200 fps. Even then, the bullet can exhibit penetration problems if the shot is too close.

The stories of Frederick Courteney Selous from the late 19th century are illuminating. Selous would hunt elephants with a muzzleloading four-bore rifle stoked with a lead ball weighing 1/4 pound, propelled by over 500 grains of blackpowder. That gives you an idea of how the early projectile directly affected the choice of bore diameter; you simply needed to compensate for a lack of penetration with sheer mass.

At moderate velocity typical of the .30-30 Winchester or .45-70 Government, or most of the classic handgun cartridges like the .38 Special and .45 Colt, a lead projectile will work well, giving a good blend of expansion and penetration. Many of these cartridges are still loaded with lead projectiles today, and they perform superbly. For some of the faster cartridges like the .44 Magnum, lead bullets can be hardened by adding a specific amount of antimony to the molten lead while casting, resulting in a harder alloy and better terminal ballistics.

In light of the velocity increases that smokeless powder brought to the table, there needed to be an advance in the construction of projectiles. It was Lt. Col. Eduard Rubin of Switzerland who, in 1882, had the ingenious idea of jacketing the lead bullets in a layer of copper—a metal hard enough to avoid the issues associated with heavy lead deposits in the barrel, yet soft enough to work perfectly with the steel rifling of the barrel. Rubin completely covered the spitzer projectile, leaving no exposed lead, creating the first 'full metal jacket' or FMJ as we all know it today.

The lead bullets that had previously been used in combat had such a terrible effect on soldier's bodies. Think about the photos and accounts from the Civil War and how some of those large-caliber lead bullets and balls would not only inflict horrible flesh wounds, but would sometimes tear limbs off at the bone. The advent of the FMJ made total sense as a weapon of war. Indeed, many countries of the world felt that the horrific wounds of injured soldiers could be minimized by the use of the non-expanding projectiles. The Hague Convention of 1899, in Declaration III, specifically prohibited the use of any expanding projectiles in international warfare, though many incorrectly attribute this prohibition to the Geneva Convention. For the record, the United States did not agree to the treaty. This decision included so-called Dum-Dum bullets: those FMJs that had any exposed lead, or a cross-slot cut into the nose for expansion. (An interesting note is that Dum-Dum bullets were named after the British military facility near Dum-Dum, West Bengal, India. It was here that Captain Neville Bertie-Clay developed the Dum-Dum bullet, an expanding projectile designed for the .303 British cartridge, with a radical hollowpoint. The expansion of this bullet could be best described as violent, and I can only imagine the devastating result of using this projectile in combat.)

The result of adding a copper jacket to the traditional lead projectile completely changed the hunting world as well. Not only could these new projectiles be driven to much higher velocity and with fantastic accuracy, but by manipulating the amount of exposed lead at the nose, or meplat of the bullet, the amount of expansion could be *controlled*. This allowed ammunition manufacturers to tune the bullet to the velocity of the cartridge and better control the expansion/penetration ratio. The method of drawing a copper cup around the lead core results in what I have referred to elsewhere in this book as a cup-and-core bullet.

There were failures early on. The copper cup would often separate from the lead core upon impacting a game animal, and penetration was severely affected. Attempts were made to

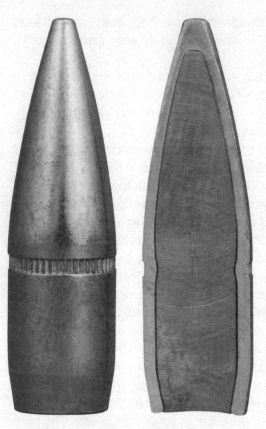

The military-approved full metal jacket.

better keep the bullets together during the terminal ballistics phase. Remington's 1939 Core-Lokt bullet used a cannelure that stepped the copper jacket into the lead core to better keep the bullet in one piece. A tapering copper jacket, thicker toward the rear, made an appreciable difference in controlling—that is, slowing—the amount of expansion so that the necessary penetration could be obtained.

In the first half of the 20th century, hunters pretty much had two choices, especially for the dangerous game of Africa: a soft-point bullet with a bit of exposed lead at the nose with a copper jacket that covered the remainder of the bullet, or a full metal jacket bullet—commonly referred to as a solid—which offered no expansion whatsoever, but would provide fantastic penetration against those animals with extremely thick hides and huge, tough bones. There were volumes of material written about the effectiveness (or lack thereof) of the waves of new cartridges being released by British, German and American ammunition and firearms companies. If you are a fan of firearms and cartridge development (and by picking up this book I would assume you are) there are plenty of articles and books available that give a good glimpse into the situation at various points throughout the first half of the 20th century. People like Elmer Keith, Jack O'Connor, John "Pondoro" Taylor, W.D.M. Bell and John Hunter authored many of these works, and these gentlemen all had huge amounts of hands-on experience with the tools of their day. In reading their works one can get a definite feel for the opinions they garnered through trial and error, and these opinions are still heralded today.

However, the reader must also appreciate the fact that many of the opinions generated by these now-famous authors were directly influenced by the terminal performance of the projectiles of their era. One of my favorite volumes, written by John 'Pondoro' Taylor—an Irishman who tramped all over southern and eastern Africa—is *African Rifles and Cartridges*, a treatise on firearms and cartridges commonly used throughout the Dark Continent from 1920 until 1948 or thereabouts. Taylor had, according to his own accounts, used the vast majority of popular cartridges, from the .22 Long Rifle up to and including the behemoth .600 Nitro Express. He recounted his experiences with those cartridges on all sorts of African game, from the diminutive antelope up to the gigantic elephant. While few may have the opportunity to hunt Africa, this cross-section of game taken by Taylor includes many that are similar to our North American species.

Jack O'Connor was a fantastic author, known for championing the .270 Winchester, and was a proponent of the lighter calibers using bullets at higher velocities. Elmer Keith, an Idaho rancher with an extensive background in firearms, was responsible for the development of several highly popular handgun cartridges, as well as participating in the development of rifle cartridges that went on to influence future developments. These two gentlemen were both very well respected, yet had diametrically opposed views on what made a suitable hunting cartridge for various species. Keith believed in much heavier bullets than did O'Connor. But I firmly believe that their respective points of view were inarguably based on the terminal performance of the projectiles from their era much more than the potential of the cartridges by which they so strongly swore.

Walter Dalrymple Maitland Bell, a Scotsman whose adventures in early 20th century Africa are heralded to this day, was a proponent of the use of small-bore rifles (the 7x57mm Mauser being the most used) for big game, especially on the 1,000+ elephants he took in his hunting career. Bell, who was an excellent shot, especially under the pressure of being in close proximity of truly dangerous game, made the claim that his "barrel had never been polluted by a soft-point bullet." He came to rely solely on full metal jacketed bullets, which had the nose portion strengthened by steel, placed under the layer of copper gilding metal. While I don't think that any Professional Hunter alive today would recommend or even accept the 7x57mm Mauser as an appropriate dangerous game cartridge, Bell was not a hunting client in today's sense. He had no legal requirements regarding rifle caliber and was literally in uncharted waters with respect to ballistic boundaries. Bell found that 173 grains of bullet properly placed would work just as effectively as 500 grains. If either bullet were placed incorrectly, Bell contended, they were equally ineffective. We can agree that a cartridge as small as the 7mm Mauser is not the best choice for dangerous game, but Bell's point was that a bullet, if properly constructed, could amaze a hunter as to its actual capabilities. In a very short period of time, the four-bore lead cannonball weighing in at 1/4 pound had effectively been matched with a 173-grain steel and copper jacketed 7mm slug. The terminal ballistics experimentation of Bell (who also used a 6.5x54mm Mannlicher-Schoenaur and a .318 Westley Richards) gave quite a bit of insight into the importance of bullet construction and its correlation to terminal ballistics.

All of these hunters had an irrefutable effect on the reputations of our favorite cartridges on both ends of the spectrum. And many of those endorsements, based on the projectiles available to them at the time, carry on to this day. Today, however, some of these viewpoints need to be revised.

The cup-and-core bullets of the first half of the 20th century were tweaked in many different ways to achieve the consummate blend of expansion and penetration. The Remington Bronze Point was an early release which used a hollowpoint design, capped with a sharp, bronze tip that would not only prevent the meplat of the bullet from being battered under recoil, but would act as a wedge to initiate expansion. It was met with mixed reviews. Some hunters found it to work wonderfully, giving great expansion and hydraulic shock. Others reported that the bullet failed to give any expansion at all—acting just like a solid and giving caliber-size entry and exit wounds. Most folks just used the standard cup-and-core bullets, with varying levels of satisfaction.

All that changed in 1948 when John Nosler went moose hunting. His chosen rifle (and a fine one at that) was the .300 Holland & Holland Magnum, a perfect choice for the distances at which moose may be taken, and a caliber with an excellent reputation for big game. I'm not sure which brand of projectile Nosler was using, but the story as I've heard it goes as follows. Nosler had a moose at relatively close range, and while he placed his shots well, right on the beast's shoulder, the bullets just wouldn't penetrate. His cup-and-core bullets, driven to a muzzle velocity of just over 3,000 fps, simply were breaking up on the tough muscles and shoulder bones of the huge moose. This left him perplexed. He knew he had done his part, and that there must be a better solution to the problem of bullet construction. Once he got home, he put on his thinking cap and came up with an idea: a bullet divided in two, separated by a partition of copper, which would be made integral with the copper jacket. He took a copper rod of proper dimension, drilled out either end, inserted a lead core, and fashioned the front portion into a spitzer profile. The idea was to allow the front portion of the bullet to expand for the tissue destruction necessary for a quick kill, yet keep the rear portion intact for deep penetration. The idea worked perfectly, and the Nosler Partition was born. It did exactly what Nosler intended, giving nearly the penetration of a solid, yet the front expanded properly. Naturally, the performance of this bullet caused it to catch on quickly, and to this day the Nosler Partition remains a favorite of hunters around the globe.

What John Nosler really did was single-handedly kick-start what would become the premium bullet industry. The premium bullet designs that have come onto the market have been nothing short of amazing. In the post-WWII years, many premium or boutique bullet companies popped up, once the raw materials became available once again. There were huge surpluses of powder, and some eager entrepreneurs began to show their wares, resulting in what are household names today: Joyce Hornady, Vernon Speer, Sierra Bullet Company, just to name a few. They gave us the projectiles that, while of standard construction, allowed hunters to develop their own handloaded ammunition with reliable and predictable results. Over the decades, these companies would hone their crafts and continue to push the boundaries of bullet technology.

The Barnes Bullet company dates back to the 1930s, when Fred Barnes was making his own custom bullets in his basement. He sold the company three decades later and, following a succession of sales, the company ended up in the hands of Randy and Coni Brooks. The Brooks' kept Barnes on for a bit as a consultant, but it was they who had the revolutionary idea. Randy

Brooks had experienced bullet failure in the past, and while he was sitting on a high perch in Alaska glassing for spring brown bear and thoughts wandering, he had an epiphany. As he explained it to me, he thought, why not take out the lead. The result: He had designed the all-copper expanding X-Bullet, which solved the problem of jacket/core separation, and led to an entire school of thought known as the monometal expanding bullet. This was a huge development in terminal ballistics. The scored hollowpoint would open upon impact to form an X. The retained weight of the bullet was unprecedented. Brooks also developed a monometal solid for the African heavyweights that remains one of the best on the market even today.

Swift Bullets, hailing from Kansas, has also set an impressive benchmark in the terminal ballistics world. Improving, if you will, on the partitioned bullet design, Bill Hober's company uses a thicker jacket for their A-Frame bullet, as well as chemically bonding the jacket to the front lead core, further slowing expansion. The A-Frame is a great choice for thick-skinned animals and is ideal for any critter smaller than elephant. When recovered from game animals, it proves to hold its weight very well—often in the 90-95 percent range—and shows good expansion on the front end, displaying the classic A-Frame rivet just behind the partition. I've often described the Swift A-Frame as "meat-resistant," meaning the more meat you hit, the greater the resistance to the bullet, the more the A-Frame will expand. On big game, such as bison and Cape buffalo, it will expand to around twice its caliber, yet on smaller game that number diminishes, often whistling clear through ... still killing, yet not leaving you with a whole bunch of bloodshot meat. I especially like this bullet when using a big-bore rifle, say a .375 or one of the .40 calibers, for hunting plains game in a dangerous game block, or when chasing elk or moose in an area known to be inhabited by grizzly. Swift makes this bullet not just for the bolt-action rifles (in a semi-spitzer design), but in a flat meplat designed for use in the popular lever-action cartridges, as well as for the hunting revolver cartridges. Were I to choose just one bullet for all of my hunting beside the elephant, it would be the Swift A-Frame. I've used it on dozens of different species, and its terminal ballistics make it my personal favorite, even though I know I'm giving up a little bit of ballistic coefficient.

There are now many different bullet designs on the market that feature a sharp polymer tip, serving to act much like the Remington Bronze Tip I discussed earlier. The polymer tip of the bullet is designed to increase the ballistic coefficient, yet upon impact the tip acts like a wedge, initiating expansion. The polymer tip has been incorporated into many different bullet designs: The Barnes TTSX, the all-copper hollowpoint with a tip to promote expansion; the Swift Scirocco II, a heavy jacketed boattail bullet with a bonded core; and the Hornady SST, a standard cup-and-core design. Nosler alone has three tipped models, the Ballistic Tip, AccuBond and E-Tip, and all three are constructed differently.

There are specially designed varmint bullets engineered to give an almost explosive terminal performance. These feature very thin jackets and soft lead cores, and are as frangible as can be, delivering all sorts of hydraulic shock. Some are hollowpoints, while others are polymer tipped, but all have come a long way toward their specific goal: creating the red mist that varmint hunters are after.

Lastly, the most recent developments in big game rifle bullet technology are some real eye openers. The Woodleigh Bullet Company of Australia has released their Hydrostatically Stabilized Solid, a non-expanding monometal with a small cup at the nose. This bullet creates a supercavitation bubble, destroying tissue along the way, yet exiting at caliber dimension. This design worked perfect for me in Africa on game from impala to elephant, offering all the penetration anyone would want, in addition to quick, humane kills.

The Pennsylvania-based company Cutting Edge Bullets produces monometal projectiles (either all-copper or all-brass) that are turned on a lathe for extremely tight tolerances. Their Raptor bullets are a hollowpoint design, available either with or without a polymer tip, and the ogive of the bullet is skived, so upon impact the front half breaks into little blades that cause the initial trauma in a star-shaped pattern. It's a very interesting concept, and one that has proven itself around the world for me.

Peregrine Bullets, hailing from South Africa, are producing a fine monometal bullet too, in several different configurations. One I find most interesting is the Bush Master bullet, which uses a bronze plunger in the hollowpoint with a slight bit of air space underneath it. The plunger sits flush with the meplat of the bullet and, upon impact, forces the bullet to expand as the air trapped inside the hollowpoint can't be compressed, resulting in force that opens up the nose of the bullet. Designed with a thick wall and an almost flat nose, the Bush Master imparts its energy much like a flat-nose or round-nose, yet retains almost all of its weight, making it a great design for truly big game like moose, bear or any buffalo.

As you can see, the rifle bullet has had a long and complex journey when it comes to terminal ballistics, and we haven't yet cracked the surface.

Revolver and pistol bullets have gone through much the same development, and many of the designs I've described are offered in a handgun configuration. Bonded cores, thick jackets, monometals, skived hollowpoints—they've all made their way into the handgun bullet market. The lead pistol bullet of yesteryear still gives good performance, but today's designers have imparted their wisdom to the handgun projectile so as to give some rather stunning results. The idea of jacketing a handgun bullet is as old as the jacketed rifle bullet itself. The same Hague Convention decree applied to handgun bullets, so the full metal jacket bullet is certainly a popular configuration, and its terminal ballistics have been proven in a pair of World Wars. The still-popular ball ammunition offers no expansion whatsoever, but provides fantastic penetration. Ballistic engineers have long sought the consummate balance between bullet expansion and penetration, seeking to give just enough penetration to neutralize a threat, yet not too much, which could injure or kill unintended parties.

There are some great pistol bullets that fit this bill using a hollowpoint design and varying jacket types. Some have the jacket locked in with a cannelure, others lock the copper jacket around the mouth of the hollowpoint. Some of these designs include the Hornady XTP and XTP Mag, Speer Gold Dot, and the Federal Hydro-Shok, Guard Dog and HST.

Monometal bullets have been adapted to a self-defense role. The Cutting Edge Bullets line

The Barnes TSX is an update of the original model and is an all-copper hollowpoint.

of Personal Home Defense ammunition comes immediately to mind, offering many of the same benefits of the rifle bullets of same design: lighter throw weight and correlative higher velocity, stout construction, and reliable expansion. When it comes to a self-defense handgun projectile, a flat trajectory is not a major concern, but accuracy and terminal ballistics are paramount.

On the hunting side of things, the evolution of the bullet has led to some impressive terminal performance. Yes, hardcast lead bullets, usually in a flat-point configuration will still make a dependable choice at most hunting handgun ranges, especially in the heavy-for-caliber weights, but the premium bullets will truly allow the hunting revolver to shine. The Swift A-Frame, with its copper partition and front bonded core, gives fantastic terminal performance. With weight retention often above 85 percent—even at the high velocities associated with the speedy .454 Casull and bone-crushing .460 Smith & Wesson—the hollowpoint front core will expand to a diameter of just around 1.5 times caliber dimension. Barnes has also adapted their X-bullet technology, resulting in their XPB handgun bullet. Being an all-copper, hollowpoint design, the XPB gives the terminal performance handgun hunters desire: good expansion, with the deep penetration associated with the monometal bullets.

It's time for a detailed look into the terminal performance of different bullet types. When we're done, don't be surprised if you feel the need to rethink some old opinions—I know I did!

CHAPTER 15

Sectional Density, Penetration And Retained Weight

We first discussed sectional density, or SD in the interior ballistics section, but I firmly believe its most important function is in the terminal phase of the bullet's flight. To briefly reiterate, sectional density is the ratio of the bullet's weight in pounds to the square of the diameter in inches.

$$SD = \text{(Bullet weight in pounds)}/\text{Bullet diameter}^2$$

This mathematical figure expresses only the weight and diameter of the bullet, not the shape or construction materials, so it's a guide, but a useful one. There is actually a debate raging that the above formula is incorrect for properly determining the actual SD of a bullet, and that the proper method for this figure should be as follows:

$$SD = \text{(Bullet weight in pounds)}/(\pi \times \text{Radius}^2)$$

I first came across the new equation in Pierre van der Walt's *African Dangerous Game Cartridges*—a book you should definitely own—and while I completely agree with his reasons for the variance in our common method for deriving sectional density values, for this book I will adhere to the first method shown so as to correlate my ideas to the published values throughout the industry.

Let's compare and contrast some common .30 caliber bullets to get a feel for SD. Bullets in this caliber range from 100 to 250 grains on the extreme ends, but I've had much experience using 125-, 150-, 165-, 180- and 220-grain slugs in my .30-caliber cartridges.

125-grain .308 SD = 0.185

150-grain .308 SD = 0.226

165-grain .308 SD = 0.248

180-grain .308 SD = 0.271

220-grain .308 SD = 0.331

The petite 125 grain—which is available in some rather stout designs, should you choose to use them for lighter game—has an SD figure of .185, rather anemic when compared to the 180-grain's figure of 0.271, or the beefy 220-grainer with an SD of 0.331. The 165-grain bullet, often considered the best middle-of-the-road choice for many of the medium-sized .30-caliber cases, has an SD of 0.248, so you can use that as a good basis for decision-making. The SD figure, within the range of bullets for a given caliber, can be used to loosely predict which projectiles within that range which will penetrate deepest (due to the additional length and weight) and which will give rapid expansion (due to the lower length/diameter ratio). Many Professional Hunters who pursue dangerous game prefer a bullet with an SD figure at or exceeding 0.300 to ensure deep penetration. In the .30-caliber bullets, that would be a projectile weighing 200 grains (SD 0.301); in .375 caliber, a 300-grain slug (SD 0.305); and in .416 caliber

The Cutting Edge Safari Raptor in .404 Jeffery.

at least a 370-grain bullet (SD 0.305), while the popular 400-grain bullets in that caliber give an SD figure of 0.330.

If you're a varmint hunter, you'll want bullets with a low SD figure to achieve the quick expansion that gives the hydraulic shock to deliver quick kills on the smaller animals. Deer hunters tend to stay in the middle—like the aforementioned 165-grain .308-inch bullet—to get a good blend of expansion (to generate shock, an effective tool when it comes to whitetail) and sufficient penetration (to reach those vital organs from any angle). Elk, bear and moose hunters lean heavier, like the 180-grain in .308, as the size of the animal being hunted generally warrants a bit more bullet to plow through the additional bone and tissue.

These points have been the general standard for decades, and those SD figures could easily be interpolated for 7mm or .338 calibers. But there is a catch: the accepted figures were based on the experiences of 20th-century hunters, using (primarily) cup-and-core bullets. You need to take a look at the new construction methods and see how things have changed—and I can guarantee you that things have changed.

I was turned onto Cutting Edge Bullets, a Pennsylvania company making lathe-turned all-copper hollowpoints. I was familiar with monometal bullets (Barnes has been around for years delivering the goods), but I hadn't experienced the kind of consistency as delivered by Cutting Edge. My good pal Dave deMoulpied and I had used the Cutting Edge projectiles in a .416 Rigby and .404 Jeffery, respectively, in South Africa and Zimbabwe, and I wanted to try them on plains game in my .300 Winchester Magnum. I was heading to the Limpopo Province with my wife Suzie to break the 11-year kudu curse. Now, a mature kudu bull isn't all that much smaller than a bull elk, and while a .300 Winchester is a perfectly capable cartridge for both species, most hunters would choose a bullet of at least 165 grains, with the larger percentage opting for a 180- or 200-grain slug. Knowing the type of terminal performance the Cutting Edge bullets provide—the skived hollowpoint breaks into small blades upon impact for severe impact trauma while the base remains at caliber dimension for deep penetration—I opted for the 150-grain Safari Raptor, leaning on bullet construction to hold things together for deep penetration, while taking advantage of the lighter bullet's flatter trajectory and lower recoil. The plan worked out just fine. I took several species on that safari, including a handsome 55-inch kudu bull, yet only managed to recover one of the Raptors. It was a going-away neck shot on the bull, which dropped him in his tracks, and the base of the recovered bullet weighed 107.3 grains—not too shabby when you consider the polymer tip and the walls of the ogive are designed to break away. A Safari Raptor also accounted for a very nice waterbuck bull from about 220 yards, taking him cleanly through the heart. My Professional Hunter Nick Prinsloo was most amazed at the performance of the light-for-caliber bullet, and I may have made a convert of him.

So, how much bullet do you actually need? That's a difficult question to answer. So-called traditionally established ideas on caliber/bullet weight are in desperate need of revision and reexamination. As mentioned, John Nosler, the godfather of premium bullets, experienced true bullet failure when the cup-and-core bullets (make unknown, but prior to his own designs) he delivered from a .300 Holland & Holland Magnum failed to penetrate the shoulder of a big bull moose. Were I forced to hunt an animal the size of a moose with a cup-and-core bullet using that same .30-caliber rifle, I would consider 180 grains to be the minimum and would be more comfortable with a 200-grain slug. However, I am absolutely certain that in a premium bullet, say a Swift A-Frame, Barnes TSX or Cutting Edge Raptor, you could drop down to 165 grains and be confident that you'll have your bull if you do your part. Even though the sectional density figure drops a bit, the construction of the bullet guarantees good penetration.

What's the difference? The fact that the bullet won't come apart or prematurely expand. Most of the accepted recommendations are based on the fact that a cup-and-core bullet will expand and shed its weight to a certain degree. The hunters of my father's and grandfather's generation observed that the longer, heavier bullets performed better because they held together during the expansion/penetration phase. When Nosler developed the now-famous Partition—which uses two lead cores, separated by a copper partition to ensure the rear core stays intact—he totally revolutionized the game. In fact, the Partition is still a great choice for any game smaller than elephant, and it's a bullet that I use often, especially for bear.

The Barnes X was probably the next huge leap in bullet technology, being a rather radical design which removed the lead core, resulting in a bullet made of all copper. Randy Brooks, who owns Barnes Bullets and is responsible for the design, created the first monomental hollowpoint that would expand upon impact and cause all sorts of damage to the vital organs of a game animal, but removed the risk of bullet breakup. Being made of copper, which is less dense than lead, monometal bullets are longer than the typical cup-and-core bullet of the same weight. The SD figure won't change—it's based on weight and diameter—but monometal bullets do have a different set of rules. Being longer they tend to take up a bit more room in the case (keeping the same Cartridge Overall Length), and their center of gravity moves a bit in comparison to a lead core bullet, but the terminal performance is wonderful. Today's Barnes bullets, such as the Triple Shock X and Tipped Triple Shock X, provide even better performance than did the original design; they've been revised to keep pressures lower and copper fouling to a minimum, while giving reliable expansion and all sorts of penetration. Weight retention is, more often than not, above 90 percent.

Chemically bonding the copper jacket to the lead core is another means of preventing premature bullet breakup. There are many bonded-core designs available today, and they are a fantastic choice. They will often retain 85-90 percent of their original weight, indicating that the bullet has held together during its terminal phase. The Swift Scirocco and A-Frame, Hornady Interbond, Norma Oryx and Nosler Accubond are all good examples of this style of bullet. The bonding process slows down the expansion, yet holds things in place even with the tremendous impact pressures that the wicked-fast magnums of today can generate. A .300 Remington Ultra Magnum can push a 180-grain bullet over 3,300 fps without issue, and that's enough to test the mettle of any cup-and-core bullet. Imagine the destruction resulting from a shot less than 100 yards! Use a premium bullet, and you'll be much better served.

Retained Weight

There is an ongoing debate that is as old as the hills: do you, as a hunter, want your bullet to completely pass through a game animal, or do you want it to remain against the offside skin, imparting all of its energy within the animal? My answer: It just depends.

Firstly, let's not lose sight of the goal. As a hunter, you want to quickly dispatch your intended quarry, causing a quick, humane kill. It's rather obvious that a pass-through shot will provide a better blood trail, should there be need to follow up a wounded animal, yet the 'kinetic energy' camp makes the case that all of the bullet's energy should stay within the animal to cause the most shock damage possible. A bow-hunter wants the pass through; he or she is not depending on the energy shockwave to kill but rather upon traumatic hemorrhaging. As long as your projectile does its job, quickly dispatching the animal, I'm OK with it.

There are, however, certain situations where a pass-through shot is undesirable. If you're hunting a whitetail buck, which is slowly cruising through the woods looking for his paramour, a pass-through poses no issue. If (like me) you live to pursue the Cape buffalo, which is primarily a herd animal, a pass-through can pose an issue: the gun you'll be using (.375 H&H or bigger) has the power to completely pass through a bull buff, wounding or killing an animal behind him. That's a tricky situation. You need enough velocity and bullet weight to properly wreck his vitals, but not so much that a pass through is a guarantee. This is one area where the Swift A-Frame's qualities shine. Such a bullet expands enough to slow things down once inside the game, retains enough weight (usually 90 percent plus) to properly penetrate, yet is often found just against the offside skin. I recovered both of my shots from my Zambian bull, and you could feel them lying right against the offside shoulder. Perfect job, in my opinion.

Secondly, I have customers tell me on a regular basis that certain bullets have failed. When I ask them to describe their situation, most stories involve a bullet retrieved from the animal during a post-mortem examination that weighs very little when compared to its original weight. I then set the hook: "You recovered the bullet from the animal, which was dead, right?"

"Well, yes."

"Did you need to shoot the animal again?"

"Well, no. I tracked it up and found it dead."

"I don't think the bullet failed, it just didn't give the results you expected."

"But I wanted my deer to drop in its tracks."

"We all do."

Terminal ballistics are a funny thing. Two shots at the same relative distance, using the same bullet and cartridge, will drop one animal as if the hand of God came down from the heavens, yet the second animal will need to be tracked for some distance. Why is that? Assuming that both shots were properly placed into the vitals, why would one fall and one run? There are great debates about the physical reasons that an animal falls or runs, theories that include hitting the heart at the instant a particular chamber is filled with blood (think about shooting a milk jug filled with water), or empty (much less dramatic). In my experience, which covers about two

Today's Barnes bullets are actually better than the original design, not an easy feat to accomplish.

dozen big game species at the time of this writing, a bullet has only failed when it does not kill a game animal within a reasonable distance and time from a properly placed shot. That can happen either from premature breakup or a failure to penetrate and destroy the vital organs. There are certain tools for certain jobs, and I like to hedge my bets by using what may be more bullet than necessary. In today's world, bullet choice has almost superseded cartridge choice.

I try to recover bullets from game animals, and keep notes and form opinions based upon real-world situations rather than depending upon theoretical data. It's a long road and requires a whole bunch of time and dedication, not to mention the fact that bullets and animals don't always do what you'd like them to do. My grandfather had a favorite phrase: "You don't live long enough to make all the mistakes on your own, so learn from other people's mistakes." He was right.

What do you want your chosen bullet to look like, were you to recover it from your chosen game animal? Do you prefer a wide mushroom, and say 50-60 percent weight retention, knowing that the vitals were destroyed (my ideal deer bullet)? Or do you subscribe to the "swatting a fly with a sledgehammer" theory like I often do for larger species, choosing a bullet more than tough enough that'll retain nearly all of its weight, but might be unrecoverable? That decision is ultimately up to you. Let's take a look at which types of bullets fall into these categories, so you can make a better decision for your hunting situation.

The Nosler Partition in cross section after impact.

Cup-and-Core Bullets

The cup-and-core bullets, like Sierra's GameKing and ProHunter, Hornady's Interlock, Remington's Core-Lokt and similar open up quickly to impart shock and ruin vital tissue. These bullets come in many shapes and sizes, and their performance is what helped form the opinions of many early gun writers. Using our .30-caliber example, a 150-grain bullet would certainly make a good deer and pronghorn bullet, but may not make a wise choice for elk or moose; there simply isn't enough bullet length (sectional density) to allow for the weight lost during impact. Now, that's not to say that the bullet won't eventually kill an animal the size of an elk, but it may be due to a superficial wound, or from infection; it'll be difficult to recover an animal shot in that manner. Hence, the recommendations of heavy-for-caliber bullets, and Elmer Keith's love of heavy-bore rifles. The same theory of high SD bullets can be applied to the lighter bores when used for big game. The classics, like the 7x57mm Mauser, 6.5x54 Mannlicher-Schoenauer and 6.5x55 Swedish Mauser made their reputations on larger game by using long, heavy, round-nosed bullets. The 6.5mm 160-grain (SD 0.328) and the 173-grain 7mm bullet (SD 0.310) worked just perfectly on deer-sized game, as well as some of the African antelope that equal the weight of an elk or moose. Blayney Percival, a Professional Hunter and Game Ranger in Kenya in the early 20th century preferred the light 6.5x54 for his work; he even used it for rogue lions.

However, impact velocity can be the undoing of the cup-and-core bullet, as Elmer Keith found out early on. Keith preferred the heavier bullets mainly because he knew they would get the job done. It was mainly due to wildcat cartridges he'd developed like the .333 OKH that the .338 Winchester Magnum became a staple of elk hunters. A .338-inch 250-grain bullet (SD 0.313), driven to a muzzle velocity of about 2,650 fps will certainly take any elk, moose or bear that ever lived, but it is not the requirement, even with some of the thicker jacketed cup-and-core bullets. But, in Keith's day, it gave him more confidence than would the lighter 130-grain .270 bullets promoted by contemporaries like Jack O'Connor. When it comes to a traditional bullet, I lean more toward Keith than O'Connor on that question, especially when I'm using a magnum cartridge.

When shooting a .308 Winchester or 7x57 Mauser, impact velocities are one thing, but bump those cartridges up to a .300 Weatherby or 7mm Remington Magnum and things get very interesting. Simply increasing the muzzle velocity—and theoretically the impact velocity—by 400 fps or so will definitely stress the best of the cup-and-core bullets. The Hornady Interlock and Remington Core-Lokt use a cannelure to help keep things together, but very few of the Sierra bullets employ this feature. Perusing the Sierra catalog, you'll find some bullets have thicker jackets than others. For instance, the .308 165-grain GameKing hollowpoint boattail was designed to shoot like its MatchKing counterpart, but features a thicker-than-normal jacket, one that will stand up to magnum impact velocities. I've used this bullet for years, in both a .308 Winchester and .300 Winchester Magnum, and it's served me very well. I'd be completely confident choosing this for a black bear bullet, or even for elk. Hawk Bullets, hailing from New Jersey, is a semi-custom bullet shop that allows you to choose the jacket thickness for the job at hand. I really like that option, especially for some of the more obscure calibers, like my .318 Westley Richards.

There have been attempts at marketing a cup-and-core delayed-expansion bullet. Winchester's original Silver Tip used an aluminum cap on the meplat of the bullet to prevent premature expansion, and the thing worked. I still have a handful that my dad bought me for bear hunting with my .30-30 WCF. They worked well for deer, too, but I still haven't happened across a bear while carrying them. The Remington Bronze Point was designed with a bronze tip—more to prevent meplat deformation than for controlled expansion, I believe—but I would venture to say that it did help to control violent expansion a bit.

The original Speer Grand Slam bullet used a lead core of different hardness to ensure proper penetration. And while that bullet is not nearly as popular as it once was, it still performs wonderfully. I've loaded it for clients headed on bear hunts, and it's worked just fine on big bruin, whether bayed by hounds or over bait.

The polymer tipped cup-and-core bullets work much like a hollowpoint, with the exception of having the tip that not only increases the ballistic coefficient, but also acts as a wedge to forcefully open the point for positive expansion. Nosler's Ballistic Tip and the Hornady SST are good examples. And like others of sufficient weight and length, these work well as a big game bullet. So, it's apparent that some examination and planning is warranted when choosing a cup-and-core bullet so you end up with the proper balance of expansion, penetration and retained weight.

Bonded Core Bullets

Bonded core bullets are a different story altogether; they simply hold together under stress, yet many of them will maintain a profile like the best of the cup-and-core designs. The highly popular boattail/polymer tip combination is well represented in the bonded-core lineup of projectiles, providing an excellent long range combination for the larger, tougher animals. Bullets like the Nosler AccuBond, which pays homage to the Ballistic Tip profile, and the AccuBond Long Range, which provides an even higher ballistic coefficient, greedily hold onto as much of the velocity generated as possible during flight to deliver it onto the animal, thus the terminal qualities of these bullets are excellent. The process of chemically bonding the lead core to the copper jacket allows for much more retained weight, as well as better penetration. Nosler has made this bullet a bit softer up front than some other designs to initiate expansion even at lower impact velocities (longer range shots), yet the rear portion stays intact to drive through the vitals. The Swift Scirocco II is another bullet utilizing the polymer tip/boattail combo, but features a very thick jacket toward the base. As mentioned previously, I've come to love this bullet for a number of reasons: it's accurate, bullet-to-bullet tolerances are very tight (when I weigh them on a scale they are usually within ½ grain of the listed weight) and they hit very hard. I've personally used the bullet on a thick-bodied bear and on whitetails. I've loaded the bullet for clients for their elk and moose hunts; all have been successful. My bear was taken at less than 50 yards, and I gave him two shots, both passed through. It was a 180-grain bullet from my .308 Winchester (muzzle velocity of 2,525 fps), so it wasn't exactly screaming fast, but it's a testament to the Scirocco's strength that both shots were pass throughs. The bear didn't go more than 15 yards. The one Scirocco that a client did recover from his elk weighed in at 162.5 grains, for a weight retention of 90 percent; that was delivered from a .300 Remington Ultra Magnum at 85 yards with a muzzle velocity of 3,360 fps. I think you can see why I'm a huge fan of this bullet; it delivers the goods in all sorts of calibers, from 6mm up to .338, and does it with authority. When I'm looking for a bullet that best combines the long-range capabilities of a high BC design, and the penetrative qualities needed for reaching the vitals reliably, I generally reach for either the Nosler AccuBond or the Swift Scirocco II.

Hornady's Interbond is another similar design, with the tell-tale red tip, and delivers a similar performance. Hornady loads this bullet in their Superformance line of ammunition, making for a great high velocity/strong bullet combination. I've not personally hunted with it, but I've loaded it for a number of clients, who've all had good results.

All of these bullets yield a similar level of performance, expanding roughly 2.5 times their original caliber in diameter, and the high weight retention that is indicative of good terminal performance, even if bones are struck. I like this style of bullet for an all-around choice. It performs well on close shots, yet is configured to retain energy downrange and give the best blend of terminal performance across a wide spectrum of hunting situations.

There are other bonded-core choices, though, and depending on your style of hunting these may serve you better. I'm referring to the semi-spitzer bonded-core bullets, which perhaps don't have the high BC figures of the boattails, but definitely make up the difference by hitting a bit harder. It's a difficult phenomenon to explain, but I've noticed that a semi-spitzer or round-nose bullet seems to make an animal shudder when hit, and you can actually see a difference once you connect. Such bullets in a bonded-core configuration are among my favorites for hunting situations where I'm hunting truly big game with shots inside of 300 yards. Among these designs, I can name three favorites that will absolutely give great penetration and reliable expansion.

The Swift A-Frame was, until recently, the only bullet I'd used in Africa for my first three safaris. With that bullet in three different cartridges I've cleanly taken animals from the size of the diminutive steenbok up to and including eland and Cape buffalo. It's very similar to the Nosler Partition in that it uses two lead cores separated by a wall of copper. The front core is bonded to the thick jacket to prevent premature expansion. The classic form of the recovered A-Frame is a good mushroom up front at twice caliber dimension, and a riveting of the shank just behind that wall of copper, with a weight retention well into the 90-percentile range. I've often described this bullet as meat-resistant, in that the bigger the animal you hit, the more it will open—actually improving chances of recovery. When you hit the smaller animals with an A-Frame, it tends to pass through. The A-Frame is a classic example of a strong bullet with which you can confidently drop down a bit in bullet weight/sectional density, yet still be confident that you'll reach the vitals. It opens up reliably, and I've used it on some long shots, out where things slow down, still with positive results. For example, take that eland hunt I mentioned when discussing the effects of wind drift. While it was difficult enough to just make that shot, I was concerned about expansion. That 300-grain A-Frame at that muzzle velocity out at 400 yards would slow down to somewhere around 1,650 fps—not exactly optimum for an antelope weighing between 1,800 and 2,000 pounds—but when I heard the thunk of the bullet connecting, I could clearly see I had nothing to worry about. I didn't recover the bullet from the follow-up shot, but we did find the first one. It weighed 287.4 grains, for 95.8 percent weight retention. That's why I love that bullet so much. Swift makes it in calibers from .25 up to the big .500s, like the .505 Gibbs and .500 Jeffery. Also, the bullet is golden in a cartridge that may be considered marginal, like using the 6.5-284 Norma for elk; load it with a good 140-grain A-Frame, and you're good to go.

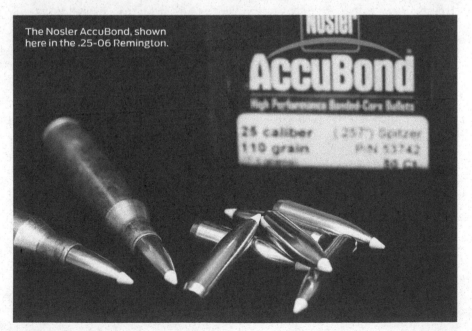

The Nosler AccuBond, shown here in the .25-06 Remington.

The North Fork semi-spitzer is another bullet that yields incredible terminal performance. Constructed of a pure copper jacket chemically bonded to a lead core—the core sits in the forward two-thirds of the bullet—it has small grooves in the shank of the bullet to keep pressures nice and low. The bullet is designed to keep weight forward, by using a lead core that sits forward, and the semi-spitzer profile. The North Fork soft point delivers full, straight-line penetration; in other words, the bullet likes to pass clear through. The folks at North Fork explained it to me like this: "Imagine a rear-wheel drive car in the snow: when resistance is met, the rear of the car tends to push out to one side or the other. A front-wheel drive will tend to pull itself through the resistance. And that's the concept behind our bullets—their weight-forward design greatly aids in deep penetration, and here in Oregon we appreciate the exit wound for a larger blood-trail." My experience with this bullet is that it performs exactly as designed, and the only one I've been able to recover was a 175-grain 7mm slug from a 7x57 Mauser that was a straight-on shot. I've become a huge fan of it. Penetration is never an issue.

The Norma Oryx is a great little bullet, which is sort of a hybrid design to provide a good balance of expansion and penetration. It's a copper-jacketed, semi-spitzer with a lead core, but the rear shank of the bullet has the jacket chemically bonded to the core. Upon impact, the nose section opens like a conventional bullet creating a classic mushroom, yet the bonding process at its base prevents it from coming apart, keeps it driving through the vitals. I've had nothing but positive experiences with the Oryx. In fact, my 6.5-284 Norma drove a 156-grainer through a big-bodied eight-point whitetail for the most dramatic one-shot kill I've ever had. At the shot, he flipped over onto his back, legs fully extended like an upside down table, and stayed there in that position. I only wish I could've recovered the bullet for observation, but it gave a complete pass-through. However, I'll take those results every time. If you're looking for just a bit more than what a conventional bullet has to offer, I'd highly recommend the Oryx, especially if shot distances are within 200 yards.

Monometal Bullets

Monometal expanding bullet construction is a fantastic method of preventing premature breakup. The Barnes X bullet was nothing short of revolutionary, in the fact that it had no lead core whatsoever. The all-copper design did pose some issues though, like increased copper fouling, and the fact that the bullets were longer than their lead core counterparts and took up a bit more room in the case, but Lord!—did they penetrate. The newer TSX and TTSX designs eliminated a good portion of the copper fouling issue, and penetrate like gangbusters. I can honestly say that with a bullet of this style (the Hornady GMX, Federal Trophy Copper and Nosler E-Tip can certainly be included in this bunch) you'll be able to get away with a bit less sectional density to achieve the same terminal effect. I used a little .243 Winchester in a Savage Lightweight Hunter with an 85-grain Trophy Copper to absolutely crumple a Texas buck; it was a 125-yard shot, and one of those few instances where the animal literally fell in his tracks. Oddly, the bullet hit a rib, and turned 90 degrees upward, to smash into his spine—hence the instant drop—but everything in the bullet's pathway was destroyed.

Bullet Disadvantages

Now, cup-and-core bullets—which I don't want you to think I dislike, it's just that I have come to appreciate the benefits of the premiums in the penetration department—come with their own set of issues. Many of my rifles have excellent accuracy with spitzer boattail bullets of traditional design. However, I've found these bullets have a tendency to shed their copper jackets, especially when impact velocities are on the higher side of the spectrum. That is why I've traditionally used the higher SD bullets, especially in magnum cartridges. I also believe that this idea had an undeniable influence on the Elmer Keith/Jack O'Connor arguments that set the benchmarks for our established minimum cartridges on particular sizes of game animals.

Retained Sectional Density

If the radically expanded bullet doesn't penetrate as well as a bullet which stays closer to original caliber diameter, and a bullet that doesn't expand much fails to destroy enough tissue, how should you balance penetration with expansion? I mean, if penetration were the key, we'd all shoot the solids used by African buffalo and elephant hunters. And if expansion alone did the trick every time, we'd all be shooting varmint-style bullets with low SD figures and thin jackets, right? There has to be a balance, and it will take some research to figure out what will work for you.

The idea of retained sectional density correlates retained weight to expanded diameter. Again, sectional density is the ratio of bullet diameter to bullet weight. If you expand the bullet's diameter (as it does after impact) and retain 100 percent of its weight, you will obviously lower the SD figure. If you shed bullet weight (again, that happens more often than not) you will further lower the SD figure. So, there needs to be a balance between the two, especially when the game size exceeds that of the common deer species.

The Swift A-Frame

I have probably taken more species of game with a Swift A-Frame than any other bullet. I've used it all over Africa and North America, with nothing less than stellar results. I've used it in calibers from 6.5mm to .308 to .375 and .416, and it's been an accurate bullet in all of my rifles. Again, the A-Frame is a partitioned bullet, with a thick jacket, and the front core is chemically bonded to that jacket. It is a semi-spitzer profile with a flat base. While the BC fig-

The Swift A-Frame bullet is like the Nosler Partition and among the toughest premium hunting bullets.

ures are better than the hemispherical round-nosed bullets and flat points, the A-Frame doesn't hold a candle to the sleek, spitzer boattail bullets that are associated with true long-range work. However, it does make a good choice for safari where shots rarely exceed 250 yards, as well as North American hunts at similar ranges. The A-Frames that I've recovered have a similar, signature shape: the front core is expanded to right around 2 times the caliber dimension, and there is a bulge, or rivet just behind the partition. Many of the A-Frame bullets I've recovered have retained over 90 percent of their weight.

Let's look at what happens to the bullet once it expands. Assuming a 180-grain bullet weight, in .308 caliber, that's a sectional density figure of 0.271, and upon expansion to twice diameter reduces that figure to 0.068. Using the formula for sectional density: 180 grains converted to pounds = 0.0257; divided by the square of 0.616 (the twice expanded diameter) yields a figure of 0.068, rather bleak in comparison to the original figure. But, that expanded bullet does all sorts of damage on the way to its resting place, and a .616-inch hole is much bigger than a .308-inch hole.

The Cutting Edge Raptor

Here's another bullet I've come to love in a wide variety of calibers. Cutting Edge makes the Raptor in a 150-grain configuration, and it has worked very well in the field. Its nose or ogive section breaks into small blades upon impact, delivering the impact trauma we hunters love, while the base of the all-copper bullet remains at caliber dimension. It starts out with a SD figure of 0.226, much less than the 180-grainer's 0.271. My own recovered bullet, taken from a large kudu bull in South Africa, weighed 107.3 grains—71.5 percent weight retention—but stayed at exact caliber dimension. At this retained weight, the base has a retained SD of 0.162, explaining why the base of the lighter bullet will often completely penetrate a large game animal, even on a frontal shot.

This illustrates how and why the terminal performance of different types of bullets can and will vary, especially with some of the newer designs. Unlike the traditional cup-and-core designs that we've come to know so well and learned so much about from the classic gun writers, these new bullets—only two of which I've given example—will take some getting used to and require additional experimentation to fully prove in the game fields. So far, though, the results are pretty hard to argue with.

The Woodleigh Hydrostatically Stabilized Solid

However, there is one more bullet that takes things even further: the Woodleigh Hydrostatically Stabilized Solid. This concept is way out of left field, but I'll be damned if it doesn't work well. The bullet, developed by the Australian firm of Woodleigh Bullets, is a monometal solid, designed to give zero expansion, destroy the vital organs and tissues, and all the penetration anyone would want. The solid has a small cup at the front of the bullet, which uses the concept of cavitation to destroy the blood-rich tissues of the vital organs. Upon impact, the cup at the

North Fork semi-spitzers yield incredible terminal performance.

The 175-grain North Fork, recovered from a frontal shot on a whitetail deer.

meplat creates an air bubble in front of the bullet, helping to keep it in a straight line as it penetrates through the game rupturing blood vessels in an 8- to 12-inch cylinder around the path of the bullet.

I've had the opportunity to use this bullet on a variety of game, varying in size from impala (a bit smaller than our whitetail deer) to blue wildebeest (slightly smaller than our elk, but no less tenacious) up to and including the African elephant. I have yet to recover one of these bullets, and all the animals went down very quickly. The Hydro kills by rupturing and destroying the cell walls of the tissue within that cylinder of destruction. Not to be gross, but my elephant's lungs were simply jellified by two lung shots, as was the upper portion of the heart. Heart/lung shots on an animal the size of an African elephant are not like a deer or elk; there is simply no way to generate enough shock to put an animal this big down. You'd need a 155mm Howitzer, and even then it would be questionable. However, with two Professional Hunters standing beside me slack-jawed over a bullet that nearly put the great beast down on his haunches with the first shot was rather interesting. There was doubt in both their eyes at the start of the safari, looking at these strangely configured projectiles, but with two quick shots from my .404 Jeffery, I had converts instead of doubters. I believe this bullet will be the wave of the future. It's available in calibers from 7mm up to the behemoth .577, and could really change the game. Imagine a good .30-caliber Hydro, in a .30-06, fully capable of taking a grizzly bear, because you've got the consummate blend of tissue destruction and deep penetration. Or what about the capabilities of the .338 Winchester Magnum with a 225-grain Hydro! It'd require some testing, but I believe you'd take Cape buffalo with that combination. There certainly are good things to come with the Woodleigh Hydro, and based upon the way my Heym .404 Jeffery shoots this bullet, it won't be the last time I use it. Federal Premium wisely includes it in their lineup, so it's not just a component bullet for reloaders. If you're headed after dangerous game, give this bullet a whirl.

Penetrative Qualities of Modern Bullets

What makes for good penetration? Why will one bullet penetrate while another won't? What qualities are desirable to achieve the necessary penetration for a quick kill?

As we discussed above, with a cup-and-core bullet, high impact velocities will definitely test the integrity of the classic design. To combat this, companies have used thicker copper jackets to slow the expansion of lead core bullets. An example is the Sierra GameKing hollowpoint, which has a very thick jacket and, even though it's a hollowpoint—a bullet style normally associated with frangibility and rapid expansion—it will definitely stand up to magnum impact velocities. I use it in my .300 Winchester Magnum and 6.5-284 Norma with good results. Some boutique bullet companies offer a variety of jacket thicknesses (such as Hawk Bullets from New Jersey) so you can tailor the bullet to the job. Deer hunter? A thinner jacket will work for you. Bear/elk/moose on the menu? A thicker jacket and perhaps more weight (equaling more length) would make a wise choice.

However, does the conformation matter? Does one nose profile give better penetrative qualities than another? Yes, it does matter. And there are some choices that are better than others.

In my experience, there is a big difference in visual impact between round-nosed and flat-nosed bullets, and the spitzers. That's not to say that the spitzers are in any way bad, but a round-nosed bullet will make an animal shudder when hit, imparting energy better. But, we've also seen via the wind and trajectory values that the round-nose bullets are inferior at longer distances. So therein lays the dichotomy, at least in my mind. I love the long-range ballistics of the spitzer boattails, but I really adore the terminal ballistics of the flat- and round-nose bullets. Generally speaking, when the game is large and the distances are short, I prefer to take advantage of the penetrative qualities of the less-than-sleek profile bullets, yet when I know I'm after thin-skinned quarry, or on a hunt where the distances may exceed 200 yards, I prefer spitzers. If I have a hunt where I can't exactly determine what shot I'll have, spitzers again get the nod, hedging my bets in the event of a long shot, and depending on the size of the game, may be a bonded-core bullet.

There are situations where penetration is paramount. Perhaps a game animal has the potential to rip, bite, claw or stomp you to pieces. Hunting dangerous game animals is a totally different experience. While I'm not an adrenaline junkie (I have an incurable fear of heights, as well as flying), I do love the thrill of dangerous game and the adventures in the wild places that are still left on earth. In my opinion, you owe it not only to the game animal, but to your family, to see that the animal is dispatched quickly and cleanly, and that you and your hunting party return unharmed. You therefore need a rifle/bullet combination that will get the job done.

I have friends and colleagues that have used traditional cup-and-core spitzer bullets to take Cape buffalo and huge grizzly bear; the trophies are on the wall and no one was harmed. I also have heard tales of poor penetration, premature bullet breakup and other terminal ballistic woes. Let's back up for a minute and reexamine the whole process. Death is caused by severe tissue trauma and blood loss—unless it's a brain shot, where the plug is pulled—and for millennia the bow and arrow has accounted for some of the nastiest beasts on the planet. Modern archers take big game including elephant each year with high-tech compound bows and arrows tipped with the strongest of broadheads. But, though death will invariably ensue for an animal with its vital tissue destroyed, what happens in that period of time between the wounding of that animal and its death can be catastrophic to the hunting party. It can be bad for your health. A grizzly can maul you in a matter of seconds. A heartshot elephant can close in on you in the blink of an eye. Point here is, there are proper tools for the job, and when it comes to dangerous game, you want the best you can get.

Reading some of the classic ballistics books that relate the terminal capabilities of our centerfire cartridges, like John Taylor's *African Rifle and Cartridges*, you can get a feel for why some ballistic formulas have the reputation they do, but there are some misconceptions that need to be addressed. Remember, any sectional density figure is a simple ratio of mass to diameter, and doesn't take into account the bullet's shape or structural integrity at all. With that in mind, the generalizations regarding the relationship between SD and penetration must be taken with a grain of salt. For example, comparing two 180-grain .30 caliber bullets, each will have an SD figure of 0.271; yet if one were a pure lead cast bullet and the other an all-copper solid, you could easily imagine the difference in penetrative qualities. Should the shoulder bones of an elk be struck, that pure lead bullet would quickly deform and penetration would invariably be poor. Yet, the modern monometal solid would whistle on through, without any expansion. So, SD does play a role in penetration, but it's only one part of the equation.

We've looked at the various construction methods, getting an idea of why modern bullets perform the way they do, but we must also look at how the nose profile of a bullet affects

Cup-and-core boattail bullets can separate upon impact.

the penetration path. Going back to the North Fork concept of keeping the bullet's weight forward for straight-line penetration, you'll find that African Professional Hunters tend to prefer a round-nose or flat meplat bullet, as such facilitates straight-line penetration. Why would this profile work better than a spitzer?

First of all, bullets are fired at a rotational rate that is optimized for the atmosphere (air), not for hide, tissue and bone. As the bullet contacts an animal, the rotation must be affected, as the medium has become considerably thicker. Striking nose-first, the bullet's rotation is upset. Depending on where the center of gravity is, the bullet may do some funny things. Going back to Pierre van der Walt's *African Dangerous Game Cartridges*, testing proved that a non-expanding spitzer bullet will tend to flip directions, and exit with the rear of the bullet facing forward. Just like the example of a rear-wheel drive vehicle in snow, the rearward center of gravity combined with the resistance of the newly introduced medium (flesh and bone) causes the bullet to veer off of its course, with the nose deflecting in some direction. Van der Walt demonstrates this concept well, confirming that a flat- or round-nosed projectile will tend to hold its direction and alignment. This idea makes an awful lot of sense and lends credence to the oft-repeated concept that the military 5.56mm NATO bullet will tumble or bounce around within the human body. It is more likely that the full metal jacket bullet skews once resistance is met, actually exiting rear-end first. I've had monometal copper bullets do the same thing. I told you of that buck in Texas which I'd hit with the little .243 Winchester using an 85-grain Federal Trophy Copper bullet. Why would a bullet heading at a slight downhill angle decide to change course at right angles and smash into the spine? I suspect it hit a rib and was deflected by bone, but I also think the deflection may have been enhanced by a rearward center of gravity and high impact velocity as the shot was only 125 yards.

Once a bullet begins to expand, its center of gravity shifts, and the sectional density changes. The mushrooming effect slows the velocity while destroying tissue along the way. Too little mushrooming, and your bullet will behave like a solid, too much and it stops before it can effectively ruin sufficient tissue. Compound that with the fact that tissue is a flexible medium and that a wound channel will expand and contract, and you'll understand why the hunters of yesteryear were fans of bigger bore diameters: the bigger the hole, the more trauma would be induced. Lower velocity round-nosed bullets helped to keep penetration in a straight line. The classic full patch or solid bullet was one way to guarantee that a bullet would give adequate penetration on the African heavyweights, and for years the Professional Hunters who were guiding for Cape buffalo recommended them exclusively. Penetration was paramount. Elephant hunters needed the best penetrating bullets they could get; the skin at the shoulder can be well over an inch thick, and a frontal brain shot requires getting that bullet through 18-20 inches of honeycombed bone. Even today, almost all of the bullets that get that job done best are round-nosed or flat-nosed, giving a clear idea of how important the nose profile can be when it comes to penetration.

This is counterproductive though when it comes to sending that same projectile over long distances through the air. African hunting is predominately done at close range, with a 250-yard shot being on the long side. In the terminal phase, lower BC profiles are preferred to the aerodynamic shapes better suited to long-range shots.

This is why companies push the envelope when it comes to bullet development, and abandon traditional ideas. Jack Carter's Trophy Bonded Bear Claw is not a new design, but it is a fantastic one. Using a smaller lead core located at the front of the bullet, and a rear section of all copper, the Bear Claw keeps its weight forward, yet maintains a spitzer design. The solid copper shank behind that lead core stays intact to ensure good penetration, yet the nose is soft enough to give good expansion. The Bear Claw is currently loaded in the Federal Premium line, and I am a huge fan of the bullet for all kinds of hunting. But there are newer kids on the block, who are fully embracing their own respective schools of thought.

One of these companies is Peregrine Bullets, from South Africa. Another is the aforementioned Cutting Edge Bullets. Both have radical designs that deviate from the cup-and-core principal and take the monometal concept to new heights.

Peregrine has embraced both schools of thought, offering fantastic monometal bullets in a couple different configurations. Their engineers recognize not only the need for a monometal projectile that opens reliably and regularly, but see the difference between the camps who prefer the flat, "bush" meplat and those looking for a sleek spitzer bullet for longer shots. I've loaded and used both styles of bullets, and they are fantastic. Let's look at the "bush" bullets first.

The Peregrine BushMaster VRG-3 is a dichotomy in the eyes of most ballistic engineers. It's a flat-meplat bullet, constructed of copper (the very grain structure of which has been manipulated and designed for optimum performance), yet features a boattail for an increased BC figure. In addition, its hollowpoint cavity is filled with a brass insert that sits flush with the nose. A cavity of air is left below the brass insert, acting like a plunger to initiate expansion. Because air is difficult to compress—more so than metal—once the brass plunger meets resistance it will be forced to move rearward. The air pocket resists compression, forcing the sidewalls of the bullet outward in a radial fashion. The combination of a larger wound channel from the flat meplat and the forced expansion causing tissue damage results in a bullet capable of awesome terminal ballistics. The construction methods ensure highly uniform tolerances, and the accuracy of the bullets reflect that. I've loaded the VRG-3s in Dave deMoulpied's .416 Rigby, and have seen him print ¾-inch groups. They perform much the same in my .404 Jeffery, and in the Heym Model 89 in .450/400 3-inch NE double rifle. Such bullets solve the problem of reliable expansion and wound channel size when it comes to a monometal, and at the same time give the huge energy transfer for which round- and flat-nosed bullets are famous. VRG-3s are an excellent choice for buffalo hunters, and work perfectly on the larger plains game species like kudu and eland. I am privileged to call Kristof Aucamp, the public relations manager for Peregrine a personal friend. We've spent a considerable amount of time discussing these designs. I inquired about the origins of the plunger concept and how it affected the terminal ballistics.

"This is the brainchild of Adriaan Rall, who was the creator of the plunger and cavity concept for Peregrine copper bullets," Aucamp revealed. "The cavity has multiple functions. First, it acts as a shock absorber if the bullet hits bone very soon after entering the skin, thus contributing to the conservation of retained weight of the bullet. In other words, it helps to keep the formation of the mushroom intact and inhibit the shedding of weight in the form of petals or broken off copper pieces. In effect, it also helps to maintain straight-line penetration whenever the plunger is able to conserve and control the mushroom formation. This is vitally important when hunting tough and dangerous animals. Of course, there never is a guarantee that the mushroom will be perfect after hitting bone in big animals, but we found that the cavity in the plunger design is a big plus, more so with the big bore calibers. The air cavity also assists with the controlled expansion of the bullet in three stages."

So, the design keeps the bullet intact for straight-line penetration, yet handles the tough shoulder bones of dangerous game? I'm on board.

Looking at the Peregrine VRG4 PlainsMaster spitzer, you'll see a recognizable profile, but in a metallic composition that expands even as velocity dips to as low as 1,600 fps—absolutely perfect for long-range shots. This bullet has all the features you'd want to see in a monometal: driving bands for low friction and reduced copper fouling, and a sensible profile for accuracy and retained energy within hunting distances, yet nothing so radical as to pose a problem for reloaders. It shoots very well in the common medium calibers that are used here in the States— my .300 Winchester and 6.5-285 Norma simply love it—and for an African application I can totally see a Kalahari hunt where the springbok and gemsbok are across the pan and require the high BC that the PlainsMaster provides.

This plunger technology—the idea that a specific nose material needs to be used to initiate expansion—is not new. Think about the Remington Bronze Point, or any of the polymer-tipped bullets that have become so popular over the last three decades. But Peregrine has revolutionized the concept. All field reports indicate positive results. Both Professional Hunters and their clients alike are more than satisfied with the terminal ballistics of the Peregrine design.

Aucamp further explained the research and development that went into the Peregrine line, in particular the PlainsMaster bullet.

"Many hours went into the design of the Extreme Long Range bullets including highly theoretical analysis using the best possible science and engineering simulation tools for such a project," he said. "No test firing happened at all during the first year as the focus was solely on creating aerodynamic related building blocks for CFD (Computational Fluid Dynamics) modeling as well as 6 Degree of Freedom calculations of bullet flight. Once a proper foundation was laid, it was possible to make steady progress from theory to reality and shooting the first test models to validate the engineering calculations and in-flight predictions.

"We did not want to fall into the trap of exotic or outrageously high BC bullets ... due to the fact that either the nose or the boattail is too long and therefore the bullets are simply not accurate or they are difficult to shoot as a result of extreme sensitivity for that perfect but elusive optimum load.

"Today's rifles are predominantly manufactured for lead-core bullets. In our opinion, there will come a day when lead will be banned worldwide. This we believe is inevitable, and Peregrine would like to steadily grow into the market and be ready to ease the pain of transition into the lead-free future as much as possible. Ultimately, copper will remain as a viable alternative and is by far the most likely long-term solution. With this in mind, we have created high BC bullets that can be used as a drop-in replacement for lead core on existing rifle platforms. And we have created bullets for the long-range fanatic who wants to fit a designer barrel with a slightly faster twist and a chamber to match his favorite monolithic bullet.

"To complement the long-range bullets we have also created a limited series of extreme long-range hunting bullets."

So, you have a bullet with excellent terminal capabilities, which will more than suffice in the exterior ballistics department. Peregrine is definitely onto something here. I load them for my own rifles, when pursuing Cape buffalo and hippo, and I believe in their abilities, as much if not more than other designs.

Cutting Edge Bullets, brainchild of Dan Smitchko, takes the polar opposite approach. The bullet is designed to be frangible—at least to a point. From the medium calibers all the way up to the safari calibers, the bullet has been engineered to provide a delicate balance of impact trauma and straight-line penetration, which is crossways to the traditional school of thought regarding expansion and penetration. It features a particular nose profile CEB calls the BBW#13 that has demonstrated the best penetration qualities, and undoubtedly they have something right. There have been many hands in the development of the Cutting Edge line. For example, I have it on good authority that BBW stands for Bastard Bullet Works, with the nose profile being developed by using a bastard file and experimenting with varying angles until the desired result had been achieved. Indeed, those hands have succeeded in developing a bullet that works very, very well.

The bullet is designed to break apart, with the walls of the hollowpoint fragmenting into what CEB calls blades. Those blades cause a significant amount of impact trauma, traveling 8-10 inches deep into the animal in a spiraling pattern. They radiate 6-10 inches from the center of impact, but the base of the bullet—left at caliber dimension once the walls of the hollowpoint have broken off—continues to penetrate the animal. This may sound like a sketchy scenario, but I've seen the bullet work perfectly on a number of species, and at a bullet weight lighter than would be normally called upon for a particular application. Between whitetails and a half-dozen or so African plains game species, the Raptor has proved itself in a number of different calibers for me.

Many times, while performing the post-mortem autopsy in the skinning shed, all that will be recovered are the blades, as the base of the bullet frequently exits the animal, irrespective of angle. As in the story I related earlier in this chapter, where I used the Raptor in my .300 Winchester Magnum at 150 grains, I've loaded this bullet in .375 caliber at 235 grains, in .416 caliber at 325 grains, and in my .404 at 325 and 350 grains. None of these bullets have let me down. In fact, I wouldn't hesitate to recommend them to any client who wanted a good bullet for their rifle. I've used the .30-caliber bullet to crumple a kudu on the run as well as to ruin a nice waterbuck's day, as he was lying down, 225 yards away. At the shot, the waterbuck stood, reeled for 10 yards, and fell down as dead as a doornail. That was a small target (with the vitals all squashed as he was lying down), but the bullet was accurate and gave fantastic terminal performance. Watching a 325-grain .416 bullet penetrate a big-bodied zebra from stem to stern, with the bullet base exiting out of the rear of the animal, engenders a whole lot of confidence.

Curious about that BBW#13 nose profile and its origins, I asked Michael McCourry, who had a huge hand in the development of this nose profile, to explain it further. McCourry set out to build a better mouse trap.

"Early in 2006, I took the first 50 B&M Prototype rifle to South Africa for a test run on plains game," McCourry explained. "This was a 2-inch RUM case at .500 inch actual diameter. We were testing bullets common to the .500 S&W at the time, 500-grain Hornady at 1,800 fps, 400-grain Sierra at 2,100 fps, 375-grain Barnes X at 2,300 fps, and a few others. Along with these was a 400-grain round-nose solid that JD Jones and I had done by David Fricke of Lehigh Bullets. At the velocities everything ran, results actually exceeded expectations; no doubt that .500 caliber was coming into play here, and far, far ahead of anything I had seen in .45/70. The big ugly disappointment was the round-nose solid, a turned brass bullet. On several occasions—on kudu and eland—the solid would veer off course as much as 90 degrees and not reach its destination.

"This led me into the search for a perfect solid, which was successful in the end. I needed a solid to work with these .500 caliber rifles. That led to an incredibly tedious process of test work. In the beginning, we basically took a similar design to the then newer Barnes Banded Flat Nose Solid. This was very successful in the new 2.25-inch .500 caliber 50 B&M rifles. I used the bullet on a couple of elephants and five Cape buffalo in 2007 with extreme success and great depth of penetration, and above all, dead straight-line penetration. However, the search continued to improve even upon this success. At that time I was running this bullet at 2,025 fps in the 18-inch barrel of the 50 B&M.

"JD Jones and I continued to play around with a few different designs over the next couple of years, and I continued to test and look at all other big-bore calibers from .416 to .510 and different designs of solids. Every single solid manufactured and available was tested, and we began to learn a great deal of what factors are involved with solid penetration, what did the driving.

"Sometime in either late 2009 or early 2010 I met a fellow named Sam Rose. Sam was extremely interested in bullet technology, and we shared many of the same desires for a solid. Sam is a talented machinist, and the fact that he had his own lathe ended up being a huge boost to our study here. Sam and I came up with some of the wildest-designed solids one can imagine, and we were testing nearly four to five sessions a week for months on end.

"During these studies we conducted one of the most important studies done with solids, a meplat size test to understand at what point we got total stability, simply because of meplat size. We tested a .500-caliber bullet, basically Barnes Flat Nose profile from a round-nose up to 80 percent of caliber meplat size, as I recall. What we learned is that everything up to 65 percent meplat of caliber was not completely stable during terminal penetration. We started seeing some stability at 60 percent meplat size, but at 65 percent meplat we got total stability and the deepest straight line penetration. At 70 percent meplat we still had dead-straight penetration, but depth of penetration began to decrease, and the same for 75 and 80 percent. We found 65 percent meplat of caliber perfect.

"During this process we also learned that twist rate did have an effect as well. Faster twist gave more stability. But twist rate only came into effect with lesser meplat size, less than 65 percent. Faster twists would stabilize lesser meplat size for added straight-line depth, it would not fully stabilize for the entire depth of penetration, but it would increase straight-line stability. Twist rate had no effect on proper-sized meplat, 65 percent or better. In fact, I had some oversized barrels here that we tested 65-70 percent meplat size, no engraving on the bullets at all, and meplat size alone stabilized them during terminal penetration up to and sometimes exceeding 90 percent of the total depth of penetration, and this is with no engraving on the bullets at all.

"We also learned that nose profile made a difference, as well. Some nose profiles did better than others, and some more stable than others, while certain nose profiles increased penetration. And, a radius edge instead of a sharp edge on the meplat made a huge difference as well, not only in depth, but stability at the very end of penetration.

"We were literally testing hundreds of solids a week, and every small step of the way learning new things about how a solid actually works. Listed below are the absolute known factors involved with terminal penetration of solids, in order of importance to straight-line penetration and depth of penetration in either aqueous test material or animal tissue.

#1. Meplat Percentage of Caliber

#2. Nose Profile

#3. Construction & Material

#4. Nose Projection

#5. Radius Edge of Meplat

Above factors related to bullet design

#6. Velocity

#7. Barrel Twist Rate

#8. Sectional Density

"Now the old diehard convention wisdom always says SD is No.1. This is not true at all, and we can prove it time after time, in any caliber. (Author's note: this comment is in reference to solid, or non-expanding bullets.) If a solid is not stable, it will not penetrate in a straight line; it will veer off course and penetrate less, every single time, as opposed to a properly designed solid. The one and only time that SD becomes a factor at all is when all of the other factors are dead equal, all the way down the line. Take for instance the very fact that a properly designed 325-grain .458-caliber solid will double the depth of penetration of a 500-grain round-nose .458-caliber solid. SD has little to do with the penetration of solids, unless all else is equal.

"Along the way, JD had sent several different designs he was working with in both .458 and .500 as well. One of these was derived from some of his old-time cast bullets that he had used in various JDJs over the years, but now in a .500-caliber copper solid. I had tested this bullet many times and always found it gave 100 percent dead straight-line penetration. One day I handed one of these to Sam Rose and asked him to measure the degree of the angle off the nose, and for him to make a series of different degrees for us to test.

"Sam went home, measured this bullet and found it was right at a 15-degree angle off the nose. The meplat measured slightly above 72 percent. As I recall, Sam made a variety from 10 degrees all the way to 20 degrees off the nose and we tested.

"All tested well until we got above a 15-degree angle, and then things got a little squirrely. We found that everything between 11 and 15 degrees did very well, was stable. A smaller meplat size of 65 to 67 percent depth of penetration was incredible compared to other tests we had done. In the end, we picked the 13-degree angle, which was basically in the middle. Now during all this time, teasing Sam, I accused him of making bullets with a 'bastard file' as a joke. He was sending several different designs of some really wild stuff weekly.

"The bastard file joke ended up evolving into Bastard Bullet Works, or BBW.

"We also started working very closely with Dan Smitchko of Cutting Edge Bullets. Dan was instrumental in making the changes we desired, to complete the study with CNC-machined bullets. After many months and many thousands of rounds fired during the test work, we declared the 13-degree angle nose and 67 percent meplat size bullet the best solid we had ever tested,

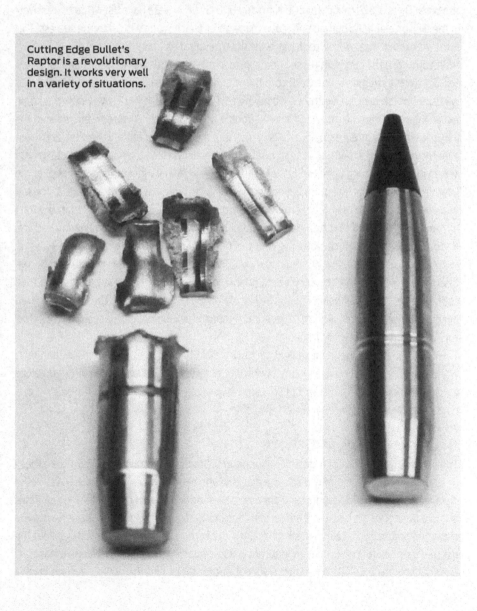

Cutting Edge Bullet's Raptor is a revolutionary design. It works very well in a variety of situations.

and the most consistent in all calibers tested. Our mission had been a great success, and it was decided to give the design to Dan at CEB and let him run with it. In the beginning, he asked what we wanted to name it, I said BBW #13—"Bastard Bullet Works," with the #13 after the angle off the nose. Later, a more proper name was given by CEB, the Safari Solid.

"Having a variety of .500 caliber rifles, including lever guns, BBW #13s were designed for all of my .500 caliber cartridges, from lever to the larger 500 MDM. BBW#13s are available from 375 grains to 550 grains in .500 caliber. Now, #13s can be had in all major large bore calibers up to the big 900 grain .620 caliber for 600 Nitro and 600 OverKill. #13's have been used extensively in the field on elephant, buffalo and hippo many times over now, all with extreme success. This is the go-to solid when absolute straight-line deep penetration is required.

"If you notice the bands on these bullets, please take note this was a special area of study, too. Sam was extremely interested in double rifles, and in particular a bullet band design that was safe for doubles. I have the capability here of doing pressure work. We hooked a strain gauge 4 inches from the muzzle of several double rifles and other rifles, as well, reduced the loads to where the strain gauge would only measure the passing of any given bullet, and measure the amount of expansion in the barrel as that bullet passed that point. The design you see, in both the Cutting Edge Bullets and the North Fork Bullets gave the least barrel strain overall of any and most all other bullets. We needed the three full diameter bands at the top and one at the rear to maintain accuracy. The more bands that were added, the barrel strain increased. We learned that barrel strain is affected by bullet diameter and bearing surface. Reduce the bearing surface, you have reduced barrel strain; reduce the diameter, you again reduce the barrel strain. But at some point, you can only go down so far in diameter before affecting other areas like accuracy, stability and so forth. Brass gives less barrel strain than copper in most cases, all being equal. The North Fork bullets are equal to the CEB in this area because of their reduced bearing surface, even though they are copper-based. The main factors are bearing surface and diameter."

McCourry's testing sheds much light on how bullets behave in both test media and real-world scenarios. I don't have as many opportunities to test the solids in the field (dangerous game safaris are very expensive), but I'm glad we have folks like Michael McCourry who have a passion for developing the best bullets available.

Defensive Handgun Bullets

The penetrative qualities of a defensive handgun bullet are even more important than those of a hunting rifle; your life may be on the line, and you need it to perform properly. While the distances at which handguns are used are invariably shorter than those of a rifle, and variations in impact velocities are less, there are certain concerns that need to be addressed. Certainly, you expect handgun bullets to penetrate sufficiently to neutralize a threat to life and limb, but the risk of over-penetration—where an innocent person might be wounded or killed—is a reality. Defensive handgun bullets have their work cut out for them, and the bullet developers have spent copious amounts of time to get the balance just right. Our military has been forced to depend on the full metal jacket design, as prescribed by the Hague Convention, and while FMJs work in a battle situation, they're not optimal for civilian needs.

Years ago, we pretty much had three choices: lead, jacketed or full metal jacket. Yes, they will all still work (the footage of Jack Ruby killing Lee Harvey Oswald with a round-nosed lead slug from a .38 Special at spitting distance is an example), but there are better choices. Premium handgun bullets have been designed for reliable expansion and proper penetration, and the tests prove just that. There are numerous choices, including the Federal Guard Dog and HST, Hornady XTP and XTP Magnum, Speer's Gold Dot, Winchester's Defender and more, but they all have the same common goal: saving your bacon.

The Woodleigh Hydrostatically Stabilized Solid, on the ear of the bull elephant it dispatched so neatly.

Handgun barrels can be almost as finicky as rifle barrels, and it may take a bit of experimentation to find the load that is most agreeable with your own gun. But look at the penetration tests for each load before settling on a brand. Some bullets employ the same construction techniques as premium rifle projectiles: bonded core, polymer tips, etc. However, not all premium handgun bullets are created equal.

I had an eye-opening experience as a guest at the Federal Premium plant, testing three different models of Federal .45 ACP defensive ammunition into ballistic gel. We had a sweet Kimber pistol that was plenty accurate and an absolute pleasure to shoot. There were boxes of 230-grain Hydra-Shok, 185-grain Guard Dog and 230-grain HST ammunition, and clean gel blocks to observe penetration and expansion. The Hydra-Shok is Federal's classic hollowpoint, skived to promote expansion and features a small post in the center of the cavity. Guard Dog is designed for indoor situations; it has a rubber insert filling the hollow cavity, and the whole bullet is plated so as to appear like a flat-nosed FMJ. The HST bullet is also a skived hollowpoint, designed to expand into a sharp, flower-like pattern, and the high antimony core holds well to the heavy copper jacket. These bullets were fired into three types of test media: gel alone, gel covered with clothing layers, and then through two pieces of drywall and into the gel.

All three of the bullets performed very well into bare ballistic gel. Weight retention for the Hydra-Shok was 222 grains, Guard Dog retained a good amount of its weight, coming in at 164 grains, and the HST did as well, weighing 228 grains after expansion. Expansion was consistent, with the Hydra-Shok measuring 0.65 inches, the Guard Dog 0.72 inches, and the HST opening up to an even inch. Penetration was between 12 and 13 inches for the HST and Hydra-Shok, and 6 ¼ inches for the Guard Dog, so I really didn't have a favorite (yet).

The clothing test revealed a different story. The Guard Dog expanded reliably, to 0.70 inches, and retained 163 out of 185 grains, but penetration was cut down to 8 ¼ inches. The Hydra-Shok retained 227 grains, but expansion was reduced to 0.65 inches and penetration was 13 inches. However, the HST retained 227 grains, expanded to 0.82 inches and penetrated 14 inches of gel. At that point I was starting to form an opinion.

The drywall test sealed the deal for me. The Hydra-Shok didn't expand at all, and the bullet could more than likely be re-fired. The weight after recovery was 232 grains, as it was filled with gypsum. The bullet penetrated 24 inches of gel block, and was recovered downrange about 15 yards. The Guard Dog expanded to the same dimension of 0.70 inches, and weighed 170 grains, but didn't penetrate more than 8 ½ inches, completely in line with the design of the bullet and loading. The HST weighed in at 228 grains, despite the wallboard, and expanded to 0.81 inches, with a full 8 inches of penetration. It was the jagged edges of the expanded HST, along with the nasty wound channel created in the gel that made me favor this bullet. If I was forced to shoot indoors, and over-penetration was an issue, I think the Guard Dog line of ammo might be your baby. But for an overall self-defense bullet, in the Federal line I prefer the HST, for the reason of the expanded shape. While the Guard Dog was very reliable, the HST, with those razor sharp petals, will undoubtedly decimate the enemy and "chastise with extreme prejudice," to borrow a military expression. I carry this ammunition confidently.

Cutting Edge has adapted their fragmenting bullet concept for handguns in the Handgun Raptor. It's available in both component form and the Personal Handgun Defense (PHD) line of loaded ammunition. Using a bullet weight that is much lighter than normal at a higher velocity, the Handgun Raptor causes that same upfront trauma from its blades, while the caliber-sized base drives deep penetration. I've tested these in 9mm Luger (90 grains), .40 S&W (120 grains) and .45 ACP (150 grains). They work as prescribed, with the nose section reliably breaking off upon impact and the base giving 8-12 inches of penetration, depending upon the caliber and the test media. If you're a fan of higher velocities and want dependable penetrative qualities, I recommend you try these bullets and test them for yourself. I like them, and believe that they will quickly and handily neutralize a threat, in spite of the lower SD figures. It would be worthwhile to do some informal penetration tests with your chosen load, even if it's just shooting into some wet phonebooks or tightly packed newspaper, so you have an idea of the penetration capabilities.

Handgun Hunting Bullets

When it comes to hunting with a handgun, reliable penetration is paramount. I like the more powerful revolvers like the .357 Magnum, .44 Magnum and .45 Colt. Bump up to the bigger cases, like the .454 Casull, .460 S&W, .500 Linebaugh and .500 S&W, and you'll see the obvious need for a bullet of high sectional density, if it is of cup-and-core construction or traditional hardcast lead. Companies like Buffalo Bore, DoubleTap and Garrett Cartridges have long offered hardcast hunting bullets for these cartridges and, at moderate velocities—usually below 2,000 fps—they work just fine and penetrate wonderfully. However, as we have shown with other examples in the rifle calibers, impact velocity can be the downfall of penetration, especially with expanding bullets.

Many of the rifle bullet companies offer handgun choices, which work as well as do their big brothers. Swift's A-Frame is available in most popular revolver calibers from .357 upward, as is the Barnes XPB monometal. Cutting Edge offers the Handgun Raptor as a configuration optimized for the handgun hunter, and these happen to be a favorite of my pal and fellow gun writer Matthew Cosenzo. He started using CEB Raptors in his .44 Magnums.

"Over the years of hunting with pistol-caliber rifles—specifically the old .44 Magnum carbines by Ruger—I have developed strong opinions on bullets choices, which translated over when hunting with handguns," said Cosenzo. "Within those particular rifles you should only shoot jacketed bullets due to the gas system, so when you are pushing a pistol bullet to higher velocity you need to be aware of its limitations. I always shot the 280-grain Speer Deep Curl soft point, an extremely tough bullet as well as accurate, in my particular rifle, consistently shooting ¾-inch groups. It is my opinion that this particular bullet is too tough for pistols to achieve reliable expansion. Over the years, seeing unimpressive results from jacketed pistol bullets I looked

RIFLE BULLET PENETRATION: THE HIGHLIGHTS

> Sectional density is a good indicator of a bullet's length, but it is only one factor. The bullet's construction must be taken into account, as well.

> High retained weight aids in good penetration, yet expansion is required for the destruction of vital tissue. What you are looking for (in the big game world) is the consummate blend of both qualities.

> Modern construction techniques have truly changed the game. Bonded-core, partitioned and monometal designs have a structural integrity superior to the traditional cup-and-core ammunition.

> Traditional cup-and-core bullets work fine if of suitable length (sectional density) and impact velocities aren't too high for the bullet's construction. For long-range work, the bullet slows down considerably, but close shots can make a mess of things.

> Round- and flat-nosed bullets—with a larger contact diameter— can facilitate better energy transfer, and that difference can be seen upon impacting a game animal.

> Round- and flat-nosed bullets have demonstrated an advantage in straight-line penetration, but suffer in the exterior ballistics department due to low BC. A compromise must be made if your hunting ranges are past 200 yards.

> The newer, more radical designs, like the Woodleigh Hydrostatically Stabilized Solid, Peregrine BushMaster and Cutting Edge Bullets' Raptor deviate from traditional thinking, but they warrant a place among the best bullets available— further proof that bullet technology is at the forefront of evolving hunting gear.

for a better mouse trap. Nearly all pistol bullets expand in the same manner, creating a mushroom, which in turn slows the bullet down as it penetrates, not always giving you two holes.

"The guys over at Cutting Edge Bullets and their Raptor line of handgun bullets are what you will see me load when I am out chasing game. While I have always been a heavy-for-caliber cast-bullet guy, the Raptors have changed my opinion of what is necessary, in regard to weight. My initial introduction to these bullets was in the .44 Magnum and what was available was a 200- and 150-grain Raptor, in addition to a 240-grain solid. I immediately knew the 150 had to be too light, though Dan Smitchko, president of Cutting Edge, made me eat my words that season. He shot a nice-sized doe at about 100 yards and the base as well as the blades exited on this whitetail. The bullet was traveling roughly 1,800 fps from a Thompson/Center Contender. So, even with the lighter weight, depth of penetration was not a factor, nor was the terminal effectiveness, if applied properly. Since all theses bullets are machined on CNC lathes, they have the advantage of consistency and repeatability not matched by any other form of manufacturing. When it comes to jacketed bullets in revolvers you need that bullet to function exactly the same way every time; this is a common gripe by many seasoned handgunners. Raptors give me that uniform performance."

Now, Cosenzo is no stranger to hunting with a handgun. And he has grown to swear by the Cutting Edge Handgun Raptor, in several different calibers, including the .500 Linebaugh. While the bullet runs light-for-caliber (lower sectional density) in comparison to hardcast lead projectiles—as most all-copper bullets do—it has the structural integrity necessary to make a quick kill.

CHAPTER 16

Kinetic Energy and Killing Power

W e hunters simply love to quantify things, right down to the last detail. We're also fond of assigning minimums, rules, absolutes, quotable lore, and arguing over these points. Kinetic energy figures are no exception. And while there is merit to using enough gun with sufficient kinetic energy, these figures can be misleading.

First of all, the kinetic energy of a bullet is measured in units of foot-pounds. The equation to derive the energy of a particular bullet is as follows:

$$KE = (M \times V^2)/450,435$$

Whereas KE = Kinetic energy in ft.-lbs., M = the mass of the bullet in grains, V = bullet velocity in fps, and the denominator of 450,435 being a product of gravitational acceleration (32.173 fps^2) multiplied by 7,000 (to convert grains into pounds) and doubled.

An example: Nosler's Trophy Grade ammunition in .30-06 Springfield launches a 180-grain AccuBond bullet at 2,750 fps, so the calculation is as follows:

$$(180 \times 2,750^2)/450,435 = 3,022 \text{ ft.-lbs.}$$

What does that bullet have left at 200 yards? Nosler indicates that it will slow down to 2,400 fps at that range, so crunching the numbers again will yield:

$$(180 \times 2,400^2)/450,435 = 2,302 \text{ ft.-lbs.}$$

Let's take it out to 400 yards, where Nosler indicates a velocity of 2,078 fps, so:

$$(180 \times 2,078^2)/450,435 = 1,726 \text{ ft.-lbs.}$$

At 600 yards—past my own personal hunting limits—the AccuBond is still traveling at 1,782 fps, therefore:

$$(180 \times 1,782^2)/450,435 = 1,269 \text{ ft.-lbs.}$$

However, while these figures are absolutely correct, do they translate directly into killing power? In reality, they give a good representation of the potential, but favor velocity. Allow me to explain.

If you take a .45-70 Government loaded with a 405-grain flat-nosed slug moving at 1,330 fps—à la Remington's load—you can crunch those numbers and arrive at 1,590 ft.-lbs. of energy. If you then look at a .22-250 Remington, driving a 55-grain bullet at 3,680 fps—like Hornady's Varmint Express ammo—you will see 1,654 ft.-lbs of kinetic energy. Facing an enraged grizzly bear in an Alaskan willow thicket, which bullet is going to kill that bear quicker? I can confidently say that almost anyone would opt for the .45-70, unless you are the bear whisperer. So where do you go wrong with your dependence on kinetic energy figures? Or, does speed truly kill, and all is right in the world with these numbers?

I personally only see the flaws in dealing with kinetic energy values, as the above example clearly demonstrates. I'm not the only one who has noticed the issue; a gentleman with much more experience dealing with big rifles and bigger animals developed a newer system before my father was born. That man was John Taylor, author of *African Rifles and Cartridges*. Taylor spent most of his adult life in wild Africa, mostly in Portuguese East Africa (modern day Mozambique), and was privileged to experiment with a large number of calibers and projectiles on all sorts of game, for an unparalleled collection of ballistic experiences. I like several things about Taylor. Aside from the fact that he was a major inspiration for my near-addiction to African big game hunting, he too was a lifelong student of ballistics. He was also a bold soul, abandoning the traditional system of measuring the striking capabilities of cartridges by using solely kinetic energy, and developed his own Taylor Knock-Out Factor. This formula varies from the kinetic energy equation in that the gravitational acceleration is removed and the bullet's diameter introduced. The Taylor Knock-Out Factor formula works as follows:

$$\text{Taylor KO} = (M \times V \times D)/7,000$$

Whereas M = mass of the bullet in grains, V = velocity in fps, and D = diameter of the bullet in inches, and dividing that product by 7,000 converts grains into pounds. The Taylor KO factor is a unitless figure, used to compare the potential killing capability of a variety of cartridges. However, the method does have flaws, as it heavily leans on bullet diameter, and I sort of understand why. In Taylor's day, there was a serious divide between the small-bore-at-hyper-velocity crowd, and the as-big-as-you-can-launch-at-a-moderate-velocity camp. In a time when even P.O. Ackley was touting the .220 Swift as the greatest thing since sliced bread, and Walter Bell's 7x57mm Mauser had already accounted for the majority of his 1,100 elephant bulls, there were people stretching the limits of bullet weight/construction/velocity boundaries. Bell used only solids. I believe he uttered the phrase, "my barrel has never been polluted by a soft-point bullet." The soft points of his day were questionable, especially on dangerous game, and survived his time among the elephants unscathed. But no one today would try that stunt, even with super bullets like the Woodleigh Hydro Solid. So Taylor compiled his formula to represent how he felt; it is scientifically skewed, but is a little bit better than the kinetic energy ideas. Let's look at why.

Using Taylor's formula and muzzle velocities, the .30-06 Springfield has a TKO value of 21.8, while the .45-70 Government is 35.2. I get the fact that the heavier bullet and increased frontal diameter have an effect, but I don't know about a 62 percent increase in performance. Even the .35 Remington, launching a 200-grain bullet at 2,100 fps, yields a TKO rating of 21.1, essentially putting it on plane with the .30-06, and I don't see that as correct. I understand Taylor's intentions, but the flaws of his equation are hard to ignore.

Looking at the quantifications even further, there is no method available that takes the bullet construction into account. Certainly, if you were to compare the same .30-06 Springfield, shooting 150-grain bullets at a particular game animal (let's just pick a mule deer for demonstrative purposes) and used two different styles of bullets, you would definitely have different results. Assuming a good bonded-core spitzer, like the Swift Scirocco II, I'd feel confident taking a shot from just about any angle offered, knowing the bullet's construction is no issue. Swap that bullet out for a Sierra 150-grain MatchKing, a bullet celebrated for its accuracy but marginal terminal ballistics, and you'd have good cause for concern—likely breaking apart on the first bone encountered. Now, that's not to suggest that mule deer are bulletproof, but it goes a long way to show that some methods of measuring killing power can be a huge waste of time, especially when it comes to making an argument for or against one cartridge over another. Invariably, the kinetic energy method is the most common today, so I'll concede the fact and use it to draw some conclusions.

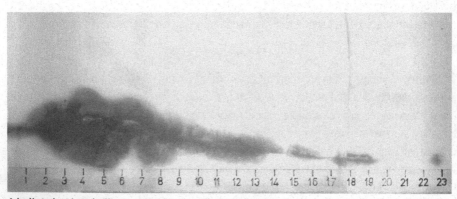

A bullet shot into ballistic gelatin can easily demonstrate the energy transfer imparted by a projectile; note the large disruption just after impact at the left side of the gel block. Photo: Hornady

There are established minimums, figures that someone—I truly have no idea from where or whom these originate—set for various game animals. You've heard these before: 1,000 ft.-lbs. for a deer, 2,000 ft.-lbs. for an elk or moose, 4,000 ft.-lbs. for Cape buffalo, elephant and other dangerous African game. Back to the need to quantify things, and the fact that a line had to be drawn somewhere, I can see that perhaps these figures aren't exactly out to lunch, but they are certainly not absolutes. A modern big game compound bow, set up for hunting grizzly bear, uses an arrow weighing a total of 500 grains, give or take a few, launched at 250 fps. Based upon the formula for kinetic energy, this combination generates a whopping 55.5 ft.-lbs. of energy. Yet we all know if that arrow is properly placed it will most certainly kill the grizzly. So, I think it's also fair to bring the aspect of tissue destruction into the mix. Returning to the .30-06 Springfield on a mule deer hunt example. Imagine the difference in tissue destruction if you compared that Swift Scirocco II with an average expansion rate of just over twice the caliber dimension (assuming a shot somewhere between 100 and 200 yards), and a full metal jacket bullet offering all sorts of penetration yet absolutely no expansion. Both bullets have the same kinetic energy figures, as well as the same sectional density figures. But I still think hunters prefer the bonded core expanding bullet.

Instead of subscribing to the hard-lined minimums and basing your facts and decisions on decades-old bullet technology, you should blend all the aspects discussed thus far and come to a common sense conclusion. You need to use the kinetic energy figures as a baseline, thinking about bore diameter, bullet configuration and construction, sectional density figures, etc., and police yourself. In other words, would the .243 Winchester make a good elk or moose cartridge? At 100 grains of bullet weight, I don't think so. I know people who've killed elk with the little 6mm, but I don't think it's an ideal, or even a wise choice. Do you need a .338 Winchester Magnum to kill that elk? Not necessarily, but I'd definitely prefer the larger cartridge over the smaller.

Bringing everything we've discussed into play, from trajectory and wind deflection values, to bullet stability factors, to sectional density and all other penetrative dimensions, to the skewed means we have on hand to determine the killing power of a bullet, you need to look at the whole gem, instead of one facet at a time. For most hunting situations, one of the classic cartridges will more than likely fulfill all of your needs. While the .30-06 Springfield has been used, is used and shall be used by an enormous amount of hunters (because it just plain works), if the .300 Dakota, .308 Norma Magnum or .300 Winchester Short Magnum floats your boat, there's no problem with that. There are availability issues, but all of those cartridges will push a .30-caliber bullet to respectable velocities and give perfectly suitable field performance. If you prefer the 6.5 Creedmoor over a traditional 6.5x55 Swede, so be it, as the performance is relatively similar. Just don't expect to ask a .25-06 Remington to do the work of a .338 Magnum; you can only push the envelope so far. There's an awful lot of overlap in our modern cartridges, and I hope that with the information I've covered thus far will not only help you recognize that fact, but also help you make an informed choice of cartridge.

There is one place where the line has been drawn, and unfortunately it's a legal line, so there's no fighting it. However, like all lines drawn, there are reasons to question it, and there are shortcomings to the logic. Most of the African continent has a law stating that a .375 bore shall be the legal minimum for hunting all dangerous game. While I understand the *intent* of this law, it does a couple of silly things.

First off, it precludes the use of the 9.3mm (.366-inch diameter) cartridges; classics like the 9.3x62mm, 9.3x64mm and 9.3x74R that have long given reliable performance on the biggest animals on the Dark Continent. Secondly, while the intent of the law (I assume) was to create a minimum performance level, as represented by the .375 H&H Magnum, it doesn't specify any sort of energy or momentum levels. So, in theory, you'd be perfectly legal using a lever-action Winchester 94 Big Bore chambered in .375 Winchester pushing a 220-grain bullet at 2,200 fps. Yet, you'd be technically breaking the law by using a 9.3x64mm Brenneke, driving a 293-grain bullet to a muzzle velocity of 2,580 fps; a formula very, very close to the .375 H&H setup of a 300-grain bullet at 2,550 fps.

Add some other oddballs into the mix, like the .405 Winchester, which Theodore Roosevelt loved so much. It uses a 300-grain .411-inch diameter bullet (of relatively low SD) at 2,200 fps, and while it does make the legal minimum for dangerous game, it doesn't make the wisest of choices for Cape buffalo, and certainly not for elephant. Pick a cartridge that uses a bullet of sensible sectional density, preferably over 0.300, of suitable caliber and velocity. African game can be rather, well, unforgiving, and your safety is paramount.

The reason that the .375 bore was chosen for the benchmark was more for its performance level than its diameter. And you'd do well to make sure you choose a cartridge that can at least mimic that power level. The commonly accepted energy level for dangerous game is 4,000 ft.-lbs. (the energy level of the .375 H&H using 300-grain bullets) and upward. I can agree with that figure so long as the bullet has a decent sectional density. African dangerous game is one area where bigger is most definitely better.

Back to the idea of a minimum energy level for common game like deer, I'm not quite sure the old adage of 1,000 ft.-lbs. as a minimum holds water. Considering that a deer is highly susceptible to shock and that modern bullet construction has changed radically, any given energy figure may be misleading. I also feel that these minimum energy rules we all consider to be gospel can be skewed to make the case for extreme long-range hunting. Federal Premium's 180-grain .300 Remington Ultra Magnum load yields 1,040 ft.-lbs. of energy at 950 yards, but that is certainly no excuse to shoot game at that distance. In addition, bullet construction plays no part in that minimum energy level figure, though it does play a huge part in the terminal ballistic phase of the equation.

The same can be said for the elk figure of 2,000 ft.-lbs., which is odd considering that the elk is considerably larger—up to five times that of a deer—and somewhere along the line someone figured that 2,000 ft.-lbs. seemed a good number to settle upon. Looking at the Federal load in 7mm Remington Magnum, using the tried-and-true 160-grain Nosler Partition bullet, you'll

The Federal Premium Punch handgun line gives fine accuracy and an affordable bonded-core projectile with excellent energy transfer and deep penetration.

see that at about 325 yards the energy levels drop below the 2,000 ft.-lb. mark. I know many people who have very effectively taken elk with a 7mm Mag. at distances past 400 yards, where the energy figures would have dropped off to less than 1,700 ft.-lbs. yet the animal was as dead as a doornail.

The point? Energy figures are a *means*, but not the definitive means, of measuring the killing power of a particular bullet/velocity combination. Speed does contribute to the killing ability of a bullet, but only to a certain point. Bullet diameter is another contribution, so long as it has the sectional density to allow the bigger projectile to penetrate properly. There's always a happy medium to be found for any game animal; and that's why the classics are the classics. Be sensible about it, and don't try to kill an elephant with a sewing needle, nor swat a fly with a sledgehammer.

SECTION

IV

TOOLS
& TIPS

SECTION IV GUNDEX®

CHAPTER 17
Tools for Better Ballistics

E ven though you're now armed with all this knowledge, you're still going to need the right tools to get the job done. I'm assuming your rifle is in working order, and that all is as it should be. Providing that the platform functions properly, your bullet—whether a round-nosed hunting slug or the most modern hybrid ogive match bullet—will tell the true story once it's sent on its merry way. The pressure will drive it down the barrel, and it will go where you've told it to go. Where you tell it to go is largely a matter of your skills. But, there have always been aids or methods of fine-tuning the ability to place a bullet accurately.

I remember as a young man hunting deer with my dad. The first gun I used was his old Stevens break-action single-barrel shotgun, loaded with Foster-style slugs. It had a 30-inch barrel and a silver bead on the end, and kicked like the hammers of hell. Recoil aside, and excluding the fact that Ol' Grumpy Pants' shotgun action was as loose as a goose, the aiming system sucked. Holding that bead on the bullseye, I could maybe, just maybe, keep my shots in a pie plate at 30 yards. But, as GP said, "you'll be sitting in the thick stuff, so they'll be close."

Switching to an iron-sighted Winchester Model 94 in .30-30 WCF made a world of difference. The traditional front post and buckhorn rear sight seemed precise in comparison to the silver bead on the shotgun, and I was pretty good to 75 yards. Scoping the rifle—it was one of the AE, or angled eject models, so mounting a scope over the center of the bore was no problem—enabled even farther shots. I was shooting minute-of-softball at 125 yards with a fixed 4x scope, and now had a deer gun that would do respectable work in the woods of the Northeast. Thus began my addiction to optics. If you take a .45-70 Government loaded with a 405-grain flat-nosed slug moving at 1,330 fps—à la Remington's load—you can crunch those numbers and arrive at 1,590 ft.-lbs. of energy. If you then look at a .22-250 Remington, driving a 55-grain bullet at 3,680 fps—like Hornady's Varmint Express ammo—you will see 1,654 ft.-lbs of kinetic energy. Facing an enraged grizzly bear in an Alaskan willow thicket, which bullet is going to kill that bear quicker? I can confidently say that almost anyone would opt for the .45-70, unless you are the bear whisperer. So where do you go wrong with your dependence on kinetic energy figures? Or, does speed truly kill, and all is right in the world with these numbers?

Riflescopes

Don't get me wrong, there is absolutely nothing wrong with iron sights; I still use them, and actually prefer them for dangerous game like elephants or follow-ups on Cape buff, or game hunted at close distance such as black bear over bait. But invariably, I am a better shot when shooting a rifle with a scope onboard. For serious target work, there's no debating the fact: you'll want the best scope you can afford, and as distances increase, necessary options follow suit. You need to properly see the target in order to hit it, and there are actually physical issues involved at longer ranges if your riflescope isn't calibrated correctly. A riflescope is so much more than just a magnifying glass screwed to the top of your rifle; it is a measuring tool, and a precise means of aiming that removes the focal issues involved with iron sights. Trying to focus three objects simultaneously—front sight, rear sight and target—becomes much more difficult as your eyes age. I know that at 45 years old my eyes are most certainly not what they were when I was 18 or 20, and I'll take any advantage I can get when it comes to precise aiming.

Today's riflescopes are leaps and bounds above those of 50 years ago. The variable power range scopes of yesteryear were plagued with all sorts of issues. Chief among them was a shifting point of aim as you changed the magnification level. Add to that a lack of structural integrity, with heavy-recoiling rifles causing them to lose zero, and you'll easily understand why early telescopic sights were shunned by some experienced hunters of the mid-20th century. I remember reading one of Hemingway's hunting stories, in which another hunter suggested the use of a riflescope. "Those things are for nuns and virgins," Papa said. In his book, Horn of the Hunter, Robert Ruark had such trouble with his scope shifting point of aim that he took it off the rifle mid-safari, and left it off for good.

Fixed-power riflescopes were much more dependable than their variable-powered brothers, and for years the fixed 2.5x and 4x ones were standard issue for hunters, with the target and varmint crowd embracing the 6x, 8x and 10x fixed-powers. If you've ever tried to use a riflescope from the 1940s or 1950s, you'll appreciate the modern advancements in optics. With the exception of a very few, highly expensive models of that era—Unertl, Bausch & Lomb, Kahles and Swarovski—most left quite a bit to be desired. All that has changed. Even today's inexpensive optics offer quite a value to the hunter or recreational target shooter, and the high-end models are nothing shy of amazing. Let's look at the dynamics of the modern riflescope, and correlate all that information to help you get your bullet properly placed.

A riflescope contains a series of lenses, designed to provide two things: first, some amount of magnification; second to superimpose an aiming system onto the target so that the target and aiming system are all on one plane. The lenses are contained in an aluminum tube (some older models used steel), with a means of adjusting the horizontal and vertical positioning of the aiming system. That aiming system, known as a reticle, is a set of crosshairs, or occasionally a post or centered dot. All lens systems have an inherent problem if not precisely focused. This condition is known as parallax, and will cause the image to be seen at one reference point within the riflescope, when in reality it truly lies at another point. This phenomenon will cause all sorts of problems at longer ranges, unless your riflescope has an adjustment to compensate for the change in focal point. Most modern riflescopes are equipped with an adjustable objective lens or parallax adjustment knob, or are set to be parallax free at 150 yards, and that will cover a considerable amount of your hunting and shooting duties. When distance stretches out beyond 200 yards, the parallax can become a problem. Just like choosing a bullet that best suits your shooting distances, you'll need to think about the optics system that works best for you.

The same can be said about the reticle. These days, reticles come in all shapes and sizes, some illuminated for use in low-light situations or on a black target like a Cape buffalo or black bear, while others resemble a World War II submarine periscope, with all sorts of tick marks, graduations, numbers, dots, additional crosshairs, and more. Some have so much going on in there that they look like abstract art. But, they all serve a purpose, which we'll see shortly. How much or how little you need depends on what you're asking of your rig.

The original crosshairs, two simple wires running horizontally and vertically, have taken a back seat to the duplex reticle, where the thin, inner wires change into a thicker wire as you move away from the center. Most of my rifles are equipped with this style of reticle, and it works just fine for most of my hunting duties. However, other than using the point on the wire where the thin transforms into the thick, there's not a lot of measuring capability with a duplex reticle.

The Ballistic Drop Compensated or BDC reticle is becoming increasingly popular, refining the early developments that gave the hunter a little bit more than the traditional crosshairs. The modern BDC sports a series of graduations on the lower post of the vertical wire, in some increment of measure, to aid you in holdover, compensating for the trajectory drop. Additionally, you will find models with graduations on the horizontal wire, used for measuring an amount of wind deflection, or for obtaining a proper lead on a moving target. Some of the graduations are mil-dots, or a series of dots subtending one milliradian—a military measure of angle equal to one one-thousandth of a radian. You'll see mil-dot reticles, as well as those using minutes for a measuring system. While minute of angle, or MOA and the divisions thereof are the most common method of measuring angles in riflescope adjustment, many of the so-called tactical riflescopes have their adjustments in 1/10th mil, rather than in MOA.

Either method is perfectly acceptable. You just have to understand how the measurements correlate to your target. Both measure the amount of angle that will be subtended by a specific distance on the reticle, and that same mathematical relationship applies to the adjustments on your riflescope. A minute of angle is 1/60th of one degree of a circle, while a milliradian is 1/1000th of a radian. To bring you back to geometry class, a radian is that portion of a circle where the arc length is equal to the radius. To put it in a different light, there are 21,600 minutes of angle in a complete circle, while there are (approximately) 6,283 milliradians in a full circle. So, the milliradian is equal to 3.44 MOA. Putting this in real-world terms, one MOA at 100 yards will subtend 1.047 inches, while one milliradian will subtend 3.60 inches. Looking at a mil-dot reticle, you can see how knowing the distance between the dots (derived by multiplying the sine of the angle by the distance to the target) will greatly aid in adjusting your hold for a particular wind call, or adjusting for drop caused by gravity at longer distances.

These same graduations are located within your adjustment turrets. The turrets will be marked in a particular fraction of angular measurement. In MOA-graduated scopes, the most popular graduations are ¼ MOA, though I've seen 1/8 MOA on the finer varmint/target styles, and many of the low-power 'safari' type scopes still have ½ MOA graduations. Mil scope turret graduations are more likely to be 1/10 mil, or about 0.36-inch at 100 yards. The ¼ MOA graduations are a bit finer than the 1/10 mil, but both are precise. I've worked as a licensed land surveyor since I was 11 years old, so my mind thinks in terms of minutes of angle. I can convert into mils without too much trouble, but for me it's like speaking a second language; I'm constantly translating it in my head. I'll explain both systems, in reference to the graduations on a riflescope, but don't be surprised if you see my preference for minutes over mils.

Let's use the ¼ MOA graduation as an example for the purposes of sighting in your riflescope. Assuming you're shooting at 100 yards, where 1 MOA subtends 1.047 inches (we can round this off to an even inch) you'll need four clicks to make one minute and move the crosshairs one inch. However many inches you need to move your crosshairs at 100 yards, simply multiply by four, as ¼ MOA is equal to ¼-inch at this distance. At 200 yards, the inch value doubles, where

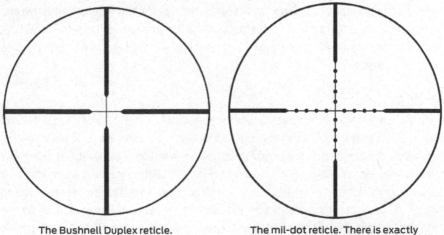

The Bushnell Duplex reticle.

The mil-dot reticle. There is exactly one milliradian between the centers of each dot; it can easily be used to make accurate trajectory and wind calls.

¼ MOA is equal to ½-inch, and so on and so forth. In mils, you'll change the value to 1/3-inch at 100 yards for every 1/10th mil click. At 200 yards, 1/10th mil is equal to 2/3rds of an inch, and on and on. Now, while you may be familiar with adjusting a riflescope, as the methods haven't really changed in 75 years, there are some different ways of measuring with a scope's reticle to adjust for both wind and holdover.

Thus far, I've given you the trajectory and wind deflection values in inches, as it's our common unit of measure, but many of the long-range shooters measure in minutes or mils, and make the adjustments by using the turrets of their scopes, rather than estimating distance within the reticle. I learned holdover for distant targets by knowing the drop of my particular load and adjusting that amount of elevation based on the size of my target, whether a game animal or paper target; my method isn't nearly as accurate as using a Ballistic Drop Compensated reticle or having target turrets to dial up the necessary amount of minutes or mils. In all fairness, when I started shooting, I couldn't afford the premium riflescopes. With a good dope card or a Kestrel Elite handheld unit, the trajectory and wind deflection values can be represented in minutes or mils, so you can adjust the riflescope a prescribed amount, and hold the crosshairs directly on the target—rather than my method of elevating the crosshairs, which is really the only possible method with a duplex reticle. Or, if you have one of the reticles I'm about to describe, you can look at your trajectory as a function of minutes. Instead of thinking "I'm 6 inches low at 300 yards," you can view it in a different light: "this rifle is 2 minutes low at 300 yards," and hold an alternate crosshair or dot to completely and quickly measure with a modern reticle, and a good target turret.

Target turrets are much larger than traditional ones and do provide a firm grip. Many of the modern models have large, easily visible numbers, for precise adjustments. As is evident, these newer riflescopes have evolved into a totally different animal, with parallax adjustments, high magnification and larger turrets for on-the-fly adjustment of both elevation and windage. Compared to my grandfather's fixed 4x, this is a quantum leap in technology. Let's look at several of these reticles, and delve into how they can help you get that little bullet onto the distant target.

Modern Reticles

There is a fundamental difference in variable scopes, which is very important to understand before using a graduated reticle. Those are first focal plane and second focal plane reticles. Both have a place in the shooting world. Boiled down, the first focal plane reticle will increase or decrease in size as the magnification is raised or lowered, and if there are graduations on the reticle, they can be used at any magnification level. The graduations remain constant relative to the size and distance of the target, but are difficult to see at the lowest magnification. Second focal plane reticles are the most common in the United States, and this style leaves the reticle the same size throughout the magnification range. This is the style of riflescope of which I'm most accustomed, but it comes with a caveat: It must be used at a specific magnification value

Yds	Moa	Clks 1/4	Inch Drop	Wind@10 MOA-Inch		MOA	200 HZD	Yards
100	Zero	Zero	-2.00	0.50	1			
150	0.75	3	-1.75	0.75	1	1.8		270
200	2.00	8	0	1.00	3	3.6		330
250	3.25	13	3	1.25	4	5.4		390
300	4.50	18	8	1.50	5	7.2		445
350	6.00	24	15	1.75	7	9		495
400	7.50	30	23	2.00	9	10.8		545
450	9.25	37	34	2.25	11	12.6		595
500	11.00	44	47	2.75	15	14.4		640
550	12.75	51	62	3.00	18	16.2		685
600	14.50	58	79	3.25	20			
650	16.50	66	99	3.50	23		Philip Massaro	
675	17.50	70	110	3.75	25		Full X Only! Double Wind	
700	18.50	74	121	4.00	28		Holds to end Bar Full X	

The FTW range card—detailed enough for any use, but easy to read and understand. This is the author's dope card for the 6.5-284 Norma, with a Swarovski Z5 BRX reticle.

or the calibration will be way out of whack. Typically, such scopes are calibrated to be used at maximum power, but I've seen a few that use a slightly lower value, and were clearly marked to reflect that.

The type you choose is entirely up to you. First focal plane reticles allow you to use the graduations at any magnification, but when the magnification is set low—like you'd use on a close shot—the graduations aren't really needed. At long ranges, you'd be inclined to adjust for trajectory or wind deflection. And you'll have your scope dialed to a higher magnification, so it's kind of a push in comparison to a second focal plane. Playing devil's advocate, second focal plane scopes somehow like to find their way to a different zoom level. Maybe it's just me, or maybe Murphy was a distant relative of mine, but it seems that if something can go wrong with a piece of gear in my hands, it will. Either way, once you've made your choice, read and re-read the literature available for the scope, so you can fully utilize its potential.

There are many different styles of modern reticles, but I'll highlight some of those that I find the most useful. It's no slight to other models, but there's only so much room here. Bushnell's G2M reticle, found in the Elite Long Range Hunter, makes a heck of a lot of sense to me. It's a first focal plane duplex reticle featuring 2 MOA graduations on the horizontal crosshair for 24 MOA either side of center, and a series of holdover crosshairs on the lower vertical wire for 32 MOA. The scope features a 30mm tube, allowing better light transmission, and has a side-mounted parallax adjustment knob. The windage adjustment is underneath a traditional screw-on cap, but the elevation adjustment features a large knob with clearly marked increments so you can dial up for distant targets. However, I like the clearly identifiable graduations on the crosshair, too. The lower vertical wire is numbered in 4 MOA increments, while the right horizontal wire is marked in 8 MOA increments, so 'counting hairs' is kept to a minimum. Because I grew up adjusting my hold within the parameters of the reticle, I am very comfortable using a reticle that doesn't require me to dial a turret. The G2M is a perfect example of one that works for hunters and target shooters alike. Your wind holds are very easy to adjust for using this reticle, and the magnification range is perfect for most hunting scenarios. If you're looking to play the long-range game, I think this scope warrants a good, long look. It sits on my Legendary Arms Works Professional in .308 Winchester, and works perfectly.

My Swarovski Z5 3.5-18x44P with BRX reticle is another scope that has worked very well for me. It rests atop a Savage Model 116 6.5-284 Norma and allows me to take full advantage of the attributes of the rifle and cartridge. It is a second focal plane scope, with what many would call a "Christmas Tree" reticle, in that the smaller crosshairs below the main crosshair—used for holdover—get wider as they get lower, to help adjust for the increasing effects of wind deflection as distances and time of flight increase. The scope is actually set up for milliradians, but a quick conversion isn't too difficult when you need to make a range card. Any good ballistics program will give you the values in distance (inches), milliradians or MOA. This scope also features a side-mounted parallax knob, yet uses the smaller hunter-style turrets; the traditional type under the caps. It's a nice, trim scope, with a 1-inch tube, yet the 44mm objective allows in all sorts of light. At its lowest magnification, I've used this scope in the woods for the close shots around home. Yet, I've also cranked up to 18x magnification to hit steel plates at 1,200 yards. Below the main crosshair there are five lower ones, interspersed by four mil-dots, in an alternating pattern. These are in ½ mil increments, with the dots being 1 mil apart. Each lower bar has a hash mark for wind calls, midway to the end of the bar. Well thought out, the BRX reticle is easy to use once you get a dope card built, and you can easily memorize holds out to 400 yards. Conveniently, the wind adjustment marks are located on the lower horizontal hairs, making for more accurate holds.

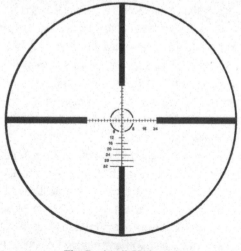

The Bushnell G2M reticle in a first focal plane scope.

I have two dope cards for this scope, one using a 200-yard zero, the other for a 250-yard zero; I use both, depending on the hunt. The fine crosshairs allow for accurate holds, and the focus adjustment lets me make sure the crosshairs are perfectly focused, which can make a huge difference when superimposing the image on targets, especially in mirage and other difficult conditions.

I have a Vortex Razor-HD 3-15x42mm scope, 1-inch tube, with the HSR-4 reticle. In addition to crystal clear glass in a nice, lightweight package, the reticle is concise, yet totally useable. Constructed in a German 3P configuration, the HSR-4 has thicker areas on the ends of the horizontal wires and no vertical wire above the center point. The lower wire has no thickening, but has graduated hash marks in 2 MOA increments. All the graduations are marked numerically, in 8 MOA increments. This type of reticle centers the eye very quickly, and in spite of the lack of conventional crosshairs, feels very natural. I appreciate the center crosshairs, as they are the finest of any in the reticle. For the target shooter who likes to focus on the smallest part of a paper target, this reticle is absolutely perfect. The Razor uses the traditional hunting turrets, at ¼ MOA per click. I'm quite OK with that, as the HSR-4 reticle is detailed enough to allow me to holdover without having to worry about dialing. Vortex has a great package here, offering plenty of magnification and a very useable reticle. Plus it's a concise profile that won't adversely affect the balance of your rifle.

Many of my other riflescopes use the duplex reticle. My Leupold VX-6 2-12x44 is as clear as any I've ever used, and while it has a plain but crisp duplex reticle, precise holdover can be an issue. I use this scope on my Winchester Model 70 Classic Stainless in .300 Winchester Magnum, which I keep zeroed at 250 yards. In spite of the fact that there is no real measuring system on the reticle (I don't really use this rifle for a target gun) it's one of my main hunting rifles. I can hold dead on to about 275 yards and, on most game animals I hunt, have a very good idea how to adjust the hold based on the size of the animal. Keep in mind, I'm not really comfortable with shots much past 400 yards at unwounded game, so there isn't a huge amount of thought needed, as it's a pretty flat shooter.

My Heym .404 Jeffery wears a Leupold Compact 2.5x fixed-power scope with a duplex reticle, and the adjustments in one-MOA visual increments (no clicks). Though it's only 2.5x, I've used this little optic to hit steel plates out to 275 yards. I am pretty comfortable using this rig on big game out to 250 yards, as I've spent a considerable amount of time with it. Point being that there are many different reticles available, and each and every one has a specific application.

The Dial-Up Method

Modern scopes, when mated with a good dope card or ballistic computer,

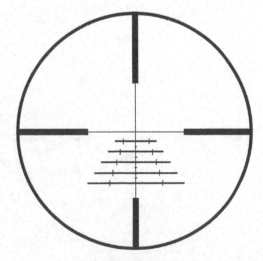

The Swarovski BRX reticle in the Z5 3.5-18x44.

can easily be used to hit targets at longer ranges by dialing-up a specific amount of elevation, and using the center crosshairs to precisely place the shot on the target. The process is relatively simple, though it may seem foreign at first. Zero your rifle at a prescribed distance—we'll use 100 yards for our example—and adjust the elevation turret for the proper hold for shots at any farther distance. The amount of adjustment necessary will need to be recorded; this is the dope card that so many shooters carry, and sometimes you'll even see it taped to the side of the rifle. I like to have the chart indicate the necessary holds at 50-yard increments so I can interpolate the curve for anything in between those reference points. The good folks at the FTW Ranch provide a common sense card that is well laid out and gives me the necessary information for both the dial-up method, as well as the ability to properly correlate my reticle to my trajectory curve if I decide to hold over instead of dial. You can set the elevation and windage turrets to read zero when you're properly sighted in, and no matter what adjustments you make during the course of your shooting session, you can always return your scope to that 100-yard zero. The same can be said for wind adjustments. If you want to dial your wind hold, a good, clearly marked turret will allow you to make adjustments and return to your no-wind zero.

Weaver and Swarovski now have a hybrid system, which I think will make a great compromise for hunters who appreciate the dial-up technique and the ability to always shoot the center crosshair, but don't want to carry charts or dope cards. It works in similar fashion to a bow sight, in that a series of color-coded markers are installed on the elevation turret, and once the distance to the target or animal is confirmed, the correlative color marker is dialed for the shot. It's a relatively simple, quick system; one I find works perfectly on a hunting rifle. Combined with a good rangefinder and some time at the target range to verify where your chosen load is hitting—preferably out to 400 yards—you can set one color for each 100-yard increment and interpolate for shots in between. Genius move!

There are even scopes with dial-up turrets designed for rimfire rifles. Bushnell's Rimfire Optics line includes a nice 3-9x40mm scope that comes with a pair of trajectory-compensated turrets. These best approximate the trajectory curve of the .22 Long Rifle and .17 Hornady Magnum Rimfire cartridges. The .22 Long Rifle turret is marked in yardage increments, from 75 yards—a popular zero setting for this cartridge—out to just about 175 yards. The turret dial is numerically marked in 25-yard increments, with interspersing hash marks

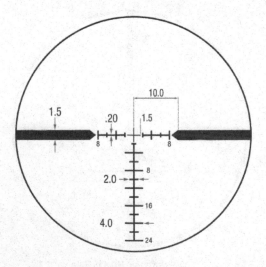

The Vortex HSR-4 reticle.

for precise shooting in between those distances. My pal Manny Vermilyea and I put this system to the test at our backyard range, and I'm happy to report that it worked as advertised. Our test rifle was a Savage Mark II BRJ, actually a very accurate bolt gun that belongs to my wife Suzie, and after setting zero at the prescribed 75 yards we engaged a series of plates, paper targets and other metallic doodads from 50 out to 200 yards. A laser rangefinder verified the distance, the Bushnell scope tracked perfectly, and all hits were well within the margin of accuracy that the ammunition provided. At 9x, this rig would definitely take squirrels and rabbits out to 100 yards, maybe more, making for a fun little rifle that will change the rules of small game hunting. You may have to make minor adjustments if you're shooting the hyper-velocity .22 LR ammo, but the calibration worked perfectly for the standard loads.

The .17 Hornady Magnum Rimfire turret takes advantage of the cartridge's higher velocity and flatter trajectory, giving you the opportunity to accurately dial up for ranges from 25 out to 275 yards. It's the same procedure as the .22 LR, as it maintains the same ¼ MOA shift per click value, but you'll easily see how the flatter trajectory requires much less adjustment for the faster cartridge as well as offering the capability to make hits at longer distances than will the .22 Long Rifle. Bushnell also provides a third turret, marked in ¼ MOA increments. That gives you a total 15 MOA of adjustment in one revolution for use of different cartridges, and to prepare your own dope chart.

This scope also comes with the all-important parallax adjustment knob, keeping distant targets perfectly focused. As a side note, this type of scope on a .22 Long Rifle makes for an excellent practice tool for sharpening your skills; there is no recoil and little report, and you can easily turn a 100-yard backyard range into a miniature long-range situation, strategically placing spinner targets or scaled-down plates at various ranges. Think mini-golf for shooters!

I opted for a rimfire scope with the BDC reticle for my own .22 Long Rifle, a Bushnell A22 scope with three mil-dots on the lower post. When my rifle is zeroed for 50 yards, the three lower dots give me aiming points for 75, 100 and 125 yards. While this system is not as refined as Suzie's, it sure makes hits past 50 yards much easier than guesstimating with a traditional duplex reticle. Bushnell also provides a turret with markings for 50, 75, 100 and 125 yards, if I were to choose to dial up but I don't use it often; actually, I installed it to check if it worked and haven't touched it since.

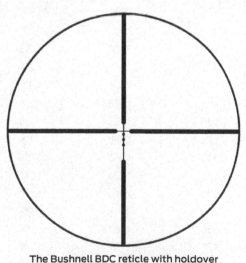

The Bushnell BDC reticle with holdover marks for 75, 100 and 125 yards.

I guess I'm just not a dialer. This scope is built with an adjustable objective lens, the adjustment ring being on the end of the scope so I can focus clearly on those gray squirrels way up in the oak trees.

Using a good ballistics calculator, many of which can be found on ammunition company websites, you can find the trajectory data for your given load in MOA, mils and inches. If you know the distance between the graduations on your reticle, you can easily correlate the values and establish where on the trajectory curve those graduations will cross. For example, using

Range (yds.)	Velocity (fps)	Energy (ft.-lb.)	Trajectory (in.)	ComeUp (MOA)
0	2,580	2,070	-1.75	0
25	2,545	2,015	-0.2893	-1.1052
50	2,511	1,961	0.8337	1.5923
75	2,477	1,908	1.6128	2.0536
100	2,443	1,857	2.0384	1.9467
125	2,410	1,806	2.1003	1.6046
150	2,376	1,756	1.7875	1.1381
175	2,343	1,707	1.0913	0.5955
200	2,310	1,660	0	0
225	2,277	1,613	-1.4988	-0.6362
250	2,245	1,567	-3.4157	-1.3048
275	2,212	1,522	-5.7625	-2.0012
300	2,180	1,478	-8.5537	-2.7229
325	2,148	1,435	-11.8016	-3.4678
350	2,116	1,392	-15.5195	-4.2346
375	2,084	1,351	-19.7216	-5.0224
400	2,052	1,310	-24.4248	-5.8314
425	2,021	1,270	-29.6425	-6.6609
450	1,990	1,231	-35.3907	-7.5107
475	1,958	1,193	-41.6884	-8.3816
500	1,927	1,155	-48.5516	-9.2734
525	1,896	1,118	-55.9986	-10.1864
550	1,865	1,081	-64.0494	-11.1213
575	1,834	1,046	-72.7245	-12.0786
600	1,802	1,010	-82.0449	-13.0589
625	1,771	975	-92.0322	-14.0626
650	1,740	941	-102.714	-15.0911
675	1,709	908	-114.111	-16.1446
700	1,677	875	-126.251	-17.2243

the Hornady 4DOF (4 Degrees of Freedom) Ballistics Calculator, I plugged the following data into the program.

Bullet: 140-grain Hornady ELD-Match, G1 BC of 0.610

Muzzle Velocity: 2,580 fps (low for this cartridge, but where the accuracy lies)

Zero Range: 200 Yards

Wind speed/angle: 10mph, 90 degrees

This is the information that 4DOF spit back at me:

Wind Drift (in.)	Wind Drift (MOA)	Spin Drift (in.)	Spin Drift (MOA)	TOF (sec.)
0	0	0	0	0
0.0348	0.1329	-0.0027	-0.0102	0.0293
0.1396	0.2666	-0.0108	-0.0206	0.0589
0.3158	0.4021	-0.0246	-0.0313	0.089
0.5649	0.5395	-0.0441	-0.0421	0.1195
0.8886	0.6789	-0.0696	-0.0532	0.1504
1.2887	0.8205	-0.1013	-0.0645	0.1817
1.7665	0.964	-0.1392	-0.076	0.2135
2.3239	1.1097	-0.1837	-0.0877	0.2458
2.9628	1.2575	-0.2347	-0.0996	0.2785
3.6849	1.4076	-0.2927	-0.1118	0.3116
4.4918	1.5599	-0.3577	-0.1242	0.3453
5.386	1.7145	-0.4299	-0.1369	0.3794
6.3697	1.8717	-0.5097	-0.1498	0.4141
7.445	2.0314	-0.5971	-0.1629	0.4493
8.6144	2.1938	-0.6924	-0.1763	0.485
9.8806	2.359	-0.7958	-0.19	0.5213
11.2458	2.527	-0.9076	-0.2039	0.5581
12.7126	2.6979	-1.0279	-0.2181	0.5955
14.284	2.8718	-1.1572	-0.2327	0.6335
15.9625	3.0488	-1.2956	-0.2475	0.6721
17.7517	3.2291	-1.4434	-0.2626	0.7113
19.6555	3.4129	-1.6008	-0.278	0.7512
21.678	3.6004	-1.7681	-0.2937	0.7918
23.8232	3.7919	-1.9455	-0.3097	0.833
26.0954	3.9874	-2.1333	-0.326	0.875
28.4996	4.1873	-2.3319	-0.3426	0.9177
31.0398	4.3916	-2.5414	-0.3596	0.9612
33.721	4.6005	-2.7623	-0.3769	1.0055

The Competition Electronics chronograph that met its untimely demise at the hands of a .505 Gibbs.

This is good information, providing you with anything you could want for accurate long-range shooting. The Swarovski riflescope I have on this rifle uses the BRX reticle, with lower gradua-tions in 1.8 MOA increments, so I'd need to interpolate to figure out where those graduations will strike along the trajectory curve, telling me where to hold in the field. Doing some math, I came up with much the same info as did the folks down at FTW, as described in chapter 8. You can do the same thing for your rifle/cartridge/scope reticle combination, using a ballistic calculator and some interpolation. The nice thing about these programs, and other means I'll describe here shortly, is that they give all the data necessary to compute trajectories for either holding over with a BDC reticle, or for dialing.

I know many hunters who prefer the dial-up technique, but I feel more comfortable using a BDC reticle; it goes to show that there is more than one way to skin a cat, and no matter which method you choose—so long as it allows you to become a more accurate shot—is fine.

Measuring Muzzle Velocity

An important factor in predicting trajectory curves and wind deflection values is the muzzle velocity of the projectile. Almost all of today's ammunition comes with the proposed muzzle velocity clearly marked on the box, but I've seen that value be off by a considerable amount, sometimes 100 fps or more. If you handload, muzzle speeds are listed in the reloading manual for each powder charge weight, but just like the factory ammunition those values can be af-fected by barrel length, construction and other factors. If you intend to play the long-range game and invest in proper bullets, optics and triggers, you absolutely need to know what the muzzle velocity of your load is in order to establish a valid trajectory curve. A chronograph is the tool you need for measuring muzzle velocity of any projectile, whether it be fired from handgun, rifle, muzzleloader or bow. Knowing how to use one will save you tons of ammunition and time. Modern chronographs utilize a series of sensors to measure the time of flight of the projectile as triggered by the shadow of the bullet passing over them. The chronograph needs at least two sensors to measure the time difference between the crossing, and establishing the velocity of the projectile.

Like all kinds of gear, there are worthy chronographs, and unworthy ones. I've had both, and a chronograph is like a riflescope: buy the best you can afford. I had a Competition Electronics ProChrono Digital machine that served me well for a number of years until one day when the muzzle blast of a .505 Gibbs kind of scrambled its brains. It was an accurate machine, but it didn't like muzzle brakes, which would cause inaccurate readings. One fateful day, when I put it out in front of the big elephant gun, well, that was the end. I tried a couple of similarly priced models, all having two screens, when I found what I consider to be the best balance of affordability, value and accuracy, the Holy Grail of chronographs: the Oehler Model 35P. This rig uses three sensors, three skyscreens and has long cables to connect the sensors to the readout unit so the electronics aren't exposed to the muzzle blast. The three-screen setup works like this: placed at 2-foot intervals, the sensors measure the time of bullet flight between sensors one and two and then again between sensors one and three, averaging the results. The 35P comes with an onboard printer, which is a nice way to keep records of your various loads' velocities, and to pay attention to your shooting instead of worrying about recording the velocities by hand.

The Oehler 35P chronograph.

Muzzle velocity most definitely needs to be ascertained for long-range shooting. Comparing the dope from the example given above, and changing muzzle velocity by exactly 100 fps from 2,580 to 2,680, you'll see that the long-range drop changes significantly.

Range (yds.)	Velocity (fps)	Energy (ft.-lb.)	Trajectory (in.)	ComeUp (MOA)
0	2,680	2,234	-1.75	0
25	2,645	2,175	-0.3822	-1.4601
50	2,609	2,118	0.6735	1.2863
75	2,575	2,061	1.4109	1.7966
100	2,540	2,007	1.8209	1.739
125	2,506	1,953	1.8938	1.4469
150	2,472	1,900	1.6214	1.0323
175	2,438	1,849	0.9934	0.5421
200	2,405	1,798	0	0
225	2,371	1,748	-1.3684	-0.5808
250	2,338	1,700	-3.1218	-1.1925
275	2,305	1,652	-5.2739	-1.8315
300	2,272	1,606	-7.8327	-2.4934
325	2,240	1,560	-10.8137	-3.1776
350	2,207	1,515	-14.2264	-3.8818
375	2,175	1,471	-18.0842	-4.6054
400	2,143	1,428	-22.4008	-5.3482
425	2,111	1,386	-27.1904	-6.1098
450	2,079	1,344	-32.4671	-6.8902
475	2,048	1,304	-38.2454	-7.6893
500	2,016	1,264	-44.5402	-8.5072
525	1,985	1,225	-51.3712	-9.3447
550	1,953	1,187	-58.7512	-10.2014
575	1,922	1,149	-66.7006	-11.0781
600	1,891	1,112	-75.2375	-11.9753
625	1,860	1,076	-84.3807	-12.8934
650	1,829	1,040	-94.1508	-13.833
675	1,797	1,005	-104.57	-14.7948
700	1,766	970	-115.662	-15.7796

At the 700-yard mark, the drop is off by 10 inches, enough to cause all sorts of issues. While the hunting dope doesn't radically change things inside 400 yards, considering the size of a big game animal's vital area I can see where the long-range crowd would be highly concerned about having an accurate muzzle velocity. Find a chronograph within your budget, and make it your friend.

One last piece of advice: always be cognizant of the placement of your chronograph. I've see them blown to bits by shooters who forgot their scope is placed 1.75 inches above the bore line, and I've seen units totally smashed by the plastic sabots of muzzleloading rifles. Many times the skyscreens and their metal support rods can be replaced easily enough, but if your chronograph has internal electronics, it may be headed for the recycle bin if it takes a direct hit.

Wind Drift (in.)	Wind Drift (MOA)	Spin Drift (in.)	Spin Drift (MOA)	TOF (sec.)
0	0	0	0	0
0.0332	0.1267	-0.0025	-0.0096	0.0282
0.1327	0.2535	-0.0101	-0.0193	0.0567
0.3	0.382	-0.023	-0.0292	0.0857
0.5363	0.5121	-0.0413	-0.0394	0.115
0.843	0.6441	-0.0652	-0.0498	0.1447
1.2213	0.7776	-0.095	-0.0605	0.1748
1.6729	0.9129	-0.1308	-0.0714	0.2054
2.1994	1.0502	-0.1727	-0.0825	0.2364
2.8022	1.1894	-0.221	-0.0938	0.2678
3.4831	1.3305	-0.2757	-0.1053	0.2996
4.2441	1.4739	-0.3371	-0.1171	0.332
5.0865	1.6192	-0.4054	-0.1291	0.3647
6.0127	1.7668	-0.4808	-0.1413	0.398
7.0241	1.9166	-0.5635	-0.1538	0.4317
8.1228	2.0686	-0.6537	-0.1665	0.4659
9.3114	2.2231	-0.7516	-0.1794	0.5007
10.5922	2.3801	-0.8574	-0.1927	0.5359
11.9675	2.5398	-0.9713	-0.2061	0.5717
13.4397	2.7021	-1.0937	-0.2199	0.6081
15.0112	2.8671	-1.2246	-0.2339	0.645
16.6853	3.0351	-1.3645	-0.2482	0.6825
18.4638	3.206	-1.5135	-0.2628	0.7206
20.3502	3.3799	-1.672	-0.2777	0.7593
22.3479	3.557	-1.8401	-0.2929	0.7986
24.4608	3.7376	-2.0182	-0.3084	0.8386
26.693	3.9218	-2.2065	-0.3242	0.8793
29.0486	4.1098	-2.4052	-0.3403	0.9206
31.5323	4.3019	-2.6147	-0.3567	0.9627

Rangefinders, Weather Stations and Handheld Ballistic Devices

As a shooter, I like all the gadgets and gizmos associated with it, but I always do my best to make sure I can still make things work when the batteries die, if you will. Dope charts, memorization, preparation; I try to keep things as free from an electronic error as possible. I do carry a rangefinder, as it's become a huge aid in establishing the proper hold for the specific range, rather than trying to guess. However, as we learned in the density altitude section (chapter 11), the surrounding weather conditions can also affect your bullet's flight path, so if you can develop an adjusted dope chart for changing environments, it'd be a no-brainer to include a device that will do just that in your hunting pack. If I had to limit my electronics to just two pieces, they'd be a good laser rangefinder capable of measuring out to 1,000 yards and a quality ballistic device. I've used different models, but have settled on a pair that sealed the deal for me. First, the rangefinders.

Rangefinders

Knowing the distance to your target is imperative. Just a quick glance at the chart shown for my 6.5-284 Norma will show you that the drop between 400 and 450 yards is over 11 inches. That's more than enough to cause a missed plate or shoot underneath a game animal, not to mention a missed wind deflection hold. I've told you before that I am a licensed land surveyor, and measuring distances is what we do in the field. My Dad and I are partners, and play the same how-far-do-you-think-that-is game every day, and then we measure the distance with a Geodetic Total Station, down to 1/16 of an inch. 30 years of playing this game has proved to me that I can routinely be wrong by at least 50 yards, especially when distances become greater than 300 yards. Since beyond that range is where knowing the distance really becomes crucial, visual range estimation amounts to just a guess, at best.

Using a laser rangefinder is a great method of getting closer to the truth. Yes, in a perfect world, there would be no obstructions between you and your game animal, and that animal would pose statue still as if being photographed for the cover shot of a magazine. However, I'm sure you understand that this isn't always the case, and that you may need to range a tree nearby the animal, or a mound in front of or behind said animal. Owning a laser rangefinder that works well in a number of different light and vegetation conditions makes a whole lot of sense. I like the Bushnell rangefinders; we've used them on the job for decades to measure streams, hedgerows and other features that don't require a ridiculous level of surveying precision and they've been rock solid. We test them often for dependability as well as for fun, measuring distances in comparison to our survey transit, and they've been very accurate. The older models were simple, just offering the measured distance between the unit and the target, irrespective of slope angle.

The Bushnell 1 Mile ConX rangefinder, which conveniently interfaces with the Kestrel Elite computer/weather station. The Kestrel Elite will greatly aid the shooter in projecting trajectory and wind drift.

They have come an awful long way since those days, with many useful features that will aid in making the shot. I have a Bushnell Elite 1Mile ARC ConX, which is much more than just a measuring device. This tool establishes slope and level distances—both useful for establishing wind calls and trajectory drop, respectively—out to one mile. It will interface with a Kestrel Elite ballistic computer (we'll discuss that awesome tool below), relaying the information observed to the ballistic computer, and then receiving data from the computer and displaying it within the rangefinder. Pretty sweet deal, especially for the solo hunter or the target shooter who doesn't have a spotter. I've checked the accuracy of this unit for both measurement of distance and slope angle against a surveying instrument, and it's surprisingly good, holding measurements of distance to within a yard, and angle to within a degree. It's not the most affordable model on the market, but if that sheep of a lifetime is 400-and-something yards up the steep scree slope, the cost of the unit is well worth knowing the exact distance. It features 7x magnification and even works well in the rain, which is where some other rangefinders have failed me. There are similar models that don't have Bluetooth connectivity that are a bit more affordable, but use the same measuring systems for those who don't wish to use the Kestrel computer.

Anemometers and Ballistic Computers

The Kestrel Elite 5700 Weather Meter with Applied Ballistics is a godsend to the long-range shooter, global hunter or serious competitive shooter. It is, at the same time, an Anemometer or, weather meter—giving complete weather data at your location—with a built-in ballistics computer. The Kestrel Elite utilizes the highly powerful Applied Ballistics software, developed by Bryan Litz, an Aerospace Engineer who is perhaps one of the greatest living ballisticians and a man for whom I have great respect. Litz now heads up research for Berger Bullets, as well as Applied Ballistic Munitions, the factory-loaded ammunition featuring Berger projectiles. Using a Kestrel Elite is relatively simple. With the information provided in this book, the possible parameters needed for input into the Kestrel, you can build a trajectory curve for your particular firearm and have it adjust for a change in location and elevation. Spin drift, Coriolis, trajectory, even wind deflection can be calculated quickly and accurately. It has several popular long-range cartridges and their parameters pre-loaded, plus the capability of loading the parameters of your chosen bullet, in both G1 and G7 drag models.

This handheld wonder can even compute custom drag curves for bullets that have a sketchy BC value, ones needing to be redefined with a curve that works. The power of this unit needs to be seen in order to be truly appreciated. I've used it for days on end in the field, shooting at targets from 100 to 1,400 yards in changing weather conditions. The FTW Ranch in Texas has a variety of terrain, and the weather can change from cool in the mornings to blazing hot and windy by late afternoon. The Kestrel adjusted the trajectory curve for my rifle, based on the changing weather conditions, as well as being a huge aid in making wind calls. You see, the weather station side of the device observes magnetic bearing (necessary for adjusting the Coriolis Effect), wind speed, temperature, chill factor, humidity, heat index, dew point, a wet bulb reading, barometric pressure, altitude and density altitude. Wind direction is also measured to correlate the amount of the wind value that should be taken in comparison to the direction of the target. You can include a couple of baseline wind values for comparison to the actual wind speeds observed along the bullet's flight path.

You can build your rifle, or several rifles, or several loads, which will be stored in the unit. The whole shebang runs on a single AA battery, securely housed in its own compartment so that the electronics are safe should a battery leak. There is a battery meter displayed when the unit is powered up that keeps an eye on power levels during the course of a hunt. The Kestrel allows you to input data in metric or English units and has the choice of several different output units, such as true MOA or shooter MOA (rounded off a bit), clicks or mils. It isn't hard to modify the trajectory curve to match the observed field data. You can calibrate the muzzle velocity of your rifle by feeding the device the observed amount of drop in inches, true MOA, or mils at a certain distance, so that the drag curve may be adjusted properly. This process is generally known as truing a rifle, and the further away from the muzzle you can observe repeatable data, the more accurate your results will be.

Keeping this idea in mind, we put the Kestrel to the test at the FTW. Dave Fulson of Safari Classics Productions and I were spotting for Nate Lee, a talented young shooter who knew his 6.5 Creedmoor very well. We had observed the muzzle velocity of the Hornady Match ammo Lee was using, and the FTW staff had plugged all the parameters into their ballistic computer program to develop a dope card for him. However, getting out to 900 yards or so, we noticed that the drop figure (in minutes) was off. An extra 1.25 minutes was needed to center-punch the plate. Instructor Doug 'Dog' Pritchard and I simply built the rifle profile in the Kestrel Elite and fed it the revised hold at 900 yards. The electronic wonder adjusted the trajectory on the fly for the new data and revised the curve. Lee rang the 1,400-yard steel plates without much trouble at all.

Where I can see that the Kestrel will truly show its worth is in the hands of the traveling sportsman. Atmospheric conditions are much different when hunting elk at 9,000 feet in Wyoming than they are hunting deer on the shores of the Hudson River at 50 feet above mean sea level. Likewise, things change when hunting in the hot, dry conditions of South Africa in comparison to the wet, cold forests of New Hampshire. A device like the Kestrel Elite adjusts for these changes in elevation and atmospheric condition, keeping you informed of the changes in your rifle's performance. It may just help you bag the trophy of a lifetime. My Elite has the LiNK feature, which allows it to Bluetooth connect with my Bushnell ConX rangefinder. That way, the unit can stay by my side, feeding the holdover data directly into the display of the rangefinder. Simply click the rangefinder and you'll see the hold in the units of your choosing. This combination makes for a slick setup in the field, whether you want to ring steel or hit that prairie dog out there at 400 yards.

Essentially, if you have the means of accurately measuring bullet length, twist rate and muzzle velocity, you can arrive at all of the data I've explained in equation form by using the Kestrel Elite, and you can do it on the go in any condition at any feasible range. Hell, for those who really want to take shots at extreme ranges, the Kestrel even has the ability to create a custom trajectory curve for a bullet once it goes into the trans-sonic and subsonic phases, where things can get truly weird.

Online Ballistic Calculators

The Kestrel Elite is a wonderful tool and well worth the financial investment, but I know there have been times in my life where the budget simply would not allow for a purchase of this magnitude—the wife would've skinned me alive. So, you can adapt and overcome by preparing your own dope cards and charts based upon some of the excellent ballistic calculators available for free online. I've mentioned the Berger Twist Rate Calculator, to make sure your bullet is stable in flight, and I've demonstrated how the Hornady 4 Degrees of Freedom program can give you some really good data, but they're not the only ones. Federal and Winchester have their own programs, too. In addition to the bullet and ammunition companies, the optics companies offer excellent programs as well. I like the Vortex site, as it allows you to save your load profiles.

In my opinion, the more data you are allowed to input, the better the data coming back out will be. Hornady's 4 Degrees of Freedom uses the drag coefficient for a particular bullet, rather than the G1 or G7 model comparisons, and that may result in some different data. I've found it to be rather accurate, especially when using the Hornady bullets available in the program, or the other popular long-range projectiles involved in this new offering.

The Federal program has settings for all of their factory ammo, but with the ability to change the curve based upon your observed muzzle velocity. This a great feature if you're shooting factory ammo but want better dope than what is available from a generalized muzzle velocity. Simply run your Federal ammunition through a chronograph, and apply the revised muzzle velocity to generate a customized dope chart for your gun.

If you have a smartphone, there are quite a few ballistic apps available for download, at a minimal cost, if not free. Winchester has their ballistic calculator as a free app for the iPhone and iPad, and the Strelok calculator is an affordable option for a smartphone. Here's a list of some cool sites and apps, by no means complete. A quick Internet search will yield a whole bunch from which to choose, but these are the ones I've used over time.

hornady.com/ballistics-resource/4dof

bergerbullets.com/ballistics/

federalpremium.com/ballistics_calculator/

apps.vortexoptics.com/lrbc/

appszoom.com/android_applications/tools/shooter_fqyd.html

play.google.com/store/apps/details?id=com.borisov.strelok&hl=en

winchester.com/learning-center/ballistics-calculator/Pages/ballistics-calculator-iphone.aspx

Triggers

Without giving a dissertation on gunsmithing, I can tell you that a great rifle can easily be ruined by having a lousy trigger. I am not a light trigger freak. But a trigger that breaks at over 5 pounds can be a severe hindrance to accuracy. I like a trigger to break cleanly, with as little creep and overtravel as possible, so that I can place my shots in a consistent manner. I've had some rifles (that later turned out to be gems) that wouldn't shoot well at all out of the box, due to

A Timney replacement trigger about to improve a Ruger tang safety in the Model 77.

heavy trigger pull. Some of the Ruger Model 77 Mk II rifles of the late 90s had terrible, non-adjustable triggers, and I nearly gave up on one such rifle until I switched out the factory trigger for a Timney. What a world of difference that made! My .22-250 went from punching groups of 1 ¼ inches to printing 3/8-inch groups, without touching the load. I don't mean to sound like I'm beating up on those Ruger rifles—the newer Hawkeye models have a trigger that is a vast improvement—but I've used a trigger scale to measure the pull weight on several of those older models, and some are approaching 10 pounds and even more. That, to me, is unacceptable for any rifle that is expected to deliver accurate results. I have a couple Legendary Arms Works rifles, and that company was wise enough to use Timney triggers right out of the factory. They are an absolute pleasure to shoot.

Timney isn't the only replacement trigger out there—Jewell, Wilson Combat, Geisselle—there are many, and sometimes a replacement will give a rifle a new lease on life. Though many triggers can be installed with simple tools, I recommend having a replacement trigger installed by a competent gunsmith to avoid any potential safety issues such as accidental discharges. Your rifle may have an adjustable trigger right out of the factory—the Savage AccuTrigger comes quickly to mind—and you can find good instructional information on the respective manufacturer's websites regarding safe adjustment of trigger pull. If, however, you have any doubts, it is definitely worth the money to have your gunsmith do the work and avoid trouble.

Scope Rings and Bases

Scope rings and bases are just a simple means of attaching your riflescope to the rifle, but I've seen misaligned and improperly installed ones cause all sorts of accuracy issues. For long-range shooting there are bases and rings that provide additional elevation to the riflescope, extending the range of adjustment necessary for those long shots.

You need a rock-solid setup when mounting your scope, so that there is no movement whatsoever, and so that you have as much contact as possible between the scope and the rings so your scope can go to sleep. I've used a bunch of different brands, and there are plenty of good ones from which to choose. These days, I'm a huge fan of Talley rings, as they are manufactured to very tight tolerances. The design uses the least amount of moving parts. I use the Talley removable rings on my dangerous game rifles, as they can be screwed on and off the rifle. That allows me to use the iron sights on the follow-up of a wounded animal and the scope can then be reinstalled without a zero shift. I also use the standard Talleys on many of my hunting rifles; my Savage 6.5-284 Norma wears them, as does Suzie's Legendary Arms Works .375 H&H Magnum.

I like the Leupold rings and bases, but prefer the dual dovetail to the older-style system that uses two screws to hold the rear ring in place. Too many times I've had that come loose on a hunt; by contrast, Leupold's dual dovetail system keeps things right where I put them. My Winchester 70 Classic Stainless in .300 Winchester Magnum has the dual dovetail rings and bases, and the Leupold VX-6 2-12x44 has never moved or lost zero, despite some tough hunts in punishing terrain. I also like Leupold's Quick Release system, which uses a post to attach the rings to the bases, kept in place via a hemispherical cutout in the post, and a locking lever that rolls a matching piece into that cutout. My Winchester Model 70 Safari Express in .416 Remington Magnum is equipped with this system, and for years I carried two scopes, pre-zeroed in rings, on safari with me. Should something happen to my primary scope, I could easily remove it and install the backup in the field so the hunt could continue.

If you are going for distance, you may run out of scope adjustment for those truly long shots. Or you may discover that a scope may not give true adjustments when at the extreme limits of its adjustment range. There are means of correcting the issue to make your life a bit easier. A 20 MOA base provides you additional elevation range, as it is tapered to rise toward the rear of the rifle, allowing you to take better advantage of the elevation adjustment of your scope. Warne makes a great 20 MOA base, and there are others; just realize that installing one of these will raise your point of impact by 20 inches at 100 yards, so you may want to make sure your reticle has the option to hold under, using hash marks on the upper post of the vertical hair, or that the adjustment range of your scope will allow you to dial down that far.

Burris came up with a cool design to solve the problem—their XTR Signature Rings. These use a concentric insert to properly align the scope, resolving some issues with bases that mount slightly off-center, but also are available in 5, 10 and 20 MOA adjustments. Using them there's no need for a tapered base, and the inserts allow you to achieve combinations of up to 40 MOA of adjustment. Pretty slick idea.

Spotting Scopes

If you're serious about long-range shooting, a spotting scope can become your new best friend. Seeing distant targets is a necessity, and calling shots for a buddy can be almost as much fun as pulling the trigger. Owning a good spotting scope can make your life easier, not to mention saving your legs.

You need to measure the wind, especially at the longer ranges, and while a high-magnification riflescope is an excellent aid, a spotting scope can quickly become an invaluable tool. Seeing mirage is a definite benefit, and the quick adjustments of a spotting scope can help you focus in front of and behind the target in order to make the mirage more visible. As with any optics in the shooting world, the better models are usually pricier, but then again, you get what you pay for. I've used several good models from Swarovski, Leupold, Meopta and Bushnell.

I prefer a model with the straight-on rear lens assembly, as opposed to the offset style. I find them easier to aim at the target. I also like a quick-locking mechanism to keep the scope where I want it pointed, and a good, strong tripod, preferably height-adjustable for those times I'm shooting alone.

The 6.8 Western is an excellent all-around cartridge, but it is especially suited for long-range shooting, so it greatly benefits from Leupold's CDS scope turret.

Leupold's CDS: Gamechanger for Long-Range Work

Adjusting for trajectory is as old as shooting itself. Like the archer's bow, the rifleman needs to raise or lower the rifle's barrel to compensate for the effects of gravity at various distances. Adjustment methods have been varied and numerous throughout time, including good ol' guesstimation, elevated iron sights (some radical, like the Mauser 98 'rollercoaster' sight, calibrated to 2,000 meters), riflescope reticles with compensated holdover markings on the crosshairs and external adjustment turrets of riflescopes.

The latter is far and away the most accurate, for once you determined the amount of drop at a given distance, you converted that elevation adjustment to some portion of an arc, whether measured in minutes of angle (MOA) or milliradians (MIL). You often prepared a chart correlating the distance from the target to the angle adjustment needed to compensate for the bullet's drop. In the more modern era, a ballistic calculator—the Kestrel unit with the Applied Ballistics software is popular—handles the mathematics for trajectory compensation: You range the target, consult the chart, dial the necessary adjustment on the turret and engage the target.

Leupold has an even faster solution and 'skipped the middle man' with its CDS (Compensated Dial System). In my opinion, it's an ingenious idea whose time has come. The concept is simple: You provide Leupold with critical data on your chosen load. Leupold cuts an elevation dial (marked in yardage instead of increments of angle), giving you instant trajectory compensation.

For example, I have a particular load built around a 200-grain Nosler AccuBond for a .300 Holland & Holland Magnum that the rifle likes, which I can use as an all-around choice. I give Leupold the needed information, including the cartridge, bullet weight and type, ballistic coefficient, muzzle velocity, scope height, zero distance, and the average temperature and altitude. Leupold then provides a dial marked in yardage for that load. If I had a bull elk at 375 yards, I dial that number on the turret, and I've got a dead hold for elevation. The turret saves a huge step in the equation, as you obtain the distance to the target via rangefinder, dial the distance and hold directly on the target, making only adjustments for wind deflection.

Long-range shots become much easier when dialing the elevation with a custom yardage-marked turret for your specific load and holding dead on.

For the casual target shooter, this system might not have as strong an appeal as it will for those who regularly participate in the numerous shooting competitions where both time and accuracy are paramount or for the hunter, for whom quick and accurate adjustments can mean the difference between a long, happy pack out and tag soup. I love this system on a hunting rifle and use it frequently on my Browning X-Bolt in 6.8 Western, a cartridge capable of making accurate hits as far as I can hold steady.

Compared to a compensated reticle, the Leupold CDS works at any magnification level, requiring little more than a duplex reticle—you may want hashmarks for wind correction—keeping the image in the scope as uncluttered as possible, and I'm all for that.

The Leupold CDS turret has demystified the art of adjusting for trajectory, and I've used it on several hunts and shoots and have never been happier when taking shots at longer ranges. Leupold offers one free turret with each of its riflescopes set up for the system (it's not available on all Leupold scopes; consult the website or call customer service), and should you want to use multiple loads for the same rifle, you can order extra turrets. The Leupold CDS is the most innovative aiming aid in years and can make long-range shooting much more fun.

leupold.com or 1-800-LEUPOLD

Leupold offers a free custom CDS dial for any of its scopes designed for this system. The user sends in the necessary data, and Leupold returns a customized turret for your load. Then, you can get right to work.

CHAPTER 18

Choosing a Cartridge

All the ballistic knowledge in the world won't help if you don't choose a cartridge that will deliver what you're after. And with all the new cartridge developments in recent decades, things can get downright confusing. Depending on your hunting or shooting style and location, your choice of cartridge can vary quite a bit. While there are many universal choices, you need not try to make a silk purse out of a sow's ear if you don't have to.

As both a writer and a handloader, I get many calls and emails regarding the choice of cartridge, and whether some truly deliver what the advertising promises. I'll address all kinds of centerfires, from rimfire rifles to small, medium and big game calibers, to hunting and defensive handguns. All have a purpose, but it's ultimately up to you to decide what your needs and expectations are, and make the choice that best suits you.

To briefly illustrate, let's say you're a hunter who sticks close to home, and like so many of us pursues game in the deer/hog/coyote class. Would you be best served by a .338 Winchester Magnum? Probably not. While that cartridge will undoubtedly take all of those animals with power to spare, that level of recoil is not justifiable for those hunting needs.

Conversely, if you own a good .270 Winchester, one that has served you well for decades, does that make a sound choice for an Alaskan grizzly bear hunt? Again, probably not, as the grizzly may require a bit more bullet weight and horsepower to end the argument. Yes, it's been done before, but the cost of traveling to hunt, in addition to the difficulty of obtaining tags, ought to suggest trying a bigger, more authoritative cartridge.

Do you need a new rifle for an African plains game safari? That'll depend on what you're currently shooting. Does your .25-06 Remington make a good elk gun? Well, while I do know folks who, with very careful bullet placement and the patience to wait for the perfect shot opportunity, do use the .25-06 and similar cartridges for elk, I personally feel there are better choices, especially for those who may only have a seven-day hunt. If you're planning an elk hunt, I firmly believe that a bigger bore with a bullet heavier than those available in .25 caliber would better outfit you for that big bull elk.

While I'll also touch on the pros and cons of defensive handgun calibers, I'm sure that my arguments won't settle the 9mm Luger vs. .45 ACP debate, but I will shed as much light on the topic as I can.

Let's start with the rimfire rifles.

Rimfire Cartridges

So many of us learned how to shoot with a good ol' .22 Long Rifle that it's very difficult to count this old-timer out. It's relatively inexpensive (when available at all!) and so mild in both report and recoil that it remains a solid choice for small game, garden pests and the smaller furbearers. The smaller .22 rimfires—the .22 Short and .22 Long—seem to be fading into obscurity, though in our circle of friends we still have a couple of cool rifles chambered for them.

But what about the other rimfire cartridges? Where do the .17 Mach II, .17 HMR, .22 WMR and .17 WSM fall into the mix, and does their performance warrant the purchase of a new firearm? I had the opportunity to put many of these rimfire cartridges through the ringer on a South Dakota prairie dog hunt. It was with the folks from Vista Outdoors, a huge company that had under its roof at the time Federal Premium ammunition, American Eagle ammunition, CCI ammunition, Savage rifles and Bushnell Optics and more, so we weren't lacking for options. Friend and colleague J.J. Reich had brought a slew of different rifles, many of them in varying rimfire calibers. We had no shortage of targets, either, as we were situated on some of the biggest prairie dog towns I've ever had the privilege to hunt. There were dogs at 50 yards, and dogs at 450 yards, and dogs everywhere in between. The .22 LR handled the close range work as you'd expect, and I even got to stretch it out to 200 yards and beyond. Shots from 200 to 250 yards were not easy in the prairie wind, and I missed more than I hit. While a .22 LR is great for squirrel hunting in the hardwoods, and for woodchucks in the garden, it didn't exactly make the optimum prairie dog rifle.

The .22 Magnum—with its increased velocity—resisted wind drift a bit more, and flattened out the trajectory, but the blunt nose bullets we had weren't exactly fantastic, either. Now, in all of my experiences with the .22 Magnum, it gave an obvious advantage over the .22 LR with respect to velocity, wind deflection and striking power. But it wasn't a show-stopper in the South Dakota winds. I do like it for hunting coyote and fox here in New York, especially in the woods where the shots are relatively close, say within 100 paces, and where the wind isn't a huge factor. The .22 Mag will definitely ruin a woodchuck's day as well, but it pales in comparison to any of the .22 centerfires, even the Hornet. If you don't like the report and additional costs of the centerfire small bores, there's absolutely nothing wrong with owning a good .22 WMR; just make sure you practice diligently with it so you'll know exactly what the drop will be on the distant shots. Personally, I really like the CCI V-Max load, which uses a 30-grain polymer-tipped bullet at a muzzle velocity of 2,200 fps; this has proven to be very accurate in several different

The .17 Hornet will work perfectly for distant prairie dogs and coyotes alike.

rifles, accounting for many crop-raiding woodchucks and egg-thieving raccoons.

Back to the prairie and how I made friends with the .17 caliber rimfires. We had the two larger .17s on hand: the .17 Hornady Magnum Rimfire, and the .17 Winchester Super Magnum. I liked both of them, but for different applications. The .17 HMR is the .22 Magnum case necked down to hold .172 bullets, pushing a 17-grainer to 2,550 fps. It's an accurate little cartridge, perfect for minimizing pelt damage on a furbearer, yet having enough energy to create the red mist on a prairie dog. The .17 WSM is a whole different ball of wax. Based on a .27-caliber nail gun blank, Winchester set out to develop the fastest rimfire cartridge ever developed, and succeeded. The .17 WSM will drive a 20-grain .17-caliber bullet to a muzzle velocity of 3,000 fps, and this combination works out very well. I used the WSM to take dogs out to 325 yards, even in gusting winds. Just like the fast centerfires, at 3,000 fps the WSM barrel can heat up quickly, especially in a rapid-fire scenario so typical of a prairie dog hunt. However, if you're looking for a hot-rodded rimfire, this is your baby.

I've spent a bit of time with the .17 Mach II, which is the .22 LR Stinger case though just a bit longer than a standard .22 LR case necked down to .172 caliber. It's the slowest of the .17 rimfires, driving a 17-grain bullet to a muzzle velocity of 2,100 fps, just a bit ahead of the .22 Magnum, but with less than half the bullet weight. It does offer an advantage over the .22 LR in that the trajectories are flatter. But the light bullet combined with the slower muzzle velocity falls prey to wind drift. Some shooters love the Mach II, but I personally feel the HMR is a better choice, with its 450 fps velocity gain. None of these rimfire cartridges have enough recoil to bother any shooter, of any stature.

Taking all this into consideration, which of the rimfires suits your needs? I feel every shooter needs a .22 Long Rifle, as they are simply too useful and too much fun to overlook. But if you're looking for a bit more range, then I'd recommend one of the faster .17s, and I'll confess to being enamored with the .17 WSM. Its field performance isn't all that far behind the .17 Hornet (another really cool cartridge), and if you like the rimfire game, you can take this cartridge out farther than any other. I'd like to pair my Ruger 77/22 in .22 LR with a good Savage B-Mag in .17 WSM, to cover all aspects of the rimfire spectrum.

Small-Bore Centerfires

Centerfire cartridges between .17 caliber and the .25s could be defined as small bore centerfires. These cartridges fall into two categories: the varmint/small deer class, and the small bore target rifles. Actually, we should split the varmint and antelope/small deer cartridges in two, for three categories. If you're a varmint or predator hunter, there's plenty here for you; you'll see most serious varminters with a rifle in this class. If you prefer to own a rifle that will do double-duty on deer and predators, there are many solid choices within this group, cartridges that can easily wear two hats. And for the target crowd, this group contains some of the most accurate cartridges ever invented.

First, the varmint cartridges. If you want to snipe varmints at distances measured in football fields, you'll need some velocity in addition to a frangible bullet. While some of the classic, lower velocity cartridges like the .22 Hornet and .218 Bee are still a ton of fun to shoot, the newer, faster designs make for some serious "reach-out-and-touch-'em." Cartridges like the .17 Remington, .204 Ruger, .22-250 Remington and the .220 Swift all launch a bullet over 3,500 fps without much trouble and make great choices for a varmint rig. Although, referring back to the ideas discussed in the chapters about wind deflection and twist rate, the .22-250 and the Swift have their shortcomings in a traditional barrel. A good .223 Remington still makes a sound choice as a varmint/predator rifle and can, in most instances, handle the longer, heavier bullets that give the advantage in the wind. If you're looking for something out of the ordinary, a .17 Hornet is a really cool varmint cartridge, pushing a polymer-tipped 20-grain bullet at 3,000 fps. I've used this combination to absolutely smoke some prairie dogs and woodchucks. It's as accurate as it is hard-hitting.

The .243 Winchester makes a good choice if you want a rifle for more than one purpose, as it will work well as a deer cartridge, but it's a great varmint cartridge, too. Loaded with lighter bullets, like the Nosler Ballistic Tip 55-grain or a frangible Speer hollowpoint, it makes a great 'chuck gun, and with some medium weights—like a 75- or 80-grain pill—will absolutely hammer coyotes and foxes. The same can be said for the 6mm Remington and the .243 WSSM: they're fast, accurate and versatile.

Jumping up to the .25 bores, you'll find that the bullet weights increase, as does recoil. For a long session over a prairie dog town, this much gun may not be the best choice, as even the .250-3000 Savage can wear on you after a long day, let alone a good hammering from the .25-06 Remington or the mighty .257 Weatherby Magnum. If you have a good quarter-bore and you wish to pursue coyotes or other furbearers where the shooting isn't as hot and heavy (as it would be over a dog town or a woodchuck field) there's nothing wrong with using it, but I don't know too many varminters who choose cartridges larger than 6mm for long duration shooting sessions.

So what's the thought process? If you'd like to have a dedicated varmint/predator rifle—if you're serious about the little critters—I'd recommend something between the .204 Ruger and the .22-250 Remington, depending on your location and quarry. Faster cartridges make longer shots easier, but will heat up a barrel during all-day shoots and lead to throat erosion. Bullet weight isn't necessarily a huge consideration for the terminal phase of things, as animals in this class tend to be smaller and thin-skinned, but considering the wind conditions and distances, the heavier bullets (with higher BC values) will make it easier to connect in difficult conditions. My own favorite rifle for this work is a Ruger Model 77 MkII in .22-250 Remington. It sports a Hogue Overmolded stock, and is topped with a Leupold Vari-X III 6.5-20x44mm scope. Although it has the 1:12 twist rate—limiting the rifle to 55-grain bullets or lighter—I can take coyotes out to 400 yards, and my handloaded ammunition maintains sub-MOA accuracy out to those distances. My buddy Donnie Thorne swears by his Remington 700 in .17 Remington, and though the bullets generally weigh between 20 and 30 grains, they are moving at over 4,000 fps. I've seen him absolutely flatten coyotes, even the big-bodied males we have here in the Northeast. Assess your hunting situation, as well as your intended use, and you'll come up with what's right for you.

Switching gears to the cartridges that you'll want to serve as deer/antelope medicine—in addition to performing adequately on the furbearers—you'll want to look at the 6mm cartridges and larger, as they have enough throw weight to handle larger game. This is where cartridges like the .243 Winchester, 6mm Remington, .25-06 Remington, .257 Roberts and .257 Weatherby Magnum truly shine. They are light enough in the recoil department (when compared to the .300 Magnums) yet heavy enough to effectively handle whitetails, pronghorn antelope, or the light African plains game species. Looking back to the wind deflection values, you'll see that they aren't quite as effective as their larger siblings, but still can get the job done in the field, especially within responsible hunting ranges. As I've said, they can be loaded with light-for-caliber bullets for use on varmints and predators, but earn their keep in the lighter big game department, too.

I don't like using .22 centerfires for deer or antelope, as they are a bit light in the bullet weight department, unless you're using one of the heavy-for-caliber premium bullets, and by that I mean something over 60 or 65 grains, and even those need to be very carefully placed. I know, many disagree with that statement, but I've seen deer lost—even the small-bodied ones in Texas—following a good shot from light .22-caliber bullets that either broke up prematurely or simply failed to penetrate. I much prefer the .243 Winchester as a minimum for deer; it hits with much more authority and is more forgiving on a marginal shot.

For target shooters, there are some cartridges in .22 and 6mm that have shattered records. Lou Palmisano's 6mm PPC and .22 PPC, based on the obscure .220 Russian cartridge, produce "one ragged hole" groups, as does the 6mmBR Remington and 6mmBR Norma. These short, fat cartridges don't have a whole ton of recoil, but are ridiculously accurate. Matter of fact, the 6mm PPC cartridge was recently used by Jim Carmichael to break the record group size for Light Varmint category in Benchrest competition. If I was after a serious small bore target rifle, I'd look to one of these four cartridges.

In addition, the .223 Remington (as well as the 5.56mm NATO), .222 Remington and the .22-250 Remington make excellent target cartridges. While designed for other purposes (namely hunting or military use), they can and will deliver superb accuracy in a well-tuned rifle using match-grade ammunition.

Medium-Bore Centerfires

Medium bore centerfire cartridges are the most common group, being used for most of our popular big game hunting. Even on an African safari, you'll probably end up spending more time with a medium rifle in your hand than your big bore, unless you're on a dedicated hunt for elephant or buffalo. Here I include cartridges ranging from 6.5mm to .358-inch diameter. When things get larger than that you're into the big bores, though as you'll see there will be some crossover.

If any group of cartridges has benefitted from modern bullet technology, it is this group, and that's a good thing. It is guns chambered in cartridges representing this middle group of which we ask the most—be it a deer rifle, a long-range sheep gun, bear stopper or target platform. There are quite a few choices, and your hunting style may require more than one of these. All of mine have a purpose, and get used regularly.

Within this category there are just a few universal answers to a variety of questions. There are also some age-old debates that still rage on, and probably won't be resolved anytime soon, as well as a plethora of new cartridges that have come into the mix. The choice of a cartridge in this category is going to depend on exactly what you're going to ask it to do for you. Is it a deer

The .257 Weatherby is a big case; too big for all day shooting sessions.

The .223 Remington and 69-grain Hornady Match bullets are a great choice for target shooting.

rifle, which will only see a few days in the field each year? Or is it a rifle you want to cover a multitude of species, in different environments? Exactly which species do you intend to hunt? Like I've said, there are some universal answers, and opinions differ.

Same can be said for target cartridges, in that the application will most definitely influence the choice. In addition, availability and expense of ammunition will play into the decision-making process. The ballistics of the .338 Lapua and now the .300 Norma are undeniably wonderful, but does the expense of these two target rounds make them a viable choice? Can you serve your needs with a 6.5 Creedmoor or .300 Winchester Magnum, both of which are readily available at a fraction of the cost? That's up to you in the end.

In the hunting world, we have volumes available regarding the established minimum calibers and energy figures, which have been memorialized for decades. However, the modern advancements in bullet technology—higher BC figures and tougher construction, namely—have changed the game. I can only imagine what Col. Townsend Whelen would say about a mono-metal hollowpoint or a bonded core, polymer tipped boattail. If the gun writers of yesteryear could have a whirl with our premium bullets and slow-burning powders, I think they'd form different opinions than what they put into print years ago. While Elmer Keith felt that the .30-06 Springfield was under-gunned for elk and ridiculed Jack O'Connor for using the "puny .270," I know hunters who cleanly take elk each year with a 6.5 Creedmoor and a 140-grain premium bullet. Does that make the .338 Winchester Magnum an obsolete elk gun? Not at all! If you shoot it well, it will still take an elk as cleanly as it did in the late 1950s. But it might mean that if you have a good '06 or 7mm Remington Magnum, you have a damned-fine elk gun right in your hands. The same can be said for bear cartridges. If you're heading to Kodiak Island, I feel comfortable recommending the biggest cartridge you can handle effectively as the coastal brown bear is a force to be reckoned with, but for black bear and interior grizzly, your deer rifle, if mated with a heavy, premium bullet, might just get the job done well.

For long-range deer, sheep and caribou hunting, the high BC bullets we've been talking about throughout this book will definitely give that old .270 Winchester or .30-06 Springfield a facelift and make hitting the vitals easier. Perhaps you're interested in one of the new short, squat magnum designs. There is a lot to be said for the shape of a particular powder column, but remember that a .308-inch diameter 165-grain bullet has no idea about the case from which it was launched, and as long as the cartridge has proven its accuracy at the target range, velocity is ... velocity. I've read arguments about the so-called huge difference between the field performance of the .300 H&H Magnum vs. the .300 Winchester Magnum vs. the .300 Weatherby Magnum. In all sincerity, we are talking about a difference of about 150 to 200 fps at best, and as long as .30you have done your part to make that distant shot (knowing your trajectory, reading the wind, etc.) I highly doubt that any game animal would be able to tell the difference. If they did, and the energy figures were that crucial, it might be wiser to jump to a larger bore diameter with a bit more striking energy rather than split hairs. Again, I'm not going to advocate hunting large bears with a .243 Winchester or go on the record as saying you need a .35 Whelen to kill a deer, but if you stay within logical boundaries, you'll be a happy hunter.

Looking at the light medium calibers such as 6.5mm and .270, you'll see many choices that can give a hunter years of positive results. These days the 6.5s are all the rage, and with good reason: they yield excellent ballistics without a whole lot of recoil. I've been telling you about my 6.5-284 Norma, which I've fallen in love with as a medium game cartridge. The 6.5 Creedmoor is also gaining quite the reputation in the field, and we've had the 6.5x55 Swedish Mauser for over a century, a cartridge sadly overlooked. The .260 Remington has no flies on it, and the fast 6.5s—the .264 Winchester Magnum, .26 Nosler and 6.5-300 Weatherby Magnum—drive some of the flattest trajectories available in their class.

While the magnum-class 6.5mm cartridges are certainly designed for long-range work, even the 6.5x55 Mauser makes a good hunting cartridge, fully capable of using a range of bullet styles and weights that will handle most of the average hunter's needs. With a high BC bullet in the 140-grain range, like the Hornady ELD-X or Nosler AccuBond Long Range, you have quite the shooter in your hands. If you spend most of your time in the woods, where shots are within the 200-yard mark, there are some good 156- and 160-grain bullets, like the Hornady InterLock and Norma Oryx that will handle deer, bear and hogs without an issue. Their high sectional density figures will ensure

The 30 Nosler, .300 Winchester and .30-06 Springfield will all launch a bullet at respectable velocities.

proper penetration, and their round-nose or semi-spitzer conformation is no handicap at the shorter ranges. The twist rate of most 6.5mm barrels is 1:8 or 1:9 at worst, so bullet stability is no problem, unless you get into the truly long-for-caliber projectiles. These features are why the 6.5mms are making their resurgence, sometimes in newer guises like the 6.5 Creedmoor or the .260 Remington, but I chuckle a bit when I compare them to the Swedish Mauser and wonder why we Americans didn't see the writing on the wall decades ago like the Scandinavians did. I often run my 6.5-284 Norma at Swede velocities for much of my local hunting, and it works just fine. Of course, by handloading the ammo, I can also choose to bring it up to full-house velocity for even longer ranges.

The .270 calibers, whether Winchester, Winchester Short Magnum or Weatherby Magnum, all make good all-around big game choices, especially with today's premium bullets. Load a 150-grain Swift A-Frame or Nosler Partition in your rifle, and you've got a bullet that will withstand the high impact velocities of a close-up shot, yet still open up at longer distances. If you prefer the better wind performance of the spitzer boattails—and there's no reason not to like them—there are all sorts of choices for these three cartridges. The Federal Trophy Bonded Tip, Swift Scirocco II, Barnes TTSX and others help retain the high velocities generated by the .270s as well as maintain structural integrity to reach the vitals on bigger game. I know Professional Hunters in Africa who use a .270 Winchester with premium bullets for animals such as eland (which can approach one ton on the hoof) with great success. They pick their shots carefully and keep the distances as close as possible, but it works like a charm. Those same bullets will handle elk and moose because of the controlled expansion. For deer and smaller cervids, the standard cup-and-core bullets will do a good job, but beware the close shots, especially with the high BC spitzer boattails, as they have a tendency to separate jacket and core when impact velocities get too high.

For target shooters, there are a few really good choices in the 6.5mm class, with the 6.5-284 Norma leading the pack. I chose this cartridge for a hunting round, based upon its performance at 1,000-yard targets, as well as its velocity capabilities. Many F-Class shooters choose to use this case combined with a 28- or 30-inch barrel to wring as much velocity from the case as possible. With this combination you can drive a 140-grain bullet to 3,000 fps and get highly consistent results. I'm sold on the 6.5-284 Norma because of its accuracy; my own rifle with a 25-inch barrel will maintain 1/3 MOA out to 500 yards or so, which is much more than I would ever expect from a hunting gun. The Creedmoor and Grendel also exhibit fantastic accuracy, and I'd comfortably recommend either for a target gun. All the 6.5 cartridges have the ability for excellent accuracy, even the 6.5 Carcano, whose inaccuracy claims lie more with the rifle than with the cartridge. The bullet selections for the 6.5s are what make them shine, and I think they are going to stay at the top of the heap for years to come.

Moving upward to the 7mm- and .30-caliber cartridges, there's an amazing amount of choices, with a whole ton of overlap. In addition, the differences between 7mm and .30 are minimal, and often the decision comes down to personal choice. Yes, the .30-caliber cartridges can use heavier bullets than can the 7mms, but the advancements in bullet construction have narrowed the performance gap, at least terminally. I like to break these cartridges into three categories: standard, magnum and super magnum.

Which will best serve your needs? Again, it's a subjective answer, with many shooters being fervent defenders of their choice. I look at it this way: with the exception of some of the lever-action choices, like the venerable .30/30 WCF and 7-30 Waters (which are still great choices, in their element) you can choose just about any of the popular 7mm or .30 calibers and get the job done. Even the older rimless designs, like the 7x57mm Mauser, .30-40 Krag and .300 Savage can still be used very effectively as hunting cartridges, benefitting from the modern bullet designs and advancements in powder technology. From a hunting perspective, almost all of these cartridges (minus the lever gun cartridges) can be zeroed at 200 yards with even the slowest posting acceptable, if not stellar trajectories when using modern bullets.

In the Sevens, you've got the 7x57 Mauser, 7mm-08 Remington, 7x64 Brenneke and .280 Remington in the standard class, and all make a good choice, especially for the recoil sensitive. The oldest, the 7x57 Mauser, suffers from what I call "old rifle syndrome," in that there are many 19th century rifles still in service, and many of the factory loads are adjusted for the older, weaker steel of those rifles. However, as a handloaded cartridge, the 7x57 is a hidden hero. The 7mm-08 is a bit limited in case capacity, often precluding some of the longest, highest BC bullets, but with proper bullet selection it can be a wonderful hunting round and performs very similar to its

The Creedmoor and Grendel cases deliver top-notch accuracy.

The 7x57 Mauser still delivers, well over a century later.

big brother, the .308 Winchester. The .280 Remington has become a bit of a sleeper these days for reasons I just don't understand. As the .30-06 necked down to hold 7mm bullets, it gives ample case capacity for the longest of 175-grain bullets, and has always been an accurate cartridge. It's not really far behind the velocities of the 7mm Remington Magnum, yet has quite a bit less recoil. With 140-grain bullets, the .280 makes a great deer cartridge, for all conditions, yet with the 160- and 175-grain premium bullets it will neatly handle elk and moose, as well as African plains game. The 7x64 Brenneke falls slightly behind the .280 Remington in the velocity department, but still offers enough to the hunter to make a good choice for an all-around rifle. If you want a standard-class 7mm, any of these will make you happy. If you're into the classics, owning a 7x57 Mauser is a good way to get back to roots, and with modern bullets you won't feel handicapped at all. Actually, the 7x57 has taken all kinds of game, including African elephants, though there are better choices for the truly big game. I'd personally opt for the .280 Remington, as it offers the most flexibility of the lot.

Heading into the magnum-class you'll find more than a few offerings. The 7mm Remington Magnum leads the pack—even having unseated the .264 Winchester Magnum in its early years—but there are others in the same power range. The 7mm WSM, 7mm Remington Short Action Ultra Magnum, .28 Nosler, 7mm Dakota and 7mm Weatherby Magnum are all similar in performance to the 7mm Remington Magnum, with varying levels of availability. The Remington version pushes a 150-grain bullet to about 3,100 fps and the 175-grainers to right around 2,900 fps. This velocity gives ample performance in windy conditions, as well as a respectable trajectory. The premium bullets cause good penetration and expansion.

The super-magnums give a boost in the velocity department, pushing the 150s to 3,300 fps, and 175s to 3,100 fps or so. The 7mm STW and the 7mm Remington Ultra Magnum are huge cases, holding in excess of 95 grains of powder, and while the performance is unparalleled, the recoil is as well. Unless you've got a muzzle brake on these shoulder pounders, the recoil can easily become too much for the average shooter.

Looking at the .30-caliber cartridges, you can lump them into the same three groups, but there are more choices. Let's face it. Americans simply love .30 caliber. And the amount of cartridges available for it are staggering. In the standard class I'm going to include the .300 Savage, .30 T/C, .308 Marlin Express, .308 Winchester, .30-40 Krag, and .30-06 Springfield. Yes, I'm aware of the raging argument between supporters of the .30-06 and those behind the .308 Winchester, but I've often felt it's a moot point. There is maybe 100 to 125 fps difference between the two and, again, I don't think that game animals can tell the difference. Yes, the .30-06 uses heavier bullets a bit better and is a welcome addition to just about any hunting camp, anywhere. But the shorter cartridges were all (generally) designed to mimic the .30-06's performance, with varying degrees of success. I'm not about to pick on anyone's choice of cartridge, but this many redundant designs—with only minor dimensional variations—means some of them will be put out to pasture, and that's unfortunate if you own one. Like the WSSM series, where ammo is rare at best, some of these are headed for obscurity. At any rate, it is the performance of the .30-06 Springfield that has become the benchmark against which all other cartridges have been measured, for the last century.

Take things up to the 'magnum-class' and you'll find some highly respected cartridges like the .300 H&H Magnum, .300 Winchester Magnum, .308 Norma Magnum and .300 Weatherby Magnum. Some of the recent developments in this class include the .300 WSM, .300 Remington Short Action Ultra Magnum, .300 Ruger Compact Magnum and 30 Nosler. Generally speaking, these cartridges give a 150 to 300 fps increase over the .30-06 Springfield, pushing a 180-grain bullet somewhere between 2,900 fps and 3,150 fps. Such cartridges are among my favorites in this class, and as you can tell from the examples I've given in this book I'm rather partial to the .300 Winchester Magnum. To me, it represents a blend of acceptable recoil and good ballistics, being fully capable of using the full spectrum of .30-caliber bullets, without being too awful rough on a barrel. I also like the .300 H&H Magnum—though more for its nostalgic aura than anything else—even though it's at the bottom of the velocity list for the magnums. It has a sweet recoil, if you will, being much easier on the shoulder than say a .300 Weatherby, yet makes a very effective hunting round. Professional Hunters in Africa smile when you uncase a .300 H&H (or Super .30 as it's also known) as they know how that round will perform on plains game.

The .30-caliber super-magnums, like the .300 Remington Ultra Magnum and the huge-cased .30-378 Weatherby Magnum, are a whole different level of cartridge. Both will drive a 180-grain bullet to 3,350 fps and can generate some soul-crushing recoil. If you're looking to really move a bullet, these are your guys, but you're going to want a muzzle brake. I've only shot one rifle in this class, a Remington Model 700 AWR in .300 RUM, that didn't ring my bell.

So among the choices in the two most popular calibers for an all-around rifle, how does one choose what is best? Try them, and try as many as you can. If you've paid attention to the science involved with a bullet's flight path outlined and explained earlier in this book, you can easily see that the case—so long as it gives consistent, desired results—is not the biggest player in the game. Among these cartridges, I like to look at two things: my anticipated ranges, and the required horsepower. If I'm hunting in a situation that may require a longer shot, say out past 300 yards, I appreciate the trajectory and wind deflection qualities of my .300 Winchester Magnum. However, if I'm hunting the woods and mountains around home, where I know my shots are rarely over 100 paces, I'm fine with the .308 Winchester, as it's a nice, compact rifle that provides plenty of accuracy. The ballistics for a woods rifle are a different consideration than for long range. The .308 Winchester represents a great blend of accuracy and mild velocity, so you're not stressing the bullets out with super-high impact velocities. I have, and will use my .308 Winchester in the woods. I just try and match the projectile to the job, so I don't end up with premature bullet breakup, or an excess of bloodshot meat.

If you don't want to own a bunch of different caliber rifles, the .30-06 Springfield makes a great universal compromise, giving the best balance of both worlds, as well as being readily available. The '06 is popular because it's readily available, and it's readily available because it works so well. The same ideas will translate into the 7mm world (if you haven't figured it out yet, I'm a bit more partial to .30 than 7mm). If you keep your shots relatively short, there's no real reason to exceed the .280 Remington's performance, but there's nothing saying a 7mm Remington Magnum won't work up close. If you choose a caliber for use in the wide, open places, the 7mm Remington Magnum may suit you better. The super-magnums are a different story.

I load a lot of super-magnums for different clients, and I understand the mentality: they want the fastest, flattest shooting, hardest hitting cartridge money can buy. However, these cartridges will definitely test the mettle of a cup-and-core bullet, and can make a god-awful mess on close shots. I'm not going to say that I dislike them, but I'm more comfortable with the 7mm Remington or .300 Winchester than I am with a 7 STW or .30-378 Weatherby. With the lighter cartridge, I can still make hits out to my own self-imposed distance limits, and the wear and tear on both shooter and gear is much less.

Some of these cartridges also make fantastic target cartridges, for obvious reasons: They utilize the benefits of the heavier, higher BC bullet. The .308 Winchester is a darling in the target community, as is the .300 Winchester Magnum. The .300 WSM also holds its own on long-range targets. The ability to launch high BC bullets at a decent velocity, more than conformation, is the key.

Getting above .30 caliber, you'll find the 8mm cartridges, which have a limited following these days. Bullet weight usually ranges between 150 and 220 grains, at .323-inch diameter, and they don't offer much more than any .30 caliber. While there's no denying the impeccable reputation of the 8x57mm Mauser, truth is the 8mm Remington Magnum and .325 Winchester Short Magnum are fast becoming obscure and ammunition a rarity. If you have a good 8mm rifle, there's no reason to retire it, but unless it's an 8x57, you'd better be a diligent shopper or reload your own.

The cartridges between .338 diameter and .358 diameter are reserved for larger game, like grizzly, moose, elk, etc. There are some cartridges still thriving that are best suited for deer like the .35 Remington. But many of these are big game specialists. There are some cartridges in this group based on the .308 Winchester case such as the .338 Federal and .358 Winchester, and others based on the .30-06 Springfield like the .338-06 A-Square and .35 Whelen. Then there are cartridges based on the .375 H&H Magnum case, shortened to varying degrees. The .350 Remington Magnum is the shortest, while the .358 Norma and .338 Winchester Magnum proudly wear the family belt, as does the .340 Weatherby Magnum. Between the two bore diameters, there seems to be a ballistic advantage with the .338 cartridges, as the maximum bullet weight between the two is (generally) 250 grains, thus the better SD and BC figures tip the scales in favor of the .338. Not unlike my thought pattern with the 7mms and .30s, the cartridge that suits you will depend on your recoil tolerance and anticipated distances. The cartridges in this class—even the diminutive cases of the .338 Federal and .358 Winchester—offer a considerable increase in frontal diameter over the .30 calibers, and the heavier bullet weight will generate more kinetic energy. But, that increase comes at a cost, and that's increased recoil. While I find the .338 Federal, .338-06 A-Square, .358 Winchester and .35 Whelen to be sweet-shooting (and fully capable of taking just about any North American species), the .338 Winchester Magnum and .340 Weatherby can be tough, especially at the bench. If you're looking for a bigger bore to pair with your 7mm or .30 perhaps to take to Alaska, I'm a fan of the .338-06 A-Square and the .338 Winchester Magnum. These two cartridges are very versatile, using good bullets weighing between 180 and 250 grains. The .338-06 sort of mimics the venerable .318 Westley Richards, pushing the big 250-grain bullets to just about 2,400 fps, while the .338 Winchester Magnum betters that figure by another 250 fps. Recoil rises dramatically, though, and gets even worse with the .340 Weatherby and its bigger sibling, the .338-378 Weatherby. I'd highly advise you to 'try-before-you-buy' with the latter two cartridges, and make sure you can handle the heat. I've tried them, and they're not for the faint of heart.

The various .35s are not a bad choice, but give up some critical BC and SD values to the slimmer .338s of the same weights. If they suit your needs, go for it, but I think you'll find the ranges of the .35 calibers are a bit limited in comparison.

Some .30-caliber cartridges. Left to right: .300 RUM, .300 Winchester Magnum, .300 WSM, .30-06 Springfield and .308 Winchester.

The beastly .338 Lapua is a true long-range cartridge. It's based on the .416 Rigby necked down to .338.

For the target crowd, this group contains one of the nastiest available: the .338 Lapua. Based on the .416 Rigby case necked down to use .338 bullets, the .338 Lapua will definitely reach out and touch someone, in a very dramatic fashion. There are some fantastic 300-grain match bullets available, as well as lighter ones that will retain velocity very well. Look for a good muzzle brake on a rifle chambered for this cartridge, as the recoil is brutal without it.

The Big Bores

Stepping up the ladder to the big bores—those cartridges designed for taking the largest game on earth—there are all sorts of choices, from the 9.3mm and .375 bores, to the lower .40s and .45s, up to the big .470s, .500s and above. While most of these are associated with African dangerous game hunting, there are some American offerings that have become classics.

If you're serious about dangerous game, you'll need a rifle of at least .375-inch diameter, though there are a few spots where the 9.3mms are acceptable. Tanzania requires a .375 or bigger for all dangerous game, including lion and leopard, while other countries only require them for elephant, buffalo, hippo and lion. The .375 is just the minimum, and there are some good choices above the .375, but I'm willing to go on the record saying this: for a global hunter, the .375 H&H Belted Magnum is the most useful cartridge ever invented. Yup, I said it. You can literally hunt anything on the planet with a good .375 H&H, and I suppose the same can be said for the .375 Ruger. With bullets ranging from 235 to 350 grains, and a trajectory that mimics a .30-06 Springfield, the .375 H&H has been used on 20-lb. steenbok, 100-lb. impala, 600-lb. kudu, 1,500-lb. Cape buffalo and 12,000-lb. elephant, for over a century. Among the big bores, it is relatively easy on the shoulder, very accurate, and has a selection of bullet profiles that will allow it to shine on 20-yard shots, as well as 400-yard shots. I've used it in both North America and Africa, and it makes just about one of the best bear guns ever, for both black and brown.

Getting this right out of the way, if you're looking for a bigger rifle to pair with your medium, it makes all the sense in the world to make it a .375 H&H. Comparing the ballistics, it will push a 250-grain (obviously of less sectional density) to a faster muzzle velocity than the .338 Winchester Magnum, and with the heavy 350-grain Woodleigh round-nose bullets at 2,150 fps, will cleanly dispatch an elephant. I've had several .375s, including a Winchester Model 70 that I love and an excellent Legendary Arms Works Big Five, which my wife snapped up as her own (when I'm good, I still get to shoot it), and both print sub-MOA groups with many different types of bullets. The fact that it is the legal minimum for Africa makes it such a viable choice there, but as an elk or moose gun, it'll push a 260-grain Nosler AccuBond to almost 2,750, so it really isn't a short-range thumper like a .458 Winchester or .458 Lott.

That aside, for the true heavyweights like Cape buffalo and elephant, there are larger choices that just might get the job done even better. Having hunted both, I can say that more bullet weight translates to a quicker kill. Regarding buffalo, a .375 H&H will definitely kill them, but a cartridge in the lower .40s—like the .416 Rigby, .450/400 3-Inch NE, .416 Remington, .416 Ru-

The .375 Holland & Holland Rimless Belted Magnum—in the author's opinion the most useful cartridge ever devised.

ger and .404 Jeffery—will have a noticeably different effect, stunning the bulls, if you will. The .416s push a 400-grain bullet to 2,400 fps, the Jeffery about 100 fps slower and the .450/400 will drive them to just under 2,100. These cartridges handle elephant quite nicely, as the lower recoil (compared to the .45s and .500s) allow you to place the shots accurately, and the high SD figures promote all kinds of penetration (remember those Woodleigh Hydro solids?). Among the big bores, this class of cartridge is my personal favorite, as they blend the hard-hitting attributes of the bigger calibers with the long-distance capabilities of the .375 H&H. Among these, I like the .404 Jeffery—my Heym Express is my favorite rifle—the .416 Remington Magnum in a bolt rifle, and the .450/400 3-Inch NE in a double rifle.

While I like the lower .40s for my own use, there's no denying that the larger calibers, the .458s and .500s, will stop a charging animal better thanks to a heavier bullet and larger frontal diameter. These are the truly big sticks, and require serious practice to master. The recoil of the .458 Lott and others like it (especially off the shooting bench) can be really nasty. I recommend that once rifles in this class are sighted in, get off the bench and do your practicing off of shooting sticks or off hand. There are quite a few to choose from, including the .458 Winchester Magnum, .458 Lott, .450 Rigby, .450 3 ¼-Inch NE, .470 NE, .505 Gibbs, .500 Jeffery and .500 NE, depending on whether or not you prefer a double rifle or bolt-action gun. The .45s launch a 480- to 500-grain bullet at velocities between 2,100 fps and 2,400 fps, for over 5,000 ft.-lbs. of kinetic energy. The .500s use a 525- to 535-grain bullet at similar velocities.

While I'm aware the market for this kind of rifle is limited, as they don't have a great trajectory, they nonetheless work very well up close. They're specialty rifles for sure, but they serve their purpose.

Those American big bores I was talking about? The .45-70 Government, .38-55 Winchester, and .444 Marlin are all popular with the lever-gun community, and while they're short-range affairs, they have devoted followers. If you like things on the larger side of average, they can be a bunch of fun to shoot and hunt with, and will work for even the largest game, if the range is right.

Making the Choice

So, if you know your hunting or shooting expectations, I hope this guide will help point you in the right direction in choosing a rifle cartridge. Here's what I use, and I don't offer it up so you mimic my choices, but to explain why I chose them.

Like many shooters, my first rifle was a .22 LR, a Ruger 77/22 that I still shoot three decades later. My first big game rifle was a .30-30 Winchester 94, a gift from my dad. After that I moved up to a Ruger 77 Mk II in .308 Winchester, a great deer rifle that has taken many good bucks and a black bear. I took it on a moose hunt where I decided I needed a much bigger cartridge (not exactly correct, but I digress). I ended up with a Winchester Model 70 in .375 H&H Magnum, as my goal was to head to Alaska for moose and grizzly bear. I ended up in Africa instead.

I added a .300 Winchester Magnum into the mix for a long-range gun, and I used it and my .375 on my first safari with great success. Shortly after, I got into calling coyotes and invested in a Ruger 77 in .22-250 Remington, as I wanted a dedicated predator rifle. It has accounted for many coyotes and foxes, as well as varmints. At an SCI dinner, I won a raffle for a Winchester 70 in the caliber of my choice, and as I had booked a Cape buffalo hunt, ordered it in .416 Remington Magnum, and loved it. I used this lineup for quite a while, until I became a gun writer and had a chance to experiment with many different calibers. I fell immediately in love with the 6.5-284 Norma and ordered one from the Savage Custom Shop. But, it was the loaner rifle I received from Heym, for a combination plains game/elephant safari, which spun my head around. It was the Martini Express rifle, in .404 Jeffery, and it was the sweetest bolt gun I've ever used. I took a pretty impala ram and a nice wildebeest bull, but the non-export elephant I took at 16 paces was far and away one of the best hunting moments of my career. That gun fits as if it were built for me (Heym rifles are made to order), and the .404 Jeffery is as cool and nostalgic as a cartridge gets. I loved it so much that I sent a check instead of returning the rifle. I'm also in the process of building a .318 Westley Richards, as I adore the classic African cartridges.

So there you have it. A good .22 LR, a predator rifle, a 6.5-284 for lighter game, a trio of .30s for short- and long-range work, a .318 just because, a .375 H&H for anything at all, and a .416 Remington and .404 Jeffery for the heavyweights. There are other guns, but they don't mean as much to me as do these.

Handgun Cartridges

No less fervent than the rifle cartridge debate, handgun cartridge choices are backed by hordes of fervent supporters; each makes their case and believes firmly in their cause. Whether it's a defensive handgun or a hunting rig, there's something for everyone. Let's tackle the defensive handguns first.

Deciding on a cartridge to defend yourself is no easy task. You want the ability to neutralize a threat and get to safety, but there are many different schools of thought. I've always subscribed to the "bigger is better" mentality, but the aspect of size and the ability to conceal the pistol becomes an issue, too. Reading the works and advice of trailblazers like Col. Jeff Cooper, you'll find a definite recommendation for the .45 ACP, and with good cause. I know of few other pistol cartridges—save perhaps the 10mm Auto—that will equal the .45 ACP's performance. However, there are a multitude of choices that, while perhaps not as powerful as the .45, are easily carried and will reliably save your bacon. The 9mm Luger is an obvious choice, as are the .38 Special and .357 Magnum. There is nothing wrong with the .40 Smith & Wesson or the .327 Federal. You'll have to find a cartridge that is available in a handgun that suits your style, has enough power to get you out of trouble, and that you can shoot effectively. The largest magnum in the world does you no good if you can't hit what you're aiming at.

While volumes have been written about the penetration tests of different calibers, and there are Internet forums that would have you thinking that anything less than the cartridge du jour would simply bounce off of an attacker, I personally wouldn't want to be shot by any handgun, including a .22 LR. It would be wise to see if you could try some of the varying handgun

The venerable .45 ACP is, arguably, the king of defensive handgun cartridges.

cartridges before you make a purchase to verify that you are comfortable with your decision. I know many grown men who, when handed a lightweight alloy revolver chambered in .357 Magnum, wince at the recoil from the first shot. Some guns just aren't comfortable. I personally prefer revolvers, as I grew up shooting Dad's Ruger Single Six and the feel of a wheelgun comes naturally to me, but I also appreciate the autoloaders. My own carry gun is a .38 Special Smith & Wesson Model 36, a five-shot revolver with a 1-7/8-inch barrel. I chose it for its reliability and small size; it has a nice set of Pachmayer grips that fit my hand perfectly, and for my purposes the short barrel poses no handicap at all. While the .38 Special is no powerhouse cartridge, it will send a 158-grain bullet at over 800 fps, for a combination that is perfect for me. It's not the .357 Magnum, and it's not the .45 ACP, but it has served law enforcement well for decades, and I know it will do the same for me. The recoil is more than manageable, but the report with the lighter 110-grain bullets at +P velocities can ring your bell, and I have tinnitus already so I prefer the heavy and slow school of thought. I can accurately place my shots out to 15 or 20 yards and don't expect to have to use this handgun any farther than that. Again, this is just my choice; I can use the good defensive ammunition, or I can handload wadcutters or cast lead bullets for practice and plinking.

I sat down with a couple good friends who teach defensive handgun classes, and got their take on the age-old self-defense caliber debate. Mark Nazi and his dad Lek own Double Eagle

Tactical Training (www.DoubleEagleTactical.com), a school for all levels of handgun instruction. Both father and son have extensive experience with a variety of handguns, from classic wheelguns to the latest polymer-frame autoloaders, in addition to providing safety and accuracy training to quite a few people each month. I've spent time in their classroom, as well as on the range, and there's no doubt in my mind that these two know what they're talking about when it comes to defensive handguns and cartridges.

We sat at the table, when all the guns were cleaned and put away, and that's when the debate began to kindle, slowly at first, like the first lick of flame on a piece of paper. It then began to rage, as the fuel took the flame, and before I knew it, father and son were in a vein-popping exchange that rivaled firearms debates I've had with my own father. You see, Lek, having many more years of experience than Mark, leans heavily on the tried and true .45 ACP and its heavy bullet weight as a defensive weapon. Mark, meanwhile, is a law enforcement officer trained with the lighter calibers, and is more of a 9mm guy. I totally get the dichotomy, and sat back while the two bickered, taking in the points of each argument. This debate is nothing new; it is as old as the .30-06 Springfield vs. .308 Winchester argument. One side insists that the .45 ACP is the only viable option and that any lesser cartridge is simply a waste of time. The other looks at energy figures, modern propellants and bullet technology, and the size and weight of the handguns for these smaller choices.

"The .45 ACP is the way to go when it comes to concealed carry," asserted Lek. "Simply put, the bigger the round, the bigger the hole. If there is a guy coming at you and you have to choose between 19 golf balls or 8 bricks to stop him ... I'm going to choose the brick every time."

"You had better make those 8 bricks count!" replied Mark.

"You know I can, boy."

And with those opening volleys the debate commenced.

"When it comes to concealed carry, I'm going to go 9mm Luger every time," Mark retorted. "With all of the advancements in modern ammunition, the 9mm is right on the heels of the .45 ACP in a lot of factors. If I'm going to get into a gunfight, I'm going to take the reduced recoil for follow up shots and the extra magazine capacity that allows me to hold off on that first mag exchange. Not to mention the cheaper cost; the 9mm is the Honda Civic of rounds—everyone makes some version of it."

But the elder Lek would have none of that.

"When it comes to the .45 think of it as a big, slow-moving brick," Lek said. "It may not penetrate as far as a 9mm+p will but the massive amount of trauma will take the threat out of the fight quick and in a hurry. The more vital organs you can damage the quicker the fight is going to be over, the faster they bleed, the quicker they die."

"Size does not always matter, it's more technique!" Mark said. "And that's all fine and dandy—and I have to agree with you that the .45 is a devastating round—but the wound cavity created from a modern 9mm bullet at +p velocity will take a person out of the fight just the same. The 9mm will penetrate more than the .45 due to its small diameter and you can apply

The modern 9mm loads are highly effective. Just ask any fan of the 9mm, they'll tell you.

that to ballistic vests, sheet metal, and bodies. The 9mm makes up for what it lacks in size with velocity."

The debate isn't over, nor will it ever be, as both make good points. I generally lean more toward the heavy .45 camp, but I understand the 9mm point of view, too. Modern bullets do, in fact, make a huge difference is terminal performance. Like I said, I carry a .38 Special, which is not all that far from the ballistics of a 9mm, if it does have a bit more bullet weight, and I carry it confidently.

While I sat with my friends and let them duke it out intellectually about a topic that is older than the hills, I realized the choice of a defensive caliber really comes down to confidence. I'm not about to say that a high-energy cartridge like the .45 ACP or 10mm Auto is too much gun, because in certain situations there is no such thing as too much gun. However, carrying a handgun that you have confidence in, one that you shoot well, is a huge factor in the self-defense equation. Remember, you're not invading Normandy; you want a cartridge that is going to get you out of trouble and into a safe situation. That will require training, good ammunition and tons of practice. If it's with a .357 Magnum, so be it. If it's a .40 Smith & Wesson, it's all good. I think we can all agree that the bigger, the better, but it doesn't necessarily need to be the biggest.

Hunting handgun cartridge choices are a different story, as you'll need enough killing power to quickly dispatch the game you're after. There are traditional choices, like the .357 Magnum, .41 Magnum and .44 Magnum, as well as the .45 Colt and.454 Casull, but things keep getting bigger. Then there are the giants—.500 Linebaugh, .460 Smith & Wesson, and the .500 Smith & Wesson.

Even the 10mm Auto has made a recent splash in the hunting fields. Just before submitting this manuscript, my colleague Razor Dobbs took two Cape buffalo in South Africa with a Dan Wesson 10mm Auto! That's quite a feat, but goes to show how powerful these handguns can be. The 10mm is one of the few autoloader cartridges that make a good hunting cartridge.

Invariably, the predominant form of a hunting handgun is the revolver. It gives you a very strong action, and the positive headspacing of a rimmed cartridge. Smaller game can easily be dispatched with a good .22 Long Rifle revolver, and it's a challenge to fill the pot with rabbits and squirrels taken with one.

Big game is a different story. I find the .357 Magnum to be a sensible minimum for a deer hunting cartridge, while the .41 and .44 Magnums, as well as the .45 Colt make excellent bear cartridges. Those bigger guns will take just about any game at sensible ranges.

CHAPTER 19

Revisionist Cartridges— Changes for the Better

I f you've ever spoken to a rock musician about writing a song, they might tell you, "It's all been done." While the numerous combinations of the twelve musical notes and endless rhythmic possibilities have not all been explored, much of our music shows its roots and influences. Many shooters feel the same way about cartridges. Since the inception of the metallic centerfire cartridge in the 1800s, the shooting industry has pretty much done it all, from small varmint

The modern crop of cartridges primarily accommodates longer bullets.

cartridges up to those designed for dangerous game and long-range target shooting, the latter of which continues to push the envelope when it comes to distance.

Where many of the designs of the 1950s and 1960s were centered around achieving yet-unprecedented velocities using larger case designs (often based on some variation of the belted Holland & Holland case) with increased powder capacity, the late 1980s and the 1990s saw a new level of larger

The 6.5 PRC offers a definite velocity advantage over the 6.5 Creedmoor, making it a more effective long-range target and hunting round.

cases in the Remington Ultra Magnum family. Looking at one of the more popular designs—the .300 Winchester Magnum—the shoulder was moved forward, and the neck was reduced in length for more powder capacity. But after the turn of the 21st century, things began to change, with Hornady's 6.5 Creedmoor being the most glaring example.

Where the .260 Remington was a darling cartridge at the turn of the 21st century, the 6.5 Creedmoor looked suspiciously similar; both were derived (even if loosely, in the Creedmoor's case) from the .308 Winchester, though the Creedmoor's case is shorter than that of the .260 Remington. While that may seem counterintuitive when you look at the velocity game, Hornady's goal was to use a bullet with an enhanced ballistic coefficient value for better downrange performance. A shorter case allowed for a bullet with a longer ogive to be seated at the case mouth yet still function in the prescribed magazine length. Hornady proved to the shooting world that a sleeker projectile at a lower velocity would perform better at long ranges than a faster cartridge with a lesser bullet. And with the Creedmoor, we started down the path of shorter case/longer bullet combinations that resulted in some of the best designs of the 21st century.

Hornady would follow up the Creedmoor with another 6.5mm cartridge with more case capacity, but still designed to be housed in a short-action magazine. The 6.5 PRC (Precision Rifle Cartridge) may resemble one of the Winchester Short Magnum family, but make no mistake: it is designed to house some of the longest 6.5mm bullets and will drive them to respectable velocities. It's based on a shortened .375 Ruger case, headspacing off the shoulder for chamber concentricity. The 6.5 PRC is a fine target cartridge and makes a better hunting choice than the 6.5 Creedmoor, as it gives a higher velocity range for those who want to use a 6.5mm projectile on larger game. It has a 250 fps advantage over the Creedmoor, with slightly heavier projectiles.

Hornady followed the 6.5 PRC with the .300 PRC, a magnum-length cartridge with magnum-level performance. Still based on the .375 Ruger case, the .300 PRC is designed to work with the heaviest weights of .30-caliber Hornady projectiles, like the 212-grain ELD-X softpoint hunting

The .300 PRC is a magnum-length cartridge that pushes a heavy-for-caliber bullet at respectable velocities.

bullet, the 225-grain ELD Match and the 190-grain CX copper monometal. Velocities are higher than the .300 Winchester Magnum, roughly on par with the .300 Weatherby Magnum; the difference is the higher BC of the .300 PRC.

Filling out the family tree, Hornady's 7mm PRC is a long-action cartridge with velocity figures roughly on par with the highly popular 7mm Remington Magnum. Again, staying with the scheme, the case measures 2.28 inches, compared to the 7mm Remington Magnum's 2.500-inch case, allowing for 175- and 180-grain bullets of higher BC values. In my opinion, the 7mm PRC is a realization of everything the 7mm Remington Magnum wanted to be. It is a sound design, and of the three PRC cartridges, I like it the best for a dual-purpose hunting/target design.

But case length is not the only parameter that has changed of late; the twist rate of specific bore diameters has been modified to give a different level of performance. Federal used a tighter twist rate for its .224 Valkyrie—1:7, to be precise—to use .22-caliber bullets as heavy as 90 grains. Nosler uses a 1:8.5 twist rate for its 27 Nosler to use bullets heavier than those generally associated with the .277-inch bore diameter. Driving a 165-grain AccuBond Long Range to a muzzle velocity of 3,158 fps, the 27 Nosler certainly has changed the potential of the .277-inch bore diameter. The Winchester/Browning development of the 6.8 Western takes the same bore diameter even further from the classic .270 Winchester formula, using a blend of improved twist rate and shortened case length (it is based on a shortened .270 WSM) to give all sorts of flexibility. Using a 1:8 twist in the Winchester barrels and a 1:7.5 twist in the

Hornady's 7mm PRC might be the most well-balanced cartridge of the PRC family, being equally at home on the long-range target range as in the hunting fields.

Federal's .224 Valkyrie uses a tighter twist rate to deliver heavy .22-caliber projectiles.

Browning barrels, the 6.8 Western uses bullets as heavy as the 175-grain Sierra Tipped GameKing; this finally puts the .277-inch bore diameter on par with the 7mm bore diameter and gives the hunter a range of bullet weights that the .270 Winchester should have always had.

The belted Holland & Holland case design has been abandoned among new case designs, and I predict it will stay that way. While I love, still use, and will continue to use classic cartridges like the .300 H&H Magnum, .375 H&H Magnum, and .300 Winchester Magnum, the newer rimless designs give better chamber concentricity, as they headspace off the shoulder. That also means less case stretching—the belted cases are notorious for stretching just above the belt—and enhanced case life. And with the price of ammunition and components, that's a good thing.

Both the 6.8 Western and the 27 Nosler use a faster-than-normal twist rate, affording the .277-caliber additional heavier bullets.

CHAPTER 20

Advancements in Projectiles

S ince the original publication of this manuscript, the bullet design trend has been toward long, sleek ogives and severe boattails. Engineers realized that the ballistic coefficient of a bullet is more important than 100 to 150 fps of muzzle velocity when it comes to downrange performance.

Let's not assume that classic projectiles like the Sierra MatchKing, Nosler Partition, Remington Core-Lokt or Hornady InterLock have become obsolete. However, things are evolving. In conjunction with shortened cartridges offering more room within the magazine, the industry has answered the call with bullets to fit the bill.

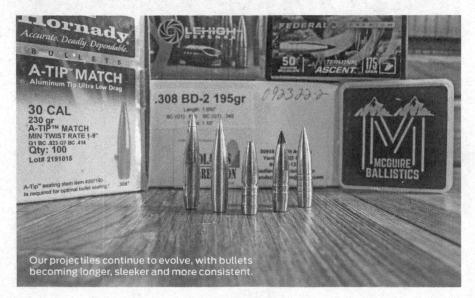

Our projectiles continue to evolve, with bullets becoming longer, sleeker and more consistent.

The Terminal Ascent has a short lead core bonded to a thick copper jacket. It is effective at close hunting ranges and for longer shots.

Federal first expanded the Trophy Bonded Bear Claw line to include the Trophy Bonded Tip—a fine bullet with a polymer tip and boattail, rock solid on game—but took things even further with the Edge TLR and, finally, the Terminal Ascent. Staying true to the family lineage, these bullets have a short lead core at the nose with a long copper shaft in the rearward section. However, Federal also elongated the ogive and engineered the grooves in the shank to minimize the effect of atmospheric drag. Like their predecessors, the Edge TLR and Terminal Ascent bullets are tough but give the flattest trajectory of any projectile in the family, enhancing downrange performance by increasing retained velocity and energy.

Hornady's ELD-X and ELD Match are a couple of the most popular bullets of modern design, and with good reason: they have a tip that doesn't deform during flight, keeping the BC consistent. Though the polymer tip was not a new concept for the folks at Hornady, they are always willing to push the boundaries and improve their products when possible. It was during Doppler Radar testing of polymer-tipped bullets when Hornady found an anomaly—a marked degradation in ballistic coefficient values at a certain point in flight (see chart). Basically, the bullet became less efficient and pointy and wasn't cutting through the atmosphere as easily. Signs pointed to the polymer tip as the weakest link or the only different variable from the hollowpoint match bullets, which didn't exhibit this phenomenon. In short, Hornady found the friction of atmospheric flight was melting, or at least deforming, the polymer tip and changing the bullet's BC value.

According to Hornady, "While analyzing the radar data on the new bullet, Hornady engineers noticed something that was puzzling. In Drag Coefficient versus Mach (Cd vs Mach) graphs, they saw that the new projectile was gaining drag shortly after leaving the barrel, which affected the performance of that bullet for the rest of its flight path. Simply put, the bullet acted like it had one particular BC for the first 100 to 150 yards, then transitioned to a lower BC for the rest of its flight path. Further testing was done with other bullets, including BTHP match and A-Max bullets. While the BTHP bullets' Cd vs. Mach charts looked as expected, the A-Max bullets were showing the same increase in drag that the prototype hunting bullet did. It was as if the bullet was changing shape in flight.

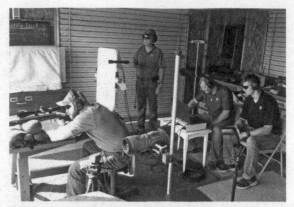

Data analysis allowed Hornady ballisticians and engineers to discover how bullet tip construction and heat deformity affect BC.

"Further testing was done to confirm suspicions that the polymer tip was the culprit. Aerodynamically efficient, high-BC bullets at high velocity were suffering from polymer tips softening and deforming in flight. Further testing proved that it happens to all conventional polymer-tipped bullets, regardless of manufacturer. Tipped varmint bullets and conventional low- to medium-BC (sub-.550 G1) bullets are not significantly affected. They simply do not hold a high velocity long enough for the aerodynamic heating to significantly affect their tip."

Hornady changed its polymer tip formula to a more rugged and heat-resistant recipe, and the ELD-X and ELD Match bullets were born, featuring the new Heat Shield tip. Federal's SlipStream polymer tip follows the concept, utilizing a heat-

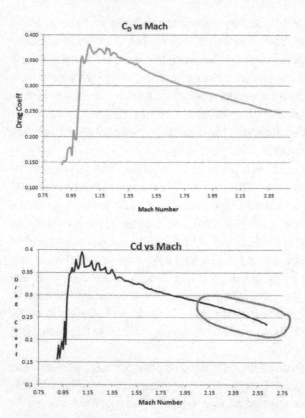

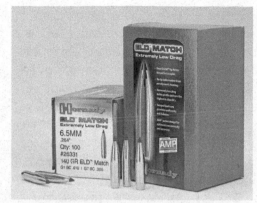

Hornady's Heat Shield tip on the ELD-X and ELD Match bullets solved the problem of deformed polymer tips during flight.

Hornady's A-Tip Match is one of the finest match-grade bullets on the market; they are packaged sequentially as they come off the line to optimize lot consistency. With a sleek ogive and an aluminum tip making for a near-seamless transition, the bullet is consistent in weight and length.

resistant formula, and Hornady extended the use of the Heat Shield tip to the monometal CX bullet line. The ELD (Extremely Low Drag) softpoint and match bullets revolutionized the long-range market.

If those bullets make great choices for hunting and target work, respectively, Hornady stepped up its game with the A-Tip Match. Using an aluminum tip instead of polymer, the A-Tip is longer than the polymer designs, resulting in a slight shift in center of gravity. Hornady packages A-Tip Match bullets sequentially as they come off the machine, with the machining oil still on the projectile; they even provide a polishing cloth to clean these component bullets before loading. The sequential packaging, in theory, should result in the most uniform lot of projectiles available. In my experience, this bullet ranks among the best match bullets I've ever used.

If you plan to use the Hornady A-Tip Match projectiles or any other precision, match-grade bullet, use a VLD bullet seating stem in your seating die so you don't mar the bullet's meplat. I also recommend using a VLD chamfer tool to make your cartridge case mouth smooth so the jackets are not scratched during seating. Long-range testing shows that scratches in the bullet jacket can affect the BC, resulting in a less-than-desirable performance with a (previously inexplicable) vertical impact shift. This seemingly minor attention to detail can be a problem solver for those who shoot long-range competition or are serious about long-distance precision shooting in any capacity.

The rise of the boutique bullet continues, with many new and exciting designs coming to market. Companies like McGuire Ballistics, Badlands Precision, and Lehigh Defense offer quality monometal hunting and match bullets for their excellent terminal performance and the lead-free motif taking root in many areas. McGuire's Copper Rose and Badlands' Super Bulldozer 2 offer superb bullet profiles and high BC values, while their construction can handle various impact velocities. My 6.8 Western printed ½-MOA groups with the Badlands Precision 140-grain Super Bulldozer 2, and while a muzzle velocity of over 3,100 fps would make an excellent long-range hunting load for sheep, pronghorn, or caribou, I used it to fill the freezer on a whitetail buck just 95 yards from the stand. With a severe quartering shot, the Super Bulldozer 2 penetrated over 3 feet of deer, resting just inches under the hide of the offside rear quarter.

McGuire's Copper Rose, shown after expansion.

Lehigh Defense's Controlled Chaos projectile is a monometal hollowpoint design, engineered so the ogive section breaks into small petals, creating an immediate energy spike and significantly

McGuire Ballistics' Copper Rose monometal bullet is an excellent lead-free design with a high-BC value.

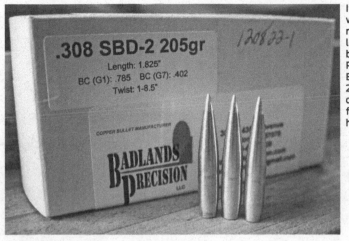

If you run barrels with tighter-than-normal twist rates, long monometal bullets like Badlands Precision's Super Bulldozer 2 205-grain in .30 caliber are perfect for long-range hunting shots.

damaging the entry site. At the same time, the base of the bullet remains at caliber diameter and penetrates deep into vital tissue. In addition to the devastating terminal performance, Lehigh's factory ammo is accurate, averaging under ¾-MOA in my rifle.

The last five years have seen excellent bullet designs for long-range competitors and hunters. One thing is for sure: the ballisticians have been busy, and I don't see a slowdown anytime soon.

Lehigh Defense's Controlled Chaos projectile is designed so its ogive section breaks into small petals; the bullet has shown to be accurate.

CHAPTER 21
Reading the Wind

'Ve shown you charts, discussed the choices of cartridge and bullet that will best perform in windy conditions, but no matter what you're shooting, you need to know how to read the wind. It's certainly not an easy prospect, especially as the distances get long. Yes, a Kestrel weather meter or similar device will accurately indicate both the wind speed and direction in relation to the target. This is definitely good information, but it is only a part of the puzzle. There will invariably be shooting situations where the wind at the target is completely different from the wind at your location. Couple that with variations in terrain, elevation and weather conditions, and you've got quite a chore on your hands.

Reading wind is no easy task. As mentioned in previous chapters, I recently had the honor of spending quite a bit of time beside Doug "Dog" Prichard, an ex-Navy Seal who is not only one helluva shot, but an expert at calling wind. I got to play the role of both shooter and spotter with him, as I wanted to concentrate on learning to call wind for other shooters as much as shoot the long distances available at the FTW Ranch. It didn't take long for me to figure out what Prichard was basing his calls on, and why.

We'd look through the spotting scopes, observing several key indicators and comparing them to the wind directions and values we were feeling at our location. Prichard explained how he unravels the mystery, using little clues presented by nature, as well as knowledge of terrain and how winds behave in canyons and valleys. I can't imagine a more difficult set of scenarios than those that are presented at the FTW Ranch. Tim Fallon & Company have handpicked some incredible shooting challenges that present steep angles, long distances and impossible wind conditions. Some of these targets combine all three factors—to an extreme degree—and really test the skill set of any experienced shooter.

The Barksdale area of Texas is canyon country, and the daily temperature differentials cause the winds to swirl, gust, calm down, and pick back up in a matter of minutes. We had to use every available piece of evidence to determine the correct call. We'd look for blowing grass, fluttering leaves; hell, we'd even use the butterflies to find out what was going on. Mirage, if it

'Dog' Prichard helps out Dave Fulson
with the dope on a 1,400-yard shot.

was present, was a definite help, as was the flight pattern of buzzards and other birds riding the winds and thermals.

Mirage is a phenomenon is which light rays are bent due to the heat difference of the ground and the air; if you've ever seen the heat shimmer on a hot asphalt road, you've seen mirage. You can use those bent light rays and the direction in which they are moving (if they're moving at all) to help you with your wind observations. Looking through your spotting scope, if you see the lines of mirage boiling or running vertically, you can assume a zero to 3 mph wind value. Should you find that mirage running at 45 degrees or thereabouts, you can assume a 3 to 5 mph wind value. If the mirage looks as if it's running horizontally, but slightly broken up, your wind value will be 5 to 8 mph, and if you see it running horizontally in a straight, consistent manner, you've got 8 mph and up, and will be able to determine the factor with other methods. Mirage is most visible on a bright, sunny day. At FTW, when we would have trouble picking up mirage, we would use the spotting scope to focus on a point closer to the target, and like magic the mirage would appear. Even so, mirage is a useful tool only evident under certain conditions, so you need other clues to help make the correct wind call.

Grass is always helpful, as it is easily moved by the slightest winds. A 3 mph wind will move the grass, and a 5 mph will move grass significantly. Leaves are another aid that can really save the day. If you're hunting in an area like Texas, where much of the vegetation holds onto its leaves year-round, you have many good indicators, but what if you're hunting the Tioga, or the wide-open crop fields of the northern U.S.? Odds are, there will always be something to gauge the wind velocity, even if it's the remnants of last autumn's leaves or the top of one of the stunted evergreens that grow at higher latitudes. If you're a traveling hunter, and you've found yourself in a new environment where the foliage and vegetation seem foreign to you, a handheld

USING MIRAGE TO ESTIMATE WIND VALUES

No Wind
Straight Up, or "Boil"

1 - 3 MPH
Slight Bend, left to right

4 - 6 MPH
45° Run, left to right

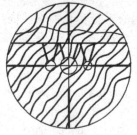

8 - 10 MPH
Running Flat, left to right

weather station will come in very handy. If you watch the wind's effects on the new flora, and measure that value with your wind meter, it will give you a much better idea of what the values will be while you are hunting. Cedar trees are a great indicator, as the tops act like a wind flag, and if you know what the wind speed is for certain movements you'll more than likely be right.

If you've got some trees with full leaves, you can quickly ascertain wind direction—even in light winds—by determining if there is movement on one side of the tree or the other. Prichard and I were discussing, well, debating—OK we were nearly arguing—about a particular shot and what the wind values should be. I had (I thought) followed all the proper procedures, and made a call of no wind and had instructed the shooter to hold the left edge of the 6-inch plate, to give the proper adjustment for spin drift at that distance.

"Nope, have him go right at it. You've got some right-to-left down there; it'll compensate for the spin drift."

I looked again and again, and it wasn't there. I saw a butterfly float by, just as happy as could be, about half way to the target, and I couldn't pick up any mirage, so I didn't know what he was getting at.

"Where are you seeing wind, Dog? I got nuthin'."

"See that live oak, about 15 yards left of and above the plate? Watch those leaves just on the right edge; they're blowing ever so slightly at the top. Because of the bullet arc (the target was 700 yards out), that slight right-to-left wind will cancel the spin drift."

Dammit, I didn't see it, and in my effort to shine in front of the Professor, I truly didn't think to look at the top of the tree in order to compensate for the entire trajectory arc of the bullet. The shooter held for the center of the plate, and I watched the paint splatter one-inch to the left of center. Professor Dog had given a clinic, and I learned my lesson. My wind call would've pushed that bullet off the left side of the plate.

Calling wind into or across a valley can pose an entire different set of problems. If you're hunting or shooting in canyon country, wind can behave much like water. You may see the tell-tale signs of the wind on the top of the hills, and though it may appear dead calm at the bottom of the valley, there may be wind acting much like a waterfall—rushing over one edge and creating an eddy of moving air along the wall of the canyon. I learned this difficult lesson at the ranch when we were set up on a range that predominately worked perpendicular to the bottom of the valley, but had two targets that ran pretty much parallel to the valley wall. The most difficult shot was an 18-inch plate at 585 yards along that wall. Where that plate was placed, the wall of the canyon got steeper than where we were shooting. The winds were just everywhere, if that makes any sense. Looking from our shooting position, it was clear the winds were hard, right to left, coming into the canyon, but I saw the slight left to right just in front of the target. It was a compound wind, in that it was definitely two different scenarios on the way to the target. I was shooting for this particular exercise, but Prichard insisted that I call my own wind. I looked and studied the scene, studied and looked some more, and decided that the predominant right to left wind would take precedence and adjusted my hold into that right wind, and touched one off. In proud fashion Prichard announced a miss, two feet off the right edge of the plate. The wind, hauling ass over that canyon wall, was curling much like water at the bottom of the valley, and rolling left to right. Once it was explained to me, I shot the plate with no issue, but had that been a game animal, I'd have either completely missed it or—worse yet—wounded it.

These ideas, and other visual clues in the hunting fields, are what the SAAM course at the FTW is all about. Other shooting situations there, especially on the longer shooting ranges, employed a multitude of flags to indicate both wind direction and intensity. It's quite easy to understand what a great aid this is to any shooter, especially when you've got a good dope card or Kestrel unit at your side.

RANGE FLAG WIND READING

The range flags pictured below indicate a 3 o'clock wind. Wind forces of varying degrees are shown. Winds of any force from 11, 1, 5, or 7 o'clock will have half the effect on the bullet as a 3 or 9 o'clock wind of the same force. Winds from 6 and 12 o'clock usually will have no measurable effect on the bullet in requalification firing.

FLAG STRAIGHT OUT WIND FORCE: MEDIUM TO HEAVY 15 TO 25 MPH		WINDAGE EFFECT 200 METERS—2 TO 3 CLICKS 300 METERS—3 TO 5 CLICKS 500 METERS—5 TO 8 CLICKS
FLAG 30° TO 45° OUT WIND FORCE: LIGHT TO MEDIUM 7 TO 11 MPH		WINDAGE EFFECT 200 METERS—0 TO 2 CLICKS 300 METERS—2 TO 3 CLICKS 500 METERS—3 TO 4 CLICKS
FLAG 8° TO 10° OUT WIND FORCE: NONE TO LIGHT 2 TO 5 MPH		WINDAGE EFFECT 200 METERS—0 CLICKS 300 METERS—0 TO 1 CLICK 500 METERS—1 TO 2 CLICKS

Figure 10.

21

Marine Corps wind flags indicate wind direction and intensity.

Wind, The Great Equalizer By Frank Galli

O n the range, people describe the wind as the great equalizer. Next to your drop, drift from wind is the second most important consideration for the long range precision rifle shooter. Unlike drop, which is predictable, the wind is a constantly changing factor.

So how do we get a handle on the wind? What are some tools, tips and tricks we can use to manage this element of long range shooting?

Starting out, we are going to look at the wind in two ways: the science department and the art department. By breaking it down this way, we'll begin to understand the complexities of reading the wind out in the field.

This is where the art and science of long range shooting meet. How the wind acts, how terrain affects it, and how we can estimate it to put rounds on target.

Science Department

What wind is most important?

This is probably the number one question asked by a new shooter, and even some very experienced shooters. The answer will vary depending on who you talk to and how detailed they want to get. The short answer is, "all of them." However, we want to get a little more precise than that, because just saying all of them doesn't help you become a better shooter. So, where do we start? Well, of course, we start with you, the shooter.

The wind is dynamic; it does not move in a straight line or at a constant value. We use the tools available to determine an average based on our observations.

Wind at the Shooter

There are several reasons we can look to wind at the shooter as the most important. The first being, the time of flight. Understand once the bullet is blown off course it stays off course and will never return. Wind at the muzzle has the longest amount of time to move the bullet off target. The flight of the bullet is angular. Distance and time increase that angle away from the intended target.

The next reason is a bit more physical. It is the only place along the bullet's path you can actually measure the wind to better than 1 mph. This is important because even a 1-mph error, especially at long distances, can be the difference between a hit and miss. A 1-mph wind blows a 175-grain SMK from a .308 10 inches at 1,000 yards. I call it the science department because here we can hold a Kestrel Wind Meter in our hand and read the actual wind speed with a scientific instrument.

Then we have the shooter. It all has to start somewhere, and that place is with us. The moment we hit the range or enter the field we begin analyzing our surroundings. We are using our sense of touch; we feel the wind on our bodies. Our sense of sight, we see what the wind is doing to objects around us. Our hearing, we can hear the changes in the wind with our ears. The wind gusts resonate, so we can use that information. Combine these factors and this is why we call wind at the shooter the science department.

Using a local wind meter, we can determine the speed at the shooter. Wind at the shooter is the foundation for all calls.

Reading the wind over time to better than 1 mph helps us establish a baseline. A foundation for all our wind calls moving forward.

The only place we can do that with any chance of accuracy is at the shooter. Understand everything else is just a guess. We'll discuss how to fine-tune that guess, but first let's start by analyzing the conditions at the shooter.

The Argument Against Wind at the Shooter

We established that wind at the shooter is the best place to start, however there are always exceptions to the rule. There are times when wind at the shooter will not work. Some of the drawbacks to using wind at the shooter are:

Our position is blocked from the wind. It is possible our position is not open to the prevailing winds, a prime example of this is having the shooter inside a structure. So, we will be forced to look downrange. In this case, we have to rely on our experience to project what we know; to use what we can see downrange. How are things like trees being affected? That is our only source of information, the visual indicators.

Downrange is where our final focus is. We want to use our initial call based off the wind at the shooter. But adjustments to that call might be based off what is observed downrange. That is where we are looking. In this case, hopefully we are just favoring slightly because we found a solid average with the Kestrel at the shooter. It's a common practice.

It's not uncommon to see 12- to 18-mph winds during the author's precision rifle classes. Students come from all over the world to dope these winds.

Max ordinate, when shooting beyond 600 meters, the bullet is arcing. A 175-grain SMK will be traveling approximately 15 feet above the line of sight for a 1,000-yard shot. Because the wind is experiencing less friction higher off the ground, it might increase in speed beyond what is read at ground level. Still we can base that call off what we know from what we read at the shooter.

Limitations of the Science Department

Many shooters point to the conditions downrange, and this is where the science department has its limitations. Because the bullet will be affected by wind during the entire flight, conditions read at the shooter can be too small a piece of the puzzle. This is where the art of precision rifle shooting comes into play.

We cannot read the wind to better than 1 mph out to distance. As well, the wind does not flow in a straight and even manner. We have to use our experience to figure out the changes based off what we see. It becomes highly subjective at this point, as no two people will read the conditions the same way.

Shooting is a cause-and-effect activity, if X happens, Y will be the result. Wind at the shooter might only give you one branch of the X while the conditions downrange fill in the other three branches.

But it is possible to calibrate and condition our senses to educate our guesses. After all, everything we can't read with a wind meter is just a guess. Some shooters have educated their guesses, but that takes time, especially for guys who are used to shooting on one particular range.

The more experience we have shooting, and reading the wind, the farther downrange our accuracy will become. This not only applies to our shooting, but to the wind calls we make. You cannot buy success. You can fool yourself and lease it, but you cannot outright buy it with the latest gadget or by using a wind-cheating caliber. At some point, nature will throw a curve at you.

Educate yourself, focus on the fundamentals, success will follow.

Most people underestimate their wind calls. It's not uncommon for people who are using the trial-and-error method to walk shots in. This is definitely one approach, but not always a very effective one. Recording your data can help expose faults in your calls. If you see a pattern appear where the first shot on a target always has you underestimating the wind, you might have to recalibrate your senses. It's possible your 8 mph is really a 10 mph and your 5 mph call is closer to 7 mph. Your data book will help you answer this question and allow you to diagnose your calls.

The Art Department

Once we get past the muzzle, everything else downrange is the art department. I call it the art department because it is subjective; no two people read the conditions downrange the same way. Let's look at the elements for reading the wind downrange and how these elements will affect our shot.

Wind Midrange

We have already noted that wind across the entire flight of the bullet matters. Each cause has an effect. We need to account for as many of these as physically possible. Once you move beyond the shooter, everything gets much harder, as we can no longer consistently estimate the wind speed and even direction down to that 1-mph threshold we are looking for.

The more experience you get, the farther downrange you can successfully estimate your calls.

Looking at the midrange wind, this is where a lot of high-power shooters turn for information. With a square range situation there are less obstacles to deal with, and many of these shooters will stick to a single range, or only a handful of ranges. They learn to account for any hiccups in the terrain that their particular range might have. It's their home-field advantage that helps with their success. Calling wind midrange works for this particular style of shooting. Generally, they are not dealing with unpredictable scenarios; it's pretty consistent how wind blows across a square range. There is, however, one important element to midrange wind we want to look at and that is max ordinate.

Max Ordinate

Maximum ordinate is the highest point the trajectory reaches between the muzzle of the weapon and the target. Why is this important? Well, because of wind gradients. We want to know how high above the line of sight the bullet is traveling so we can consider the increase in wind speed the bullet will experience. Basically, as the vertical height increases, the horizontal wind speed will increase due to less friction from the ground. The higher the bullet is above the ground, the more wind velocity the bullet will be subjected to.

In the past, people rationalized the changes to the slowing of the bullet. However, we know the bullet is not going "that slow" to be overly affected. Yes, it is going slower, but it is still supersonic, and the ballistic coefficient is giving an overall average, which accounts for this slowing. What actually happens is the bullet is subjected to higher wind speeds, which effect the shot. In some cases, the changes can be quite significant.

Locating midrange for your shot is quite simple. Most people use the halfway plus 10 percent solution to establish where max ordinate will be. After finding out where max ord will be for your shot, you can then subtract the Mil reading for the shot distance, from the Mil reading for the max ord range and that difference above the line of sight is where the bullet will be flying.

A 1,000-yard dope equals 11.2 MRAD minus 3.9 MRAD (550) equals 7.3 MRAD.

Looking at this in the reticle, you can begin to see where your bullet is actually flying for the shot being made. Well above the ground.

Now a midrange call will work very well for a shooter working inside 600 meters. Why? Because the height of the bullet is not enough to get effected by max ordinate. Extend that same shot out beyond 600, 800 even 1,000 meters and max ordinate becomes a factor that a midrange call might not be able to account for.

Midrange calls are a very good average; you can look at them like the Rule of Thumb formulas. They will give you a single place to look and one number that might not be off enough to miss the target. Using a ballistic computer with multiple winds enabled, the shooter can read the wind, note the value at midrange and then increase the wind speed with the understanding that the bullet will be affected by the wind-gradient increase. An example of this: You are making a 1,000-yard shot; the wind read at the shooter is 8 mph; and we know by observing the wind we have at least a 2-mph swing, so we dope the midrange call as 10 mph. That little increase in our call is often enough to fix any errors from attempting to estimate a downrange call by visually noted objects being moved by the wind alone.

Difficulties With a Midrange Call

Let's face it, wind is invisible. Sure, we can see what it is doing to objects downrange, but those objects are rarely calibrated. So, calling wind downrange presents a lot of trouble, especially to new and inexperienced shooters. You'll always hear old-timers talk about what they see on the ground, the grass moving, the mirage. We need to recognize all this, observing what is being done under the bullet. If the shot is going beyond 600 meters, odds are the bullet is a full wind gradient over that, so the value needs to be increased. By understanding this, we can dope the wind at the shooter, observe the midrange direction and changes and then add to our initial call based on that information.

Another problem arises when looking for this call in the field. When the shot is going across a canyon or from ridgeline to ridgeline with a valley below, the shooter might be several hundred feet above the valley floor, so we have nothing but empty space. Add to this the bullet is still above the line of sight and you won't have a mirage between the shooter and target, no change

Sniper's Hide field matches use natural terrain as the obstacles. Here in the rolling hills the wind moves in all directions.

in air layers to cause it. So how do you use a midrange call in this case? Well, you can't. Which is why knowing about the wind gradients and increase in horizontal wind velocity is important. You can estimate a call based on this knowledge even though there is nothing to observe.

If the terrain and the shot give you information midrange, use it, but know what it will do when that information is missing.

Downrange Wind Observation Values

Here are some common wind speeds for downrange observations. People will key off trees, grass and dust, and over the years they have provided a rough value to these observations. However, understand these are highly subjective and not accurate to within our goal of 1 mph accuracy. I am including these references points only as a historical reference, as I don't think I have ever used these numbers to success. I would much rather have a Kestrel in my hand.

0 to 3 mph: Wind barely felt on face and smoke lightly drifts

3 to 5 mph: Wind felt lightly on the face and ears

5 to 8 mph: Trees and leaves in constant motion

8 to 12 mph: Raises dust and loose paper

12 to 15 mph: Small trees sway

15 to 20 mph: Small trees and bushes are in constant motion

20 to 25 mph: Large trees sway

Some ranges have no wind indicators. It's important to use a weather meter to dope the wind speed as nothing on this range tells you the true story.

Trajectory µCard - Wind Only					
Range	6.0 mph		12.0 mph		18.0 mph	
(yd)	(mil)	(MOA)	(mil)	(MOA)	(mil)	(MOA)
100	0.1	0.3	0.2	0.7	0.3	1.0
200	0.2	0.7	0.4	1.3	0.6	2.0
300	0.3	1.0	0.6	2.1	0.9	3.1
350	0.4	1.2	0.7	2.5	1.1	3.7
400	0.4	1.4	0.8	2.9	1.2	4.3
450	0.5	1.6	0.9	3.3	1.4	4.9
500	0.5	1.8	1.1	3.7	1.6	5.5
525	0.6	1.9	1.1	3.9	1.7	5.8
550	0.6	2.1	1.2	4.1	1.8	6.2
575	0.6	2.2	1.3	4.3	1.9	6.5
600	0.7	2.3	1.3	4.6	2.0	6.8
625	0.7	2.4	1.4	4.8	2.1	7.2
650	0.7	2.5	1.5	5.0	2.2	7.5
675	0.8	2.6	1.5	5.3	2.3	7.9
700	0.8	2.8	1.6	5.5	2.4	8.3
725	0.8	2.9	1.7	5.7	2.5	8.6
750	0.9	3.0	1.7	6.0	2.6	9.0
775	0.9	3.1	1.8	6.3	2.7	9.4
800	0.9	3.3	1.9	6.5	2.8	9.8

Wind charts are an excellent way to reference the wind speeds measured with a Kestrel.

As you can see, these are very coarse, rough estimates for the wind. I highly recommend you calibrate your own observations backed up with actual readings from a wind meter. We want to build a personal database by training our observations. You can even write down what you see or take a picture of a wind flag on your local range and place it in your data book. This is much easier to work with than the common observations above. A 5-mph swing is a pretty rough estimate.

Square Range Wind Flags

If you are shooting on a high-power range that employs the use of wind flags, you can estimate the speed based on the angle of a calibrated flag. The formula for this is simple:

Angle divided by four equals wind mph.

A flag that is blowing at a 60-degree angle from the flagpole would be a 15 mph. They also sell calibrated flags for golfing that would work well for a shooter on a firing line.

These are outdated practices to base your wind off the flag angle. But flags are helpful in calibrating your senses and matching them up to a Kestrel. It's giving you a great visual on the highs and lows, but nobody is going to calculate the flag angle to determine the wind speed. This is 1978 thinking, but here we are repeating it.

Wind at the Target

Wind at the target is good to help fine-tune your call because that is where our final focus is. When we shoot, we should put 100 percent of our attention to the sights on the target. This means our focus is downrange. It gives us the opportunity to favor any significant changes we see. We can then use our reticle to hold as we know it has the same value as dialing. If the shooter, prior to breaking the shot, observes something that indicates a big change in the wind, he should react using the target wind observations.

We use several senses to determine the wind speed, direction and any changes. We see the effects it has on objects around us. We hear the increase and decrease in speed as well. We feel it on our body. All this helps us establish a call. When we understand wind across the entire bullet flight matters, we have to understand how we use these senses to adjust. Wind at the target is the hardest to successfully call to within 1 mph, which is our target goal. Any less than that can mean a miss, and it's really not easy to determine this across a long distance. Wind does not move in a straight line, nor does it move at one constant speed. We want to hone our senses and build a personal database where we can recognize these changes in time in order to make an on-the-spot correction. Wind at the target is a very useful tool here.

Another good tip for the competitive shooters out there: Watch the splash of the bullet to see what the wind is doing to the dust. If you are on a line with other shooters you can hesitate and observe their splash to see if the wind is changing. I often use the splash observed to fine-tune my downrange wind call. That splash has value in not just correcting for the shot, but for determining wind speed and direction. In fact, Field Firing Solutions has timing utility to estimate the dust movement.

Spend two minutes determining your wind speed before calculating the high value, average value and low value.

Effects of Terrain

Terrain can have as much effect on your shot, even more than just the wind alone. Wind is water, or you can say, wind can be visualized like water. Picture a river or stream, add in obstacles, rocks, branches, and it creates turbulence. Terrain features in the path of the wind will do the same thing. This turbulence can throw off your shot in an unexpected way.

Have you ever been on a high-power range with a row of flags every 100 yards? Have you ever noticed one flag blowing in the opposite direction of the rest? That is due to some terrain feature or obstacle redirecting the wind. There was not some odd spike in the prevailing winds going in the wrong direction. This was caused by a terrain feature, maybe a berm in or around that one flag. It's what we call a local phenomenon and it was isolated to that one spot. Unless the terrain feature was significant in size, and wind is very strong that day, in 95 percent of those cases you can ignore that one flag. Tip: Move to the center of the range.

Individual ranges have their quirks and there is no discounting that time and experience will help overcome the unpredictable changes presented. It's why the old-timers on that range can call it so successfully. Experience. Look for the root cause, something physical in the wind's path. The transition from woods to field can be the culprit; maybe a set of hills funneling the wind. When you recognize the effects of terrain, it helps refine your personal database to make the correct call.

Thermal Effects

Heating and cooling of the Earth's surface has a major effect on the wind. This heating and cooling also causes turbulent flow accounting for unpredictable changes in the wind patterns. We see the greatest influence of this in the early afternoon. We can see increased wind speeds and changing directions due to the area one might be operating in. We have a friction layer across the Earth that extends roughly 2,000 feet above the surface. Changes in terrain can affect the depth of this friction layer.

Mechanical Effects

Mechanical effects are when the winds encounter something solid, like terrain, trees and other obstacles, even buildings. This causes the wind to increase or decrease in speed and can cause them to change direction.

These two effects are very similar to each when viewed from the shooter's perspective. They have the same effect on the bullet, but are caused by two different things.

Winds ebb and flow, creating gusts. I picture the waves of the ocean crashing on a beach. Imagine that effect on the bullet as it passes through the wind. I use this information as a foundation for my holds. There is a high, low and average wind speed.

When I plug these numbers into my personal database or ballistic computer, I can then determine what effects my bullet will encounter. Just like the values at the shooter, midrange and at the target matter, so do the changes in speed experienced during the time of flight.

Wind Eddies From Both Mechanical and Thermal Effects

Every solid obstacle in the path of the wind will create an eddy, with its speed based on the size and composition of the solid object. They can change the wind's direction as well as effect whether they are horizontal or vertical in nature. A dust devil observed in an open field is an example of a vertical wind eddy.

Here is your visual representation on why a wind flag might be moving in a different direction relative to the rest of the flags on a square range. It's because of the eddy current created by solid objects in the wind's path.

Wind Gradients

As you rise above the Earth, the wind experiences an increase in speed. This is due to the reduced friction from the surface. Roughly every 14 feet, we have a new wind gradient. The problem with this gradient is, we can't see it. The mirage has to have a difference in temperature between layers in order to be visible, so once off the ground, the mirage will no longer help. Knowing the maximum ordinate of your bullet will help you determine where the bullet will be flying. We know at longer distances it's no longer moving across the ground, so using the mirage can cause an underestimation of the wind speed.

A good way to look at the gradient effect is to use the gusts you read on the ground. If the gusts are 2 mph, you can expect the increased effect from the gradient to be close to that value. A lot of times for a shot where I know the bullet will enter the next wind gradient, I increase my wind call to compensate.

The topography of the land controls the wind flow. Both regionally and locally. We are most concerned with the local variations caused by the terrain around us. The field shooter must have a good understanding of the obstacles in the flow pattern in order to account for them. Vegetation moving 1,000 yards away from the shooter's position might not give you an accurate representation of what the wind is doing, at the same time, neither will the wind pattern at the shooter. By observing, analyzing and recognizing the terrain features around us, we can make better estimates at distances.

The reference material used in this section was derived from wildfire material put out by groups like the Smokejumpers. For the men and women who are tasked with combating wildfires, wind is one of their biggest threats. Studying their material on the subject will help the field shooter become more proficient at recognizing the wind patterns at distance.

Gun Digest PRESENTS

Precision Rifle Marksmanship:
The Fundamentals

A Marine Sniper's Guide to
Long Range Shooting

by Frank Galli

This sidebar is an excerpt from *Precision Rifle Marksmanship: The Fundamentals*, by Frank Galli, available at GunDigestStore.com.

APPENDIX I
Cartridge Nomenclature

By Frank Barnes and W. Todd Woodard

It is difficult or impossible for the novice to follow the action without some knowledge of cartridge caliber designation. Even the individual experienced with standard American ammunition may be ignorant of British, European, and obsolete American cartridge nomenclature. The subject, regrettably, is full of inconsistencies and confusion.

With the majority of American, British, or European (metric) cartridges, the caliber (indicating bore land diameter in 1/100-inch), is the first figure given. However, there are exceptions that will be pointed out later. Caliber may be given in terms of bullet or bore diameter (the later in either land or groove), and is neither accurate nor consistent. For example, we have the .307 Winchester cartridge, which uses the same .308-inch diameter bullet as the .308 Winchester. Then there is the .458 Winchester Magnum and the .460 Weatherby Magnum, both of which are loaded with the same .458-inch diameter bullet. In the latter example, the Weatherby people didn't want anyone to get their round mixed up with the Winchester design, so they changed the figures a little. That is one reason some cartridges do not follow in normal caliber designation in the dimensional tables. There are others.

The second figure, if there is one, is usually some distinguishing feature such as case length or powder charge. Cartridges of European origin are, almost without exception, designated in metric units by caliber and case length. Obsolete American cartridges or any that have a black-powder origin are designated by caliber and powder charge weight, or caliber/powder charge/bullet weight (the last two in grain weight). Smokeless powder charges vary so widely with the powder type and grain structure that this system is no longer used. However, there are, again, such exceptions as the .30-30 Winchester and .30-40 Krag. Here, the second figure represents the original smokeless powder charge, although it no longer has anything to do with it. With black-powder cartridges, the designation ".45-70 Springfield" means a .45-caliber bullet with 70 grains of black powder. The designation ".45-70-405" spells out the same cartridge, but with a 405-grain bullet to distinguish it from such other bullet loadings as the .45-70-500. And then there was the .45-56-405 carbine load—in the same case!

The truth of the matter is the American "system" of cartridge nomenclature really hasn't any system at all to it, and what there is can only be learned through reading and experience.

Otherwise, you simply never know what is meant. For example, take the .30-06, a very popular military and sporting round. Here, the first figure shows the caliber, while the last two numbers are the date of origin. In other words, a .30-caliber cartridge—model of 1906. Or, again, the .250-3000 Savage (".25-3000" simply lacked that special "ring" the advertising folks wanted). This translates out as a .25-caliber cartridge firing a bullet at 3,000 fps muzzle velocity. Yet the bullet diameter is actually .257-inch and muzzle velocity varies with bullet weight from 2,800 to over 3,000 fps. Some of the older black-powder cartridges included the case length and type, thus, the .44-90 Sharps 2⅝-inch Necked or .45-120 Sharps 3¼-inch Straight. As you can see, cartridge nomenclature isn't a system at all—it's a *code*.

The British, to a large extent, follow the same "system" as we do. However, they add to the general confusion with such cartridges as the .577/.450 or .500/.465. Here, the second figure gives the approximate bullet diameter in 1/1,000-inch, and what is meant is that the .577 case is necked to .450-caliber, while the .500 case is necked to .465-caliber. The British may also add the case length. At this point, it is necessary to point out that some American wildcat (i.e., noncommercial), cartridges dreamed up by individual experimenters are designated by a similar, though opposite, system. Here, we have such cartridges as the 8mm-06, .30-338, and .25-06. These work out as an 8mm based on the .30-06 case, a .30-caliber based on the .338 Winchester case, and a .25-caliber based on the .30-06 case.

The Europeans have evolved the only real system of cartridge designation that is consistent and somewhat meaningful. Dimensions are in millimeters, including bore land diameter, case length, and type. The 7x57mm Mauser is a cartridge, for example, for use with a 7mm bore land size (7.21mm groove size), with a 57mm rimless case. The 9.3x74Rmm is a 9.3mm caliber with a 74mm rimmed case. The "R" denotes the rimmed type, while its absence indicates a rimless case. The name of the originator or manufacturer may follow. This is a relatively simple and straightforward system, but, unfortunately, it isn't perfect, either. The Germans used two rim types in some of their older cartridges, and this resulted in duplicate designations of cartridges that differ only in the rim (9.05x36.4R, 10.85x24.9R, etc.), and there must be at least three 9.3x72mm cartridges that differ only in case configuration. This is all something of a mess and probably too late to change. *Editor's Note: The late Frank Barnes, the original author of* Cartridges of the World, *in an effort to straighten things out (or, perhaps, add to the confusion), developed two wildcat cartridges that he designated as the .308x1½-inch and .458x2-inch.*

To further elucidate, the reader needs to know that there are two major classifications of cartridges—centerfire and rimfire. The former is fired by a primer located in the center of the case head, the latter by priming compound distributed throughout the entire inside of the rim's outer diameter. The modern centerfire cartridge primer is removable and replaceable, so that the case can be reloaded after it is fired. It is possible, but not practical, to reload rimfire cases after they have been fired. Centerfire cartridges are subdivided into two types based on the primer, Berdan and Boxer. The Berdan-primed case has the anvil as a separate protrusion or teat in the bottom of the primer pocket. The Boxer primer is completely self-contained, its anvil a part of the primer. All American-made ammunition is normally Boxer-primed, whereas much British and European ammunition is Berdan-primed. Most foreign-made ammunition manufactured for the American market has the Boxer-type primer.

Rim Types

There are four common types of centerfire cartridge cases based on rim type. These are rimmed, rimless, semi-rimmed, and belted. The British equivalents are flanged, rimless, semi-flanged, and belted. There is a fifth type, not widely used, which is the rebated rimless, in which the rim is of smaller diameter than the base of the case. Examples of cartridges with rebated rims would be the .284 Winchester and .30 Remington AR. The .41 Action Express pistol cartridge is also rebated. The purpose of the rebated rim is to allow the use of a standard diameter bolt with a larger diameter cartridge. In the past, there have been a few rimless cases without the usual extractor groove.

Both centerfire and rimfire cartridges may be of straight or necked type. Contrary to popular opinion, the necked case was *not* designed to provide greater velocity for smokeless powder cartridges. It evolved back in black-powder days, as a means of getting the same powder charge in a shorter case, thus allowing the repeating actions of the day to handle cartridges of the same power as the single-shots with their long, straight cartridges. Some of the very early rimfire cartridges were of the necked type.

The latest fad in cartridges is the caseless, or combustible type, an idea not really all that very new, as it actually dates back to the early 1800s or before. The original design used a nitrated paper or cloth container for the powder charge and, sometimes, the bullet. The entire package was loaded into the gun, and the powder and its container were consumed in firing. During World War II, the Germans began an intense research and development program to perfect caseless ammunition and design weapons to shoot it. The principal motivating factor at the time was the severe shortage of brass and other metal for cartridge cases. The Germans are known to have had at least partial success with caseless cartridges, and some insist complete success. United States military ordnance facilities, as well as private industry, have been working on the problem of caseless ammunition for the past 50 years or more. There has been considerable success in developing caseless and partially caseless artillery rounds, but there are still many problems in the small arms field. Obturation is a big problem, as is ejecting a misfired round from the chamber of a repeating action. Modern caseless ammunition usually consists of compressed powder grains fastened to the base of the bullet, or the powder may be encased in a plastic case made of the same material as the propellant. Ignition may be percussion or electrical, and there is, in some types, a booster charge extending through the center of the powder charge.

Cartridge Collectors

Though this book is not a collectors' manual, it nonetheless includes considerable material of use and interest to collectors and any serious student of cartridges and related weapons.

The tables of dimensions are organized to facilitate cartridge identification. The key to reading these tables lies in the bullet diameter and case type. The reader must understand that, in measuring cartridge dimensions, certain manufacturing tolerances must be allowed, and these can affect the last, or even the second, decimal figure. Dimensional tolerances can be rather considerable with old black-powder cartridges and the modern bottlenecked numbers. Also, the true diameter of the obsolete paper-patched bullet should include the patch, not just the lead slug protruding from it. Minor variations in dimensions should not be mistaken for errors or the existence of an unknown caliber.

The dimensional tables can also be used to identify the caliber of a gun, if the chamber dimensions are known. This can best be determined by a chamber casting. The means of doing this are explained in Chapter 3. If you own an obsolete or foreign gun for which ammunition is not available, the tables of dimensions will assist in determining whether ammunition can be made by reforming some similar, existing case.

Metallic Cartridge Development

The self-contained metallic cartridge is a fairly modern development, one perfected only about 1850. The use of black powder as a propellant in guns in the Western world goes back something like 650 years, and the knowledge of gunpowder more than 700 years. The Chinese knew about gunpowder 500 or 600 years before it was introduced to Europeans, although they used it as fireworks and not as a propellant any earlier than the Europeans.

The centerfire cartridge, a necessary prerequisite to our modern ammunition, evolved during the 1860s and '70s. Smokeless powder and high-velocity cartridges date back only to the 1890s. Improvements since the turn of the century have been more in the area of improved ignition, powder chemistry, and bullet construction, rather than cartridge design. Charles Newton designed cartridges back around 1910 that, had modern powders been available, would have equaled the performance of present-day high-velocity developments of similar caliber and type. Smokeless powder military cartridges designed between 1888 and 1915 were so good that improvement was possible only after more advanced powders became available, and many of these cartridges were still in use through World War II. As the result of this situation, many modern innovations in the gun and cartridge field turn out, after a little investigation, to be a reintroduction of something really quite old.

A few examples of the not-really-very-new among modern cartridges are worth pointing out. The .244 Remington (6mm) makes a good case with which to start. Introduced in 1955, it is based on the .257 Roberts case necked down, which, in turn, is the 7x57mm Mauser slightly modified. Back in 1895, or thereabout, the Germans had a 6x57mm, made by necking down the 7x57mm Mauser. With the exception of a slight (insignificant) difference in the shoulder angle, the .244 Remington is a carbon copy of this much older cartridge.

The 7mm Remington Magnum is another brilliant "design" that is really just a modification of a much older cartridge. It is very similar to the .275 Holland & Holland Magnum introduced around 1912 or 1913. However, the H&H round didn't have a good American smokeless powder of later development to bring out its full potential. On the other hand, there are a number of wildcat 7mm short-belted magnums practically identical to the 7mm Remington Magnum that pre-date it by quite a few years and are identical in performance.

Yet another Remington innovation is the .280 Remington, a rimless cartridge based on the .30-06 case necked down. This is a dead ringer for the 7x64mm Brenneke, introduced in 1917. It is also practically identical to the wildcat 7mm-06 developed around 1928, so there is nothing very original here. It should be noted that none of these cartridges are interchangeable.

The commercial manufacturers are not alone in their design duplication. Many individuals have inadvertently done the same thing. One of the most popular wildcat cartridges anyone has thought up is the .35 Whelen, introduced about 1922 and adopted as a commercial standard by Remington, in 1987. This is simply the .30-06 case necked-up to .35-caliber. It was originated by the late Col. Townsend Whelen, but it is a very close copy of the German 9x63mm, which dates back to about 1905. As a matter of fact, a number of wildcat cartridges are nothing more than a duplication of some much older British or European designs. In fairness, it must be stated that the originator of the wildcat version probably was completely unaware of the existence of a parallel cartridge at the time.

Some companies and wildcatters go to considerable trouble to complete the circle, often coming up with something that duplicates a long-forgotten cartridge. If they were more familiar with the history of cartridge development, they could save a lot of time. The .444 Marlin, introduced during 1964, is a good case in point. To begin with, it is a poorly disguised copy of

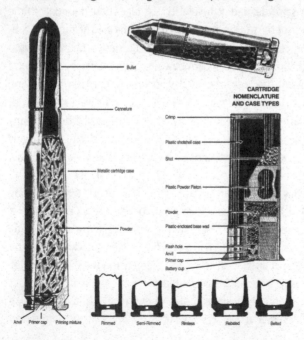

the wildcat .44 Van Houten Super that pre-dates it by at least three years. According to Parker Ackley, in his Handbook for Shooters and Reloaders, the .44 VHS is made by necking up the .30-40 Krag case, trimming it to two inches, and turning down the rim. When this is done, we end up with a near carbon copy of the 10.3x65Rmm Swiss cartridge (DWM 237A) that originated around 1900 or earlier. The only difference is in the fact that the 10.3mm case is .3-inch longer than the .44 VHS or .2-inch longer than the .444 Marlin. However, that's not all there is to the story, because the 10.3x65Rmm cartridge is based on the brass .410 shotgun shell loaded with a conical bullet and fired in a rifled barrel. It is possible to make the .444 Marlin from brass .410 cases, and the new originators could have done the same thing in the beginning.

Cartridges don't just happen; they evolve in response to some need or use requirement. Our Western frontier dictated American cartridge development for 50 years or more. Its influence is still an important factor in directing the imagination of the modern hunter. British rifle cartridges, in the main, were designed for conditions existing in other parts of the world, such as Africa and India, rather than the home island. European cartridges were developed on one hand because of hunting conditions and available game on the European continent, and on the other to compete with American and British innovations. Since the end of World War II, there has been considerable blending and standardization of the various worldwide cartridge designs. More British and European rifles and cartridges are used by American gun buffs than ever before, and they, in turn, have adopted many of our ideas.

Modern Ammunition

The most important factor influencing the ammunition available at any given time is economics. The ammunition manufacturers are willing to produce anything that will sell, but, obviously, are most reluctant to tool up and turn out something for which there is little or no demand. Military developments, as illustrated by the .30 Carbine, .30-06, 7.62mm NATO (.308 Winchester), 5.56mm (.223 Remington), .45 ACP, and that old standby, the .45-70, have almost always provided a good long-term sales record, when introduced in sporting version. For this reason, the ammunition companies have usually been quick to adopt these. They have not been quite so enthusiastic in their attitude toward cartridges developed by individuals or wildcatters. However, Remington has been the leader in introducing commercial versions of what were originally wildcat cartridges. It initiated the trend with the .257 Roberts, back in 1934, and, since 1945, have added a number of others, including the .17 Remington, .22-250 Remington, 6mm Remington, .25-06 Remington, 7mm-08, 7mm Remington Magnum, and the 8mm Remington Magnum, to name most of them. Actually, we must recognize that Winchester adopted the .22 Hornet (an original wildcat development), in 1930. Also, the .300 Winchester Magnum and possibly the .358 Winchester were around in wildcat versions before the company decided to develop something similar. The .444 Marlin is another cartridge based on a wildcat innovation. Since most of these have had good sales records, it would not be surprising to see some of the other more popular wildcats introduced in commercial version as time goes on. This is a healthy trend, and we hope it will continue.

Nostalgia is another factor that is now exerting considerable influence on ammunition and firearms trends. Shooting muzzleloading and black-powder cartridge guns of all types is a solidly established facet of the shooting game. Although there have always been a few muzzleloading clubs and a small core of black-powder devotees, the current popularity of this sport has given birth to a whole new industry specializing in the manufacture of replica arms. Muzzle-loading clubs with several hundred members are now common, and most states have special muzzleloading big-game hunting seasons. As an example of the magnitude of this development, Colt once again sold its cap-and-ball revolvers, Harrington & Richardson offered replicas of the U.S. 1873 Trapdoor cavalry carbine, Shiloh Rifle Mfg. will sell you 1874 Sharps carbines and rifles, and one can buy any number of Hawken-type muzzleloading replicas. What is mentioned here is only a very small portion of what is available to black-powder shooters. If you are interested in the full extent of the offerings in this field, I suggest you buy the latest edition of *Gun Digest* (from the same publishers that produce this book) and look in the manufacturer's web directory in the back of the book.

How does all this affect modern cartridges? The nostalgia syndrome is responsible for the reappearance of a number of long-obsolete cartridges, or at least new reloadable cases, although, admittedly, this is as yet on a rather limited or custom basis for most of the old-timers. Dixie Gun Works, for example, is offering new, reloadable cases in the old .50-70 Government caliber and has recently brought in the .41 Rimfire. The development of modern cartridges is a dynamic, rather than a static, process, although it does move in starts and stops, depending on the fads and trends of any given time. These, then, are the factors that shape our modern ammunition, and this includes some very exciting innovations (some old and some new) since the first edition of *Cartridges of the World*.

Cartridge Loading Data

Basic loading data has been furnished as part of the general information on each cartridge when available and if test rifles or cartridges were obtainable. Insofar as possible, the loads listed are for those powders that provide the most efficient velocity and energy for the caliber and bullet weight involved. With old black-powder cartridges or obsolete smokeless powder numbers, the objective has been to supply data that more or less duplicates the original factory performance figures. The cartridge loading data has been gathered from various published sources and the extensive experience of the original author and various editors. The data selected for inclusion in COTW provides a good starting point for the handloader, but there are many more good powders available for loading each cartridge than can possibly be presented here. It is, therefore, recommended that the serious reloader obtain one or more of the very fine reloading manuals published by Lyman, Speer, Hornady, Hodgdon, Sierra, Nosler, P.O. Ackley, and others. Loading data listed here does not necessarily agree with that published elsewhere, regarding the velocity obtainable with a given charge of powder, because the test conditions and equipment are not the same. There is no such thing as absolute loading data, and all published loads reflect the conditions of test firing, which include a number of important variables such as barrel length, chamber configuration, temperature, components used, test equipment, etc.

All loading data, wherever published, should be used with caution and common sense. If you are not sure or don't know what you are doing, *don't do it!* Since neither the author, editors, nor publisher has any control over the components, assembly of the ammunition, arms they are to be fired in, the degree of reloading knowledge involved, or how the resulting ammunition might be used, no responsibility, either implied or expressed, is assumed for the use of any of the cartridge loading data in this or any previous edition of *COTW*.

Cartridge Dimensional Data

The reader should understand that the cartridge schematics and the table of cartridge dimensional data at the end of this book are based either on actual cartridge measurements, SAAMI specs, or other drawings. In some instances, data is based on measurement of a single specimen. In others, it may be an average taken from several cartridges of different manufacture. The table is intended primarily to assist the reader in identifying cartridges, and its use for the purpose of chambering rifles is not recommended unless checked carefully against manufacturers' chamber dimensions. The reason? There are far greater differences in cartridge dimensions between makes and production lots than most people realize. There are differences in the third decimal place even within most 20-round boxes, in fact.

This brings up another point. From time to time, the editors will receive letters from readers complaining that their measurement of some cartridge dimension does not agree with ours and, therefore, we must be wrong. We have, for example, two letters before us—one claiming a certain figure is too high, the other stating that the very same figure is too low. The differences are all in the third decimal place. This is not a matter of anyone being wrong, but rather variances in manufacturing tolerance.

As a more specific example of the tolerance factor, I acquired a box of 10mm pistol ammunition for the Bren 10 and other semi-autos and, in measuring several rounds, found some discrepancy in the rim diameters. Just to see what the minimum and maximum figures were, I measured the entire 20-round box. It turned out that the minimum rim diameter was .419-inch and the maximum was .426-inch, or a difference of .007-inch. Is that a sufficient range to cause the pistol to malfunction? I hardly think so.

All of this is just to get the subject of cartridge dimensions into proper perspective. In any event, if your measurements don't match someone else's by a few thousandths of an inch, don't get excited and don't get the idea you may have discovered a new and heretofore unknown cartridge. You may be dealing with maximum and the other guy with minimum dimensions.—*Frank C. Barnes*

Cartridge Identification

Cartridge identification is important to anyone who works with cartridges, whatever the reason. It is of particular consequence to those involved in forensic firearms identification, military intelligence, or serious collecting. In addition to the information presented here, the collector of old, obsolete cartridges has special problems involving ignition systems and types not manufactured for 100 years or more. Much of this is beyond the scope of this book, but the basic procedures are still the same.

In teaching classes in firearms identification, I always tell my students that the easiest way to identify a cartridge is to look at the headstamp, if there is one, because in many instances that will tell you exactly what it is. Unfortunately, it isn't always that simple, since some cartridges don't have headstamps, or if it is a military or foreign round, the headstamp may not be readily decipherable. Additionally, the headstamp may be misleading. You might be dealing with a wildcat cartridge, something made by necking an original case up or down or otherwise changing the configuration. For example, the .30-06 case is used as the basis for a variety of wildcats using both military and commercial cases, so the headstamp would only indicate the original case, not the actual cartridge. Cartridge identification may range from a simple determination of caliber to the more complex ascertainment of the country of origin, date of origin, place of manufacture, and type of gun involved.

The various factors and problems involved in cartridge identification can be summarized as follows:

1. What is the caliber and/or other designation of the cartridge? For example, .38 Special, 9mm Luger, .250 Savage, 7.62x39mm (M43) Russian, .303 British, etc.
2. What type of cartridge is it: handgun, rifle, sporting, or military? Is it modern or obsolete?
3. What is the country of origin, who made it, and when was it made? The headstamp is usually the clue to these answers, but it may not do for all of them.
4. What is the functional character of the cartridge—ball, tracer, incendiary, explosive, sporting, match, etc.?
5. Is the cartridge functional? This usually requires actual testing and is important primarily to those in the forensic field. Obviously, one does not test-fire rare and valuable collectors cartridges.

Cartridges are classified on the basis of ignition type, case shape, and rim type. Combustion of the propellant charge is initiated by the primer. If the priming compound is distributed around the rim of the cartridge, it is a rimfire. If the priming compound is contained in a separate cup in the center of the case head, it is a centerfire. Until the advent of Remington's EtronX® ammunition and rifle system featuring electronic ignition in 2000, all small arms cartridges are percussion-fired. That is, the primer is detonated by the blow or impact of a hammer or firing pin. However, some military ammunition, usually of a size 20mm or greater, is electrically fired. There are two types of centerfire primers currently in general use, Boxer and Berdan. The Boxer primer is entirely self-contained with the anvil as a part of the primer. The Berdan type lacks the anvil that is produced as a small "teat" or protrusion in the primer pocket. Boxer-primed cases have a single flash hole in the center of the primer pocket, whereas Berdan-primed cases have two or more flash holes surrounding the anvil. The Boxer-type primer is used almost exclusively in the United States at the present time, although some Berdan-primed cartridges were manufactured here in the 1800s and early 1900s. The Berdan type is preferred by many European manufacturers and is usually an indication of such origin.

The cartridge base and rim type are important identifying features. These also serve an important functional purpose in feeding and extraction of the cartridge within the gun mechanism. There are five rim types: rimmed, semi-rimmed, rimless, belted and rebated.

Rimmed cartridges have a rim or extractor flange of larger diameter than the case base, often with a grooved or undercut area immediately ahead of the rim. Semi-rimmed cartridges have a rim that is only slightly larger in diameter than the base, and usually also a distinct undercut area between the rim and case base. It is sometimes difficult to recognize a semi-rimmed cartridge without actually measuring rim and base diameter, and these can easily be mistaken for a rimless case. Rimless cartridges have a rim and base of the same diameter, although the rim may actually be .001 or .002 inch larger than the base. These are the most common type of military cartridges. Belted cartridges have a distinct belt or flange at the base, just forward of the rim, and an extractor groove between the rim and the belt. Rebated cartridges have a rim of significantly smaller diameter than the case body at the base, plus a definite extractor groove between rim and base or belt. Only a few rebated cartridges have been commercialized with success, and those are usually easy to identify. In several rebated rim designs, the rim is only very slightly smaller than the case head. The .404 Jeffery and its derivatives (chiefly the Imperial and Canadian Magnums) are the best examples. These can be difficult to identify without taking careful measurements. Also, note that naming a case design "semi-rimmed" versus "rimmed" is strictly a subjective call—there is no specified difference in base diameter and rim diameter that automatically separates these two styles. However, cases described as semi-rimmed are usually visually distinguishable from similar rimless cases.

The shape or configuration of the cartridge case is also an important identifying characteristic. Cartridges can be divided into the following 12 case types, with their corresponding letter designation used in the cartridge dimensional tables at the end of each chapter:

A. Rimmed bottleneck

B. Rimmed straight	F. Belted straight	J. Rebated straight
C. Rimless bottleneck	G. Semi-rimmed bottleneck	K. Rebated belted bottleneck
D. Rimless straight	H. Semi-rimmed straight	L. Rebated belted straight
E. Belted bottleneck	I. Rebated bottleneck	It will be important to note

when referencing these letter designations that some cases described and lettered as straight are actually often tapered; case diameter can be considerably larger at the base, compared to the neck.

The bullet or projectile also provides a clue to the identity of a cartridge, its functional use, and the gun it is fired in. Based on the material or construction, bullets are divided into two major types, lead and jacketed. Lead bullets are used for low-velocity guns, such as handguns or black-powder arms. However, these may also be used for target practice in more powerful guns. Training cartridges may have wooden, fiber, composition or plastic bullets. The shape of the projectile is also important and can be round-nose, flat-nose, conical or spitzer (sharp pointed). Because of the Hague Convention, military bullets do not have lead exposed at the point and are restricted to full-metal-jacket types. Sporting ammunition or that intended for civilian use can have a variety of bullet tips with varying degrees of lead exposed, hollowpoint, plastic tips and bronze or other metal tips, to control expansion in the target.

Bullets for military use can also be classified in terms of special functional design, such as ball; tracer (T); armor-piercing (AP); incendiary (I); high explosive (HE); and observation/ranging, or spotter-tracer types. There can also be two or more of these combined in the same bullet, such as APT, API-T, HEI, or HE-T. Not all types are made in every cartridge, since their function is developed to fulfill a specific military requirement. In addition, makeup depends, to some extent, on the gun for which each is loaded. In general, ball or full metal jacket (FMJ) bullets are intended for use against personnel or unarmored vehicles. These usually have a lead core covered by a cupro-nickel jacket, or a mild steel jacket plated with some copper alloy. These can be easily identified with a magnet. At one time, the French 8mm Lebel military bullet was made of solid bronze. Tracer bullets are used for fire correction or target designation. These cannot be distinguished from ball, unless some identifying marking, such as a colored tip (usually, but not always, red), is included. Armor-piercing bullets are also similar to ball except they have a hardened steel or tungsten alloy core. They may or may not have a colored tip. Incendiary bullets contain an incendiary mixture that ignites on impact; visual identification depends on the color-coding system used. High-explosive bullets are uncommon, but do exist. These are made to explode on impact and can only be recognized by the color-coding. Observation and ranging bullets are intended to produce a flash and/or a puff of smoke to mark the point of impact. Again, these are

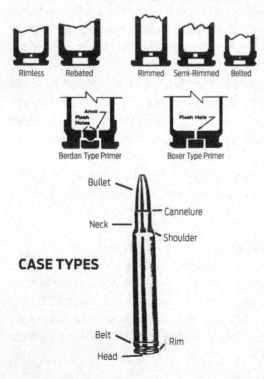

Rimless   Rebated   Rimmed   Semi-Rimmed   Belted

Berdan Type Primer   Boxer Type Primer

CASE TYPES

Bullet

Neck

Cannelure

Shoulder

Belt

Rim

Head

recognizable only when color-coded. One should handle any ammunition with a colored bullet tip with great care, as appropriate.

The headstamp is the stamped markings on the head of the cartridge. Information that can be obtained from the headstamp is extremely varied and depends on the intended purpose or use of the cartridge and who manufactured it.

Headstamps consist of one or more parts or information elements. Cartridges intended for sporting or civilian use usually have two elements. One identifies the specific chambering, the other identifies the manufacturer. Military cartridges can have from one to five elements, including cartridge, date and place of manufacture, plus other identifying markings. Some headstamps are segmented. That is, these have one or more segment lines that divide the head into two to four equal parts. This usually indicates an older cartridge, since most countries discontinued segment lines shortly after World War I. The location of the elements is most conveniently indicated by its clock-face orientation, with 12 o'clock at the top, three o'clock at the right, six o'clock at the bottom, and nine o'clock at the left. The basic U.S. military headstamp before World War II had two elements, with the factory code at 12 o'clock and the date at six o'clock. Rapid expansion of ammunition manufacturing facilities as the result of the war introduced many new designs without any effort at standardization. Some used three elements spaced equidistant from each other while others adopted a four-element system located at 12, three, six, and nine o'clock. Also, the location of the factory code was changed, in some instances, to six o'clock or another location.

Worldwide, there are more than 800 military headstamps in existence plus some 400 or more commercial headstamps that have existed at various times. Obviously, this is a complex and highly specialized field. Several volumes have been published on headstamps, including at least three by various U.S. governmental agencies. In addition, some books for cartridge collectors include headstamp data on obsolete cartridges. Since it would require another whole book to adequately cover the subject, it is quite impossible to include more than a few basics here. However, we have listed several sources for such data to assist those readers who find a need for it.

The procedure for identifying a cartridge, using the tables in Cartridges of the World, are as follows:

1. First look at the headstamp and see what, if any, information is provided there.
2. Look at the cartridge and determine what type it is: straight, necked, rimmed, rimless, etc.
3. Measure the dimensions of the cartridge and make up a table as follows:

Type (A, B, C, D, etc., as shown in the tables)	Base Diameter
Bullet Diameter	Rim Diameter
Neck Diameter	Case Length
Shoulder Diameter (if there is one)	Cartridge Length

Now go to the cartridge measurement tables in Chapter 12 or at the end of each group chapter and compare your data with the dimensional data. Check bullet diameters under the proper type, and then compare case length and, finally, other dimensions with your measurements. The type of cartridge case, caliber, and case length are the key elements to start with. For practice, two examples are shown below. See if you can identify the cartridges.

Example #1 Type: C		Example #2 Type: B	
Bullet Diameter:	.308"	Bullet Diameter:	.410"
Neck Diameter:	.340"	Neck Diameter:	.432"
Shoulder Diameter:	.441"	Shoulder Diameter:	n/a
Base Diameter:	.470"	Base Diameter:	.433"
Rim Diameter:	.473"	Rim Diameter:	.488"
Case Length:	2.490"	Case Length:	1.280"
Cartridge Length:	3.340"	Cartridge Length:	1.580"

Bear in mind that there is a certain amount of manufacturing tolerance to be allowed for and your measurements may vary .001- to .002-inch plus or minus from some dimensions in the table. The cartridge in Example 1 will be found in the chapter on modern rifle cartridges; Example 2 is in the chapter on handgun cartridges. Not every known cartridge is listed in Cartridges of the World, particularly the more obscure black-powder types. However, practically all modern sporting and military are included, so most readers will not have any difficulty. The idea here is to help you to determine what the cartridge is rather than where it originated or when.

In trying to identify cartridges, there are a couple things the reader should know. For one thing, the major ammunition manufacturers have, from time to time, made up batches of ammunition on special order with the purchaser's headstamp. Anyone can do this if your order is large enough and you have the money. Then there is the matter of commercial reloading firms that turn out ammunition for police departments and others using recycled cases of varying make and loaded with powder and bullets never used by the original company. Last, but not least, you have the individual handloader whose imagination is unbounded and who may turn out a few wondrous and non-standard products.

Headstamp Markings of the Principal American Ammunition Manufacturers

Federal Cartridge Co. - Rimfire, AL EP, G or G, HP, F, XL, XR and WM Centerfire, FC

General Electric Co. - GE plus date (military)

Newton Arms Co. - NA plus caliber (Made by Rem.)

Peters Cartridge Co. - Rimfire, P or PETERSHV Centerfire, P, PC, P.C., PCCO,

Peters E. Remington & Sons - E Remington & Sons (1870-1890)

Remington Arms Co. - U, UMC, REM, REM*, UMC, R-P, RAH

Robin Hood Ammunition Co. - R, RHA, R.H.A. Co.

Savage Arms Co. - S.A. Co. (made by U.S. Cartridge Co.)

Savage Repeating Arms Co. - S.A. Co., S.R.A.C.O.

Richard Speer Manufacturing Co. - Speer Weatherby

Union Metallic Cartridge Co. - U, UMC or R B (Purchased by Remington in 1911)

United States Cartridge Co. - US, U.S., *U.S. Cartridge CO*,U.S.C. CO. or RL (1869 to 1936)

Western Cartridge Co. - SUPER X, SUPER-X, W, WCC, W.C. Co. Western

Winchester - W, H, Super Speed, W.C. Co.

Winchester-Western - W-W, Super Speed

There were about 15 other companies that manufactured ammunition at various times, particularly during the 1860-1900 period. Also a number of private firms manufactured military ammunition during World War I and II.

United States Arsenal Headstamp Markings

Alleghany Ordnance Plant	KS plus date
Denver Ordnance Plant	DEN plus date
Des Moines Ordnance Plant	DM plus date
Eau Claire Ordnance Plant	EW plus date
Evansville Ordnance Plant	ECS plus date
Frankford Arsenal	CF plus date (45-70),
	F plus date
	FA plus date
Lake City Arsenal	LC plus date
Lowell Ordnance Plant	LM plus date
Milwaukee Ordnance Plant	M plus date
Saint Louis Ordnance Plant	SL plus date
Twin Cities Ordnance Plant	TW plus date
Utah Ordnance Plant	U plus date
	UT plus date

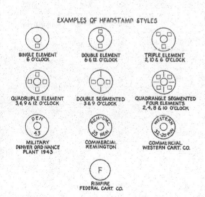

EXAMPLES OF HEADSTAMP STYLES

SINGLE ELEMENT 6 O'CLOCK

DOUBLE ELEMENT 6 & 12 O'CLOCK

TRIPLE ELEMENT 2, 10 & 6 O'CLOCK

QUADRUPLE ELEMENT 3, 6, 9 & 12 O'CLOCK

DOUBLE SEGMENTED 3 & 9 O'CLOCK

QUADRANGLE SEGMENTED FOUR ELEMENTS 2, 4, 8 & 10 O'CLOCK

MILITARY DENVER ORDNANCE PLANT 1943

COMMERCIAL REMINGTON

COMMERCIAL WESTERN CART. CO.

RIMFIRE FEDERAL CART. CO.

U.S. Small Arms Ammunition Color Codes

Bullet Tip Marking	Functional Type
Black	Armor piercing (AP)
Red	Tracer
White	Tracer, aircraft type
Blue	Incendiary

Bibliography of Cartridge Identification Publications

Jane's Directory of Military Small Arms Ammunition, by Ian V. Hogg. Jane's Publications, Inc., N.Y., N.Y., 1988.

Cartridges For Collectors, by Fred A. Datig. The Fadco Publishing Co., Vol. I, 1956 and Vol. 2, 1958.

Cartridges For Collectors, by Fred A. Datig. Borden Publishing Co., Los Angeles, Calif., Vol. 3, 1967.

Handbuch der Pistolen und Revolver Patronen, Vol. 1, by Hans A. Erlmeier und Jakob H. Brandt. E. Schwend GmbH, West Germany, 1967.

History of Modern U.S. Military Small Arms and Ammunition, by F.W. Hackley, W.H. Woodin, and E.L. Scranton. The Macmillan Co., N.Y., N.Y., 1967.

Cartridges, by Herschel C. Logan. The Stackpole Co., Harrisburg, PA, 1959.

Cartridge Guide 11/71, by Dr. Manfred R. Rosenberger, and Lilla E. Rosenberger. Sporting Goods GmbH, Bremen, West Germany, 1971.

The American Cartridge, by Charles R. Suydam. G. Robert Lawrence, Santa Ana, CA, 1960.

Centerfire Metric Pistol and Revolver Cartridges, Volume 1 of Cartridge Identification, by H.P. White and B.D. Mundhall. The Infantry Journal Press, Washington, DC, 1948.

Centerfire American and British Pistol and Revolver Cartridges, Volume 2 of Cartridge Identification, by H.P. White and B.D. Munhall. The Combat Force Press, Washington, DC, 1950.

Cartridge Headstamp Guide, by H.P. White and B.D. Munhall. H.P. White Laboratory, Bel Air, MD, 1963.

Small-Caliber Ammunition Identification Guide, Volume 1 & 2; Army Material Development and Readiness Command, DST-1160G-514-78-Vol. I & II.

Recognition Guide of Ammunition Available to, or Used by, The Viet Cong; Dept. of the Army Pamphlet #381-12, 1966.

Small Arms Ammunition Identification Guide; U.S. Army Foreign Science Technology Center, FSTC-CW-7-68, Washington, DC 20315.

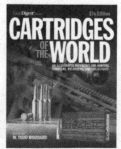

This excerpt is from *Cartridges of the World*, available at GunDigestStore.com.

APPENDIX II
Bullet Directory by Manufacturer

HORNADY

BULLET CHART

Caliber/Type	Diameter	Weight	B.C.	Item #	Caliber/Type	Diameter	Weight	B.C.	Item #
GMX®					25 Cal. SST® InterLock®	.257"	117 gr.	.390	25522
22 Cal. GMX®	.224"	50 gr.	.215	22403	6.5MM Cal. SST® InterLock®	.264"	129 gr.	.485	26202
22 Cal. GMX®	.224"	55 gr.	.270	22273	6.5MM Cal. SST® InterLock®	.264"	140 gr.	.520	26302
22 Cal. GMX®	.224"	70 gr.	.350	2281	270 Cal. SST® InterLock®	.277"	130 gr.	.460	27302
6MM GMX®	.243"	80 gr.	.300	24370	270 Cal. SST® InterLock®	.277"	140 gr.	.495	27352
25 Cal. GMX®	.257"	90 gr.	.290	25410	270 Cal. SST® InterLock®	.277"	150 gr.	.525	27402
6.5MM GMX®	.264"	120 gr.	.450	26110	7MM Cal. SST® InterLock®	.284"	139 gr.	.486	28202
270 Cal. GMX®	.277"	130 gr.	.460	27370	7MM Cal. SST® InterLock®	.284"	154 gr.	.525	28302
7MM Cal. GMX®	.284"	139 gr.	.486	28270	7MM Cal. SST® InterLock®	.284"	162 gr.	.550	28452
30 Cal. GMX®	.308"	150 gr.	.415	30370	30 Cal. SST® (300 Savage)	.308"	150 gr.	.370	30303
30 Cal. GMX®	.308"	165 gr.	.447	30470	30 Cal. SST® InterLock®	.308"	150 gr.	.415	30302
338 Cal. GMX®	.338"	185 gr.	.420	33270	30 Cal. SST® InterLock®	.308"	165 gr.	.447	30452
MonoFlex™					30 Cal. SST® InterLock®	.308"	180 gr.	.480	30702
30-30 Cal. MonoFlex™	.308"	140 gr.	.277	30310	310 Cal. SST® (7.62X39)	.310"	123 gr.	.183	3142
308 Marlin MonoFlex™	.308"	140 gr.	.335	30311	338 Cal. SST® InterLock®	.338"	200 gr.	.455	33102
45 Cal. MonoFlex™	.458"	250 gr.	.155	45010	338 Cal. SST® InterLock®	.338"	225 gr.	.515	33202
FTX®					**InterBond®**				
30 Cal. FTX® (30-30)	.308"	160 gr.	.330	30395	6MM Cal. InterBond®	.243"	85 gr.	.395	24539
308 Cal. FTX® Marlin Express	.308"	160 gr.	.395	30396	25 Cal. InterBond®	.257"	110 gr.	.390	25419
32 Win FTX®	.321"	165 gr.	.310	32005	6.5MM InterBond®	.264"	129 gr.	.485	26209
338 Cal. FTX® Marlin Express	.338"	200 gr.	.430	33104	270 Cal. InterBond®	.277"	130 gr.	.460	27309
348 Cal. FTX®	.348"	200 gr.	.320	3415	270 Cal. InterBond®	.277"	150 gr.	.525	27409
357 Cal. FTX®	.357"	140 gr.	.160	35745	7MM Cal. InterBond®	.284"	139 gr.	.486	28209
35 Cal. FTX®	.358"	200 gr.	.300	35105	7MM Cal. InterBond®	.284"	154 gr.	.525	28309
44 Mag FTX®	.430"	225 gr.	.150	44105	30 Cal. InterBond®	.308"	150 gr.	.415	30309
44 Cal. FTX® (444 Marlin)	.430"	265 gr.	.225	4305	30 Cal. InterBond®	.308"	165 gr.	.447	30459
45 Cal. FTX® (460 S&W only)	.452"	200 gr.	.145	45215	30 Cal. InterBond®	.308"	180 gr.	.480	30709
45 Colt FTX®	.452"	225 gr.	.140	45218	338 Cal. InterBond®	.338"	225 gr.	.515	33209
45 Cal. FTX® (450 Bushmaster)	.452"	250 gr.	.210	45201	**V-MAX™**				
45 Cal. FTX®	.458"	325 gr.	.230	45015	17 Cal. V-MAX™	.172"	20 gr.	.185	21710
50 Cal. FTX®	.500"	300 gr.	.200	50102	17 Cal. V-MAX™	.172"	25 gr.	.230	17105
SST®					20 Cal. V-MAX™	.204"	32 gr.	.210	22004
6MM Cal. SST® InterLock®	.243"	95 gr.	.355	24532	20 Cal. V-MAX™	.204"	40 gr.	.275	22006

Caliber/Type	Diameter	Weight	B.C.	Item #
22 Cal. V-MAX™	.224"	35 gr.	.109	22252
22 Cal. V-MAX™	.224"	40 gr.	.200	22241
22 Cal. V-MAX™	.224"	50 gr.	.242	22261
22 Cal. V-MAX™ w/Moly	.224"	50 gr.	.242	22613
22 Cal. V-MAX™	.224"	53 gr.	.290	22265
22 Cal. V-MAX™	.224"	55 gr.	.255	22271
22 Cal. V-MAX™ w/Moly	.224"	55 gr.	.255	22713
22 Cal. V-MAX™ W/C	.224"	55 gr.	.255	22272
22 Cal. V-MAX™	.224"	60 gr.	.265	22281
6MM Cal. V-MAX™	.243"	58 gr.	.250	22411
6MM Cal. V-MAX™	.243"	65 gr.	.280	22415
6MM Cal. V-MAX™	.243"	75 gr.	.330	22420
6MM Cal. V-MAX™	.243"	87 gr.	.400	22440
25 Cal. V-MAX™	.257"	75 gr.	.290	22520
6.5MM Cal. V-MAX™	.264"	95 gr.	.365	22601
270 Cal. V-MAX™ W/C	.277"	110 gr.	.370	22721
7MM Cal. V-MAX™	.284"	120 gr.	.365	22810
30 Cal. V-MAX™	.300"	110 gr.	.290	23010
NTX®				
204 Cal. NTX®	.204"	24 gr.	.170	22000
22 Cal. NTX®	.224"	35 gr.	.177	22240
Traditional Varmint				
17 Cal. HP	.172"	25 gr.	.187	1710
20 Cal. SP	.204"	45 gr.	.245	22008
22 Cal. JET	.222"	40 gr.	.104	2210
22 Cal. HORNET	.223"	45 gr.	.202	2220
22 Cal. HP BEE	.224"	45 gr.	.108	2229
22 Cal. HORNET	.224"	45 gr.	.202	2230
22 Cal. SPSX	.224"	50 gr.	.214	2240
22 Cal. SP	.224"	50 gr.	.214	2245
22 Cal. SPSX	.224"	55 gr.	.235	2260
22 Cal. SP	.224"	55 gr.	.235	2265
22 Cal. SP W/C	.224"	55 gr.	.235	2266
22 Cal. SP	.224"	60 gr.	.264	2270
22 Cal. HP	.224"	60 gr.	.271	2275
22 Cal. SP W/C	.227"	70 gr.	.296	2280
6MM Cal. HP	.243"	75 gr.	.294	2420
6MM Cal. SP	.243"	87 gr.	.327	2440

Caliber/Type	Diameter	Weight	B.C.	Item #
6MM Cal. BTHP	.243"	87 gr.	.376	2442
25 Cal. HP	.257"	75 gr.	.257	2520
25 Cal. SP	.257"	87 gr.	.322	2530
270 Cal. SP	.277"	100 gr.	.307	2710
270 Cal. HP	.277"	110 gr.	.352	2720
7MM Cal. HP	.284"	120 gr.	.334	2815
30 Cal. SJ	.308"	100 gr.	.152	3005
30 Cal. SP	.308"	110 gr.	.256	3010
30 Cal. SP	.308"	130 gr.	.295	3020
Traditional Handgun XTP® InterLock® Hunting				
6MM Cal. SP InterLock®	.243"	100 gr.	.381	2450
6MM Cal. BTSP InterLock®	.243"	100 gr.	.405	2453
25 Cal. FP	.257"	60 gr.	.101	2510
25 Cal. SP InterLock®	.257"	100 gr.	.357	2540
25 Cal. BTSP InterLock®	.257"	117 gr.	.391	2552
25 Cal. RN InterLock®	.257"	117 gr.	.243	2550
25 Cal. HP InterLock®	.257"	120 gr.	.394	2560
6.5MM Cal. SP	.264"	100 gr.	.358	2610
6.5MM Cal. SP InterLock®	.264"	129 gr.	.445	2620
6.5MM Cal. SP InterLock®	.264"	140 gr.	.465	2630
6.5MM RN	.264"	160 gr.	.283	2640
Carcano 6.5MM Cal. RN	.267"	160 gr.	.275	2645
270 Cal. SP InterLock®	.277"	130 gr.	.409	2730
270 Cal. BTSP InterLock®	.277"	140 gr.	.486	2735
270 Cal. SP InterLock®	.277"	150 gr.	.462	2740
7MM Cal. SP InterLock®	.284"	139 gr.	.392	2820
7MM Cal. BTSP InterLock®	.284"	139 gr.	.453	2825
7MM Cal. SP InterLock®	.284"	154 gr.	.433	2830
7MM Cal. BTSP InterLock®	.284"	162 gr.	.514	2845
7MM Cal. SP InterLock®	.284"	175 gr.	.462	2850
7MM Cal. RN InterLock®	.284"	175 gr.	.285	2855
30 Cal. RN	.308"	110 gr.	.150	3015
30 Cal. SP InterLock®	.308"	150 gr.	.338	3031
30 Cal. RN (30-30) InterLock®	.308"	150 gr.	.186	3035
30 Cal. BTSP InterLock®	.308"	150 gr.	.349	3033
30 Cal. SP InterLock®	.308"	165 gr.	.387	3040
30 Cal. BTSP InterLock®	.308"	165 gr.	.435	3045
30 Cal. FP (30-30) InterLock®	.308"	170 gr.	.189	3060

HORNADY

Caliber/Type	Diameter	Weight	B.C.	Item #
30 Cal. SP InterLock®	.308"	180 gr.	.425	3070
30 Cal. BTSP InterLock®	.308"	180 gr.	.452	3072
30 Cal. RN InterLock®	.308"	180 gr.	.241	3075
30 Cal. BTSP InterLock®	.308"	190 gr.	.491	3085
30 Cal. RN InterLock®	.308"	220 gr.	.300	3090
7.62 X 39MM Cal. SP	.310"	123 gr.	.252	3140
303 Cal. SP InterLock®	.312"	150 gr.	.361	3120
303 Cal. RN InterLock®	.312"	174 gr.	.262	3130
32 Cal. FP InterLock®	.321"	170 gr.	.249	3210
8MM Cal. SP InterLock®	.323"	150 gr.	.290	3232
8MM Cal. RN InterLock®	.323"	170 gr.	.217	3235
8MM Cal. SP InterLock®	.323"	195 gr.	.410	3236
338 Cal. SP-RP InterLock®	.338"	200 gr.	.361	3310
338 Cal. SP-RP InterLock®	.338"	225 gr.	.397	3320
338 Cal. SP-RP InterLock®	.338"	250 gr.	.431	3335
338 Cal. RN InterLock®	.338"	250 gr.	.291	3330
348 Cal. FP InterLock®	.348"	200 gr.	.246	3410
35 Cal. SP-SSP InterLock®	.358"	180 gr.	.248	3505
35 Cal. SP-RP InterLock®	.358"	200 gr.	.282	3510
35 Cal. RN InterLock®	.358"	200 gr.	.195	3515
35 Cal. SP-RP InterLock®	.358"	250 gr.	.375	3520
35 Cal. RN InterLock®	.358"	250 gr.	.271	3525
9.3 Cal. SP-RP InterLock®	.366	286 gr.	.400	3560
375 Cal. FP (375 Win.)	.375"	220 gr.	.217	3705
375 Cal. SP-RP InterLock®	.375"	225 gr.	.320	3706
375 Cal. SP-RP InterLock®	.375"	270 gr.	.380	3711
375 Cal. BTSP-RP InterLock®	.375"	300 gr.	.460	3725
375 Cal. RN InterLock®	.375"	300 gr.	.250	3720
405 Cal. FP InterLock®	.411"	300 gr.	.215	41050
405 Cal. SP InterLock®	.411"	300 gr.	.250	41051
416 Cal. RN InterLock®	.416"	400 gr.	.311	4165
44 Cal. FP InterLock®	.430"	265 gr.	.186	4300
45 Cal. HP	.458"	300 gr.	.197	4500
45 Cal. RN InterLock®	.458"	350 gr.	.189	4502
45 Cal. FP InterLock®	.458"	350 gr.	.195	4503
45 Cal. RN InterLock®	.458"	500 gr.	.287	4504
Full Metal Jacket				
22 Cal. BT-FMJ w/c	.224"	55 gr.	.243	2267

Caliber/Type	Diameter	Weight	B.C.	Item #
30 Cal. FMJ	.308"	110 gr.	.178	3017
30 Cal. BT-FMJ	.308"	150 gr.	.398	3037
303 Cal. BT-FMJ	.3105"	174 gr.	.470	3131
Dangerous Game™				
9.3 MM DGS®	.366"	300 gr.	.280	3565
375 Cal. DGX®	.375"	300 gr.	.275	3721
375 Cal. DGS®	.375"	300 gr.	.275	3727
400 Cal. DGX®	.410"	400 gr.	.325	4104
400 Cal. DGS®	.410"	400 gr.	.325	4103
416 Cal. DGX®	.416"	400 gr.	.319	4169
416 Cal. DGS®	.416"	400 gr.	.319	4167
423 Cal. DGX®	.423"	400 gr.	.315	4240
423 Cal. DGS®	.423"	400 gr.	.315	4241
458 Cal. DGX®	.458"	480 gr.	.285	45032
458 Cal. DGS®	.458"	480 gr.	.285	45033
458 Cal. DGX®	.458"	500 gr.	.295	4505
458 Cal. DGS®	.458"	500 gr.	.295	4507
470 Cal. DGX®	.474"	500 gr.	.290	4747
470 Cal. DGS®	.474"	500 gr.	.290	4748
505 Cal. DGX®	.505"	525 gr.	.270	5050
505 Cal. DGS®	.505"	525 gr.	.270	5051
510 Cal. DGX®	.510"	570 gr.	.295	5150
510 Cal. DGS®	.510"	570 gr.	.295	5155
BTHP Match™				
22 Cal. BTHP	.224"	52 gr.	.229	2249
22 Cal. HP	.224"	53 gr.	.218	2250
22 Cal. BTHP	.224"	68 gr.	.355	2278
22 Cal. BTHP	.224"	75 gr.	.395	2279
6MM BTHP	.243"	105 gr.	.530	2458
6.5MM BTHP	.264	140 gr.	.580	26335
6.8 Cal. BTHP w/c	.277"	110 gr.	.360	27200
7MM BTHP	.284"	162 gr.	.610	28405
30 Cal. BTHP	.308"	168 gr.	.450	30501
30 Cal. BTHP w/Moly	.308"	168 gr.	.450	30503
30 Cal. BTHP	.308"	178 gr.	.530	30715
30 Cal. BTHP	.308"	195 gr.	.550	3095
30 Cal. BTHP	.308"	208 gr.	.620	30733
30 Cal. BTHP	.308"	225 gr.	.670	30903

Caliber/Type	Diameter	Weight	B.C.	Item #
8MM BTHP	.323"	196 gr.	.525	3237
338 Cal. BTHP	.338"	250 gr.	.670	33361
338 Cal. BTHP	.338"	285 gr.	.720	3339
416 Cal. BTHP	.416"	450 gr.	.720	41691
A-MAX®				
22 Cal. A-MAX®	.224"	52 gr.	.247	22492
22 Cal. A-MAX®	.224"	75 gr.	.435	22792
22 Cal. A-MAX® w/ Moly	.224"	75 gr.	.435	22794
22 Cal. A-MAX®	.224"	80 gr.	.473	22832
6MM Cal. A-MAX®	.243"	105 gr.	.500	24562
6MM Cal. A-MAX® w/Moly	.243"	105 gr.	.500	24564
6.5MM Cal. A-MAX®	.264"	100 gr.	.390	26101
6.5MM Cal. A-MAX®	.264"	120 gr.	.465	26172
6.5MM Cal. A-MAX®	.264"	123 gr.	.510	26171
6.5MM Cal. A-MAX®	.264"	140 gr.	.585	26332
7MM Cal. A-MAX®	.284"	162 gr.	.625	28402
30 Cal. A-MAX®	.308"	155 gr.	.435	30312
30 Cal. A-MAX® w/Moly	.308"	155 gr.	.435	30314
30 Cal. A-MAX®	.308"	168 gr.	.475	30502
30 Cal. A-MAX® w/Moly	.308"	168 gr.	.475	30504
30 Cal. A-MAX®	.308"	178 gr.	.495	30712
30 Cal. A-MAX®	.308"	208 gr.	.648	30732
50 Cal. A-MAX®	.510"	750 gr.	1.050	5165
Handgun XTP®				
30 Cal. RN	.308"	86 gr.	.105	3100
30 Cal. XTP®	.308"	90 gr.	.115	31000
32 Cal. XTP®	.312"	60 gr.	.090	32010
32 Cal. XTP®	.312"	85 gr.	.145	32050
32 Cal. XTP®	.312"	100 gr.	.170	32070
9MM Cal. XTP®	.355"	90 gr.	.099	35500
9MM Cal. XTP®	.355"	115 gr.	.129	35540
9MM Cal. XTP®	.355"	124 gr.	.165	35571
9MM Cal. XTP®	.355"	147 gr.	.212	35580
38 Cal. XTP®	.357"	110 gr.	.131	35700
38 Cal. XTP®	.357"	125 gr.	.151	35710
38 Cal. FP-XTP®	.357"	125 gr.	.148	35730
38 Cal. XTP®	.357"	140 gr.	.169	35740
38 Cal. XTP®	.357"	158 gr.	.206	35750

Caliber/Type	Diameter	Weight	B.C.	Item #
38 Cal. XTP®	.357"	158 gr.	.199	35780
38 Cal. XTP®	.357"	180 gr.	.230	35771
9 X 18MM XTP®	.365"	95 gr.	.127	36500
10MM Cal. XTP®	.400"	155 gr.	.137	40000
10MM Cal. XTP®	.400"	180 gr.	.164	40040
10MM Cal. XTP®	.400"	200 gr.	.199	40060
41 Cal. XTP®	.410"	210 gr.	.182	41000
44 Cal. XTP®	.430"	180 gr.	.138	44050
44 Cal. XTP®	.430"	200 gr.	.170	44100
44 Cal. XTP®	.430"	240 gr.	.205	44200
44 Cal. CL-SIL	.430"	240 gr.	.174	4425
44 Cal. XTP®	.430"	300 gr.	.245	44280
45 Cal. XTP®	.451"	185 gr.	.139	45100
45 Cal. XTP®	.451"	200 gr.	.151	45140
45 Cal. XTP®	.451"	230 gr.	.188	45160
45 Cal. XTP® MAG™	.452"	240 gr.	.160	45220
45 Cal. XTP®	.452"	250 gr.	.146	45200
45 Cal. XTP® MAG™	.452"	300 gr.	.200	45235
45 Cal. XTP®	.452"	300 gr.	.180	45230
475 Cal. XTP® MAG™	.475"	325 gr.	.150	47500
475 Cal. XTP® MAG™	.475"	400 gr.	.182	47550
50 Cal. (50 AE) XTP® MAG™	.500"	300 gr.	.120	50101
50 Cal. XTP® MAG™	.500"	350 gr.	.145	50100
50 Cal. FP XTP®	.500"	500 gr.	.185	50105
Handgun FMJ				
9MM Cal. FMJ RN	.355"	115 gr.	.140	35557
9MM Cal. FMJ FP	.355"	124 gr.	.174	35567B
9MM Cal. FMJ RN	.355"	124 gr.	.145	35577B
10MM Cal. FMJ FP	.400"	180 gr.	.188	400471
45 Cal. FMJ SWC	.451"	185 gr.	.068	45137
45 Cal. FMJ CT	.451"	200 gr.	.115	45157B
45 Cal. FMJ RN	.451"	230 gr.	.184	45177
45 Cal. FMJ	.451"	230 gr.	.168	45187B
Handgun HAP®				
9MM Cal. HAP®	.356"	121 gr.	.147	35530B
9MM Cal. HAP®	.356"	125 gr.	.158	35721/ 35572B
10MM Cal. HAP®	.400"	180 gr.	.164	40042B
45 Cal. HAP®	.451"	230 gr.	.188	45161B

HORNADY

HORNADY

Caliber/Type	Diameter	Weight	B.C.	Item #
Frontier® Lead				
32 Cal. SWC	.314"	90 gr.	.096	10008
32 Cal. HBWC	.314"	90 gr.	.040	10028
38 Cal. Cowboy	.358"	140 gr.	.127	10078
38 Cal. HBWC	.358"	148 gr.	.047	10208
38 Cal. SWC	.358"	158 gr.	.135	10408
38 Cal. SWC/HP	.358"	158 gr.	.139	10428
38 Cal. LRN	.358"	158 gr.	.159	10508
44 Cal. Cowboy	.427"	205 gr.	.123	11208
44 Cal. Cowboy	.430"	180 gr.	.114	11058
44 Cal. SWC	.430"	240 gr.	.182	11108
44 Cal. SWC/HP	.430"	240 gr.	.204	11118
45 Cal. SWC	.452"	200 gr.	.070	12108
45 Cal. L-C/T	.452"	200 gr.	.081	12208
45 Cal. LRN	.452"	230 gr.	.207	12308
45 Cal. Cowboy	.454"	255 gr.	.117	12458

BULLET LEGEND			
BT	Boattail	GMX®	Gilding Metal eXpanding®
CL-SIL	Crimp Lock Silhouette	HAP®	Hornady Action Pistol®
DGS®	Dangerous Game™ Solid	HBWC	Hollow Base Wadcutter
DGX®	Dangerous Game™ Expanding	HP	Hollow Point
ENC	Encapsulated	IB	InterBond®
FMJ	Full Metal Jacket	L-C/T	Lead Combat Target
FP	Flat Point	LRN	Lead Round Nose
FTX®	Flex Tip® eXpanding	w/Moly	Moly Coated
		NTX®	Non Toxic eXpanding®

RN	Round Nose		
SIL	Silhouette		
SP	Spire Point		
SP-RP	Spire Point Recoil Proof		
SST®	Super Shock Tip™		
SSP	Single Shot Pistol		
SWC	Semi Wadcutter		
w/c	With Cannelure		
XTP®	eXtreme Terminal Performance®		

RIFLE AMMUNITION

Caliber		Description	Item #	Caliber		Description	Item #
17 Mach 2®	V	17 gr. V-MAX™	83177		V	55 gr. V-MAX™	8337
	V	15.5 gr. NTX™	83176		C	60 gr. SP	8039
17 HMR®	V	17 gr. V-MAX™	83170	220 Swift	V	40 gr. V-MAX™ Moly	83213
	V	15.5 gr. NTX®	83171		V	55 gr. V-MAX™	8324
	V	20 gr. XTP	83172		C	60 gr. HP	8122
17 Hornet	SV	20 gr. V-MAX™	83005	243 Winchester	SV	58 gr. V-MAX™	8343
22 WMR®	V	25 gr. NTX®	83201		V	58 gr. V-MAX™ Moly	83423
	V	30 gr. V-MAX™	83202		C	75 gr. HP	8040
22 Hornet	V	35 gr. V-MAX™	8302		SF	80 gr. GMX®	80456
204 Ruger	SV	24 gr. NTX®	83209		SF	95 gr. SST®	80463
	V	32 gr. V-MAX™	83204		C	95 gr. SST®	80464
	V	40 gr. V-MAX™	83206		C	100 gr. InterLock® BTSP	8046
	V	45 gr. SP	83208	6MM Remington	SF	95 gr. SST®	81663
5.45 x 39MM	V	60 gr. V-MAX™	8124		C	100 gr. BTSP InterLock®	8166
222 Remington	SV	35 gr. NTX®	8309	25-06 Remington	SF	90 gr. GMX®	81446
	V	40 gr. V-MAX™	8310		SF	117 gr. SST®	81453
	SV	50 gr. V-MAX™	8316		C	117 gr. SST®	81454
223 Remington	SV	35 gr. NTX®	83266		C	117 gr. BTSP InterLock®	8145
	V	40 gr. V-MAX™	8325	257 Weatherby Mag	C	90 gr. GMX®	8136
	SV	53 gr. V-MAX™	8025		C	110 gr. InterBond®	81363
	SF	55 gr. GMX®	83274	257 Roberts + P	SF	117 gr. SST®	81353
	S	55 gr. HP Steel Match™	80274		C	117 gr. BTSP InterLock®	8135
	T	55 gr. TAP®-FPD™	83278	6.5 x 55MM Swedish Mauser	VM	140 gr. BTHP Match™	85508
	V	55 gr. V-MAX™ Moly	83273		SF	140 gr. SST®	85507
	V	55 gr. V-MAX™	8327	6.5 Grendel	M	123 gr. A-MAX®	8150
	S	75 gr. BTHP Steel	80261	6.5 Creedmoor	M	120 gr. A-MAX®	81492
	T	75 gr. TAP®-FPD™	80268		SF	120 gr. GMX®	81490
	M	75 gr. BTHP	8026		F	129 gr. SST®	81496
	SM	75 gr. BTHP	80264		SF	129 gr. InterBond®	81497
5.56 NATO	SF	55 gr. GMX®	81254		M	140 gr. A-MAX®	81494
	SM	75 gr. BTHP	81264	6.8 SPC	V	110 gr. V-MAX™	8346
22-250 Remington	SV	35 gr. NTX®	8334		M	110 gr. BTHP	8146
	V	40 gr. V-MAX™	8335		C	120 gr. SST®	8347
	V	50 gr. V-MAX™	8336	270 Winchester	SF	130 gr. Interbond®	80548
	SV	50 gr. V-MAX™	83366		SF	130 gr. GMX®	8052
	V	50 gr. V-MAX™ Moly	83363		SF	130 gr. SST®	80543

HORNADY

HORNADY

Caliber		Description	Item #
	C	130 gr. SST®	8054
	C	130 gr. SP InterLock®	8055
	SF	140 gr. SST®	80563
	C	140 gr. BTSP InterLock®	8056
	C	150 gr. SP InterLock®	8058
7 x 57MM Mauser	SF	139 gr. GMX®	81556
	SF	139 gr. SST®	81553
	C	139 gr. BTSP InterLock®	8155
7MM-08 Remington	SF	139 gr. GMX®	80576
	SF	139 gr. SST®	80573
280 Remington	SF	139 gr. SST®	81583
	SF	139 gr. GMX®	81586
303 British	C	150 gr. SP InterLock®	8225
	VM	174 gr. BTHP Match™	8228
7MM Remington Mag	SF	139 gr. GMX®	80592
	SF	139 gr. SST®	80593
	C	139 gr. BTSP InterLock®	8059
	SF	154 gr. SST®	8061
	SF	154 gr. InterBond®	80628
	C	154 gr. SP InterLock®	8060
	C	154 gr. SST®	8062
	SF	162 gr. SST®	80633
	C	162 gr. BTSP InterLock®	8063
7MM Weatherby Mag	C	139 gr. GMX®	80666
	C	154 gr. InterBond®	80689
300 Whisper	C	110 gr. V-MAX™	8089
	C	208 gr. A-MAX®	80892
300 Savage	SF	150 gr. SST®	82221
30-30 Winchester	LE	140 gr. MonoFlex™	82731
	C	150 gr. RN InterLock®	8080
	LE	160 gr. FTX®	82730
	C	170 gr. FP InterLock®	8085
308 Marlin Express	LE	140 gr. MonoFlex™	82734
	LE	160 gr. FTX®	82733
308 Winchester	T	110 gr. TAP®-FPD™	80898
	SF	150 gr. GMX®	8094
	SF	150 gr. SST®	80933
	C	150 gr. SST®	8093

Caliber		Description	Item #
	C	150 gr. BTSP InterLock®	8091
	SF	150 gr. InterBond®	80938
	M	155 gr. OTM	8087N
	S	155 gr. BTHP Match™	80926
	T	155 gr. TAP®-FPD™	80928
	M	155 gr. A-MAX® Match™	8095PM
	SF	165 gr. SST®	80983
	SF	165 gr. InterBond®	80998
	SF	165 gr. GMX®	8099
	C	165 gr. BTSP InterLock®	8098
	M	168 gr. A-MAX® Match™	8096
	M	168 gr. BTHP Match™	8097
	SM	168 gr. A-MAX®	80964
	T	168 gr. TAP®-FPD™	80968
	SM	178 gr. BTHP	8077
	M	178 gr. BTHP	8105
30 Carbine	S	110 gr. FMJ	8103
30 TC	SF	150 gr. GMX®	81006
	SF	150 gr. SST®	81004
	SF	165 gr. SST®	81014
30-06 Springfield	SF	150 gr. SST®	81093
	SF	150 gr. GMX®	8112
	C	150 gr. SP InterLock®	8110
	C	150 gr. SST®	8109
	SF	150 gr. InterBond®	81098
	SF	165 gr. SST®	81153
	SF	165 gr. GMX®	8116
	C	165 gr. BTSP InterLock®	8115
	C	165 gr. SST®	81154
	SF	165 gr. InterBond®	81158
	M	168 gr. A-MAX® M1 Garand	81170
	C	180 gr. SP InterLock®	8118
	C	180 gr. SST®	81184
	SF	180 gr. SST®	81183
	SF	180 gr. InterBond®	81188
300 RCM	SF	150 gr. GMX®	82230
	SF	150 gr. SST®	82231
	SF	165 gr. GMX®	82229

Caliber		Description	Item #
	SF	165 gr. SST®	82232
	SF	180 gr. SST®	82235
	SF	180 gr. InterBond®	82228
300 H&H Mag	C	180 gr. InterBond®	8210
300 Winchester Mag	SF	150 gr. GMX®	82012
	C	150 gr. SST®	82014
	C	150 gr. BTSP InterLock®	8201
	C	165 gr. BTSP InterLock®	8202
	C	165 gr. SST®	82024
	SF	165 gr. GMX®	82026
	SF	165 gr. InterBond®	82028
	M	178 gr. A-MAX®	8203
	C	180 gr. SP InterLock®	8200
	C	180 gr. SST®	82194
	SF	180 gr. InterBond®	82198
	SF	180 gr. SST®	82193
	M	195 gr. BTHP Match™	8218
300 Weatherby Mag	C	150 gr. InterBond®	82219
	C	165 gr. GMX®	82220
	C	180 gr. SP InterLock®	8222
7.62 x 39 MM	C	123 gr. SST®	8078
7.62 x 54R	VM	174 gr. BTHP Match™ (Steel Case)	80518
32 Win Special	LE	165 gr. FTX®	82732
338 Marlin Express	LE	200 gr. FTX®	82240
338 RCM	SF	185 gr. GMX®	82238
	SF	200 gr. SST®	82237
	SF	225 gr. SST®	82236
	SF	225 gr. InterBond®	82138
338 Win Mag	SF	185 gr. GMX®	82226
	SF	200 gr. SST®	82223
	SF	225 gr. SST®	82233
	C	225 gr. SST®	82234
	SF	225 gr. InterBond®	82338
338 Lapua	M	250 gr. BTHP Match™	8230
	M	285 gr. BTHP Match™	82306
35 Remington	LE	200 gr. FTX®	82735
35 Whelen	SF	200 gr. SP InterLock®	81193
358 Winchester	C	200 gr. SP InterLock®	91318

Caliber		Description	Item #
8X57 JS	VM	196 gr. BTHP Match™	82298
9.3 x 62MM	DG	286 gr. SP-RP InterLock®	82303
9.3 X 74R	DG	286 gr. SP-RP InterLock®	82304
376 Steyr	DG	225 gr. SP InterLock®	8234
	DG	270 gr. SP-RP InterLock®	8237
375 H&H	DG	270 gr. SP-RP Superformance®	8508
	DG	270 gr. SP-RP InterLock®	82312
	DG	300 gr. DGS® Superformance®	8509
	DG	300 gr. DGS®	82322
	DG	300 gr. DGX®	82332
375 Ruger	DG	270 gr. SP-RP Superformance®	8231
	DG	300 gr. DGS® Superformance®	8232
	DG	300 gr. DGX® Superformance®	82333
404 Jeffery	DG	400 gr. DGS®	8239
	DG	400 gr. DGX®	8238
405 Winchester	C	300 gr. SP InterLock®	8241
416 Rem	DG	400 gr. DGS®	82674
	DG	400 gr. DGX®	82673
416 Rigby	DG	400 gr. DGS®	8265
	DG	400 gr. DGX®	82663
416 Ruger	DG	400 gr. DGX® Superformance®	82665
	DG	400 gr. DGS® Superformance®	82666
444 Marlin	LE	265 gr. FTX®	82744
	SF	265 gr. FP InterLock®	82453
45-70 Government	LE	250 gr. MonoFlex™	82741
	LE	325 gr. FTX®	82747
450 Marlin	LE	325 gr. FTX®	82750
	C	350 gr. FP InterLock®	8250
450/400 Nitro Express 3"	DG	400 gr. DGS®	8242
	DG	400 gr. DGX®	82433
450 Nitro Express 3¼"	DG	480 gr. DGX®	8255
	DG	480 gr. DGS®	8256
450 Bushmaster	C	250 gr. FTX®	82244
458 Win Mag	DG	500 gr. DGX® Superformance®	85833
	DG	500 gr. DGS® Superformance®	8585
458 Lott	DG	500 gr. DGX®	82613
	DG	500 gr. DGS®	8262
470 Nitro Express	DG	500 gr. DGS®	8264

HORNADY

HORNADY

Caliber		Description	Item #
	DG	500 gr. DGX®	8263
500 Nitro Express	DG	570 gr. DGS®	8269

Caliber		Description	Item #
	DG	570 gr. DGX®	8268
50 BMG	M	750 gr. A-MAX® Match™	8270

HANDGUN AMMUNITION

Caliber		Description	Item #
22 WMR®	CD	45 gr. FTX®	83200
25 Auto	C	35 gr. XTP®	90012
32 Auto	C	60 gr. XTP®	90062
380 Auto	C	90 gr. XTP®	90102
	CD	90 gr. FTX®	90080
9 MM Luger	C	115 gr. XTP®	90252
	CD	115 gr. FTX®	90250
	C	124 gr. XTP®	90242
	T	124 gr. TAP®-FPD™	90248
	S	125 gr. HAP® Steel	90275
	D	135 gr. FlexLock®	90236
	C	147 gr. XTP®	90282
9 MM Luger +P	D	135 gr. FlexLock®	90226
9x18 MM Makarov	C	95 gr. XTP®	91002
	CD	95 gr. FTX®	91000
38 Special	CD	110 gr. FTX®	90310
	C	125 gr. XTP®	90322
	C	158 gr. XTP®	90362
38 Special +P	CD	110 gr. FTX®	90311
357 Magnum	C	125 gr. XTP®	90502
	CD	125 gr. FTX®	90500
	C	140 gr. XTP®	90552
	LE	140 gr. FTX®	92755
	C	158 gr. XTP®	90562
357 SIG	C	124 gr. XTP®	9130
	C	147 gr. XTP®	9131
40 S&W	C	155 gr. XTP®	9132
	T	155 gr. TAP®-FPD™	91328
	CD	165 gr. FTX®	91340
	D	175 gr. FlexLock®	91376
	S	180 gr. HAP® Steel	91362
	C	180 gr. XTP®	9136
10 MM Auto	C	155 gr. XTP®	9122

Caliber		Description	Item #
	C	180 gr. XTP®	9126
	C	200 gr. XTP®	9129
44-40 Cowboy	C	205 gr. Cowboy	9075
44 Special	CD	165 gr. FTX®	90700
	C	180 gr. XTP®	9070
44 Remington Mag	C	180 gr. XTP®	9081
	C	200 gr. XTP®	9080
	LE	225 gr. FTX®	92782
	C	240 gr. XTP®	9085
	C	300 gr. XTP®	9088
45 Auto	C	185 gr. XTP®	9090
	CD	185 gr. FTX®	90900
	C	200 gr. XTP®	9112
	S	230 gr. HAP® Steel	90985
	C	230 gr. FMJ RN	9097
45 Auto + P	T	200 gr. TAP®-FPD™	91128
	C	200 gr. XTP®	9113
	C	230 gr. XTP®	9096
	T	230 gr. TAP®-FPD™	90958
45 Colt	CD	185 gr. FTX®	92790
	C	255 gr. Cowboy	9115
	LE	225 gr. FTX®	92792
454 Casull	C	240 gr. XTP® MAG™	9148
	C	300 gr. XTP® MAG™	9150
460 S&W	C	200 gr. FTX®	9152
475 Linebaugh	C	400 gr. XTP® MAG™	9140
480 Ruger	C	325 gr. XTP® MAG™	9138
	C	400 gr. XTP® MAG™	9144
50 AE	C	300 gr. XTP®	9245
500 S&W	C	300 gr. FTX®	9249
	C	350 gr. XTP® MAG™	9250
	C	500 gr. XTP®	9252

SHOTGUN AMMUNITION

Caliber		Description	Item #
12 Gauge	SF	12 gauge 00 Buck	86246
	T	12 gauge TAP®-FPD™ 00 Buck	86276
	CD	12 gauge 00 Buck	86240
	V	12 gauge #4 Buckshot	86243
	HM	12 gauge #4 Nickel Turkey	86242
	HM	12 gauge #5 Nickel Turkey	86241
	HM	12 gauge #6 Nickel Turkey	86244
SST® Shotgun Slug	C	20 ga. 250 gr. FTX®	86232
	C	12 ga. 300 gr. FTX®	8623

AMMUNITION LEGEND			
C	Custom™	S	Steel Match™
CD	Critical Defense®	SF	Superformance®
D	Critical DUTY™	SM	Superformance® Match™
DG	Dangerous Game™ Series	SV	Superformance® Varmint
HM	Heavy Magnum® Turkey	T	TAP® FPD™
LE	LEVERevolution®	V	Varmint Express®
M	Match™	VM	Vintage Match™

HORNADY

NOSLER

BULLET CHART

CAL	DIA	Description	SD	BC	OAL	Part #
Partition® Hunting						
22 Cal	(.224")	60 Gr. Spitzer	0.171	0.228	0.790"	16316
6mm	(.243")	85 Gr. Spitzer	0.206	0.315	0.950"	16314
6mm	(.243")	95 Gr. Spitzer	0.230	0.365	1.025"	16315
6mm	(.243")	100 Gr. Spitzer	0.242	0.384	1.065"	35642
25 Cal	(.257")	100 Gr. Spitzer	0.216	0.377	1.035"	16317
25 Cal	(.257")	115 Gr. Spitzer	0.249	0.389	1.145"	16318
25 Cal	(.257")	120 Gr. Spitzer	0.260	0.391	1.175"	35643
6.5mm	(.264")	100 Gr. Spitzer	0.205	0.326	0.962"	16319
6.5mm	(.264")	125 Gr. Spitzer	0.256	0.449	1.170"	16320
6.5mm	(.264")	140 Gr. Spitzer	0.287	0.490	1.290"	16321
270 Cal	(.277")	130 Gr. Spitzer	0.242	0.416	1.135"	16322
270 Cal	(.277")	140 Gr. Spitzer	0.261	0.432	1.190"	35200
270 Cal	(.277")	150 Gr. Spitzer	0.279	0.465	1.250"	16323
270 Cal	(.277")	160 Gr. Semi Spitzer	0.298	0.434	1.300"	16324
7mm	(.284")	140 Gr. Spitzer	0.248	0.434	1.160"	16325
7mm	(.284")	150 Gr. Spitzer	0.266	0.456	1.220"	16326
7mm	(.284")	160 Gr. Spitzer	0.283	0.475	1.270"	16327
7mm	(.284")	175 Gr. Spitzer	0.310	0.519	1.360"	35645
30 Cal	(.308")	150 Gr. Spitzer	0.226	0.387	1.100"	16329
30 Cal	(.308")	165 Gr. Spitzer	0.248	0.410	1.175"	16330
30 Cal	(.308")	170 Gr. Spitzer	0.256	0.252	1.030"	16333
30 Cal	(.308")	180 Gr. Protected Point	0.271	0.361	1.180"	25396
30 Cal	(.308")	180 Gr. Spitzer	0.271	0.474	1.260"	16331
30 Cal	(.308")	200 Gr. Spitzer	0.301	0.481	1.350"	35626
30 Cal	(.308")	220 Gr. Semi Spitzer	0.331	0.351	1.370"	16332
8mm	(.323")	200 Gr. Spitzer	0.274	0.426	1.240"	35277
338 Cal	(.338")	210 Gr. Spitzer	0.263	0.400	1.200"	16337
338 Cal	(.338")	225 Gr. Spitzer	0.281	0.454	1.300"	16336
338 Cal	(.338")	250 Gr. Spitzer	0.313	0.473	1.375"	35644
35 Cal	(.358")	225 Gr. Spitzer	0.251	0.421	1.175"	44800
35 Cal	(.358")	250 Gr. Spitzer	0.279	0.446	1.270"	44801
9.3mm	(.366")	286 Gr. Spitzer (18.5 gram)	0.307	0.482	1.375"	44750
375 Cal	(.375")	260 Gr. Spitzer	0.264	0.314	1.145"	44850
375 Cal	(.375")	300 Gr. Spitzer	0.305	0.398	1.335"	44845
416 Cal	(.416")	400 Gr. Spitzer	0.330	0.390	1.485"	45200
458 Cal	(.458")	500 Gr. Protected Point	0.341	0.389	1.443"	44745

CAL	DIA	Description	SD	BC	OAL	Part #
AccuBond® Bonded Bullets						
Caliber	Diameter	Description	SD	BC	OAL	Part #
22 Cal	(.224")	70 Gr. Spitzer	0.199	0.370	0.985"	53780
6mm	(.243")	90 Gr. Spitzer	0.218	0.376	1.085"	56357
25 Cal	(.257")	110 Gr. Spitzer	0.238	0.418	1.180"	53742
6.5mm	(.264")	130 Gr. Spitzer	0.266	0.488	1.305"	56902
6.5mm	(.264")	140 Gr. Spitzer	0.287	0.509	1.375"	57873
6.8mm	(.277")	100 Gr. Spitzer W/Cannelure	0.186	0.323	1.030"	57845
6.8mm	(.277")	110 Gr. Spitzer W/Cannelure	0.205	0.370	1.105"	54382
270 Cal	(.277")	130 Gr. Spitzer	0.242	0.435	1.230"	54987
270 Cal	(.277")	140 Gr. Spitzer	0.261	0.460	1.295"	54765
270 Cal	(.277")	150 Gr. Spitzer	0.279	0.500	1.345"	54801
7mm	(.284")	140 Gr. Spitzer	0.248	0.485	1.270"	59992
7mm	(.284")	150 Gr. Spitzer	0.266	0.493	1.290"	54951
7mm	(.284")	160 Gr. Spitzer	0.283	0.531	1.385"	54932
30 Cal	(.308")	125 Gr. Spitzer	0.188	0.366	1.080"	52165
30 Cal	(.308")	150 Gr. Spitzer	0.226	0.435	1.200"	56719
30 Cal	(.308")	165 Gr. Spitzer	0.248	0.475	1.290"	55602
30 Cal	(.308")	180 Gr. Spitzer	0.271	0.507	1.380"	54825
30 Cal	(.308")	200 Gr. Spitzer	0.301	0.588	1.485"	54618
8mm	(.323")	200 Gr. Spitzer	0.274	0.450	1.380"	54374
338 Cal	(.338")	180 Gr. Spitzer	0.225	0.372	1.240"	57625
338 Cal	(.338")	200 Gr. Spitzer	0.250	0.414	1.340"	56382
338 Cal	(.338")	225 Gr. Spitzer	0.281	0.550	1.450"	54357
338 Cal	(.338")	250 Gr. Spitzer	0.313	0.575	1.567"	57287
338 Cal	(.338")	300 Gr. Spitzer	0.375	0.720	1.750"	54851
35 Cal	(.358")	200 Gr. Spitzer (Whelen)	0.223	0.365	1.245"	54425
35 Cal	(.358")	225 Gr. Spitzer (Whelen)	0.251	0.430	1.365"	50712
9.3mm	(.366")	250 Gr. Spitzer W/Cannelure	0.267	0.494	1.375"	59756
375 Cal	(.375")	260 Gr. Spitzer W/Cannelure	0.264	0.473	1.380"	54413
375 Cal	(.375")	300 Gr. Spitzer W/Cannelure	0.305	0.485	1.520"	53662
AccuBond® Bonded Long-Range (LR)						
6.5mm	(.264")	129 Gr. Spitzer	0.264	0.530	1.370"	58943
6.5mm	(.264")	142 Gr. Spitzer	0.291	0.625	1.445"	58922
6.5mm	(.264")	150 Gr. Spitzer	0.327	0.634	1.495"	58930
270 Cal	(.277")	150 Gr. Spitzer	0.279	0.591	1.390"	58836
270 Cal	(.277")	165 Gr. Spitzer	0.307	0.620	1.515"	54827
7mm	(.284")	150 Gr. Spitzer	0.266	0.546	1.400"	58734

NOSLER

NOSLER

CAL	DIA	Description	SD	BC	OAL	Part #
7mm	(.284")	168 Gr. Spitzer	0.298	0.616	1.500"	58623
7mm	(.284")	175 Gr. Spitzer	0.310	0.648	1.540"	58517
30 Cal	(.308")	168 Gr. Spitzer	0.253	0.525	1.365"	58455
30 Cal	(.308")	190 Gr. Spitzer	0.286	0.640	1.460"	58456
30 Cal	(.308")	210 Gr. Spitzer	0.316	0.661	1.570"	58317
338 Cal	(.338")	265 Gr. Spitzer	0.331	0.732	1.700"	58454
338 Cal	(.338")	300 Gr. Spitzer	0.375	0.785	1.875"	58518
Ballistic Tip® Hunting Bullets						
6mm	(.243")	90 Gr. Spitzer (Purple Tip)	0.218	0.365	1.080"	24090
6mm	(.243")	95 Gr. Spitzer (Purple Tip)	0.230	0.379	1.120"	24095
25 Cal	(.257")	100 Gr. Spitzer (Blue Tip)	0.216	0.393	1.110"	25100
25 Cal	(.257")	115 Gr. Spitzer (Blue Tip)	0.249	0.453	1.215"	25115
6.5mm	(.264")	100 Gr. Spitzer (Brown Tip)	0.205	0.350	1.080"	26100
6.5mm	(.264")	120 Gr. Spitzer (Brown Tip)	0.246	0.458	1.220"	26120
6.5mm	(.264")	140 Gr. Spitzer (Brown Tip)	0.287	0.509	1.350"	26140
270 Cal	(.277")	130 Gr. Spitzer (Yellow Tip)	0.242	0.433	1.220"	27130
270 Cal	(.277")	140 Gr. Spitzer (Yellow Tip)	0.261	0.456	1.296"	27140
270 Cal	(.277")	150 Gr. Spitzer (Yellow Tip)	0.279	0.496	1.350"	27150
270 Cal	(.277")	170 Gr. Spitzer (Yellow Tip)	0.317	0.550	1.485"	28135
7mm	(.284")	120 Gr. Spitzer (Red Tip)	0.213	0.417	1.135"	28120
7mm	(.284")	140 Gr. Spitzer (Red Tip)	0.248	0.485	1.255"	28140
7mm	(.284")	150 Gr. Spitzer (Red Tip)	0.266	0.493	1.300"	28150
7mm	(.284")	160 Gr. Spitzer (Red Tip)	0.283	0.531	1.385"	28125
30 Cal	(.308")	125 Gr. Spitzer (Green Tip)	0.188	0.366	1.060"	30125
30 Cal	(.308")	150 Gr. Spitzer (Green Tip)	0.226	0.435	1.220"	30150
30 Cal	(.308")	165 Gr. Spitzer (Green Tip)	0.248	0.475	1.290"	30165
30 Cal	(.308")	168 Gr. Spitzer (Green Tip)	0.253	0.490	1.307"	30168
30 Cal	(.308")	180 Gr. Spitzer (Green Tip)	0.271	0.507	1.360"	30180
30 Cal	(.308")	220 Gr. Round Nose (Green Tip) Suppressor Ready	0.331	0.472	1.465"	30181
7.62x39	(.310")	123 Gr. Spitzer (Green Tip)	0.183	0.310	1.010"	30131
8mm	(.323")	180 Gr. Spitzer (Gunmetal Tip)	0.246	0.394	1.280"	32180
458 Cal	(.458")	300 Gr. Spitzer (Orange Tip)	0.204	0.250	0.960"	31456
Combined Technology® Ballistic Silvertip® Lubalox® Coated						
6mm	(.243")	95 Gr. Spitzer (Silver Tip)	0.230	0.379	1.120"	51040
25 Cal	(.257")	115 Gr. Spitzer (Silver Tip)	0.249	0.453	1.215"	51050
270 Cal	(.277")	130 Gr. Spitzer (Silver Tip)	0.242	0.433	1.220"	51075
270 Cal	(.277")	150 Gr. Spitzer (Silver Tip)	0.279	0.496	1.350"	51100
7mm	(.284")	140 Gr. Spitzer (Silver Tip)	0.248	0.485	1.255"	51105

CAL	DIA	Description	SD	BC	OAL	Part #
7mm	(.284")	150 Gr. Spitzer (Silver Tip)	0.266	0.493	1.300"	51110
30 Cal	(.308")	150 Gr. Spitzer (Silver Tip)	0.226	0.435	1.220"	51150
30 Cal	(.308")	150 Gr. Round Nose (Silver Tip)	0.226	0.232	1.066"	51165
30 Cal	(.308")	168 Gr. Spitzer (Silver Tip)	0.253	0.490	1.307"	51160
30 Cal	(.308")	180 Gr. Spitzer (Silver Tip)	0.271	0.507	1.360"	51170
338 Cal	(.338")	200 Gr. Spitzer (Silver Tip)	0.250	0.414	1.340"	51200
45 Cal	(.458")	300 Gr. Round Nose (Silver Tip)	0.204	0.191	0.900"	51834
Expansion Tip® Lead-Free Hunting						
22 Cal	(.224")	55 Gr. Spitzer	0.157	0.305	0.890"	59624
6mm	(.243")	90 Gr. Spitzer	0.218	0.403	1.180"	59165
25 Cal	(.257")	100 Gr. Spitzer	0.216	0.409	1.215"	59456
6.5mm	(.264")	120 Gr. Spitzer	0.246	0.497	1.350"	59765
6.8mm	(.277")	85 Gr. Spitzer	0.158	0.273	0.985"	59543
270 Cal	(.277")	130 Gr. Spitzer	0.242	0.459	1.345"	59298
7mm	(.284")	140 Gr. Spitzer	0.248	0.489	1.360"	59955
7mm	(.284")	150 Gr. Spitzer	0.266	0.498	1.425"	59426
300 AAC	(.308")	110 Gr. Spitzer	0.166	0.245	1.095"	59380
30/30	(.308")	150 Gr. Round Nose	0.226	0.344	1.165"	59451
30 Cal	(.308")	150 Gr. Spitzer	0.226	0.469	1.293"	59378
30 Cal	(.308")	168 Gr. Spitzer	0.253	0.503	1.415"	59415
30 Cal	(.308")	180 Gr. Spitzer	0.271	0.523	1.485"	59180
7.62x39	(.310")	123 Gr. Spitzer	0.183	0.316	1.125"	59387
8mm	(.323")	180 Gr. Spitzer	0.246	0.427	1.365"	59265
338 Cal	(.338")	200 Gr. Spitzer	0.250	0.425	1.427"	59186
338 Cal	(.338")	225 Gr. Spitzer	0.281	0.611	1.575"	59372
338 Cal	(.338")	250 Gr. Spitzer	0.313	0.627	1.680"	59385
9.3mm	(.366")	250 Gr. Spitzer	0.267	0.494	1.680"	59270
375 Cal	(.375")	260 Gr. Spitzer	0.264	0.490	1.489"	59379
Ballistic Tip® Varmint						
204 Cal	(.204")	32 Gr. Spitzer (Maroon Tip)	0.110	0.206	0.640"	35216
204 Cal	(.204")	40 Gr. Spitzer (Maroon Tip)	0.137	0.239	0.730"	52111
22 Cal	(.224")	40 Gr. Spitzer (Orange Tip)	0.114	0.221	0.705"	39510
22 Cal	(.224")	50 Gr. Spitzer (Orange Tip)	0.142	0.238	0.800"	39522
22 Cal	(.224")	55 Gr. Spitzer (Orange Tip)	0.157	0.267	0.810"	39526
22 Cal	(.224")	60 Gr. Spitzer (Orange Tip)	0.171	0.270	0.855"	34992
6mm	(.243")	55 Gr. Spitzer (Purple Tip)	0.133	0.276	0.785"	24055
6mm	(.243")	70 Gr. Spitzer (Purple Tip)	0.169	0.310	0.915"	39532
6mm	(.243")	80 Gr. Spitzer (Purple Tip)	0.194	0.329	0.990"	24080

NOSLER

NOSLER

CAL	DIA	Description	SD	BC	OAL	Part #
25 Cal	(.257")	85 Gr. Spitzer (Blue Tip)	0.183	0.329	1.015"	43004
Varmageddon						
17 Cal	(.172")	20 Gr. FBHP	0.097	0.119	0.500"	17205
17 Cal	(.172")	20 Gr. FB Tipped (Metallic Black Tip)	0.097	0.183	0.555"	17210
204 Cal	(.204")	32 Gr. FB Tipped (Metallic Black Tip)	0.110	0.204	0.600"	17220
22 Cal	(.224")	35 Gr. FB Tipped (Metallic Black Tip)	0.100	0.120	0.520"	36763
22 Cal	(.224")	40 Gr. FB Tipped (Metallic Black Tip)	0.114	0.211	0.665"	17230
22 Cal	(.224")	50 Gr. FB Tipped (Metallic Black Tip)	0.142	0.227	0.750"	17223
22 Cal	(.224")	53 Gr. FB Tipped (Metallic Black Tip)	0.152	0.303	0.830"	36523
22 Cal	(.224")	55 Gr. FB Tipped (Metallic Black Tip)	0.157	0.255	0.795"	17240
22 Cal	(.224")	62 Gr. FBHP W/Cannelure	0.176	0.251	0.770"	35631
6mm	(.243")	55 Gr. FB Tipped (Metallic Black Tip)	0.133	0.252	0.750"	17250
6mm	(.243")	70 Gr. FB Tipped (Metallic Black Tip)	0.169	0.305	0.875"	26123
6.5mm	(.264")	90 Gr. FB Tipped (Metallic Black Tip)	0.184	0.350	1.020"	26129
30 Cal	(.308")	110 Gr. FB Tipped (Metallic Black Tip)	0.166	0.293	0.920"	34057
7.62x39	(.310")	123 Gr. FB Tipped (Metallic Black Tip)	0.183	0.304	0.950"	34056
Ballistic Tip® Lead-Free™ (BTLF)						
204 Cal	(.204")	32 Gr. Spitzer (Metallic Maroon Tip)	0.110	0.228	0.745"	45140
22 Cal	(.224")	35 Gr. Spitzer (Metallic Orange Tip)	0.100	0.201	0.730"	45150
22 Cal	(.224")	40 Gr. Spitzer (Metallic Orange Tip)	0.114	0.220	0.783"	45160
22 Cal	(.224")	50 Gr. Spitzer (Metallic Orange Tip)	0.142	0.251	0.900"	45498
6mm	(.243")	55 Gr. Spitzer (Metallic Purple Tip)	0.133	0.288	0.950"	45170
Ballistic Tip® Muzzle Loader						
50 Cal	(.500")	300 Gr. Spitzer	0.204	0.250	0.960"	50300
RDF® Reduced Drag Factor						
22 Cal	(.224")	70 Gr. HPBT	0.199	0.416	0.965"	53066
22 Cal	(.224")	77 Gr. HPBT	0.219	0.454	1.070"	53452
22 Cal	(.224")	85 Gr. HPBT	0.242	0.498	1.135"	53441
6mm	(.243")	105 Gr. HPBT	0.254	0.571	1.250"	53410
6mm	(.243")	115 Gr. HPBT	0.278	0.634	1.350"	53507
6.5mm	(.264")	130 Gr. HPBT	0.266	0.615	1.333"	53505
6.5mm	(.264")	140 Gr. HPBT	0.287	0.658	1.420"	49824
7mm	(.284")	185 Gr. HPBT	0.328	0.719	1.540"	53432
30 Cal	(.308")	168 Gr. HPBT	0.253	0.505	1.320"	53182
30 Cal	(.308")	175 Gr. HPBT	0.264	0.536	1.330"	53170
30 Cal	(.308")	210 Gr. HPBT	0.316	0.707	1.516"	53434
338 Cal	(.338")	300 Gr. HPBT	0.375	0.826	1.865"	53445

CAL	DIA	Description	SD	BC	OAL	Part #
Custom Competition®						
22 Cal	(.224")	52 Gr. HPBT	0.148	0.220	0.730"	53294
22 Cal	(.224")	69 Gr. HPBT	0.196	0.305	0.900"	17101
22 Cal	(.224")	77 Gr. HPBT W/Cannelure	0.219	0.340	0.980"	53033
22 Cal	(.224")	77 Gr. HPBT	0.219	0.340	0.980"	22421
22 Cal	(.224")	80 Gr. HPBT	0.228	0.415	1.065"	25116
6mm	(.243")	107 Gr. HPBT	0.259	0.525	1.240"	49742
6.5mm	(.264")	100 Gr. HPBT	0.205	0.362	1.122"	53427
6.5mm	(.264")	123 Gr. HPBT	0.252	0.510	1.200"	53415
6.5mm	(.264")	140 Gr. HPBT	0.287	0.529	1.307"	26725
6.8mm	(.277")	115 Gr. HPBT W/Cannelure	0.214	0.375	0.965"	45357
7mm	(.284")	168 Gr. HPBT	0.298	0.520	1.290"	53418
30 Cal	(.308")	155 Gr. HPBT	0.233	0.450	1.145"	53155
30 Cal	(.308")	168 Gr. HPBT	0.253	0.462	1.200"	53164
30 Cal	(.308")	175 Gr. HPBT	0.264	0.505	1.240"	53952
30 Cal	(.308")	190 Gr. HPBT	0.286	0.530	1.343"	53417
30 Cal	(.308")	220 Gr. HPBT	0.331	0.690	1.530"	53154
8mm	(.323")	200 Gr. HPBT	0.274	0.520	1.325"	49524
338 Cal	(.338")	300 Gr. HPBT	0.375	0.800	1.725"	53515
Sporting Handgun™ Revolver						
38 Cal	(.357")	158 Gr. JHP	0.177	0.182	0.775"	44841
41 Cal	(.410")	210 Gr. JHP	0.178	0.170	0.687"	43012
44 Cal	(.429")	200 Gr. JHP	0.155	0.151	0.610"	44846
44 Cal	(.429")	240 Gr. JHP	0.186	0.173	0.710"	44842
44 Cal	(.429")	240 Gr. JSP	0.186	0.177	0.700"	44868
44 Cal	(.429")	300 Gr. JHP	0.233	0.206	0.976"	42069
45 Colt	(.451")	250 Gr. JHP	0.176	0.177	0.774"	43013
Sporting Handgun™ ASP™						
9mm	(.355")	115 Gr. JHP	0.130	0.109	0.511"	44848
9mm	(.355")	124 Gr. JHP	0.141	0.118	0.560"	43123
9mm	(.355")	147 Gr. JHP	0.167	0.156	0.630"	43258
10mm	(.400")	135 Gr. JHP	0.121	0.093	0.494"	44852
10mm	(.400")	150 Gr. JHP	0.134	0.106	0.535"	44860
10mm	(.400")	180 Gr. JHP	0.161	0.147	0.620"	44885
10mm	(.400")	200 Gr. JHP	0.179	0.163	0.674"	44952
45 Cal	(.451")	185 Gr. JHP	0.130	0.142	0.530"	44847
45 Cal	(.451")	230 Gr. JHP	0.162	0.175	0.635"	44922

NOSLER

RIFLE AMMUNITION

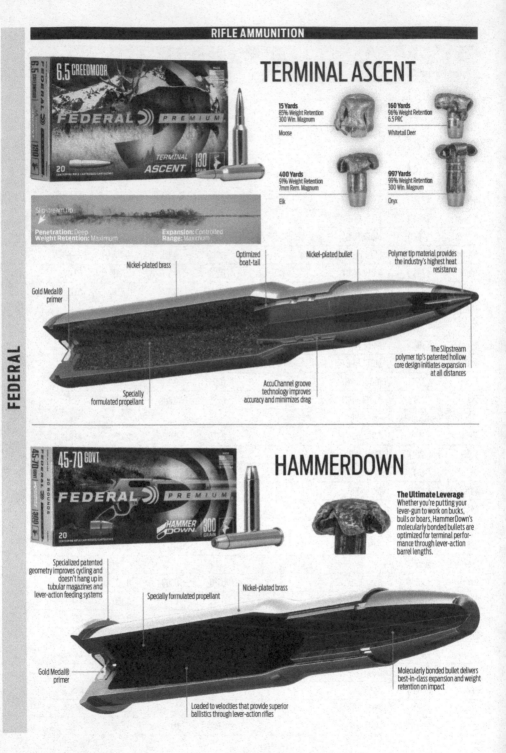

TERMINAL ASCENT

6.5 CREEDMOOR — FEDERAL PREMIUM — TERMINAL ASCENT — 130 GRAIN — 20 CENTERFIRE RIFLE CARTRIDGES/CARTOUCHES

15 Yards
85% Weight Retention
300 Win. Magnum

Moose

160 Yards
96% Weight Retention
6.5 PRC

Whitetail Deer

400 Yards
91% Weight Retention
7mm Rem. Magnum

Elk

997 Yards
99% Weight Retention
300 Win. Magnum

Oryx

Slipstream tip

Penetration: Deep
Weight Retention: Maximum
Expansion: Controlled
Range: Maximum

- Nickel-plated brass
- Optimized boat-tail
- Nickel-plated bullet
- Polymer tip material provides the industry's highest heat resistance
- Gold Medal® primer
- The Slipstream polymer tip's patented hollow core design initiates expansion at all distances
- Specially formulated propellant
- AccuChannel groove technology improves accuracy and minimizes drag

FEDERAL

HAMMERDOWN

45-70 GOVT — FEDERAL PREMIUM — HAMMER DOWN — 300 GRAIN — 20 CENTERFIRE RIFLE CARTRIDGES/CARTOUCHES

The Ultimate Leverage
Whether you're putting your lever-gun to work on bucks, bulls or boars, HammerDown's molecularly bonded bullets are optimized for terminal performance through lever-action barrel lengths.

- Specialized patented geometry improves cycling and doesn't hang up in tubular magazines and lever-action feeding systems
- Specially formulated propellant
- Nickel-plated brass
- Gold Medal® primer
- Loaded to velocities that provide superior ballistics through lever-action rifles
- Molecularly bonded bullet delivers best-in-class expansion and weight retention on impact

HORNADY ELD-X

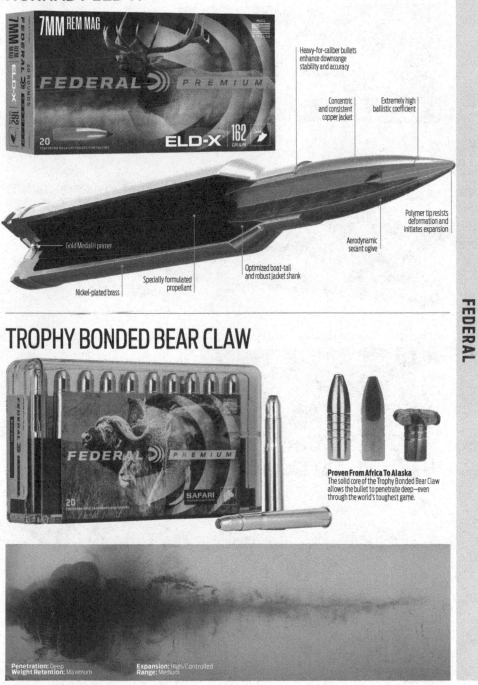

Heavy-for-caliber bullets enhance downrange stability and accuracy

Concentric and consistent copper jacket

Extremely high ballistic coefficient

Polymer tip resists deformation and initiates expansion

Aerodynamic secant ogive

Gold Medal® primer

Optimized boat-tail and robust jacket shank

Specially formulated propellant

Nickel-plated brass

TROPHY BONDED BEAR CLAW

Proven From Africa To Alaska
The solid core of the Trophy Bonded Bear Claw allows the bullet to penetrate deep—even through the world's toughest game.

Penetration: Deep
Weight Retention: Maximum
Expansion: High/Controlled
Range: Medium

FEDERAL

FEDERAL

VARMINT & PREDATOR V-MAX

Ready To Explode
The V-Max bullet's polymer tip is carefully positioned over a hollow nose cavity to initiate violent fragmentation of the jacket and swaged lead core.

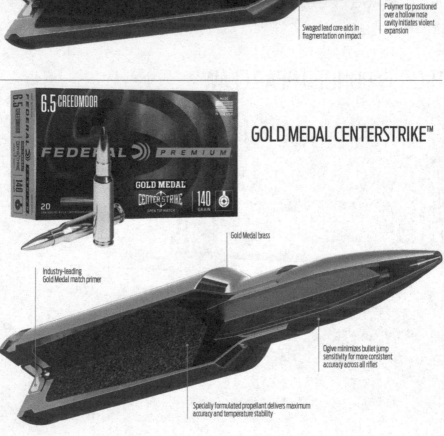

Consistent Federal® brass

Reliable primer

Swaged lead core aids in fragmentation on impact

Polymer tip positioned over a hollow nose cavity initiates violent expansion

GOLD MEDAL CENTERSTRIKE™

Gold Medal brass

Industry-leading Gold Medal match primer

Ogive minimizes bullet jump sensitivity for more consistent accuracy across all rifles

Specially formulated propellant delivers maximum accuracy and temperature stability

PISTOL AMMUNITION

HST

Consistency Counts
The exclusive HST bullet is engineered to expand extremely reliably and retain nearly all of its weight through almost every barrier. The result is consistent, nearly identical penetration and expansion in any situation, shot after shot. Bare gelatin shot with 10mm Auto HST (P10HST1S) at 10 feet.

Heavy Clothing

HYDRA-SHOK DEEP

Upset

380 Auto Redefined
Powered by the Hydra-Shok Deep design, the 380 Auto easily meets the FBI's penetration guidelines, surpassing the 12-inch mark. Bare gel shot with 380 Auto (P380HSD1) at 10 feet; 13.5 inches of penetration.

Upset

Deep Defense
A beefed-up center post and redesigned core give Hydra-Shok Deep loads the ability to hit critical depths through the most common self-defense barriers. Bare gelatin shot with 9mm Luger (P9HSD1) at 10 feet, 15 inches of penetration.

PUNCH

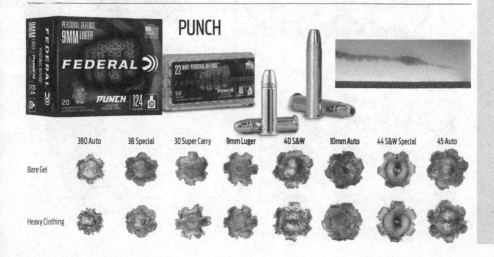

	380 Auto	38 Special	30 Super Carry	9mm Luger	40 S&W	10mm Auto	44 S&W Special	45 Auto
Bare Gel								
Heavy Clothing								

FEDERAL

FEDERAL

SYNTECH DEFENSE™

SYNTECH ACTION PISTOL®

Flat-nose Syntech bullet for better energy transfer to steel targets

TSJ® eliminates copper and lead fouling, while extending barrel life

Bullet core drastically reduces splash-back on steel targets

Clean-burning propellants minimize residue

Reduced felt recoil

Exclusive Catalyst™ lead-free primer formulation provides reliable, consistent ignition

GOLD MEDAL® ACTION PISTOL

Fully encapsulated FMJ improves accuracy and reduces airborne lead

Federal® brass

Consistent, specially formulated propellant

Loaded to our tightest accuracy specifications

Catalyst lead-free primer

SOLID CORE

Nickel-plated case

Hard lead core penetrates deep

Consistent propellant

Federal primer

Syntech jacket eliminates lead fouling and reduces friction without the complexity of wax rings and gas checks

RIFLE AMMUNITION

360 BUCKHAMMER

STRAIGHT WALL

200 Grain Core-Lokt shown.   50 yards   100 yards   200 yards

1. ULTIMATE STRAIGHT WALL CARTRIDGE
360 BHMR optimized for lever action rifles. Easy to shoot, low recoil

2. REMINGTON COMPONENTS
Reliable Remington brass, propellant, & primers carefully loaded

3. Core-Lokt Performance
High-weight retention, controlled expansion.
.358 diameter Core-Lokt bullet

4. ACCURATE 200 YARDS+
Velocity, energy and drop ideal across common hunting ranges

PREMIER LONG RANGE

1. SLIPSTREAM TIP
High ballistic coefficient for flat trajectory and ultimate accuracy. Helps initiate expansion at wide range of velocities

2. SPEER IMPACT BULLET
Chemically fused bullet jacket and core designed to stop separation and impart maximum retained energy and weight impact on target

3. AERODYNAMIC DESIGN
Boat tail bullet and rear adjusted center of gravity assists truer flight and long range accuracy

4. PREMIER COMPONENTS
Highest-quality Remington primers and propellants chosen in combination for ultimate performance across spectrum of environmental conditions

High speed videography time lapse of ballistic gel testing shows extreme energy transfer and wound channel expansion. Premier Long Range 172 grain .308 Win @ 200 yards shown.

PREMIER LONG RANGE

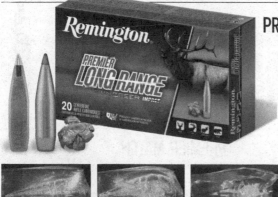

1. BIG GREEN polymer tip
Improves long-range ballistics, in-flight accuracy, and initiates rapid expansion

2. PROVEN CORE-LOKT JACKET
Tuned for optimal performance on big game

3. MATCH-GRADE ACCURACY
Rear-adjusted center of gravity and boat-tail design maximize accuracy

4. Premier Brass
Factory fresh brass built to the highest of standards

5. Advanced Propellants
Carefully chosen propellants built for a clean burn and utmost accuracy

6. Remington Primer
Steady and consistent ignition when it matters most

180 grain Core-Lokt Tipped bullet shot from 300 Win. Mag. shows extreme energy transfer and optimal penetration at 200 yards.

REMINGTON

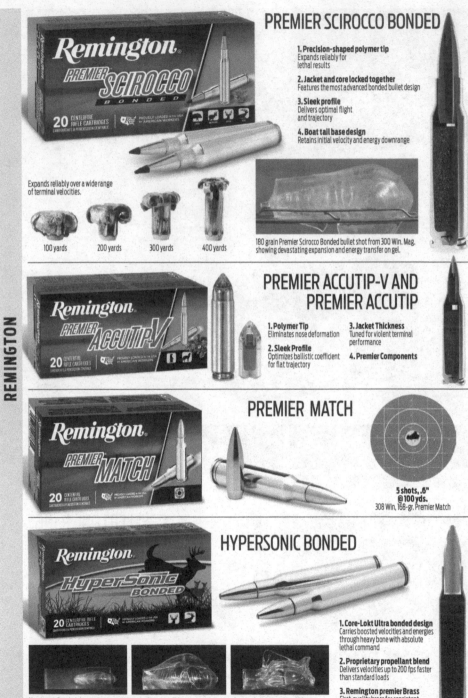

REMINGTON

PREMIER SCIROCCO BONDED

1. Precision-shaped polymer tip
Expands reliably for lethal results

2. Jacket and core locked together
Features the most advanced bonded bullet design

3. Sleek profile
Delivers optimal flight and trajectory

4. Boat tail base design
Retains initial velocity and energy downrange

Expands reliably over a wide range of terminal velocities.

100 yards   200 yards   300 yards   400 yards

180 grain Premier Scirocco Bonded bullet shot from 300 Win. Mag. showing devastating expansion and energy transfer on gel.

PREMIER ACCUTIP-V AND PREMIER ACCUTIP

1. Polymer Tip
Eliminates nose deformation

2. Sleek Profile
Optimizes ballistic coefficient for flat trajectory

3. Jacket Thickness
Tuned for violent terminal performance

4. Premier Components

PREMIER MATCH

5 shots, .6"
@ 100 yds.
308 Win, 168-gr. Premier Match

HYPERSONIC BONDED

1. Core-Lokt Ultra bonded design
Carries boosted velocities and energies through heavy bone with absolute lethal command

2. Proprietary propellant blend
Delivers velocities up to 200 fps faster than standard loads

3. Remington premier Brass
First-quality brass for consistent feeding and extraction

Hypersonic Bonded shows ultimate energy transfer on gel. 180 grain Core-Lokt Ultra Bonded bullet shot from 300 Win. Mag. shown.

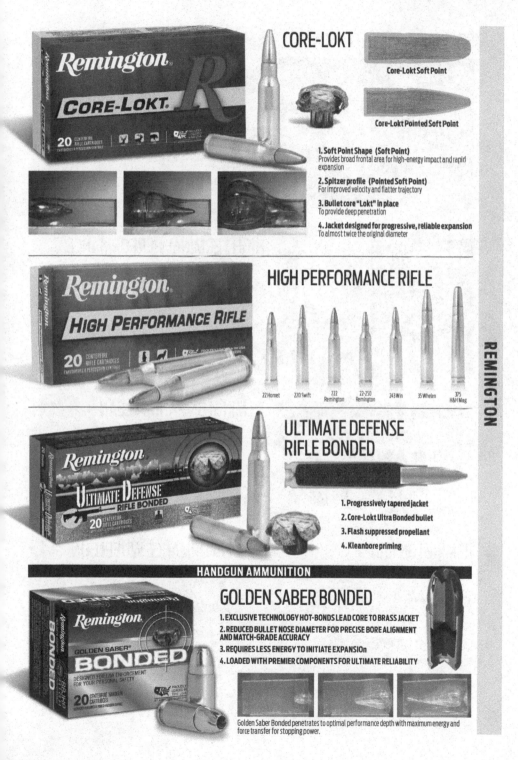

CORE-LOKT

Core-Lokt Soft Point

Core-Lokt Pointed Soft Point

1. Soft Point Shape (Soft Point)
Provides broad frontal area for high-energy impact and rapid expansion

2. Spitzer profile (Pointed Soft Point)
For improved velocity and flatter trajectory

3. Bullet core "Lokt" in place
To provide deep penetration

4. Jacket designed for progressive, reliable expansion
To almost twice the original diameter

HIGH PERFORMANCE RIFLE

22 Hornet | 220 Swift | 222 Remington | 22-250 Remington | 243 Win | 35 Whelen | 375 H&H Mag

ULTIMATE DEFENSE RIFLE BONDED

1. Progressively tapered jacket

2. Core-Lokt Ultra Bonded bullet

3. Flash suppressed propellant

4. Kleanbore priming

HANDGUN AMMUNITION

GOLDEN SABER BONDED

1. EXCLUSIVE TECHNOLOGY HOT-BONDS LEAD CORE TO BRASS JACKET

2. REDUCED BULLET NOSE DIAMETER FOR PRECISE BORE ALIGNMENT AND MATCH-GRADE ACCURACY

3. REQUIRES LESS ENERGY TO INITIATE EXPANSIOn

4. LOADED WITH PREMIER COMPONENTS FOR ULTIMATE RELIABILITY

Golden Saber Bonded penetrates to optimal performance depth with maximum energy and force transfer for stopping power.

REMINGTON

REMINGTON

GOLDEN SABER DEFENSE

Optimal Penetration & Expansion for Threat-Stopping Performance.

1. Exclusive Brass Jacket
Its precision nose cuts control expansion and optimizes energy transfer

2. Case Mouth and Primer Waterproofing
For maximum reliability

3. Nickel-Plated Cases
To reduce oxidation and improve feeding and extraction

4. Specially Treated Powders
To suppress muzzle flash

HIGH TERMINAL PERFORMANCE

Jacketed Soft Point

Jacketed Hollow Point

Semi-Jacketed Hollow Point

REMINGTON RANGE CLEAN

1. Designed for indoor ranges

2. Lead-free primer

3. Same weight as conventional loads

4. Available in 380 Auto, 9mm Luger, 40 S&W, and 45 Auto

REMINGTON RANGE

1. Proven Bullet
FMJ built to high quality standards

2. Lead Core
Manufactured from scratch

3. Factory-Firsts
Fresh brass, easily reloaded

4. Reliable Components
Loaded with quality primers and propellants

PERFORMANCE WHEELGUN

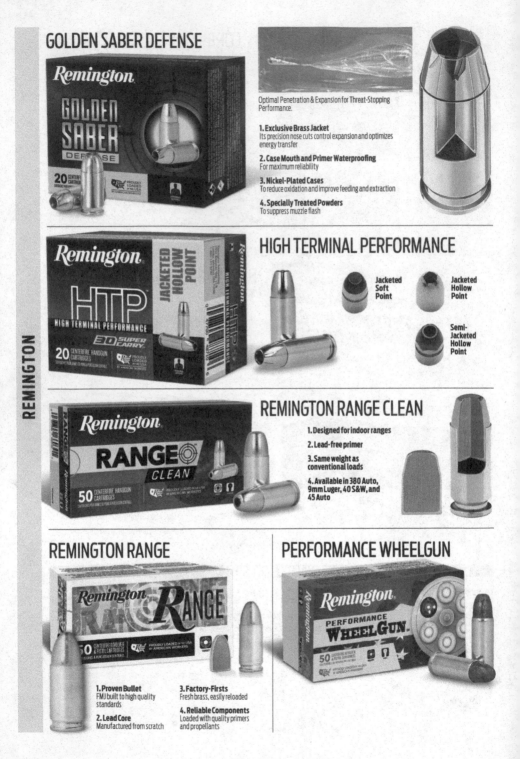

Cartridge	Index No.	Order No.	Bullet Wt. (GR.)	Bullet Type
360 Buckhammer				
NEW 360 BHMR Core-Lokt	R360BH4	R27742	180	SP
NEW 360 BHMR Core-Lokt	R360BH2	R27743	200	SP
Premier Long Range				
NEW 6.5 Creedmoor	RLR65CR	21341	140	SI
NEW 270 WIN	RLR270W	21342	150	SI
NEW 7mm REM MAG	RLR7MMR	21343	175	SI
NEW 30-06 Sprg	RLR3006	21344	172	SI
NEW 308 WIN	RLR308W	21345	172	SI
NEW 300 WIN MAG	RLR300W	21346	190	SI
NEW 300 REM Ultra Mag	RLR300UM	21347	190	SI
Core-Lokt Tipped				
243 Win	RT243WA	29015	95	CLT
6.5 Creedmoor	RT65CR1	29017	129	CLT
270 Win	RT270WA	29019	130	CLT
280 Remington	RT280RA	29020	140	CLT
7mm Remington Mag	RT7MMRB	29021	150	CLT
30-06 Sprg	RT3006A	29027	150	CLT
30-06 Sprg	RT3006B	29035	165	CLT
30-06 Sprg	RT3006C	29037	180	CLT
300 Win Mag	RT300WC	29038	180	CLT
308 Win	RT308WA	29039	150	CLT
308 Win	RT308WB	29044	165	CLT
308 Win	RT308WC	29041	180	CLT
300 WSM	RT300WSM1	29043	150	CLT
Premier Scirocco Bonded				
243 Win	PRSC243WA	29320	90	SSB
6.5 Creedmoor	PRSC65CR	29344	130	SSB
270 Win	PRSC270WA	29322	130	SSB
7mm Remington Magnum	PRSC7MMB	29316	150	SSB
7mm Remington Ultra Magnum	PRSC7UM1	29335	150	SSB
30-06 Sprg	PRSC3006B	29318	150	SSB
30-06 Sprg	PRSC3006C	29328	180	SSB
300 WSM	PRSC300WSMB	29345	180	SSB
300 Win Mag	PRSC300WB	29330	180	SSB
300 Remington Ultra Magnum	PR300UM5	27950	150	SSB

Cartridge	Index No.	Order No.	Bullet Wt. (GR.)	Bullet Type
300 Remington Ultra Magnum	PR300UM3	27936	180	SSB
308 Win	PRSC308WB	29332	165	SSB
Premier Accutip-V & Premier ACCUTIP				
17 Remington	PRA17RA	29162	20	ATV
17 Remington Fireball	PRA17FB	29165	20	ATV
204 Ruger	PRA204A	29218	32	ATV
204 Ruger	PRA204B	29220	40	ATV, BT
22 Hornet	PRA22HNA	29154	35	ATV
221 Remington Fireball	PRA221FB	29172	50	ATV, BT
222 Remington	PRA222RB	29174	50	ATV, BT
223 Remington	PRA223RB	29184	50	ATV, BT
223 Remington	PRA223RC	29192	55	AT
224 Valkyrie	PRA224VLK	21202	60	ATV
22-250 Remington	PRA2250RB	29186	50	ATV, BT
243 Win	PRA243WB	29194	75	ATV, BT
450 Bushmaster	PRA450B1	27943	260	AT
Premier Match				
NEW 6mm Creedmoor	RM6CRD	20001	107	MatchKing BTHP
223 Remington	R223R6	22106	62	HP, Match
223 Remington	RM223R1	27680	69	MatchKing BTHP
NEW 223 Remington	RM223R2R	27682	52	OTM BTHP
223 Remington	RM223R3	27686	77	MatchKing BTHP
224 Valkyrie	RM224VLK	21201	90	MatchKing
260 Remington	RM260R1	26852	140	Berger OTM
6.5 Creedmoor	RM65CRD	27661	140	MatchKing BTHP
NEW 6.5 PRC	RM65PRC01L	27673	140	Berger OTM
6.5 Grendel	RM65GDL	21205	130	Berger OTM
6.8mm Remington SPC	RM68R1	27676	115	MatchKing BTHP
300 AAC Blackout	RM300AAC6	21503	125	MatchKing
308 Win	RM308W7	21485	168	MatchKing BTHP
308 Win	RM308W8	21486	175	MatchKing BTHP
Hypersonic Bonded				
223 Remington	PRH223R4	28919	62	Core-Lokt Ultra Bonded, PSP
243 Win	PRH243WC	28923	100	Core-Lokt Ultra Bonded, PSP
270 Win	PRH270WB	28955	140	Core-Lokt Ultra Bonded, PSP
30-06 Sprg	PRH3006A	29007	150	Core-Lokt Ultra Bonded, PSP

REMINGTON

REMINGTON

Cartridge	Index No.	Order No.	Bullet Wt. (GR.)	Bullet Type
30-06 Sprg	PRH3006C	29009	180	Core-Lokt Ultra Bonded, PSP
300 Win Mag	PRH300WC	29033	180	Core-Lokt Ultra Bonded, PSP
308 Win	PRH308WA	29119	150	Core-Lokt Ultra Bonded, PSP
Core-Lokt Pointed Soft Point				
223 Remington	R223R8	22111	62	PSP, UB
6mm Creedmoor	R6CM01	29049	100	PSP
6mm Remington	R6MM4	29051	100	PSP
243 Win	R243W3	27802	100	PSP
25-06 Remington	R25062	21507	100	PSP
25-06 Remington	R25063	21515	120	PSP
25-20 Win	R25202	28364	86	PSP
250 Sav	R250SV	29077	100	PSP
6.5 x 55 Swedish	R65SWE1	29140	140	PSP
6.5 Creedmoor	R65CR1	27657	140	PSP
260 Remington	R260R1	21292	140	PSP
264 Win Mag	R264W2	29493	140	PSP
270 Win	R270W1	21325	100	PSP
270 Win	R260W2	27808	130	PSP
270 WSM	R270WSM1	28940	130	PSP
280 Remington	R280R3	28313	140	PSP
280 Remington	R280R1	29069	150	PSP
7mm-08 Remington	R7M081	21337	140	PSP
7mm Remington Magnum	R7MM4	28821	140	PSP
7mm Remington Magnum	R7MM2	29487	150	PSP
7mm Remington Magnum	R7MM3	27814	175	PSP
7mm Mauser (7x57)	R7MSR1	29031	140	PSP
7mm Remington SA UM	PR7SM2	27874	150	PSP
7mm Remington UM	R7RUM01	27759	150	PSP
7 x 64 Brenneke	R7X641	29130	140	PSP
30-40 Krag	R30402	28345	180	PSP
30-06 Sprg	R30061	21401	125	PSP
30-06 Sprg	R30062	27826	150	PSP
30-06 Sprg	R3006B	21415	165	PSP
30-06 Sprg	R30065	27828	180	PSP
300 Savage	R30SV2	21465	150	PSP
300 Win Mag	R300W1	29495	150	PSP

Cartridge	Index No.	Order No.	Bullet Wt. (GR.)	Bullet Type
300 Win Mag	R300W2	29497	180	PSP
450 Bushmaster	R450B1	27941	260	PSP
300 WSM	R300WSM1	29489	150	PSP
308 Win	R308W1	27842	150	PSP
308 Win	R308W3	21479	180	PSP
300 Weatherby Mag	R300WB1	29279	180	PSP
7.62 x 39mm	R762391	29125	125	PSP
300 Remington SA UM	PR300SM2	27954	165	PSP
300 Remington UM	R300RUM01	27641	180	PSP
30 Remington AR	R30RAR2	29485	150	PSP
338 Remington UM	PR338UM2	27942	250	PSP
338 Win Mag	R338W1	22189	225	PSP
338 Win Mag	R338W2	22191	250	PSP
NEW 35 Remington	R35R1	21491	150	PSP
35 Whelen	R35WH1	21495	200	PSP
Core-Lokt Soft Point				
257 Roberts	R257	28335	117	SP
270 Win	R270W4	27810	150	SP
280 Remington	R280R2	28417	165	SP
30 Carbine	R30CAR	28322	110	SP
30-30 Win	R30301	27818	150	SP
30-30 Win	R30302	27820	170	SP
30-30 Win	RL30301	27644	125	SP
30-06 Sprg	R30064	21407	180	SP
30-06 Sprg	R30067	27830	220	SP
308 Marlin Express	R308ME1	27848	150	SP
308 Win	R308W2	27844	180	SP
303 British	R303B1	21471	180	SP
32 Win Special	R32WS2	21489	170	SP
35 Remington	R35R2	27852	200	SP
350 Legend	R350L1	20012	180	SP
444 Marlin	R444M	29475	240	SP
45-70 Gov (FP)	R4570G1	21459	405	SP
45-70 Gov (RP)	R4570G	29473	405	SP
Core-Lokt Hollow Point				
30-30 Win	R30303	21395	170	HP

Cartridge	Index No.	Order No.	Bullet Wt. (GR.)	Bullet Type
High Performance Rifle				
17 Remington	R17R2	28460	25	HP
22 Hornet	R22HN1	28376	45	PSP
220 Swift	R220S1	21297	50	PSP
222 Remington	R222R1	21303	50	PSP
223 Remington	R223R1	28399	55	PSP
22-250 Remington	R22501	21311	55	PSP
243 Win	R243W1	27800	80	PSP
6.5 Creedmoor	R65CR2	27671	140	BTHP
6.5 Grendel	R65GR1	27649	120	BTHP
32-20 Win	R32201	28410	100	Lead
35 Whelen	R35WH3	21499	250	PSP
NEW 308 Win	R308W4	R21473	180	PSP
375 H&H Mag	R375M1	29097	270	SP
375 Remington Ultra Mag	PR375UM2	29340	270	SP
45-70 Govt (Full Pressure)	R4570L1	21463	300	SJHP
Golden Saber Bonded				
9mm Luger	GSB9MMDB	29341	124	BBJHP
9mm Luger	GSB9MMCB	29343	147	BBJHP
NEW 10MM Auto	GSB10MMAB	R21368	180	BBJHP
357 Sig	GSB357SBB	29407	125	BBJHP
40 S&W	GSB40SWAB	29363	165	BBJHP
40 S&W	GSB40SWBB	29365	180	BBJHP
45 Auto	GSB45APAB	29325	185	BBJHP
45 Auto	GSB45APBB	29327	230	BBJHP
Golden Saber Bonded				
9mm Luger	GSB9MMDB	29341	124	BBJHP
Golden Saber Defense Full Size				
380 Auto	GSD380BN	27605	102	BJHP
38 Special +P ‡	GSD38SBN	27606	125	BJHP
9mm Luger	GSD9MMBN	27601	124	BJHP
9mm Luger	GSD9MMC	27604	147	BJHP
9mm Luger +P	GSD9MMD	27603	124	BJHP
NEW 10MM Auto	GSD10MMBN	R21369	180	BJHP
357 Magnum	GSD357MA	27600	125	BJHP
40 S&W	GSD40SWA	27607	165	BJHP

Cartridge	Index No.	Order No.	Bullet Wt. (GR.)	Bullet Type
40 S&W	GSD40SWBN	27608	180	BJHP
45 Auto	GSD45APA	27609	185	BJHP
45 Auto	GSD45APBN	27612	230	BJHP
45 Auto +P	GSD45APC	27611	185	BJHP
Golden Saber Defense Compact				
380 Auto	GSC380BN	27615	102	BJHP
38 Special+P ‡	GSC38SBN	27617	125	BJHP
9mm Luger	GSC9MMBN	27613	124	BJHP
NEW 10MM Auto	GSC10MMBN	R21370	180	BJHP
40 S&W	GSC40SWBN	27618	180	BJHP
45 Auto	GSC45APBN	27619	230	BJHP
High Terminal Performance (HTP)				
NEW 30 Super Carry	RTP30C	R20019	100	JHP
9mm Luger	RTP9MM1A	28288	115	JHP
9mm Luger +P	RTP9MM6A	28293	115	JHP
9mm Luger	RTP9MM8A	28295	147	JHP
NEW 32 H&R Mag	RTP32HR	R20017	85	JHP
357 Mag	RTP357M7A	22237	110	SJHP
357 Mag	RTP357M1A	22227	125	SJHP
357 Mag	RTP357M2A	22231	158	SJHP
357 Mag	RTP357M3A	22233	158	SP
357 Mag	RTP357M10A	22239	180	SJHP
38 Spl	RTP38S16A	22293	110	SJHP
38 Spl +P	RTP38S10A	22295	110	SJHP
38 Spl +P	RTP38S21A	22303	125	SJHP
38 Spl +P	RTP38S12A	22297	158	LHP
380 Auto	RTP380A1A	22248	88	JHP
41 Rem Mag	RTP41MG1A	23000	210	JSP
44 Rem Mag	RTP44MG2A	23002	240	JHP
44 Rem Mag	RTP44MG3A	23010	240	SJHP
40 S&W	RTP40SW1A	22306	155	JHP
40 S&W	RTP40SW2A	22308	180	JHP
45 Auto	RTP45AP2A	21453	185	JHP
45 Auto	RTP45AP7A	21455	230	JHP
45 Colt	RTP45C1A	23012	230	JHP

Cartridge	Index No.	Order No.	Bullet Wt. (GR.)	Bullet Type
Remington Range Clean				
380 Auto	RC380AP2	27683	95	FNEB
9mm Luger	RC9MM11	27681	115	FNEB
40 S&W	RC40SW5	27685	180	FNEB
45 Auto	RC45AP8	27687	230	FNEB
Remington Range				
NEW 9mm Luger	T9MM3L	R27778	115	FMJ
NEW 9mm Luger	T9MM3CL	R27779	115	FMJ
NEW 9mm Luger	T9MM3BL	R23979	115	FMJ
NEW 9mm Luger	T9MM3AL	R23975	115	FMJ
NEW 9mm Luger	T9MM2L	R27780	124	FMJ
NEW 40 S&W	T40SW3L	R27781	180	FMJ
Performance Wheelgun				
NEW 32 H&R Mag	RPW32HR	20021	95	Semi Wad Cutter HP
32 S&W	RPW32SW	22206	88	Lead Round Nose
32 S&W Long	RPW32SWL	22210	98	Lead Round Nose
357 Magnum	RPW357M5	22223	158	Lead Semi Wad Cutter
38 S&W	RPW38SW	22278	146	Lead Round Nose
38 Special	RPW38S3	22267	148	Target-Master Wad Cutter
38 Special	RPW38S6	22271	158	Lead Semi Wad Cutter
38 Special	RPW38S5	22281	158	Lead Round Nose
38 Short Colt	RPW38SC	22273	125	Lead Round Nose
44 S&W Special	RPW44SW	22333	246	Lead Round Nose
45 Colt	RPW45C1	22338	225	Lead Semi Wad Cutter
45 Colt	RPW45C	22340	250	Lead Round Nose

APPENDIX III
Ballistics Tables by Manufacturer

HORNADY

	RIFLE BALLISTICS																				
	Ammo Description			Velocity (fps)						Energy (ft/lb)						Trajectory Tables (inches)					
	CARTRIDGE	BULLET	ITEM#	MUZ	100 yd	200 yd	300 yd	400 yd	500 yd	MUZ	100 yd	200 yd	300 yd	400 yd	500 yd	MUZ	100 yd	200 yd	300 yd	400 yd	500 yd
V	17 Mach 2	15.5 gr. NTX®	83176	2050	1450	1070	–	–	–	145	72	39	–	–	–	-1.5	0	-15.6	–	–	–
V	17 Mach 2	17 gr. V-MAX®	83177	2100	1531	1133	–	–	–	166	88	48	–	–	–	-1.5	0	-13.8	–	–	–
V	17 HMR	15.5 gr. NTX®	83171	2525	1830	1291	–	–	–	219	115	57	–	–	–	-1.5	0	-10	–	–	–
V	17 HMR	17 gr. V-MAX®	83170	2550	1902	1379	–	–	–	245	137	72	–	–	–	-1.5	0	-8.5	–	–	–
V	17 HMR	20 gr. XTP®	83172	2375	1755	1274	–	–	–	250	137	72	–	–	–	-1.5	0	-9.9	–	–	–
V	17 WSM	20 gr. V-MAX®	83180	3000	2504	2058	–	–	–	400	278	188	–	–	–	-1.5	0	-4.1	–	–	–
SV	17 Hornet	20 gr. V-MAX®	83005	3650	3077	2574	2122	1721	1383	592	420	294	200	132	85	-1.5	1.1	0	-6.4	-20.7	-46.9
SV	204 Ruger	24 gr. NTX® (26" Bbl)	83209	4400	3667	3046	2504	2023	1604	1032	717	494	334	218	137	-1.5	0.6	0	-4.3	-14.3	-33
SV	204 Ruger	32 gr. V-MAX® (26" Bbl)	83204	4225	3645	3137	2685	2275	1903	1268	944	699	512	368	257	-1.5	0.6	0	-4.1	-13.1	-28.9
SV	204 Ruger	40 gr. V-MAX® (26" Bbl)	83206	3900	3482	3104	2757	2435	2136	1351	1077	855	675	527	405	-1.5	0.7	0	-4.3	-13.2	-28
V	22 WMR	30 gr. V-MAX®	83202	2200	1454	1026	–	–	–	322	141	70	–	–	–	-1.5	0	-15.7	–	–	–
V	22 Hornet	35 gr. V-MAX®	8302	3070	2247	1574	1117	918	802	732	392	192	97	65	50	-1.5	2.9	0	-17.5	-62.7	-149.2
C	22 Hornet	45 gr. SP	83028	2665	2241	1858	1523	1252	1071	710	502	345	232	157	115	-1.5	2.8	0	-13	-41.2	-91.6
C	218 Bee	45 gr. HP Match	8307	2750	1974	1362	1019	867	763	756	389	185	104	75	58	-1.5	3.9	0	-23.2	-79.6	-182.3
SV	222 Rem	35 gr. NTX®	8309	3760	3148	2615	2140	1719	1369	1099	770	531	356	230	146	-1.5	1	0	-6.2	-20.1	-46
SV	222 Rem	50 gr. V-MAX®	8316	3345	2930	2553	2205	1886	1599	1242	953	723	540	395	284	-1.5	1.3	0	-6.7	-20.6	-44.3
B	5.45 x 39mm	60 gr. V-MAX® (16" Bbl)	81247	2810	2495	2202	1929	1679	1457	1052	830	646	496	376	283	-1.8	1.9	0	-9.1	-27.7	-58.6
SV	223 Rem	35 gr. NTX®	83266	4000	3353	2796	2302	1861	1483	1243	874	607	412	269	171	-1.5	0.8	0	-5.3	-17.3	-39.6
SV	223 Rem	53 gr. V-MAX®	8025	3465	3106	2776	2470	2183	1916	1413	1135	907	718	561	432	-1.5	1.1	0	-5.6	-16.9	-35.6
SF	223 Rem	55 gr. CX™	832744	3250	2849	2482	2144	1834	1557	1290	991	753	561	411	296	-1.5	0	-2.8	-11.3	-27.5	-54.1
CD	223 Rem	55 gr. FTX®	80270	3240	2690	2201	1768	–	–	1282	883	592	382	–	–	-1.5	0	-3.4	-14.1	–	–
AG	223 Rem	55 gr. HP Match	80237	3240	2802	2405	2042	1713	1429	1282	959	706	509	358	249	-1.5	1.5	0	-7.6	-23.6	-51.5
C	223 Rem	55 gr. SP	80255																		
V	223 Rem	55 gr. V-MAX®	8327	3240	2855	2502	2175	1873	1602	1282	995	764	578	429	313	-1.5	1.4	0	-7	-21.4	-45.8
B	223 Rem	62 gr. FMJ	80234	3100	2751	2428	2127	1849	1597	1323	1042	811	623	471	351	-1.5	1.6	0	-7.5	-22.7	-48.2
M	223 Rem	73 gr. ELD® Match	80269	2790	2563	2348	2143	1949	1766	1262	1065	894	744	616	505	-1.5	1.9	0	-8.2	-24	-49
CD	223 Rem	73 gr. FTX®	80260	2790	2448	2131	1839	–	–	1262	971	736	548	–	–	-1.5	0	-4.4	-16.4	–	–
B	223 Rem	75 gr. BTHP	80267	2790	2562	2345	2139	1943	1759	1296	1093	916	762	629	515	-1.5	1.9	0	-8.2	-24.1	-49.3
M	223 Rem	75 gr. BTHP	8026	2790	2562	2345	2139	1943	1759	1296	1093	916	762	629	515	-1.5	1.9	0	-8.2	-24.1	-49.3
SM	223 Rem	75 gr. BTHP	80264	2930	2695	2471	2259	2057	1866	1430	1209	1017	850	705	580	-1.5	1.7	0	-7.4	-21.6	-44
SF	5.56 NATO	55 gr. CX™ (20" Bbl)	812544	3175	2781	2420	2086	1781	1511	1231	944	715	531	388	279	-1.5	0	-3	-12.1	-29.1	-57.3

	Ammo Description			Velocity (fps)						Energy (ft/lb)						Trajectory Tables (Inches)					
	CARTRIDGE	BULLET	ITEM#	MUZ	100 yd	200 yd	300 yd	400 yd	500 yd	MUZ	100 yd	200 yd	300 yd	400 yd	500 yd	MUZ	100 yd	200 yd	300 yd	400 yd	500 yd
B	5.56 NATO	62 gr. FMJ (20" Bbl)	81263	3060	2714	2394	2095	1820	1571	1289	1014	789	604	456	340	-1.5	1.6	0	-7.7	-23.4	-49.7
SM	5.56 NATO	75 gr. BTHP (20" Bbl)	81264	2910	2676	2453	2242	2041	1851	1410	1192	1002	837	693	570	-2.4	1.2	0	-7	-21	-43.3
B	5.56 NATO	75 gr. InterLock HD SBR (20" Bbl)	81296	2310	1695	1654	1387	1179	1042	889	643	456	321	231	181	-2.5	3.3	0	-16.1	-50.5	-109.9
V	224 Valkyrie	60 gr. V-MAX® W/C	81531	3300	2924	2578	2258	1961	1690	1451	1139	885	679	512	380	-1.5	1.3	0	-6.6	-20	-42.6
B	224 Valkyrie	75 gr. BTHP W/C	81532	3000	2761	2534	2319	2114	1920	1499	1269	1070	896	744	614	-1.5	1.5	0	-7	-20.4	-41.7
M	224 Valkyrie	88 gr. ELD® Match	81534	2675	2513	2356	2205	2060	1920	1398	1234	1085	950	829	720	-1.5	2	0	-8.3	-23.7	-47.4
SV	22-250 Rem	35 gr. NTX®	8334	4450	3736	3128	2598	2125	1706	1539	1085	761	524	351	226	-1.5	0.5	0	-4.1	-13.4	-30.6
V	22-250 Rem	50 gr. V-MAX®	8336	3800	3339	2925	2548	2201	1882	1603	1238	950	721	538	393	-1.5	0.8	0	-4.9	-15.2	-32.8
SV	22-250 Rem	50 gr. V-MAX®	83366	4000	3517	3086	2696	2337	2006	1776	1373	1057	807	606	447	-1.5	0.7	0	-4.3	-13.5	-29.1
V	22-250 Rem	55 gr. V-MAX®	8337	3680	3253	2868	2514	2186	1884	1654	1293	1004	772	583	433	-1.5	0.9	0	-5.1	-15.8	-33.9
V	220 Swift	55 gr. V-MAX®	8324	3680	3253	2868	2514	2186	1884	1654	1293	1004	772	583	433	-1.5	0.9	0	-5.1	-15.8	-33.9
PH	6mm ARC	103 gr. ELD-X®	81602	2800	2623	2452	2288	2130	1979	1793	1573	1375	1197	1038	895	-1.5	1.8	0	-7.6	-21.8	-43.7
B	6mm ARC	105 gr. BTHP	81604	2750	2580	2417	2260	2108	1963	1763	1552	1362	1190	1036	898	-1.5	1.9	0	-7.8	-22.4	-44.9
M	6mm ARC	108 gr. ELD® Match	81608	2750	2582	2421	2265	2115	1971	1813	1599	1405	1230	1072	931	-1.5	1.9	0	-7.8	-22.4	-44.8
SV	243 Win	58 gr. V-MAX®	8343	3925	3465	3052	2676	2330	2010	1984	1546	1200	922	699	520	-1.5	0.7	0	-4.4	-13.8	-29.6
SV	243 Win	75 gr. V-MAX®	83433	3580	3254	2953	2672	2407	2158	2134	1764	1452	1189	965	775	-1.5	0.9	0	-4.9	-14.7	-30.5
O	243 Win	80 gr. CX™	804574	3200	2842	2513	2206	1921	1661	1819	1435	1121	864	656	490	-1.5	1.4	0	-7	-21.1	-44.8
LL	243 Win	87 gr. SST®	80466	2800	2574	2359	2155	1961	1778	1514	1280	1075	897	743	611	1.5	1.9	0	-8.1	-23.8	-48.5
C	243 Win	87 gr. V-MAX®	00468	3240	2990	2754	2530	2317	2114	2028	1727	1465	1236	1037	863	-1.5	1.2	0	-5.8	-17	-34.8
PH	243 Win	90 gr. ELD-X®	80462	3150	2911	2685	2469	2264	2069	1983	1693	1440	1219	1024	855	-1.5	1.3	0	-6.1	-18	-36.6
SF	243 Win	95 gr. SST®	80463	3185	2908	2649	2404	2172	1953	2140	1784	1480	1219	995	804	-1.5	1.3	0	-6.3	-18.6	-38.3
AW	243 Win	100 gr. InterLock® BTSP	8047	2960	2729	2509	2300	2101	1912	1945	1653	1398	1175	980	812	-1.5	1.6	0	-7.1	-20.9	-42.5
SF	6mm Rem	95 gr. SST®	81663	3235	2955	2693	2445	2211	1990	2207	1842	1530	1261	1031	835	-1.5	1.3	0	-6.1	-18	-37
V	6mm Creedmoor	87 gr. V-MAX®	81393	3210	2962	2727	2505	2292	2091	1990	1694	1437	1212	1015	844	-1.5	1.2	0	-5.9	-17.4	-35.5
SF	6mm Creedmoor	90 gr. CX™	813944	3325	3081	2851	2632	2424	2225	2209	1897	1624	1385	1174	989	-1.5	1.1	0	-5.4	-15.8	-32.1
PH	6mm Creedmoor	103 gr. ELD-X®	81392	3050	2862	2687	2514	2348	2189	2127	1874	1651	1446	1261	1096	-1.5	1.4	0	-6.2	-17.9	-35.9
B	6mm Creedmoor	105 gr. BTHP	81396	2960	2782	2612	2447	2289	2136	2043	1805	1590	1396	1221	1064	-1.5	1.5	0	-6.6	-19	-38.1
M	6mm Creedmoor	108 gr. ELD® Match	81391	2960	2784	2615	2453	2296	2144	2101	1859	1640	1443	1264	1103	-1.5	1.5	0	-6.6	-19	-38
LEV	25-35 Win	110 gr. FTX®	8277	2425	2181	1952	1738	1543	1370	1436	1162	930	738	581	458	-0.8	3.3	0	-12.5	-36.5	-75.2
C	250 Savage	100 gr. InterLock® SP	8132	2800	2542	2299	2069	1853	1652	1741	1435	1173	950	762	606	-0.9	2.2	0	-8.9	-25.9	-53.1
SF	257 Roberts +P	117 gr. SST®	81353	2946	2707	2480	2265	2060	1866	2255	1903	1598	1332	1102	905	-1.5	1.6	0	-7.3	-21.4	-43.7
SF	25-06 Rem	90 gr. CX™	814464	3350	2980	2640	2324	2031	1761	2243	1774	1393	1080	824	619	-1.5	1.2	0	-6.2	-19	-40.2
PH	25-06 Rem	110 gr. ELD-X®	8143	3140	2929	2728	2536	2351	2175	2408	2095	1817	1570	1350	1155	-1.5	1.3	0	-6	-17.3	-35
AW	25-06 Rem	117 gr. InterLock® BTSP	8144	2990	2749	2521	2304	2098	1902	2322	1963	1651	1379	1143	940	-1.5	1.6	0	-7	-20.7	-42.2
SF	25-06 Rem	117 gr. SST®	81453	3110	2862	2627	2405	2193	1992	2513	2127	1793	1502	1249	1031	-1.5	1.4	0	-6.4	-18.9	-38.6
O	257 Wby Mag	90 gr. CX™	813624	3625	3230	2871	2539	2230	1944	2626	2085	1647	1288	994	755	-1.5	0.9	0	-5.2	-15.8	-33.4
PH	257 Wby Mag.	110 gr. ELD-X®	81364	3240	3024	2819	2623	2435	2255	2564	2233	1940	1680	1448	1241	-1.5	1.2	0	-5.5	-16.1	-32.6

HORNADY

HORNADY

	CARTRIDGE	BULLET	ITEM#	MUZ	100yd	200yd	300yd	400yd	500yd	MUZ	100yd	200yd	300yd	400yd	500yd	MUZ	100yd	200yd	300yd	400yd	500yd
				Velocity (fps)						**Energy (ft/lb)**						**Trajectory Tables (inches)**					
B	6.5 Grendel	123 gr. ELD® Match	81528	2580	2409	2244	2086	1935	1791	1818	1585	1376	1189	1023	876	-1.5	2.3	0	-9.2	-26.4	-52.8
C	6.5 Grendel	123 gr. SST®	8152	2580	2410	2247	2090	1940	1796	1818	1586	1379	1193	1028	881	-1.5	2.3	0	-9.1	-26.3	-52.7
SF	6.5 x 55mm	140 gr. SST®	85507	2735	2563	2397	2237	2084	1937	2325	2041	1786	1556	1350	1166	-1.5	1.9	0	-8	-22.9	-45.9
SF	260 Rem	129 gr. SST®	8552	2930	2737	2552	2375	2204	2041	2459	2145	1865	1615	1391	1193	-1.5	1.6	0	-6.9	-20	-40.3
M	260 Rem	130 gr. ELD® Match	8553	2840	2674	2515	2361	2212	2069	2328	2064	1825	1609	1412	1235	-1.5	1.7	0	-7.2	-20.6	-41.2
V	6.5 Creedmoor	95 gr. V-MAX®	81481	3300	3023	2764	2520	2288	2068	2297	1928	1612	1339	1104	902	-1.5	1.2	0	-5.7	-16.9	-34.8
O	6.5 Creedmoor	120 gr. CX™	814874	2925	2708	2501	2303	2114	1934	2280	1953	1666	1413	1191	997	-1.5	1.6	0	-7.2	-21	-42.6
SF	6.5 Creedmoor	120 gr. CX™	814904	3050	2826	2614	2411	2217	2033	2479	2128	1821	1549	1310	1101	-1.5	1.4	0	-6.5	-19	-38.7
M	6.5 Creedmoor	120 gr. ELD® Match	81491	2910	2719	2535	2359	2190	2028	2256	1969	1713	1483	1278	1096	-1.5	1.6	0	-7	-20.3	-40.8
AW	6.5 Creedmoor	129 gr. InterLock®	81489	2820	2615	2419	2232	2053	1882	2277	1959	1676	1427	1207	1015	-1.5	1.8	0	-7.7	-22.5	-45.5
SF	6.5 Creedmoor	129 gr. SST®	81496	2950	2756	2571	2394	2223	2059	2493	2176	1894	1641	1415	1214	-1.5	1.5	0	-6.8	-19.7	-39.7
AG	6.5 Creedmoor	140 gr. BTHP Match	81482	2690	2536	2388	2245	2106	1972	2249	2000	1773	1566	1379	1209	-1.5	2	0	-8.1	-23	-45.8
M	6.5 Creedmoor	140 gr. ELD® Match	81500	2710	2564	2422	2285	2152	2023	2283	2043	1823	1622	1439	1273	-1.5	1.9	0	-7.8	-22.3	-44.4
PH	6.5 Creedmoor	143 gr. ELD-X®	81499	2700	2556	2417	2282	2151	2025	2315	2075	1855	1654	1470	1302	-1.5	1.9	0	-7.9	-22.4	-44.5
M	6.5 Creedmoor	147 gr. ELD® Match	81501	2695	2567	2443	2323	2206	2092	2370	2151	1948	1761	1587	1428	-1.5	1.9	0	-7.7	-21.9	-43.2
O	6.5 PRC	130 gr. CX™	81622	2975	2782	2597	2420	2250	2086	2555	2234	1947	1690	1461	1256	-1.5	1.5	0	-6.6	-19.2	-38.7
PH	6.5 PRC	143 gr. ELD-X®	81621	2960	2808	2661	2519	2381	2248	2782	2503	2248	2014	1800	1604	-1.5	1.5	0	-6.4	-18.2	-36.2
M	6.5 PRC	147 gr. ELD® Match	81620	2910	2775	2645	2518	2395	2275	2764	2514	2283	2069	1871	1689	-1.5	1.5	0	-6.5	-18.4	-36.5
C	264 Win Mag	140 gr. InterLock® SP	8154	2935	2734	2542	2358	2182	2013	2678	2324	2009	1729	1479	1259	-1.5	1.6	0	-7	-20.2	-40.8
C	6.8mm SPC	100 gr. CX™	834814	2550	2227	1930	1659	1421	1226	1444	1102	827	611	448	334	-1.5	2.8	0	-12.2	-37.1	-79.4
B	6.8mm SPC	110 gr. V-MAX® (16" Bbl)	83464	2575	2343	2123	1916	1722	1544	1619	1341	1101	896	724	582	-2.4	2	0	-9.7	-29	-60
C	6.8mm SPC	120 gr. SST® (16" Bbl)	8347	2460	2250	2051	1863	1687	1524	1612	1349	1121	925	758	619	-2.4	2.3	0	-10.5	-31.1	-64
O	270 Win	130 gr. CX™	805294	3000	2648	2323	2021	1744	1497	2598	2024	1557	1179	878	647	-1.5	1.7	0	-8.2	-25.1	-53.4
SF	270 Win	130 gr. CX™	80524	3190	2945	2714	2494	2285	2085	2937	2503	2126	1795	1507	1255	-1.5	1.3	0	-6	-17.6	-35.9
SF	270 Win	130 gr. SST®	80543	3200	2984	2779	2583	2396	2216	2956	2570	2229	1926	1656	1417	-1.5	1.2	0	-5.7	-16.7	-33.7
AW	270 Win	130 gr. InterLock® SP	8053	3060	2852	2653	2463	2281	2107	2703	2347	2032	1752	1502	1281	-1.5	1.4	0	-6.4	-18.4	-37.2
AW	270 Win	140 gr. InterLock® SP	80534	2940	2747	2563	2386	2216	2053	2687	2346	2042	1770	1526	1310	-1.5	1.6	0	-6.8	-19.8	-39.9
SF	270 Win	140 gr. SST®	80563	3090	2894	2707	2528	2355	2189	2968	2604	2278	1986	1724	1490	-1.5	1.3	0	-6.1	-17.6	-35.5
PH	270 Win	145 gr. ELD-X®	80536	2970	2796	2627	2465	2308	2157	2840	2516	2222	1955	1714	1497	-1.5	1.5	0	-6.5	-18.8	-37.6
O	270 WSM	130 gr. CX™	805574	3150	2907	2678	2460	2252	2054	2864	2440	2070	1747	1464	1218	-1.5	1.3	0	-6.2	-18.1	-36.9
PH	270 WSM	145 gr. ELD-X®	80558	3100	2918	2744	2576	2414	2258	3094	2741	2423	2136	1876	1641	-1.5	1.3	0	-5.9	-17.1	-34.2
C	275 Rigby	140 gr. InterLock® SP	8070	2680	2456	2242	2040	1848	1670	2217	1861	1552	1284	1054	860	-1.5	2.2	0	-9.1	-26.5	-54.2
CL	7mm-08 Rem	120 gr. SST®	80572	2675	2435	2207	1992	1790	1604	1907	1579	1298	1057	854	685	-1.5	2.2	0	-9.4	-27.5	-56.6
SF	7mm-08 Rem	139 gr. CX™	805764	2910	2694	2488	2291	2103	1925	2613	2240	1910	1620	1365	1143	-1.5	1.7	0	-7.3	-21.2	-43
AW	7mm-08 Rem	139 gr. InterLock® SP	8057	2840	2608	2387	2177	1978	1790	2489	2098	1758	1463	1207	989	-1.5	1.8	0	-7.9	-23.2	-47.5
SF	7mm-08 Rem	139 gr. SST®	80573	2950	2757	2572	2395	2224	2061	2686	2346	2042	1770	1527	1311	-1.5	1.5	0	-6.8	-19.7	-39.6
PH	7mm-08 Rem	150 gr. ELD-X®	85578	2770	2613	2461	2315	2173	2037	2555	2274	2018	1784	1573	1381	-1.5	1.8	0	-7.5	-21.6	-43

	Ammo Description			Velocity (fps)						Energy (ft/lb)						Trajectory Tables (inches)					
CARTRIDGE	**BULLET**	**ITEM#**	**MUZ**	**100 yd**	**200 yd**	**300 yd**	**400 yd**	**500 yd**	**MUZ**	**100 yd**	**200 yd**	**300 yd**	**400 yd**	**500 yd**	**MUZ**	**100 yd**	**200 yd**	**300 yd**	**400 yd**	**500 yd**
PH 280 Rem	150 gr. ELD-X®	81587	2925	2763	2607	2455	2309	2167	2849	2543	2263	2007	1775	1564	-1.5	1.5	0	-6.7	-19.1	-38
PH 280 Ackley Imp	162 gr. ELD-X®	85586	2850	2704	2562	2424	2291	2162	2921	2629	2360	2114	1888	1681	-1.5	1.6	0	-6.9	-19.8	-39.3
AW 7mm Rem Mag	139 gr. InterLock® SP	80591	3150	2933	2728	2531	2343	2162	3062	2656	2296	1977	1694	1443	-1.5	1.3	0	-5.9	-17.3	-35.1
SF 7mm Rem Mag	139 gr. SST®	80593	3240	3033	2837	2649	2469	2295	3240	2840	2484	2166	1881	1626	-1.5	1.2	0	-5.5	-15.9	-32
O 7mm Rem Mag	150 gr. CX™	806114	3000	2792	2593	2403	2221	2047	2997	2596	2240	1923	1643	1395	-1.5	1.5	0	-6.7	-19.4	-39.2
AW 7mm Rem Mag	154 gr. InterLock® SP	80590	3035	2815	2605	2405	2214	2031	3150	2709	2321	1978	1676	1411	-1.5	1.5	0	-6.6	-19.2	-38.9
SF 7mm Rem Mag	154 gr. SST®	8061	3100	2915	2737	2567	2403	2244	3286	2905	2562	2253	1974	1722	-1.5	1.3	0	-5.9	-17.2	-34.4
PH 7mm Rem Mag	162 gr. ELD-X®	80636	2975	2827	2682	2542	2406	2274	3183	2874	2588	2324	2082	1860	-1.5	1.4	0	-6.3	-17.9	-35.6
SF 7mm Rem Mag	162 gr. SST®	80633	3030	2856	2689	2527	2372	2222	3302	2933	2600	2298	2023	1775	-1.5	1.4	0	-6.2	-17.8	-35.7
O 7mm WSM	150 gr. CX™	805514	3050	2839	2639	2447	2263	2087	3098	2685	2319	1994	1705	1450	-1.5	1.4	0	-6.4	-18.6	-37.7
PH 7mm WSM	162 gr. ELD-X®	80552	3000	2849	2702	2560	2423	2290	3237	2918	2626	2358	2112	1886	-1.5	1.4	0	-6.2	-17.6	-35
LEV 7-30 Waters	120 gr. FTX®	81569	2700	2425	2167	1926	1702	1500	1942	1567	1251	988	772	599	-1.5	2.2	0	-9.7	-28.8	-59.9
PH 28 Nosler	162 gr. ELD-X®	8069	3175	3017	2866	2719	2578	2440	3626	3275	2954	2660	2390	2142	-1.5	1.2	0	-5.4	-15.5	-30.9
PH 7mm STW	162 gr. ELD-X®	80851	3050	2897	2749	2606	2468	2333	3346	3018	2718	2443	2190	1958	-1.5	1.3	0	-5.6	-17	-33.8
CD 30 Carbine	110 gr. FTX® (20" Bbl)	81030	2000	1601	1279	1067	–	–	977	626	399	278	–	–	-0.9	0	-12.9	-47.2	–	–
C 300 Blackout	110 gr. CX™ (16" Bbl)	808794	2285	2029	1791	1575	1383	1224	1275	1005	784	606	467	366	-1.5	3.5	0	-14.4	-42.9	-89.7
B 300 Blackout	110 gr. V-MAX® (16" Bbl)	80873	2375	2094	1834	1597	–	–	1378	1071	821	623	–	–	-1.5	3.2	0	-13.7	–	–
AG 300 Blackout	125 gr. HP Match (16" Bbl)	80897	2175	1932	1708	1505	–	–	1313	1036	810	609	–	–	-1.5	4	0	-15.9	–	–
C 300 Blackout	135 gr. FTX® (16" Bbl)	80881	2085	1811	1564	1350	–	–	1303	983	733	546	–	–	-1.5	4.6	0	-18.9	–	–
SUB 300 Blackout	190 gr. SUB-X™ (16" Bbl)	80877	1050	998	955	918	–	–	465	420	384	355	–	–	-1.5	0	-33.4	-104.6	–	–
B 300 Blackout	208 gr. A-MAX® (16" Bbl)	80891	1020	987	959	–	–	–	480	450	424	–	–	–	-1.5	0	-33.5	–	–	–
LEV 30-30 Win	140 gr. MonoFlex®	82731	2465	2183	1920	1679	–	–	1889	1481	1146	876	–	–	-1.5	0	-5.8	-21.2	–	–
AW 30-30 Win	150 gr. RN	80801	2390	1959	1581	1276	–	–	1902	1278	832	542	–	–	-1.5	0	-7.7	-29.6	–	–
LFV 30-30 Win	160 gr. FTX®	82730	2400	2151	1917	1700	–	–	2046	1643	1305	1027	–	–	-1.5	3	0	-12.5	–	–
SUB 30-30 Win	175 gr. SUB-X™	80809	1050	977	921	874	–	–	428	371	329	297	–	–	-1.5	0	-34.9	-110.8	–	–
SF 300 Savage	150 gr. SST®	82221	2740	2499	2272	2056	1852	1663	2500	2081	1718	1407	1143	921	-1.5	2.1	0	-8.8	-25.8	-53.1
LEV 307 Win	160 gr. FTX®	8273	2650	2386	2137	1904	1688	1492	2494	2022	1622	1287	1012	791	-1.5	2.3	0	-10	-29.6	-61.4
AW 300 Win Mag	150 gr. InterLock® SP	8204	3275	2988	2719	2466	2227	2001	3572	2973	2463	2026	1651	1333	-1.5	1.2	0	-5.9	-17.6	-36.3
SF 300 Win Mag	165 gr. CX™	820264	3260	3031	2815	2609	2412	2223	3893	3367	2903	2493	2131	1810	-1.5	1.2	0	-5.5	-16.2	-32.9
PH 300 Win Mag	178 gr. ELD-X®	82041	2960	2789	2625	2467	2314	2166	3463	3075	2723	2405	2116	1854	-1.5	1.5	0	-6.6	-18.8	-37.6
M 300 Win Mag	178 gr. ELD® Match	82043	2960	2788	2622	2462	2308	2159	3463	3071	2717	2396	2106	1843	-1.5	1.5	0	-6.5	-18.8	-37.7
O 300 Win Mag	180 gr. CX™	821974	2960	2760	2568	2385	2209	2040	3502	3044	2636	2273	1949	1663	-1.5	1.5	0	-6.8	-19.8	-39.9
AW 300 Win Mag	180 gr. InterLock® SP	82044	2960	2739	2530	2329	2138	1956	3502	2999	2557	2168	1826	1529	-1.5	1.6	0	-7	-20.4	-41.5
SF 300 Win Mag	180 gr. SST®	82193	3130	2926	2732	2546	2368	2196	3915	3422	2983	2591	2240	1928	-1.5	1.3	0	-5.9	-17.2	-34.8
M 300 Win Mag	195 gr. ELD® Match	82180	2930	2769	2615	2465	2321	2181	3717	3321	2960	2631	2332	2059	-1.5	1.5	0	-6.6	-18.9	-37.7
PH 300 Win Mag	200 gr. ELD-X®	82002	2860	2707	2558	2414	2274	2140	3632	3253	2905	2587	2297	2033	-1.5	1.6	0	-6.9	-19.9	-39.5
O 300 Wby Mag	180 gr. CX™	822124	3100	2893	2696	2507	2326	2152	3841	3345	2905	2512	2163	1852	-1.5	1.3	0	-6.1	-17.8	-35.9

HORNADY

	Ammo Description			Velocity (fps)						Energy (ft/lb)						Trajectory Tables (inches)					
	CARTRIDGE	BULLET	ITEM#	MUZ	100yd	200yd	300yd	400yd	500yd	MUZ	100yd	200yd	300yd	400yd	500yd	MUZ	100yd	200yd	300yd	400yd	500yd
PH	300 Wby Mag	200 gr. ELD-X®	82213	2960	2804	2652	2505	2363	2225	3890	3491	3123	2786	2479	2198	-1.5	1.5	0	-6.4	-18.4	-36.5
O	300 PRC	190 gr. CX™	82164	3000	2834	2675	2521	2372	2229	3797	3389	3019	2682	2375	2095	-1.5	1.4	0	-6.3	-18	-36
PH	300 PRC	212 gr. ELD-X®	82166	2860	2723	2589	2460	2334	2212	3850	3489	3156	2849	2565	2304	-1.5	1.6	0	-6.8	-19.3	-38.3
M	300 PRC	225 gr. ELD® Match	82162	2810	2692	2577	2465	2356	2250	3945	3620	3318	3036	2773	2528	-1.5	1.7	0	-6.9	-19.5	-39.4
O	300 Rem Ultra Mag	180 gr. CX™	82084	3200	2988	2787	2594	2410	2233	4093	3569	3104	2690	2321	1992	-1.5	1.2	0	-5.7	-16.5	-33.4
PH	300 Rem Ultra Mag	220 gr. ELD-X®	8209	2910	2766	2627	2492	2361	2234	4136	3738	3371	3034	2723	2438	-1.5	1.5	0	-6.5	-18.7	-37.1
PH	30-378 Wby Mag	220 gr. ELD-X®	82214	3025	2877	2735	2597	2463	2332	4470	4044	3653	3293	2962	2657	-1.5	1.4	0	-6	-17.2	-34.1
AG	7.62x39	123 gr. HP Match (20" Bbl)	80786	2350	2053	1780	1535	1324	1159	1508	1151	865	643	479	367	-1.5	3.4	0	-14.4	-43.8	-93
B	7.62x39	123 gr. SST® (20" Bbl)	80784	2350	2040	1756	1503	1290	1129	1508	1136	842	617	454	348	-1.5	3.5	0	-14.8	-45.2	-96.5
C	303 British	150 gr. InterLock® SP	8225	2685	2441	2211	1993	1789	1601	2401	1985	1628	1323	1066	854	-1.5	2.2	0	-9.3	-27.4	-56.4
LEV	32 Win Special	165 gr. FTX®	82732	2410	2144	1897	1669	–	–	2128	1685	1318	1020	–	–	-0.9	3.4	0	-13.1	–	–
VM	8x57	196 gr. BTHP	82298	2500	2338	2182	2032	1888	1751	2720	2379	2072	1797	1552	1335	-1.5	2.4	0	-9.8	-27.9	-55.9
LEV	338 Marlin Express	200 gr. FTX®	82240	2565	2365	2174	1992	1820	1659	2922	2484	2099	1763	1471	1221	-1.5	2.4	0	-9.7	-28.3	-57.3
SF	338 RCM	225 gr. SST®	82236	2750	2575	2408	2246	2091	1942	3778	3314	2896	2521	2184	1884	-1.5	1.9	0	-7.9	-22.7	-45.5
SF	338 Win Mag	200 gr. SST®	82223	3030	2820	2620	2429	2246	2071	4077	3532	3049	2621	2240	1904	-1.5	1.4	0	-6.5	-18.9	-38.3
O	338 Win Mag	225 gr. CX™	823394	2800	2615	2437	2266	2102	1945	3917	3416	2967	2566	2208	1891	-1.5	1.8	0	-7.6	-22.1	-44.4
SF	338 Win Mag	225 gr. SST®	82233	2840	2662	2491	2326	2168	2016	4029	3540	3100	2704	2348	2030	-1.5	1.7	0	-7.3	-21.1	-42.2
PH	338 Win Mag	230 gr. ELD-X®	82222	2810	2662	2519	2381	2246	2116	4032	3620	3241	2894	2576	2287	-1.5	1.7	0	-7.2	-20.5	-40.7
M	338 Lapua Mag	250 gr. BTHP	8230	2860	2722	2587	2457	2331	2208	4540	4111	3716	3351	3015	2706	-1.5	1.6	0	-6.8	-19.3	-38.3
PH	338 Lapua Mag	270 gr. ELD-X®	82313	2800	2680	2562	2447	2336	2227	4699	4304	3935	3590	3270	2973	-1.5	1.7	0	-7	-19.7	-39.9
M	338 Lapua Mag	285 gr. ELD® Match	82300	2745	2636	2530	2426	2324	2225	4768	4397	4049	3723	3418	3133	-1.5	1.8	0	-7.2	-20.3	-39.8
LEV	348 Win	200 gr. FTX®	82738	2560	2294	2044	1811	1597	1407	2910	2336	1855	1456	1133	879	-1.5	2.6	0	-10.8	-32.6	-67.9
C	350 Legend	165 gr. FTX®	81197	2200	1890	1612	1371	–	–	1773	1309	952	689	–	–	-1.5	4.2	0	-17.6	–	–
AW	350 Legend	170 gr. InterLock® SP	81196	2200	1843	1529	1271	–	–	1827	1281	882	609	–	–	-1.5	4.5	0	-19.4	–	–
SUB	350 Legend	250 gr. SUB-X™	81198	1050	969	908	857	813	774	612	521	457	408	367	332	-1.5	0	-35.5	-113.2	-238.2	-416.1
LEV	35 Rem	200 gr. FTX®	82735	2225	1963	1722	1505	–	–	2198	1711	1317	1006	–	–	-1.5	3.8	0	-15.6	–	–
C	358 Win	200 gr. InterLock® SP	91318	2475	2180	1906	1655	1434	1248	2720	2110	1612	1217	913	692	-1.5	2.9	0	-12.6	-37.9	-80.3
SF	35 Whelen	200 gr. InterLock® SP	81193	2910	2585	2283	2001	1742	1509	3760	2968	2314	1778	1347	1012	-1.5	1.9	0	-8.6	-25.9	-54.8
DG	9.3x74R	286 gr. InterLock® SP-RP	82304	2360	2155	1961	1778	1608	1453	3537	2949	2442	2008	1642	1341	-1.5	0	-6	-21.1	-47.2	-86.8
DG	9.3x62mm	286 gr. InterLock® SP-RP	82303	2360	2155	1961	1778	1608	1453	3537	2949	2442	2008	1642	1341	-1.5	0	-6	-21.1	-47.2	-86.8
DG	376 Steyr	225 gr. InterLock® SP-RP	8234	2600	2332	2079	1844	1627	1434	3377	2716	2160	1698	1323	1027	-1.5	0	-4.9	-17.9	-41.2	-77.7
DG	376 Steyr	270 gr. InterLock® SP-RP	8237	2600	2372	2156	1951	1759	1582	4052	3373	2787	2283	1855	1500	-1.5	0	-4.7	-16.9	-38.3	-70.9
O	375 H&H Mag	250 gr. CX™	823314	2700	2481	2272	2073	1885	1708	4047	3416	2865	2385	1972	1620	-1.5	2.1	0	-8.8	-25.8	-52.6
DG	375 H&H Mag	270 gr. InterLock® SP-RP SPF	8508	2800	2562	2336	2122	1919	1729	4699	3935	3272	2699	2208	1793	-1.5	0	-3.8	-14	-32	-59.4
DG	375 H&H Mag	300 gr. DGS®	82322	2530	2223	1938	1678	1448	1256	4263	3292	2503	1875	1396	1050	-1.5	0	-5.6	-20.5	-47.8	-91.9
DG	375 H&H Mag	300 gr. DGX® Bonded	82334	2530	2223	1938	1678	1448	1256	4263	3292	2503	1875	1396	1050	-1.5	0	-5.6	-20.5	-47.8	-91.9
O	375 Ruger	250 gr. CX™	823374	2800	2576	2362	2159	1966	1784	4352	3683	3098	2588	2146	1768	-1.5	1.9	0	-8.1	-23.8	-48.4

	Ammo Description			Velocity (fps)						Energy (ft/lb)						Trajectory Tables (inches)					
CARTRIDGE	BULLET	ITEM#	MUZ	100 yd	200 yd	300 yd	400 yd	500 yd	MUZ	100 yd	200 yd	300 yd	400 yd	500 yd	MUZ	100 yd	200 yd	300 yd	400 yd	500 yd
DG 375 Ruger	270 gr. InterLock® SP-RP	8231	2840	2600	2372	2156	1951	1759	4835	4052	3373	2786	2283	1855	-1.5	0	-3.7	-13.5	-30.9	-57.4
DG 375 Ruger	300 gr. DGS®	8232	2660	2344	2050	1780	1536	1328	4713	3660	2800	2110	1572	1174	-1.5	0	-4.9	-18.1	-42.3	-81.4
DG 375 Ruger	300 gr. DGX® Bonded	82336	2660	2344	2050	1780	1536	1328	4713	3660	2800	2110	1572	1174	-1.5	0	-4.9	-18.1	-42.3	-81.4
DG 450-400 Nitro Express 3"	400 gr. DGS®	8242	2050	1820	1609	1420	–	–	3732	2940	2298	1791	–	–	-0.9	0	-9.7	-32.8	–	–
DG 450-400 Nitro Express 3"	400 gr. DGX® Bonded	82432	2050	1820	1609	1420	–	–	3732	2940	2298	1791	–	–	-0.9	0	-9.7	-32.8	–	–
C 405 Win	300 gr. InterLock® SP	8241	2200	1890	1612	1371	–	–	3224	2380	1730	1252	–	–	-1.5	0	-8.3	-30.2	–	–
DG 416 Ruger	400 gr. DGS®	82666	2400	2142	1901	1678	–	–	5115	4075	3208	2500	–	–	-1.5	0	-6.1	-21.9	–	–
DG 416 Ruger	400 gr. DGX® Bonded	82667	2400	2142	1901	1678	–	–	5115	4075	3208	2500	–	–	-1.5	0	-6.1	-21.9	–	–
DG 416 Rem Mag	400 gr. DGS®	82674	2400	2142	1901	1678	–	–	5115	4075	3208	2500	–	–	-1.5	0	-6.1	-21.9	–	–
DG 416 Rem Mag	400 gr. DGX® Bonded	82672	2400	2142	1901	1678	–	–	5115	4075	3208	2500	–	–	-1.5	0	-6.1	-21.9	–	–
DG 416 Rigby	400 gr. DGS®	8265	2415	2156	1915	1691	–	–	5180	4130	3256	2540	–	–	-1.5	0	-6	-21.6	–	–
DG 416 Rigby	400 gr. DGX® Bonded	82661	2415	2156	1915	1691	–	–	5180	4130	3256	2540	–	–	-1.5	0	-6	-21.6	–	–
DG 404 Jeffery	400 gr. DGS®	8239	2300	2053	1823	1611	–	–	4698	3743	2950	2306	–	–	-1.5	0	-6.8	-24.1	–	–
DG 404 Jeffery	400 gr. DGX® Bonded	82381	2300	2053	1823	1611	–	–	4698	3743	2950	2306	–	–	-1.5	0	-6.8	-24.1	–	–
LEV 444 Marlin	265 gr. FTX®	82744	2325	1971	1654	1381	–	–	3181	2286	1609	1123	–	–	-1.5	3.8	0	-16.6	–	–
SF 444 Marlin	265 gr. InterLock® FP	82453	2400	1974	1601	1295	–	–	3389	2294	1508	987	–	–	-1.5	3.8	0	-17.5	–	–
AW 450 Bushmaster	245 gr. InterLock®	82242	2200	1742	1364	1103	–	–	2633	1651	1012	662	–	–	-1.5	5.1	0	-24	–	–
C 450 Bushmaster	250 gr. FTX® (20" Bbl)	82244	2200	1835	1515	1255	–	–	2687	1868	1274	874	–	–	-2.4	4.1	0	-19.3	–	–
B 450 Bushmaster	250 gr. FTX® (20" Bbl)	82246	2200	1835	1515	1255	–	–	2687	1868	1274	874	–	–	-2.4	4.1	0	-19.3	–	–
SUB 450 Bushmaster	395 gr. SUB-X™ (20" Bbl)	82247	1050	977	921	874	–	–	967	837	744	670	–	–	-1.5	0	-34.9	-110.8	–	–
LEV 45-70 Govt	250 gr. MonoFlex®	82741	2025	1616	1285	1068	–	–	2276	1449	917	634	–	–	-1.5	6.1	0	-27.2	–	–
LEV 45-70 Govt	325 gr. FTX®	82747	2000	1685	1413	1197	–	–	2886	2049	1441	1035	–	–	-1.5	5.5	0	-23	–	–
SUB 45-70 Govt	410 gr. SUB-X™	82742	1075	992	930	879	–	–	1052	895	787	704	–	–	-1.5	0	-33.8	-107.8	–	–
LEV 450 Marlin	325 gr. FTX®	82750	2225	1887	1587	1332	–	–	3572	2570	1816	1280	–	–	-1.5	4.2	0	-18.1	–	–
DG 450 Nitro Express 3¼"	480 gr. DGS®	8256	2150	1881	1635	1418	–	–	4927	3769	2850	2144	–	–	-1.5	0	-8.4	-29.9	–	–
DG 450 Nitro Express 3¼"	480 gr. DGX® Bonded	8257	2150	1881	1635	1418	–	–	4927	3769	2850	2144	–	–	-1.5	0	-8.4	-29.9	–	–
DG 458 Win Mag	500 gr. DGS® SPF	8585	2140	1880	1643	1432	–	–	5084	3924	2996	2276	–	–	-1.5	0	-8.4	-29.8	–	–
DG 458 Win Mag	500 gr. DGX® Bonded SPF	85834	2140	1880	1643	1432	–	–	5084	3924	2996	2276	–	–	-1.5	0	-8.4	-29.8	–	–
DG 458 Lott	500 gr. DGS®	8262	2300	2029	1778	1551	–	–	5873	4569	3509	2671	–	–	-1.5	0	-7	-25.1	–	–
DG 458 Lott	500 gr. DGX® Bonded	82614	2300	2029	1778	1551	–	–	5873	4569	3509	2671	–	–	-1.5	0	-7	-25.1	–	–
DG 470 Nitro Express	500 gr. DGS®	8264	2150	1885	1643	1429	–	–	5132	3945	2998	2267	–	–	-0.9	0	-8.9	-30.8	–	–
DG 470 Nitro Express	500 gr. DGX® Bonded	82631	2150	1885	1643	1429	–	–	5132	3945	2998	2267	–	–	-0.9	0	-8.9	-30.8	–	–
NG 500 Nitro Express 3"	570 gr. DGS®	8269	2120	1862	1626	1417	–	–	5688	4386	3346	2542	–	–	-0.9	0	-9.2	-31.6	–	–
NG 500 Nitro Express 3"	570 gr. DGX® Bonded	82689	2120	1862	1626	1417	–	–	5688	4386	3346	2542	–	–	-0.9	0	-9.2	-31.6	–	–
M 50 BMG	750 gr. A-MAX® (36" Bbl)	8270	2815	2727	2641	2557	2474	2393	13196	12386	11619	10889	10196	9538	-1.8	1.4	0	-6.4	-18.2	-35.6

All data from a 24" Bbl, unless otherwise noted.

HORNADY

HORNADY

FRONTIER® CARTRIDGE BALLISTICS

	Ammo Description		Velocity (fps)						Energy (ft/lb)						Trajectory Tables (inches)					
CARTRIDGE	BULLET	ITEM #	MUZ	100 yd	200 yd	300 yd	400 yd	500 yd	MUZ	100 yd	200 yd	300 yd	400 yd	500 yd	MUZ	100 yd	200 yd	300 yd	400 yd	500 yd
223 Rem	55 gr. FMJ (24" Bbl)	FR100	3240	2837	2468	2128	1817	1540	1282	983	744	553	403	290	-1.5	1.4	0	-7.2	-22.1	-47.7
223 Rem	55 gr. Spire Point (24" Bbl)	FR120	3240	2824	2444	2095	1777	1497	1282	974	730	536	386	274	-1.5	1.5	0	-7.3	-22.6	-49.1
223 Rem	55 gr. Hollow Point Match (24" Bbl)	FR140	3240	2853	2499	2171	1869	1597	1282	994	763	576	427	311	-1.5	1.4	0	-7	-21.5	-46
223 Rem	68 gr. BTHP Match (24" Bbl)	FR160	2960	2697	2449	2215	1993	1786	1323	1098	906	741	600	482	-1.5	1.7	0	-7.5	-22	-45.4
6.5 Grendel	123 gr. FMJ	FR700	See hornady.com for latest information																	
5.56 NATO	55 gr. FMJ (M193) (20" Bbl)	FR200	3240	2837	2468	2128	1817	1540	1282	983	744	553	403	290	-1.5	1.4	0	-7.2	-22.1	-47.7
5.56 NATO	55 gr. Hollow Point Match (20" Bbl)	FR240	3240	2853	2499	2171	1869	1597	1282	994	763	576	427	311	-1.5	1.4	0	-7	-21.5	-46
5.56 NATO	62 gr. FMJ (20" Bbl)	FR260	3060	2715	2395	2097	1822	1574	1289	1015	790	606	457	341	-1.5	1.6	0	-7.7	-23.4	-49.6
5.56 NATO	62 gr. Spire Point (20" Bbl)	FR280	3060	2702	2372	2065	1783	1531	1289	1005	774	587	438	323	-1.5	1.7	0	-7.9	-23.9	-51.1
5.56 NATO	62 gr. BTHP Match (20" Bbl)	FR300	3060	2763	2485	2223	1978	1750	1289	1051	850	680	538	421	-1.5	1.5	0	-7.2	-21.5	-44.7
5.56 NATO	68 gr. BTHP Match (20" Bbl)	FR310	2960	2697	2449	2215	1993	1786	1323	1098	906	741	600	482	-1.5	1.7	0	-7.5	-22	-45.4
5.56 NATO	75 gr. BTHP Match (20" Bbl)	FR320	2860	2603	2360	2130	1914	1712	1362	1128	928	756	610	488	-1.5	1.8	0	-8.1	-23.9	-49.2
300 Blackout	125 gr. FMJ (16" Bbl)	FR400	2175	1867	1591	1354	1169	1044	1313	968	703	509	379	302	-1.5	4.3	0	-18.1	-55.3	-118

MUZZLELOADER PROJECTILE BALLISTICS

Muzzleloader Ammo Description			Velocity (fps)						Energy (ft/lb)						Trajectory Tables (inches)					
DESCRIPTION	BULLET WT.	ITEM #	MUZ	50 yd	100 yd	150 yd	200 yd	250 yd	MUZ	50 yd	100 yd	150 yd	200 yd	250 yd	MUZ	50 yd	100 yd	150 yd	200 yd	250 yd
45 Cal. SST®-ML™ Low Drag Sabot	200 gr.	67132	2325	2171	2022	1880	1744	1616	2400	2092	1815	1569	1351	1160	-1.5	2	3	2	-1	-7.1
50 Cal. SST®-ML™ Lock-N-Load® Speed Sabot®	250 gr.	67270	2250	2031	1852	1684	1529	1389	2735	2290	1904	1574	1297	1070	-1.5	1.8	3	1.7	-2.7	-11
50 Cal. SST®-ML™ Low Drag Sabot	250 gr.	67273	2250	2031	1852	1684	1529	1389	2735	2290	1904	1574	1297	1070	-1.5	1.8	3	1.7	-2.7	-11
50 Cal. MonoFlex® Lock-N-Load® Speed Sabot®	250 gr.	67269	2250	2031	1852	1684	1529	1389	2735	2290	1904	1574	1297	1070	-1.5	1.8	3	1.7	-2.7	-11
50 Cal. MonoFlex® High Speed Low Drag Sabot	250 gr.	67274	2250	2031	1852	1684	1529	1389	2735	2290	1904	1574	1297	1070	-1.5	1.8	3	1.7	-2.7	-11
50 Cal. Bore Driver™ FTX®	290 gr.	67713	See hornady.com for latest information																	
50 Cal. SST®-ML™ Lock-N-Load® Speed Sabot®	300 gr.	67271	2130	1974	1826	1686	1554	1433	3022	2597	2221	1893	1609	1368	-1.5	1.9	3	1.6	-2.9	-11.1
50 Cal. SST®-ML™ Low Drag Sabot	300 gr.	67263	2130	1974	1826	1686	1554	1433	3022	2597	2221	1893	1609	1368	-1.5	1.9	3	1.6	-2.9	-11.1

All data developed in a stock T/C Omega inline muzzleloader with 150 gr. charges except when noted. Zero your rifle 3" high at 100 yards for a 6" shooting window to 200 yards with 3 pellets or 150 gr. charges.

SHOTGUN SLUG BALLISTICS

Shotgun Slug Description			Velocity (fps)					Energy (ft/lb)					Trajectory Tables (inches)				
AMMO DESCRIPTION	BULLET	ITEM #	MUZ	50 yd	100 yd	150 yd	200 yd	MUZ	50 yd	100 yd	150 yd	200 yd	MUZ	50 yd	100 yd	150 yd	200 yd
12 GA SST® Shotgun Slug 2¾"	300 gr. FTX®	8623	2000	1814	1641	1483	1342	2664	2192	1795	1465	1199	-1.5	1.9	2.6	0	-6.5
12 GA Superformance® Shotgun Slug 2¾"	300 gr. MonoFlex®	86236	1950	1742	1552	1383	1239	2533	2022	1605	1274	1022	-1.5	2.1	2.9	0	-7.4
12 GA Custom Lite® Shotgun Slug 2¾"	300 gr. FTX®	86230	1575	1423	1289	1178	1091	1652	1348	1107	924	793	-1.5	3.6	4.5	0	-10.7
12 GA American Whitetail® Shotgun Slug 2¾"	325 gr. InterLock®	86271	1825	1651	1491	1349	1227	2403	1966	1605	1313	1086	-1.5	0.9	0	-4.8	-14.3
12 GA American Whitetail® Rifled Slug 2¾"	1 oz. Rifled Slug	86234	1600	1210	997	882	–	2484	1420	965	754	–	-0.5	2.8	0	-11.4	–
12 GA American Gunner® Reduced Recoil Rifled Slug 2¾"	1 oz. Rifled Slug	86231	1300	1038	907	816	–	1640	1046	798	647	–	-1.5	0	-6.5	-23.6	–
20 GA SST® Shotgun Slug 2¾"	250 gr. FTX®	86232	1800	1628	1471	1331	1212	1798	1471	1201	983	815	-1.5	2.6	3.3	0	-8.2
20 GA Superformance® Shotgun Slug 2¾"	250 gr. MonoFlex®	86237	1800	1628	1471	1331	1212	1798	1471	1201	983	815	-1.5	2.6	3.3	0	-8.2
20 GA Custom Lite® Shotgun Slug 2¾"	250 gr. FTX®	86233	1600	1452	1321	1208	1118	1421	1171	968	810	694	-1.5	3.4	4.2	0	-10.1

SHOTGUN BALLISTICS

AMMO DESCRIPTION	SHOT SIZE	SHELL LENGTH	ITEM #	Velocity (fps) muzzle
12 GA Varmint Express® 2¾"	#4 Buck	2¾"	86243	1350
12 GA Critical Defense® 2¾"	00 Buck (8 Pellets)	2¾"	86240	1600
12 GA American Gunner® 2¾"	00 Buck (8 Pellets)	2¾"	86274	1350
12 GA Hornady BLACK™ 2¾"	00 Buck (8 Pellets)	2¾"	86249	1600
12 GA Heavy Magnum® Coyote 3"	BB	3"	86222	1300
12 GA Heavy Magnum® Coyote 3"	00 Buck	3"	86224	1300
410 Critical Defense® Triple Defense™	FTX® Slug & 2 round balls	2½"	86238	750

12 gauge shotgun ballistics are established with a 30" SAAMI standard test barrel. 20 gauge shotgun ballistics are established with a 26" SAAMI standard test barrel.

HORNADY

Rifle Ammunition Product Lines:								
	C	Custom™	LEV	LEVERevolution®	SUB	Subsonic	V	Varmint Express®
AG	American Gunner™	CL	Custom Lite®	M	Match™	SF	Superformance®	VM	Vintage Match™
AW	American Whitetail®	DG	Dangerous Game™ Series	O	Outfitter®	SM	Superformance® Match
CD	Critical Defense®	B	Hornady BLACK®	PH	Precision Hunter®	SV	Superformance® Varmint

HORNADY

HANDGUN BALLISTICS

	Ammo Description				Velocity (fps)			Energy (ft/lb)		
CARTRIDGE		BULLET	ITEM #	BARREL LENGTH	MUZ	50 yd	100 yd	MUZ	50 yd	100 yd
CD	22 WMR	45 gr. FTX®	83200	1⅞ V"	1000	920	857	100	85	73
CD	25 Auto	35 gr. FTX®	90014	2"	900	805	728	63	50	41
C	25 Auto	35 gr. XTP®	90012	2"	900	813	742	63	51	43
CD	32 Auto	60 gr. FTX®	90063	4"	1000	882	797	133	104	85
C	32 Auto	60 gr. XTP®	90062	4"	1000	905	833	133	109	92
CD	32 H&R	80 gr. FTX®	90060	4"	1150	1039	963	235	192	165
CD	327 Federal Mag	80 gr. FTX®	90061	See hornady.com for latest information						
AG	380 Auto	90 gr. XTP®	90104	4"	1000	912	845	200	166	143
CD	380 Auto	90 gr. FTX®	90080	4"	1000	912	845	200	166	143
CDL	9mm Luger	100 gr. FTX®	90240	4"	1125	1003	922	281	224	189
AG	9mm Luger	115 gr. XTP®	90244	4"	1155	1038	958	341	275	234
CD	9mm Luger	115 gr. FTX®	90250	4"	1135	1025	949	329	268	230
DUTY	9mm Luger +P	124 gr. FlexLock®	90216	4"	1175	1081	1012	380	322	282
AG	9mm Luger +P	124 gr. XTP®	90224	4"	1175	1074	1001	380	317	276
C	9mm Luger	124 gr. XTP®	90242	4"	1110	1027	965	339	290	257
DUTY	9mm Luger	135 gr. FlexLock®	90236	4"	1010	960	918	306	276	253
DUTY	9mm Luger +P	135 gr. FlexLock®	90226	4"	1110	1038	983	369	323	289
C	9mm Luger	147 gr. XTP®	90282	4"	975	934	899	310	285	264
SUB	9mm Luger	147 gr. XTP®	90287	4"	See hornady.com for latest information						
HH	9mm Luger +P	115 gr. MonoFlex®	90281	4"	See hornady.com for latest information						
C	357 Sig	147 gr. XTP®	9131	4"	1225	1132	1060	490	418	367
DUTY	357 Sig	135 gr. FlexLock®	91296	4"	1225	1112	1031	450	371	319
CDL	38 Special	90 gr. FTX®	90300	4"	1200	1037	938	288	215	176
CD	38 Special	110 gr. FTX®	90310	4" V	1010	939	882	249	215	190
CD	38 Special +P	110 gr. FTX®	90311	4" V	1090	996	928	290	242	210
AG	38 Special	125 gr. XTP®	90324	4" V	900	856	817	225	203	185
C	38 Special	158 gr. XTP®	90362	4" V	800	775	751	225	210	198
CD	357 Magnum	125 gr. FTX®	90500	8" V	1500	1312	1163	624	478	376
AG	357 Magnum	125 gr. XTP®	90504	8" V	1500	1313	1165	624	479	377
HH	357 Magnum	130 gr. MonoFlex®	9052	8" V	See hornady.com for latest information						
DUTY	357 Magnum	135 gr. FlexLock®	90511	8" V	1275	1150	1058	487	396	336
LEV	357 Magnum	140 gr. FTX®	92755	8" V	1440	1281	1154	645	510	414
C	357 Magnum	158 gr. XTP®	90562	8" V	1250	1149	1072	548	463	403
CD	9 x 18mm Makarov	95 gr. FTX®	91000	4"	1000	913	846	211	176	151
C	40 S&W	155 gr. XTP®	9132	4"	1180	1060	978	479	387	329

	Ammo Description				Velocity (fps)			Energy (ft/lb)		
CARTRIDGE		BULLET	ITEM #	BARREL LENGTH	MUZ	50 yd	100 yd	MUZ	50 yd	100 yd
CD	40 S&W	165 gr. FTX®	91340	3"	1045	971	914	400	345	306
DUTY	40 S&W	175 gr. FlexLock®	91376	4"	1010	948	899	396	350	314
AG	40 S&W	180 gr. XTP®	91364	4"	950	903	862	361	326	297
SUB	40 S&W	180 gr. XTP®	91369	4"	See hornady.com for latest information					
HH	40 S&W	135 gr. MonoFlex®	91361	4"	See hornady.com for latest information					
C	10mm Auto	155 gr. XTP®	9122	5"	1410	1224	1090	684	516	409
DUTY	10mm Auto	175 gr. FlexLock®	91256	5"	1160	1061	990	523	437	381
C	10mm Auto	180 gr. XTP®	9126	5"	1275	1146	1052	650	525	443
HH	10mm Auto	135 gr. MonoFlex®	91267	5"	1315	1108	985	518	368	291
LEV	41 Rem Mag	190 gr. FTX®	9078	10"	1620	1432	1272	1107	865	682
C	41 Rem Mag	210 gr. XTP®	9077	10"	1545	1383	1244	1113	892	722
C	44-40 Cowboy	205 gr. Cowboy™	9075	7½" V	725	689	655	239	216	195
CD	44 Special	165 gr. FTX®	90700	2½" V	900	847	802	297	263	235
C	44 Rem Mag	200 gr. XTP®	9080	7½" V	1500	1332	1194	999	788	633
HH	44 Rem Mag	200 gr. MonoFlex®	9083	7½" V	See hornady.com for latest information					
LEV	44 Rem Mag	225 gr. FTX®	92782	7½" V	1410	1233	1102	993	760	607
C	44 Rem Mag	240 gr. XTP®	9085	7½" V	1350	1230	1133	971	806	684
C	44 Rem Mag	300 gr. XTP®	9088	7½" V	1150	1083	1030	881	781	706
AG	45 Auto	185 gr. XTP®	90904	5"	970	911	862	386	341	305
CD	45 Auto	185 gr. FTX®	90900	3"	900	853	811	333	299	270
C	45 Auto	200 gr. XTP®	9112	5"	900	856	817	360	325	296
DUTY	45 Auto +P	220 gr. FlexLock®	90926	5"	975	927	887	464	420	384
C	45 Auto +P	230 gr. XTP®	9096	5"	950	908	871	461	421	388
SUB	45 Auto	230 gr. XTP®	90971	5"	See hornady.com for latest information					
CD	45 Colt	185 gr. FTX®	92790	3" V	920	870	826	348	311	280
C	45 Colt	255 gr. Cowboy™	9115	4¾" V	725	687	651	298	267	240
LEV	45 Colt	225 gr. FTX®	92792	4¾" V	960	903	855	460	407	366
HH	454 Casull	200 gr. MonoFlex®	9151	7½" V	See hornady.com for latest information					
C	454 Casull	240 gr. XTP® Mag	9148	7½" V	1900	1678	1478	1924	1500	1164
C	454 Casull	300 gr. XTP® Mag	9150	7½" V	1650	1490	1348	1813	1480	1210
C	460 S&W Mag	200 gr. FTX®	9152	8 3/8"	2200	1948	1715	2149	1673	1288
HH	460 S&W Mag	200 gr. MonoFlex®	9153	8 3/8"	See hornady.com for latest information					
C	480 Ruger	325 gr. XTP® Mag	9138	7½"	1350	1191	1077	1315	1024	837
C	50 AE	300 gr. XTP®	9245	6"	1475	1251	1092	1449	1043	795
C	500 S&W Mag	300 gr. FTX®	9249	8½"	1950	1653	1396	2533	1819	1298
C	500 S&W Mag	500 gr. FP-XTP®	9252	8½"	1300	1178	1085	1876	1541	1308

HORNADY

NOSLER

CARTRIDGE	BRAND	BULLET WEIGHT	BULLET STYLE	PART #	COUNT	BBL TWIST RQMT	FOR USE	LEAD-FREE	MUZ	100	200	300	400	500	600	700	800
17 Rem Fireball	VMG	20	FB Tipped	63100	20	1-10"	Varmint-Targets		4,000	3363	2811	2322	1885	1508	1214	1033	927
17 Remington	VMG	20	FBHP	65100	20	1-10"	Varmint-Targets		4,200	3230	2442	1780	1272	1002	869	774	695
	VMG	20	FB Tipped	65105	20	"	Varmint-Targets		4,200	3544	2978	2477	2029	1634	1312	1094	970
204 Ruger	VMG	32	FB Tipped	65115	20	1-12"	Varmint-Targets		4,000	3433	2934	2487	2081	1718	1408	1174	1028
	BTV	32	BTLF	61040	20	"	Varmint-Targets	XX	3,975	3459	3001	2587	2209	1865	1559	1304	1117
	BTV	40	BT	61021	20	"	Varmint-Targets		3,625	3176	2771	2399	2058	1748	1475	1252	1095
22 Hornet	VMG	35	FB Tipped	41132	50	1-16"	Varmint-Targets		3,000	2286	1683	1229	992	869	778	702	637
221 Remington Fireball	VMG	40	FBHP	65120	20	1-12"	Varmint-Targets		3,100	2510	1991	1547	1209	1016	907	826	759
	VMG	40	FB Tipped	65125	20	"	Varmint-Targets		3,100	2651	2243	1874	1549	1283	1097	985	908
222 Remington	VMG	40	FB Tipped	65135	20	1-14"	Varmint-Targets		3,400	2920	2488	2095	1742	1437	1200	1047	952
	VMG	50	FB Tipped	65137	20	"	Varmint-Targets		3,150	2721	2330	1973	1652	1378	1167	1031	943
223 Remington	BTV	35	BTLF	61042	20	1-14"	Varmint-Targets	XX	3,750	3206	2725	2291	1899	1555	1276	1087	974
	BTV	40	BTLF	61048	20	1-12"	Varmint-Targets	XX	3,625	3139	2704	2308	1947	1624	1352	1148	1021
	VMG	53	FB Tipped	65139	20	1-14"	Varmint-Targets		3,350	3024	2712	2420	2147	1892	1658	1449	1272
	BTV	55	BT	61025	20	"	Varmint-Targets		3,100	2737	2401	2090	1803	1546	1327	1156	1040
	VMG	55	FB Tipped	65145	20	"	Varmint-Targets		3,100	2725	2380	2060	1768	1508	1290	1128	1022
	ETA	55	ET	40150	20	1-10"	Deer Sized Game	XX	3,100	2785	2491	2215	1959	1722	1508	1323	1175
	VMG	62	FBHP	40223	20	1-14"	Varmint-Targets		2,950	2581	2242	1928	1645	1400	1204	1069	981
	MGA	69	HPBT	60023	20	1-9"	Targets		2,900	2594	2308	2040	1792	1567	1369	1207	1087
	MG-RDF	70	RDF	60130	20	"	Targets		2,850	2630	2419	2219	2028	1847	1673	1507	1349
	TGA	70	AB	61036	20	"	Deer Sized Game		2,750	2505	2272	2052	1845	1653	1478	1324	1196
	MGA	77	HPBT	60011	20	1-8"	Targets		2,600	2342	2099	1872	1661	1471	1306	1171	1072
22 Nosler	VMG	53	FB Tipped	65177	20	1-8"	Varmint-Targets		3,450	3101	2779	2480	2199	1937	1696	1480	1295
	BTV	55	BT	61030	20	"	Varmint-Targets		3,500	3102	2738	2403	2091	1805	1548	1328	1157
	ETA	55	ET	40140	20	"	Deer Sized Game	XX	3,500	3150	2826	2525	2243	1980	1737	1517	1327
	VMG	62	FBHP	65180	50	"	Varmint-Targets		3,250	2851	2486	2149	1840	1563	1328	1148	1029
	TGA	70	AB	60918	20	"	Deer Sized Game		2,950	2694	2451	2222	2004	1801	1612	1442	1293
	MG-RDF	70	RDF	60124	20	"	Targets		3,000	2781	2562	2354	2156	1967	1788	1616	1451
	MGA	77	CC	60016	20	"	Targets		2,950	2672	2410	2163	1931	1715	1519	1347	1204
	MG-RDF	85	RDF	60162	20	"	Targets		2,750	2563	2382	2210	2045	1887	1734	1588	1447
22-250 Remington	BTV	35	BTLF	61038	20	1-14"	Varmint-Targets	XX	4,200	3598	3073	2606	2183	1803	1474	1217	1051
	BTV	40	BTLF	61044	20	1-12"	Varmint-Targets	XX	3,950	3420	2950	2527	2141	1792	1486	1240	1072
	VMG	55	FB Tipped	65155	20	1-14"	Varmint-Targets		3,550	3135	2757	2410	2088	1793	1530	1308	1140
	BTV	55	BT	61034	20	"	Varmint-Targets		3,550	3153	2790	2455	2144	1857	1597	1373	1194
243 Winchester	VMG	55	FB Tipped	65165	20	1-10"	Varmint-Targets		3,800	3355	2954	2587	2248	1936	1653	1407	1210
	VMG	70	FB Tipped	61029	20	"	Varmint-Targets		3,500	3150	2826	2525	2243	1980	1737	1517	1327
	TGA	85	PT	60002	20	"	Deer Sized Game		3,225	2910	2617	7342	2084	1843	1622	1426	1260
	BTA	90	BT	40050	20	"	Deer/Hogs/Antelope		3,100	2842	2599	2368	2149	1942	1749	1570	1410
	TGA	90	AB	48263	20	"	Deer Sized Game		3,100	2842	2599	2368	2149	1942	1749	1570	1410
	ETA	90	ET	40030	20	1-9"	Deer Sized Game	XX	3,050	2809	2580	2362	2155	1959	1774	1603	1446
	TGA	100	PT	61046	20	1-10"	Deer Sized Game		2,950	2703	2468	2246	2035	1837	1652	1483	1334
6mm Creedmoor	VMG	70	FB Tipped	65170	20	1-10"	Varmint-Targets		3,550	3195	2869	2565	2281	2015	1769	1546	1351
	TGA	90	AB	60142	20	"	Deer Sized Game		3,200	2933	2681	2443	2218	2004	1803	1618	1449
	BTA	95	BT	40052	20	"	Deer/Hogs/Antelope		3,100	2841	2596	2365	2145	1937	1742	1563	1402
	MG-RDF	105	RDF	60135	20	1-8"	Targets		3,050	2877	2709	2546	2388	2237	2091	1950	1815
	MG-RDF	115	RDF	60170	20	1-7.5"	Targets		2,900	2748	2601	2457	2318	2184	2055	1930	1809

ENERGY (FT-LBS)									DROP IN INCHES (100 YRD ZERO)									DROP IN INCHES (200 YRD ZERO)								
MUZ	100	200	300	400	500	600	700	800	MUZ	100	200	300	400	500	600	700	800	MUZ	100	200	300	400	500	600	700	800
710	502	351	239	158	101	65	47	38	-1.5	0	-1.6	-7.7	-20.3	-42.9	-81.0	-142.7	-237.0	-1.5	0.8	0.0	-5.3	-17.1	-38.8	-76.1	-137.1	-230.6
783	463	265	141	72	45	34	27	21	-1.5	0	-1.9	-9.9	-29.3	-70.4	-146.0	-267.7	447.6	-1.5	1.0	0.0	-7.0	-25.4	-65.6	-140.3	-261.0	-439.9
783	558	394	272	183	119	76	53	42	-1.5	0	-1.3	-6.6	-17.6	-37.2	-70.0	-123.7	-200.1	-1.5	0.6	0.0	-4.6	-15.0	-33.9	-66.1	-118.6	-200.1
1137	837	612	439	308	210	141	98	75	-1.5	0	-1.5	-7.0	-18.3	-37.6	-68.9	-117.9	-192.2	-1.5	0.7	0.0	-4.8	-15.3	-33.9	-64.5	-112.8	-186.3
1123	850	640	476	347	247	173	121	89	-1.5	0	-1.4	-6.7	-17.3	-35.0	-62.9	-105.2	-168.1	-1.5	0.7	0.0	-4.6	-14.4	-31.5	-58.6	-100.2	-162.4
1167	896	682	511	376	271	193	139	106	-1.5	0	-2.0	-8.5	-21.1	-42.0	-74.4	-122.9	-185.8	-1.5	1.0	0.0	-5.5	-17.2	-37.1	-68.5	-116.0	-185.8
699	406	220	117	76	58	47	38	31	-1.5	0	-5.1	-23.0	-64.0	-140.1	-262.4	-442.2	-692.8	-1.5	2.6	0.0	-15.3	53.7	-127.3	-247.0	-424.3	-672.3
853	559	352	212	129	91	73	61	51	-1.5	0	-4.1	-17.3	-45.1	-96.9	-182.2	-309.8	-488.4	-1.5	2.1	0.0	-11.0	-36.9	-86.6	-169.8	-295.3	-471.9
853	624	447	312	213	146	107	86	73	-1.5	0	-3.5	-14.0	-34.5	-69.7	-126.1	-211.2	-332.2	-1.5	1.7	0.0	-8.7	-27.5	-60.9	-115.6	-199.0	-318.2
1026	757	550	390	269	183	127	97	80	-1.5	0	-2.6	-10.9	-27.2	-55.1	-100.0	-169.0	-269.7	-1.5	1.3	0.0	-7.0	-22.0	-48.6	-92.2	-159.9	-259.2
1101	822	603	432	303	211	151	118	99	-1.5	0	-3.2	-12.9	-31.7	-63.3	-113.4	-189.0	-297.3	-1.5	1.6	0.0	-8.1	-25.2	-55.2	-103.7	-177.7	-284.3
1092	799	577	408	280	188	126	92	74	-1.5	0	-1.9	-8.6	-21.9	-45.0	-82.7	-141.8	-230.2	-1.5	1.0	0.0	-5.7	-18.1	-40.2	-76.9	-135.1	-222.5
1166	875	649	473	336	234	162	117	92	-1.5	0	-2.1	-8.9	-22.3	-45.7	-81.1	-136.3	-217.8	-1.5	1.0	0.0	-5.8	-18.2	-39.9	-74.9	-129.1	-209.5
1330	1076	865	689	542	421	324	247	190	-1.5	0	-2.3	-9.4	-22.4	-43.0	-73.4	-116.5	-176.3	-1.5	1.2	0.0	-5.9	-17.8	-37.2	-66.5	-108.4	-167.0
1173	914	704	533	397	292	215	163	132	-1.5	0	-3.2	-12.4	-29.7	-57.7	-100.4	-163.0	-251.5	-1.5	1.6	0.0	-7.7	-23.3	-49.8	-90.9	-151.9	-238.8
1173	906	691	518	381	277	203	155	127	-1.5	0	-3.2	-12.6	-30.3	-59.1	-103.4	-168.6	-261.0	-1.5	1.6	0.0	-7.8	-23.8	-51.1	-93.8	-157.4	-248.2
1174	947	758	599	469	362	277.6	214	169	-1.5	0	-3.0	-11.6	-27.4	-52.2	-88.9	-140.9	-212.9	-1.5	1.5	0.0	-7.1	-21.4	-44.7	-79.9	-130.4	-200.9
1197	917	691	512	372	269	199	157	132	-1.5	0	-3.8	-14.5	-34.6	-67.7	-118.7	-193.6	-298.8	-1.5	1.9	0.0	-8.8	-27.1	-58.4	-107.4	-180.5	-203.0
1288	1031	816	630	492	376	287	223	181	-1.5	0	-3.7	-13.9	-32.6	-62.1	-105.9	-168.4	-254.7	-1.5	1.8	0.0	-8.4	-25.2	-52.9	-94.9	-155.4	-239.9
1262	1075	910	765	639	530	435	353	283	-1.5	0	-3.5	-13.0	-29.6	-54.7	-89.9	-137.7	-200.8	-1.5	1.8	0.0	-7.7	-22.5	45.8	79.3	-125.3	-186.7
1175	975	802	655	529	425	340	273	222	-1.5	0	-4.1	-14.9	-34.0	-63.3	-105.5	-163.6	-241.5	-1.5	2.0	0.0	-8.8	-25.9	-53.2	-93.3	-149.4	-225.3
1156	938	753	599	472	370	291	235	197	-1.5	0	-4.9	-17.7	-40.4	-75.8	-127.4	-199.4	-296.8	-1.5	2.4	0.0	-10.4	-30.7	63.7	-112.0	-182.4	-277.3
1401	1132	909	723	569	442	339	258	197	-1.5	0	-2.1	-8.8	-21.1	-40.7	-69.6	-110.6	-167.6	-1.5	1.1	0.0	-5.6	-16.9	-35.4	-63.2	-103.2	-159.1
1496	1175	916	705	534	398	292	215	163	-1.5	0	-2.1	-8.9	-21.8	-42.7	-74.3	-120.6	-186.6	-1.5	1.1	0.0	-5.7	-17.5	-37.3	-67.9	-113.1	-178.7
1496	1211	975	779	615	479	368	201	215	-1.5	0	-2.0	-8.4	-20.3	-39.1	-66.8	-106.2	-160.7	-1.5	1.0	0.0	-5.4	-16.2	-34.0	-60.8	-99.1	-152.6
1454	1119	851	636	466	336	243	181	146	-1.5	0	-2.8	-11.3	-27.3	-53.8	-94.6	-155.2	-242.1	-1.5	1.4	0.0	-7.1	-21.7	-46.8	-86.1	-145.3	-230.9
1352	1127	934	767	624	504	404	323	260	-1.5	0	-3.3	-12.4	-28.6	-53.5	-09.1	-138.2	-204.0	-1.5	1.7	0.0	-7.5	-22.0	-45.2	-79.2	-126.6	-190.8
1398	1202	1020	861	722	601	497	406	327	-1.5	0	-3.0	-11.3	-25.9	-48.0	-79.1	-121.2	-176.6	-1.5	1.5	0.0	-6.8	-19.9	-40.5	-70.1	-110.7	-164.6
1488	1220	993	800	637	503	395	310	248	-1.5	0	-3.4	-12.8	-29.7	-55.9	-94.0	-147.2	-219.7	-1.5	1.7	0.0	-7.7	-22.9	-47.4	-83.8	-135.4	-206.1
1427	1239	1071	921	789	672	568	476	395	-1.5	0	-3.8	-13.7	-30.8	-56.2	-91.4	-138.2	-198.8	-1.5	1.9	0.0	-8.0	-23.2	-46.7	-80.0	-124.9	-183.6
1370	1006	734	527	370	252	169	115	85	-1.5	0	-1.2	-6.1	-16.2	-33.7	-62.0	-106.5	-174.5	-1.5	0.6	0.0	-4.3	-13.8	-30.7	-58.4	-102.3	-169.7
1386	1038	773	567	407	285	196	136	102	-1.5	0	-1.5	-7.0	-18.0	-36.7	-66.4	-112.0	-180.2	-1.5	0.7	0.0	-4.8	-15.1	-33.0	-61.9	-106.7	-174.3
1538	1200	928	709	532	392	285	209	158	-1.5	0	-2.1	-8.7	-21.4	-42.1	-73.8	-120.3	-187.3	-1.5	1.0	0.0	-5.6	-17.3	-37.0	-67.6	-113.2	-179.1
1538	1214	950	736	561	421	311	230	174	-1.5	0	-2.0	-8.5	-20.8	-40.8	-70.8	-114.7	-177.0	-1.5	1.0	0.0	-5.5	-16.8	-35.7	-64.8	-107.6	-168.9
1763	1375	1066	817	617	457	333	241	179	-1.5	0	-1.6	-7.2	-18.1	-35.8	-62.9	-102.9	-160.5	-1.5	0.8	0.0	-4.8	-14.8	-31.8	-58.1	-97.3	-154.1
1904	1542	1241	991	782	609	469	358	274	-1.5	0	-2.0	-8.4	-20.3	-39.1	-66.8	-106.2	-160.7	-1.5	1.0	0.0	-5.4	-16.2	-34.0	-60.8	-99.1	-152.6
1962	1598	1292	1035	819	641	498	383	299	-1.5	0	-2.6	-10.3	-24.4	-46.5	-79.0	-124.7	-187.5	-1.5	1.3	0.0	-6.4	-19.2	-40.0	-71.1	-115.5	-177.0
1920	1614	1349	1120	923	754	611	492	397	-1.5	0	-2.8	-10.8	-25.0	-46.7	-77.7	-120.1	-176.6	-1.5	1.4	0.0	-6.6	-19.4	-39.7	-69.3	-110.3	-165.4
1920	1614	1349	1120	923	754	611	492	397	-1.5	0	-2.8	-10.8	-25.0	-46.7	-77.7	-120.1	-176.6	-1.5	1.4	0.0	-6.6	-19.4	-39.7	-69.3	-110.3	-165.4
1859	1576	1330	1115	928	767	629	513	418	-1.5	0	-2.9	-11.1	-25.5	-47.4	-78.4	-120.5	-176.1	-1.5	1.5	0.0	-6.7	-19.6	-40.1	-69.6	-110.2	-164.5
1932	1622	1353	1120	920	749	606	488	395	-1.5	0	-3.3	-12.3	-28.2	-52.5	-87.2	-134.7	-198.0	-1.5	1.6	0.0	-7.4	-21.6	-44.3	-77.4	-123.2	-184.9
1959	1587	1279	1022	808	631	486	371	284	-1.5	0	-1.9	-8.1	-19.5	-37.7	-64.5	-102.5	-155.2	-1.5	1.0	0.0	-5.2	-15.7	-32.9	-58.8	-95.8	-147.5
2046	1719	1436	1193	983	803	650	523	420	-1.5	0	-2.6	-10.0	-23.2	-43.5	-72.6	-112.3	-165.4	-1.5	1.3	0.0	-6.1	-18.1	-37.2	-64.9	-103.4	-155.2
2027	1702	1422	1179	970	791	640	515	415	-1.5	0	-2.8	-10.8	-25.0	-46.9	-78.0	-120.6	-177.5	-1.5	1.4	0.0	-6.6	-19.4	-39.8	-69.5	-110.7	-166.2
2169	1930	1710	1511	1330	1166	1019	887	768	-1.5	0	-2.7	-10.2	-23.0	-41.9	-67.8	-101.6	-144.6	-1.5	1.4	0.0	-6.1	-17.6	-35.1	-59.7	-92.1	-133.8
2147	1928	1727	1542	1372	1218	1078	951	835	-1.5	0	-3.1	-11.4	-25.4	-45.9	-73.6	-109.7	-155.0	-1.5	1.6	0.0	-6.7	-19.2	-38.1	-64.3	-98.8	-142.6

NOSLER

NOSLER

CARTRIDGE	BRAND	BULLET WEIGHT	BULLET STYLE	PART#	COUNT	BBL TWIST RQMT	FOR USE	LEAD-FREE	MUZ	100	200	300	400	500	600	700	800
25-06 Remington	TGA	100	PT	60005	20	1-10"	Deer Sized Game		3,300	3031	2778	2538	2312	2096	1893	1703	1529
	ETA	100	ET	40238	20	"	Deer Sized Game	XX	3,200	2957	2727	2508	2300	2102	1914	1737	1573
	BTA	115	BT	40071	20	"	Deer Sized Game		3,000	2787	2584	2390	2204	2026	1858	1699	1551
257 Roberts +P	TGA	110	AB	60010	20	1-10"	Deer Sized Game		3,050	2817	2596	2385	2184	1993	1813	1644	1489
257 WBY Mag	TGA	110	AB	60012	20	1-10"	Deer Sized Game		3,400	3151	2916	2693	2480	2278	2085	1901	1729
6.5 Grendel	VMG	90	FB Tipped	65182	20	1-9"	Varmint-Targets		2,800	2549	2311	2086	1874	1677	1497	1339	1206
	BTA	120	BT	61023	20	"	Deer/Hogs/Antelope		2,400	2216	2040	1872	1714	1566	1431	1311	1207
	MGA	123	HPBT	44501	20	"	Targets		2,400	2234	2075	1922	1777	1640	1512	1395	1290
	TGA	129	ABLR	60146	20	1-8"	Deer Sized Game		2,350	2193	2042	1896	1756	1621	1490	1364	1244
6.5x55 Swedish	TGA	140	AB	60022	20	1-9"	Deer Sized Game		2,650	2476	2309	2149	1995	1848	1708	1577	1456
260 Remington	BTA	120	BT	40056	20	1-9"	Deer/Hogs/Antelope		2,850	2649	2457	2273	2098	1930	1772	1622	1485
	ETA	120	ET	40672	20	"	Deer Sized Game	XX	2,750	2568	2394	2227	2067	1914	1769	1630	1503
	TGA	125	PT	60018	20	"	Deer Sized Game		2,800	2595	2398	2210	2031	1861	1700	1551	1415
	TGA-LR	129	ABLR	61022	20	"	Deer Sized Game		2,800	2626	2458	2296	2141	1992	1849	1710	1576
	TGA	130	AB	60024	20	"	Deer Sized Game		2,700	2518	2342	2174	2014	1861	1715	1578	1453
	MGA-RDF	130	RDF	60138	20	"	Targets		2,900	2746	2596	2450	2310	2174	2043	1916	1793
	BTA	140	BT	61027	20	"	Deer/Hogs/Antelope		2,700	2522	2351	2187	2029	1879	1736	1601	1476
6.5 Creedmoor	VGA	90	FB Tipped	65175	20	1-8"	Varmint-Targets		3,300	3019	2755	2506	2270	2047	1838	1644	1468
	BTA	120	BT	42050	20	"	Deer/Hogs/Antelope		2,900	2702	2505	2318	2138	1966	1803	1650	1508
	ETA	120	ET	40398	20	"	Deer Sized Game	XX	2,850	2669	2489	2316	2150	1991	1840	1696	1562
	TGA-LR	129	ABLR	60091	20	"	Deer Sized Game		2,850	2675	2505	2341	2184	2034	1889	1749	1614
	MGA	140	HPBT	43455	20	"	Targets		2,650	2481	2318	2161	2010	1866	1729	1599	1479
	MGA-RDF	140	RDF	60115	20	"	Targets		2,650	2518	2384	2255	2131	2010	1893	1779	1669
	BTA	140	BT	40064	20	"	Deer/Hogs/Antelope		2,650	2477	2310	2150	1997	1851	1711	1581	1460
	TGA	140	AB	60080	20	"	Deer/Elk Sized Game		2,650	2477	2310	2150	1997	1851	1711	1581	1460
	TGA	140	PT	61016	20	"	Deer/Elk Sized Game		2,650	2468	2292	2124	1963	1810	1666	1531	1408
	TGA-LR	142	ABLR	60105	20	"	Deer/Elk Sized Game		2,600	2458	2321	2188	2059	1935	1815	1699	1585
6.5 PRC	ETA	120	ET	40688	20	1-8"	Deer/Elk Sized Game	XX	3,100	2901	2711	2528	2353	2185	2024	1870	1724
	BTA	140	BT	43457	20	"	Deer/Hogs/Antelope		2,900	2714	2536	2365	2200	2042	1890	1746	1611
	TGA	140	AB	61014	20	"	Deer/Elk Sized Game		2,900	2714	2536	2365	2200	2042	1890	1746	1611
	TGA-LR	142	ABLR	61232	20	"	Deer/Elk Sized Game		2,900	2750	2603	2461	2324	2191	2062	1938	1818
264 Winchester Mag	TGA	130	AB	60019	20	1-9"	Deer/Elk Sized Game		3,100	2900	2709	2526	2350	2128	2019	1864	1718
6.5-284 Norma	TGA-LR	129	ABLR	60128	20	1-9"	Deer Sized Game		2,965	2786	2613	2445	2284	2129	1981	1838	1700
	TGA	130	AB	60021	20	"	Deer/Elk Sized Game		2,900	2709	2525	2350	2181	2019	1864	1718	1581
	TGA	140	AB	60040	20	"	Deer/Elk Sized Game		2,750	2573	2403	2239	2082	1932	1789	1653	1526
	MGA	140	HPBT	44166	20	"	Targets		2,750	2579	2414	2256	2103	1957	1817	1684	1560
26 Nosler	ETA	120	ET	40302	20	1-9"	Deer/Elk Sized Game	XX	3,450	3237	3035	2842	2657	2480	2309	2145	1989
	TGA-LR	129	ABLR	60110	20	"	Deer Sized Game		3,400	3211	3025	2845	2669	2500	2337	2180	2029
	MGA	140	CC	51288	20	"	Targets		3,200	3008	2825	2649	2480	2317	2160	2009	1865
	TGA	140	AB	60014	20	"	Deer/Elk Sized Game		3,300	3100	2908	2725	2549	2379	2216	2061	1911
	BTA	140	BT	43459	20	"	Deer/Hogs/Antelope		3,200	3001	2811	2629	2454	2286	2124	1969	1821
	TGA-LR	142	ABLR	60122	20	"	Deer/Elk Sized Game		3,300	3141	2985	2833	2684	2540	2399	2264	2133
	TGA-LR	150	ABLR	61052	20	"	Deer/Elk Sized Game		3,200	3045	2893	2745	2600	2460	2324	2193	2066
6.8 Remington SPC	MGA*	115	CC	75035	20	1-10"	Targets		2,550	2318	2099	1892	1698	1521	1364	1230	1123
270 Winchester	TGA	130	AB	60025	20	1-10"	Deer/Elk Sized Game		3,075	2852	2641	2439	2246	2062	1887	1722	1568
	BTA	130	BT	40062	20	"	Deer/Hogs/Antelope		3,075	2852	2641	2439	2246	2062	1887	1722	1568

ENERGY (FT-LBS)									DROP IN INCHES (100 YRD ZERO)									DROP IN INCHES (200 YRD ZERO)								
MUZ	100	200	300	400	500	600	700	800	MUZ	100	200	300	400	500	600	700	800	MUZ	100	200	300	400	500	600	700	800
2417	2039	1713	1431	1186	975	795	644	519	-1.5	0	-2.3	-9.1	-21.3	-40.1	-66.7	-103.2	-151.6	-1.5	1.1	0.0	-5.7	-16.7	-34.3	-59.9	-95.1	-142.4
2273	1941	1651	1397	1175	981	813	670	549	-1.5	0	-2.5	-9.7	-22.4	-41.6	-68.8	-105.5	-153.8	-1.5	1.2	0.0	-5.9	-17.4	-35.4	-61.4	-96.8	-143.8
2298	1983	1705	1458	1240	1048	881	737	614	-1.5	0	-3.0	-11.2	-25.5	-47.0	-76.9	-117.0	-169.1	-1.5	1.5	0.0	-6.7	-19.5	-39.5	-68.0	-106.5	-157.2
2272	1938	1646	1389	1165	970	803	660	542	-1.5	0	-2.9	-11.0	-25.1	-46.6	-76.9	-117.8	-171.6	-1.5	1.4	0.0	-6.6	-19.4	-39.4	-68.2	-107.7	-160.0
2823	2424	2076	1771	1502	1267	1061	883	730	-1.5	0	-2.0	-8.1	-19.0	-35.6	-58.9	-90.2	-123.1	-1.5	1.0	0.0	-5.1	-15.0	-30.6	-52.9	-83.2	-123.1
1567	1298	1067	869	702	562	448	358	291	-1.5	0	-3.9	-14.3	-32.7	-61.1	-101.9	-158.2	-234.0	-1.5	1.9	0.0	-8.5	-25.0	-51.4	-90.2	-144.7	-218.5
1534	1308	1108	934	782	653	546	458	388	-1.5	0	-5.6	-19.6	-43.5	-79.3	-129.3	-196.3	-283.5	-1.5	2.8	0.0	-11.2	-32.3	-65.3	-112.5	-176.7	-261.2
1573	1363	1176	1009	862	735	625	532	455	-1.5	0	-5.5	-19.0	-42.0	-76.1	-123.0	-185.2	-265.3	-1.5	2.7	0.0	-10.8	-31.1	-62.4	-106.6	-166.1	-243.4
1582	1377	1194	1030	883	752	636	533	443	-1.5	0	-5.7	-19.8	-43.6	-78.7	-127.1	-191.1	-273.9	-1.5	2.9	0.0	-11.2	-32.1	-64.4	-109.8	-171.0	-251.0
2182	1906	1658	1435	1237	1061	907	773	659	-1.5	0	-4.2	-14.9	-33.1	-60.1	-97.3	-146.4	-209.5	-1.5	2.1	0.0	-8.6	-24.8	-49.7	-84.8	-131.8	-192.8
2164	1870	1609	1377	1172	993	836	701	588	-1.5	0	-3.5	-12.7	-28.7	-52.6	-85.8	-130.1	-187.7	-1.5	1.7	0.0	-7.5	-21.7	-43.9	-75.4	-118.0	-173.9
2015	1758	1528	1322	1139	976	833	708	602	-1.5	0	-3.8	-13.6	-30.5	-55.5	-90.0	-135.7	-194.5	-1.5	1.9	0.0	-7.9	-22.9	-46.0	-78.7	-122.5	-179.0
2176	1868	1596	1356	1145	961	802	668	555	-1.5	0	-3.7	-13.4	-30.3	-55.6	-91.0	-138.4	-200.3	-1.5	1.8	0.0	-7.9	-22.9	-46.4	-79.9	-125.5	-185.6
2745	1975	1731	1510	1313	1137	979	838	712	-1.5	0	-3.5	-12.9	-28.8	-52.3	-84.6	-127.0	-181.4	-1.5	1.8	0.0	-7.5	-21.7	-43.4	-73.9	-114.6	-167.2
2104	1830	1583	1364	1170	999	849	719	609	-1.5	0	-4.0	-14.3	-32.0	-58.3	-94.7	-142.9	-205.1	-1.5	2.0	0.0	-8.3	-24.0	-48.4	-82.7	-128.9	-189.0
2427	2176	1945	1733	1540	1364	1204	1060	928	-1.5	0	-3.1	-11.4	-25.5	-46.1	-74.0	-110.3	-156.1	-1.5	1.6	0.0	-6.7	-19.2	-38.3	-64.7	-99.4	-143.7
2266	1977	1719	1487	1280	1097	936	797	677	-1.5	0	-4.0	-14.2	-31.8	-57.8	-93.7	-141.1	-202.2	-1.5	2.0	0.0	-8.3	-23.8	-47.9	-81.8	-127.2	-186.3
2176	1821	1516	1254	1030	838	675	540	430	-1.5	0	-2.3	-9.2	-21.7	-41.0	-68.5	-106.5	-157.3	-1.5	1.2	0.0	-5.8	-17.1	35.2	-61.6	-98.3	-148.0
2251	1944	1672	1431	1218	1030	866	726	606	-1.5	0	-3.3	-12.1	-27.4	-50.3	-82.3	-124.9	-180.4	-1.5	1.6	0.0	-7.2	-20.9	-42.2	-72.5	-113.5	-167.3
2174	1898	1651	1429	1232	1057	902	766	650	-1.5	0	-3.4	-12.4	-27.9	-50.9	-82.7	-124.8	-179.1	-1.5	1.7	0.0	-7.3	21.1	+42.5	-72.6	-113.0	-165.5
2326	2049	1797	1570	1366	1184	1022	876	746	-1.5	0	-3.4	-12.3	-27.5	-50.1	-81.1	-121.8	-174.0	-1.5	1.7	0.0	-7.2	-20.8	-41.7	-71.0	-110.1	-160.5
2183	1913	1670	1451	1256	1082	929	795	680	-1.5	0	-4.2	-14.8	-32.9	-59.6	-96.3	-144.7	-206.7	-1.5	2.1	0.0	-8.6	-24.6	-49.2	-83.9	-130.2	-190.1
2183	1970	1767	1581	1411	1256	1114	984	866	-1.5	0	-4.0	-14.1	-31.0	-55.7	-88.9	-131.8	-185.8	-1.5	2.0	0.0	-8.1	-23.1	-45.7	-76.9	-117.9	-169.8
2183	1907	1659	1437	1240	1065	910	777	663	-1.5	0	-4.2	-14.9	-33.1	-60.1	-97.2	-146.2	-209.2	-1.5	2.1	0.0	-8.6	-24.8	-49.6	-84.7	-131.6	-192.5
2183	1907	1659	1437	1240	1065	910	777	663	-1.5	0	-4.2	-14.9	-33.1	-60.1	-97.2	-146.2	-209.2	-1.5	2.1	0.0	-8.6	-24.8	-49.6	-84.7	-131.6	-192.5
2183	1892	1633	1403	1198	1019	862	729	616	-1.5	0	-4.2	-15.1	-33.6	-61.2	-99.5	-150.3	-215.9	-1.5	2.1	0.0	-8.7	-25.2	-50.7	-86.8	-135.5	-199.0
2131	1905	1698	1509	1337	1181	1039	909	792	-1.5	0	-4.3	-15.0	-33.0	-59.2	-94.7	-140.7	-198.8	-1.5	2.1	0.0	-8.6	-24.5	-48.5	-81.9	-125.8	-181.8
2560	2242	1957	1703	1475	1272	1091	931	791	-1.5	0	-2.6	-10.0	-22.8	-41.9	-68.4	-103.3	-148.1	-1.5	1.3	0.0	-6.1	-17.6	-35.4	-60.4	-94.0	-137.6
2614	2290	1999	1738	1504	1295	1111	948	807	-1.5	0	-3.2	-11.9	-26.7	-48.8	-79.2	-119.4	-171.0	-1.5	1.6	0.0	-7.0	-20.3	-40.7	-69.5	-108.1	-158.1
2614	2290	1999	1738	1504	1295	1111	948	807	-1.5	0	-3.2	-11.9	-26.7	-48.8	-79.2	-119.4	-171.0	-1.5	1.6	0.0	-7.0	-20.3	-40.7	-69.5	-108.1	-158.1
2651	2383	2137	1910	1702	1513	1341	1184	1042	-1.5	0	-3.1	-11.3	-25.3	-45.7	-73.4	-109.3	-154.4	-1.5	1.6	0.0	-6.7	-19.1	-38.0	-64.1	-98.4	-142.0
2773	2427	2118	1841	1594	1373	1176	1003	852	-1.5	0	-2.6	-10.0	-22.9	-42.0	-68.5	-103.5	-148.5	-1.5	1.3	0.0	-6.1	-17.6	-35.4	-60.6	-94.2	-137.9
2518	2223	1955	1712	1494	1298	1124	967	827	-1.5	0	-3.0	-11.1	-25.0	-45.6	-73.8	-111.0	-158.4	-1.5	1.5	0.0	-6.6	-19.0	-38.1	-64.9	-100.5	-146.5
2427	2118	1841	1593	1372	1176	1003	852	721	-1.5	0	-3.2	-11.9	-27.0	-49.3	-80.2	-121.0	-173.7	-1.5	1.6	0.0	-7.1	-20.5	-41.2	-70.4	-109.7	-160.8
2350	2058	1794	1558	1347	1160	995	849	724	-1.5	0	-3.8	-13.6	-30.3	-55.0	-89.2	-134.0	-192.0	-1.5	1.9	0.0	-7.9	-22.8	-45.7	-77.9	-121.0	-176.8
2350	2067	1812	1582	1375	1190	1026	882	756	-1.5	0	-3.7	-13.4	-30.0	-54.4	-87.9	-131.9	-188.2	-1.5	1.9	0.0	-7.8	-22.5	-45.1	-76.7	-118.9	-173.3
3171	2792	2455	2152	1881	1638	1420	1226	1054	-1.5	0	-1.8	-7.4	-17.3	-32.2	-52.7	-79.7	-114.3	-1.5	0.9	0.0	-4.7	-13.7	-27.6	-47.2	-73.3	-107.0
3311	2952	2621	2318	2041	1790	1564	1361	1179	-1.5	0	-1.9	-7.6	-17.5	-32.4	-52.8	-79.6	-113.8	-1.5	0.9	0.0	-4.7	-13.8	-27.7	-47.2	-73.1	-106.3
3183	2813	2480	2181	1911	1668	1450	1255	1081	-1.5	0	-2.3	-9.1	-20.7	-38.0	-61.9	-93.1	-133.0	-1.5	1.2	0.0	-5.5	-16.0	-32.2	-54.8	-84.9	-123.7
3385	2987	2629	2308	2019	1760	1527	1320	1136	-1.5	0	-2.1	-8.4	-19.3	-35.6	-58.0	-87.5	-125.3	-1.5	1.0	0.0	-5.2	-15.0	-30.3	-51.6	-80.0	-116.8
3183	2799	2456	2148	1871	1624	1402	1205	1031	-1.5	0	-2.4	-9.1	-20.9	-38.5	-62.8	-94.8	-135.7	-1.5	1.2	0.0	-5.6	-16.2	-32.6	-55.7	-86.5	-126.3
3433	3110	2809	2529	2271	2033	1815	1616	1434	-1.5	0	-2.0	-8.0	-18.2	-33.3	-53.8	-80.3	-113.7	-1.5	1.0	0.0	-4.9	-14.2	-28.3	-47.7	-73.3	-105.6
3410	3087	2787	2508	2251	2015	1799	1601	1421	-1.5	0	-2.3	-8.7	-19.7	-35.9	-57.8	-86.2	-121.8	-1.5	1.1	0.0	-5.3	-15.2	-30.2	-51.0	-78.3	-112.7
1660	1372	1124	913	736	591	475	386	322	-1.5	0	-5.0	-17.9	-40.6	-75.3	-125.2	-193.8	-285.4	-1.5	2.5	0.0	-10.4	-30.6	-62.9	-110.2	-176.3	-265.5
2729	2348	2013	1717	1456	1227	1027	856	710	-1.5	0	-2.8	-10.6	-24.2	-44.7	-73.4	-112.0	-162.2	-1.5	1.4	0.0	-6.4	-18.6	-37.8	-65.1	-102.2	-151.1
2729	2348	2013	1717	1456	1227	1027	856	710	-1.5	0	-2.8	-10.6	-24.2	-44.7	-73.4	-112.0	-162.2	-1.5	1.4	0.0	-6.4	-18.6	-37.8	-65.1	-102.2	-151.1

NOSLER

NOSLER

CARTRIDGE	BRAND	BULLET WEIGHT	BULLET STYLE	PART#	COUNT	BBL TWIST RQMT	FOR USE	LEAD-FREE	MUZ	100	200	300	400	500	600	700	800
	ETA	130	ET	40031	20	"	Deer/Elk Sized Game	XX	2,950	2744	2548	2361	2181	2009	1846	1692	1548
	TGA	130	PT	61024	20	"	Deer/Elk Sized Game		3,050	2816	2594	2382	2181	1989	1808	1639	1484
	BTA	140	BT	40055	20	"	Deer/Hogs/Antelope		2,900	2712	2531	2358	2191	2032	1879	1734	1598
	TGA-LR	150	ABLR	60125	20	"	Deer/Elk Sized Game		2,850	2693	2540	2392	2249	2111	1979	1850	1726
	TGA	150	PT	61235	20	"	Deer/Elk Sized Game		2,800	2601	2411	2229	2055	1889	1732	1586	1451
270 WSM	ETA	130	ET	40142	20	1-10"	Deer/Elk Sized Game	XX	3,200	2984	2777	2580	2391	2210	2038	1874	1719
	TGA	140	AB	60030	20	"	Deer/Elk Sized Game		3,100	2903	2715	2534	2361	2194	2034	1882	1737
	TGA-LR	150	ABLR	60114	20	"	Deer/Elk Sized Game		3,050	2887	2729	2575	2426	2282	2143	2009	1880
270 WBY Magnum	TGA-LR	150	ABLR	60150	20	1-10"	Deer/Elk Sized Game		3,080	2917	2757	2603	2453	2308	2168	2033	1903
27 Nosler	TGA	150	AB	61026	20	1-8.5"	Deer/Elk Sized Game		3,250	3044	2847	2658	2478	2304	2138	1978	1826
	TGA-LR	165	ABLR	61237	20	"	Deer/Elk Sized Game		3,158	3000	2846	2696	2549	2408	2271	2138	2010
280 Remington	TGA	140	AB	48545	20	1-9.5"	Deer/Elk Sized Game		3,000	2803	2615	2434	2261	2095	1936	1785	1642
	BTA	140	BT	40073	20	"	Deer/Hogs/Antelope		3,000	2803	2615	2434	2261	2095	1936	1785	1642
	ETA	140	ET	40511	20	"	Deer/Elk Sized Game	XX	2,925	2731	2545	2366	2195	2030	1873	1725	1586
7mm-08 Remington	BTA	120	BT	40060	20	1-9.5"	Deer/Hogs/Antelope		3,000	2772	2555	2349	2152	1965	1788	1623	1472
	BTA	140	BT	40059	20	"	Deer/Hogs/Antelope		2,825	2636	2454	2280	2113	1953	1801	1658	1525
	ETA	140	ET	40033	20	"	Deer/Elk Sized Game	XX	2,850	2662	2481	2307	2141	1983	1831	1687	1553
	TGA	140	AB	60042	20	"	Deer/Elk Sized Game		2,825	2636	2454	2280	2113	1953	1801	1658	1525
	TGA-LR	150	ABLR	61020	20	"	Deer/Elk Sized Game		2,750	2583	2421	2265	2116	1972	1833	1699	1570
7x57 Mauser	TGA	140	AB	47118	20	1-9.5"	Deer/Elk Sized Game		2,700	2516	2339	2170	2007	1852	1706	1569	1443
	ETA	140	ET	40481	20	"	Deer/Elk Sized Game	XX	2,700	2521	2344	2173	2010	1854	1707	1569	1441
280 Ackley Improved	TGA	140	AB	60043	20	1-9.5"	Deer/Elk Sized Game		3,200	2991	2792	2602	2420	2245	2077	1917	1765
	BTA	140	BT	43504	20	"	Deer Sized Game		3,200	2991	2792	2602	2420	2245	2077	1917	1765
	ETA	140	ET	40067	20	"	Deer/Elk Sized Game	XX	3,200	2993	2796	2607	2426	2252	2085	1926	1774
	TGA-LR	150	ABLR	60116	20	"	Deer/Elk Sized Game		2,930	2757	2590	2428	2272	2122	1978	1839	1705
	TGA	160	AB	60076	20	"	Deer/Elk Sized Game		2,950	2770	2597	2430	2269	2115	1967	1825	1690
	TGA	160	PT	60044	20	"	Deer/Elk Sized Game		2,950	2751	2561	2379	2205	2037	1878	1727	1586
7mm SAUM	TGA	160	AB	60045	20	1-9.5"	Deer/Elk Sized Game		2,850	2676	2508	2347	2192	2042	1899	1762	1633
7mm Remington Magnum	TGA	140	AB	60033	20	1-9.5"	Deer/Elk Sized Game		3,125	2920	2724	2537	2357	2185	2019	1862	1713
	BTA	150	BT	40045	20	"	Deer/Hogs/Antelope		3,050	2852	2662	2480	2306	2138	1977	1824	1680
	ETA	150	ET	40032	20	"	Deer/Elk Sized Game	XX	3,000	2808	2625	2449	2280	2118	1963	1815	1675
	BTA	160	BT	43461	20	"	Deer/Hogs/Antelope		3,000	2818	2643	2474	2312	2156	2006	1862	1726
	TGA	160	AB	47284	20	"	Deer/Elk Sized Game		3,000	2818	2643	2474	2312	2156	2006	1862	1726
	TGA	160	PT	61054	20	"	Deer/Elk Sized Game		2,950	2749	2557	2372	2196	2027	1866	1713	1571
	TGA-LR	168	ABLR	60108	20	"	Deer/Elk Sized Game		2,880	2728	2580	2436	2297	2163	2034	1909	1787
7mm STW	TGA	140	PT	60046	20	1-9.5"	Deer/Elk Sized Game		3,300	3065	2843	2631	2429	2236	2052	1877	1713
	TGA	160	AB	60047	20	"	Deer/Elk Sized Game		3,075	2892	2716	2547	2385	2228	2077	1932	1794
	TGA-LR	175	ABLR	60104	20	"	Deer/Elk Sized Game		2,950	2803	2661	2522	2387	2256	2130	2008	1889
7mm RUM	TGA	160	AB	60048	20	1-9.5"	Deer/Elk Sized Game		3,225	3035	2854	2680	2512	2351	2195	2046	1902
	TGA-LR	175	ABLR	60120	20	"	Deer/Elk Sized Game		3,040	2891	2746	2605	2468	2334	2205	2081	1960
28 Nosler	ETA	150	ETA	40039	20	1-9"	Deer/Elk Sized Game	XX	3,250	3054	2859	2674	2496	2324	2160	2002	1851
	BTA	160	BT	43463	20	"	Deer/Hogs/Antelope		3,200	3009	2826	2651	2482	2320	2163	2013	1869
	TGA	160	AB	60035	20	"	Deer/Elk Sized Game		3,300	3114	2930	2753	2583	2420	2262	2110	1964
	TGA	160	PT	61010	20	"	Deer/Elk Sized Game		3,250	3035	2830	2634	2446	2267	2095	1930	1774
	MGA	168	CC	51287	20	"	Targets		3,075	2894	2715	2542	2376	2217	2063	1916	1776
	TGA-LR	175	ABLR	60155	20	"	Deer/Elk Sized Game		3,125	2975	2827	2684	2544	2409	2277	2150	2028

ENERGY (FT-LBS)									DROP IN INCHES (100 YRD ZERO)									DROP IN INCHES (200 YRD ZERO)								
MUZ	100	200	300	400	500	600	700	800	MUZ	100	200	300	400	500	600	700	800	MUZ	100	200	300	400	500	600	700	800
2511	2174	1875	1609	1373	1165	983	826	692	-1.5	0	-3.1	-11.6	-26.3	-48.4	-79.1	-120.0	-173.1	-1.5	1.6	0.0	-6.9	-20.1	-40.6	-69.7	-109.0	-160.6
2685	2288	1942	1638	1372	1142	943	775	635	-1.5	0	-2.9	-11.0	-25.2	-46.7	-77.1	-118.1	-172.1	-1.5	1.4	0.0	-6.6	-19.4	-39.5	-68.4	-108.0	-160.6
2613	2286	1992	1728	1493	1283	1097	935	794	-1.5	0	-3.2	-11.9	-26.8	-49.0	-79.6	-120.1	-172.1	-1.5	1.6	0.0	-7.0	-20.4	-40.9	-69.9	-108.8	-159.2
2705	2414	2148	1905	1684	1484	1304	1140	992	-1.5	0	-3.3	-12.0	-26.8	-48.4	-77.9	-116.3	-164.8	-1.5	1.6	0.0	-7.0	-20.7	-40.2	-68.0	-104.7	-151.6
2611	2254	1936	1655	1407	1189	999	837	701	-1.5	0	-3.6	-13.3	-29.9	-54.8	-89.5	-135.8	-195.9	-1.5	1.8	0.0	-7.8	-22.6	-45.7	-78.5	-123.0	-181.3
2956	2569	2226	1921	1650	1410	1199	1014	853	-1.5	0	-2.4	-9.3	-21.5	-39.8	-65.1	-98.9	-142.6	-1.5	1.2	0.0	-5.7	-16.7	-33.7	-57.9	-90.5	-132.9
2986	2619	2291	1996	1733	1497	1286	1100	937	-1.5	0	-2.6	-10.0	-22.8	-41.8	-68.0	-102.7	-147.2	-1.5	1.6	0.0	-6.0	-17.5	-35.2	-60.1	-93.5	-136.7
3098	2776	2480	2208	1960	1734	1529	1344	1177	-1.5	0	-2.7	-10.0	-22.6	-41.1	-66.3	-99.1	-140.5	-1.5	1.3	0.0	-6.0	-17.3	-34.4	-58.3	-89.7	-129.8
3159	2833	2532	2256	2003	1773	1565	1376	1206	-1.5	0	-2.6	-9.8	-22.1	-40.2	-64.8	-96.8	-137.3	-1.5	1.3	0.0	-5.9	-16.9	-33.7	-57.0	-87.7	-126.9
3517	3085	2698	2353	2044	1768	1522	1303	1110	-1.5	0	-2.3	-8.8	-20.3	-37.4	-61.2	-92.5	-132.7	-1.5	1.1	0.0	-5.4	-15.8	-31.8	-54.4	-84.6	-123.7
3653	3297	2967	2662	2381	2123	1888	1675	1481	-1.5	0	-2.4	-9.0	-20.5	-37.3	-60.1	-89.6	-126.8	-1.5	1.2	0.0	-5.5	-15.7	-31.4	-53.0	-81.4	117.3
2797	2442	2126	1842	1589	1364	1165	990	839	-1.5	0	-2.9	-10.9	-24.8	-45.5	-74.2	-112.1	-162.3	-1.5	1.5	0.0	-6.6	-19.0	-38.2	-65.4	-101.9	-149.3
2797	2442	2126	1842	1589	1364	1165	990	839	-1.5	0	-2.9	-10.9	-24.8	-45.5	-74.2	-112.1	-162.3	-1.5	1.5	0.0	-6.6	-19.0	-38.2	-65.4	-101.9	-149.3
2659	2318	2012	1740	1497	1281	1091	925	782	-1.5	0	-3.2	-11.7	-26.5	-48.5	-78.9	-119.3	-171.4	-1.5	1.6	0.0	-7.0	-20.1	-40.6	-69.4	-108.2	-158.7
2397	2047	1740	1470	1234	1028	852	702	577	-1.5	0	-3.0	-11.4	-26.1	-48.3	-79.5	-121.7	-177.0	-1.5	1.5	0.0	-6.9	-20.0	-40.7	-70.4	-111.0	-164.9
2480	2159	1872	1616	1388	1186	1008	854	722	-1.5	0	-3.5	-12.8	-28.8	-52.6	-85.5	-129.1	-185.4	-1.5	1.8	0.0	-7.5	-21.8	-43.8	-75.0	-116.8	-171.4
2525	2202	1914	1655	1425	1222	1042	885	750	-1.5	0	-3.4	-12.5	-28.0	-51.3	-83.4	-125.8	-180.5	-1.5	1.7	0.0	-7.4	-21.3	-42.8	-73.1	-113.9	-167.0
2480	2159	1872	1616	1388	1186	1008	854	722	-1.5	0	-3.5	-12.8	-28.8	-52.6	-85.5	-129.1	-185.4	-1.5	1.8	0.0	-7.5	-21.8	-43.8	-75.0	-116.8	-171.4
2518	2221	1952	1709	1491	1295	1119	962	820	-1.5	0	-3.7	-13.4	-29.8	-54.0	-87.2	-130.7	-186.4	-1.5	1.9	0.0	-7.8	-22.4	-44.7	-76.1	-117.7	-171.5
2265	1967	1701	1463	1252	1067	905	765	647	-1.5	0	-4.0	-14.4	-32.1	-58.5	-95.1	-143.6	-206.2	-1.5	2.0	0.0	-8.4	-24.1	-40.5	-83.1	-129.6	-190.2
2276	1976	1707	1468	1255	1068	905	765	646	-1.5	0	-4.0	-14.3	-32.0	-58.3	-94.8	-143.2	-205.8	-1.5	2.0	0.0	-8.3	-24.0	-48.4	-82.8	-129.3	-189.9
3183	2781	2424	2105	1820	1566	1341	1142	968	-1.5	0	-2.4	-9.2	-21.2	-39.2	-64.0	-97.0	-139.4	-1.5	1.2	0.0	-5.7	-16.5	-33.2	-56.9	-88.6	-129.8
3183	2781	2424	2105	1820	1566	1341	1142	968	-1.5	0	-2.4	-9.2	-21.2	-39.2	-64.0	-97.0	-139.4	-1.5	1.2	0.0	-5.7	-16.5	-33.2	-56.9	-88.6	-129.8
3183	2784	2429	2112	1879	1576	1351	1153	979	-1.5	0	-2.4	-9.2	-21.2	-39.1	-63.8	-96.6	-138.7	-1.5	1.2	0.0	-5.6	-16.4	-33.1	-56.7	-88.2	-129.2
2859	2532	2233	1963	1719	1500	1303	1126	968	-1.5	0	-3.1	-11.3	-25.5	-46.4	-75.1	-112.6	-160.5	-1.5	1.5	0.0	-6.7	-19.4	-38.7	-65.9	-101.9	-148.2
3091	2725	2395	2097	1829	1589	1374	1183	1015	-1.5	0	-3.0	-11.2	-25.3	-46.2	-74.8	-112.5	-160.6	-1.5	1.5	0.0	-6.7	-19.3	-38.6	-65.7	-101.9	-148.4
3091	2686	2331	2011	1727	1475	1253	1060	893	-1.5	0	-3.1	-11.5	-26.1	-47.8	-77.9	-117.9	-169.5	-1.5	1.5	0.0	-6.9	-19.9	-40.0	-68.6	-107.0	-157.1
2885	2543	2235	1957	1706	1482	1281	1103	948	-1.5	0	-3.4	-12.3	-27.5	-49.9	-80.7	-121.2	-172.8	-1.5	1.7	0.0	-7.2	-20.7	-41.5	-70.6	-109.4	-159.4
3035	2650	2307	2000	1727	1483	1268	1078	912	-1.5	0	-2.6	-9.9	-22.5	-41.5	-67.7	-102.5	-147.4	-1.5	1.3	0.0	-6.0	-17.4	-35.0	-60.0	-93.5	-137.1
3098	2708	2360	2048	1770	1522	1302	1109	940	-1.5	0	-2.8	-10.5	-23.8	-43.7	-71.3	-107.7	-154.6	-1.5	1.4	0.0	-6.3	-18.3	-36.8	-62.9	-98.0	-143.5
2997	2627	2295	1998	1731	1494	1283	1097	934	-1.5	0	-2.9	-10.9	-24.6	-45.1	-73.3	-110.6	-158.5	-1.5	1.5	0.0	-6.5	-18.8	-37.8	-64.6	-100.4	-146.8
3197	2820	2481	2175	1899	1651	1429	1232	1058	-1.5	0	-2.9	-10.8	-24.3	-44.4	-71.9	-108.1	-154.4	-1.5	1.4	0.0	-6.4	-18.5	-37.2	-63.3	-98.1	-142.9
3197	2820	2481	2175	1899	1651	1429	1232	1058	-1.5	0	-2.9	-10.8	-24.3	-44.4	-71.9	-108.1	-154.4	-1.5	1.4	0.0	-6.4	-18.5	-37.2	-63.3	-98.1	-142.9
3091	2684	2322	1999	1713	1459	1236	1043	877	-1.5	0	-3.1	-11.5	-26.2	-48.0	-78.4	-118.7	-170.9	-1.5	1.6	0.0	-6.9	-20.0	-40.2	-69.0	-107.8	-158.5
3094	2775	2482	2214	1968	1745	1543	1359	1191	-1.5	0	-3.2	-11.6	-25.8	-46.7	-75.0	-111.7	-158.0	-1.5	1.6	0.0	-6.8	-19.5	-38.8	-65.5	-100.6	-145.3
3384	2920	2512	2152	1834	1555	1309	1095	912	-1.5	0	-2.2	-8.7	-20.3	-37.7	-62.1	-94.8	-137.4	-1.5	1.1	0.0	-5.4	-15.9	-32.2	-55.5	-87.1	-128.6
3358	2971	2621	2305	2020	1763	1532	1326	1143	-1.5	0	-2.7	-10.0	-22.8	-41.6	-67.5	-101.5	-144.7	-1.5	1.3	0.0	-6.0	-17.5	-35.0	-59.5	-92.1	-134.1
3381	3053	2750	2470	2213	1977	1762	1566	1387	-1.5	0	-2.9	-10.8	-24.1	-43.5	-69.8	-103.7	-146.3	-1.5	1.5	0.0	-6.4	-18.2	-36.2	-61.0	-93.4	-134.5
3694	3273	2894	2551	2242	1964	1712	1487	1286	-1.5	0	-2.3	-8.8	-20.2	-37.1	-60.3	-90.7	-129.5	-1.5	1.1	0.0	-5.4	-15.7	-31.4	-53.5	-82.8	-120.4
3591	3248	2930	2636	2366	2117	1890	1682	1493	-1.5	0	-2.7	-9.9	-22.3	-40.5	-65.0	-96.6	-136.3	-1.5	1.3	0.0	-5.9	-17.0	-33.8	-57.0	-87.3	-125.7
3530	3105	2723	2381	2074	1799	1553	1334	1141	-1.5	0	-2.2	-8.7	-20.1	-37.0	-60.4	-91.3	-130.9	-1.5	1.1	0.0	-5.4	-15.6	-31.5	-53.7	-83.5	-121.9
3637	3216	2837	2496	2189	1912	1663	1440	1241	-1.5	0	-2.3	-9.0	-20.7	-38.0	-61.8	-93.0	-132.8	-1.5	1.2	0.0	-5.5	-16.0	-32.1	-54.7	-84.8	-123.4
3883	3444	3049	2693	2371	2080	1818	1582	1371	-1.5	0	-2.1	-8.3	-19.0	-35.0	-57.0	-85.9	-122.6	-1.5	1.1	0.0	-5.1	-14.9	-29.8	-50.8	-78.6	-114.2
3752	3271	2844	2464	2126	1825	1558	1323	1118	-1.5	0	-2.3	-8.9	-20.6	-38.0	-62.3	-94.5	-136.0	-1.5	1.1	0.0	-5.5	-16.0	-32.3	-55.4	-86.5	-126.9
3541	3124	2749	2411	2106	1833	1587	1369	1176	-1.5	0	-2.7	-10.0	-22.8	-41.7	-67.7	-101.9	-145.6	-1.5	1.3	0.0	-6.1	-17.5	-35.1	-59.8	-92.6	-135.0
3794	3438	3106	2799	2515	2254	2015	1797	1597	-1.5	0	-2.4	-9.2	-20.8	-37.8	-60.8	-90.5	-127.7	-1.5	1.2	0.0	-5.6	-16.0	-31.7	-53.5	-82.0	-118.0

NOSLER

NOSLER

CARTRIDGE	BRAND	BULLET WEIGHT	BULLET STYLE	PART #	COUNT	BBL TWIST RQMT	FOR USE	LEAD-FREE	MUZ	100	200	300	400	500	600	700	800
	MG-RDF	185	RDF	60141	20	"	Targets		2,950	2816	2685	2557	2433	2312	2195	2081	1971
300 AAC Blackout	VMG*	110	FB Tipped	40127	20	1-8"	Varmints-Targets		2,200	1930	1681	1460	1273	1130	1031	961	906
	ETA*	110	ET	40660	20	"	Deer/Hogs	XX	2,300	1970	1672	1413	1205	1063	972	904	850
	BTA*	125	BT	61032	20	"	Deer/Hogs		2,250	2031	1826	1636	1464	1314	1189	1095	1025
	BTA*	220	BT RN	61050	20	"	Deer/Hogs		1,020	989	962	937	915	894	875	857	840
	MGA*	220	CC	51275	20	"	Targets		1,020	989	962	937	915	894	875	857	840
30-30 Winchester	BTA	150	BT RN	40065	20	1-12"	Deer/Hogs/Antelope		2,100	1778	1494	1261	1097	992	917	858	807
	ETA	150	ET RN	40670	20	"	Deer/Hogs/Antelope	XX	2,250	2024	1805	1603	1423	1268	1144	1054	988
7.62x39mm	VMG	123	FB Tipped	60176	20	1-9.45"	Varmints-Targets		2,350	2081	1841	1612	1410	1241	1112	1023	957
	BTA	123	BT	40069	20	"	Deer/Hogs		2,350	2089	1845	1622	1423	1255	1125	1034	967
	ETA	123	ET	40040	20	"	Deer/Hogs	XX	2,350	2099	1865	1649	1455	1288	1154	1058	988
308 Winchester	VMG	110	FB Tipped	40272	20	1-10"	Varmints-Targets		3,150	2818	2510	2222	1953	1706	1485	1297	1151
	BTA	125	BT	40061	20	"	Deer/Hogs/Antelope		3,100	2836	2587	2351	2128	1918	1722	1541	1381
	BTA	150	BT	61028	20	"	Deer/Hogs/Antelope		2,800	2588	2386	2193	2009	1834	1670	1519	1382
	TGA	150	AB	60056	20	"	Deer/Elk Sized Game		2,875	2662	2459	2265	2080	1904	1738	1584	1442
	ETA	150	ET	40034	20	"	Deer/Elk Sized Game	XX	2,750	2558	2374	2198	2030	1870	1718	1576	1446
	MGA	155	HPBT	60052	20	"	Targets		2,850	2645	2450	2262	2083	1913	1752	1601	1463
	BTA	165	BT	40063	20	"	Deer/Hogs/Antelope		2,800	2608	2424	2247	2078	1917	1764	1620	1487
	TGA	165	AB	60049	20	"	Deer/Elk Sized Game		2,800	2608	2424	2247	2078	1917	1764	1620	1487
	TGA	165	PT	60053	20	"	Deer/Elk Sized Game		2,800	2578	2367	2166	1975	1795	1627	1473	1336
	TGA-LR	168	ABLR	60101	20	"	Deer/Elk Sized Game		2,750	2577	2409	2248	2094	1945	1803	1665	1531
	MGA	168	HPBT	60054	20	"	Targets		2,750	2555	2368	2189	2018	1855	1701	1558	1427
	ETA	168	ET	40035	20	"	Deer/Elk Sized Game	XX	2,750	2570	2398	2232	2073	1920	1775	1638	1511
	MGA	175	HPBT	60072	20	"	Targets		2,600	2425	2256	2095	1940	1792	1653	1523	1404
	MGA-RDF	175	RDF	60132	20	"	Targets		2,650	2489	2329	2175	2027	1884	1747	1614	1485
30-06 Springfield	BTA	125	BT	40068	20	1-12"	Deer/Hogs/Antelope		3,100	2836	2587	2351	2128	1918	1722	1541	1381
	TGA	150	PT	60055	20	"	Deer/Elk Sized Game		3,000	2755	2523	2302	2093	1895	1710	1539	1387
	TGA	165	AB	60057	20	"	Deer/Elk Sized Game		2,950	2749	2557	2372	2196	2027	1866	1713	1571
	BTA	165	BT	40043	20	"	Deer/Hogs/Antelope		2,950	2749	2557	2372	2196	2027	1866	1713	1571
	TGA	165	PT	61018	20	"	Deer/Elk Sized Game		2,950	2718	2497	2287	2088	1898	1720	1556	1407
	TGA-LR	168	ABLR	60102	20	"	Deer/Elk Sized Game		2,800	2625	2456	2293	2137	1987	1842	1703	1568
	ETA	168	ET	40036	20	"	Deer/Elk Sized Game	XX	2,800	2618	2444	2276	2115	1961	1814	1675	1545
	BTA	180	BT	40072	20	"	Deer/Hogs/Antelope		2,750	2572	2400	2236	2078	1926	1782	1646	1519
	ETA	180	ET	40037	20	"	Deer/Elk/Moose Sized Game	XX	2750	2578	2412	2252	2098	1952	1811	1677	1552
	TGA	180	AB	46134	20	"	Deer/Elk/Moose Sized Game		2,750	2572	2400	2236	2078	1926	1782	1646	1519
	TGA	180	PT	46142	20	"	Deer/Elk/Moose Sized Game		2,750	2559	2377	2202	2035	1875	1724	1583	1453
300 SAUM	TGA	165	PT	60061	20	1-10"	Deer/Elk Sized Game		3,025	2789	2565	2352	2149	1956	1775	1606	1452
	TGA	180	PT	60062	20	"	Deer/Elk/Moose Sized Game		2,950	2749	2556	2371	2194	2025	1864	1711	1569
300 WSM	TGA	180	AB	60063	20	1-10"	Deer/Elk/Moose Sized Game		2,950	2761	2580	2407	2240	2079	1926	1779	1641
	ETA	180	ET	40152	20	"	Deer/Elk/Moose Sized Game	XX	2,900	2719	2545	2378	2217	2062	1914	1773	1639
	TGA-LR	190	ABLR	60106	20	"	Deer/Elk Sized Game		2,875	2718	2566	2419	2277	2139	2007	1879	1755
300 Winchester Magnum	TGA	180	AB	60059	20	1-10"	Deer/Elk/Moose Sized Game		2,950	2763	2585	2413	2248	2089	1937	1793	1656
	TGA	180	PT	61056	20	"	Deer/Elk/Moose Sized Game		2,950	2749	2556	2371	2194	2025	1864	1711	1569
	BTA	180	BT	40053	20	"	Deer/Hogs/Antelope		2,950	2763	2585	2413	2248	2089	1937	1793	1656
	ETA	180	ET	40038	20	"	Deer/Elk/Moose Sized Game	XX	2,950	2770	2596	2430	2269	2115	1968	1827	1692
	TGA-LR	190	ABLR	60126	20	"	Deer/Elk Sized Game		2,870	2714	2562	2414	2272	2135	2003	1875	1751

ENERGY (FT-LBS)									DROP IN INCHES (100 YRD ZERO)									DROP IN INCHES (200 YRD ZERO)								
MUZ	100	200	300	400	500	600	700	800	MUZ	100	200	300	400	500	600	700	800	MUZ	100	200	300	400	500	600	700	800
3574	3257	2961	2686	2431	2196	1979	1779	1596	-1.5	0	-2.9	-10.6	-23.6	-42.5	-67.9	-100.6	-142.1	-1.5	1.4	0.0	-6.3	-17.9	-35.3	-59.3	-90.5	-129.7
1182	909	690	521	396	312	260	225	200	-1.5	0	-7.9	-28.2	-64.9	-123.0	-208.4	-326.5	-482.3	-1.5	4.0	0.0	-16.3	-49.1	-103.3	-184.7	-298.9	-450.7
1292	948	683	487	355	276	231	200	176	-1.5	0	-7.5	-27.6	-65.3	-126.9	-219.2	-348.3	-520.0	-1.5	3.8	0.0	-16.3	-50.2	-108.0	-196.6	-321.9	-489.8
1404	1145	926	743	595	479	392	332	291	-1.5	0	-7.0	-24.4	-54.8	-101.5	-168.4	-259.8	-380.2	-1.5	3.5	0.0	-13.9	-40.9	-84.1	-147.5	-235.4	-352.4
508	478	452	429	408	390	374	359	344	-1.5	0	-34.0	-106.0	-217.0	-370.0	-566.0	-808.0	-1098.0	-1.5	17.0	0.0	-54.6	-149.0	-285.0	-464.0	-689.0	-961.0
508	478	452	429	408	390	374	359	344	-1.5	0	-34.0	-106.0	-217.0	-370.0	-566.0	-808.0	-1098.0	-1.5	17.0	0.0	-54.6	-149.0	-285.0	-464.0	-689.0	-961.0
1469	1053	743	530	401	328	280	245	217	-1.5	0	-9.6	-35.0	-82.2	-158.3	-269.7	-422.5	-622.6	-1.5	4.8	0.0	-20.5	-63.0	-134.2	-240.8	-388.8	-584.2
1698	1364	1085	856	674	535	436	370	325	1.5	0	-7.0	-24.8	-56.1	-104.7	-174.9	-271.7	-399.7	-1.5	3.5	0.0	-14.2	-42.1	-87.1	-153.8	-247.1	-371.6
1508	1194	925	710	543	420	338	286	250	-1.5	0	-6.5	-23.3	-53.6	-101.4	-171.9	-270.4	-402.1	-1.5	3.2	0.0	-13.6	-40.6	-85.2	-152.4	-247.6	-376.1
1508	1191	930	718	553	430	346	292	256	-1.5	0	-6.5	-23.3	-53.4	-100.7	-170.1	-267.0	-396.4	-1.5	3.3	0.0	-13.5	-40.3	-84.4	-150.6	-244.2	-370.4
1508	1204	950	742	578	453	364	305	267	-1.5	0	-6.4	-22.9	-52.2	-98.1	-164.9	-257.8	-381.8	-1.5	3.2	0.0	-13.3	-39.4	-82.0	-145.6	-235.3	-356.1
2423	1939	1538	1206	932	711	539	411	323	-1.5	0	-2.9	-11.3	-26.9	-51.6	-88.3	-140.8	-214.0	-1.5	1.4	0.0	-7.0	-21.1	-44.3	-79.6	-130.7	-202.5
2667	2232	1857	1534	1257	1021	823	659	529	-1.5	0	-2.8	-10.9	-25.2	-47.3	-78.9	-122.2	-180.2	-1.5	1.4	0.0	-6.6	-19.6	-40.2	-70.3	-112.2	-168.8
2611	2231	1896	1601	1344	1120	929	768	636	-1.5	0	-3.7	-13.5	-30.6	-56.3	-92.4	-141.0	-204.6	-1.5	1.9	0.0	-8.0	-23.2	-47.1	-81.3	-128.0	-189.8
7752	2360	2014	1709	1441	1207	1006	835	693	-1.5	0	-3.4	-12.6	-28.5	-52.6	-86.2	-131.3	-190.4	-1.5	1.7	0.0	-7.5	-21.7	-44.0	-75.9	-119.4	-176.7
2519	2180	1877	1609	1372	1165	983	827	696	-1.5	0	-3.8	-13.8	-31.0	-56.7	-92.3	-139.7	-201.2	-1.5	1.9	0.0	-8.1	-23.4	-47.1	-80.8	-126.4	-185.9
2795	2408	2065	1762	1494	1259	1056	882	736	-1.5	0	-3.5	-12.8	-28.8	-52.9	-86.6	-131.6	-190.1	-1.5	1.7	0.0	-7.5	-21.9	-44.3	-76.2	-119.4	-176.2
2871	2491	2152	1850	1582	1346	1139	961	810	-1.5	0	-3.6	-13.2	-29.6	-54.1	-88.1	-133.3	-191.7	-1.5	1.8	0.0	-7.7	-22.4	-45.1	-77.2	-120.6	-177.2
2871	2491	2152	1850	1582	1346	1139	961	810	-1.5	0	-3.6	-13.2	-29.6	-54.1	-88.1	-133.3	-191.7	-1.5	1.8	0.0	-7.7	-22.4	-45.1	-77.2	-120.6	-177.2
2871	2435	2053	1719	1429	1180	969	795	654	-1.5	0	-3.7	-13.7	-31.1	-57.4	-94.6	-144.9	-211.3	-1.5	1.9	0.0	8.1	-23.0	-48.1	-83.3	-131.8	-196.3
2820	2476	2165	1885	1635	1412	1212	1034	875	-1.5	0	-3.7	-13.5	-30.1	-54.7	-88.5	-133.0	-190.1	-1.5	1.9	0.0	-7.9	-22.6	-45.3	-77.2	-119.9	-175.1
2820	2434	2091	1787	1519	1283	1080	906	760	-1.5	0	-3.8	-13.9	-31.2	-57.1	-93.1	-141.1	-203.5	-1.5	1.9	0.0	8.1	-23.5	-47.5	-81.6	-127.7	-188.1
2820	2464	2145	1858	1602	1375	1175	1001	852	-1.5	0	-3.8	-13.6	-30.4	-55.3	-89.7	-135.1	-193.5	-1.5	1.9	0.0	-7.9	-22.9	-45.9	-78.4	-121.9	-178.4
2626	2284	1978	1705	1462	1248	1062	901	766	-1.5	0	-4.4	-15.7	-34.9	-63.3	-102.6	-154.7	-221.8	-1.5	2.2	0.0	-9.1	-26.0	-52.3	-89.4	-139.2	-204.1
2740	2408	2107	1838	1596	1380	1186	1012	857	-1.5	0	-4.1	-14.7	-32.5	-58.9	-95.1	-142.7	-203.7	-1.5	2.1	0.0	-8.5	-24.3	-48.6	-82.8	-128.3	-187.2
2667	2232	1857	1534	1257	1021	823	659	529	-1.5	0	-2.8	-10.9	-25.2	-47.3	-78.9	-122.2	-180.2	-1.5	1.4	0.0	-6.6	-19.6	-40.2	-70.3	-112.2	-168.8
2997	2527	2119	1765	1459	1196	973	589	640	-1.5	0	-3.1	-11.7	-26.8	-49.0	82.7	-127.5	-186.9	-1.5	1.5	0.0	-7.0	-20.6	-42.2	-73.5	-116.7	-174.6
3188	2768	2394	2062	1766	1505	1275	1075	904	-1.5	0	-3.1	-11.5	-26.2	-48.0	-78.4	-118.7	-170.9	-1.5	1.6	0.0	-6.9	-20.0	-40.2	-69.0	-107.8	-158.5
3188	2768	2394	2062	1766	1505	1275	1075	904	3.1	0	-11.5	-26.2	-48.0	-78.4	-118.7	-170.9		-1.5	1.6	0.0	-6.9	-20.0	-40.2	-69.0	-107.8	-158.5
3188	2706	2285	1917	1596	1320	1084	887	725	-1.5	0	-3.2	-12.0	-27.5	-51.0	-84.1	-129.0	-188.4	-1.5	1.6	0.0	-7.2	-21.1	-42.9	-74.5	-117.8	-175.5
2924	2570	2249	1961	1703	1472	1266	1082	918	-1.5	0	-3.6	-12.9	-28.8	-52.4	-84.8	-127.5	-182.1	-1.5	1.8	0.0	-7.5	-21.7	-43.5	-74.1	-115.0	-167.9
2924	2557	2228	1933	1669	1434	1227	1046	890	-1.5	0	-3.6	-13.0	-29.1	-53.0	-86.0	-129.5	-185.5	-1.5	1.8	0.0	-7.6	-21.9	-44.1	-75.2	-117.0	-171.2
3022	2643	2303	1998	1725	1483	1269	1082	922	-1.5	0	-3.8	-13.6	-30.3	-55.2	-89.4	-134.6	-192.6	-1.5	1.9	0.0	-7.9	-22.8	-45.8	-78.1	-121.4	-177.6
3022	2655	2324	2026	1760	1522	1311	1124	963	-1.5	0	-3.7	-13.5	-30.1	-54.6	-88.2	-132.4	-189.1	-1.5	1.9	0.0	-7.9	-22.6	-45.2	-77.0	-119.4	-174.1
3022	2643	2303	1998	1725	1483	1269	1082	922	-1.5	0	-3.8	-13.6	-30.3	-55.2	-89.4	-134.6	-192.6	-1.5	1.9	0.0	-7.9	-22.8	-45.8	-78.1	-121.4	-177.6
3022	2618	2258	1938	1655	1405	1188	1001	843	-1.5	0	-3.8	-13.8	-30.9	-56.5	-92.0	-139.2	-200.3	-1.5	1.9	0.0	-8.1	-23.3	-47.0	-80.5	-125.8	-185.0
3352	2849	2410	2026	1691	1402	1154	944	772	-1.5	0	-3.0	-11.3	-25.8	-48.0	-79.2	-121.5	-177.4	-1.5	1.5	0.0	-6.8	-19.9	-40.5	-70.3	-111.1	-165.5
3478	3019	2610	2247	1924	1639	1388	1170	983	-1.5	0	-3.1	-11.5	-26.2	-48.1	-78.4	-118.8	-171.1	-1.5	1.6	0.0	-6.9	-20.0	-40.3	-69.1	-107.9	-158.7
3478	3047	2661	2315	2004	1728	1482	1265	1077	-1.5	0	-3.1	-11.4	-25.7	-46.9	-76.2	-114.9	-164.6	-1.5	1.5	0.0	-6.8	-19.5	-39.2	-67.0	-104.2	-152.4
3361	2954	2589	2260	1964	1700	1464	1256	1074	-1.5	0	-3.2	-11.8	-26.5	-48.4	-78.4	-117.9	-168.5	-1.5	1.6	0.0	-7.0	-20.1	-40.3	-68.7	-106.7	-155.7
3487	3117	2778	2468	2186	1930	1699	1489	1299	-1.5	0	-3.2	-11.7	-26.1	-47.3	-76.1	-113.5	-160.7	-1.5	1.6	0.0	-6.9	-19.7	-39.3	-66.4	-102.2	-147.9
3477	3052	2671	2328	2020	1745	1500	1284	1096	-1.5	0	-3.1	-11.3	-25.6	-46.7	-75.8	-114.2	-163.4	-1.5	1.5	0.0	-6.7	-19.4	-39.0	-66.6	-103.5	-151.2
3477	3019	2610	2247	1924	1639	1388	1170	983	-1.5	0	-3.1	-11.5	-26.2	-48.1	-78.4	-118.8	-171.1	-1.5	1.6	0.0	-6.9	-20.0	-40.3	-69.1	-107.9	-158.7
3477	3052	2671	2328	2020	1745	1500	1284	1096	-1.5	0	-3.1	-11.3	-25.6	-46.7	-75.8	-114.2	-163.4	-1.5	1.5	0.0	-6.7	-19.4	-39.0	-66.6	-103.5	-151.2
3478	3065	2694	2360	2058	1788	1547	1333	1144	-1.5	0	-3.0	-11.2	-25.3	-46.2	-74.8	-112.5	-160.6	-1.5	1.5	0.0	-6.7	-19.3	-38.6	-65.7	-101.8	-148.4
3474	3106	2768	2459	2178	1923	1692	1483	1293	-1.5	0	-3.2	-11.8	-26.3	-47.5	-76.4	-113.9	-161.4	-1.5	1.6	0.0	-6.9	-19.8	-39.4	-66.7	-102.6	-148.5

NOSLER

NOSLER

CARTRIDGE	BRAND	BULLET WEIGHT	BULLET STYLE	PART#	COUNT	BBL TWIST RQMT	FOR USE	LEAD-FREE	MUZ	100	200	300	400	500	600	700	800
	TGA	200	PT	60069	20	"	Deer/Elk/Moose Sized Game		2,750	2562	2382	2210	2044	1886	1737	1597	1467
	MGA-RDF	210	RDF	60158	20	"	Targets		2,750	2617	2488	2363	2241	2123	2009	1898	1790
300 H&H Magnum	TGA	180	AB	60060	20	1-10"	Deer/Elk/Moose Sized Game		2,950	2763	2585	2413	2248	2089	1937	1793	1656
308 Norma Magnum	TGA	180	AB	60093	20	1-10"	Deer/Elk/Moose Sized Game		2,975	2787	2608	2435	2269	2110	1957	1811	1673
300 WBY Magnum	TGA	180	AB	48643	20	1-10"	Deer/Elk/Moose Sized Game		3,175	2979	2791	2612	2439	2273	2113	1960	1814
	ETA	180	ET	40012	20	"	Deer/Elk/Moose Sized Game	XX	3,050	2865	2688	2517	2353	2196	2044	1898	1760
	TGA-LR	210	ABLR	60131	20	"	Deer/Elk/Moose Sized Game		2,825	2685	2548	2415	2286	2161	2041	1924	1811
30 Nosler	TGA	180	AB	60117	20	1-10"	Deer/Elk/Moose Sized Game		3,200	3004	2815	2635	2462	2295	2135	1982	1836
	ETA	180	ET	40330	20	"	Deer/Elk/Moose Sized Game	XX	3,100	2918	2737	2563	2396	2235	2081	1932	1791
	MGA	190	CC	60029	20	"	Targets		3,050	2874	2698	2530	2367	2211	2060	1916	1778
	TGA	200	AB	61012	20	"	Deer/Elk/Moose Sized Game		3,000	2835	2676	2523	2374	2231	2092	1959	1831
	TGA	200	PT	61230	20	"	Deer/Elk/Moose Sized Game		3,000	2799	2607	2423	2246	2077	1916	1762	1618
	TGA-LR	210	ABLR	60118	20	"	Deer/Elk/Moose Sized Game		3,000	2855	2714	2577	2443	2313	2188	2066	1949
300 RUM	TGA	165	PT	60064	20	1-10"	Deer/Elk Sized Game		3,350	3099	2862	2638	2424	2220	2026	1843	1671
	TGA	180	AB	60065	20	"	Deer/Elk/Moose Sized Game		3,250	3050	2860	2678	2502	2334	2172	2016	1868
	TGA	180	PT	60066	20	"	Deer/Elk/Moose Sized Game		3,200	2989	2789	2597	2413	2237	2068	1906	1754
	ETA	180	ET	40144	20	"	Deer/Elk/Moose Sized Game	XX	3,200	3009	2826	2650	2481	2318	2162	2011	1867
	TGA	200	AB	60165	20	"	Deer/Elk/Moose Sized Game		3,050	2885	2726	2573	2424	2282	2144	2010	1882
	TGA-LR	210	ABLR	60129	20	"	Deer/Elk/Moose Sized Game		2,920	2777	2638	2502	2371	2244	2120	2001	1885
30-378 WBY Magnum	TGA	180	AB	60094	20	1-10"	Deer/Elk/Moose Sized Game		3,400	3193	2997	2809	2628	2455	2288	2128	1974
	TGA-LR	210	ABLR	60133	20	"	Deer/Elk/Moose Sized Game		3,040	2895	2752	2614	2479	2348	2221	2099	1980
8x57 JS Mauser	ETA	180	ET	40643	20	1-10"	Deer/Elk/Moose Sized Game	XX	2,550	2346	2151	1966	1791	1627	1477	1342	1226
325 WSM	ETA	180	ET	40146	20	1-10"	Deer/Elk/Moose Sized Game	XX	3,050	2782	2529	2290	2064	1852	1656	1477	1321
	TGA	200	AB	60077	20	"	Deer/Elk/Moose Sized Game		2,900	2693	2495	2306	2125	1953	1789	1636	1494
8mm Remington Magnum	TGA	180	BT	60160	20	1-10"	Deer/Elk/Moose Sized Game		3,100	2850	2614	2390	2177	1976	1786	1609	1449
	TGA	200	AB	60095	20	"	Deer/Elk/Moose Sized Game		3,000	2788	2586	2393	2209	2032	1864	1706	1559
338 Winchester Magnum	TGA	210	PT	61058	20	1-10"	Deer/Elk/Moose Sized Game		2,950	2715	2492	2280	2079	1888	1709	1544	1395
	TGA	225	AB	60074	20	"	Deer/Elk/Moose Sized Game		2,750	2585	2427	2274	2126	1984	1849	1719	1597
	ETA	225	ET	40154	20	"	Deer/Elk/Moose Sized Game	XX	2,750	2602	2459	2320	2186	2057	1932	1812	1697
	TGA	250	AB	60086	20	"	Deer/Elk/Moose Sized Game		2,650	2496	2347	2203	2065	1931	1803	1682	1567
	TGA	250	PT	60082	20	"	Deer/Elk/Moose Sized Game		2,600	2415	2238	2069	1907	1754	1610	1478	1358
338 RUM	TGA	225	AB	60083	20	1-10"	Deer/Elk/Moose Sized Game		2,975	2802	2636	2475	2321	2171	2028	1890	1759
	TGA	250	AB	48952	20	"	Deer/Elk/Moose Sized Game		2,850	2689	2533	2384	2239	2099	1964	1835	1711
	TGA	300	AB	60123	20	"	Deer/Elk/Moose Sized Game		2,600	2478	2359	2243	2131	2022	1916	1814	1716
340 WBY Magnum	TGA	300	AB	60112	20	1-10"	Deer/Elk/Moose Sized Game		2,540	2419	2302	2188	2077	1970	1866	1766	1670
338 Lapua Magnum	MGA	300	HPBT	43136	20	1-10"	Targets		2,650	2533	2420	2309	2202	2097	1995	1896	1801
	TGA	300	AB	49323	20	"	Deer/Elk/Moose Sized Game		2,650	2526	2406	2289	2176	2066	1959	1855	1755
33 Nosler	TGA	225	AB	60098	20	1-10"	Deer/Elk/Moose Sized Game		3,025	2856	2687	2525	2369	2218	2072	1933	1799
	ETA	225	ET	40042	20	"	Deer/Elk/Moose Sized Game	XX	2,975	2823	2671	2524	2382	2244	2111	1983	1859
	TGA	250	PT	60134	20	"	Deer/Elk/Moose Sized Game		2,750	2557	2372	2195	2025	1863	1710	1568	1437
	TGA-LR	265	ABLR	60099	20	"	Deer/Elk/Moose Sized Game		2,775	2649	2527	2407	2291	2178	2069	1962	1859
	MGA	300	CC	60031	20	"	Targets		2,550	2445	2339	2235	2134	2036	1940	1847	1758
35 Whelen	TGA	225	AB	60081	20	1-16"	Deer/Elk/Moose Sized Game		2,700	2490	2290	2099	1918	1747	1588	1442	1313

ENERGY (FT-LBS)									DROP IN INCHES (100 YRD ZERO)									DROP IN INCHES (200 YRD ZERO)								
MUZ	100	200	300	400	500	600	700	800	MUZ	100	200	300	400	500	600	700	800	MUZ	100	200	300	400	500	600	700	800
3357	2915	2520	2168	1856	1580	1340	1132	956	-1.5	0	-3.8	-13.7	-30.8	-56.2	-91.4	-138.1	-198.5	-1.5	1.9	0.0	-8.0	-23.2	-46.7	-80.0	-124.8	-183.3
3526	3194	2886	2603	2341	2101	1881	1679	1493	-1.5	0	-3.6	-12.8	-28.2	-50.6	-80.6	-119.3	-167.7	-1.5	1.8	0.0	-7.4	-21.0	-41.6	-69.9	-106.8	-153.4
3477	3052	2671	2328	2020	1745	1500	1284	1096	-1.5	0	-3.1	-11.3	-25.6	-46.7	-75.8	-114.2	-163.4	-1.5	1.5	0.0	-6.7	-19.4	-39.0	-66.6	-103.5	-151.2
3536	3105	2718	2371	2058	1779	1531	1311	119.5	-1.5	0	-3.0	-11.1	-25.0	-45.8	-74.3	-111.9	-160.2	-1.5	1.5	0.0	-6.6	-19.1	-38.3	-65.4	-101.5	-148.3
4028	3546	3114	2726	2378	2065	1785	1536	1316	-1.5	0	-2.4	-9.3	-21.3	-39.1	-63.7	-96.1	-137.5	-1.5	1.2	0.0	-5.7	-16.5	-33.1	-56.4	-87.6	-127.8
3717	3281	2887	2533	2214	1927	1669	1440	1238	-1.5	0	-2.7	-10.3	-23.3	-42.7	-69.2	-104.1	-148.6	-1.5	1.4	0.0	-6.2	-17.9	-35.8	-61.0	-94.5	-137.7
3721	3360	3026	2719	2436	2178	1942	1726	1528	-1.5	0	-3.3	-12.0	-26.7	-48.0	-76.7	-113.8	-160.4	-1.5	1.7	0.0	-7.0	-20.0	-39.7	-66.8	-102.2	-147.1
4092	3606	3168	2774	2422	2105	1822	1570	1347	-1.5	0	-2.4	-9.1	-20.9	-38.4	-62.5	-94.3	-134.9	-1.5	1.2	0.0	-5.6	-16.2	-32.5	-55.4	-86.0	-125.4
3856	3402	2993	2625	2294	1997	1730	1492	1282	-1.5	0	-2.6	-9.8	-22.4	-41.0	-66.5	-100.1	-143.1	-1.5	1.3	0.0	-5.9	-17.2	-34.5	-58.8	-91.1	-132.7
3940	3483	3071	2699	2364	2062	1791	1548	1334	-1.5	0	-2.7	-10.2	-23.1	-42.3	-68.6	-103.0	-147.0	-1.5	1.4	0.0	-6.1	-17.7	-35.5	-60.4	-93.5	-136.1
3996	3569	3179	2825	2503	2210	1944	1704	1489	-1.5	0	-2.8	-10.5	-23.7	-43.0	-69.3	-103.6	-147.0	-1.5	1.4	0.0	-6.3	-18.0	-35.9	-60.8	-93.7	-135.6
3996	3479	3018	2607	2241	1916	1629	1379	1163	-1.5	0	-2.9	-11.0	-25.0	-45.9	-74.9	-113.4	-163.1	-1.5	1.5	0.0	-6.6	-19.1	-38.6	-66.1	-103.1	-151.3
4196	3801	3434	3095	2782	2494	2231	1990	1770	-1.5	0	-2.8	-10.3	-23.0	-41.5	-66.6	-98.9	-139.4	-1.5	1.4	0.0	-6.1	-17.5	-34.6	-50.3	-89.3	-128.4
4110	3518	3001	2549	2152	1806	1504	1244	1023	-1.5	0	-2.1	-8.5	-19.9	-37.2	-61.6	-94.5	-137.6	-1.5	1.1	0.0	-5.3	-15.6	-31.9	-55.2	-87.0	-129.1
4220	3719	3269	2866	2503	2177	1885	1625	1394	-1.5	0	-2.2	-8.7	-20.1	-37.0	-60.3	-91.0	-130.2	-1.5	1.1	0.0	-5.4	-15.6	-31.4	-53.6	-83.1	-121.2
4092	3571	3108	2696	2327	2000	1709	1453	1229	-1.5	0	-2.4	-9.3	-21.3	-39.3	-64.3	-97.4	-140.1	-1.5	1.2	0.0	-5.7	-16.5	-33.3	-57.1	-89.0	-130.5
4092	3618	3191	2807	2460	2148	1868	1617	1394	-1.5	0	-2.3	-9.0	-20.7	-38.0	-61.8	-93.0	-132.9	-1.5	1.2	0.0	-5.5	-16.0	-32.2	-54.8	-84.8	-123.5
4130	3696	3301	2941	2612	2313	2041	1795	1573	-1.5	0	-2.7	-10	-22.6	-41.2	-66.4	-99.2	-140.5	-1.5	1.3	0	-6	-17.3	-34.5	-58.3	-89.8	-129.8
3975	3596	3244	2920	2621	2347	2096	1867	1657	-1.5	0	-3.0	-11.0	-24.6	-44.3	-71.0	-105.4	-148.5	-1.5	1.5	0.0	-6.5	-18.6	-36.8	-62.0	-94.9	-136.5
4619	4076	3589	3153	2761	2409	2093	1810	1558	-1.5	0	-1.9	-7.7	-17.9	-33.1	-54.1	-81.8	-117.1	-1.5	1	0	-4.8	-14.1	-28.4	-48.4	-75.1	-109.5
4309	3906	3532	3185	2865	2570	2301	2054	1020	-1.5	0	-2.1	-9.9	-22.2	-40.2	-64.5	-95.9	-135.2	-1.5	1.3	0.0	-5.9	-16.9	-33.6	-56.6	-86.6	-124.6
2599	2199	1849	1544	1281	1058	871	720	601	-1.5	0	-4.8	-17.2	-38.6	-70.9	-116.3	-177.7	-258.5	-1.5	2.4	0.0	-10.0	-28.9	-58.8	-101.8	-160.8	-239.2
3717	3093	2557	2097	1703	1371	1096	872	690	-1.5	0	-3.0	-11.5	-26.6	-49.9	-83.3	-129.5	-191.7	-1.5	1.5	0.0	-7.0	-20.6	-42.3	-74.3	-119.0	-179.7
3734	3220	2765	2362	2006	1693	1422	1188	992	-1.5	0	-3.3	-12.2	-27.6	-50.8	-83.0	-126.3	-182.5	-1.5	1.7	0.0	-7.2	-21.0	-42.5	-73.2	-114.7	-169.2
3840	3247	2731	2283	1895	1560	1274	1035	839	-1.5	0	-2.8	-10.7	-24.7	-46.0	-76.3	-117.5	-172.2	-1.5	1.4	0.0	-6.5	-19.1	-39.0	-67.9	-107.8	-161.1
3996	3452	2971	2544	2166	1834	1543	1293	1079	-1.5	0	-3.0	-11.2	-25.4	-46.8	-76.7	-116.5	-168.4	-1.5	1.5	0.0	-6.7	-19.5	-39.4	-67.7	-106.1	-156.4
4057	3437	2896	2425	2015	1662	1362	1111	908	-1.5	0	-3.2	-12.1	-27.6	-51.2	-84.6	-129.9	-189.9	-1.5	1.6	0.0	-7.2	-21.1	-43.1	-74.9	-118.6	--177.0
3777	3339	2942	2583	2259	1968	1707	1477	1274	-1.5	0	-3.7	-13.3	-29.7	-53.7	-86.6	-129.6	-184.5	-1.5	1.9	0.0	-7.8	-22.3	-44.4	-75.5	-116.7	-169.7
3778	3382	3021	2689	2387	2113	1865	1641	1439	-1.5	0	-3.6	-13.0	-28.9	-52.0	-83.4	-124.0	-175.4	-1.5	1.8	0.0	-7.6	-21.6	-43.0	-72.5	-111.3	-160.8
3897	3458	3058	2695	2366	2070	1805	1570	1363	-1.5	0	-4.1	-14.5	-32.1	-57.8	-92.9	-138.6	-196.7	-1.5	2.0	0.0	-8.4	-23.9	-47.6	-80.6	-124.3	-180.3
3751	3238	2781	2376	2019	1708	1440	1212	1023	-1.5	0	-4.5	-15.9	-35.4	-64.6	-105.0	-158.9	-228.7	-1.5	2.2	0.0	-9.2	-26.5	-53.4	-91.6	-143.3	-210.8
4421	3922	3470	3061	2691	2356	2054	1785	1545	-1.5	0	-2.9	-10.9	-24.5	-44.6	-72.0	-108.0	-153.6	-1.5	1.5	0.0	-6.5	-18.6	-37.2	-63.2	-97.7	-141.9
4508	4013	3563	3154	2782	2445	2141	1869	1626	-1.5	0	-3.3	-12.0	-26.9	-48.7	-78.4	-117.1	-166.2	-1.5	1.7	0.0	-7.1	-20.3	-40.4	-68.5	-105.5	-152.9
4502	4089	3707	3353	3026	2724	2447	2193	1963	-1.5	0	-4.2	-14.6	-31.9	-56.9	-90.4	-133.3	-186.8	-1.5	2.1	0.0	-8.3	-23.6	-46.5	-77.9	-118.7	-170.2
4296	3899	3531	3190	2875	2586	2320	2078	1858	-1.5	0	-4.4	-15.4	-33.7	-60.0	-95.3	-140.6	-179.0	-1.5	2.2	0.0	-8.8	-24.8	-48.9	-82.0	-125.0	-179.2
4677	4275	3901	3553	3230	2929	2652	2396	2161	-1.5	0	-3.9	-13.8	-30.1	-53.7	-85.1	-125.3	-175.2	-1.5	2.0	0.0	-7.9	-22.3	-43.9	-73.4	-111.6	-159.5
4677	4251	3857	3492	3154	2842	2555	2293	2053	-1.5	0	-3.9	-13.9	-30.5	-54.4	-86.5	-127.6	-178.9	-1.5	2.0	0.0	-8.0	-22.6	-44.5	-74.7	-113.8	-163.1
4589	4074	3608	3185	2803	2457	2145	1866	1617	-1.5	0	-2.8	-10.4	-23.4	-42.6	-69.0	-103.4	-147.1	-1.5	1.4	0.0	-6.2	-17.9	-35.7	-60.7	-93.7	-136.1
4437	3980	3564	3182	2834	2516	2226	1964	1727	-1.5	0	-2.9	-10.6	-23.8	-43.2	-69.4	-103.5	-146.4	-1.5	1.4	0.0	-6.3	-18.1	-36.0	-60.8	-93.4	-134.9
4197	3629	3122	2673	2275	1927	1624	1364	1145	-1.5	0	-3.8	-13.8	-31.1	-56.8	-92.6	-140.3	-202.2	-1.5	1.9	0.0	-8.1	-23.4	-47.3	-81.2	-126.9	-186.9
4530	4129	3755	3409	3087	2791	2517	2265	2032	-1.5	0	-3.5	-12.4	-27.3	-48.8	-77.7	-114.7	-160.7	-1.5	1.7	0.0	-7.2	-20.4	-40.2	-67.3	-102.6	-146.9
4343	3981	3643	3327	3033	2760	2507	2273	2057	-1.5	0	-4.3	-15.0	-32.6	-57.9	-91.6	-134.5	-187.6	-1.5	2.2	0.0	-8.5	-24.0	-47.1	-78.6	-119.4	-170.3
3642	3098	2620	2202	1838	1524	1259	1039	861	-1.5	0	-4.1	-14.9	-33.6	-61.7	-101.3	-154.7	-224.9	-1.5	2.1	0.0	-8.7	-25.3	-51.4	-88.9	-140.3	-208.4

NOSLER

BRAND LEGEND

BTA	Ballistic Tip Ammunition	ETA	Expansion Tip Ammunition	TGA	Trophy Grade Ammunition
BTV	Ballistic Tip Varmint Ammunition	MGA	Match Grade Ammunition	TGA-LR	Trophy Grade (LONG RANGE) Ammunition
DEFENSE	Defense Ammunition	SAFARI	Safari Dangerous Game Ammunition	VMG	Varmageddon Ammunition

NOSLER

CARTRIDGE	BRAND	BULLET WEIGHT	BULLET STYLE	PART #	COUNT	BBL TWIST RQMT	FOR USE	VELOCITY (FPS)						
								MUZZLE	50	100	150	200	250	300
9.3x62 Mauser	TGA	250	AB	48634	20	1-10"	Bear/Moose	2,550	2462	2376	2291	2208	2127	2048
	ETA	250	ET	40393	20	"	Bear/Moose	2,425	2338	2253	2170	2088	2008	1930
	SAFARI	286	PT	40602	20	"	Bear/Moose- Dangerous Game	2,350	2263	2179	2096	2015	1936	1859
	SAFARI	286	SD	40604	20	"	Dangerous Game	2,400	2280	2163	2050	1941	1835	1733
375 Flanged	TGA	300	PT	40610	20	1-12"	Bear/Moose- Dangerous Game	2,400	2294	2191	2091	1993	1898	1806
	SAFARI	300	SD	40612	20	"	Dangerous Game	2,400	2260	2125	1995	1870	1750	1636
375 H&H Magnum	ETA	260	ET	40395	20	1-12"	Bear/Moose- Dangerous Game	2,700	2606	2514	2423	2335	2248	2163
	TGA	260	PT	60090	20	"	Bear/Moose- Dangerous Game	2,750	2605	2466	2330	2199	2072	1949
	TGA	300	AB	60070	20	"	Bear/Moose- Dangerous Game	2,400	2313	2228	2144	2063	1983	1905
	TGA	300	PT	40606	20	"	Bear/Moose- Dangerous Game	2,450	2343	2239	2137	2038	1942	1849
	TGA	300	SD	40608	20	"	Dangerous Game	2,550	2405	2265	2130	2000	1874	1754
404 Jeffery	SAFARI	400	SD	40614	20	1-14"	Dangerous Game	2,350	2181	2020	1866	1720	1584	1458
416 Remington Magnum	TGA	400	PT	40616	20	1-14"	Bear/Moose- Dangerous Game	2,400	2292	2187	2084	1985	1889	1795
	SAFARI	400	PT	40618	20	"	Dangerous Game	2,400	2255	2115	1980	1851	1728	1611
416 Rigby	SAFARI	400	PT	40620	20	1-14"	Bear/Moose- Dangerous Game	2,400	2292	2187	2084	1985	1889	1795
	SAFARI	400	SD	40622	20	"	Dangerous Game	2,400	2255	2115	1980	1851	1728	1611
458 Winchester Magnum	SAFARI	500	PT	40624	20	1-14"	Bear/Moose- Dangerous Game	2,100	1999	1902	1808	1717	1630	1547
	SAFARI	500	SD	40626	20	"	Dangerous Game	2,100	1943	1793	1652	1521	1401	1294
458 Lott	SAFARI	500	PT	40628	20	1-14"	Bear/Moose- Dangerous Game	2,300	2194	2091	1991	1894	1801	1710
	SAFARI	500	SD	40630	20	"	Dangerous Game	2,300	2134	1975	1824	1682	1548	1426
470 Nitro Express	SAFARI	500	SD	40632	10	1-16"	Dangerous Game	2,100	1937	1782	1637	1502	1380	1272
450 Rigby	SAFARI	500	PT	40634	10	1-14"	Bear/Moose- Dangerous Game	2,350	2243	2139	2037	1939	1844	1752
500/416 Nitro Express	SAFARI	400	PT	40642	10	1-14"	Bear/Moose- Dangerous Game	2,300	2194	2092	1992	1895	1802	1712
500 Jeffery	SAFARI	570	SD	40636	10	1-20"	Dangerous Game	2,300	2136	1979	1830	1688	1556	1434
500 Nitro Express	SAFARI	570	SD	40638	10	1-20"	Dangerous Game	2,100	1944	1797	1657	1527	1408	1301
505 Gibbs	SAFARI	525	SD	40640	10	1-16"	Dangerous Game	2,200	2061	1927	1799	1678	1563	1456

BIG BORE AND SAFARI LOADINGS, IRON SIGHT ZERO — **VELOCITY (FPS)**

CARTRIDGE	BRAND	BULLET WEIGHT	BULLET STYLE	PART #	COUNT	FOR USE	VELOCITY (FPS)		ENERGY (FT-LBS)	
							MUZZLE	25yd	MUZZLE	25yd
9mm Luger	MGA	115	JHP	51285	20	Targets	1,170	1,090	350	303
	MGA	115	JHP	51017	50	Targets	1,170	1,090	350	303
	MGA	124	JHP	51286	20	Targets	1,150	1,080	364	321
	MGA	124	JHP	51054	50	Targets	1,150	1,080	364	321
	MGA	147	JHP	51290	20	Targets	950	924	295	278
	MGA	147	JHP	51325	50	Targets	950	924	295	278
9mm Luger +P	DEFENSE	124	B-JHP	38432	20	Personal Defense	1,200	1,119	396	345
	DEFENSE	124	T-BND	37151	20	Personal Defense	1,200	1,119	396	345
40 S&W	MGA	150	JHP	51283	20	Targets	1,110	1,042	410	361
	MGA	150	JHP	51181	50	Targets	1,110	1,042	410	361
	MGA	180	JHP	51279	20	Targets	1005	970	404	377
	MGA	180	JHP	51212	50	Targets	1005	970	404	377

HANDGUN AMMUNITION

ENERGY (FT-LBS)							DROP IN INCHES 50YD ZERO IRON SIGHT							DROP IN INCHES 100YD ZERO IRON SIGHT						
MUZZLE	50	100	150	200	250	300	MUZZLE	50	100	150	200	250	300	MUZZLE	50	100	150	200	250	300
710	502	351	239	158	101	65	-1.5	0	-1.6	-7.7	-20.3	-42.9	-81.0	-1.5	0.8	0.0	-5.3	-17.1	-38.8	-76.1
783	463	265	141	72	45	34	-1.5	0	-1.9	-9.9	-29.3	-70.4	-146.0	-1.5	1.0	0.0	-7.0	-25.4	-65.6	-140.3
783	558	394	272	183	119	76	-1.5	0	-1.3	-6.6	-17.6	-37.2	-70.0	-1.5	0.6	0.0	-4.6	-15.0	-33.9	-66.1
1137	837	612	439	308	210	141	-1.5	0	-1.5	-7.0	-18.3	-37.6	-68.9	-1.5	0.7	0.0	-4.8	-15.3	-33.9	-64.5
1123	850	640	476	347	247	173	-1.5	0	-1.4	-6.7	-17.3	-35.0	-62.9	-1.5	0.7	0.0	-4.6	-14.4	-31.5	-58.6
1167	896	682	511	376	271	193	-1.5	0	-2.0	-8.5	-21.1	-42.0	-74.4	-1.5	1.0	0.0	-5.5	-17.2	-37.1	-68.5
699	406	220	117	76	58	47	-1.5	0	-5.1	-23.0	-64.0	-140.1	-262.4	-1.5	2.6	0.0	-15.3	-53.7	-127.3	-247.0
853	559	352	212	129	91	73	-1.5	0	-4.1	-17.3	-45.1	-96.9	-182.2	-1.5	2.1	0.0	-11.0	-36.9	-86.6	-169.8
853	624	447	312	213	146	107	-1.5	0	-3.5	-14.0	-34.5	-69.7	-126.1	-1.5	1.7	0.0	-8.7	-27.5	-60.9	-115.6
1026	757	550	390	269	183	127	-1.5	0	-2.6	-10.9	-27.2	-55.1	-100.0	-1.5	1.3	0.0	-7.0	-22.0	-48.6	-92.2
1101	822	603	432	303	211	151	-1.5	0	-3.2	-12.9	-31.7	-63.3	-113.4	-1.5	1.6	0.0	-8.1	-25.2	-55.2	-103.7
1092	799	577	408	280	188	126	-1.5	0	-1.9	-8.6	-21.9	-45.0	-82.7	-1.5	1.0	0.0	-5.7	-18.1	-40.2	-76.9
1166	875	649	473	336	234	162	-1.5	0	-2.1	-8.9	-22.3	-45.7	-81.1	-1.5	1.0	0.0	-5.8	-18.2	-39.9	-74.9
1330	1076	865	689	542	421	324	-1.5	0	-2.3	-9.4	-22.4	-43.0	-73.4	-1.5	1.2	0.0	-5.9	-17.8	-37.2	-66.5
1173	914	704	533	397	292	215	-1.5	0	-3.2	-12.4	-29.7	-57.7	-100.4	-1.5	1.6	0.0	-7.7	-23.3	-49.8	-90.9
1173	906	691	518	381	277	203	-1.5	0	-3.2	-12.6	-30.3	-59.1	-103.4	-1.5	1.6	0.0	-7.8	-23.8	-51.1	-93.8
1174	947	758	599	469	362	277.6	-1.5	0	-3.0	-11.6	-27.4	-52.2	-88.9	-1.5	1.5	0.0	-7.1	-21.4	-44.7	-79.9
1197	917	691	512	372	269	199	-1.5	0	-3.8	-14.5	-34.6	-67.7	-118.7	-1.5	1.9	0.0	-8.8	-27.1	-58.4	-107.4
1288	1031	816	638	492	376	287	-1.5	0	-3.7	-13.9	-32.6	-62.1	-105.9	1.5	1.8	0.0	-8.4	-25.2	-52.9	-94.9
1262	1075	910	765	620	530	435	-1.5	0	-3.5	-13.0	-29.6	-54.7	-89.9	-1.5	1.8	0.0	-7.7	-22.5	-45.8	-79.3
1175	975	802	655	529	425	340	-1.5	0	-4.1	-14.9	-34.0	-63.3	-105.5	-1.5	2.0	0.0	-8.8	-25.9	-53.2	-93.3
1156	938	753	599	472	370	291	-1.5	0	-4.9	-17.7	-40.4	-75.8	-127.4	-1.5	2.4	0.0	-10.4	-30.7	-63.7	-112.8
1401	1132	909	723	569	442	339	-1.5	0	-2.1	-8.8	-21.1	-40.7	-69.6	-1.5	1.1	0.0	-5.6	-16.9	-35.4	-63.2
1496	1175	916	705	534	398	292	-1.5	0	-2.1	-8.9	-21.8	-42.7	-74.3	-1.5	1.1	0.0	-5.7	-17.5	-37.3	-67.9
1496	1211	975	779	615	479	368	-1.5	0	-2.0	-8.4	-20.3	-39.1	-66.8	-1.5	1.0	0.0	-5.4	-16.2	-34.0	-60.8
1454	1119	851	636	466	336	243	-1.5	0	-2.8	-11.3	-27.3	-53.8	-94.6	-1.5	1.4	0.0	-7.1	-21.7	-46.8	-86.1

NOSLER

HANDGUN AMMUNITION							VELOCITY (FPS)		ENERGY (FT-LBS)	
CARTRIDGE	BRAND	BULLET WEIGHT	BULLET STYLE	PART #	COUNT	FOR USE	MUZZLE	25yd	MUZZLE	25yd
	DEFENSE	200	B-JHP	39123	20	Personal Defense	900	878	360	343
	DEFENSE	200	T-BND	39515	20	Personal Defense	900	878	360	343
10mm Auto	MGA	180	JHP	51400	20	Targets	1,150	1,092	529	477
	MGA	180	JHP	51412	50	Targets	1,150	1,092	529	477
	DEFENSE	200	B-JHP	39156	20	Personal Defense	1,000	970	444	417
45 ACP (AUTO)	MGA	185	JHP	51278	20	Targets	980	948	395	369
	MGA	185	JHP	51271	50	Targets	980	948	395	369
	MGA	230	JHP	51277	20	Targets	850	833	368	354
	MGA	230	JHP	51284	50	Targets	850	833	368	354
45 ACP (AUTO) +P	DEFENSE	230	B-JHP	39645	20	Personal Defense	950	926	461	438
	DEFENSE	230	T-BND	39873	20	Personal Defense	950	926	461	438

FEDERAL

RIFLE BALLISTICS

ATT.	USAGE	FEDERAL LOAD NO.	CARTRIDGE	BULLET WEIGHT IN		Bullet Style	GOLD MEDAL PRIMER	BALLISTIC COEFFICIENT		VELOCITY IN FEET PER SECOND (TO NEAREST 10 FPS)					
				GRAINS	GRAMS			G1	G7	MUZZLE	100 YDS.	200 YDS.	300 YDS.	400 YDS.	500 YDS.
FEDERAL PREMIUM BIG GAME															
◊	12	P223TC1	223 Rem.	55	3.56	Trophy Copper	X	0.305		3240	2915	2613	2330	2066	1819
◊	2	P223S	223 Rem.	55	3.56	Barnes Triple-Shock X	X	0.209		3200	2738	2320	1940	1604	1323
◊	2	P223Q	223 Rem.	60	3.89	Nosler Partition	X	0.227		3160	2737	2350	1998	1679	1403
◊	2	P22250G	22-250 Rem.	60	3.89	Nosler Partition	X	0.227		3500	3043	2630	2253	1908	1601
◊	2	P224VLKBTSX1	224 Valkyrie	78	5.05	Barnes Triple-Shock X	X	0.383		2850	2611	2385	2170	1966	1774
◊	2	P243TC1	243 Win.	85	5.51	Trophy Copper	X	0.391		3200	2947	2708	2481	2265	2061
◊	2	P243K	243 Win.	85	5.51	Barnes Triple-Shock X	X	0.333		3200	2904	2628	2367	2122	1891
◊	2	P243SS1	243 Win.	90	5.83	Swift Scirocco II	X	0.419		3100	2869	2649	2440	2240	2050
◊	2	P243BCH1	243 Win.	95	6.16	Berger Hybrid Hunter	X	0.434	0.223	3050	2829	2619	2418	2226	2043
◊	2	P243E	243 Win.	100	6.48	Nosler Partition	X	0.384		2850	2612	2386	2171	1968	1776
◊	2	P2506H	25-06 Rem.	100	6.48	Barnes Triple-Shock X	X	0.336		3210	2916	2641	2382	2138	1908
◊	2	P2506TC1	25-06 Rem.	100	6.48	Trophy Copper	X	0.409		3210	2967	2737	2519	2311	2113
◊	2	P2506E	25-06 Rem.	115	7.45	Nosler Partition	X	0.389		3030	2785	2553	2333	2124	1925
◊	2	P65CRDTC1	6.5 Creedmoor	120	7.78	Trophy Copper	X	0.453		2875	2689	2510	2338	2174	2015
◊	23	P65CRDTA1	6.5 Creedmoor	130	8.42	Terminal Ascent	X	0.532	0.263	2800	2629	2464	2305	2152	2005
◊	2	P65CRDBTSX1	6.5 Creedmoor	130	8.42	Barnes Triple-Shock X	X	0.365		2825	2576	2341	2118	1906	1711
◊	2	P65CRDSS1	6.5 Creedmoor	130	8.42	Swift Scirocco II	X	0.571		2800	2640	2486	2337	2193	2054
◊	2	P65PRCTC1	6.5 PRC	120	7.78	Trophy Copper	X	0.497		3050	2856	2671	2493	2322	2158
◊	23	P65PRCTA1	6.5 PRC	130	8.42	Terminal Ascent	X	0.532	0.263	3000	2821	2649	2483	2324	2170
◊	2	P270L	270 Win.	130	8.42	Barnes Triple-Shock X	X	0.374		3060	2804	2562	2333	2115	1909
◊	2	P270BCH1	270 Win.	140	9.07	Berger Hybrid Hunter	X	0.528	0.271	2950	2772	2600	2435	2276	2123
◊	23	P270TA1	270 Win.	136	8.81	Terminal Ascent	X	0.493	0.247	3000	2807	2622	2445	2274	2111
◊	2	P270P	270 Win.	130	8.42	Nosler Partition	X	0.416		3060	2829	2610	2401	2202	2012
◊	2	P270TC1	270 Win.	130	8.42	Trophy Copper	X	0.459		3060	2850	2650	2459	2275	2100
◊	2	P270TT1	270 Win.	130	8.42	Trophy Bonded Tip	X	0.44		3060	2841	2633	2434	2244	2063
◊	2	P270SS1	270 Win.	130	8.42	Swift Scirocco II	X	0.45		3050	2837	2633	2439	2253	2075
◊	2	P270TT3	270 Win.	140	9.07	Trophy Bonded Tip	X	0.455		2950	2744	2547	2358	2177	2004
◊	2	P270E	270 Win.	150	9.72	Nosler Partition	X	0.466		2830	2634	2446	2266	2093	1928
◊	2	P270WSMTC1	270 Win. Short Magnum	130	8.42	Trophy Copper	X	0.459		3280	3059	2850	2650	2458	2275
◊	2	P270WSMTT1	270 Win. Short Magnum	130	8.42	Trophy Bonded Tip	X	0.44		3280	3050	2832	2624	2426	2236
◊	23	P270WSMTA1	270 Win. Short Magnum	136	8.81	Terminal Ascent	X	0.493	0.247	3240	3036	2842	2655	2477	2305
◊	2	P270WSMBCH1	270 Win. Short Magnum	140	9.07	Berger Hybrid Hunter	X	0.528	0.271	3200	3011	2830	2657	2489	2328
◊	2	P270WSMTT3	270 Win. Short Magnum	140	9.07	Trophy Bonded Tip	X	0.455		3200	2982	2774	2575	2385	2204
◊	2	P708C	7mm-08 Rem.	140	9.07	Barnes Triple-Shock X	X	0.394		2820	2589	2370	2162	1963	1777
◊	2	P708TC2	7mm-08 Rem.	140	9.07	Trophy Copper	X	0.489		2800	2614	2435	2264	2100	1942
◊	2	P708TT2	7mm-08 Rem.	140	9.07	Trophy Bonded Tip	X	0.43		2800	2589	2388	2196	2012	1838
◊	2	P280TT2	280 Rem.	140	9.07	Trophy Bonded Tip	X	0.43		2950	2732	2524	2326	2136	1956
◊	2	P280A	280 Rem.	150	9.72	Nosler Partition	X	0.457		2890	2687	2494	2308	2130	1960
◊	2	P280AITC1	280 Ackley Improved	140	9.07	Trophy Copper	X	0.489		3075	2877	2688	2506	2332	2165
◊	34	P280AITA1	280 Ackley Improved	155	10.04	Terminal Ascent	X	0.586	0.3	2930	2770	2615	2465	2321	2181
◊	2	P280AIBCH1	280 Ackley Improved	168	10.89	Berger Hybrid Hunter	X	0.566	0.29	2830	2668	2511	2360	2214	2073
◊	2	P7RG	7mm Rem. Magnum	140	9.07	Nosler Partition	X	0.434		3150	2924	2709	2504	2308	2122
◊	2	P7RTC2	7mm Rem. Magnum	140	9.07	Trophy Copper	X	0.489		3150	2949	2756	2572	2395	2226

ENERGY IN FOOT-POUNDS (TO NEAREST 5 FOOT-POUNDS)						WIND DRIFT IN INCHES 10 MPH CROSSWIND					HEIGHT OF BULLET TRAJECTORY IN INCHES ABOVE OR BELOW LINE OF SIGHT IF ZEROED AT ⊕ YARDS. SIGHTS 1.5 INCHES ABOVE BORE LINE. AVERAGE RANGE				LONG RANGE						TEST BARREL LENGTH
MUZZLE	100 YDS.	200 YDS.	300 YDS.	400 YDS.	500 YDS.	100 YDS.	200 YDS.	300 YDS.	400 YDS.	500 YDS.	50 YDS.	100 YDS.	200 YDS.	300 YDS.	50 YDS.	100 YDS.	200 YDS.	300 YDS.	400 YDS.	500 YDS.	INCHES
1282	1038	834	663	521	404	0.9	3.7	8.8	16.6	27.5	-0.3	⊕	-2.6	-10.3	0.4	1.3	⊕	-6.4	-19.3	-40.2	24
1250	915	657	460	314	214	1.3	5.8	14.1	27.7	47.5	-0.3	⊕	-3.2	-12.9	0.5	1.6	⊕	-8.1	-25.8	-57.5	24
1330	998	736	532	375	262	1.2	5.3	13.1	25.2	42.9	-0.2	⊕	-3.2	-12.7	0.5	1.6	⊕	-8	-24.8	-54.4	24
1632	1234	922	676	485	341	1.1	4.7	11.3	21.6	36.9	-0.3	⊕	-2.3	-9.6	0.2	1.1	⊕	-6.2	-19.3	-42.4	24
1407	1181	985	815	669	545	0.9	3.4	8.2	15.2	24.9	-0.2	⊕	-3.6	-13.4	0.7	1.8	⊕	-8	-23.3	-47.7	24
1933	1639	1384	1162	969	801	0.7	2.9	6.8	12.5	20.5	-0.3	⊕	-2.5	-9.8	0.3	1.3	⊕	-6	-17.6	-36.2	24
1933	1592	1303	1057	850	675	0.8	3.5	8.1	15.2	24.9	-0.3	⊕	-2.7	-10.3	0.4	1.3	⊕	-6.3	-19	-39.2	24
1920	1644	1402	1189	1003	840	0.6	2.8	6.5	12.1	19.7	-0.3	⊕	-2.8	-10.4	0.4	1.4	⊕	-6.3	-18.5	-37.6	24
1962	1688	1446	1233	1045	880	0.6	2.8	6.4	11.9	19.3	-0.2	⊕	-2.9	-10.8	0.5	1.4	⊕	-6.5	-18.9	-38.4	24
1803	1515	1264	1047	860	701	0.9	3.4	8.2	15.2	24.8	-0.2	⊕	-3.6	-13.4	0.7	1.8	⊕	-8	-23.3	-47.6	24
2288	1888	1549	1260	1015	808	0.8	3.4	7.9	15	24.5	-0.3	⊕	-2.6	-10.2	0.4	1.3	⊕	-6.3	-18.8	-38.7	24
2288	1955	1664	1409	1185	991	0.7	2.7	6.4	11.8	19.3	-0.3	⊕	-2.5	-9.6	0.3	1.2	⊕	-5.9	-17.2	-35.2	24
2344	1981	1665	1390	1152	946	0.7	3.1	7.3	13.7	22.2	-0.2	⊕	-3	-11.3	0.5	1.5	⊕	-6.8	-20.1	-40.9	24
2202	1926	1679	1457	1259	1082	0.7	2.6	6	11.1	17.9	-0.2	⊕	-3.3	-12.1	0.6	1.7	⊕	-7.1	-20.8	-41.6	24
2263	1995	1752	1533	1337	1160	0.7	2.5	5.8	10.7	17.2	-0.2	⊕	-3.5	-12.8	0.7	1.8	⊕	-7.5	21.6	-43.1	24
2303	1916	1581	1294	1049	845	0.9	3.7	8.8	16.2	76.9	0.2	⊕	-3.7	-13.9	0.8	1.9	⊕	-8.3	-24.2	-50	24
2263	2012	1784	1576	1388	1218	0.6	2.4	5.3	9.9	15.9	-0.3	⊕	-3.5	-12.5	0.7	1.7	⊕	-7.3	-21.1	-42.1	24
2478	2174	1901	1656	1436	1241	0.5	2.4	5.6	10.1	16.5	-0.3	⊕	-2.8	-10.5	0.4	1.4	⊕	-6.3	-18	-36.5	24
2598	2297	2025	1700	1558	1359	0.5	2.3	5.3	9.6	15.6	-0.2	⊕	-2.9	-10.7	0.5	1.5	⊕	-6.4	-18.4	-36.9	24
2703	2269	1895	1571	1292	1052	0.7	3.2	7.5	14.1	23	-0.2	⊕	-2.9	-11.2	0.5	1.5	⊕	-6.7	-20	-40.8	24
2705	2388	2102	1843	1610	1401	0.6	2.4	5.4	9.9	16.2	-0.2	⊕	-3.1	-11.2	0.5	1.5	⊕	-6.6	-19.1	-38.5	24
2718	2379	2076	1805	1562	1345	0.6	2.5	5.7	10.5	17.1	-0.2	⊕	-2.9	-10.9	0.5	1.5	⊕	-6.5	-18.8	-38	24
2703	2310	1966	1664	1399	1168	0.7	2.9	6.6	12.4	20.2	-0.2	⊕	-2.9	-10.8	0.5	1.4	⊕	-6.5	-19.1	-38.8	24
2703	2345	2027	1745	1494	1273	0.6	2.6	6	11	18	-0.3	⊕	-2.8	-10.5	0.4	1.4	⊕	-6.3	-18.4	-37.3	24
2703	2330	2001	1711	1454	1228	0.6	2.7	6.3	11.6	18.9	-0.3	⊕	-2.8	-10.6	0.5	1.4	⊕	-6.4	-18.7	-38	24
2685	2322	2001	1717	1465	1242	0.6	2.7	6.1	11.4	18.5	-0.2	⊕	-2.9	-10.7	0.5	1.4	⊕	-6.4	-18.7	-37.9	24
2705	2340	2016	1728	1473	1249	0.7	2.8	6.3	11.9	19.2	-0.2	⊕	-3.1	-11.6	0.6	1.6	⊕	-6.9	-20.1	-40.6	24
2667	2310	1992	1709	1459	1238	0.7	2.8	6.6	12.3	19.7	-0.2	⊕	-3.5	-12.8	0.7	1.7	⊕	-7.6	-22	-44.1	24
3105	2702	2344	2026	1744	1494	0.6	2.3	5.5	10.1	16.3	-0.3	⊕	-2.2	-8.7	0.2	1.1	⊕	-5.4	-15.8	-31.9	24
3105	2685	2315	1988	1699	1443	0.6	2.4	5.8	10.5	17.1	-0.3	⊕	-2.2	-8.8	0.2	1.1	⊕	-5.5	-16	-32.4	24
3170	2783	2438	2129	1852	1604	0.5	2.2	5.2	9.4	15.2	-0.3	⊕	-2.3	-8.9	0.3	1.2	⊕	-5.5	-15.9	-31.9	24
3183	2818	2490	2194	1926	1685	0.5	2.1	4.9	8.9	14.3	-0.3	⊕	-2.3	-9	0.3	1.2	⊕	-5.6	-16	-32	24
3183	2763	2391	2062	1768	1509	0.6	2.4	5.7	10.4	17.1	-0.3	⊕	-2.4	-9.4	0.3	1.2	⊕	-5.8	-16.7	-33.8	24
2472	2084	1746	1452	1198	982	0.9	3.4	8.1	14.9	24.4	-0.2	⊕	-3.7	-13.6	0.8	1.8	⊕	-8.1	-23.6	-48.1	24
2437	2124	1844	1593	1370	1172	0.7	2.7	6.4	11.8	18.9	-0.2	⊕	-3.6	-13	0.7	1.8	⊕	-7.7	-22.2	-44.4	24
2437	2084	1772	1498	1258	1050	0.8	3.1	7.4	13.6	22.1	-0.1	⊕	-3.7	-13.5	0.8	1.8	⊕	-8	-23.2	-46.8	24
2705	2320	1980	1681	1419	1189	0.7	2.9	6.8	12.7	20.5	-0.2	⊕	-3.2	-11.8	0.6	1.6	⊕	-7	-20.6	-41.6	24
2782	2405	2071	1774	1511	1279	0.7	2.9	6.5	12.2	19.6	-0.2	⊕	-3.3	-12.2	0.6	1.7	⊕	-7.2	-21.1	-42.4	24
2939	2573	2246	1953	1691	1457	0.5	2.4	5.5	10.2	16.6	-0.3	⊕	-2.7	-10.2	0.4	1.4	⊕	-6.1	-17.8	-36	24
2954	2640	2353	2092	1854	1637	0.5	2.2	4.9	8.9	14.5	-0.2	⊕	-3.1	-11.2	0.6	1.5	⊕	-6.6	-18.8	-37.7	24
2987	2655	2352	2078	1829	1604	0.6	2.3	5.3	9.8	15.8	-0.2	⊕	-3.4	-12.2	0.7	1.7	⊕	-7.2	-20.7	-41.3	24
3084	2657	2281	1949	1656	1399	0.6	2.6	6.1	11.3	18.5	-0.3	⊕	-2.6	-9.9	0.4	1.3	⊕	-6	-17.6	-35.8	24
3084	2703	2362	2057	1783	1540	0.5	2.3	5.4	9.8	16	-0.3	⊕	-2.5	-9.6	0.3	1.3	⊕	-5.9	-16.9	-34.1	24

FEDERAL

FEDERAL

ATT.	USAGE	FEDERAL LOAD NO.	CARTRIDGE	GRAINS	GRAMS	Bullet Style	GOLD MEDAL PRIMER	G1	G7	MUZZLE	100 YDS.	200 YDS.	300 YDS.	400 YDS.	500 YDS.
◊	2	P7RTT2	7mm Rem. Magnum	140	9.07	Trophy Bonded Tip	X	0.43		3150	2922	2705	2499	2301	2113
◊	3	P7RTC3	7mm Rem. Magnum	150	9.72	Trophy Copper	X	0.498		3025	2833	2649	2472	2302	2139
◊	3	P7RSS1	7mm Rem. Magnum	150	9.72	Swift Scirocco II	X	0.515		3050	2863	2684	2511	2345	2186
◊	23	P7RTA1	7mm Rem. Magnum	155	10.04	Terminal Ascent	X	0.586	0.3	3000	2837	2680	2528	2382	2240
◊	3	P7RTT1	7mm Rem. Magnum	160	10.37	Trophy Bonded Tip	X	0.52		2900	2721	2549	2383	2224	2070
◊	3	P7RF	7mm Rem. Magnum	160	10.37	Nosler Partition	X	0.475		2950	2752	2563	2381	2207	2040
◊	3	P7RN	7mm Rem. Magnum	160	10.37	Barnes Triple-Shock X	X	0.392		2940	2702	2476	2261	2057	1863
◊	2	P7RBCH1	7mm Rem. Magnum	168	10.89	Berger Hybrid Hunter	X	0.566	0.29	2870	2706	2549	2396	2249	2107
◊	2	P3030TC1	30-30 Win.	150	9.72	Trophy Copper	X	0.222		2300	1943	1625	1354	1150	1021
◊	2	P3030G	30-30 Win.	150	9.72	Barnes Triple-Shock X	X	0.184		2220	1803	1447	1178	1017	919
◊	2	P3030D	30-30 Win.	170	11.02	Nosler Partition	X	0.254		2200	1894	1619	1380	1191	1060
◊	2	P308S	308 Win.	150	9.72	Nosler Partition	X	0.387		2840	2604	2380	2168	1966	1776
◊	2	P308V	308 Win.	150	9.72	Barnes Triple-Shock X	X	0.369		2820	2574	2341	2120	1911	1717
◊	2	P308TC3	308 Win.	150	9.72	Trophy Copper	X	0.469		2820	2625	2439	2260	2089	1925
◊	2	P308TC2	308 Win.	165	10.69	Trophy Copper	X	0.503		2700	2510	2329	2155	1988	1829
◊	2	P308TT2	308 Win.	165	10.69	Trophy Bonded Tip	X	0.45		2700	2503	2314	2133	1960	1797
◊	3	P308H	308 Win.	165	10.69	Barnes Triple-Shock X	X	0.398		2650	2430	2220	2021	1833	1659
◊	2	P308SS1	308 Win.	165	10.69	Swift Scirocco II	X	0.47		2700	2511	2329	2156	1990	1830
◊	2	P308BCH1	308 Win.	168	10.89	Berger Hybrid Hunter	X	0.489	0.251	2700	2518	2343	2176	2015	1860
◊	23	P308TA1	308 Win.	175	11.34	Terminal Ascent	X	0.52	0.258	2600	2432	2271	2116	1967	1824
◊	3	P308E	308 Win.	180	11.66	Nosler Partition	X	0.474		2570	2388	2213	2045	1885	1734
◊	2	P308TT1	308 Win.	180	11.66	Trophy Bonded Tip	X	0.5		2620	2445	2277	2116	1960	1812
◊	2	P3006TT2	30-06 Spring.	165	10.69	Trophy Bonded Tip	X	0.45		2800	2598	2405	2221	2044	1875
◊	2	P3006AD	30-06 Spring.	165	10.69	Nosler Partition	X	0.409		2830	2607	2395	2193	2000	1818
◊	2	P3006AF	30-06 Spring.	165	10.69	Barnes Triple-Shock X	X	0.398		2800	2573	2356	2151	1955	1771
◊	2	P3006SS1	30-06 Spring.	165	10.69	Swift Scirocco II	X	0.47		2800	2607	2421	2244	2074	1910
◊	2	P3006BCH1	30-06 Spring.	168	10.89	Berger Hybrid Hunter	X	0.489	0.251	2800	2614	2435	2264	2100	1942
◊	23	P3006TA1	30-06 Spring.	175	11.34	Terminal Ascent	X	0.52	0.258	2730	2558	2391	2232	2078	1930
◊	3	P3006F	30-06 Spring.	180	11.66	Nosler Partition	X	0.474		2700	2512	2332	2160	1995	1837
◊	2	P3006TT1	30-06 Spring.	180	11.66	Trophy Bonded Tip	X	0.5		2700	2522	2351	2186	2029	1877
◊	3	P3006TC1	30-06 Spring.	180	11.66	Trophy Copper	X	0.523		2700	2530	2366	2208	2056	1910
◊	3	P3006AE	30-06 Spring.	180	11.66	Barnes Triple-Shock X	X	0.453		2700	2504	2316	2137	1965	1802
◊	2	P300WR	300 Win. Magnum	165	10.69	Barnes Triple-Shock X	X	0.398		3050	2810	2582	2365	2159	1963
◊	2	P300WK	300 Win. Magnum	165	10.69	Nosler Partition	X	0.409		3050	2816	2594	2382	2180	1989
◊	2	P300WTT2	300 Win. Magnum	165	10.69	Trophy Bonded Tip	X	0.45		3050	2837	2633	2439	2253	2075
◊	2	P300WTC2	300 Win. Magnum	165	10.69	Trophy Copper	X	0.503		3050	2859	2675	2499	2330	2167
◊	3	P300WTT1	300 Win. Magnum	180	11.66	Trophy Bonded Tip	X	0.5		2960	2771	2591	2417	2250	2089
◊	3	P300WTC1	300 Win. Magnum	180	11.66	Trophy Copper	X	0.523		2960	2780	2606	2439	2279	2124
◊	3	P300WD2	300 Win. Magnum	180	11.66	Nosler Partition	X	0.361		2960	2701	2456	2224	2005	1799
◊	3	P300WP	300 Win. Magnum	180	11.66	Barnes Triple-Shock X	X	0.453		2960	2752	2554	2364	2182	2009
◊	23	P300WSS1	300 Win. Magnum	180	11.66	Swift Scirocco II	X	0.52		2950	2769	2595	2428	2266	2112
◊	2	P300WBCH1	300 Win. Magnum	185	11.99	Berger Hybrid Hunter	x	0.533	0.273	2950	2773	2603	2440	2282	2130
◊	23	P300WTA1	300 Win. Magnum	200	12.96	Terminal Ascent	X	0.608	0.304	2810	2660	2514	2373	2236	2105
◊	3	P300WSMTT2	300 Win. Short Magnum	165	10.69	Trophy Bonded Tip	X	0.45		3130	2913	2706	2508	2319	2138
◊	2	P300WSMTC2	300 Win. Short Magnum	165	10.69	Trophy Copper	X	0.503		3120	2926	2739	2561	2389	2224

FEDERAL

ENERGY IN FOOT-POUNDS (TO NEAREST 5 FOOT-POUNDS)						WIND DRIFT IN INCHES 10 MPH CROSSWIND					HEIGHT OF BULLET TRAJECTORY IN INCHES ABOVE OR BELOW LINE OF SIGHT IF ZEROED AT ⊕ YARDS. SIGHTS 1.5 INCHES ABOVE BORE LINE. AVERAGE RANGE				LONG RANGE						TEST BARREL LENGTH
MUZZLE	100 YDS.	200 YDS.	300 YDS.	400 YDS.	500 YDS.	100 YDS.	200 YDS.	300 YDS.	400 YDS.	500 YDS.	50 YDS.	100 YDS.	200 YDS.	300 YDS.	50 YDS.	100 YDS.	200 YDS.	300 YDS.	400 YDS.	500 YDS.	INCHES
3084	2654	2275	1941	1646	1388	0.6	2.7	6.2	11.4	18.7	-0.3	⊕	-2.6	-10	0.4	1.3	⊕	-6.1	-17.6	-35.9	24
3047	2673	2337	2035	1765	1524	0.6	2.4	5.6	10.2	16.7	-0.3	⊕	-2.9	-10.7	0.5	1.4	⊕	-6.4	-18.4	-37.1	24
3098	2730	2399	2101	1832	1592	0.5	2.3	5.3	9.7	15.8	-0.3	⊕	-2.8	-10.3	0.4	1.4	⊕	-6.2	-17.8	-36	24
3097	2770	2472	2200	1952	1727	0.5	2.1	4.7	8.6	13.9	-0.2	⊕	-2.9	-10.5	0.5	1.4	⊕	-6.2	-17.9	-35.7	24
2988	2630	2308	2017	1757	1523	0.6	2.5	5.6	10.4	16.9	-0.2	⊕	-3.2	-11.7	0.6	1.6	⊕	-6.9	-20	-40.2	24
3091	2691	2333	2014	1730	1479	0.6	2.7	6	11.3	18.2	-0.2	⊕	-3.1	-11.5	0.6	1.6	⊕	-6.8	-19.8	-40	24
3071	2593	2178	1816	1503	1234	0.8	3.2	7.6	14.2	23	-0.2	⊕	-3.3	-12.2	0.6	1.6	⊕	-7.3	-21.5	-43.7	24
3072	2732	2423	2141	1886	1656	0.6	2.3	5.2	9.6	15.5	-0.2	⊕	-3.3	-11.8	0.6	1.6	⊕	-6.9	-20	-40	24
1762	1258	880	611	441	347	2	8.9	21.5	41	67	0.2	⊕	-7.9	-29	2.2	3.9	⊕	-17.2	-53.8	-117	24
1641	1083	697	462	344	281	2.6	11.5	28.4	53.2	84.2	0.3	⊕	-9.4	-35.8	2.7	4.7	⊕	-21.7	-68.6	-147.8	24
1827	1354	990	719	535	424	1.8	8.1	19.4	36.7	59.9	0.3	⊕	-8.4	-30	2.4	4.2	⊕	-17.4	-53.5	-114.4	24
2686	2259	1887	1565	1287	1050	0.9	3.4	8.2	15.1	24.7	-0.2	⊕	-3.6	-13.4	0.7	1.8	⊕	-8	-23.4	-47.8	24
2648	2207	1825	1497	1217	982	0.9	3.6	8.7	16	26.6	-0.2	⊕	-3.7	-13.9	0.8	1.9	⊕	-8.3	-24.2	-49.9	24
2648	2296	1981	1701	1453	1234	0.7	2.8	6.6	12.2	19.7	-0.2	⊕	-3.5	-12.9	0.7	1.8	⊕	-7.6	-22.2	-44.4	24
2671	2309	1986	1701	1448	1225	0.7	2.9	7.1	13	20.9	-0.1	⊕	-4	-14.5	0.9	2	⊕	-8.5	-24.5	-49	24
2671	2294	1961	1667	1408	1182	0.7	3.1	7.4	13.6	22.1	-0.1	⊕	-4.1	-14.7	0.9	2	⊕	-8.6	-24.7	-49.9	24
2573	2163	1806	1497	1231	1008	0.8	3.7	8.7	16	26.7	-0.1	⊕	-4.4	-15.9	1	2.2	⊕	-9.3	26.9	-55.4	24
2671	2310	1988	1702	1450	1227	0.7	2.9	7	13	20.9	-0.1	⊕	-4	-14.5	0.9	2	⊕	-8.5	-24.5	-48.9	24
2719	2365	2048	1766	1514	1291	0.7	2.8	6.7	12.3	19.9	-0.1	⊕	-4	-14.4	0.9	2	⊕	8.4	-24.1	-48.1	24
2627	2299	2004	1740	1503	1292	0.6	2.8	6.7	12.1	19.6	-0.1	⊕	-4.4	-15.6	1	2.2	⊕	-9	-25.6	-51.2	24
2640	2278	1957	1672	1420	1202	0.7	3.2	7.5	13.6	22.5	-0.1	⊕	-4.7	-16.4	1.1	2.3	⊕	9.4	-26.9	-54.7	24
2743	2389	2072	1789	1536	1313	0.6	2.9	6.9	12.5	20.3	-0.1	⊕	-4.3	-15.4	1	2.2	⊕	-8.9	-25.5	-51.1	24
2872	2473	2119	1806	1531	1288	0.8	2.9	7	12.9	20.9	-0.2	⊕	-3.6	-13.3	0.8	1.8	⊕	-7.9	-22.8	-45.8	24
2934	2490	2101	1761	1465	1210	0.8	3.2	7.7	14.2	23.1	-0.2	⊕	-3.6	-13.3	0.7	1.8	⊕	-7.9	-23	-46.8	24
2872	2425	2034	1694	1400	1149	0.9	3.4	8.1	14.9	24.4	-0.1	⊕	-3.7	-13.8	0.8	1.9	⊕	-8.2	-23.8	-48.7	24
2872	2489	2148	1844	1575	1337	0.7	2.8	6.7	12.3	19.8	-0.2	⊕	-3.6	-13.2	0.7	1.8	⊕	-7.8	-22.5	-45	24
2924	2549	2212	1912	1644	1406	0.7	2.7	6.4	11.8	18.9	-0.2	⊕	-3.6	-13	0.7	1.8	⊕	-7.7	-22.2	-44.4	24
2896	2542	2222	1935	1678	1447	0.7	2.6	6.2	11.4	18.2	-0.1	⊕	-3.8	-13.7	0.8	1.9	⊕	-8.1	-23.1	-45.9	24
2913	2523	2174	1865	1591	1348	0.7	2.9	7	12.9	20.7	-0.1	⊕	-4	-14.5	0.9	2	⊕	-8.5	-24.4	-48.7	24
2913	2542	2208	1911	1644	1408	0.7	2.7	6.6	12	19.4	-0.1	⊕	-3.9	-14.3	0.9	2	⊕	-8.4	-23.9	-47.7	24
2913	2557	2236	1948	1689	1457	0.6	2.6	6.2	11.5	18.4	-0.1	⊕	-3.9	-14.1	0.9	2	⊕	-8.3	-23.6	-46.9	24
2913	2506	2144	1824	1543	1297	0.7	3.1	7.3	13.5	21.9	-0.1	⊕	-4	-14.7	0.9	2	⊕	-8.6	-24.7	-49.7	24
3408	2892	2442	2049	1707	1411	0.7	3	7	13.2	21.4	-0.2	⊕	-2.9	-11	0.5	1.5	⊕	-6.6	-19.6	-39.9	24
3408	2905	2464	2078	1742	1449	0.7	3	6.8	12.8	20.8	-0.2	⊕	-2.9	-10.9	0.5	1.5	⊕	-6.6	-19.4	-39.5	24
3408	2948	2540	2179	1859	1577	0.6	2.7	6.1	11.4	18.5	-0.2	⊕	-2.9	-10.7	0.5	1.4	⊕	-6.4	-18.7	-37.9	24
3408	2994	2622	2289	1989	1721	0.5	2.4	5.5	10	16.3	-0.3	⊕	-2.8	-10.4	0.4	1.4	⊕	-6.3	-18	-36.3	24
3502	3070	2682	2334	2023	1745	0.6	2.5	5.7	10.5	17.1	-0.2	⊕	-3.1	-11.2	0.5	1.5	⊕	-6.6	-19.3	-38.9	24
3502	3088	2715	2378	2075	1803	0.6	2.4	5.4	10	16.3	-0.2	⊕	-3	-11.1	0.5	1.5	⊕	-6.6	-19	-38.3	24
3502	2915	2411	1978	1607	1294	0.9	3.5	8.3	15.4	25.3	-0.2	⊕	-3.3	-12.3	0.6	1.6	⊕	-7.4	-21.9	-45	24
3502	3027	2607	2233	1904	1612	0.7	2.8	6.3	11.8	19.2	-0.2	⊕	-3.1	-11.5	0.6	1.6	⊕	-6.8	-20	-40.4	24
3478	3064	2691	2355	2053	1782	0.6	2.4	5.5	10.1	16.4	-0.2	⊕	-3.1	-11.2	0.6	1.5	⊕	-6.6	-19.2	-38.7	24
3575	3159	2784	2445	2139	1864	0.6	2.4	5.3	9.8	16	-0.2	⊕	-3	-11.2	0.5	1.5	⊕	-6.6	-19.1	-38.3	24
3506	3141	2806	2500	2221	1967	0.6	2.2	4.9	9.1	14.8	-0.2	⊕	-3.4	-12.3	0.7	1.7	⊕	-7.2	-20.6	-41.1	24
3589	3108	2682	2305	1970	1675	0.6	2.6	5.9	10.9	17.9	-0.3	⊕	-2.6	-10	0.4	1.3	⊕	-6	-17.6	-35.7	24
3566	3135	2749	2403	2091	1813	0.5	2.3	5.3	9.6	15.7	-0.3	⊕	-2.6	-9.8	0.4	1.3	⊕	-5.9	-17.1	-34.5	24

FEDERAL

ATT.	USAGE	FEDERAL LOAD NO.	CARTRIDGE	GRAINS	GRAMS	Bullet Style	PRIMER	G1	G7	MUZZLE	100 YDS.	200 YDS.	300 YDS.	400 YDS.	500 YDS.
◇	2	P300WSMG	300 Win. Short Magnum	165	10.69	Barnes Triple-Shock X	X	0.398		3130	2885	2653	2433	2224	2024
◇	3	P300WSMTT1	300 Win. Short Magnum	180	11.66	Trophy Bonded Tip	X	0.5		2960	2771	2591	2417	2250	2089
◇	3	P300WSMB	300 Win. Short Magnum	180	11.66	Nosler Partition	X	0.474		2980	2780	2589	2406	2231	2063
◇	3	P300WSMTC1	300 Win. Short Magnum	180	11.66	Trophy Copper	X	0.523		2960	2780	2606	2439	2279	2124
◇	23	P300WSMSS1	300 Win. Short Magnum	180	11.66	Swift Scirocco Ii	X	0.52		2960	2779	2604	2436	2275	2120
◇	2	P300WSMBCH1	300 Win. Short Magnum	185	11.99	Berger Hybrid Hunter	x	0.533	0.273	2950	2773	2603	2440	2282	2130
◇	23	P300WSMTA1	300 Win. Short Magnum	200	12.96	Terminal Ascent	X	0.608	0.304	2810	2660	2514	2373	2236	2105
◇	3	P338FTC2	338 Federal	200	12.96	Trophy Copper	X	0.425		2630	2424	2228	2041	1863	1697
◇	3	P338FTT2	338 Federal	200	12.96	Trophy Bonded Tip	X	0.44		2630	2431	2241	2060	1887	1725
◇	3	P338LTC1	338 Lapua Magnum	250	16.2	Trophy Copper	X	0.625		2850	2702	2559	2420	2286	2156
◇	3	P375T4	375 H&H Magnum	250	16.2	Trophy Bonded Bear Claw	X	0.34		2670	2412	2169	1940	1728	1534
◇	4	P375F	375 H&H Magnum	300	19.44	Nosler Partition	X	0.398		2440	2230	2031	1841	1666	1504
◇	3	P4570T4	45-70 Government	300	19.44	Trophy Bonded Bear Claw	X	0.215		1850	1612	1401	1227	1099	1011
FEDERAL PREMIUM HAMMERDOWN™															
◇	2	LG327F1	327 FEDERAL MAGNUM	127	8.23	Bonded Hollow Point	X	0.195		1650	1341	1120	990	905	838
◇	2	LG45C1	45 COLT	250	16.2	Bonded Hollow Point	X	0.165		1400	1125	975	881	808	746
◇	2	LG30301	30-30 WIN.	150	9.72	Bonded Hollow Point	X	0.268		2390	2086	1805	1553	1337	1167
◇	2	LG3571	357 MAGNUM	170	11.02	Bonded Hollow Point	X	0.185		1610	1296	1084	963	881	815
◇	2	LG35R1	35 REM.	220	14.26	Bonded Hollow Point	X	0.286		1990	1734	1505	1309	1155	1048
◇	2	LG441	44 REM. MAGNUM	270	17.5	Bonded Hollow Point	X	0.193		1715	1390	1150	1006	916	846
◇	3	LG444M1	444 MARLIN	270	17.5	Bonded Hollow Point	X	0.193		2250	1848	1500	1225	1049	945
◇	2	LG45701	45-70 GOVERNMENT	300	19.44	Bonded Hollow Point	X	0.29		1850	1612	1401	1227	1099	1011
FEDERAL PREMIUM SAFARI															
◇	4	P9362SA	9.3X62 MAUSER	286	18.53	Swift A-Frame	X	0.385		2360	2147	1945	1756	1582	1423
◇	4	P9362WH	9.3X62 MAUSER	286	18.53	Woodleigh Hydro	X	0.26		2360	2049	1763	1509	1295	1133
◇	4	P9374SA	9.3X74 R	286	18.53	Swift A-Frame	X	0.385		2360	2147	1945	1756	1582	1423
◇	4	P9374WH	9.3X74 R	286	18.53	Woodleigh Hydro	X	0.26		2360	2049	1763	1509	1295	1133
◇	4	P370SA	370 SAKO MAGNUM	286	18.53	Swift A-Frame	X	0.385		2550	2328	2117	1916	1730	1557
◇	4	P370WH	370 SAKO MAGNUM	286	18.53	Woodleigh Hydro	X	0.26		2450	2132	1839	1576	1349	1172
◇	4	P375SA	375 H&H MAGNUM	300	19.44	Swift A-Frame	X	0.325		2450	2194	1953	1730	1527	1349
◇	4	P375T1	375 H&H MAGNUM	300	19.44	Trophy Bonded Bear Claw	X	0.342		2400	2159	1932	1721	1529	1359
◇	4	P375T2	375 H&H MAGNUM	300	19.44	Trophy Bonded Sledgehammer Solid	X	0.253		2440	2115	1815	1548	1321	1147
◇	4	P375WH	375 H&H MAGNUM	300	19.44	Woodleigh Hydro	X	0.26		2500	2179	1881	1614	1380	1195
◇	4	P416SA	416 RIGBY	400	25.92	Swift A-Frame	X	0.367		2350	2128	1917	1722	1542	1381
◇	4	P416T1	416 RIGBY	400	25.92	Trophy Bonded Bear Claw	X	0.374		2300	2084	1880	1691	1517	1362
◇	4	P416T2	416 RIGBY	400	25.92	Trophy Bonded Sledgehammer Solid	X	0.273		2370	2073	1798	1551	1339	1171
◇	4	P416WH	416 RIGBY	400	25.92	Woodleigh Hydro	X	0.26		2400	2086	1797	1539	1319	1149
◇	4	P416RSA	416 REM. MAGNUM	400	25.92	Swift A-Frame	X	0.367		2400	2175	1962	1763	1580	1413
◇	4	P416RT1	416 REM. MAGNUM	400	25.92	Trophy Bonded Bear Claw	X	0.373		2400	2179	1969	1772	1591	1426
◇	4	P416RT2	416 REM. MAGNUM	400	25.92	Trophy Bonded Sledgehammer Solid	X	0.273		2400	2100	1823	1574	1357	1185
◇	4	P416RWH	416 REM. MAGNUM	400	25.92	Woodleigh Hydro	X	0.26		2400	2086	1797	1539	1319	1149
◇	4	P458T1	458 WIN. MAGNUM	400	25.92	Trophy Bonded Bear Claw	X	0.353		2250	2025	1813	1619	1442	1290
◇	4	P458T2	458 WIN. MAGNUM	500	32.4	Trophy Bonded Bear Claw	X	0.282		2090	1822	1580	1369	1198	1076

ENERGY IN FOOT-POUNDS (TO NEAREST 5 FOOT-POUNDS)						WIND DRIFT IN INCHES 10 MPH CROSSWIND					HEIGHT OF BULLET TRAJECTORY IN INCHES ABOVE OR BELOW LINE OF SIGHT IF ZEROED AT ⊕ YARDS, SIGHTS 1.5 INCHES ABOVE BORE LINE. AVERAGE RANGE				LONG RANGE						TEST BARREL LENGTH
MUZZLE	100 YDS.	200 YDS.	300 YDS.	400 YDS.	500 YDS.	100 YDS.	200 YDS.	300 YDS.	400 YDS.	500 YDS.	50 YDS.	100 YDS.	200 YDS.	300 YDS.	50 YDS.	100 YDS.	200 YDS.	300 YDS.	400 YDS.	500 YDS.	INCHES
3589	3049	2579	2169	1811	1501	0.7	2.9	6.8	12.7	20.7	-0.3	⊕	-2.7	-10.3	0.4	1.4	⊕	-6.3	-18.4	-37.7	24
3502	3070	2682	2334	2023	1745	0.6	2.5	5.7	10.5	17.1	-0.2	⊕	-3.1	-11.2	0.5	1.5	⊕	-6.6	-19.3	-38.9	24
3549	3089	2680	2314	1989	1700	0.6	2.6	6	11.1	18	-0.2	⊕	-3	-11.2	0.5	1.5	⊕	-6.6	-19.4	-39.1	24
3502	3088	2715	2378	2075	1803	0.6	2.4	5.4	10	16.3	-0.2	⊕	-3	-11.1	0.5	1.5	⊕	-6.6	-19	-38.3	24
3502	3085	2710	2372	2068	1796	0.6	2.4	5.5	10.1	16.4	-0.2	⊕	-3	-11.1	0.5	1.5	⊕	-6.6	-19.1	-38.4	24
3575	3159	2784	2445	2139	1864	0.6	2.4	5.3	9.8	16	-0.2	⊕	-3	-11.2	0.5	1.5	⊕	-6.6	-19.1	-38.3	24
3506	3141	2806	2500	2221	1967	0.6	2.2	4.9	9.1	14.8	-0.2	⊕	-3.4	-12.3	0.7	1.7	⊕	-7.2	-20.6	-41.1	24
3071	2610	2205	1850	1541	1279	0.8	3.5	8.1	15	24.8	-0.1	⊕	-4.5	-15.9	1	2.2	⊕	-9.2	-26.6	-54.6	24
3071	2625	2231	1884	1581	1321	0.7	3.3	7.9	14.4	23.7	-0.1	⊕	-4.4	-15.8	1	2.2	⊕	-9.2	-26.3	-53.6	24
4508	4053	3635	3252	2901	2581	0.6	2.1	4.7	8.7	14	-0.2	⊕	-3.3	-11.8	0.6	1.6	⊕	-6.9	-19.8	-39.4	24
3957	3230	2612	2089	1657	1305	1	4.4	10.2	19.4	32.1	-0.1	⊕	-4.5	-16.4	1.1	2.3	⊕	-9.6	-28.6	-59.4	24
3966	3313	2747	2259	1850	1506	1	4.2	9.7	18.5	30	⊕	-0.1	-5.7	-19.7	0.1	⊕	-5.5	-19.3	-43.9	-80.5	24
2280	1731	1307	1003	804	681	2.3	8.7	20.6	37.6	59.3	0.7	⊕	-11.9	-41.6	3.7	5.9	⊕	-23.8	-70.9	-146.5	24
768	507	354	276	231	198	3.5	14.9	33.2	57.1	85.9	1.2	⊕	-18	-63.4	5.7	9	⊕	-36.4	-107	-217.6	20
1088	703	528	431	362	308	4.7	17.6	37	62	92.4	2.1	⊕	-25.7	-86.9	8.5	12.8	⊕	-48.4	-139.7	-281.7	20
1902	1449	1085	803	595	453	1.6	6.6	16.2	30.8	51.1	0.1	⊕	-6.5	-23.9	1.7	3.2	⊕	-14.2	-42.8	-91.5	24
970	634	444	350	293	251	3.8	15.9	34.9	59.6	89.2	1.4	⊕	-19.3	-67.7	6.2	9.7	⊕	-38.7	-113.3	-230.2	20
1934	1469	1106	837	652	537	1.9	8	19.2	35.7	57.3	0.5	⊕	-10.1	-35.8	3.1	5	⊕	-20.6	-61.6	-128.8	24
1703	1158	792	607	503	429	3.4	14.7	33.2	57.6	86.8	1.1	⊕	-16.7	-59.6	5.2	8.3	⊕	-34.5	-102.2	-208.7	20
3035	2047	1349	900	660	535	2.4	10.7	26.3	49.7	79.5	0.3	⊕	-8.9	-33.5	2.5	4.4	⊕	-20.2	-63.9	-130.4	24
2280	1731	1307	1003	804	681	2.3	8.7	20.6	37.6	59.3	0.7	⊕	-11.9	-41.6	3.7	5.9	⊕	-23.8	-70.9	-146.5	24
3537	2928	2403	1959	1589	1285	1.2	4.5	10.8	20.2	32.9	0.1	⊕	-6	-21.3	1.6	3	⊕	-12.3	-36.1	-73.4	24
3537	2666	1974	1446	1065	815	1.7	7.1	17.1	32.6	53.9	0.1	⊕	-6.8	-24.9	1.9	3.4	⊕	-14.7	-45	-96.5	24
3537	2928	2403	1959	1589	1285	1.2	4.5	10.8	20.2	32.9	0.1	⊕	-6	-21.3	1.6	3	⊕	-12.3	-36.1	-73.4	24
3537	2666	1974	1446	1065	815	1.7	7.1	17.1	32.6	53.9	0.1	⊕	-6.8	-24.9	1.9	3.4	⊕	-14.7	-45	-96.5	24
4129	3440	2845	2331	1899	1540	0.9	4.1	9.4	17.9	29.4	0	⊕	-5	-17.6	1.2	2.5	⊕	-10.1	-30	-61.5	24
3812	2887	2147	1578	1156	872	1.6	6.6	16.2	30.9	51.5	0.1	⊕	-6.1	-22.8	1.6	3.1	⊕	-13.6	-41.3	-88.7	24
3998	3206	2541	1994	1553	1213	1.3	5.2	12.4	23.3	38.6	0.1	⊕	-5.7	-20.7	1.5	2.9	⊕	-12.1	-35.8	-74.8	24
3837	3105	2486	1974	1557	1230	1.3	5	12.1	22.6	37.3	-0.2	⊕	-6.3	-21.9	0.1	⊕	-5.9	-21.3	-48.5	-90.7	24
3966	2978	2194	1597	1163	877	1.7	6.9	16.9	32.2	53.6	0.1	⊕	-6.3	-23.4	1.7	3.1	⊕	-13.9	-42.6	-91.6	24
4163	3161	2357	1735	1269	951	1.5	6.4	15.8	30	50.1	0.1	⊕	-5.8	-21.7	1.5	2.9	⊕	-13	-39.4	-84.6	24
4905	4021	3264	2633	2111	1693	1.2	4.7	11.5	21.5	35.2	⊕	-0.3	-6.6	-22.6	0.1	⊕	-6.1	-21.9	-49.4	-91.6	24
4698	3859	3139	2540	2043	1647	1.2	4.8	11.6	21.6	35.4	0.2	⊕	-6.4	-23	1.8	3.2	⊕	-13.3	-38.6	-79.3	24
4988	3815	2870	2137	1591	1217	1.6	6.6	16.1	30.5	50.5	0.1	⊕	-6.6	-24.2	1.8	3.3	⊕	-14.3	-43.1	-91.8	24
5115	3865	2867	2103	1545	1173	1.7	6.8	16.7	31.9	52.8	0.1	⊕	-6.5	-24	1.7	3.2	⊕	-14.2	-43.4	-92.9	24
5115	4202	3419	2760	2216	1774	1.2	4.7	11.1	20.9	34.1	-0.2	⊕	-6.2	-21.3	0.1	⊕	-5.8	-20.8	-47.1	-87.1	24
5115	4215	3443	2789	2248	1806	1.2	4.6	10.9	20.5	33.4	0.1	⊕	-5.8	-20.6	1.5	2.9	⊕	-11.9	-35.1	-71.8	24
5115	3918	2951	2200	1636	1246	1.6	6.5	15.8	29.9	49.7	0.1	⊕	-6.4	-23.5	1.7	3.2	⊕	-13.9	-41.9	-89.2	24
5115	3865	2867	2103	1545	1173	1.7	6.8	16.7	31.9	52.8	0.1	⊕	-6.5	-24	1.7	3.2	⊕	-14.2	-43.4	-92.9	24
4496	3641	2919	2327	1846	1478	1.3	5.3	12.9	23.8	39.2	0.2	⊕	-7	-24.8	1.9	3.5	⊕	-14.3	-41.6	-86.3	24
4849	3684	2773	2080	1594	1285	1.7	7.7	18.3	34.4	55.8	0.4	⊕	-9.2	-32.2	2.7	4.6	⊕	-18.5	-55.8	-117.6	24

FEDERAL

FEDERAL

ATT.	USAGE	FEDERAL LOAD NO.	CARTRIDGE	GRAINS	GRAMS	Bullet Style	GOLD MEDAL PRIMER	G1	G7	MUZZLE	100 YDS.	200 YDS.	300 YDS.	400 YDS.	500 YDS.
◇	4	P458T3	458 WIN. MAGNUM	500	32.4	Trophy Bonded Sledgehammer Solid	X	0.328		1950	1729	1528	1352	1205	1096
◇	4	P458WH	458 WIN. MAGNUM	500	32.4	Woodleigh Hydro	X	0.26		2050	1764	1510	1296	1133	1025
◇	4	P458SA	458 WIN. MAGNUM	500	32.4	Swift A-Frame	X	0.361		2090	1878	1683	1503	1345	1212
◇	4	P458LT1	458 LOTT	500	32.4	Trophy Bonded Bear Claw	X	0.282		2300	2016	1755	1520	1319	1161
◇	4	P458LT2	458 LOTT	500	32.4	Trophy Bonded Sledgehammer Solid	X	0.328		2300	2055	1825	1616	1427	1267
◇	4	P458LWH	458 LOTT	500	32.4	Woodleigh Hydro	X	0.26		2250	1947	1672	1430	1232	1090
◇	4	P470SA	470 NITRO EXPRESS	500	32.4	Swift A-Frame	X	0.364		2150	1936	1738	1555	1391	1251
◇	4	P470T1	470 NITRO EXPRESS	500	32.4	Trophy Bonded Bear Claw	X	0.299		2150	1892	1657	1445	1268	1131
◇	4	P470T2	470 NITRO EXPRESS	500	32.4	Trophy Bonded Sledgehammer Solid	X	0.28		2150	1875	1627	1406	1226	1094
◇	4	P470WH	470 NITRO EXPRESS	500	32.4	Woodleigh Hydro	X	0.26		2150	1855	1591	1361	1180	1056
◇	4	P500NSA	500 NITRO EXPRESS	570	36.94	Swift A-Frame	X	0.306		2100	1851	1625	1422	1252	1122
◇	4	P500NWH	500 NITRO EXPRESS	570	36.94	Woodleigh Hydro	X	0.26		2100	1809	1550	1328	1156	1040

FEDERAL PREMIUM VARMINT & PREDATOR

ATT.	USAGE	FEDERAL LOAD NO.	CARTRIDGE	GRAINS	GRAMS	Bullet Style	GOLD MEDAL PRIMER	G1	G7	MUZZLE	100 YDS.	200 YDS.	300 YDS.	400 YDS.	500 YDS.
◇	1	P22D	22 HORNET	30	1.94	SPEER TNT GREEN	X	0.09		3150	2154	1387	990	828	715
◇	1	P222D	222 REM.	43	2.79	SPEER TNT GREEN	X	0.151		3400	2745	2176	1683	1290	1048
◇	1	P22250D	22-250 REM.	43	2.79	SPEER TNT GREEN	X	0.151		4000	3252	2618	2065	1590	1224

FEDERAL PREMIUM GOLD MEDAL®

ATT.	USAGE	FEDERAL LOAD NO.	CARTRIDGE	GRAINS	GRAMS	Bullet Style	GOLD MEDAL PRIMER	G1	G7	MUZZLE	100 YDS.	200 YDS.	300 YDS.	400 YDS.	500 YDS.
	5	GM223M	223 REM.	69	4.47	SIERRA MATCHKING BTHP	X	0.301	0.165	2950	2642	2353	2084	1832	1604
	5	GM223BH73	223 REM.	73	4.73	BERGER BT TARGET	X	0.348	0.178	2800	2541	2296	2065	1847	1648
	5	GM223M3	223 REM.	77	4.99	SIERRA MATCHKING BTHP	X	0.372	0.188	2720	2481	2255	2041	1838	1652
	5	GM223OTM3	223 Rem.	77	4.99	CENTERSTRIKE OTM	X	0.356	0.183	2720	2471	2235	2012	1803	1612
◇	5	GM224VLKBH2	224 VALKYRIE	80.5	5.22	BERGER BT TARGET	X	0.441	0.226	2925	2713	2512	2318	2134	1958
	5	GM224VLK1	224 VALKYRIE	90	5.83	SIERRA MATCHKING BTHP	X	0.563	0.274	2700	2542	2388	2241	2098	1961
	5	GM6CRDBH1	6MM CREEDMOOR	105	6.8	BERGER HYBRID	X	0.536	0.275	3025	2846	2674	2509	2350	2196
◇	5	GM6CRDM1	6MM CREEDMOOR	107	6.93	SIERRA MATCHKING BTHP	X	0.547	0.271	3000	2826	2658	2497	2341	2191
	5	GM6CRDLRHT1	6mm Creedmoor	109	7.06	Berger Hybrid	X	0.568	0.292	2975	2808	2647	2492	2342	2197
◇	5	GM65CRDBH130	6.5 CREEDMOOR	130	8.42	BERGER HYBRID OTM	X	0.56	0.287	2825	2661	2503	2351	2204	2062
◇	5	GM65CRD1	6.5 CREEDMOOR	140	9.07	SIERRA MATCHKING BTHP	X	0.535	0.261	2675	2509	2350	2196	2048	1905
	5	GM65CRDBH2	6.5 Creedmoor	140	9.07	Berger Hybrid	X	0.607	0.311	2725	2577	2434	2295	2161	2031
	5	GM65CRDOTM1	6.5 Creedmoor	140	9.07	CENTERSTRIKE OTM	X	0.554	0.285	2675	2515	2360	2211	2068	1929
	5	GM65PRCBH1	6.5 PRC	140	9.07	BERGER HYBRID	X	0.607	0.311	2925	2770	2621	2476	2336	2201
	5	GM308M	308 WIN.	168	10.89	SIERRA MATCHKING BTHP	X	0.462	0.224	2650	2460	2277	2103	1936	1778
	5	GM308OTM1	308 Win.	168	10.89	CENTERSTRIKE OTM	X	0.45	0.221	2650	2455	2268	2089	1918	1758
	5	GM308OTM2	308 Win.	175	11.34	CENTERSTRIKE OTM	X	0.505	0.257	2600	2427	2262	2102	1949	1803
	5	GM308M2	308 WIN.	175	11.34	SIERRA MATCHKING BTHP	X	0.505	0.25	2600	2427	2262	2102	1949	1803
	5	GM308BH185	308 WIN.	185	11.99	BERGER JUGGERNAUT OTM	X	0.552	0.283	2600	2442	2289	2143	2001	1864
	5	GM3006M	30-06 SPRING.	168	10.89	SIERRA MATCHKING BTHP	X	0.463	0.224	2700	2508	2324	2148	1980	1819
	5	GM300WM	300 WIN. MAGNUM	190	12.31	SIERRA MATCHKING BTHP	X	0.533	0.275	2900	2725	2557	2395	2239	2089
	5	GM300WMBH1	300 WIN. MAGNUM	215	13.93	BERGER HYBRID	X	0.691	0.354	2825	2692	2563	2437	2315	2196
	5	GM338LM	338 LAPUA MAG	250	16.2	SIERRA MATCHKING BTHP	X	0.587	0.318	2950	2789	2634	2484	2339	2199
	5	GM338LM2	338 LAPUA MAG	300	19.44	SIERRA MATCHKING BTHP	X	0.768	0.387	2580	2466	2355	2248	2143	2040

ENERGY IN FOOT-POUNDS (TO NEAREST 5 FOOT-POUNDS)						WIND DRIFT IN INCHES 10 MPH CROSSWIND					HEIGHT OF BULLET TRAJECTORY IN INCHES ABOVE OR BELOW LINE OF SIGHT IF ZEROED AT ⊕ YARDS. SIGHTS 1.5 INCHES ABOVE BORE LINE. AVERAGE RANGE				LONG RANGE						TEST BARREL LENGTH
MUZZLE	100 YDS.	200 YDS.	300 YDS.	400 YDS.	500 YDS.	100 YDS.	200 YDS.	300 YDS.	400 YDS.	500 YDS.	50 YDS.	100 YDS.	200 YDS.	300 YDS.	50 YDS.	100 YDS.	200 YDS.	300 YDS.	400 YDS.	500 YDS.	INCHES
4221	3320	2593	2028	1613	1333	1.8	7.2	16.9	31.2	50.2	0.6	⊕	-10.2	-35.3	3.1	5.1	⊕	-20.1	-59.2	-122.6	24
4665	3455	2530	1864	1425	1167	2	0.6	20.7	38.7	62	0.5	⊕	-9.8	-35	2.9	4.9	⊕	-20.4	-61.6	-129.9	24
4849	3916	3144	2508	2009	1631	1.2	5.9	13.7	25.7	41.8	⊕	-0.7	-9.9	-31.1	0.3	⊕	-8.5	-29.2	-65.5	-121.1	24
5873	4514	3419	2566	1933	1496	1.6	6.7	16.1	30.5	50.3	0.2	⊕	-7.1	-25.6	2	3.6	⊕	-14.9	-45.2	-95.7	24
5873	4689	3699	2900	2260	1782	1.4	5.6	13.6	25.2	41.7	0.2	⊕	-6.7	-24.1	1.8	3.3	⊕	-14.1	-41.2	-86	24
5620	4209	3105	2269	1686	1320	1.7	7.6	18.2	34.7	56.9	0.2	⊕	-7.8	-28	2.2	3.9	⊕	-16.3	-50	-107	24
5132	4163	3353	2685	2148	1736	1.2	5.5	13.2	24.4	39.9	⊕	-0.6	-9	-29	0.3	⊕	-7.9	-27.3	-61	-113	24
5132	3973	3047	2318	1784	1419	1.5	7	16.4	31	50.6	0.3	⊕	-8.4	-29.3	2.4	4.2	⊕	-16.7	-50.5	-106.1	24
5132	3902	2937	2195	1669	1329	1.6	7.5	17.8	33.5	54.7	0.3	⊕	-8.6	-30.2	2.5	4.3	⊕	-17.3	-52.6	-111.3	24
5132	3819	2809	2057	1546	1238	1.8	8.1	19.4	36.7	59.6	0.3	⊕	-8.8	-31.3	2.5	4.4	⊕	-18.1	-55.4	-117.8	24
5581	4336	3342	2559	1985	1594	1.5	7	16.5	31	50.5	⊕	-0.7	-10.2	-32.8	0.3	⊕	-8.8	-30.7	-70.1	-131.9	24
5581	4143	3041	2232	1691	1369	1.8	8.4	20.1	37.7	60.8	0.4	⊕	-9.3	-33.1	2.7	4.6	⊕	-19.2	-58.3	-123.7	24
661	309	128	65	46	34	3.5	17.5	46.9	88.9	140.9	-0.1	⊕	-6.6	-32.7	1.5	3.3	⊕	-22.8	-78.7	-179.7	24
1104	719	452	270	159	105	1.8	7.9	20	40.4	70.7	-0.3	⊕	-3.2	-14	0.5	1.6	⊕	-9.2	-31.4	-75.9	24
1528	1010	654	407	241	143	1.5	6.4	15.9	31.9	56.7	-0.4	⊕	-1.8	-8.9	0	0.9	⊕	-6.1	-20.8	-50.5	24
1333	1069	848	665	514	394	1	4.3	10.3	19.3	32.4	-0.2	⊕	-3.5	-13.3	0.7	1.7	⊕	-8.1	-24.1	-51	24
1271	1046	854	691	553	440	1	3.9	9.4	17.4	29.1	-0.1	⊕	-3.9	-14.4	0.8	1.9	⊕	-8.6	-25.2	-52.6	24
1265	1053	869	712	578	466	0.9	3.8	9	16.7	27.9	-0.1	⊕	-4.2	-15.2	0.9	2.1	⊕	-9	-26.1	-54.1	24
1265	1044	854	692	556	444	0.9	4	9.5	17.7	29.5	-0.1	⊕	-4.2	-15.4	0.9	2.1	⊕	-9.1	-26.7	-55.5	24
1529	1316	1127	961	814	685	0.7	2.9	6.7	12.5	20.1	-0.2	⊕	-3.2	-11.9	0.6	1.6	⊕	-7.1	-20.8	-42	24
1457	1291	1140	1003	880	768	0.6	2.4	5.7	10.6	16.9	-0.1	⊕	-3.8	-13.9	0.8	1.9	⊕	-8.1	-23.2	-45.9	24
2133	1889	1668	1468	1287	1124	0.5	2.2	5.1	9.4	15.3	-0.2	⊕	-2.8	-10.5	0.5	1.4	⊕	-6.7	-18	-36.1	24
2138	1897	1679	1481	1302	1140	0.5	2.2	5.2	9.3	15.1	-0.2	⊕	-2.9	-10.7	0.5	1.4	⊕	-6.4	-18.2	-36.6	24
2142	1908	1696	1503	1327	1168	0.5	2.2	5	9	14.6	-0.2	⊕	-2.9	-10.8	0.5	1.5	⊕	-6.4	-18.3	-36.8	24
2303	2044	1809	1595	1402	1227	0.6	2.3	5.4	10	16.1	-0.2	⊕	-3.4	-12.3	0.7	1.7	⊕	-7.2	-20.9	-41.6	24
2224	1957	1716	1499	1303	1128	0.6	2.6	6.2	11.3	18.1	-0.1	⊕	-4	-14.4	0.9	2	⊕	-8.4	-23.9	-47.5	24
2308	2064	1841	1637	1452	1283	0.6	2.2	5.2	9.6	15.4	-0.1	⊕	-3.7	-13.3	0.8	1.9	⊕	-7.7	-22.2	-44	24
2224	1966	1732	1520	1329	1157	0.6	2.5	5.9	10.9	17.4	-0.1	⊕	-4	-14.3	0.9	2	⊕	-8.3	-23.7	-47	24
2659	2386	2135	1906	1696	1506	0.5	2.1	4.8	8.6	13.9	-0.2	⊕	-3.1	-11.1	0.6	1.5	⊕	-6.6	-18.7	-37.5	24
2619	2257	1935	1650	1398	1179	0.7	3.1	7.4	13.4	22	-0.1	⊕	-4.3	-15.3	1	2.1	⊕	-8.9	-25.5	-51.5	24
2619	2248	1918	1628	1373	1152	0.7	3.2	7.6	13.8	22.8	-0.1	⊕	-4.3	-15.4	1	2.1	⊕	-9	-25.7	-52.1	24
2627	2290	1987	1717	1476	1264	0.6	2.9	6.9	12.5	20.3	-0.1	⊕	-4.4	-15.7	1	2.2	⊕	-9.1	-25.8	-51.8	24
2627	2290	1987	1717	1476	1264	0.6	2.9	6.9	12.5	20.3	-0.1	⊕	-4.4	-15.7	1	2.2	⊕	-9.1	-25.8	-51.8	24
2777	2449	2153	1886	1644	1428	0.6	2.6	6.2	11.3	18.2	-0.1	⊕	-4.3	-15.4	1	2.2	⊕	-8.9	-25.2	-50	24
2719	2346	2015	1721	1462	1234	0.7	3	7.2	13.2	21.3	-0.1	⊕	-4	-14.6	0.9	2	⊕	-8.5	-24.5	-49.2	24
3548	3133	2758	2420	2115	1841	0.6	2.4	5.5	10.1	16.4	-0.2	⊕	-3.2	-11.6	0.6	1.6	⊕	-6.9	-19.9	-39.9	24
3810	3459	3135	2835	2558	2303	0.5	1.9	4.3	7.8	12.7	-0.2	⊕	-3.3	-11.8	0.7	1.7	⊕	-6.9	-19.7	-39.1	24
4830	4318	3851	3426	3037	2685	0.5	2.1	4.9	8.8	14.3	-0.2	⊕	-3	-11	0.5	1.5	⊕	-6.5	-18.5	-37.1	24
4434	4052	3696	3365	3058	2772	0.4	1.8	4.3	8	12.8	-0.1	⊕	-4.2	-14.7	1	2.1	⊕	-8.5	-23.8	-46.6	24

FEDERAL

FEDERAL

ATT.	USAGE	FEDERAL LOAD NO.	CARTRIDGE	GRAINS	GRAMS	Bullet Style	MUZZLE	100 YDS.	200 YDS.	300 YDS.	400 YDS.	500 YDS.
FEDERAL POWER·SHOK®												
	1	222A	222 REM.	50	3.24	SP	3140	2626	2166	1755	1408	1152
	1	223A	223 REM.	55	3.56	SP	3240	2800	2400	2035	1705	1420
	2	223L	223 REM.	64	4.15	SP	3050	2682	2342	2027	1740	1485
	1	22250A	22-250 REM.	55	3.56	SP	3650	3136	2679	2264	1888	1558
	2	243AS	243 WIN.	80	5.18	SP	3330	3051	2790	2543	2309	2088
	2	2438SLFA	243 WIN.	85	5.51	COPPER HP	3200	2783	2403	2054	1737	1459
	2	243B	243 WIN.	100	6.48	SP	2960	2697	2448	2213	1991	1783
	2	6B	6MM REM.	100	6.48	SP	3100	2827	2571	2329	2100	1883
	2	2506BS	25-06 REM.	117	7.58	SP	3030	2767	2519	2283	2061	1851
	2	65CRDB	6.5 Creedmoor	140	9.07	SP	2725	2522	2327	2142	1964	1796
	2	6555B	6.5X55 SWEDISH	140	9.07	SP	2650	2450	2258	2075	1900	1736
	2	270A	270 WIN.	130	8.42	SP	3060	2803	2560	2329	2111	1904
	2	270130LFA	270 WIN.	130	8.42	COPPER HP	3060	2729	2422	2135	1867	1625
	2	270B	270 WIN.	150	9.72	SPRN	2830	2486	2166	1871	1606	1374
	2	270WSME	270 WIN. SHORT MAGNUM	130	8.42	SP	3250	2978	2722	2480	2251	2034
	2	7B	7MM MAUSER	140	9.07	SP	2660	2454	2256	2069	1889	1722
	2	7A	7MM MAUSER	175	11.34	SPRN	2390	2090	1812	1564	1348	1177
	2	708CS	7MM-08 REM.	150	9.72	SP	2650	2438	2235	2043	1859	1689
	2	280B	280 REM.	150	9.72	SP	2890	2667	2455	2253	2060	1877
	2	7RA	7MM REM. MAGNUM	150	9.72	SP	3110	2841	2587	2347	2120	1905
	3	7RB	7MM REM. MAGNUM	175	11.34	SP	2860	2646	2441	2246	2060	1882
	2	7WSME	7MM WIN. SHORT MAGNUM	150	9.72	SP	3100	2831	2578	2338	2112	1898
	1	30CA	30 CARBINE	110	7.13	SPRN	1990	1564	1231	1031	919	839
	2	300BLK120LFA	300 BLACKOUT	120	7.78	COPPER HP	2100	1799	1533	1307	1136	1024
	2	300BLKB	300 Blackout	150	9.72	SP	1900	1685	1490	1320	1181	1079
	2	76239B	7.62X39MM SOVIET	123	7.97	SP	2350	2055	1783	1539	1329	1164
	1	3030C	30-30 WIN.	125	8.1	HP	2570	2083	1656	1309	1079	952
	2	3030A	30-30 WIN.	150	9.72	SPFN	2390	2019	1686	1399	1179	1037
	2	3030B	30-30 WIN.	170	11.02	SPRN	2200	1894	1619	1380	1191	1060
	2	300A	300 SAVAGE	150	9.72	SP	2630	2353	2094	1850	1629	1430
	2	300B	300 SAVAGE	180	11.66	SP	2350	2137	1934	1745	1571	1412
	2	308A	308 WIN.	150	9.72	SP	2820	2532	2261	2007	1771	1557
	2	308150LFA	308 WIN.	150	9.72	COPPER HP	2820	2497	2195	1915	1661	1434
	2	308B	308 WIN.	180	11.66	SP	2570	2345	2131	1929	1740	1565
	1	3006CS	30-06 SPRING.	125	8.1	SP	3140	2779	2446	2136	1850	1593
	2	3006A	30-06 SPRING.	150	9.72	SP	2910	2616	2340	2081	1839	1619
	2	3006150LFA	30-06 SPRING.	150	9.72	COPPER HP	2910	2580	2273	1988	1725	1491
	2	3006B	30-06 SPRING.	180	11.66	SP	2700	2470	2252	2045	1848	1667
	2	3006HS	30-06 SPRING.	220	14.26	SP	2400	2120	1859	1623	1412	1238
	2	300WGS	300 WIN. MAGNUM	150	9.72	SP	3150	2898	2661	2435	2221	2017
	3	300WBS	300 WIN. MAGNUM	180	11.66	SP	2960	2746	2542	2346	2160	1982
	3	300W180LFA	300 WIN. MAGNUM	180	11.66	COPPER HP	2960	2693	2441	2203	1979	1769
	3	300WSMC	300 WIN. SHORT MAGNUM	180	11.66	SP	2980	2736	2504	2284	2075	1877
	3	300WSM180LFA	300 WIN. SHORT MAGNUM	180	11.66	COPPER HP	2950	2684	2432	2195	1971	1761
	2	303B	303 BRITISH	150	9.72	SP	2690	2442	2208	1988	1780	1590
	2	303AS	303 BRITISH	180	11.66	SP	2460	2206	1966	1744	1542	1363
	2	32A	32 WIN. SPECIAL	170	11.02	SPFN	2250	1923	1630	1376	1179	1047

FEDERAL

| ENERGY IN FOOT-POUNDS (TO NEAREST 5 FOOT-POUNDS) | | | | | | WIND DRIFT IN INCHES 10 MPH CROSSWIND | | | | | HEIGHT OF BULLET TRAJECTORY IN INCHES ABOVE OR BELOW LINE OF SIGHT IF ZEROED AT ⊕ YARDS. SIGHTS 1.5 INCHES ABOVE BORE LINE. AVERAGE RANGE | | | | LONG RANGE | | | | | | TEST BARREL LENGTH |
MUZZLE	100 YDS.	200 YDS.	300 YDS.	400 YDS.	500 YDS.	100 YDS.	200 YDS.	300 YDS.	400 YDS.	500 YDS.	50 YDS.	100 YDS.	200 YDS.	300 YDS.	50 YDS.	100 YDS.	200 YDS.	300 YDS.	400 YDS.	500 YDS.	INCHES
1095	765	521	342	220	147	1.6	6.9	17.2	34	58.9	-0.2	⊕	-3.6	-14.8	0.7	1.8	⊕	-9.3	-30.4	-70.1	24
1282	957	703	505	355	246	1.2	5.3	12.9	25	42.6	-0.3	⊕	-3	-12	0.5	1.5	⊕	-7.6	-23.8	-52.3	24
1322	1022	779	584	430	313	1.2	4.9	11.8	22.6	38.2	-0.2	⊕	-3.3	-13.1	0.6	1.7	⊕	-8.1	-24.7	-53.2	24
1627	1201	876	626	435	296	1.2	4.9	11.9	22.9	39.4	-0.4	⊕	-2.1	-9	0.1	1	⊕	-5.9	-18.7	-41.8	24
1970	1654	1382	1148	947	774	0.7	3	6.9	12.8	21.1	-0.3	⊕	-2.2	-9	0.2	1.1	⊕	-5.6	-16.6	-34.2	24
1933	1462	1090	796	569	402	1.2	5.1	12.4	23.9	40.5	-0.3	⊕	-3	-12.1	0.5	1.5	⊕	-7.6	-23.6	-51.4	24
1945	1615	1331	1087	880	706	0.9	3.6	8.4	15.8	25.9	-0.2	⊕	-3.3	-12.4	0.6	1.6	⊕	-7.5	-22.1	-45.4	24
2134	1775	1468	1204	979	787	0.8	3.4	7.9	14.8	24.1	-0.3	⊕	-2.9	-11	0.5	1.4	⊕	-6.7	-19.9	-40.7	24
2385	1989	1648	1354	1104	890	0.8	3.4	8	14.9	24.4	-0.2	⊕	-3.1	-11.6	0.5	1.5	⊕	-7	-20.8	-42.5	24
2308	1977	1683	1426	1199	1003	0.8	3.1	7.5	13.8	22.5	-0.1	⊕	-4	-14.4	0.9	2	⊕	-8.5	-24.4	-49.4	24
2183	1865	1585	1338	1122	937	0.7	3.3	7.8	14.3	23.6	-0.1	⊕	-4.3	-15.5	1	2.2	⊕	-9	-25.9	-52.8	24
2703	2267	1891	1566	1286	1046	0.8	3.2	7.6	14.2	23.1	-0.2	⊕	-3	-11.2	0.5	1.5	⊕	-6.7	-20	-40.9	24
2703	2150	1693	1315	1006	763	1	4.3	10.3	19.3	32.6	-0.2	⊕	-3.2	-12.4	0.6	1.6	⊕	-7.6	-22.7	-48.4	24
2667	2057	1563	1166	859	629	1.3	5.4	12.8	24.9	41.7	-0.1	⊕	-4.2	-15.7	0.9	2.1	⊕	-9.4	-29.2	-62.6	24
3049	2559	2138	1775	1462	1194	0.7	3	7.1	13.2	21.7	-0.3	⊕	-2.4	-9.6	0.3	1.2	⊕	-5.9	-17.5	-36	24
2199	1871	1583	1330	1109	922	0.8	3.4	8	14.7	24.3	-0.1	⊕	-4.3	-15.5	1	2.1	⊕	-9	-25.9	-53.1	24
2219	1697	1276	950	706	538	1.6	6.5	16	30.2	50.2	0.1	⊕	-6.5	-23.7	1.7	3.2	⊕	-14.1	-42.4	-90.4	24
2339	1979	1664	1390	1151	950	0.8	3.5	8.3	15.3	25.4	-0.1	⊕	-4.4	-15.7	1	2.2	⊕	-9.2	-26.5	-54.4	24
2782	2369	2008	1690	1414	1173	0.8	3.1	7.3	13.6	22	-0.2	⊕	-3.4	-12.6	0.7	1.7	⊕	-7.5	-21.9	-44.2	24
3221	2687	2229	1834	1497	1209	0.8	3.3	7.7	14.5	23.6	-0.3	⊕	-2.8	-10.8	0.4	1.4	⊕	-6.6	-19.6	-40.1	24
3178	2720	2316	1961	1649	1377	0.8	3	7.2	13.3	21.4	-0.2	⊕	-3.5	-12.8	0.7	1.7	⊕	-7.6	-22.1	-44.6	24
3200	2669	2213	1821	1486	1199	0.8	3.3	7.7	14.5	23.7	-0.3	⊕	-2.9	-10.9	0.5	1.4	⊕	-6.6	-19.7	-40.4	24
967	597	370	260	206	172	3.5	15.1	35.8	63.7	97.4	0.7	⊕	-13	-49.1	3.9	6.5	⊕	-29.7	-90.9	-190.2	18
1175	863	626	455	344	279	1.9	8.7	20.9	39.2	63.2	0.4	⊕	-9.4	-33.7	2.7	4.7	⊕	-19.6	-59.9	-127.1	16
1202	946	739	580	465	388	1.9	7.4	17.4	31.9	51	0.6	⊕	-10.8	-37.3	3.3	5.4	⊕	-21.2	-62.4	-128.7	24
1508	1153	868	646	482	370	1.6	6.7	16.2	30.7	50.8	0.2	⊕	-6.7	-24.6	1.8	3.4	⊕	-14.5	-43.9	-93.3	20
1833	1204	761	476	323	252	2.3	10.2	25.6	49.9	81.6	0.1	⊕	-6.7	-26.4	1.7	3.3	⊕	-16.4	-53.7	-120.6	24
1902	1358	947	652	463	358	2	8.6	20.8	40	65.9	0.1	⊕	-7.2	-26.7	1.9	3.6	⊕	-15.9	-50.1	-109.4	24
1827	1354	990	719	535	424	1.8	8.1	19.4	36.7	59.9	0.3	⊕	-8.4	-30	2.4	4.2	⊕	-17.4	-53.5	-114.4	24
2304	1844	1460	1140	884	681	1.1	4.9	11.5	22.1	36.4	-0.1	⊕	-4.8	-17.5	1.2	2.4	⊕	-10.2	-31.1	-64.8	24
2207	1825	1495	1217	986	797	1.2	4.5	10.9	20.5	33.3	0.1	⊕	-6.1	-21.6	1.6	3	⊕	-12.5	-36.5	-74.4	24
2648	2134	1702	1341	1044	807	1.1	4.4	10.4	19.7	32.9	-0.1	⊕	-3.9	-14.7	0.8	2	⊕	-8.8	-26.3	-55.2	24
2648	2076	1605	1221	918	685	1.2	5	12	23	38.4	-0.1	⊕	-4.1	-15.4	0.9	2.1	⊕	-9.2	-28.3	-59.9	24
2640	2197	1816	1486	1209	979	0.9	4.1	9.4	17.8	29.4	0	⊕	-4.9	-17.3	1.2	2.4	⊕	-10	-29.5	-60.7	24
2736	2143	1660	1267	949	704	1	4.5	10.8	20.4	34.6	-0.3	⊕	-3	-11.9	0.5	1.5	⊕	-7.4	-22.3	-48	24
2820	2279	1823	1442	1126	873	1	4.2	10	18.7	31.4	-0.2	⊕	-3.6	-13.6	0.7	1.8	⊕	-8.2	-24.4	-51.3	24
2820	2217	1721	1316	991	740	1.2	4.8	11.5	21.9	36.7	-0.2	⊕	-3.7	-14.3	0.8	1.9	⊕	-8.7	-26.2	-55.7	24
2913	2439	2026	1671	1365	1111	0.9	3.7	8.8	16.2	27	-0.1	⊕	-4.2	-15.3	1	2.1	⊕	-9	-26.2	-54	24
2813	2196	1688	1286	974	748	1.5	5.9	14.6	27.3	45.4	0.1	⊕	-6.2	-22.7	1.7	3.1	⊕	-13.5	-40	-84.5	24
3305	2798	2358	1975	1643	1355	0.7	3	6.9	12.9	21.1	-0.3	⊕	-2.7	-10.2	0.4	1.3	⊕	-6.2	-18.3	-37.5	24
3502	3013	2582	2200	1864	1570	0.7	2.9	6.6	12.3	20	-0.2	⊕	-3.1	-11.6	0.6	1.6	⊕	-6.9	-20.3	-41	24
3502	2898	2382	1940	1565	1250	0.9	3.6	8.6	16	26.4	-0.2	⊕	-3.3	-12.5	0.6	1.6	⊕	-7.5	-22.2	-45.8	24
3549	2991	2506	2084	1721	1408	0.8	3.2	7.6	14.2	23	-0.2	⊕	-3.2	-11.9	0.6	1.6	⊕	-7.1	-21	-42.7	24
3478	2878	2364	1925	1552	1240	0.9	3.6	8.6	16.1	26.5	-0.2	⊕	-3.3	-12.6	0.6	1.7	⊕	-7.6	-22.4	-46.2	24
2410	1987	1624	1316	1055	842	0.9	4.1	9.7	18	30	-0.1	⊕	-4.4	-15.9	1	2.2	⊕	-9.3	-27.4	-56.9	24
2418	1944	1545	1215	950	742	1.2	5.1	12.2	23	37.9	0.1	⊕	-5.7	-20.4	1.5	2.8	⊕	-11.9	-35.3	-73.6	24
1911	1395	1002	715	524	414	1.8	8.4	20.1	38.3	62.5	0.2	⊕	-8.1	-29.3	2.3	4	⊕	-17.2	-53.1	-114.4	24

FEDERAL

ATT.	USAGE	FEDERAL LOAD NO.	CARTRIDGE	BULLET WEIGHT IN GRAINS	GRAMS	Bullet Style	VELOCITY IN FEET PER SECOND (TO NEAREST 10 FPS) MUZZLE	100 YDS.	200 YDS.	300 YDS.	400 YDS.	500 YDS.
	2	338FJ	338 FEDERAL	200	12.96	SP	2700	2484	2278	2082	1895	1721
	2	8A	8MM MAUSER	170	11.02	SP	2250	2025	1814	1620	1444	1292
	2	C357G	357 MAGNUM	180	11.66	HP	1550	1282	1095	982	904	841
	2	35A	35 REM.	200	12.96	SPRN	2080	1697	1374	1138	999	910
	2	350LA	350 LEGEND	180	11.66	SP	2100	1793	1520	1292	1123	1013
		360BHAS	360 BuckHammer	180	11.66	SP	2,374	1,917	1,522	1,216	1,031	924
		360BHBS	360 BuckHammer	200	12.96	SP	1,197	1,777	1,421	1,157	1,003	908
	3	375A	375 H&H MAGNUM	270	17.5	SP	2690	2418	2162	1922	1700	1500
	3	375B	375 H&H MAGNUM	300	19.44	SP	2530	2267	2021	1790	1581	1394
	2	C44A	44 REM. MAGNUM	240	15.55	HP	1760	1387	1123	978	885	813
	2	4570AS	45-70 GOVERNMENT	300	19.44	HP	1850	1612	1400	1226	1097	1010
	2	450BMB	450 BUSHMASTER	300	19.44	SP	1900	1602	1346	1153	1028	945

FEDERAL VARMINT & PREDATOR

ATT.	USAGE	FEDERAL LOAD NO.	CARTRIDGE	GRAINS	GRAMS	Bullet Style	MUZZLE	100 YDS.	200 YDS.	300 YDS.	400 YDS.	500 YDS.
	1	AE17H20TVP	17 HORNET	20	1.3	TIPPED VARMINT	3610	3042	2541	2092	1694	1361
	1	AE22H35TVP	22 HORNET	35	2.27	TIPPED VARMINT	3000	2188	1526	1094	908	795
	1	V204VM32	204 RUGER	32	2.07	HORNADY® V-MAX®	4100	3536	3040	2596	2193	1827
	1,5	AE22350VP	223 REM.	50	3.24	JHP	3325	2839	2402	2006	1653	1355
	1	V223VM53	223 REM.	53	3.43	HORNADY V-MAX	3400	3046	2720	2416	2132	1868
	1	V224VLKM60	224 VALKYRIE	60	3.89	HORNADY V-MAX	3300	2923	2577	2255	1958	1687
	1	V22250VM2	22-250 REM.	55	3.56	HORNADY V-MAX	3670	3244	2858	2504	2176	1873
	1,5	AE22250VP	22-250 REM.	50	3.24	JHP	3850	3303	2819	2384	1990	1639
	1	AE24375VP	243 WIN.	75	4.86	JHP	3375	2943	2551	2191	1861	1569
	1	V243VM75	243 WIN.	75	4.86	HORNADY V-MAX	3425	3111	2819	2545	2286	2044
	1	AE65GDL90VP	6.5 GRENDEL	90	5.83	SPEER TNT	3000	2641	2309	2002	1721	1472
	1	V65CRDVM95	6.5 CREEDMOOR	95	6.16	HORNADY V-MAX	3300	3023	2763	2518	2285	2065
	1	AE6890VP	6.8 SPC	90	5.83	JACKETED HOLLOW POINT	2990	2651	2335	2043	1772	1530
	1	V308VM110	308 WIN.	110	7.13	HORNADY V-MAX	3300	2954	2635	2336	2058	1799
	1	AE308130VP	308 WIN.	130	8.42	JHP	3050	2691	2359	2052	1769	1516
	1	V76239VP1	7.62X39MM SOVIET	130	8.42	JACKETED HOLLOW POINT	2300	1997	1720	1473	1269	1116

AMERICAN EAGLE

ATT.	USAGE	FEDERAL LOAD NO.	CARTRIDGE	GRAINS	GRAMS	Bullet Style	MUZZLE	100 YDS.	200 YDS.	300 YDS.	400 YDS.	500 YDS.
	5	AE5728A	5.7x28 MM	40	2.59	TMJ	2250	1606	1151	942	825	735
	1,5	AE223G	223 Rem.	50	3.24	JHP	3325	2839	2402	2006	1653	1355
	5	AE223	223 Rem.	55	3.56	FMJ BT	3240	2874	2536	2222	1931	1667
	5	AE223N	223 Rem.	62	4.02	FMJ BT	3020	2713	2426	2156	1904	1674
	5	AE223T75	223 Rem.	75	4.86	TMJ	2775	2550	2336	2132	1938	1756
	5	AE224VLK1	224 Valkyrie	75	4.86	TMJ	3000	2763	2539	2325	2122	1929
	1,5	AE22250G	22-250 Rem.	50	3.24	JHP	3850	3303	2819	2384	1990	1639
	5	AE65GDL1	6.5 Grendel	120	7.97	OTM	2580	2410	2246	2089	1938	1794
	5	AE65CRD2	6.5 Creedmoor	120	7.78	OTM	2900	2680	2470	2270	2079	1897
	5	AE68A	6.8 SPC	115	7.45	FMJ	2675	2442	2221	2012	1815	1633
	5	AE65CRD3	6.5 Creedmoor	120	7.78	TMJ	2900	2672	2455	2248	2052	1865
	5	AE65CRD4	6.5 Creedmoor	123	7.97	OTM	2875	2667	2468	2277	2096	1922
	5	AE30CB	30 Carbine	110	7.13	FMJ	1990	1564	1231	1031	919	839
	5	AE300BLK1	300 Blackout	150	9.72	FMJ BT	1900	1724	1561	1411	1282	1174
	5	AE300BLKSUP2	300 Blackout	220	14.26	OTM	1000	970	944	920	897	876
	5	A76239A	7.62x39mm Soviet	124	8.04	FMJ	2350	2078	1824	1595	1392	1224
	5	AE308D	308 Win.	150	9.72	FMJ BT	2820	2597	2385	2183	1990	1808
	5	A7625IM1A	7.62x51mm	168	10.89	OTM	2650	2459	2276	2101	1933	1774

FEDERAL

ENERGY IN FOOT-POUNDS (TO NEAREST 5 FOOT-POUNDS)						WIND DRIFT IN INCHES 10 MPH CROSS WIND					HEIGHT OF BULLET TRAJECTORY IN INCHES ABOVE OR BELOW LINE OF SIGHT IF ZEROED AT ⊕ YARDS. SIGHTS 1.5 INCHES ABOVE BORE LINE. AVERAGE RANGE				LONG RANGE						TEST BARREL LENGTH
MUZZLE	100 YDS.	200 YDS.	300 YDS.	400 YDS.	500 YDS.	100 YDS.	200 YDS.	300 YDS.	400 YDS.	500 YDS.	50 YDS.	100 YDS.	200 YDS.	300 YDS.	50 YDS.	100 YDS.	200 YDS.	300 YDS.	400 YDS.	500 YDS.	INCHES
3237	2740	2304	1824	1594	1313	0.8	3.4	8.2	15	24.9	-0.1	⊕	-4.1	-15	0.9	2.1	⊕	-8.8	-25.5	-52.2	24
1911	1548	1242	991	786	630	1.3	5.3	12.8	23.7	39.1	0.2	⊕	-6.9	-24.8	1.9	3.5	⊕	-14.3	-41.6	-86.1	24
960	657	479	385	326	283	3.5	14.2	31.2	53.4	79.9	1.5	⊕	-19.7	-68.1	6.4	9.9	⊕	-38.5	-111.9	-225.7	18
1921	1278	838	575	443	368	2.8	12	29.1	53.5	83.6	0.5	⊕	-10.7	-40.2	3.2	5.4	⊕	-24.1	-75.1	-159.2	24
1762	1284	924	668	504	410	2	8.9	21.6	40.4	64.9	0.4	⊕	-9.4	-34.1	2.8	4.7	⊕	-20	-61	-129.6	16
2,252	1,468	926	591	425	341	2.5	11.2	28	53.3	85.3	0.2	⊕	-8.1	-31.5	-	-	-	-	-	-	20
2,144	1,402	896	595	447	366	2.7	12	29.3	54.6	86	0.4	⊕	-9.7	-36.9	-	-	-	-	-	-	20
4338	3505	2803	2214	1733	1348	1	4.6	10.7	20.4	33.9	-0.1	⊕	-4.5	-16.4	1	2.3	⊕	-9.6	-28.9	-60.3	24
4263	3424	2720	2135	1665	1294	1.2	5	11.8	22.5	37.1	0	⊕	-5.3	-19.1	1.3	2.6	⊕	-11.1	-33.5	-69.5	24
1651	1025	672	509	417	352	3.9	16.5	37.1	64	96.4	1	⊕	-16.8	-60.9	5.2	8.4	⊕	-35.6	-106	-217.7	20
2280	1730	1305	1001	802	679	2.3	8.8	20.7	37.8	59.5	0.7	⊕	-11.9	-41.7	3.7	5.9	⊕	-23.9	-71	-146.8	24
2405	1708	1208	885	703	595	2.7	10.8	25.6	46.5	72.4	0.7	⊕	-12.2	-43.7	3.7	6.1	⊕	-25.4	-77.1	-160.6	24
579	411	287	194	127	82	1.3	5.7	14	27.5	47.7	-0.4	⊕	-2.3	-10.1	0.2	1.1	⊕	-6.6	-21.4	-49.1	24
699	372	181	93	64	49	3	14.4	38.3	74.2	118.8	-0.1	⊕	-6.1	-28.3	1.4	3.1	⊕	-19.1	-66.9	-152.6	24
1194	888	657	479	342	237	1	4.2	10.2	19.4	32.8	-0.4	⊕	-1.3	-6.4	-0.1	0.6	⊕	-4.4	-14.1	-31.1	24
1227	895	640	447	303	204	1.3	5.6	13.8	27.1	46.5	-0.3	⊕	-2.8	-11.8	0.4	1.4	⊕	-7.5	-24	-53.7	24
1360	1092	871	687	535	410	0.9	3.7	8.7	16.5	27.3	-0.3	⊕	-2.3	-9.2	0.2	1.1	⊕	-5.8	-17.7	-37.1	24
1451	1138	884	678	511	379	1	4.3	10.2	19.3	32.4	-0.3	⊕	-2.6	-10.4	0.3	1.3	⊕	-6.5	-20	-42.8	24
1645	1285	998	766	578	428	0.9	3.9	9.2	17.5	29.1	-0.4	⊕	-1.8	-7.0	0.7	0.9	⊕	-5.7	-16	-34.1	24
1645	1211	882	631	439	298	1.1	4.7	11.3	21.9	37.5	-0.4	⊕	-1.7	-7.8	0	0.9	⊕	-5.3	-16.8	-37.5	24
1897	1443	1084	800	577	410	1.1	4.8	11.5	21.9	37.3	-0.3	⊕	-7.5	-10.5	0.3	1.3	⊕	-6.7	-20.6	-45.1	24
1953	1612	1323	1078	871	696	0.8	3.2	7.5	13.9	23	-0.3	⊕	-2.1	-8.6	0.2	1	⊕	-5.5	-16.3	-33.8	24
1798	1394	1065	801	592	433	1.2	4.9	11.9	22.8	38.3	-0.2	⊕	-3.5	-13.6	0.7	1.7	⊕	-8.3	-25.5	-54.6	24
2297	1928	1610	1337	1101	900	0.7	3	7	13	21.4	-0.3	⊕	-2.3	-9.2	0.3	1.2	⊕	-5.7	-16.9	-34.9	24
1786	1404	1090	834	628	468	1.1	4.6	11.2	21.2	35.7	-0.2	⊕	-3.5	-13.4	0.7	1.7	⊕	-8.2	-24.7	-52.6	24
2660	2132	1695	1333	1034	791	0.9	3.9	9.1	17.2	28.6	-0.3	⊕	-2.5	-10	0.3	1.3	⊕	-6.2	-19	-39.9	24
2685	2090	1606	1215	903	664	1.1	4.7	11.5	21.8	36.8	-0.2	⊕	-3.3	-12.9	0.6	1.7	⊕	-8	-24.3	-52	24
1527	1151	854	627	464	359	1.8	7.3	17.5	33.2	54.8	0.2	⊕	-7.3	-26.4	2	3.6	⊕	-15.5	-47.1	-101.1	20
450	229	118	79	60	48	4.4	20.2	48	84.7	129.1	0.5	⊕	-12.6	-51.3	3.6	6.3	⊕	-32.4	-101.1	-216.1	24
1227	895	640	447	303	204	1.3	5.6	13.8	27.1	46.5	-0.3	⊕	-2.8	-11.8	0.4	1.4	⊕	-7.5	-24	-53.7	24
1282	1008	785	603	455	339	1	4.3	10.2	19.4	32.7	-0.3	⊕	-2.7	-10.9	0.4	1.4	⊕	-6.8	-20.6	-44.2	24
1255	1013	810	640	499	386	1	4	9.7	18.1	30.4	-0.2	⊕	-3.2	-12.4	0.6	1.6	⊕	-7.6	-22.6	-47.6	24
1282	1083	908	757	625	514	0.8	3.4	8.1	14.9	24.6	-0.1	⊕	-3.8	-14.1	0.8	1.9	⊕	-8.4	-24.2	-49.6	24
1499	1272	1073	900	750	619	0.7	3.1	7.2	13.4	21.8	-0.2	⊕	-3.1	-11.5	0.5	1.5	⊕	-6.9	-20.4	-41.3	24
1645	1211	882	631	439	298	1.1	4.7	11.3	21.9	37.5	-0.4	⊕	-1.7	-7.8	0	0.9	⊕	-5.3	-16.8	-37.5	24
1818	1586	1378	1192	1026	879	0.6	2.9	6.9	12.5	20.3	-0.1	⊕	-4.5	-16	1.1	2.3	⊕	-9.2	-26.1	-52.5	24
2241	1913	1626	1373	1152	959	0.8	3.1	7.2	13.3	21.5	-0.2	⊕	-3.3	-12.4	0.6	1.7	⊕	-7.4	-21.6	-43.5	24
1827	1523	1260	1034	841	681	0.9	3.8	9.1	16.9	28	-0.1	⊕	-4.4	-15.8	1	2.2	⊕	-9.2	-27	-55.8	24
2241	1902	1606	1347	1122	927	0.8	3.2	7.5	13.9	22.5	-0.2	⊕	-3.4	-12.5	0.7	1.7	⊕	-7.5	-21.9	-44.3	24
2257	1942	1663	1416	1199	1009	0.8	2.9	6.8	12.7	20.5	-0.2	⊕	-3.4	-12.5	0.7	1.7	⊕	-7.4	-21.6	-43.4	24
967	597	370	260	206	172	3.5	15.1	35.8	63.7	97.4	0.7	⊕	-13	-49.1	3.9	6.5	⊕	-29.7	-90.9	-190.2	18
1202	990	811	663	547	459	1.6	6.1	13.7	25.3	40.6	0.6	⊕	-10.3	-34.7	3.2	5.1	⊕	-19.3	-56.3	-114.5	16
488	460	435	413	393	375	0.7	3.3	7.2	12.5	19.1	3.7	⊕	-35.6	-110.4	12.6	17.8	⊕	-56.9	-154.7	-294.9	16
1520	1189	916	701	533	412	1.5	6	14.7	27.6	45.7	0.1	⊕	-6.5	-23.8	1.8	3.3	⊕	-14	-41.5	-87.5	20
2648	2246	1894	1586	1319	1089	0.8	3.3	7.8	14.4	23.3	-0.2	⊕	-3.6	-13.5	0.8	1.8	⊕	-8	-23.3	-47.2	24
2619	2255	1932	1646	1394	1174	0.7	3.1	7.4	13.5	22.1	-0.1	⊕	-4.3	-15.3	1	2.1	⊕	-8.9	-25.5	-51.6	24

FEDERAL

ATT.	USAGE	FEDERAL LOAD NO.	CARTRIDGE	BULLET WEIGHT IN GRAINS	GRAMS	Bullet Style	VELOCITY IN FEET PER SECOND (TO NEAREST 10 FPS) MUZZLE	100 YDS.	200 YDS.	300 YDS.	400 YDS.	500 YDS.
	5	AE3006M1	30-06 Spring.	150	9.72	FMJ BT	2740	2522	2314	2116	1928	1751
	5	AE3006N	30-06 Spring.	150	9.72	FMJ BT	2910	2683	2466	2260	2064	1877
FUSION												
	2	F223FS1	223 Rem.	62	4.02	Fusion	3000	2697	2413	2148	1898	1671
	2	F224VLKMSR1	224 Valkyrie	90	5.83	Fusion	2700	2491	2291	2101	1919	1749
	2	F22250FS1	22-250 Rem.	55	3.56	Fusion	3600	3108	2667	2267	1902	1580
	2	F243FS1	243 Win.	95	6.16	Fusion	2980	2730	2493	2268	2056	1854
	2	F2506FS1	25-06 Rem.	120	7.78	Fusion	2980	2778	2585	2399	2222	2052
	2	F65CRDFS1	6.5 Creedmoor	140	9.07	Fusion	2725	2522	2327	2142	1964	1796
	2	F65PRCFS1	6.5 PRC	140	9.07	Fusion	2925	2713	2510	2316	2131	1954
	3	F6555FS1	6.5x55 Swedish	140	9.07	Fusion	2530	2336	2150	1973	1804	1648
	2	F6555FS12	6.5x55 Swedish	156	10.11	Fusion	2500	2326	2159	1999	1845	1702
	2	F260FS1	260 Rem.	120	7.78	Fusion	2950	2710	2483	2266	2061	1866
	2	F270FS1	270 Win.	130	8.42	Fusion	3050	2811	2584	2368	2163	1968
	2	F270FS2	270 Win.	150	9.72	Fusion	2850	2655	2468	2289	2117	1953
	2	F270WSMFS1	270 Win. Short Magnum	150	9.72	Fusion	3060	2867	2682	2504	2333	2169
	2	F708FS2	7mm-08 Rem.	120	7.78	Fusion	3000	2719	2455	2206	1971	1753
	2	F708FS1	7mm-08 Rem.	140	9.07	Fusion	2850	2615	2393	2181	1980	1791
	2	F280FS1	280 Rem.	140	9.07	Fusion	2990	2794	2607	2427	2255	2089
	3	F7RFS1	7mm Rem. Magnum	150	9.72	Fusion	3050	2861	2680	2505	2338	2177
	3	F7RFS2	7mm Rem. Magnum	175	11.34	Fusion	2760	2592	2430	2274	2123	1978
	2	F76239FS1	7.62x39mm Soviet	123	7.97	Fusion	2350	2077	1823	1593	1389	1222
	2	F3030FS1	30-30 Win.	150	9.72	Fusion	2390	2086	1805	1553	1337	1167
	2	F3030FS2	30-30 Win.	170	11.02	Fusion	2200	1950	1719	1510	1329	1182
	2	F308FS1	308 Win.	150	9.72	Fusion	2820	2600	2391	2191	2001	1821
	2	F308FS2	308 Win.	165	10.69	Fusion	2700	2501	2310	2128	1954	1789
	2	F308FS3	308 Win.	180	11.66	Fusion	2600	2427	2260	2101	1947	1801
	2	F3006FS1	30-06 Spring.	150	9.72	Fusion	2900	2674	2459	2254	2059	1874
	2	F3006FS2	30-06 Spring.	165	10.69	Fusion	2790	2590	2399	2217	2042	1875
	2	F3006FS3	30-06 Spring.	180	11.66	Fusion	2700	2521	2349	2185	2026	1874
	2	F300WFS1	300 Win. Magnum	150	9.72	Fusion	3200	2958	2729	2512	2304	2107
	2	F300WFS2	300 Win. Magnum	165	10.69	Fusion	3080	2865	2660	2464	2276	2097
	2	F300WFS3	300 Win. Magnum	180	11.66	Fusion	2960	2766	2580	2401	2230	2065
	2	F300WSMFS3	300 Win. Short Magnum	150	9.72	Fusion	3250	3005	2774	2555	2345	2146
	2	F300WSMFS1	300 Win. Short Magnum	165	10.69	Fusion	3100	2885	2680	2484	2296	2116
	2	F300WSMFS2	300 Win. Short Magnum	180	11.66	Fusion	2950	2756	2570	2391	2220	2055
	2	F338FFS2	338 Federal	200	12.96	Fusion	2700	2487	2284	2090	1905	1733
	2	F35FS1	35 Whelen	200	12.96	Fusion	2800	2537	2289	2055	1835	1634
	2	F350LFS1	350 Legend	160	10.37	Fusion	2300	1993	1712	1463	1257	1107
	2	F4570FS1	45-70 Government	300	19.44	Fusion	1850	1612	1401	1227	1099	1011
	2	F450BMFS1	450 BUSHMASTER	260	16.85	Fusion	2200	1777	1419	1155	1002	907
FUSION MSR												
	2	F223MSR1	223 Rem.	62	4.02	Fusion	2750	2463	2194	1942	1710	1500
	2	F224VLKMSR1	224 Valkyrie	90	5.83	Fusion	2700	2491	2291	2101	1919	1749
	2	F65GDLMSR1	6.5 Grendel	120	7.78	Fusion	2600	2346	2107	1881	1674	1485
	2	F68MSR2	6.8 SPC	90	5.83	Fusion	2850	2524	2221	1939	1682	1453
	2	F68MSR1	6.8 SPC	115	7.45	Fusion	2470	2248	2037	1838	1654	1485
	2	F300BMSR2	300 Blackout	150	9.72	Fusion	1900	1685	1490	1320	1181	1079
	2	F308MSR1	308 Win.	150	9.72	Fusion	2770	2553	2345	2148	1960	1782
	2	F338FMSR2	338 Federal	185	11.99	Fusion	2680	2447	2226	2016	1819	1636

	ENERGY IN FOOT-POUNDS (TO NEAREST 5 FOOT-POUNDS)					WIND DRIFT IN INCHES 10 MPH CROSSWIND					HEIGHT OF BULLET TRAJECTORY IN INCHES ABOVE OR BELOW LINE OF SIGHT IF ZEROED AT ⊕ YARDS. SIGHTS 1.5 INCHES ABOVE BORE LINE. AVERAGE RANGE				LONG RANGE						TEST BARREL LENGTH
MUZZLE	100 YDS.	200 YDS.	300 YDS.	400 YDS.	500 YDS.	100 YDS.	200 YDS.	300 YDS.	400 YDS.	500 YDS.	50 YDS.	100 YDS.	200 YDS.	300 YDS.	50 YDS.	100 YDS.	200 YDS.	300 YDS.	400 YDS.	500 YDS.	INCHES
2500	2118	1783	1492	1238	1021	0.8	3.4	8	14.7	24.3	-0.1	⊕	-4	-14.5	0.9	2	⊕	-8.6	-24.7	-50.5	24
2820	2397	2026	1701	1419	1173	0.8	3.2	7.4	13.7	22.2	-0.2	⊕	-3.3	-12.4	0.6	1.7	⊕	-7.4	-21.7	-43.8	24
1239	1001	802	635	496	384	1	4	9.7	18.1	30.4	-0.2	⊕	-3.3	-12.6	0.6	1.6	⊕	-7.7	-22.8	-48	24
1457	1240	1049	882	736	611	0.8	3.3	7.9	14.5	23.8	-0.1	0	-4.1	-14.9	0.9	2	0	-8.8	-25.2	-51.4	24
1583	1179	869	627	442	305	1.1	4.8	11.6	22.3	38.3	-0.4	⊕	-2.1	-9.2	0.2	1.1	⊕	-6	-18.8	-41.8	24
1873	1572	1311	1085	891	725	0.8	3.3	7.8	14.6	23.7	-0.2	⊕	-3.2	-11.9	0.6	1.6	⊕	-7.2	-21.2	-43.2	24
2366	2056	1780	1534	1315	1122	0.6	2.6	6	11.3	18.3	-0.2	⊕	-3	-11.2	0.5	1.5	⊕	-6.7	-19.5	-39.3	24
2308	1977	1683	1426	1199	1003	0.8	3.1	7.5	13.8	22.5	-0.1	⊕	-4	-14.4	0.9	2	⊕	-8.5	-24.4	-49.4	24
2659	2287	1958	1667	1411	1187	0.7	2.9	6.7	12.5	20.2	-0.2	⊕	-3.2	-12	0.6	1.6	⊕	-7.1	-20.8	-42	24
1990	1696	1437	1210	1012	844	0.8	3.6	8.3	15.3	25.3	0	⊕	-4.9	-17.4	1.2	2.5	⊕	-9.9	-28.7	-58.7	24
2165	1874	1614	1384	1179	1003	0.7	3.3	7.7	13.7	22.7	0	⊕	-5	-17.5	1.2	2.5	⊕	-10	-28.3	-57.5	24
2319	1957	1642	1369	1132	928	0.8	3.3	7.6	14.2	23	-0.2	⊕	-3.2	-12.1	0.6	1.6	⊕	-7.3	-21.4	-43.4	24
2685	2280	1927	1618	1350	1117	0.7	3	7	13.1	21.3	-0.2	⊕	-2.9	-11	0.5	1.5	⊕	-6.6	-19.6	-39.8	24
2705	2347	2029	1745	1493	1270	0.7	2.8	6.5	12	19.3	-0.2	⊕	-3.4	-12.6	0.7	1.7	⊕	-7.4	-21.6	-43.3	24
3118	2737	2395	2088	1813	1567	0.5	2.4	5.5	10	16.3	-0.3	⊕	-2.8	-10.3	0.4	1.4	⊕	-6.2	-17.9	-36.1	24
2398	1970	1605	1296	1035	819	0.9	3.7	8.8	16.5	27.3	-0.2	⊕	-3.2	-12.2	0.6	1.6	⊕	-7.4	-22	-45.6	24
2525	2126	1779	1479	1219	997	0.9	3.4	8	14.9	24.3	-0.2	⊕	-3.6	-13.3	0.7	1.8	⊕	-7.9	-23.2	-47.2	24
2779	2427	2113	1831	1580	1357	0.6	2.5	5.8	10.7	17.5	-0.2	⊕	-3	-11	0.5	1.5	⊕	-6.5	-19.1	-38.5	24
3098	2726	2391	2091	1820	1578	0.5	2.3	5.4	9.8	16	-0.3	⊕	-2.8	-10.4	0.4	1.4	⊕	-6.2	-17.9	-36.1	24
2960	2610	2294	2008	1751	1521	0.7	2.5	5.8	10.0	17.4	0.1	⊕	-3.6	-13.2	0.8	1.8	⊕	-7.8	-22.3	-44.5	24
1508	1178	907	693	527	407	1.5	6	14.8	27.7	45.9	0.1	⊕	-6.5	-23.8	1.8	3.3	⊕	-14	-41.6	-87.7	24
1902	1449	1085	803	595	453	1.6	6.6	16.2	30.8	51.1	0.1	⊕	-6.5	-23.9	1.7	3.2	⊕	-14.2	-42.8	-91.5	24
1827	1435	1115	860	666	527	1.4	6.3	15.1	28.5	46.7	0.3	⊕	-7.7	-27.2	2.2	3.9	⊕	-15.6	-46.8	-97.8	24
2648	2252	1903	1599	1333	1104	0.8	3.2	7.6	14.1	22.9	-0.2	⊕	-3.6	-13.4	0.7	1.8	⊕	-8	-23.1	-46.9	24
2671	2291	1955	1660	1399	1173	0.7	3.1	7.5	13.7	22.3	-0.1	⊕	-4.1	-14.7	0.9	2	⊕	-8.6	-24.8	-50.1	24
2702	2354	2042	1763	1515	1296	0.6	2.9	6.9	12.6	20.4	-0.1	⊕	-4.4	-15.7	1	2.2	⊕	-9.1	-25.8	-51.9	24
2801	2382	2014	1693	1412	1169	0.8	3.1	7.4	13.7	22.2	-0.2	⊕	-3.4	-12.5	0.7	1.7	⊕	-7.5	-21.8	-44.1	24
2852	2458	2109	1800	1527	1287	0.8	2.9	7	12.9	20.7	-0.1	⊕	-3.7	-13.4	0.8	1.8	⊕	-7.9	-22.9	-46	24
2913	2540	2206	1907	1640	1403	0.7	2.7	6.6	12.1	19.4	-0.1	⊕	-4	-14.3	0.9	2	⊕	-8.4	-23.9	-47.8	24
3410	2915	2481	2101	1769	1479	0.6	2.7	6.4	11.8	19.4	-0.3	⊕	-2.5	-9.6	0.3	1.2	⊕	-5.9	-17.3	-35.4	24
3475	3006	2591	2223	1898	1610	0.6	2.6	6.1	11.2	18.3	-0.3	⊕	-2.8	-10.4	0.4	1.4	⊕	-6.3	-18.3	-37.1	24
3502	3057	2659	2304	1987	1704	0.6	2.6	5.9	10.9	17.7	-0.2	⊕	-3.1	-11.3	0.6	1.5	⊕	-6.7	-19.5	-39.4	24
3518	3008	2563	2173	1832	1534	0.6	2.7	6.3	11.6	18.9	-0.3	⊕	-2.4	-9.3	0.3	1.2	⊕	-5.7	-16.7	-34.2	24
3521	3048	2630	2260	1931	1641	0.6	2.6	6	11.1	18.1	-0.3	⊕	-2.7	-10.2	0.4	1.4	⊕	-6.2	-18	-36.5	24
3478	3035	2639	2285	1969	1688	0.6	2.6	5.9	11	17.9	-0.2	⊕	-3.1	-11.4	0.6	1.5	⊕	-6.8	-19.7	-39.7	24
3237	2746	2316	1940	1612	1334	0.8	3.4	8.1	14.8	24.4	-0.1	⊕	-4.1	-15	0.9	2.1	⊕	-8.8	-25.3	-51.9	24
3481	2858	2327	1876	1495	1185	1	4	9.5	17.7	29.6	-0.1	⊕	-3.9	-14.5	0.8	2	⊕	-8.7	-25.4	-53	24
1879	1411	1041	760	562	435	1.8	7.4	17.8	33.9	55.8	0.2	⊕	-7.3	-26.6	2	3.7	⊕	-15.6	-47.8	-102.4	16
2280	1731	1307	1003	804	681	2.3	8.7	20.6	37.6	59.3	0.7	⊕	-11.9	-41.6	3.7	5.9	⊕	-23.8	-70.9	-146.5	24
2794	1823	1162	770	579	475	2.7	12	29.5	54.9	86.4	0.4	⊕	-9.7	-177.1	2.8	4.9	⊕	-22.5	-71.2	-152.8	24
1041	835	663	519	402	310	1.1	4.6	10.9	20.8	34.6	-0.1	⊕	-4.3	-15.7	1	2.1	⊕	-9.3	-28.1	-58.8	16
1457	1240	1049	882	736	611	0.8	3.3	7.9	14.5	23.8	-0.1	⊕	-4.1	-14.9	0.9	2	⊕	-8.8	-25.2	-51.4	24
1801	1467	1183	943	747	588	1	4.5	10.6	20.2	33.3	0	⊕	-4.9	-17.5	1.2	2.4	⊕	-10.1	-30.5	-63.1	24
1623	1273	986	751	565	422	1.2	5	11.8	22.7	37.8	-0.1	⊕	-4	-15	0.9	2	⊕	-9	-27.6	-58.4	16
1558	1290	1059	862	699	563	1	4.3	10.1	19.3	31.5	0	⊕	-5.4	-19.1	1.4	2.7	⊕	-11	-32.7	-66.8	16
1202	946	739	580	465	388	1.9	7.4	17.4	31.9	51	0.6	⊕	-10.8	-37.3	3.3	5.4	⊕	-21.2	-62.4	-128.7	16
2555	2170	1832	1536	1279	1058	0.8	3.3	7.8	14.4	23.6	-0.1	⊕	-3.8	-14.1	0.8	1.9	⊕	-8.3	-24.1	-48.9	20
2950	2459	2035	1670	1358	1100	0.9	3.8	9	16.8	28	-0.1	⊕	-4.3	-15.7	1	2.2	⊕	-9.2	-26.8	-55.5	20

FEDERAL

FEDERAL

HANDGUN BALLISTICS											
			BULLET WEIGHT IN				VELOCITY IN FEET PER SECOND (TO NEAREST 10 FPS)				
USAGE	FEDERAL LOAD NO.	CARTRIDGE	GRAINS	GRAMS	BULLET STYLE	MUZ	25 YDS.	50 YDS.	75 YDS.	100 YDS.	
FEDERAL PREMIUM PERSONAL DEFENSE HST®											
6	P380HST1S	380 AUTO	99	6.42	HST	1030	986	948	915	885	
6	P327HST1S	327 FEDERAL MAGNUM	104	6.74	HST	1525	1080	895	781	690	
6	P30HST1S	30 SUPER CARRY	100	6.48	HST	1250	1185	1129	1081	1041	
6	P9HST1S	9MM LUGER	124	8.04	HST	1150	1095	1049	1010	977	
6	P9HST3S	9MM LUGER +P	124	8.04	HST	1200	1136	1083	1039	1002	
6	P9HST2S	9MM LUGER	147	8.04	HST	1000	976	953	933	914	
6	P357HST1S	357 MAGNUM	154	9.98	HST	1340	1127	999	914	848	
6	P357SHST1S	357 SIG	125	8.1	HST	1360	1275	1200	1136	1083	
6	P40HST1S	40 S&W	180	11.66	HST	1010	980	954	930	908	
6	P10HST1S	10MM AUTO	200	12.96	HST	1130	1051	991	943	902	
6	P45HST2S	45 AUTO	230	14.9	HST	890	872	856	840	824	
6	P45HST1S	45 AUTO +P	230	14.9	HST	950	929	909	890	873	
FEDERAL PREMIUM PERSONAL DEFENSE PRACTICE & DEFEND											
6	P9HST1TM100	9MM LUGER	124	8.04	HST	1150	1095	1049	1010	977	
6	P9HST2TM100	9MM LUGER	147	9.53	HST	1000	976	953	933	914	
6	P40HST1TM100	40 S&W	180	11.66	HST	1010	980	954	930	908	
6	P45HST2TM100	45 AUTO	230	14.9	HST	890	872	856	840	824	
FEDERAL PREMIUM PERSONAL DEFENSE HYDRA-SHOK DEEP®											
6	P380HSD1	380 AUTO	99	6.42	HYDRA-SHOK DEEP	975	929	888	853	820	
6	P9HSD1	9MM LUGER	135	8.75	HYDRA-SHOK DEEP	1060	1026	996	970	946	
6	P38HSD1	38 SPECIAL +P	130	8.42	HYDRA-SHOK JHP	900	877	856	836	816	
6	P40HSD1	40 S&W	165	10.69	HYDRA-SHOK DEEP	100	1011	978	949	922	
6	P45HSD1	45 AUTO	210	13.61	HYDRA-SHOK DEEP	980	952	927	903	882	
FEDERAL PREMIUM PERSONAL DEFENSE® HYDRA-SHOK®											
6	P32HS1	32 AUTO	65	4.21	HYDRA-SHOK	925	892	862	834	808	
6	PD380HS1 H	380 AUTO	90	5.83	HYDRA-SHOK	1000	953	914	879	847	
6	P9HS1	9MM LUGER	124	8.04	HYDRA-SHOK	1120	1070	1028	993	961	
6	PD38HS3 H	38 SPECIAL	110	7.13	HYDRA-SHOK	980	943	911	882	855	
6	P38HS1	38 SPECIAL +P	129	8.36	HYDRA-SHOK	950	926	904	884	865	
6	P357HS1	357 MAGNUM	158	10.24	HYDRA-SHOK	1240	1187	1139	1098	1063	
6	P40HS3	40 S&W	165	10.69	HYDRA-SHOK	980	950	924	899	876	
6	P44HS1	44 REM. MAGNUM	240	15.55	HYDRA-SHOK	1210	1152	1102	1060	1024	
6	P45HS1	45 AUTO	230	14.9	HYDRA-SHOK	900	882	865	848	832	
FEDERAL PREMIUM HUNTING HANDGUN											
2	P327SA	327 FEDERAL MAGNUM	100	6.47	SWIFT A-FRAME	1500	1411	1329	1254	1189	
3 4	P9SHC1	9MM LUGER	147	9.53	SOLID CORE	1120	1082	1048	1019	993	
2	P357XB1	357 MAGNUM	140	9.07	BARNES EXPANDER	1400	1326	1257	1196	1143	
2	P357SA	357 MAGNUM	180	11.66	SWIFT A-FRAME	1130	1086	1049	1016	988	
3 4	P357SHC1	357 MAGNUM	180	11.66	SOLID CORE	1400	1333	1270	1214	1163	
3 4	P40SHC1	40 S&W	200	12.96	SOLID CORE	1000	976	953	933	914	
3	P10T1	10MM AUTO	180	11.66	TROPHY BONDED JSP	1275	1192	1123	1067	1021	
3 4	P10SHC1	10MM AUTO	200	12.96	SOLID CORE	1200	1143	1095	1054	1019	

ENERGY IN FOOT-POUNDS (TO NEAREST 5 FOOT-POUNDS)					TRAJECTORY SIGHTS .9 INCHES ABOVE BORE LINE				TEST BARREL LENGTH
MUZ	25 YDS.	50 YDS.	75 YDS.	100 YDS.	25 YDS.	50 YDS.	75 YDS.	100 YDS.	INCHES
233	213	197	184	172	⊕	-1.3	-5.1	-11.4	3.75
537	270	185	141	110	⊕	-0.9	-4.4	-11.2	4
347	312	283	260	241	⊕	-0.6	-3	-7.2	4
364	330	303	281	263	⊕	-0.9	-3.8	-8.8	4
396	355	323	297	277	⊕	-0.8	-3.4	-8	4
326	311	297	284	273	⊕	-1.4	-5.2	-11.5	4
614	434	341	286	246	⊕	-0.8	-3.7	-9.2	4
513	451	400	358	326	⊕	-0.4	-2.4	-6	4
408	384	364	346	329	⊕	-1.4	-5.1	-11.4	4
567	490	436	395	361	⊕	-1.1	-4.3	-10	5
404	389	374	360	347	⊕	-2.0	-6.9	-15.0	5
461	440	422	405	389	⊕	-1.6	-5.9	-12.8	5
364	330	303	281	263	⊕	-0.9	-3.8	-8.8	4
326	311	297	7R4	273	⊕	-1.4	-5.2	-11.5	4
408	384	364	346	329	⊕	-1.4	-5.1	-11.4	4
404	389	374	360	347	⊕	-2	-6.9	-15	5
209	189	173	160	148	⊕	-1.6	-6	-13.3	3.75
337	316	298	282	268	⊕	-1.2	-4.5	-10.2	4
234	222	211	202	192	⊕	-1.9	-6.9	-14.9	4-V
404	375	350	330	311	⊕	-1.2	-4.7	-10.6	4
448	423	400	381	363	⊕	-1.5	-5.5	-12.2	5
123	115	107	100	94	⊕	-1.8	-6.6	-14.5	4
200	182	167	154	143	⊕	-1.5	-5.6	-12.5	3.75
345	315	291	271	255	⊕	-1.0	-4.0	-9.3	4
235	217	203	190	179	⊕	-1.5	-5.7	-12.6	4-V
258	246	234	224	214	⊕	-1.6	-5.9	-13	4-V
539	494	455	423	396	⊕	-0.6	-3.0	-7.1	4-V
352	331	312	296	281	⊕	-1.5	-5.6	-12.3	4
780	707	647	599	559	⊕	-0.7	-3.3	-7.7	4-V
414	397	382	367	354	⊕	-1.9	-6.7	-14.6	5
500	442	392	349	314	⊕	-0.2	-1.6	-4.4	4-V
409	382	359	339	322	⊕	-1.0	-3.9	-8.9	4
609	546	491	445	406	⊕	-0.3	-2.0	-5.3	6-V
510	471	439	413	390	⊕	-0.9	-3.9	-8.9	6-V
783	710	645	589	541	⊕	-0.3	-2	-5.1	4-V
444	423	404	386	371	⊕	-1.4	-5.2	-11.5	4
650	568	504	455	417	⊕	-0.6	-3.0	-7.2	5
639	580	532	493	461	⊕	-0.8	-3.3	-7.9	5

FEDERAL

FEDERAL

USAGE	FEDERAL LOAD NO.	CARTRIDGE	BULLET WEIGHT IN		BULLET STYLE	VELOCITY IN FEET PER SECOND (TO NEAREST 10 FPS)				
			GRAINS	GRAMS		MUZ	25 YDS.	50 YDS.	75 YDS.	100 YDS.
1 2	P10SA	10MM AUTO	200	12.96	SWIFT A-FRAME	1100	1062	1030	1001	975
2	P41XB1	41 REM. MAGNUM	180	11.66	BARNES EXPANDER	1340	1262	1193	1134	1084
2	P41SA	41 REM. MAGNUM	210	13.61	SWIFT A-FRAME	1360	1289	1224	1167	1118
2	P44XB1	44 REM. MAGNUM	225	14.58	BARNES EXPANDER	1280	1209	1147	1096	1052
2	P44SA	44 REM. MAGNUM	280	18.14	SWIFT A-FRAME	1170	1107	1056	1013	977
3 4	P44SHC1	44 REM. MAGNUM	300	19.44	SOLID CORE	1300	1230	1169	1117	1073
3 4	P45SHC1	45 AUTO +P	240	15.55	SOLID CORE	1000	973	949	926	906
2	P454XB1	454 CASULL	250	16.2	BARNES EXPANDER	1530	1423	1326	1239	1165
2	P454SA	454 CASULL	300	19.44	SWIFT A-FRAME	1520	1410	1311	1223	1149
2	P460XB1	460 S&W	275	17.82	BARNES EXPANDER	1670	1595	1522	1453	1388
2	P460SA	460 S&W	300	19.44	SWIFT A-FRAME	1750	1625	1506	1397	1300
2	P500XB1	500 S&W	275	17.82	BARNES EXPANDER	1660	1544	1435	1337	1249
3	P500SA	500 S&W	325	21.06	SWIFT A-FRAME	1800	1677	1559	1449	1350
FEDERAL PREMIUM GOLD MEDAL®										
7	GM38A	38 SPECIAL	148	9.59	LW MATCH	690	650	610	570	540
7	GM45B	45 AUTO	185	11.99	FMJ-SWC MATCH	770	740	700	670	640
7	GM45A	45 AUTO	230	14.90	FMJ MATCH	860	840	830	810	800
FEDERAL PREMIUM GOLD MEDAL® ACTION PISTOL										
5	GM9AP1	9MM LUGER	147	9.53	FMJ MATCH	900	883	866	851	836
5	GM40AP1	40 S&W	180	11.66	FMJ MATCH	950	926	904	884	865
FEDERAL POWER·SHOK®										
2	C357G	357 MAGNUM	180	11.66	JHP	1080	1050	1020	1000	970
2	C41A	41 Rem. Magnum	210	13.61	JHP	1230	1170	1120	1080	1040
2	C44B	44 Rem. Magnum	180	11.66	JHP	1460	1340	1240	1160	1090
2	C44A	44 Rem. Magnum	240	15.55	JHP	1230	1170	1120	1070	1040
FEDERAL PERSONAL DEFENSE PUNCH™										
6	PD22L1	22 Long rifle	29	1.87	SOLID	1070	1020	978	843	912
6	PD22WMR1	22 WMR	45	2.91	JHP	1000	961	933	905	880
6	PD380P1	380 Auto	85	5.51	JHP	1000	949	907	869	835
6	PD30P1	30 SUPER CARRY	103	6.67	JHP	1130	1082	1042	1008	978
6	PD9P1	9mm Luger	124	8.04	JHP	1150	1095	1049	1010	977
6	PD38P1	38 Special +P	120	7.78	JHP	1000	949	907	869	835
6	PD40P1	40 S&W	165	10.69	JHP	1130	1078	1035	999	967
6	PD10P1	10MM Auto	200	12.96	JHP	1100	1075	1052	1031	1012
6	PD44SP1	44 Special	180	11.66	JHP	815	795	777	759	741
6	PD45P1	45 Auto	230	14.9	JHP	890	872	856	840	824
FEDERAL PERSONAL DEFENSE REVOLVER										
6	C32HRB	32 H&R Magnum	85	5.51	JHP	1120	1070	1020	990	950
5	C44SA	44 Special	200	12.96	SWHP	870	850	830	810	790
5	WM5233	45 Auto	230	14.9	FMJ	845	829	814	800	786
FEDERAL TRAIN+PROTECT™										
5 6	TP380VHP1	380 Auto	85	5.51	JHP	1000	953	914	879	847
6, 7	TP9VHP1	9mm Luger	115	7.45	JHP	1180	1110	1050	1000	960
5 6	TP38VHP1	38 Special	158	10.24	SWHP	830	816	802	789	776
6	TP357VHP1	357 Magnum	125	8.1	JHP	1440	1335	1240	1161	1096

ENERGY IN FOOT-POUNDS (TO NEAREST 5 FOOT-POUNDS)					TRAJECTORY SIGHTS .9 INCHES ABOVE BORE LINE				TEST BARREL LENGTH
MUZ	25 YDS.	50 YDS.	75 YDS.	100 YDS.	25 YDS.	50 YDS.	75 YDS.	100 YDS.	INCHES
537	501	471	445	423	⊕	-1.0	-4.1	-9.3	5
718	636	569	514	470	⊕	-0.5	-2.5	-6.1	6-V
862	775	698	635	582	⊕	-0.4	-2.3	-5.7	6-V
818	730	658	600	553	⊕	-0.6	-2.8	-6.9	6-V
851	762	693	638	594	⊕	-0.9	-3.7	-8.6	6-V
1126	1008	911	831	766	⊕	-0.5	-2.7	-6.5	4-V
533	505	480	457	437	⊕	-1.4	-5.2	-11.6	5
1299	1123	976	852	753	⊕	-0.2	-1.6	-4.4	5.7-V
1539	1324	1145	996	879	⊕	-0.2	-1.7	-4.6	5.7-V
1703	1553	1415	1289	1177	⊕	0.1	-0.8	-2.7	8.4-V
2040	1758	1510	1300	1125	⊕	0.1	-0.8	-2.8	8.4-V
1682	1455	1257	1091	952	⊕	0.0	-1.1	-3.4	8.4-V
2338	2028	1754	1515	1315	⊕	0.1	-0.6	-2.4	8.4-V
155	140	120	110	95	⊕	-4.3	-14.4	-31.2	4-V
245	220	205	185	170	⊕	-3.1	-10.6	-23.0	5
380	365	350	340	325	⊕	-2.2	-7.5	-16.1	5
264	254	245	236	228	⊕	-1.9	-6.7	-14.5	4
361	343	327	312	299	⊕	-1.6	-5.9	-13	4
465	440	415	395	380	⊕	-1.1	-4.2	-9.6	4-V
705	640	585	545	505	⊕	-0.7	-3.1	-7.3	4-V
850	720	615	535	470	⊕	-0.3	-2	-5.4	4-V
805	730	665	615	570	⊕	-0.7	-3.1	-7.4	4-V
74	67	62	57	54	⊕	-0.61	-3.5	-8.9	2
100	93	87	82	77	0.4	⊕	-2.9	-8.48	2
189	170	155	143	132	⊕	-1.5	-5.7	-12.7	3.75
292	268	248	232	219	⊕	-1	-3.9	-9	4
364	330	303	281	263	⊕	-0.9	-3.8	-8.8	4
266	240	219	201	186	⊕	-1.5	-5.7	-12.7	4-V
468	426	392	365	342	⊕	-1	-4	-9.1	4
537	513	491	472	454	⊕	-1	-3.9	-8.9	5
265	253	241	230	220	⊕	-2.5	-8.7	-18.6	4-V
404	389	374	360	347	⊕	-2	-6.9	-15	5
235	215	195	185	170	⊕	-1	-4.1	-9.4	5
335	320	305	290	275	⊕	-2.1	-7.4	-16	4-V
365	351	339	327	315	⊕	-2.3	-7.8	-16.6	5
189	172	158	146	135	⊕	-1.5	-5.6	-12.5	3.75
355	310	280	255	235	⊕	-0.9	-3.7	-8.7	4
242	233	226	218	211	⊕	-2.3	-8	-17.3	4-V
575	494	427	374	333	⊕	-0.3	-2.1	-5.4	4-V

FEDERAL

FEDERAL

USAGE	FEDERAL LOAD NO.	CARTRIDGE	BULLET WEIGHT IN GRAINS	BULLET WEIGHT IN GRAMS	BULLET STYLE	MUZ	25 YDS.	50 YDS.	75 YDS.	100 YDS.
6, 7	TP40VHP1	40 S&W	180	11.66	JHP	1000	970	950	920	900
5 6	TP10VHP1	10mm Auto	180	11.66	JHP	1175	1122	1077	1039	1006
6	TP45VHP1	45 Auto	230	14.9	JHP	850	830	820	800	790
FEDERAL CHAMPION™										
5	C32HRA	32 H&R Magnum	95	6.16	LSW	1020	970	930	890	860
5	WM5199	9mm Luger	115	7.45	FMJ	1125	1063	1013	972	936
5	WM5221	10MM AUTO	180	11.66	FMJ	1200	1129	1073	1035	980
5	WM5223	40 S&W	180	11.66	FMJ	1000	972	946	923	901
5	C44SA	44 Special	200	12.96	SWHP	870	850	830	810	790
5	WM5233	45 Auto	230	14.9	FMJ	845	829	814	800	786
FEDERAL MILITARY GRADE										
5	C9N882	9mm Luger	124	8.04	FMJ	1260	1187	1126	1074	1032
SYNTECH RANGE™										
5	AE380SJ1	380 Auto	95	6.16	TSJ	1000	953	914	879	847
5	AE9SJ1	9mm Luger	115	7.45	TSJ	1130	1105	1083	1062	1043
5	AE9SJ2	9mm Luger	124	8.04	TSJ	1050	1011	978	949	922
5	AE38SJ1	38 special	148	9.59	TSJ	880	858	838	819	800
5	AE40SJ1	40 S&W	165	10.69	TSJ	1050	1027	1007	988	970
5	AE45SJ1	45 Auto	230	14.9	TSJ	830	821	812	803	795
5	AE10SJ1	10mm Auto	205	13.28	TSJ	1150	1101	1059	1023	992
SYNTECH ACTION PISTOL™										
5	AE9SJAP1	9mm Luger	150	9.72	TSJ	870	854	839	824	810
5	AE40SJAP1	40 S&W	205	13.28	TSJ	830	813	797	782	767
5	AE45SJAP1	45 Auto	220	14.26	TSJ	810	795	780	766	752
SYNTECH PCC™										
5	AE9SJPC1	9mm Luger	130	8.42	TSJ	1130	1078	1035	999	967
SYNTECH TRAINING MATCH®										
5	AE9SJ4	9mm Luger	124	8.04	TSJ	1150	1064	1000	949	907
5	AE9SJ3	9mm Luger	147	9.53	TSJ	1000	976	953	933	914
5	AE40SJ2	40 S&W	180	11.66	TSJ	1010	958	914	876	842
5	AE45SJ2	45 Auto	230	14.9	TSJ	890	855	824	794	767
SYNTECH DEFENSE™										
6	S9SJT2	9mm Luger	138	8.94	SHP	1050	989	940	899	862
6	S40SJT2	40 S&W	175	11.34	SHP	1000	950	907	870	836
6	S45SJT2	45 Auto	205	13.28	SHP	970	926	887	853	821
AMERICAN EAGLE										
5	AE5728A	5.7x28MM	40	2.59	TMJ	1655	1514	1387	1275	1179
5	AE25AP	25 Auto	50	3.24	FMJ	760	738	717	697	677
5	AE32AP	32 Auto	71	4.6	FMJ	900	872	846	821	798
5	AE327A	327 Federal Magnum	85	5.51	JSP	1400	1306	1221	1150	1091
6	AE327	327 Federal Magnum	100	6.48	JSP	1500	1408	1324	1248	1181
5	AE380AP	380 Auto	95	6.16	FMJ	980	937	899	865	835
5	AE30SCA	30 Super Carry	100	6.48	FMJ FP	1250	1185	1129	1081	1041
5	AE9DP	9mm Luger	115	7.45	FMJ	1180	1106	1048	1001	961
5	AE9AP	9mm Luger	124	8.04	FMJ	1150	1095	1049	1010	977

ENERGY IN FOOT-POUNDS (TO NEAREST 5 FOOT-POUNDS)					TRAJECTORY SIGHTS .9 INCHES ABOVE BORE LINE				TEST BARREL LENGTH
MUZ	25 YDS.	50 YDS.	75 YDS.	100 YDS.	25 YDS.	50 YDS.	75 YDS.	100 YDS.	INCHES
400	375	360	340	325	⊕	-1.4	-5.3	-11.6	4
552	503	463	431	404	⊕	-0.8	-3.5	-8.2	5
370	355	345	330	320	⊕	-2.2	-7.7	-16.4	5
220	200	180	170	155	⊕	-1.4	-5.3	-12	5
323	288	262	241	224	⊕	-1	-4.1	-9.6	4
576	509	460	428	383	⊕	-1.4	-4.7	-10.1	5
400	377	358	340	324	⊕	-1.4	-5.3	-11.6	4
335	320	305	290	275	⊕	-2.1	-7.4	-16	4-V
365	351	339	327	315	⊕	-2.3	-7.8	-16.6	5
437	388	349	318	293	⊕	-0.6	-3	-7.2	4
211	192	176	163	151	⊕	-1.5	-5.6	-12.5	3.75
326	312	299	288	278	⊕	-0.9	-3.6	-8.3	4
304	282	263	248	234	⊕	-1.2	-4.7	-10.6	4
254	242	231	220	210	⊕	-2.1	-7.2	-15.6	4-V
404	387	371	357	345	⊕	-1.2	-4.4	-10	4
352	344	337	329	322	⊕	-2.3	-7.9	-16.8	5
602	551	510	477	448	⊕	-0.9	-3.7	-8.6	5
252	243	234	226	219	⊕	-2.1	-7.3	-15.6	4
314	301	289	278	267	⊕	-2.4	-8.1	-17.5	4
320	309	297	287	277	⊕	-2.5	-8.6	-18.5	5
369	336	309	288	270	⊕	-1	-4	-9.1	16
364	312	275	248	226	⊕	-1	-4.2	-9.8	4
326	311	297	284	273	⊕	-1.4	-5.2	-11.5	4
408	367	334	307	283	⊕	-1.5	-5.5	-12.4	4
404	374	346	322	300	⊕	-2.1	-7.3	-16	5
338	300	271	248	228	⊕	-1.3	-5.1	-11.5	4
389	350	320	294	272	⊕	-1.5	-5.6	-12.7	4
428	390	358	331	307	⊕	-1.6	-6	-13.4	5
243	204	171	144	124	⊕	0	-1.2	-3.8	4.8
64	60	57	54	51	⊕	-3.1	-10.4	-22.1	2
128	120	113	106	100	⊕	-2	-7	-15.2	4
370	322	281	250	225	⊕	-0.4	-2.2	-5.7	4-V
500	440	389	346	310	⊕	-0.2	-1.6	-4.5	4-V
203	185	170	158	147	⊕	-1.6	-5.8	-13	3.75
347	312	283	260	241	⊕	-0.6	-3	-7.2	4
356	312	280	256	236	⊕	-0.9	-3.7	-8.7	4
364	330	303	281	263	⊕	-0.9	-3.8	-8.8	4

FEDERAL

FEDERAL

USAGE	FEDERAL LOAD NO.	CARTRIDGE	BULLET WEIGHT IN		BULLET STYLE	VELOCITY IN FEET PER SECOND (TO NEAREST 10 FPS)				
			GRAINS	GRAMS		MUZ	25 YDS.	50 YDS.	75 YDS.	100 YDS.
5	AE9FP	9mm Luger	147	9.53	FMJ FP	1000	976	953	933	914
5	AE38S3	38 Super +P	115	7.45	JHP	1130	1067	1016	974	938
5	AE357S2	357 Sig	125	8.1	FMJ	1350	1266	1192	1130	1078
5	AE38K	38 Special	130	8.42	FMJ	890	870	852	834	817
5	AE38B	38 Special	158	10.24	LRN	770	758	745	733	722
5	AE357A	357 Magnum	158	10.24	JSP	1240	1187	1139	1098	1063
5	AE40R2	40 S&W	155	10.04	FMJ	1160	1095	1043	1000	963
5	AE40R3	40 S&W	165	10.69	FMJ	1130	1078	1035	999	967
5	AE40R1	40 S&W	180	11.66	FMJ	1000	972	946	923	901
5	AE10A	10mm Auto	180	11.66	FMJ	1030	998	970	945	921
5	AE44A	44 Rem. Magnum	240	15.55	JHP	1230	1169	1117	1073	1035
5	AE45A	45 Auto	230	14.9	FMJ	1090	1045	1007	974	945
5	AE45LC	45 Colt	225	14.58	JSP	860	844	828	813	799
AMERICAN EAGLE IRT										
5	AE9N1	9mm Luger	124	8.04	TMJ	1120	1070	1028	993	961
5	AE9N2	9mm Luger	147	9.53	TMJ	1000	976	953	933	914
5	AE40N1	40 S&W	180	11.66	TMJ	1000	972	946	923	901
5	AE45N1	45 Auto	230	14.9	TMJ	850	834	819	804	790
AMERICAN EAGLE IRT LEAD FREE										
5	AE380LF1	380 Auto	70	4.54	RHT	1110	1035	977	930	890
5	AE9LF1	9mm Luger	70	4.54	RHT	1625	1457	1312	1190	1096
5	AE38LF1	38 Special	100	6.48	RHT	960	935	913	892	872
5	AE40LF1	40 S&W	120	7.78	RHT	1330	1199	1099	1026	970
5	AE45LF1	45 Auto	137	8.88	RHT	1200	1136	1083	1039	1002
FUSION										
2	F357FS1	357 Magnum	158	10.24	Fusion SP	1240	1187	1139	1098	1063
2	F10FS1	10mm Auto	200	12.96	Fusion SP	1200	1147	1102	1063	1030
2	F41FS1	41 Rem. Magnum	210	13.61	Fusion SP	1230	1172	1122	1079	1043
2	F44FS1	44 Rem. Magnum	240	15.55	Fusion SP	1290	1221	1162	1110	1067
2	F454FS1	454 Casull	260	16.85	Fusion SP	1350	1266	1192	1130	1078
2	F460FS1	460 S&W	260	16.85	Fusion SP	1600	1495	1397	1309	1229
2	F500FS2	500 S&W	325	21.06	Fusion SP	1450	1357	1272	1198	1134
2	F50AEFS1	50 Action Express	300	19.44	Fusion SP	1550	1451	1361	1278	1205

ENERGY IN FOOT-POUNDS (TO NEAREST 5 FOOT-POUNDS)					TRAJECTORY SIGHTS .9 INCHES ABOVE BORE LINE				TEST BARREL LENGTH
MUZ	25 YDS.	50 YDS.	75 YDS.	100 YDS.	25 YDS.	50 YDS.	75 YDS.	100 YDS.	INCHES
326	311	297	284	273	⊕	-1.4	-5.2	-11.5	4
326	290	264	242	225	⊕	-1	-4.1	-9.5	5
506	445	395	354	323	⊕	-0.5	-2.4	-6.1	4
229	219	209	201	193	⊕	-2	-7	-15.1	4-V
208	201	195	189	183	⊕	-2.9	-9.8	-20.7	4-V
539	494	455	423	396	⊕	-0.6	-3	-7.1	4-V
463	413	374	344	319	⊕	-0.9	-3.8	-8.9	4
468	426	392	365	342	⊕	-1	-4	-9.1	4
400	377	358	340	324	⊕	-1.4	-5.3	-11.6	4
424	398	376	357	339	⊕	-1.3	-4.9	-10.9	5
806	729	665	613	571	⊕	-0.7	-3.1	-7.4	4-V
488	449	417	390	367	⊕	-2	-6.9	-15	5
369	356	343	330	319	⊕	-2.2	-7.5	-16.1	4
345	315	291	271	255	⊕	-1	-4	-9.3	4
326	311	297	284	273	⊕	-1.4	-5.2	-11.5	4
400	377	358	340	324	Ø	1.4	5.3	11.6	4
369	355	343	330	319	⊕	-2.2	-7.7	-16.4	5
191	166	148	135	123	⊕	-1.1	-4.5	-10.4	3.75
410	330	268	220	187	⊕	-0.1	-1.5	-4.4	4
205	194	185	177	169	⊕	-1.6	-5.8	-12.7	4-V
471	383	322	280	251	⊕	-0.6	-3	-7.4	4
438	393	357	329	306	⊕	-0.8	-3.4	-8	5
539	494	455	423	396	⊕	-0.6	-3	-7.1	4-V
639	585	539	502	471	⊕	-0.8	-3.3	-7.7	5
705	641	587	543	507	⊕	-0.7	-3.1	-7.3	4-V
887	795	719	657	607	⊕	-0.6	-2.7	-6.7	4-V
1052	925	821	737	671	⊕	-0.5	-2.4	-6.1	5.7-V
1478	1289	1126	989	872	⊕	-0.1	-1.3	-3.7	8.4-V
1517	1329	1168	1035	929	⊕	-0.3	-1.9	-5	8.4-V
1600	1402	1233	1088	967	⊕	-0.1	-1.5	-4.1	6

FEDERAL

FEDERAL

WATERFOWL

LOAD NO.	GAUGE	SHELL LENGTH	VELOCITY	PAYLOAD	SHOT
FEDERAL PREMIUM BLACK CLOUD® FS STEEL					
PWBX107	10	3-1/2	1375	1-5/8	BB, 2
PWBX134	12	3-1/2	1500	1-1/2	BBB, BB, 1, 2, 3, 4
PWBX142	12	3	1450	1-1/4	BBB, BB, 1, 2, 3, 4
PWBX147	12	2-3/4	1500	1-1/8	2, 3, 4
PWBX209	20	3	1350	1	1, 2, 3, 4
PWBX285	28	3	1400	3/4	3, 4
FEDERAL PREMIUM BLACK CLOUD TSS					
PWBTSSX142 7BB	12	3	1450	1-1/4	BB FS Steel/7 TSS
PWBTSSX142 39	12	3	1450	1-1/4	3 FS Steel/9 TSS
PWBTSSX209 39	20	3	1350	1	3 FS Steel/9 TSS
FEDERAL PREMIUM BLACK CLOUD FS STEEL HIGH VELOCITY					
PWBXH143	12	3	1635	1-1/8	BB, 1, 2, 3, 4
SPEED·SHOK® WATERFOWL					
WF107	10	3-1/2	1450	1-1/2	T, BBB, BB, 2
WF133	12	3-1/2	1550	1-3/8	T, BBB, BB, 1, 2, 3, 4
WF134	12	3-1/2	1500	1-1/2	T, BBB, BB, 1, 2
WF143	12	3	1550	1-1/8	T, BBB, BB, 1, 2, 3, 4,
WF142	12	3	1450	1-1/4	T, BBB, BB, 1, 2, 3, 4
WF145	12	2-3/4	1500	1-1/8	BB, 2, 3, 4
WF168	16	2-3/4	1350	15/16	2, 4
WF209	20	3	1550	7/8	1, 2, 3, 4
WF208	20	2-3/4	1425	3/4	4, 6, 7
WF283	28	2-3/4	1350	5/8	6
WF413	0.41	3	1400	3/8	6

BUCKSHOT

LOAD NO.	GAUGE	SHELL LENGTH	VELOCITY	PAYLOAD
FEDERAL PREMIUM BUCKSHOT WITH FLITECONTROL® WAD				
PFC157 00	12	3	1325	12 Pellets - 00 Buck
PFC154 00	12	2-3/4	1325	9 Pellets - 00 Buck
FEDERAL PREMIUM BUCKSHOT				
P108F 00	10	3-1/2	1100	18 Pellets - 00 Buck
P135F 00	12	3-1/2	1100	18 Pellets - 00 Buck
P158 4B	12	3	1100	41 Pellets - 4 Buck
P158 00	12	3	1100	15 Pellets - 00 Buck

BUCKSHOT

LOAD NO.	GAUGE	SHELL LENGTH	VELOCITY	PAYLOAD
P158 000	12	3	1225	10 Pellets - 000 Buck
P154 00	12	2-3/4	1325	9 Pellets - 00 Buck
P154 1B	12	2-3/4	1325	16 Pellets - 1 Buck
P156 00	12	2-3/4	1290	12 Pellets - 00 Buck
P258 2B	20	3	1100	18 Pellets - 2 Buck
P256 3B	20	2-3/4	1175	20 Pellets - 3 Buck
POWER·SHOK® BUCKSHOT				
F131 00	12	3	1210	15 Pellets - 00 Buck
F131 4B	12	3	1210	41 Pellets - 4 Buck
F127 000	12	2-3/4	1325	8 Pellets - 000 Buck
F127 00	12	2-3/4	1325	9 Pellets - 00 Buck
F127 1B	12	2-3/4	1325	16 Pellets - 1 Buck
F127 4B	12	2-3/4	1325	27 Pellets - 4 Buck
F130 00	12	2-3/4	1290	12 Pellets - 00 Buck
F164 1B	16	2-3/4	1225	12 Pellets - 1 Buck
F207 2B	20	3	1100	18 Pellets - 2 Buck
F203 3B	20	2-3/4	1200	20 Pellets - 3 Buck
POWER·SHOK BUCKSHOT - LOW RECOIL				
H132 00	12	2-3/4	1140	9 Pellets - 00 Buck
PERSONAL DEFENSE SHOTSHELL WITH FLITECONTROL				
PD132	12	2-3/4	1145	9 Pellets - 00 Buck
FORCE X2 PERSONAL DEFENSE SHOTSHELL				
PD12FX2 00	12	2-3/4	1245	9 Pellet FX2 00 Buckshot
FORCE X2 PERSONAL DEFENSE SHORTY SHOTSHELL				
PD129FX2 00	12	1-3/4	1245	6 Pellet FX2 00 Buckshot
PERSONAL DEFENSE SHOTSHELL				
PD156	12	2-3/4	1100	34 Pellets - 4 Buck
PD256	20	2-3/4	1100	24 Pellets - 4 Buck
PERSONAL DEFENSE .410 HANDGUN				
PD413JGE 000		3	775	5 pellets–000 Buck
PD413JGE 4B		3	950	9 pellets–4 Buck
PD412JGE 000		2-1/2	850	4 pellets - 000 Buck
PD412JGE 4		2-1/2	950	7/16 ounce - 4 Shot

FEDERAL

FEDERAL

TURKEY

LOAD NO.	GAUGE	SHELL LENGTH	VELOCITY	PAYLOAD	SHOT
FEDERAL PREMIUM 3RD DEGREE® WITH FLITECONTROL FLEX® WAD					
PTDX139 567	12	3-1/2	1250	2	5/6/07
PTDX157 567	12	3	1250	1-3/4	5/6/07
PTDX258 567	20	3	1100	1-1/2	5/6/07
FEDERAL PREMIUM GRAND SLAM® WITH FLITECONTROL FLEX WAD					
PFCX101F	10	3-1/2	1200	2	4, 5
PFCX139F	12	3-1/2	1200	2	4, 5, 6
PFCX157F	12	3	1200	1-3/4	4, 5, 6
PFCX156F	12	2-3/4	1200	1-1/2	5
PFCX258F	20	3	1185	15/16	5
FEDERAL PREMIUM HEAVYWEIGHT® TSS WITH FLITECONTROL FLEX WAD					
PTSSX195F	12	3-1/2	1000	2-1/2	9-Jul
PTSSX191F	12	3-1/2	1200	2-1/4	7, 9
PTSSX197F	12	3	1150	2	9-Jul
PTSSX193F	12	3	1200	1-3/4	7, 9
PTSSX295F	20	3	1000	1-5/8	9-Jul
PTSSX259F	20	3	1100	1-1/2	7, 9
PTSSX257F	20	2-3/4	1000	1-1/8	9
PTSS419F	0.41	3	1100	1-3/16	9

UPLAND & WATERFOWL

LOAD NO.	GAUGE	SHELL LENGTH	VELOCITY	PAYLOAD	SHOT
FEDERAL PREMIUM HEVI-BISMUTH					
PHBX138	12	3	1450	1-3/8	3, 4, 5
PHBX144	12	2-3/4	1350	1-1/4	3, 4, 5
PHBX244	20	3	1350	1-1/8	3, 4, 5

UPLAND

LOAD NO.	GAUGE	SHELL LENGTH	VELOCITY	PAYLOAD	SHOT
FEDERAL PREMIUM HI-BIRD®					
HVF12H	12	2-3/4	1330	1-1/4	5, 6, 7.5
HVF12	12	2-3/4	1275	1-1/8	7.5, 8
FEDERAL PREMIUM HI-BIRD FIBER WAD					
HVF12HW	12	2-3/4	1330	1-1/4	5
FEDERAL PREMIUM UPLAND MAGNUM					
P156	12	2-3/4	1315	1-1/2	4, 6
P165	16	2-3/4	1260	1-1/4	4, 6
P258	20	3	1300	1-1/4	5, 6
FEDERAL PREMIUM UPLAND HIGH VELOCITY					
P129	12	3	1350	1-5/8	4, 5, 6
P128	12	2-3/4	1500	1-1/8	4, 6, 7.5
P138	12	2-3/4	1500	1-3/8	4, 5, 6
P283	28	2-3/4	1295	3/4	6, 7.5, 8
FEDERAL PREMIUM UPLAND PHEASANTS FOREVER HIGH VELOCITY					
PF154	12	2-3/4	1500	1-1/4	4, 5, 6, 7.5

UPLAND

LOAD NO.	GAUGE	SHELL LENGTH	VELOCITY	PAYLOAD	SHOT
PF163	16	2-3/4	1425	1-1/8	4, 5, 6
PF204	20	2-3/4	1350	1	4, 5, 6, 7.5
FEDERAL PREMIUM PRAIRIE STORM® FS LEAD					
PFX129FS	12	3	1350	1-5/8	4, 5, 6
PFX154FS	12	2-3/4	1500	1-1/4	4, 5, 6
PFX164FS	16	2-3/4	1425	1-1/8	4, 5, 6
PFX258FS	20	3	1300	1-1/4	4, 5, 6
PFX204FS	20	2-3/4	1350	1	4, 5, 6
PFX289FS	28	2-3/4	1300	13/16	6
FEDERAL PREMIUM PRAIRIE STORM FS STEEL					
PFSX143FS	12	3	1600	1-1/8	3, 4
PFSX147FS	12	2-3/4	1500	1-1/8	3, 4
PFSX207FS	20	3	1500	7/8	3, 4
FEDERAL PREMIUM PAPER FLYER					
P154	12	2-3/4	1330	1-1/4	7.5, 8
Upland Steel					
USH122	12	2-3/4	1375	1	6, 7.5
USH12	12	2-3/4	1400	1-1/8	6, 7.5
USH20	20	2-3/4	1500	3/4	6, 7.5
USH28	28	2-3/4	1350	5/8	6, 7.5
USH410	.410	3	1400	3/8	6, 7.5
UPLAND STEEL WITH PAPER WAD					
USH122W	12	2-3/4	1330	1	7.5
GAME LOAD – HI-BRASS					
H126	12	2-3/4	1330	1-1/4	4, 5, 6, 7.5
H163	16	2-3/4	1295	1-1/8	4, 6, 7.5
H204	20	2-3/4	1220	1	4, 5, 6, 7.5
H258	20	3	1300	1-1/4	5, 6
N124	24	2-1/2	1280	11/16	8
H289	28	2-3/4	1220	1	5, 6, 7.5
N132	32	2-1/2	1260	1/2	8
H413	.410	3	1135	11/16	4, 5, 6, 7.5
H412	.410	2-1/2	1200	1/2	6, 7.5
GAME LOAD – HEAVY FIELD					
H123	12	2-3/4	1255	1-1/8	4, 6, 7.5, 8
H125	12	2-3/4	1220	1-1/4	4, 5, 6, 7.5
H202	20	2-3/4	1165	1	6, 7.5, 8
GAME LOAD					
H121	12	2-3/4	1290	1	6, 7.5, 8
H160	16	2-3/4	1165	1	6, 7.5, 8
H200	20	2-3/4	1210	7/8	6, 7.5, 8

FEDERAL

FEDERAL PREMIUM SABOT SLUG

USAGE	FEDERAL LOAD NO.	GAUGE	SHELL LENGTH		SLUG TYPE	SLUG WEIGHT	
			INCHES	MM		OUNCES	GRAINS

FEDERAL PREMIUM TROPHY® COPPER (FULLY RIFLED SLUG BARREL)

USAGE	LOAD NO.	GAUGE	INCHES	MM	SLUG TYPE	OUNCES	GRAINS
2	P151 TC	12	3	76	Trophy Copper Slug	0.69	300
2	P152 TC	12	2¾	70	Trophy Copper Slug	0.69	300
2	P209 TC	20	3	76	Trophy Copper Slug	0.63	275
2	P208 TC	20	2¾	70	Trophy Copper Slug	0.63	275

Note: For optimum slug performance, we recommend matching the chamber length to the slug length. For example, use a 3-inch slug in a 3-inch chamber.

FEDERAL PREMIUM SMOOTHBORE SLUG

USAGE	FEDERAL LOAD NO.	GAUGE	SHELL LENGTH		SLUG TYPE	SLUG WEIGHT	
			INCHES	MM		OUNCES	GRAINS

FEDERAL PREMIUM TRUBALL® RIFLED SLUGS (SMOOTHBORE BARREL)

USAGE	LOAD NO.	GAUGE	INCHES	MM	SLUG TYPE	OUNCES	GRAINS
2	PB127 LRS*	12	2¾	70	TruBall Rifled Slug	1	438
2	PB127 RS	12	2¾	70	TruBall Rifled Slug	1	438
2	PB131 RS	12	3	76	TruBall Rifled Slug	1	438
2	PB203 RS	20	2¾	70	TruBall Rifled Slug	¾	328
2	PB209 RS	20	3	76	TruBall Rifled Slug	¾	328

FEDERAL PREMIUM TRUBALL DEEP PENETRATOR RIFLED SLUGS (Smoothbore Barrel)

USAGE	LOAD NO.	GAUGE	INCHES	MM	SLUG TYPE	OUNCES	GRAINS
3	PB127 DPRS	12	2¾	70	TruBall Rifled Slug	1	438

* Low-recoil load

FEDERAL SLUG

USAGE	FEDERAL LOAD NO.	GAUGE	SHELL LENGTH		SLUG TYPE	SLUG WEIGHT	
			INCHES	MM		OUNCES	GRAINS

FEDERAL POWER·SHOK® SABOT SLUG (FULLY RIFLED SLUG BARREL)

USAGE	LOAD NO.	GAUGE	INCHES	MM	SLUG TYPE	OUNCES	GRAINS
2	F127 SS2	12	2-3/4	70	Sabot HP	1	438
2	F203 SS2	20	2-3/4	70	Sabot HP	7/8	383

FEDERAL POWER·SHOK RIFLED SLUG (SMOOTHBORE BARREL)

USAGE	LOAD NO.	GAUGE	INCHES	MM	SLUG TYPE	OUNCES	GRAINS
2	F103F RS	10	3-1/2	89	HP	1-3/4	766
2	F131 RS	12	3	76	HP	1-1/4	547
2	F127 RS	12	2-3/4	70	HP	1	438
2	F130 RS	12	2-3/4	70	HP	1-1/4	547
2	F164 RS	16	2-3/4	70	HP	4/5	350
2	F203 RS	20	2-3/4	70	HP	3/4	328
2	F412 RS	0.41	2-1/2	64	HP	1/4	109

FEDERAL

VELOCITY IN FEET PER SECOND (TO NEAREST 10 FPS)						ENERGY IN FOOT-POUNDS (TO NEAREST FOOT-POUND)						HEIGHT OF SLUG TRAJECTORY IN INCHES ABOVE OR BELOW LINE OF SIGHT IF ZEROED AT ⊕ YARDS. SIGHTS .5 INCHES ABOVE BORE LINE.					TEST BARREL LENGTH
MUZ	25 YDS.	50 YDS.	100 YDS.	150 YDS.	200 YDS.	MUZ	25 YDS.	50 YDS.	100 YDS.	150 YDS.	200 YDS.	25 YDS.	50 YDS.	100 YDS.	150 YDS.	200 YDS.	INCHES
2000	1900	1800	1620	1450	1310	2665	2400	2160	1745	1400	1135	1.3	2.6	2.9	⊕	-7.1	30
1900	1800	1710	1530	1380	1240	2405	2165	1945	1565	1260	1030	1.7	2.9	3.3	⊕	-7.9	30
1900	1790	1690	1500	1340	1200	2205	1965	1750	1380	1090	875	1.6	3	3.4	⊕	-8.3	30
1700	1600	1510	1340	1200	-	1765	1570	1390	1100	885	-	1	1.7	⊕	-6.5	-	30

VELOCITY IN FEET PER SECOND (TO NEAREST 10 FPS)				ENERGY IN FOOT-POUNDS (TO NEAREST FOOT-POUND)				HEIGHT OF SLUG TRAJECTORY IN INCHES ABOVE OR BELOW LINE OF SIGHT IF ZEROED AT ⊕ YARDS. SIGHTS .5 INCHES ABOVE BORE LINE.			TEST BARREL LENGTH
MUZ	25 YDS.	50 YDS.	100 YDS.	MUZ	25 YDS.	50 YDS.	100 YDS.	25 YDS.	50 YDS.	100 YDS.	INCHES
1300	1150	1040	910	1640	1275	1055	805	0.6	⊕	-7.4	30
1600	1370	1180	970	2485	1810	1355	915	0.3	⊕	-5.7	30
1700	1450	1240	1000	2805	2040	1505	970	0.3	⊕	-5.1	30
1600	1390	1220	1010	1865	1410	1090	745	0.3	⊕	-5.3	30
1700	1480	1290	1040	2105	1595	1215	795	0.3	⊕	-4.8	30
1350	1200	1090	950	1775	1400	1150	875	0.5	⊕	-6.8	30

VELOCITY IN FEET PER SECOND (TO NEAREST 10 FPS)						ENERGY IN FOOT-POUNDS (TO NEAREST FOOT-POUND)						HEIGHT OF SLUG TRAJECTORY IN INCHES ABOVE OR BELOW LINE OF SIGHT IF ZEROED AT ⊕ YARDS. SIGHTS .5 INCHES ABOVE BORE LINE.					TEST BARREL LENGTH
MUZ	25 YDS.	50 YDS.	75 YDS.	100 YDS.	125 YDS.	MUZ	25 YDS.	50 YDS.	75 YDS.	100 YDS.	125 YDS.	25 YDS.	50 YDS.	75 YDS.	100 YDS.	125 YDS.	INCHES
1500	1420	1350	1280	1220	1170	2190	1970	1775	1600	1455	1330	1.4	2.1	1.7	⊕	-3.2	30
1450	1350	1260	1180	1120	1070	1785	1550	1350	1190	1065	965	1.6	2.5	2	⊕	-3.8	30
1280	1170	1090	1020	970	930	2785	2325	2000	1770	1600	1465	0.5	⊕	-2.4	-6.8	-13.6	32
1600	1460	1330	1220	1130	1060	3110	2570	2140	1800	1545	1360	0.3	⊕	-1.5	-4.5	-9.1	30
1610	1470	1340	1230	1140	1070	2520	2090	1745	1470	1260	1110	0.3	⊕	-1.5	-4.4	-8.9	30
1520	1390	1270	1170	1090	1030	2805	2330	1950	1660	1445	1290	0.3	⊕	-1.7	-4.9	-10	30
1600	1380	1210	1080	1000	930	1990	1490	1135	910	770	675	0.3	⊕	-1.8	-5.4	-11.2	28
1600	1430	1280	1160	1070	1000	1865	1480	1190	975	830	730	0.3	⊕	-1.6	-4.8	-10	26
1775	1540	1340	1180	1060	980	760	575	430	335	270	235	0.2	⊕	-1.4	-4.4	-9.3	26

FEDERAL

FEDERAL

TARGET

LOAD NO.	GAUGE	SHELL LENGTH	VELOCITY	DRAM	PAYLOAD	SHOT
		FEDERAL PREMIUM HIGH OVER ALL™				
HOA1224H	12	2-3/4	1335	3-1/4	24 gram	7.5, 9
HOA12L	12	2-3/4	1145	2-3/4	8-Nov	7.5, 8, 9
HOA12H	12	2-3/4	1200	3	8-Nov	7.5, 8
HOA12HC	12	2-3/4	1250	HDCP	8-Nov	7.5, 8
HOA12L1	12	2-3/4	1200	2-3/4	1	7.5, 8
HOA12H1	12	2-3/4	1250	3	1	7.5, 8
HOA12HC1	12	2-3/4	1290	3-1/4	1	7.5, 8, 8.5
HOA20	20	2-3/4	1200	2-1/2	7/8	7.5, 8
HOA20H	20	2-3/4	1275	3	7/8	7.5, 8
HOA28	28	2-3/4	1250	2	¾	8, 8.5, 9
HOA28H	28	2-3/4	1300	2-1/4	¾	8, 9
HOA410	0.41	2-1/2	1200	MAX	½	8, 8.5, 9
HOA410H	0.41	2-1/2	1275	MAX	½	8.5, 9
		FEDERAL PREMIUM GOLD MEDAL PAPER				
GMT111	12	2-3/4	1290	3-1/4	1	7.5, 8
GMT175	12	2-3/4	1180	2-3/4	1	8
GMT117	12	2-3/4	1145	2-3/4	8-Nov	7.5, 8
GMT118	12	2-3/4	1200	3	8-Nov	7.5, 8
GMT171	12	2-3/4	1235	HDCP	8-Nov	7.5, 8

CENTERFIRE RIFLE BALLISTICS

CARTRIDGE	INDEX/ EDI NO.	RAMAC	WT (GR)	BULLET STYLE	PRIMER NO.	SIGHT HEIGHT (INCHES)	ZERO (YARDS)
17 Remington Fireball	PRA17FB	29165	20	AccuTip-V	7½	1.5	200
	L17FBV	28472	25	Jacketed Hollow Point	7½	1.5	200
17 Remington	PRA17RA	29162	20	AccuTip-V	7½	1.5	200
	R17R2	28460	25	Hollow Point	7½	1.5	200
204 Ruger	PRA204A	29218	32	AccuTip-V	7½	1.5	200
	PRA204B	29220	40	AccuTip-V Boat Tail	7½	1.5	200
22 Hornet	PRA22HNA	29154	35	AccuTip-V	6½	1.5	100
	R22HN1	28376	45	Pointed Soft Point	6½	1.5	100
	R22HN2	28378	45	Hollow Point	6½	1.5	100
220 Swift	R220S1	21297	50	Pointed Soft Point	9½	1.5	200
221 Remington Fireball	PRA221FB	29172	50	AccuTip-V Boat Tail	7½	1.5	200
222 Remington	R222R1	21303	50	Pointed Soft Point	7½	1.5	200
	PRA222RB	29174	50	AccuTip-V Boat Tail	7½	1.5	200
223 Remington	L223R3	23711	55	Full Metal Jacket	7½	1.5	200
	L223R7	23748	45	Jacketed Hollow Point	7½	1.5	200
	L223R8	23812	50	Jacketed Hollow Point	7½	1.5	200
	PRA223RB	29184	50	AccuTip-V Boat Tail	7½	1.5	200
	PRA223RC	29192	55	AccuTip-V	7½	1.5	200
	R223R8	22111	62	Core-Lokt Ultra Bonded PSP	7½	2.5	200
	R223R1	28399	55	Pointed Soft Point	7½	1.5	200
	RD223R4	22107	62	Core-Lokt Ultra Bonded PSP	7½	2.5	200
	PRH223R4	28919	62	Core-Lokt Ultra Bonded PSP	7½	1.5	200
	R223R6	22106	62	Open Tip Match	7½	2.5	200
	RM223R1	27680	69	MatchKing BTHP ††††	7½	2.5	200

TARGET

LOAD NO.	GAUGE	SHELL LENGTH	VELOCITY	PAYLOAD	SHOT
			TOP GUN TARGET		
TG12EL	12	2-3/4	1200	7/8	8
TG121	12	2-3/4	1180	1	7.5, 8
TGSF128	12	2-3/4	1330	1	7.5, 8
TGSH12	12	2-3/4	1300	1	7.5, 8
TGS128	12	2-3/4	1250	1	7.5, 8
TG12	12	2-3/4	1200	1-1/8	7.5, 8
TGL12	12	2-3/4	1145	1-1/8	7.5, 8, 9
TGL12US	12	2-3/4	1145	1-1/8	8
TGL12P	12	2-3/4	1145	1-1/8	8
TG20	20	2-3/4	1210	7/8	7.5, 8, 9
TGS224	20	2-3/4	1250	7/8	7.5, 8
TGS2821	28	2-3/4	1330	3/4	7.5, 8, 9
TGS41214	.410	2-1/2	1330	1/2	7.5, 8, 9
		TOP GUN® WITH PAPER WAD			
TG12W	12	2-3/4	1200	1-1/8	7.5, 8
		TOP GUN TARGET – STEEL WITH PAPER WAD			
TG12WS1	12	2-3/4	1250	1	7.5
TG12WS2	12	2-3/4	1300	1	7.5
		SHORTY SHOTSHELLS			
SH129 4B	12	1-3/4	1200	15 Pellet	4 Buck
SH129 RS	12	1-3/4	1200	1	Rifled slug
SH129 8	12	1-3/4	1145	15/16	8

FEDERAL

VELOCITY (FPS)						ENERGY (FT-LB)						TRAJECTORY (INCHES)						
MUZ	100	200	300	400	500	MUZ	100	200	300	400	500	MUZ	100	200	300	400	500	BC
4000	3380	2840	2360	1930	1555	710	507	358	247	165	107	-1.5	0.8	0.0	-5.1	-16.6	-37.6	0.185
3850	3273	2767	2313	1905	1547	823	595	425	297	201	133	-1.5	0.9	0.0	-5.5	-17.6	-39.3	0.193
4250	3594	3028	2529	2081	1684	802	574	407	284	192	126	-1.5	0.6	0.0	-4.4	-14.4	-32.5	0.185
4040	3420	2881	2402	1972	1594	906	649	461	320	216	141	-1.5	0.8	0.0	-5.0	-16.1	-36.3	0.187
4225	3645	3137	2683	2272	1899	1268	944	699	512	367	256	-1.5	0.6	0.0	-4.1	-13.1	-29.0	0.210
3900	3482	3103	2755	2433	2133	1351	1077	855	674	526	404	-1.5	0.7	0.0	-4.3	-13.2	-28.1	0.275
3100	2271	1590	1126	–	–	747	401	197	99	–	–	-1.5	0.0	-5.6	-25.5	–	–	0.109
2690	2044	1505	1130	–	–	723	417	226	128	–	–	-1.5	0.0	-7.1	-30.0	–	–	0.130
2690	2044	1505	1130	–	–	723	417	226	128	–	–	-1.5	0.0	-7.1	-30.0	–	–	0.130
3780	3158	2617	2135	1710	1357	1586	1107	760	506	325	204	-1.5	1.0	0.0	-6.2	-20.1	-46.1	0.175
2995	2605	2246	1917	1621	1368	996	753	560	408	292	208	-1.5	1.8	0.0	-8.8	-27.1	-58.8	0.238
3140	2601	2121	1697	1347	1105	1094	751	499	320	202	136	-1.5	1.9	0.0	-9.7	-31.8	-73.1	0.175
3140	2743	2380	2045	1740	1471	1094	835	629	464	336	240	-1.5	1.6	0.0	-7.8	-23.9	-51.7	0.242
3240	2759	2325	1933	1586	1300	1282	929	660	456	307	206	-1.5	1.6	0.0	-8.1	-25.6	-57.1	0.202
3550	2953	2430	1963	1559	1241	1259	871	590	385	243	154	-1.5	1.3	0.0	-7.3	-23.7	-54.7	0.173
3425	2899	2430	2007	1633	1324	1302	933	655	447	296	195	-1.5	1.3	0.0	-7.3	-23.4	-52.7	0.192
3410	2989	2605	2252	1928	1635	1291	992	753	563	413	297	-1.5	1.2	0.0	-6.4	-19.7	-42.4	0.242
3240	2854	2500	2172	1871	1598	1282	995	763	576	427	312	-1.5	1.4	0.0	-7.0	-21.4	-45.9	0.255
3100	2700	2328	1986	1678	1411	1323	1004	746	543	388	274	-2.5	1.2	0.0	-7.6	-24.2	-53.2	0.234
3240	2747	2304	1904	1554	1270	1282	921	648	443	295	197	-1.5	1.6	0.0	-8.2	-26.2	-58.7	0.197
3100	2700	2328	1986	1678	1411	1323	1004	746	543	388	274	-2.5	1.17	0.0	-7.6	-24.2	-53.2	0.234
3260	2841	2458	2105	1784	1501	1465	1112	832	610	438	310	-1.5	1.4	0.0	-7.2	-22.4	-48.6	0.234
3025	2572	2162	1792	1471	1218	1260	911	644	442	298	204	-2.5	1.4	0.0	-8.9	-28.9	-65.0	0.205
3000	2720	2456	2208	1974	1756	1379	1133	924	747	597	472	-2.5	1.1	0.0	-6.9	-21.0	-44.0	0.336

REMINGTON

CENTERFIRE RIFLE BALLISTICS

CARTRIDGE	INDEX/ EDI NO.	RAMAC	WT (GR)	BULLET STYLE	PRIMER NO.	SIGHT HEIGHT (INCHES)	ZERO (YARDS)
	RM223R3	27686	77	MatchKing BTHP †††	7½	2.5	200
22-250 Remington	L22503	23750	45	Jacketed Hollow Point	9½	1.5	200
	L22504	23813	50	Jacketed Hollow Point	9½	1.5	200
	PRA2250RB	29186	50	AccuTip-V Boat Tail	9½	1.5	200
	HTP2250R1	27726	50	Barnes TSX FB	9½	1.5	200
	R22501	21311	55	Pointed Soft Point	9½	1.5	200
224 Valkyrie	L224VLK	21203	75	Full Metal Jacket	7½	1.5	100
	RM224VLK	21201	90	MatchKing OTM	7½	1.5	100
	PRA224VLK	21202	60	AccuTip-V	7½	1.5	100
6mm Remington	R6MM4	29051	100	Core-Lokt Pointed Soft Point	9½	1.5	200
6mm Creedmoor	RM6CRD	20001	107	Matchking OTM	9½	1.5	200
	R6CM01	29049	100	Core-Lokt Pointed Soft Point	9½	1.5	200
243 Win	PRA243WB	29194	75	AccuTip-V Boat Tail	9½	1.5	200
	R243W1	27800	80	Pointed Soft Point	9½	1.5	200
	PRSC243WA	29320	90	Swift Scirocco Bonded	9½	1.5	200
	RT243WA	29015	95	Core-Lokt Tipped	9½	1.5	200
	PRH243WC	28923	100	Core-Lokt Ultra Bonded PSP	9½	1.5	200
	R243W3	27802	100	Core-Lokt Pointed Soft Point	9½	1.5	200
25-06 Remington	R25062	21507	100	Core-Lokt Pointed Soft Point	9½	1.5	200
	R25063	21515	120	Core-Lokt Pointed Soft Point	9½	1.5	200
25-20 Win	R25202	28364	86	Core-Lokt Pointed Soft Point	6½	0.9	100
250 Savage	R250SV	29077	100	Core-Lokt Pointed Soft Point	9½	1.5	200
257 Roberts	R257	28335	117	Core-Lokt Pointed Soft Point	9½	1.5	200
6.5 Creedmoor	PRSC65CR	29344	130	Swift Scirocco Bonded	9½	1.5	200
	R65CR2	27671	140	BTHP	9½	1.5	200
	R65CR1	27657	140	Core-Lokt Pointed Soft Point	9½	1.5	200
	RT65CR1	29017	129	Core-Lokt Tipped	9½	1.5	200
	RM65CRD	27661	140	Matchking OTM	9½	1.5	200
	RLR65CR	R21341	140	Speer Impact	9½	1.5	200
6.5x55 Swedish	R65SWE1	29140	140	Core-Lokt Pointed Soft Point	9½	1.5	200
6.5 Grendel	R65GR1	27649	120	BTHP	9½	1.5	100
	RM65GDL	21205	130	Berger OTM	9½	1.5	100
6.5 PRC	RM65PRC01	27673	140	Berger OTM			
260 Remington	R260R1	21292	140	Core-Lokt Pointed Soft Point	9½	1.5	200
	RM260R1	26852	142	Matchking OTM	9½	1.5	200
264 Win Mag	R264W2	29493	140	Core-Lokt Pointed Soft Point	9½ M	1.5	200
6.8 Remington SPC	L68R2	24035	115	Full Metal Jacket	9½	2.5	200
	RM68R1	27676	115	MatchKing BTHP	9½	2.5	200
270 Win	RT270WA	29019	130	Core-Lokt Tipped	9½	1.5	200
	R270W1	21325	100	Core-Lokt Pointed Soft Point	9½	1.5	200
	R270W2	27808	130	Core-Lokt Pointed Soft Point	9½	1.5	200
	PRSC270WA	29322	130	Swift Scirocco Bonded	9½	1.5	200
	PRH270WB	28955	140	Core-Lokt Ultra Bonded PSP	9½	1.5	200
	R270W4	27810	150	Core-Lokt Soft Point	9½	1.5	200
	RLR270W	R21342	150	Speer Impact	9½	1.5	200
270 WSM	R270WSM1	28940	130	Core-Lokt Pointed Soft Point	9½ M	1.5	200
280 Remington	RT280RA	29020	140	Core-Lokt Tipped	9½	1.5	200
	R280R3	28313	140	Core-Lokt Pointed Soft Point	9½	1.5	200
	R280R1	29069	150	Core-Lokt Pointed Soft Point	9½	1.5	200
	R280R2	28417	165	Core-Lokt Soft Point	9½	1.5	200
7mm-08 Remington	R7M082	28827	120	Hollow Point	9½	1.5	200

VELOCITY (FPS)						ENERGY (FT-LB)						TRAJECTORY (INCHES)						BC
MUZ	100	200	300	400	500	MUZ	100	200	300	400	500	MUZ	100	200	300	400	500	BC
2790	2539	2304	2081	1871	1676	1329	1102	907	740	598	480	-2.5	1.5	0.0	-8.0	-24.1	-50.2	0.362
4000	3340	2770	2267	1820	1441	1598	1114	767	513	331	207	-1.5	0.8	0.0	-5.4	-17.7	-40.7	0.173
3820	3245	2739	2286	1878	1523	1620	1169	833	580	392	258	-1.5	0.9	0.0	-5.6	-18.0	-40.3	0.192
3800	3339	2925	2546	2198	1878	1603	1238	949	720	536	392	-1.5	0.8	0.0	-4.9	-15.2	-32.8	0.242
3830	3267	2771	2326	1924	1570	1629	1185	853	601	411	274	-1.5	0.9	0.0	-5.5	-17.5	-39.0	0.197
3680	3136	2654	2220	1829	1490	1654	1201	860	602	409	271	-1.5	1.0	0.0	-6.0	-19.2	-42.9	0.197
3000	2763	2539	2325	2122	1929	1499	1272	1073	900	750	619	-1.5	0.0	-3.1	-11.5	--	--	0.400
2700	2542	2388	2241	2098	1961	1457	1291	1140	1003	880	768	-1.5	0.0	-3.8	-13.9	--	--	0.274
3300	2923	2577	2255	1958	1687	1451	1138	884	678	511	379	-1.5	0.0	-2.6	-10.4	--	--	0.265
3100	2829	2574	2333	2104	1890	2133	1777	1471	1208	983	793	-1.5	1.4	0.0	-6.7	-19.8	-40.8	0.356
3000	2826	2658	2497	2341	2191	2138	1897	1679	1481	1302	1140	-1.5	1.4	0.0	-6.4	-18.2	-36.6	0.547
3000	2656	2337	2041	1768	1524	1999	1567	1214	925	695	516	-1.5	1.7	0.0	-8.1	-24.7	-52.4	0.272
3375	3065	2775	2504	2248	2008	1897	1564	1282	1044	842	671	-1.5	1.1	0.0	-5.6	-16.8	-35.0	0.330
3350	2955	2593	2258	1949	–	1993	1550	1194	906	675	–	-1.5	1.3	0.0	-6.5	-19.8	–	0.255
3120	2871	2635	2411	2199	1997	1946	1647	1388	1162	966	797	-1.5	1.4	0.0	-6.4	-18.7	-38.4	0.390
3140	2866	2608	2364	2134	1916	2189	1823	1510	1241	1011	815	-1.5	1.4	0	-6.5	-19.2	-39.7	0.355
3120	2860	2614	2382	2161	1952	2162	1817	1518	1260	1037	847	-1.5	1.4	0.0	-6.5	-19.1	-39.2	0.373
2960	2697	2449	2215	1993	1786	1945	1615	1332	1089	882	708	-1.5	1.7	0.0	-7.5	-22.0	-45.4	0.356
3230	2892	2579	2286	2013	1760	2316	1857	1476	1160	899	688	-1.5	1.3	0.0	-6.6	-19.9	-41.8	0.292
2990	2730	2484	2252	2032	1825	2382	1985	1644	1351	1100	887	-1.5	1.0	0.0	-7.2	-21.4	-43.9	0.362
1460	1194	1030	–	–	–	407	272	202	–	–	–	-0.9	0.0	-23.5	–	–	–	0.190
2820	2504	2209	1935	1684	–	1765	1392	1084	831	629	–	-1.5	2.0	0.0	-9.2	-27.8	–	0.285
2650	2291	1961	1663	1404	1199	1824	1363	999	718	512	373	-1.5	2.6	0.0	-11.7	-36.1	-78.20	0.240
2750	2585	2426	2273	2125	1982	2183	1929	1699	1491	1303	1135	-1.5	1.9	0.0	-7.8	-22.3	-44.5	0.547
2700	2548	2400	2258	2120	1988	2267	2018	1792	1585	1398	1228	-1.5	1.9	0.0	-8.0	-22.8	-45.3	0.586
2700	2484	2278	2082	1896	1721	2267	1918	1613	1347	1117	921	-1.5	2.1	0.0	-8.8	-25.6	-52.2	0.410
2945	2751	2566	2388	2217	2053	2484	2168	1885	1633	1407	1207	-1.5	1.6	0.0	-6.8	-19.8	-39.8	0.485
2700	2548	2400	2258	2120	1988	2267	2018	1792	1585	1398	1228	-1.5	1.9	0.0	-8.0	-22.8	-45.3	0.586
2715	2546	2382	2225	2073	1927	2293	2015	1764	1538	1335	1154	-1.5	1.9	0	-8.1	-23.2	-46.4	0.526
2550	2353	2164	1984	1814	1654	2021	1720	1456	1224	1023	850.00	-1.5	2.4	0.0	-9.8	-27.0	-57.80	0.435
2590	2401	2221	2048	1883	1728	–	–	–	–	–	–	-1.5	0.0	-4.5	-16.1	-36.0	-65.8	0.460
2400	2251	2108	1969	1836	1711	1663	1463	1282	1119	973	845	-1.5	2.7	0.0	-10.4	-29.7	-59.8	0.560
2750	2544	2347	2158	1979	1812	2351	2011	1712	1448	1217	1021	-1.5	1.9	0.0	-8.3	-24.0	-48.7	0.435
2750	2602	2459	2320	2187	2057	2384	2135	1907	1698	1507	1334	-1.5	1.8	0.0	-7.5	-21.7	-43.0	0.611
3030	2782	2548	2325	2113	1913	2854	2406	2017	1680	1388	1137	-1.5	1.5	0.0	-6.9	-20.2	-41.3	0.384
2625	2329	2053	1797	1565	1363	1759	1385	1076	825	625	474	-2.5	2.0	0.0	-10.3	-31.4	-66.8	0.292
2625	2365	2119	1889	1676	1484	1759	1428	1147	911	717	562	-2.5	1.9	0.0	-9.7	-29.1	-61.0	0.333
3080	2864	2658	2461	2273	2093	2738	2367	2039	1748	1491	1264	-1.5	1.4	0.0	-6.3	-18.4	-37.2	0.447
3320	2923	2559	2223	1914	--	2248	1897	1455	1098	813	--	-1.5	1.3	0.0	-6.6	-20.4	--	0.252
3060	2776	2509	2258	2021	1799	2702	2224	1817	1471	1179	935	-1.5	1.5	0.0	-7.1	-21.0	-43.4	0.336
3060	2838	2627	2425	2232	2049	2704	2326	1992	1698	1439	1212	-1.5	1.4	0.0	-6.5	-18.8	-38.2	0.433
2975	2714	2468	2235	2015	1812	2751	2290	1893	1553	1262	1020	-1.5	1.6	0.0	-7.3	-21.7	-43.7	0.360
2850	2504	2183	1887	1619	1386	2705	2088	1587	1186	873	640	-1.5	2.0	0.0	-9.4	-28.6	-61.2	0.261
3285	2986	2707	2444	2196	1963	3114	2573	2114	1724	1392	1112	-1.5	1.2	0	-6	-17.8	-36.8	0.336
3020	2823	2635	2455	2282	2115	2835	2478	2159	1873	1618	1391	-1.5	1.4	0.0	-6.4	-18.7	-37.6	0.486
3000	2757	2528	2309	2102	1905	2797	2363	1986	1657	1373	1128	-1.5	1.5	0.0	-7.0	-20.5	-42.0	0.390
2890	2624	2373	2136	1914	1706	2781	2293	1876	1520	1219	970	-1.5	1.8	0.0	-8.0	-23.6	-48.8	0.346
2820	2509	2219	1949	1700	1478	2913	2307	1804	1391	1059	800	-1.5	2.0	0.0	-9.1	-27.5	-57.9	0.290
3000	2725	2467	2223	1992	1777	2398	1979	1621	1316	1058	842	-1.5	1.6	0.0	-7.3	-21.7	-44.9	0.343

REMINGTON

REMINGTON

CENTERFIRE RIFLE BALLISTICS

CARTRIDGE	INDEX/ EDI NO.	RAMAC	WT (GR)	BULLET STYLE	PRIMER NO.	SIGHT HEIGHT (INCHES)	ZERO (YARDS)
	R7M081	21337	140	Core-Lokt Pointed Soft Point	9½	1.5	200
	PRA7M08RB	29216	140	AccuTip Boat Tail	9½	1.5	200
7mm Remington Magnum	R7MM4	28821	140	Core-Lokt Pointed Soft Point	9½ M	1.5	200
	RT7MMRB	29021	150	Core-Lokt Tipped	9½ M	1.5	200
	R7MM2	29487	150	Core-Lokt Pointed Soft Point	9½ M	1.5	200
	PRSC7MMB	29316	150	Swift Scirocco Bonded	9½ M	1.5	200
	PRH7MMRC	28979	160	Core-Lokt Ultra Bonded PSP	9½ M	1.5	200
	R7MM3	27814	175	Core-Lokt Pointed Soft Point	9½ M	1.5	200
	RLR7MMR	R21343	175	Speer Impact	9½ M	1.5	200
7mm Mauser (7x57)	R7MSR1	29031	140	Core-Lokt Pointed Soft Point	9½	1.5	200
7 x 64 Brenneke	R7X641	29130	140	Core-Lokt Pointed Soft Point	9½	1.5	200
7mm Remington SA Ultra Mag	PR7SM2	27874	150	Core-Lokt Pointed Soft Point	9½ M	1.5	200
7mm Remington Ultra Mag	PRSC7UM1	29335	150	Swift Scirocco Bonded	9½ M	1.5	200
	R7RUM01	27759	150	Core-Lokt Pointed Soft Point	9½ M	1.5	200
30 Carbine	L30CR1	23712	110	Full Metal Jacket	6½	0.9	100
	R30CAR	28322	110	Core-Lokt Soft Point	6½	0.9	100
300 AAC Blackout	L300AAC1	21421	120	Open Tip Flat Base	7½	2.5	100
	RM300AAC6	21503	125	MatchKing Flat Base	7½	2.5	100
	L300AAC2	26854	150	Full Metal Jacket	7½	2.5	100
	S300AAC4	28430	220	OTFB	7.5	2.5	100
	L300AAC4	21422	220	Open Tip Flat Base	7½	2.5	100
30 Remington AR	R30RAR2	29485	150	Core-Lokt Pointed Soft Point	7½	2.5	200
30-30 Win	R30301	27818	150	Core-Lokt Soft Point	9½	0.9	100
	RL30301	27644	125	Core-Lokt Soft Point	9½	0.9	100
	R30302	27820	170	Core-Lokt Soft Point	9½	0.9	100
	R30303	21395	170	Core-Lokt Hollow Point	9½	0.9	100
30-40 Krag	R30402	28345	180	Core-Lokt Pointed Soft Point	9½	1.5	200
30-06 Sprg	R30061	21401	125	Core-Lokt Pointed Soft Point	9½	1.5	200
	L30062	27622	150	Full Metal Jacket	9½	1.5	200
	RT3006A	29027	150	Core-Lokt Tipped	9½	1.5	200
	R30062	27826	150	Core-Lokt Pointed Soft Point	9½	1.5	200
	PRSC3006C	29318	150	Swift Scirocco Bonded	9½ M	1.5	200
	PRH3006A	29007	150	Core-Lokt Ultra Bonded PSP	9½	1.5	200
	RT3006B	29035	165	Core-Lokt Tipped	9½	1.5	200
	RLR3006	R21344	172	Speer Impact	9½	1.5	200
	R3006B	21415	165	Core-Lokt Pointed Soft Point	9½	1.5	200
	RT3006C	29037	180	Core-Lokt Tipped	9½	1.5	200
	R30064	21407	180	Core-Lokt Soft Point	9½	1.5	200
	R30065	27828	180	Core-Lokt Pointed Soft Point	9½	1.5	200
	PRSC3006B	29328	180	Swift Scirocco Bonded	9½	1.5	200
	PRH3006C	29009	180	Core-Lokt Ultra Bonded PSP	9½	1.5	200
	R30067	27830	220	Core-Lokt Soft Point	9½	1.5	200
300 Savage	R30SV2	21465	150	Core-Lokt Pointed Soft Point	9½	1.5	200
300 Win Mag	R300W1	29495	150	Core-Lokt Pointed Soft Point	9½ M	1.5	200
	RT300WC	R29038	180	Core-Lokt Tipped	9½ M	1.5	200
	PRSC300WB	29330	180	Swift Scirocco Bonded	9½ M	1.5	200
	PRH300WC	29033	180	Core-Lokt Ultra Bonded PSP	9½ M	1.5	200
	R300W2	29497	180	Core-Lokt Pointed Soft Point	9½ M	1.5	200
	RLR300W	R21346	190	Speer Impact	9½ M	1.5	200
300 WSM	R300WSM1	29489	150	Core-Lokt Pointed Soft Point	9½ M	1.5	200
	RT300WSM1	29043	150	Core-Lokt Tipped	9½ M	1.5	200

VELOCITY (FPS)						ENERGY (FT-LB)						TRAJECTORY (INCHES)						BC
MUZ	100	200	300	400	500	MUZ	100	200	300	400	500	MUZ	100	200	300	400	500	
2860	2625	2402	2189	1988	1798	2542	2142	1793	1490	1228	1005	-1.5	1.8	0.0	-7.8	-22.9	-46.9	0.390
2860	2670	2489	2314	2146	1986	2542	2216	1925	1664	1432	1225	-1.5	1.7	0.0	-7.3	-21.1	-42.5	0.486
3175	2923	2684	2458	2243	2039	3133	2655	2240	1878	1564	1292	-1.5	1.3	0	-6.1	-18	-36.9	0.390
3130	2945	2767	2597	2432	2274	3262	2888	2550	2245	1970	1722	-1.5	1.3	0	-5.8	-16.8	-33.6	0.530
3110	2831	2568	2321	2087	1867	3221	2669	2197	1793	1450	1161	-1.5	1.4	0	-6.7	-19.9	-41.1	0.346
3110	2927	2751	2582	2419	2262	3222	2854	2521	2221	1949	1705	-1.5	1.3	0	-5.9	-17	-34	0.533
3000	2774	2557	2350	2152	1965	3203	2734	2323	1962	1646	1372	-1.5	1.5	0	-6.9	-20	-40.7	0.415
2860	2645	2440	2244	2057	1879	3178	2718	2312	1956	1643	1372	-1.5	1.7	0	-7.6	-22.1	-44.9	0.427
2660	2435	2221	2018	1827	1648	2199	1843	1533	1266	1037	844	-1.5	2.2	0.0	-9.3	-27.1	-55.4	0.390
2950	2710	2483	2266	2061	1867	2705	2283	1916	1597	1320	1083	-1.5	1.6	0.0	-7.3	-21.3	-43.6	0.390
3110	2831	2568	2321	2087	1867	3221	2669	2197	1793	1450	1161	-1.5	1.4	0.0	-6.7	-19.9	-41.1	0.346
3325	3132	2948	2771	2602	2438	3683	3269	2896	2559	2255	1980	-1.5	1.0	0.0	-5	-14.6	-29.3	0.533
3230	2943	2674	2421	2181	1955	3476	2886	2382	1952	1585	1274	-1.5	1.2	0.0	-6.1	-18.2	-37.7	0.346
1990	1566	1235	1034	–	–	967	599	372	261	–	–	-0.9	0.0	-13.6	-50.0	–	–	0.166
1990	1566	1235	1034	–	–	967	599	372	261	–	–	-0.9	0.0	-13.6	-50.0	–	–	0.166
2200	1937	1695	1479	1294	–	1290	1000	766	583	446	–	-2.5	0.0	-6.8	-25.8	-60.8	–	0.297
2215	1977	1755	1552	1373	–	1362	1084	854	669	523	–	-2.5	0.0	-6.4	-24.2	-56.5	–	0.330
1905	1721	1551	1398	–	–	1209	986	801	651	–	–	-2.5	0.0	-9.3	-33.1	–	–	0.390
940	918	897	877	858	841	433	412	393	376	360	345	-2.5	0.0	-38.8	-120.7	–	–	0.680
1015	985	958	934	–	–	503	474	448	426	–	–	-2.5	0.0	-33.3	-104.5	–	–	0.680
2575	2302	2047	1812	1591	–	2708	1765	1395	1093	843	–	-2.5	0.0	0.0	-10.4	-31.5	–	0.314
2390	1973	1606	1304	–	–	1902	1297	859	567	–	–	-0.9	0.0	-8.2	-30.0	–	–	0.193
2175	1820	1508	1255	1082	975	1313	919	631	437	325	264	-0.9	0.0	-9.1	-33.7	–	–	0.215
2200	1895	1619	1380	–	–	1827	1355	989	719	–	–	-0.9	0.0	-8.9	-31.1	–	–	0.254
2200	1895	1619	1380	–	–	1827	1355	989	719	–	–	-0.9	0.0	-8.9	-31.1	–	–	0.254
2430	2213	2006	1815	1632	1467	2360	1956	1609	1316	1064	860	-1.5	2.8	0.0	-11.5	-33.6	-68.8	0.383
3140	2780	2448	2139	1854	1596	2736	2145	1663	1270	954	707	-1.5	1.5	0.0	-7.4	-22.4	-47.5	0.268
2910	2617	2342	2083	1842	1621	2820	2280	1826	1445	1130	875	-1.5	1.8	0.0	-8.2	-24.4	-50.9	0.314
2930	2705	2491	2287	2093	1909	2859	2437	2067	1742	1459	1213	-1.5	1.6	0.0	-7.2	-21.2	-43.0	0.415
2910	2617	2342	2083	1842	1621	2820	2280	1826	1445	1130	875	-1.5	1.8	0.0	-8.2	-24.4	-50.9	0.314
2910	2696	2492	2298	2112	1934	2821	2422	2070	1759	1485	1247	-1.5	1.7	0.0	-7.3	-21.1	-42.8	0.435
3035	2748	2479	2226	1988	1766	3069	2517	2048	1651	1316	1038	-1.5	1.56	0.0	-7.2	-21.5	-44.7	0.331
2820	2616	2421	2234	2056	1886	2913	2507	2147	1829	1548	1303	-1.5	1.8	0.0	-7.7	-22.5	-45.4	0.447
2825	2650	2481	2319	2162	2012	3048	2681	2351	2053	1785	1545	-1.5	1.7	0	-7.4	-21.2	-42.6	0.522
2800	2534	2283	2047	1826	1622	2872	2352	1910	1535	1221	963	-1.5	2.0	0.0	-8.7	-25.7	-53.1	0.339
2745	2558	2378	2206	2041	1883	3011	2615	2260	1945	1664	1417	-1.5	1.9	0.0	-8.1	-23.3	-46.9	0.480
2700	2348	2023	1727	1467	1252	2913	2203	1636	1192	860	627	-1.5	2.4	0.0	-11.0	-33.8	-72.8	0.248
2700	2469	2250	2041	1845	1662	2913	2436	2022	1665	1360	1104	-1.5	2.1	0.0	-9.0	-26.4	-54.0	0.383
2700	2522	2351	2186	2028	1878	2914	2543	2209	1911	1645	1409	-1.5	2.0	0.0	-8.3	-23.9	-47.9	0.500
2830	2605	2389	2184	1989	1805	3206	2713	2282	1907	1581	1302	-1.5	1.8	0.0	-7.9	-23.1	-47.2	0.402
2410	2130	1870	1632	1421	1246	2837	2216	1708	1301	987	758	-1.5	3.1	0.0	-13.1	-39.4	-82.9	0.294
2630	2354	2095	1853	1631	1433	2303	1845	1462	1144	886	684	-1.5	2.4	0.0	-10.4	-30.9	-64.6	0.314
3290	2950	2634	2340	2065	1813	3605	2897	2311	1823	1420	1094	-1.5	1.3	0.0	-6.3	-19.0	-39.8	0.294
2980	2783	2594	2413	2239	2073	3549	3095	2689	2327	2004	1717	-1.5	1.5	0.0	-6.7	-19.3	-38.9	0.481
2960	2774	2595	2424	2259	2100	3503	3076	2693	2349	2040	1763	-1.5	1.5	0.0	-6.7	-19.3	-38.7	0.507
3120	2880	2651	2433	2225	2028	3897	3316	2809	2366	1980	1644	-1.5	1.4	0.0	-6.3	-18.5	-37.8	0.402
2960	2715	2484	2263	2054	1857	3501	2946	2465	2047	1687	1379	-1.5	1.6	0.0	-7.3	-21.3	-43.7	0.383
2885	2727	2577	2430	2289	2153	3506	3138	2800	2492	2210	1955	-1.5	1.6	0	-6.8	-19.5	-38.9	0.596
3320	2977	2660	2364	2087	1830	3671	2952	2356	1861	1451	1116	-1.5	1.2	0.0	-6.2	-18.6	-39.0	0.294
3340	3093	2860	2639	2428	2227	3715	3186	2724	2319	1963	1652	-1.5	1.1	0.0	-5.3	-15.7	-31.9	0.415

REMINGTON

REMINGTON

CENTERFIRE RIFLE BALLISTICS

CARTRIDGE	INDEX/ EDI NO.	RAMAC	WT (GR)	BULLET STYLE	PRIMER NO.	SIGHT HEIGHT (INCHES)	ZERO (YARDS)
	PRSC300WSMB	29345	180	Swift Scirocco Bonded	9½ M	1.5	200
308 Marlin Express	R308ME1	27848	150	Core-Lokt Pointed Soft Point	9½	1.5	200
308 Win	L308W4	23715	150	Full Metal Jacket	9½	1.5	200
	R308W1	27842	150	Core-Lokt Pointed Soft Point	9½	1.5	200
	PRH308WA	29119	150	Core-Lokt Ultra Bonded PSP	9½	1.5	200
	RT308WA	29039	150	Core-Lokt Tipped	9½	1.5	200
	RT308WB	29044	165	Core-Lokt Tipped	9½	1.5	200
	RT308WC	29041	180	Core-Lokt Tipped	9½	1.5	200
	PRSC308WB	29332	165	Swift Scirocco Bonded	9½	1.5	200
	RM308W7	21485	168	MatchKing BTHP	9½	1.5	200
	RLR308W	R21345	172	Speer Impact	9½	1.5	200
	RM308W8	21486	175	MatchKing BTHP	9½	1.5	200
	R308W4	R21473	180	Pointed Soft Point Boattail	9½	1.5	200
	R308W2	27844	180	Core-Lokt Soft Point	9½	1.5	200
	R308W3	21479	180	Core-Lokt Pointed Soft Point	9½	1.5	200
300 Wby Mag	R300WB1	29279	180	Core-Lokt Pointed Soft Point	9½ M	1.5	200
303 British	L303B1	23701	174	Full Metal Jacket	9½	1.5	100
	R303B1	21471	180	Core-Lokt Soft Point	9½	1.5	100
7.62 x 39	L762391	23709	123	Full Metal Jacket	9½	2.0	100
	R762391	29125	125	Core-Lokt Pointed Soft Point	9½	2.0	100
300 Remington SA Ultra Mag	PR300SM2	27954	165	Core-Lokt Pointed Soft Point	9½ M	1.5	200
300 Remington Ultra Mag	PR300UM5	27950	150	Swift Scirocco Bonded	9½ M	1.5	200
	R300RUM01	27641	180	Core-Lokt Pointed Soft Point	9½ M	1.5	200
	RLR300UM	R21347	190	Speer Impact	9½ M	1.5	200
	PR300UM3	27936	180	Swift Scirocco Bonded	9½ M	1.5	200
32-20 Win	R32201	28410	100	Lead	6½	0.9	100
32 Win Special	R32WS2	21489	170	Core-Lokt Soft Point	9½	0.9	100
338 Marlin Express	R338ME1	22184	250	Soft Point	9½	1.5	200
338 Win Mag	R338W1	22189	225	Core-Lokt Pointed Soft Point	9½ M	1.5	200
	R338W2	22191	250	Core-Lokt Pointed Soft Point	9½ M	1.5	200
338 Remington Ultra Mag	PR338UM2	27942	250	Core-Lokt Pointed Soft Point	9½ M	1.5	200
338 Lapua Mag	RM338LMR1	27944	250	Scenar Match	9½ M	1.5	200
35 Remington	R35R2	27852	200	Core-Lokt Soft Point	9½	1.5	100
	R35R2	27852	200	Core-Lokt Soft Point	9½	1.5	100
35 Whelen	R35WH1	21495	200	Core-Lokt Pointed Soft Point	9½ M	1.5	200
	R35WH3	21499	250	Pointed Soft Point	9½ M	1.5	200
350 Legend	R350L1	20012	180	Core-Lokt Soft Point	7½	1.5	100
360 Buckhammer	R360BH4	R27742	180	Core-Lokt Soft Point	9½	1.5	100
	R360BH2	R27743	200	Core-Lokt Soft Point	9½	1.5	100
9.3 x 62	R93x621	28276	286	Pointed Soft Point	9½	1.5	200
375 H&H Mag	R375M1	29097	270	Soft Point	9½ M	1.5	200
375 Remington Ultra Mag	PR375UM2	29340	270	Soft Point	9½ M	1.5	200
444 Marlin	R444M	29475	240	Core-Lokt Soft Point	9½	0.9	100
45-70 Gov't	R4570G	29473	405	Core-Lokt Soft Point †	9½	0.9	100
	R4570G1	21459	405	Core-Lokt Soft Point ††	9½	0.9	100
	R4570L1	21463	300	Semi-Jacketed Hollow Point ††	9½	0.9	100
450 Bushmaster	R450B1	27941	260	Core-Lokt Pointed Soft Point	7½	2.5	100
	L450BM1	23661	260	Full Metal Jacket	7½	2.5	100
	PRA450B1	27943	260	AccuTip	7½	2.5	100

VELOCITY (FPS)						ENERGY (FT-LB)						TRAJECTORY (INCHES)						BC
MUZ	100	200	300	400	500	MUZ	100	200	300	400	500	MUZ	100	200	300	400	500	
2980	2793	2614	2442	2276	2117	3550	3119	2731	2383	2071	1791	-1.5	1.5	0.0	-6.6	-19	-38.1	0.507
2725	2275	1871	1519	1239	–	2473	1724	1166	768	511	–	-1.5	2.7	0.0	-12.7	-40.8	–	0.193
2820	2532	2262	2009	1774	1560	2648	2136	1704	1344	1048	810	-1.5	2.0	0.0	-8.8	-26.3	-54.8	0.314
2820	2532	2262	2009	1774	1560	2648	2136	1704	1344	1048	810	-1.5	2.0	0.0	-8.8	-26.3	-54.8	0.314
2925	2644	2381	2134	1901	1686	2848	2330	1889	1517	1204	947	-1.5	1.8	0.0	-7.9	-23.5	-48.7	0.331
2840	7620	2410	2210	2019	1839	2686	2285	1934	1626	1358	1126	-1.5	1.8	0.0	-7.8	-22.7	-46.2	0.415
2700	2501	2311	2129	1956	1792	2670	2292	1957	1661	1401	1176	-1.5	2.0	0.0	-8.6	-24.8	-50.1	0.447
2640	2457	2282	2113	1952	1799	2785	2413	2080	1785	1523	1293	-1.5	2.1	0.0	-8.8	-25.4	-51.2	0.480
2680	2493	2314	2143	1979	1823	2631	2277	1962	1682	1434	1217	-1.5	2.1	0.0	-8.6	-24.7	-49.7	0.475
2680	2494	2315	2143	1979	1823	2679	2319	1999	1713	1461	1240	-1.5	2.1	0.0	-8.6	-24.7	-49.7	0.475
2635	2467	2305	2149	1999	1856	2652	2324	2029	1763	1526	1315	-1.5	2.1	0	-8.7	-24.9	-49.8	0.522
2610	2434	7265	2103	1947	1799	2647	2302	1993	1718	1473	1257	-1.5	2.2	0.0	-9.0	-25.8	-51.9	0.496
2615	2395	2185	1985	1797	1622	2735	2293	1907	1575	1291	1052	-1.5	2.3	0	-9.6	-28	-57.3	0.393
2620	2274	1956	1667	1415	–	2743	2067	1528	1110	800	–	-1.5	2.6	0.0	-11.8	-36.3	–	0.248
2620	2393	2177	1973	1781	1603	2743	2288	1895	1556	1268	1027	-1.5	2.3	0.0	-9.7	-28.3	-57.9	0.383
3120	2866	2627	2399	2184	1979	3890	3283	2757	2301	1905	1565	-1.5	1.4	0.0	-6.4	-18.9	-38.7	0.383
2475	2209	1960	1730	1521	1339	2366	1886	1484	1156	893	692	-1.5	0.0	-5.7	-20.4	-46.9	-88.4	0.315
2460	2125	1819	1544	1313	–	2418	1805	1322	953	689	–	-1.5	0.0	-6.3	-23.1	-54.7	–	0.247
2365	2060	1780	1529	1315	1150	1577	1159	865	638	472	361	-2.0	0.0	-6.3	-23.6	-55.9	-108.3	0.266
2365	2061	1782	1531	–	–	1552	1179	881	651	–	–	-2.0	0.0	-6.2	-23.5	–	–	0.267
3075	2792	2527	2277	2041	1820	3464	2856	7339	1899	1525	1213	-1.5	1.5	0.0	-7.0	-20.6	-42.7	0.339
3450	3208	2980	2763	2556	2358	3965	3429	2958	2542	2176	1853	-1.5	0.9	0	-4.9	-14.3	-29.1	0.435
3175	2922	2679	2449	2231	2024	4030	3405	2863	2392	1984	1633	-1.5	1.3	0	-6.2	-18.1	-37.1	0.383
3130	2965	2806	2653	2504	2361	4133	3708	3321	2968	2646	2351	-1.5	1.2	0	-5.6	-16.2	-32.4	0.596
3250	3048	2856	2672	2495	2325	4182	3679	3229	2825	2462	2137	-1.5	1.1	0	-5.4	-15.7	-31.5	0.5
1210	1021	913	–	–	–	325	232	185	–	–	–	-0.9	0.0	-32.3	–	–	–	0.166
2250	1922	1627	1373	–	–	1911	1394	999	712	–	–	-0.9	0.0	-8.6	-30.5	–	–	0.239
2215	1946	1698	1477	1289	--	2723	2101	1601	1211	922	--	-1.5	3.9	0.0	-16.0	-48.0	--	0.291
2780	2572	2374	2184	2004	1832	3860	3305	2815	2384	2005	1677	-1.5	1.9	0.0	-8.1	-23.4	-47.5	0.435
2660	2456	2261	2075	1898	1731	3977	3348	2837	2389	1999	1663	-1.5	2.1	0.0	-9.0	-26.0	-52.7	0.431
2860	2647	2443	2249	2063	1887	4540	3888	3313	2807	2363	1976	-1.5	1.7	0.0	-7.6	-22.0	-44.7	0.431
2960	2820	2683	2551	2423	2299	4863	4412	3996	3613	3259	2932	-1.5	1.4	0.0	-6.3	-17.9	-35.4	0.675
2080	1697	1374	1138	–	–	1921	1278	838	575	–	–	-1.5	0.0	-8.4	-31.7	–	–	0.192
2080	1697	1374	1138	--	--	1921	1278	838	575	--	--	-1.5	0	-10.7	-40.1	--	--	0.192
2675	2378	2100	1842	1607	1400	3177	2511	1959	1507	1147	870	-1.5	2.3	0.0	-10.3	-30.9	-65.0	0.294
2400	2197	2005	1823	1652	1496	3197	2681	2232	1845	1516	1243	-1.5	2.9	0.0	-11.5	-33.6	-68.4	0.409
2100	1793	1520	1292	1123	1013	1762	1284	924	668	504	410	-1.5	0.0	-9.4	-34.1	--	--	0.245
2374	1917	1522	1216	2252	1468	926	591	-1.5	0.0	-8.1	-31.5	0.174						
2197	1777	1421	1157	2144	1402	896	595	-1.5	0.0	-9.7	-36.9	0.181						
2360	2155	1960	1777	1607	1451	3536	2948	2440	2005	1639	1337	-1.5	3.0	0.0	-12.1	-35.2	-71.8	0.400
2690	2363	2059	1780	1530	1317	4337	3347	2542	1900	1403	1039	-1.5	2.4	0.0	-10.6	-32.4	-69.0	0.267
2900	2558	2240	1946	1677	1441	5041	3921	3008	2269	1686	1244	-1.5	1.9	0.0	-8.9	-27.1	-57.7	0.267
2350	1816	1376	1087	–	–	2942	1758	1009	630	–	–	-0.9	0.0	-10.0	-38.5	–	–	0.146
1330	1169	1056	978	–	–	1590	1228	1002	860	–	–	-0.9	0.0	-24.5	-80.2	–	–	0.281
1600	1385	1210	1084	–	–	2303	1726	1318	1057	–	–	-0.9	0.0	-17.3	-58.3	–	–	0.281
1900	1574	1304	1111	–	–	2405	1651	1134	823	–	–	-0.9	0.0	-13.3	-47.1	–	–	0.213
2040	1621	1285	1066	--	--	2402	1517	952	656	--	--	-1.5	0.0	-12.0	-45.2	--	--	0.172
2040	1651	1330	1106	--	--	2402	1574	1021	706	--	--	-1.5	0.0	-11.5	-42.7	--	--	0.186
2180	1664	1261	1026	--	--	2743	1598	918	608	--	--	-2.5	0.0	-10.4	-42.8	--	--	0.144

REMINGTON

REMINGTON

MUZZLELOADER BALLISTICS

CARTRIDGE	INDEX/EDI NO.	RAMAC	WT (GR)	BULLET STYLE	SIGHT HEIGHT (INCHES)
50 Caliber	RBMLR2A	30610	250	AccuTip FB	1.5

SHOTSHELL

PRODUCT NAME	INDEX/EDI NO.	RAMAC	GAUGE	LENGTH (IN)	DRAM EQUIV.	VELOCITY	OZ. OF SHOT	VELOCITY
Premier TSS Turkey	TSS10359	28033	10	3.5"	N/A	1050	2-1/2	9
	TSS1237	28043	12	3"	N/A	1200	1-3/4	7
	TSS1239	28045	12	3"	N/A	1200	1-3/4	9
	TSS1237A	28086	12	3"	N/A	1000	2	7
	TSS1239A	28087	12	3"	N/A	1000	2	9
	TSS12357	28089	12	3.5"	N/A	1100	2-1/4	7
	TSS12359	28091	12	3.5"	N/A	1100	2-1/4	9
	TSS2037	28063	20	3"	N/A	1100	1-1/2	7
	TSS2039	28065	20	3"	N/A	1100	1-1/2	9
	TSS2037A	28074	20	3"	N/A	1000	1-5/8	7
	TSS2039A	28078	20	3"	N/A	1000	1-5/8	9
	TSS41039	28069	410	3"	N/A	1100	13/16	9
Premier High Velocity	PHV12M4A	28029	12	3"	N/A	1300	1-3/4	4
Magnum Turkey	PHV12M5A	28031	12	3	N/A	1300	1-3/4	5
	PHV1235M4A	28039	12	3-1/2	N/A	1300	2	4
	PHV1235M5A	28041	12	3-1/2	N/A	1300	2	5
	PHV20M5A	20119	20	3	N/A	1300	1-1/8	5
Premier Magnum Turkey	P10HM4A	24395	10	3-1/2	N/A	1210	2-1/4	4
	P12XHM4A	26801	12	3	N/A	1175	2	4
	P12XHM5A	26803	12	3	N/A	1175	2	5
	P12XHM6A	26805	12	3	N/A	1175	2	6
	P1235M4A	26833	12	3-1/2	N/A	1150	2-1/4	4
	P20XHM6A	26859	20	3	N/A	1185	1-1/4	6
Nitro Turkey	NT12H4A	26669	12	3	N/A	1210	1-7/8	4
	NT12H5A	26671	12	3	N/A	1210	1-7/8	5
	NT12H6A	26673	12	3	N/A	1210	1-7/8	6
	NT12354A	26707	12	3-1/2	N/A	1300	2	4
	NT12355A	26709	12	3-1/2	N/A	1300	2	5
	NT12356A	26711	12	3-1/2	N/A	1300	2	6
	NT20M5A	26731	20	3	N/A	1185	1-1/4	5
Nitro Pheasant	NP124	28620	12	2-3/4	N/A	1400	1-1/4	4
	NP125	28622	12	2-3/4	N/A	1400	1-1/4	5
	NP126	28624	12	2-3/4	N/A	1400	1-1/4	6
	NP12M4	28632	12	2-3/4	N/A	1300	1-3/8	4
	NP12M5	28634	12	2-3/4	N/A	1300	1-3/8	5
	NP12M6	28636	12	2-3/4	N/A	1300	1-3/8	6
	NP205	28646	20	2-3/4	N/A	1300	1	5
	NP206	28648	20	2-3/4	N/A	1300	1	6
	NP20M5	28651	20	3	N/A	1185	1-1/4	5
	NP20M6	28653	20	3	N/A	1185	1-1/4	6
Nitro Magnum	NM12S2	26676	12	2-3/4	N/A	1260	1-1/2	2
	NM12S4	26678	12	2-3/4	N/A	1260	1-1/2	4
	NM124	26674	12	3	N/A	1280	1-5/8	4
	NM126	20376	12	3	N/A	1280	1-5/8	6

	VELOCITY (FPS)						ENERGY (FT-LB)						TRAJECTORY (INCHES)						
MUZ	50	100	150	200	300	MUZ	50	100	150	200	300	MUZ	50	100	150	200	300	BC
2400	2188	1987	1797	1621	1319	3198	2658	2191	1793	1459	966	-1.5	0.09	1.49	0.0	-4.28	-23.57	0.195

SHOTSHELL

PRODUCT NAME	INDEX/EDI NO.	RAMAC	GAUGE	LENGTH (IN)	DRAM EQUIV.	VELOCITY	OZ. OF SHOT	VELOCITY
	NM12H2	26682	12	3	N/A	1210	1-7/8	2
	NM12H4	26684	12	3	N/A	1210	1-7/8	4
	NM12H6	26685	12	3	N/A	1210	1-7/8	6
	NM20S4	20664	20	2-3/4	N/A	1175	1-1/8	4
	NM20S6	20666	20	2-3/4	N/A	1175	1-1/8	6
	NM20H4	20672	20	3	N/A	1185	1-1/4	4
	NM20H6	20674	20	3	N/A	1185	1-1/4	6
Express XLR	SP122	20143	12	2-3/4	N/A	1330	1-1/4	2
Extra Long Range	SP124	20145	12	2-3/4	N/A	1330	1-1/4	4
	SP125	20147	12	2-3/4	N/A	1330	1-1/4	5
	SP126	20149	12	2-3/4	N/A	1330	1-1/4	6
	SP1275	20151	12	2-3/4	N/A	1330	1-1/4	7-1/2
	NEHV125	20167	12	2-3/4	N/A	1450	1-1/8	5
	NEHV126	20168	12	2-3/4	N/A	1450	1 1/8	6
	NEHV1275	20169	12	2-3/4	N/A	1450	1-1/8	7-1/2
	SP164	28003	16	2-3/4	N/A	1295	1-1/8	4
	SP166	28007	16	2-3/4	N/A	1295	1-1/8	6
	SP1675	28009	16	2-3/4	N/A	1295	1-1/8	7-1/2
	SP204	20333	20	2-3/4	N/A	1220	1	4
	SP205	20335	20	2-3/4	N/A	1220	1	5
	SP206	20337	20	2-3/4	N/A	1220	1	6
	SP2075	20339	20	2-3/4	N/A	1220	1	7-1/2
	NEHV206	20181	20	2-3/4	N/A	1350	7/8	6
	NEHV2075	20183	20	2-3/4	N/A	1350	7/8	7-1/2
	SP286	28047	28	2-3/4	N/A	1295	3/4	6
	SP2875	28049	28	2-3/4	N/A	1295	3/4	7-1/2
	SP4104	20743	410	2-1/2	N/A	1250	1/2	4
	SP4106	20745	410	2-1/2	N/A	1250	1/2	6
	SP41075	20747	410	2-1/2	N/A	1250	1/2	7-1/2
	SP4134	20771	410	3	N/A	1135	11/16	4
	SP4136	20775	410	3	N/A	1135	11/16	6
	SP41375	20777	410	3	N/A	1135	11/16	7-1/2
Heavy Dove Loads	RHD1275	28755	12	2-3/4	N/A	1255	1-1/8	7-1/2
	RHD128	28757	12	2-3/4	N/A	1255	1-1/8	8
	RHD2075	28777	20	2-3/4	N/A	1165	1	7-1/2
	RHD208	28779	20	2-3/4	N/A	1165	1	8
Pheasant Loads	PL124	20046	12	2-3/4	N/A	1330	1-1/4	4
	PL125	20024	12	2-3/4	N/A	1330	1-1/4	5
	PL126	20048	12	2-3/4	N/A	1330	1-1/4	6
	PL127	20050	12	2-3/4	N/A	1330	1-1/4	7-1/2
	PL166	20054	16	2-3/4	N/A	1295	1-1/8	6
	PL204	20058	20	2-3/4	N/A	1220	1	4
	PL205	20018	20	2-3/4	N/A	1220	1	5
	PL206	20060	20	2-3/4	N/A	1220	1	6

REMINGTON

REMINGTON

SHOTSHELL

PRODUCT NAME	INDEX/EDI NO.	RAMAC	GAUGE	LENGTH (IN)	DRAM EQUIV.	VELOCITY	OZ. OF SHOT	VELOCITY
Game Loads	GL126	20028	12	2-3/4	N/A	1290	1	6
	GL127	20030	12	2-3/4	N/A	1290	1	7-1/2
	GL128	20032	12	2-3/4	N/A	1290	1	8
	GL166	20034	16	2-3/4	N/A	1200	1	6
	GL167	20036	16	2-3/4	N/A	1200	1	7-1/2
	GL168	20038	16	2-3/4	N/A	1200	1	8
	GL206	20040	20	2-3/4	N/A	1225	7/8	6
	GL207	20042	20	2-3/4	N/A	1225	7/8	7-1/2
	GL208	20044	20	2-3/4	N/A	1225	7/8	8
	GL4106	20014	410	2-1/2	N/A	1200	1/2	6
Express Magnum Buckshot	12SB00	20632	12	2-3/4	N/A	1290	12 pel	00
	12HB000	20408	12	3	N/A	1225	10 pel	000
	12HB00	20636	12	3	N/A	1225	15 pel	00
	12HB4	20640	12	3	N/A	1225	41 pel	4
	1235B00	20280	12	3-1/2	N/A	1125	18 pel	00
Express Buckshot	12B000	20406	12	2-3/4	N/A	1325	8 pel	000
	12B00	20620	12	2-3/4	N/A	1325	9 pel	00
	12B0	20622	12	2-3/4	N/A	1275	12 pel	0
	12B1	20624	12	2-3/4	N/A	1250	16 pel	1
	12B4	20626	12	2-3/4	N/A	1325	27 pel	4
	20B3	20630	20	2-3/4	N/A	1220	20 pel	3
	12B00A	20411	12	2-3/4	N/A	1325	9 pel	00
	12B00B	20413	12	2-3/4	N/A	1325	9 pel	00
Managed Recoil Buckshot	RL12BK00	20282	12	2-3/4	N/A	1200	8 pel	00 BK
Ultimate Defense	12B009HD	20713	12	2-3/4	N/A	1325	9 pel	00 BK
	12B008RRHD	20711	12	2-3/4	N/A	1200	8 pel	00 BK
	12HB00HD	20633	12	3	4	1225	15 pel	00
	12HB4HD	20639	12	3	4	1225	41 pel	4
	12BRR4HD	20637	12	2-3/4	N/A	1200	21 pel	4
	20BRR3HD	20681	20	2-3/4	N/A	1140	17 pel	3
	410B000HD	20697	410	2-1/2	N/A	1225	4 pel	000 BK
	413B000HD	20707	410	3	N/A	1125	5 pel	000 BK
Wingmaster HD	RW12S4	20693	12	2-3/4	N/A	1325	1-1/4	4
	RW12S6	20695	12	2-3/4	N/A	1325	1-1/4	6
	RW122	20871	12	3	N/A	1450	1-1/4	2
	RW124	20873	12	3	N/A	1450	1-1/4	4
	RW126	20875	12	3	N/A	1450	1-1/4	6
	RW12M2	20685	12	3	N/A	1450	1-3/8	2
	RW12M4	20687	12	3	N/A	1450	1-3/8	4
	RW12M6	20689	12	3	N/A	1450	1-3/8	6
	RW12HM2	20903	12	3	N/A	1300	1-1/2	2
	RW12HM4	20905	12	3	N/A	1300	1-1/2	4
	RW1235MB	20655	12	3-1/2	N/A	1300	1-3/4	BB
	RW1235M2	20657	12	3-1/2	N/A	1300	1-3/4	2
	RW1235M4	20659	12	3-1/2	N/A	1300	1-3/4	4
	RW20M4	20763	20	3	N/A	1300	1-1/8	4
Premier Bismuth	RHB12M2	R20500	12	3	N/A	1400	1-3/8	2
	RHB12M5	R20501	12	3	N/A	1400	1-3/8	5
	RHB12S2	R20503	12	2-3/4	N/A	1400	1-1/4	2
	RHB12S5	R20505	12	2-3/4	N/A	1400	1-1/4	5

SHOTSHELL

PRODUCT NAME	INDEX/EDI NO.	RAMAC	GAUGE	LENGTH (IN)	DRAM EQUIV.	VELOCITY	OZ. OF SHOT	VELOCITY
	RHBZOM2	R20507	20	3	N/A	1400	1-1/8	2
	RHBZOM5	R20508	20	3	N/A	1400	1-1/8	5
	RHBZOS5	R20509	20	2-3/4	N/A	1300	1	5
	RHB16M4	R20511	16	2-3/4	N/A	1300	1-1/8	4
	RHBZ8M4	R20513	28	2-3/4	N/A	1250	7/8	4
	RHB4104	R20514	410	3	N/A	1200	5/8	4
Hypersonic Steel	HSS10C	26724	10	3-1/2	N/A	1500	1-1/2	BBB
	HSS10B	26726	10	3-1/2	N/A	1500	1-1/2	BB
	HSS102	26728	10	3-1/2	N/A	1500	1-1/2	2
	HSS12B	26741	12	3	N/A	1700	1-1/8	BB
	HSS122	26743	12	3	N/A	1700	1-1/8	2
	HSS124	26745	12	3	N/A	1700	1-1/8	4
	HSS17MB	26769	12	3	N/A	1700	1-1/4	BB
	HSS12M1	26771	12	3	N/A	1700	1-1/4	1
	HSS12M2	26775	12	3	N/A	1700	1-1/4	2
	HSS12M3	26776	12	3	N/A	1700	1-1/4	3
	HSS12M4	26777	12	3	N/A	1700	1-1/4	4
	HSS1235B	26793	12	3-1/2	N/A	1700	1-3/8	BB
	HSS12352	26795	12	3-1/2	N/A	1700	1-3/8	2
	HSS12354	26799	12	3-1/2	N/A	1700	1-3/8	4
	HSS20M2	26823	20	3	N/A	1600	7/8	2
	HSS20M4	26825	20	3	N/A	1600	7/8	4
Nitro Steel	NS110M2	20853	10	3-1/2	N/A	1450	1-1/2	2
	NS12HVS4	20803	12	2-3/4	N/A	1390	1-1/8	4
	NS12SB	20650	12	2-3/4	N/A	1275	1-1/4	BB
	NS12S2	20654	12	2-3/4	N/A	1275	1-1/4	2
	NS12S4	20658	12	2-3/4	N/A	1275	1-1/4	4
	NS12MB	20794	12	3	N/A	1450	1-1/4	BB
	NS12M1	20796	12	3	N/A	1450	1-1/4	1
	NS12M2	20798	12	3	N/A	1450	1-1/4	2
	NS12M3	20800	12	3	N/A	1450	1-1/4	3
	NS12M4	20802	12	3	N/A	1450	1-1/4	4
	NS12HMT	20852	12	3	N/A	1300	1-3/8	T
	NS12HMB	20856	12	3	N/A	1300	1-3/8	BB
	NS12HM2	20860	12	3	N/A	1300	1-3/8	2
	NS12HM4	20864	12	3	N/A	1300	1-3/8	4
	NSI1235BB	20837	12	3-1/2	N/A	1500	1-1/2	BB
	NSI12352	20839	12	3-1/2	N/A	1500	1-1/2	2
	NS16HV2	20941	16	2-3/4	N/A	1300	15/16	2
	NS16HV4	20943	16	2-3/4	N/A	1300	15/16	4
	NS120M4	20769	20	3	N/A	1400	1	4
Sportsman Hi-Speed Steel	SSTHV10B	26605	10	3-1/2	N/A	1500	1-3/8	BB
	SSTHV102	26607	10	3-1/2	N/A	1500	1-3/8	2
	SST126	20005	12	2-3/4	N/A	1365	1	6
	SST127	20007	12	2-3/4	N/A	1365	1	7
	SST12S2	20934	12	2-3/4	N/A	1375	1-1/8	2
	SST12S4	20936	12	2-3/4	N/A	1375	1-1/8	4
	SSTHV12HB	20973	12	3	N/A	1550	1-1/8	BB
	SSTHV12H2	20977	12	3	N/A	1550	1-1/8	2
	SSTHV12H4	20981	12	3	N/A	1550	1-1/8	4

REMINGTON

REMINGTON

SHOTSHELL

PRODUCT NAME	INDEX/EDI NO.	RAMAC	GAUGE	LENGTH (IN)	DRAM EQUIV.	VELOCITY	OZ. OF SHOT	VELOCITY
	SSTHV12HMB	20987	12	3	N/A	1400	1-1/4	BB
	SSTHV12HM1	20791	12	3	N/A	1400	1-1/4	1
	SSTHV12HM2	20989	12	3	N/A	1400	1-1/4	2
	SSTHV12HM3	20795	12	3	N/A	1400	1-1/4	3
	SSTHV12HM4	20991	12	3	N/A	1400	1-1/4	4
	SST12HMB	20900	12	3	N/A	1300	1-3/8	BB
	SST12HM2	20904	12	3	N/A	1300	1-3/8	2
	SSTHV1235B	20997	12	3-1/2	N/A	1550	1-3/8	BB
	SSTHV12352	20999	12	3-1/2	N/A	1550	1-3/8	2
	SST207	20009	20	2-3/4	N/A	1425	3/4	7
	SST20M2	20879	20	3	N/A	1300	1	2
	SST20M4	20881	20	3	N/A	1300	1	4
Premier STS	STS12LR7	20240	12	2-3/4	2-1/2	1100	1-1/8	7.5
	STS12LR8	20242	12	2-3/4	2-1/2	1100	1-1/8	8
	STS1218	20155	12	2-3/4	2-3/4	1185	1	8
	STS12L7	20110	12	2-3/4	2-3/4	1145	1-1/8	7-1/2
	STS12L8	20112	12	2-3/4	2-3/4	1145	1-1/8	8
	STS12L85	20114	12	2-3/4	2-3/4	1145	1-1/8	8-1/2
	STS12L9	20116	12	2-3/4	2-3/4	1145	1-1/8	9
	STS12LH7	20250	12	2-3/4	3	1200	1-1/8	7-1/2
	STS12LH8	20252	12	2-3/4	3	1200	1-1/8	8
	STS20SC8	28059	20	2-3/4	2-1/2	1200	7/8	8
	STS209	20217	20	2-3/4	2-1/2	1200	7/8	9
	STS20NSC7	28860	20	2-3/4	3	1300	7/8	7-1/2
	STS28SC8	28057	28	2-3/4	2	1250	3/4	8
	STS289	28053	28	2-3/4	2	1250	3/4	9
	STS28NSC7	28868	28	2-3/4	2	1300	3/4	7-1/2
	STS410NSC8	28879	410	3-1/2	MAX	1300	1/2	8
	STS4109	20750	410	3-1/2	MAX	1275	1/2	9
Premier Nitro Sporting Clays	STS12NSC17	28850	12	2-3/4	MAX	1350	1	7-1/2
	STS12NSC7	20264	12	2-3/4	MAX	1300	1-1/8	7-1/2
	STS12NSC8	20266	12	2-3/4	MAX	1300	1-1/8	8

SS SLUG BALLISTICS

GAUGE/BORE	INDEX/EDI NO.	RAMAC	LENGTH (INCHES)	WEIGHT	SLUG STYLE	SIGHT HEIGHT (INCHES)
410	SP41RS	20618	2-1/2	1/5 oz.	Rifled Slug	1.5
16	SP16RS	20614	2-3/4	4/5 oz.	Rifled Slug HP	1.5
20	PRA20	20496	2-3/4	260 gr.	Power Port Tip	1.5
	PRA20M	20498	3	260 gr.	Power Port Tip	1.5
	SPHV20RS	28608	2-3/4	1/2 oz.	Rifled Slug	1.5
	PR20CS	20824	2-3/4	5/8 oz.	Copper Solid HP	1.5
	SP20RS	20616	2-3/4	5/8 oz.	Rifled Slug HP	1.5
12	PR12CS	20716	2-3/4	1 oz.	Copper Solid HP	1.5
	PR12MCS	20718	3	1 oz.	Copper Solid HP	1.5
	PRA12	20727	2-3/4	385 Ggr.	Power Port Tip	1.5
	PRA12M	20731	3	385 gr.	Power Port Tip	1.5
	SPHV12RS	28600	2-3/4	7/8 oz.	Rifled Slug	1.5
	SPHV12MRS	28604	3	7/8 oz.	Rifled Slug	1.5
	RL12RS	20290	2-3/4	1 oz.	Rifled Slug	1.5
	SP12RS	20300	2-3/4	1 oz.	Rifled Slug	1.5
	S12SRS	20302	2-3/4	1 oz.	Rifled Slug	1.5
	S12MRS	20270	3	1 oz.	Rifled Slug	1.5

SHOTSHELL

PRODUCT NAME	INDEX/EDI NO.	RAMAC	GAUGE	LENGTH (IN)	DRAM EQUIV.	VELOCITY	OZ. OF SHOT	VELOCITY
	STS20NSC7	28860	20	2-3/4	3	1300	7/8	7-1/2
	STS28NSC7	28868	28	2-3/4	2	1300	3/4	7-1/2
	STS410NSC8	28879	410	3-1/2	MAX	1300	1/2	8
Premier Nitro 27 Handicap	STS12NH17	20227	12	2-3/4	HDCP	1290	1	7-1/2
	STS12NH7	20222	12	2-3/4	HDCP	1235	1-1/8	7-1/2
	STS17NH8	20224	12	2-3/4	HDCP	1235	1-1/8	8
American Clay & Field	HT1275	20344	12	2-3/4	3	1200	1-1/8	7-1/2
	HT128	20346	12	2-3/4	3	1200	1-1/8	8
	HT129	20348	12	2-3/4	3	1200	1-1/8	9
	HT12L8	20356	12	2-3/4	2-3/4	1200	1	8
	HT12L9	20358	12	2-3/4	2-3/4	1200	1	9
	HT2075	20377	20	2-3/4	2-1/2	1200	7/8	7-1/2
	HT208	20379	20	2-3/4	2-1/2	1200	7/8	8
	HT209	20381	20	2-3/4	2-1/2	1200	7/8	9
	HT288	20492	28	2-3/4	N/A	1250	3/4	8
	HT289	20494	28	2-3/4	N/A	1250	3/4	9
	HT4108	20497	410	2-1/2	MAX	1275	1/2	8
	HT4109	20499	410	2-1/2	MAX	1275	1/2	9
Gun Club Cure	GCC12L8	R20029	12	2-3/4	2-3/4	1145	1-1/8	8
	GC12LR8A	R20031	12	2-3/4	2.5	1100	1-1/8	8
Gun Club	GC12LR8	20241	12	2-3/4	7.5	1150	1	8
	GC12LR8A	20243	12	2-3/4	2.5	1100	1-1/8	8
	GC1218	20081	12	2-3/4	2-3/4	1185	1	8
	GC12LJ	20244	12	2-3/4	2-3/4	1145	1-1/8	7-1/2
	GC12L8	20230	12	2-3/4	2-3/4	1145	1-1/8	8
	GC12L9	20248	12	2-3/4	2-3/4	1145	1-1/8	9
	GC127	20232	12	2-3/4	3	1200	1-1/8	7-1/2
	GC128	20234	12	2-3/4	3	1200	1-1/8	8
	GC207	20239	20	2-3/4	2-1/2	1200	7/8	7-1/2
	GC208	20235	20	2-3/4	2-1/2	1200	7/8	8
	GC209	20236	20	2-3/4	2-1/2	1200	7/8	9

VELOCITY (FPS)			ENERGY (FT-LB)			TRAJECTORY (INCHES)			
MUZ	50	100	MUZ	50	100	50	100	150	BC
1830	1335	1040	654	348	211	0	-3.5	--	0.064
1600	1175	965	1989	1072	724	0	-4.8	--	0.063
1850	1610	1399	1976	1496	1130	0	-1.9	-8.2	0.144
1900	1655	1438	2084	1581	1193	2.5	3.4	0	0.144
1800	1800	1321	1037	1575	848	0	-2.2	--	0.13
1500	1360	1240	1444	1187	986	0	-3.2	--	0.206
1580	1240	1034	1513	931	648	0	-4.2	--	0.081
1450	1320	1208	2040	1689	1417	0	-3.5	-12.9	0.211
1550	1408	1283	2331	1923	1597	0	-2.9	-11.1	0.211
1850	1611	1401	2925	2218	1677	2.7	3.6	0	0.145
1900	1656	1439	3086	2344	1771	2.5	3.4	0	0.145
1800	1252	978	2751	1517	813	0	-4.1	--	0.055
1875	1302	998	2989	1442	847	0	-3.7	--	0.055
1200	988	873	1397	948	739	0	-7.4	--	0.068
1560	1203	1004	2361	1403	976	0	-4.5	--	0.075
1680	1285	1045	2378	1605	1059	0	-3.8	--	0.075
1760	1345	1075	3005	1753	1121	0	-3.4	--	0.075

REMINGTON

REMINGTON

HANDGUN BALLISTICS

CARTRIDGE	INDEX/EDI NO.	RAMAC	WT (GR)	BULLET STYLE	PRIMER NO.	SIGHT HEIGHT (INCHES)
5.7x28mm	L5728MM1	R23986	40	Full Metal Jacket	0.9	25
25 Auto (6.35mm Browning)	L25AP	23716	50	Full Metal Jacket	1-1/2	0.9
30 Super Carry	L30SC	R20015	100	Full Metal Jacket	550	0.9
	RTP30SC	R20019	100	Jacketed Hollow Point	205	0.9
32 S&W	RPW32SW	22206	88	Lead Round Nose	1-1/2	0.9
32 S&W Long	RPW32SWL	22210	98	Lead Round Nose	1-1/2	0.9
32 Auto (7.65mm Browning)	L32AP	23704	71	Full Metal Jacket	1-1/2	0.9
32 H&R Mag	RTP32HR	R20017	85	Jacketed Hollow Point	5-1/2	0.9
RPW32HR	20021	95	Lead	Semi-Wadcutter	1-1/2	0.9
327 Federal Magnum	L327	R20016	100	Jacketed Soft Point	5-1/2	0.9
357 Mag**	RTP357M7A	22237	110	Semi-Jacketed Hollow Point	5-1/2	0.9
	HD357MA	28920	125	Brass Jacketed Hollow Point	5-1/2	0.9
	RTP357M1A	22227	125	Semi-Jacketed Hollow Point	5-1/2	0.9
	L357M12	23738	125	Jacketed Soft Point	5-1/2	0.9
	RTP357M2A	22231	158	Semi-Jacketed Hollow Point	5-1/2	0.9
	RTP357M3A	22233	158	Soft Point	5-1/2	0.9
	RPW357M5	22223	158	Lead Semi-Wadcutter	5-1/2	0.9
	RTP357M10A	22239	180	Semi-Jacketed Hollow Point	5-1/2	0.9
357 Sig	GSB357SBB	29407	125	Bonded Brass Jacketed Hollow Point	5-1/2	0.9
	L357S1	23734	125	Full Metal Jacket	5-1/2	0.9
	L357S2	23692	125	Jacketed Hollow Point	5-1/2	0.9
9mm Luger	RTP9MM1A	28288	115	Jacketed Hollow Point	1-1/2	0.9
	RTP9MM6A	28293	115	Jacketed Hollow Point +P ‡	1-1/2	0.9
	L9MM1B	23753	115	Jacketed Hollow Point	1-1/2	0.9
	L9MM3	23728	115	Full Metal Jacket	1-1/2	0.9
	LL9MM11	23785	115	Flat Nose Enclosed Base	1-1/2	0.9
	LL9MM2	23811	124	Flat Nose Enclosed Base	1-1/2	0.9
	GSB9MMDB	29341	124	Bonded Brass Jacketed Hollow Point +P ‡	1-1/2	0.9
	HD9MMBN	28935	124	Brass Jacketed Hollow Point	1-1/2	0.9
	HD9MMD	28948	124	Brass Jacketed Hollow Point +P ‡	1-1/2	0.9
	CHD9MMBN	28963	124	Brass Jacketed Hollow Point	1-1/2	0.9
	L9MM2	23718	124	Full Metal Jacket	1-1/2	0.9
	GSB9MMCB	29343	147	Bonded Brass Jacketed Hollow Point	1-1/2	0.9
	RTP9MM8A	28295	147	Jacketed Hollow Point	1-1/2	0.9
	HD9MMC	28946	147	Brass Jacketed Hollow Point	1-1/2	0.9
	L9MM9	23732	147	Full Metal Jacket	1-1/2	0.9
	S9MM9	28435	147	Flat Nose Enclosed Base	1-1/2	0.9
	LL9MM9	23749	147	Flat Nose Enclosed Base	1-1/2	0.9
	T9MM3L	R27778	115	Full Metal Jacket	1-1/2	0.9
	T9MM3A	R23975	115	Full Metal Jacket	1-1/2	0.9
	T9MM3B	R23972	115	Full Metal Jacket	1-1/2	0.9
	T9MM3CL	R27779	115	Full Metal Jacket	1-1/2	0.9
	T9MM2L	R27780	124	Full Metal Jacket	1-1/2	0.9
	T40SW3L	27781	180	Full Metal Jacket	1-1/2	0.9
380 Auto	RTP380A1A	22248	88	Jacketed Hollow Point	1-1/2	0.9

ZERO (YARDS)	VELOCITY (FPS)			ENERGY (FT-LB)			TRAJECTORY (INCHES)		BARREL LENGTH	BC
	MUZ	25	50	MUZ	25	50	25	50		
1655	1514	1387	243	204	171	0.0	-0.0	4.8		0.064
25	760	733	707	64	60	56	0.0	-3.2	2	0.088
25	1250	1185	1129	347	312	283	-0.7	-2.9	4	0.144
25	1235	1170	1115	339	304	276	-0.7	-3	4	0.144
25	680	662	644	90	86	81	0.0	-4.1	3	0.114
25	705	687	669	108	103	97	0.0	3.7	4	0.119
25	905	879	854	129	122	115	0.0	-1.9	4	0.131
25	1120	1067	1023	235	215	195	0.0	1.0	5	0.100
25	1020	970	928	220	200	180	0.0	1.4	5	0.14
25	1500	1408	1324	500	440	389	-0.5	-2.1	4	0.145
25	1295	1182	1093	410	341	292	0.0	0.7	4**	0.098
25	1220	1095	1009	413	333	283	0.0	-0.9	4**	0.073
25	1450	1338	1240	583	497	427	0.0	-0.3	4**	0.125
25	1450	1338	1240	583	497	427	0.0	-0.3	4**	0.125
25	1235	1164	1104	535	475	428	0.0	-0.7	4**	0.145
25	1235	1164	1104	535	475	428	0.0	-0.7	4**	0.145
25	1235	1164	1104	535	475	428	0.0	-0.7	4**	0.145
25	1145	1095	1052	524	479	443	0.0	-0.9	8-3/8**	0.163
25	1350	1245	1157	506	430	372	0.0	4		
25	1350	1238	1146	506	425	365	0.0	-0.5	4	0.110
25	1350	1245	1157	506	430	372	0.0	-0.5	4	0.118
25	1145	1092	1048	335	304	280	0.0	-0.9	4	0.155
25	1250	1175	1113	399	353	316	0.0	-0.7	4	0.143
25	1145	1092	1048	335	304	280	0.0	-0.9	4	0.155
25	1145	1092	1048	335	304	280	0.0	-0.9	4	0.155
25	1145	1092	1048	335	304	280	0.0	-0.9	4	0.155
25	1110	1069	1031	339	314	292	0.0	-1.0	4	0.173
25	1125	1074	1031	348	317	293	0.0	-1.0	4	0.149
25	1125	1074	1031	348	317	293	0.0	-1.0	4	0.149
25	1180	1131	1089	383	352	326	0.0	-0.8	4	0.189
25	1020	992	967	286	271	258	0.0	-1.3	2.7	0.189
25	1110	1069	1031	339	314	292	0.0	-1.0	4	0.173
25	990	964	941	320	304	289	0.0	-1.4	4	0.182
25	990	965	941	320	304	289	0.0	-1.4	4	0.182
25	990	964	941	320	304	289	0.0	-1.4	4	0.182
25	990	965	941	320	304	289	0.0	-1.4	4	0.182
25	945	923	903	292	278	266	0.0	-1.7	4	0.183
25	990	965	941	320	304	289	0.0	-1.4	4	0.182
25	1145	1092	1048	335	304	280	0.0	-0.9	4	0.155
25	1145	1092	1048	335	304	280	0.0	-0.9	4	0.155
25	1145	1092	1048	335	304	280	0.0	-0.9	4	0.155
25	1145	1092	1048	335	304	280	0.0	-0.9	4	0.155
25	1110	1069	1031	339	314	292	0.0	-1.0	4	0.173
25	990	964	940	392	371	353	0.0	-1.4	4	0.178
25	990	954	923	191	178	166	0.0	-1.5	4	0.13

REMINGTON

HANDGUN BALLISTICS

REMINGTON

CARTRIDGE	INDEX/EDI NO.	RAMAC	WT (GR)	BULLET STYLE	PRIMER NO.	SIGHT HEIGHT (INCHES)
	L380AP	23720	95	Full Metal Jacket	1-1/2	0.9
	LL380AP2	23805	95	Flat Nose Enclosed Base	1-1/2	0.9
	HD380BN	28937	102	Brass Jacketed Hollow Point	1-1/2	0.9
	CHD380BN	28964	102	Brass Jacketed Hollow Point	1-1/2	0.9
38 Super Auto +P	L38SUP	23722	130	Full Metal Jacket +P‡	1-1/2	0.9
38 S&W	RPW38SW	22278	146	Lead Round Nose	1-1/2	0.9
38 Spl**	RTP38S10A	22295	110	Semi-Jacketed Hollow Point +P‡	1-1/2	0.9
	RTP38S16A	22293	110	Semi-Jacketed Hollow Point	1-1/2	0.9
	RTP38S21A	22303	125	Semi-Jacketed Hollow Point +P‡	1-1/2	0.9
	HD38SBN	28938	125	Brass Jacketed Hollow Point +P‡	1-1/2	0.9
	CHD38SBN	28965	125	Brass Jacketed Hollow Point +P‡	1-1/2	0.9
	LL38S17	23789	125	Flat Nose Enclosed Base	1-1/2	0.9
	L38S2B	23771	125	Jacketed Hollow Point +P‡	1-1/2	0.9
	L38S11	23730	130	Full Metal Jacket	1-1/2	0.9
	RPW38S3	22267	148	TMWC	1-1/2	0.9
	RPW38S6	22271	158	Lead SWC	1-1/2	0.9
	RPW38S5	22281	158	Lead Round Nose	1-1/2	0.9
	RTP38S12	22301	158	Lead Hollow Point +P‡	1-1/2	0.9
	L38S5	23724	158	Lead Round Nose	1-1/2	0.9
38 Short Colt**	RPW38SC	22273	125	Lead Round Nose	1-1/2	0.9
40 S&W	RTP40SW1A	22306	155	Jacketed Hollow Point	1-1/2	0.9
	L40SW4	23746	165	Full Metal Jacket	1-1/2	0.9
	GSB40SWAB	29363	165	Bonded Brass Jacketed Hollow Point	1-1/2	0.9
	HD40SWA	28957	165	Brass Jacketed Hollow Point	1-1/2	0.9
	HD40SWBN	28939	180	Brass Jacketed Hollow Point	1-1/2	0.9
	CHD40SWBN	28966	180	Brass Jacketed Hollow Point	1-1/2	0.9
	GSB40SWBB	29365	180	Bonded Brass Jacketed Hollow Point	1-1/2	0.9
	RTP40SW2A	22308	180	Jacketed Hollow Point	1-1/2	0.9
	L40SW2B	23687	180	Jacketed Hollow Point	1-1/2	0.9
	L40SW3	23742	180	Full Metal Jacket	1-1/2	0.9
	LL40SW5	23791	180	Flat Nose Enclosed Base	1-1/2	0.9
10mm Auto	L10MM6	23706	180	Full Metal Jacket	2-1/2	0.9
	R21368		180	Bonded Brass Jacketed Hollow Point	2/1/02	0.9
	R21369		180	Brass Jacketed Hollow Point	2/1/02	0.9
	R21370		180	Brass Jacketed Hollow Point	2/1/02	0.9
	RTP10MM					
41 Remington Mag	RTP41MG1A	23000	210	Jacketed Soft Point	2-1/2	0.9
44 Remington Mag**	L44MG7	23744	180	Jacketed Soft Point	2-1/2	0.9
	RTP44MG2A	23002	240	Jacketed Soft Point	2-1/2	0.9
	RTP44MG3A	23010	240	Semi-Jacketed Hollow Point	2-1/2	0.9
44 S&W Spl**	RPW44SW	22333	246	Lead Round Nose	2-1/2	0.9
45 Colt	HD45C410**	28927	230	Brass Jacketed Hollow Point	2-1/2	0.9
	RPW45C1	22338	225	Lead SWC	2-1/2	0.9
	RPW45C	22340	250	Lead Round Nose	2-1/2	0.9
45 Auto	RTP45AP2A	21453	185	Jacketed Hollow Point	2-1/2	0.9

ZERO (YARDS)	VELOCITY (FPS)			ENERGY (FT-LB)			TRAJECTORY (INCHES)		BARREL LENGTH	BC
	MUZ	25	50	MUZ	25	50	25	50		
25	955	904	860	192	172	156	0.0	-1.8	4	0.077
25	955	904	860	192	172	156	0.0	-1.8	4	0.077
25	940	920	901	200	192	184	0.0	-1.7	4	0.195
25	815	801	787	265	256	247	0.0	-2.5	2.7	0.195
25	1215	1152	1099	426	383	348	0.0	-0.7	4	0.158
25	685	668	652	152	145	138	0.0	-4.0	4	0.126
25	995	958	926	242	224	210	0.0	-1.5	4**	0.128
25	950	919	890	220	206	194	0.0	-1.7	4**	0.126
25	945	921	898	248	235	224	0.0	-1.7	4**	0.162
25	975	950	927	264	250	238	0.0	-1.5	4**	0.177
25	895	876	857	222	213	204	0.0	-1.9	1.875**	0.174
25	850	836	822	201	184	188	0.0	-2.2	4**	0.211
25	945	921	898	248	235	224	0.0	-1.7	4**	0.162
25	800	787	775	185	179	173	0.0	-2.6	4**	0.213
25	710	671	634	166	148	132	0.0	-3.9	4**	0.056
25	755	739	723	200	191	183	0.0	-3.1	4**	0.148
25	755	739	723	200	191	183	0.0	-3.1	4**	0.148
25	890	872	855	278	267	256	0.0	-2.0	4**	0.187
25	755	739	723	200	191	183	0.0	-3.1	4**	0.148
25	730	708	686	148	139	131	0.0	-3.4	6**	0.101
25	1205	1146	1095	500	452	413	0.0	-0.8	4	0.163
25	1150	1040	964	485	396	339	0.0	-1.1	4	0.068
25	1150	1089	1040	484	435	396	0.0	-0.9	4	0.135
25	1150	1089	1040	484	435	396	0.0	-0.9	4	0.135
25	1015	986	960	412	388	368	0.0	-1.3	4	0.177
25	785	770	756	246	237	228	0.0	-2.8	3.6	0.174
25	1015	986	960	412	388	368	0.0	-1.3	4	0.177
25	1015	986	960	412	388	368	0.0	-1.3	4	0.177
25	1015	986	960	412	388	368	0.0	-1.3	4	0.177
25	990	964	940	392	371	353	0.0	-1.4	4	0.178
25	990	964	940	392	371	353	0.0	-1.4	4	0.178
25	1150	1103	1063	528	486	451	0.0	-0.9	4	0.180
25	1160	1111	1070	538	494	457	0	-0.8	5	0.177
25	1160	1111	1070	538	494	457	0	-0.8	5	0.177
25	1080	1040	1008	464	433	406	0	-1.1	3.78	0.174
25	1300	1226	1162	788	701	629	0.0	-0.5	4**	0.159
25	1610	1482	1366	1036	878	745	0.0	-0.1	4**	0.123
25	1180	1126	1081	742	676	623	0.0	-0.8	4**	0.172
25	1180	1126	1081	742	676	623	0.0	-0.8	4**	0.172
25	755	740	725	311	299	287	0.0	-3.1	4**	0.158
25	850	830	811	369	352	335	0.0	-2.3	4**	0.149
25	830	804	780	344	323	304	0.0	-2.5	4**	0.101
25	750	733	717	312	298	285	0.0	-3.1	4**	0.142
25	1000	968	939	411	385	362	0.0	-1.4	4	0.149

REMINGTON

HANDGUN BALLISTICS

CARTRIDGE	INDEX/EDI NO.	RAMAC	WT (GR)	BULLET STYLE	PRIMER NO.	SIGHT HEIGHT (INCHES)
	L45AP1	23818	185	Full Metal Jacket	2-1/2	0.9
	HD45APA	28971	185	Brass Jacketed Hollow Point	2-1/2	0.9
	HD45APC	28973	185	Brass Jacketed Hollow Point +P ‡	2-1/2	0.9
	GSB45APAB	29325	185	Bonded Brass Jacketed Hollow Point	2-1/2	0.9
	GSB45APBB	29327	230	Bonded Brass Jacketed Hollow Point	2-1/2	0.9
	RTP45AP7A	21455	230	Jacketed Hollow Point	2-1/2	0.9
	HD45APBN	28942	230	Brass Jacketed Hollow Point	2-1/2	0.9
	CHD45APBN	28967	230	Brass Jacketed Hollow Point	2-1/2	0.9
	L45AP4	23726	230	Full Metal Jacket	2-1/2	0.9
	S45AP4	28428	230	Flat Nose Enclosed Base	2-1/2	0.9
	L45AP7B	23689	230	Jacketed Hollow Point	2-1/2	0.9
	LL45AP8	23793	230	Flat Nose Enclosed Base	2-1/2	0.9
45 GAP	L45GAP4	23691	230	Full Metal Jacket	2-1/2	0.9

RIMFIRE BALLISTICS

CARTRIDGE	INDEX/EDI NO.	RAMAC	WT (GR)	BULLET STYLE	VELOCITY (FPS)				
					MUZ	50	100	150	200
22 Short	1022 1000*	21000 21001	29	Plated Round Nose	1095	986	903	829	–
	1722 1700* YJ225	21074 21280 21233	33	Plated Truncated Cone HP	1500	1243	1075	983	–
	1922 1900* VP225	21080 21288 21239	36	Plated Truncated Cone Solid	1410	1186	1056	976	–
	CY-22HP***	21222	36	Lead Hollow Point	1280	1104	1010	939	–
	1622 1600* 1622E** 1622C** 1622B****	21008 21278 21229 21250 21231	36	Plated Hollow Point	1280	1104	1010	939	–
	1522 1500*	21006 21276	40	Plated Round Nose	1255	1103	1017	952	–
	TB-22A TB-22B***	21238 21241	40	Lead Round Nose	1255	1103	1017	952	–
	6122 6100*	21022 21284	40	Lead Round Nose	1150	1046	976	916	w–
	SUB22HP SUB22HP1* SS225	21135 21137 21249	40	Plated Hollow Point	1050	950	867	793	–
	CB-22L100*	21119	33	Plated Truncated Cone HP	740	687	638	592	–
17 HMR	PR17HM1	28464	17	AccuTip-V BT	2550	2212	1901	1620	1378
	R17HM1	20023	17	JHP	2530	2150	1804	1502	–
	R17HM2	20025	20	PSP	2375	2051	1754	--	–
22 Win Mag	PR22M1	21184	33	AccuTip-V BT	2000	1730	1495	1289	1135
	R22M1	21170	40	JHP	1910	1610	1355	1160	1032
	R22M2	21172	40	PSP	1910	1600	1340	1143	1018

ZERO (YARDS)	VELOCITY (FPS)			ENERGY (FT-LB)			TRAJECTORY (INCHES)		BARREL LENGTH	BC
	MUZ	25	50	MUZ	25	50	25	50		
25	1015	981	951	423	395	371	0.0	-1.4	4	0.149
25	1015	981	951	423	395	372	0.0	-1.4	4	0.149
25	1140	1086	1042	534	485	446	0.0	-0.9	4	0.150
25	1015	981	951	423	395	372	0.0	-1.4	4	0.149
25	875	853	833	391	372	354	0.0	-2.1	4	0.148
25	835	817	800	356	341	326	0.0	-2.4	4	0.161
25	875	853	833	391	372	354	0.0	-2.1	4	0.148
25	725	710	695	210	201	193	0.0	-3.4	3	0.149
25	835	817	800	356	341	326	0.0	-2.4	5	0.161
25	830	812	795	352	337	323	0.0	-2.4	5	0.159
25	835	817	800	356	341	326	0.0	-2.4	5	0.161
25	835	817	800	356	341	326	0.0	-2.4	5	0.161
25	880	860	841	395	378	361	0.0	-2.0	5	0.162

ENERGY (FT-LB)					TRAJECTORY (INCHES)					BC
MUZ	50	100	150	200	MUZ	50	100	150	200	
77	63	52	44	–	0.3	0	-7.4	-25.5	–	0.084
165	113	85	71	–	-0.2	0	-4.1	-15.0	–	0.095
159	112	89	76	–	-0.1	0	-4.7	-17.1	–	0.103
131	97	82	71	–	0.0	0	-5.6	-19.7	–	0.104
131	97	82	71	–	0.0	0	-5.6	-19.7	–	0.104
140	108	92	80	–	0.0	0	-5.6	-19.6	–	0.116
140	108	92	80	–	0.0	0	-5.6	-19.6	–	0.116
117	97	85	75	–	0.2	0	-6.4	-22.0	–	0.116
98	80	67	56	–	-1.5	0	-8.2	-27.9	–	0.079
40	35	30	26	–	1.4	0	-16.9	-55.2	–	0.095
246	185	136	99	72	-1.5	0.2	zero	-2.6	-8.5	0.125
242	174	123	85	--	-1.5	0.2	0.0	-2.9	--	0.110
250	187	137	--	--	-1.5	0.3	0.0	--	--	0.125
293	220	163	122	94	-1.5	0.7	zero	-4.6	-14.5	0.136
324	230	163	119	95	-1.5	0.9	zero	-5.7	-17.8	0.117
324	228	159	116	78	-1.5	1	zero	-5.8	-18.3	0.113

REMINGTON

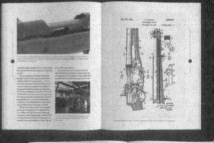